Walking with a Saint

Morning Walks and Conversations 2008

with Śrīla Bhaktivedānta Nārāyaṇa Gosvāmī Mahārāja

Contributors

There were many contributors to the completion of *Walking with a Saint – Morning Walks and Conversations 2008* in the form of transcribers, translators, editors, designers, proofreaders, typists, and typesetters. Their names are listed here: Śrīpāda Mādhava Mahārāja, Śrīpāda Vaikhānas Mahārāja; Anaṅga-mohinī dāsī, Ānitā dāsī, Anupama dāsa, Bhānumati dāsī, Brajanātha dāsa, Devānanda dāsa, Govinda-priya dāsī, Hari-vallabha dāsī, Jagat-kartā dāsa, Jāhnavā dāsī, Jānakī dāsī, Jayantī dāsī, Jayaśrī dāsī, Kṛṣṇa-kāminī dāsī, Kṛṣṇa-vallabha dāsī, Lalit-kiśorī dāsī, Madana-mohinī dāsī, Mahā-mantra dāsa, Nandinī dāsī, Rādhā-kānta dāsa, Rādhikā dāsī, Śānti dāsī, Sudevī dāsī, Sundara-gopāla dāsa, Śyāmarāṇī dāsī, Vaijayantī-mālā dāsī, Vasanti dāsī, Veṇu-gopāla dāsa, Viṣṇurāta dāsa, and Yasodānandana dāsa.

Also so many devotees helped with filling in names, when we couldn't recognize voices.

Special thanks to Īśa dāsa of purebhakti.tv, for providing most of the sound-files.

Graphic and cover design by Anupama dāsa
Cover photo by Anurādhā dāsī
Other photos by Anurādhā dāsī, Jagannātha dāsa, Madhuvrata dāsa, Nārāyaṇa dāsa, Vasanti dāsī, and Viśvarūpa dāsa.

www.purebhakti.com
for news, updates, and free downloads of books and lectures

www.harikatha.com
to receive, by email, the lectures and videos of
Śrīla Bhaktivedānta Nārāyaṇa Gosvāmī Mahārāja on his world tours

www.purebhakti.tv
to watch and hear classes online, or get links and schedule updates
for live webcasts

www.backtobhakti.com
for the latest, up-to-date news on IPBYS,
the International Pure Bhakti Yoga Society

Walking with A Saint - Morning Walks and Conversations 2008
by Śrī Śrīmad Bhaktivedānta Nārāyaṇa Gosvāmī Mahārāja

ISBN 978-1-935428-26-8
First printing: October 2010 (5,000 copies)
Printed by: Spectrum Printing Press (P) Ltd., New Delhi, India

Śrī Śrīmad
Bhaktivedānta Nārāyaṇa Gosvāmī Mahārāja

Śrī Śrīmad
Bhaktivedānta Vāmana Gosvāmī Mahārāja

Śrī Śrīmad
Bhaktivedānta Svāmī Mahārāja

Śrī Śrīmad
Bhakti Prajñāna Keśava Gosvāmī Mahārāja

Śrī Śrīmad
Bhaktisiddhānta Sarasvatī Prabhupāda

Table of contents

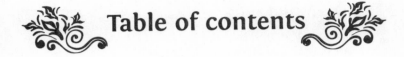

Foreword

For whatever we aspire to become, it is inspiring to associate with a master. This holds true for those of us who dream to be great athletes, musicians, artists, or businessmen.

Moreover, nowadays many of us are waking up to an understanding that we are spiritual beings; somewhere along the path of realizing that the purpose of human life is more than just survival and material accomplishments. We are beginning to see that we are souls, not just mechanical bodies. We see all around us the allure of material life, but our hearts are yearning for a deeper, richer, fuller experience. We want to taste God. We want to be whole and fulfilled, not for five minutes or five hours, but forever – and for that attainment, inspiring masters are also available.

These days we are very fortunate, because we have so much access to information through books and the internet. We also have access to the Vedas, the ancient scriptures, a vast opus compiled thousands of years ago in India by great sages in order to benefit mankind to progress along the path of self-realization.

However, there is such an enormous diversity of information available from these timeless books of wisdom, with so many interpretations, that choice can lead to confusion. Thus, we become like starving children entering a sumptuous restaurant. There is so much available, but what would be good for us to eat? What will really nourish us?

With our hearts yearning for truth in a world offering a myriad of solutions, the spiritual master, the *sādhu*, or saint, plays an essential role. The word *sādhu* is derived from the Sanskrit word *sat*, or *sattva*, which means the 'ever-existing Supreme Absolute Truth, the Supreme Personality of Godhead.' The *sādhu* is fully surrendered to that Absolute Truth, and is in essence a manifestation of that Truth, who is revealed in the Vedic scriptures as Śrī Kṛṣṇa.

It is stated in the Vedas: "The symptoms of a *sādhu*, or saint, are that he is tolerant, merciful, and friendly to all living entities. He has no enemies, he is peaceful, he abides by the scriptures, and all his characteristics are sublime."

The *sādhu* is tolerant, without being disturbed. For example, Lord Jesus Christ was tolerant. Even when he was being crucified, he prayed to God, "Forgive them, Father, for they know not what they do." Another example is the child-saint Prahlāda Mahārāja.

Prahlāda's demonic father tried to torture him in many ways: by hurling him off a cliff, at the feet of a wild elephant, into a fire, and in a pit of snakes; but Prahlāda was never disturbed. His father forced him to drink poison, and he drank it, but he was not at all disturbed.

We learn that part of the core process of progressing in God-realization is *sādhu-saṅga*, which means 'association with a *sādhu*,' and which the ancient Vedas tell us offers unfathomable benefits: "If a person gets the chance to attentively hear from elevated saints about the activities and character of Śrī Kṛṣṇa, which are like a flowing river of nectar, he will forget the necessities of life, namely hunger and thirst, and become immune to all kinds of fear, lamentation, and illusion" (*Śrīmad-Bhāgavatam* 4.29.40).

And further, "Association with wise devotees makes what was empty full. It turns death into immortality. It turns calamity into good fortune" (*Vasiṣṭha-śāstra*).

The great self-realized soul, Śrīla Bhaktivinoda Ṭhākura, who lived in India in the nineteenth century, explains in a poetic song that there is no one in this entire world more dear than a *sādhu*. Worldly fathers, mothers, and other relatives are dear, but not as dear as that *sādhu*. These worldly relationships may sometimes bring us suffering, but a *sādhu* takes away all our sufferings. For this reason the scriptures tell us that by even a moment's association with a pure *sādhu* one can attain all success.

The Sādhu of This Book

After rising as early as three a.m., uttering *mantras* and prayers and chanting the various names and glories of Kṛṣṇa, it was a part of Śrīla Bhaktivedānta Nārāyaṇa Gosvāmī Mahārāja's morning practice to take a brisk walk for up to one hour. This was a time when those seeking his association could walk with him, and also hear from him, for at times he would stop and spontaneously share his realizations.

A sublime and elevated personality, his relationships and interactions with people on a one-to-one basis are intimate and sweet. Hundreds of thousands of people take his association, and yet he is always able to tailor his communication for the person who asks a question, even if that person has never met him before. To one inquirer he might express himself with joking irony, to another with gravity, to another in a playful way, to another with sternness, to another with a tone of sympathy, to another with subtle philosophical intricacies, and to another with deliberate simplicity. Sometimes what he says is applicable for the moment, and sometimes for eternity. Sometimes his replies apply to a specific individual, and sometimes to the entire audience, but in both cases his words enlighten all.

He personally replies most of the time, and on occasion he calls on a *sannyāsī* (renunciant) or other senior disciples to reply. Sometimes he expresses appreciation for his disciples' replies, and sometimes he corrects them. There is a saying in India that a mother teaches her daughter-in-law by teaching her daughter. In other words, the mother will most readily give corrective instruction to her own daughter, but that instruction will apply equally to the less accessible daughter-in-law. Similarly, on his morning walks Śrīla Mahārāja trains his disciple/preachers to speak and understand with great precision and clarity the established truths of Vedic philosophy; and by this he also wants to inspire all people of the world, all of whom he considers as his spiritual children. He wants to inspire them with the understanding that correct philosophical thought elevates one on his or her path to perfection, whereas a philosophical misunderstanding can derail one from the path and keep one chained in the darkness of material and spiritual confusion.

In 2008 his eighty-seventh birthday was celebrated, yet he not only walked briskly but with great elegance and refinement. One could not help but be struck by his warmth, ease, compassion, and gravitas, and one was struck by even a slight sense of his unconditional, ever-fresh love and affection for all.

We learn from spiritual masters that whenever a saint speaks, atoms of *prema* (transcendental love of God) emanate from his glance and from every pore of his divine body, and these atoms fall upon all those who are fortunate enough to be in his presence. Everyone starts somewhere, and he accepts all with an unfathomable open heart.

We wish we could put a video of these morning walks and *darśanas* on each page of this book so that you would be able to see his sweet smiles, hear his laughter, and hear his voice full of unending care and compassion. You may download these videos, if you wish, on www.purebhakti.tv.

The Making

It was in Odessa, Ukraine, in September of 2008 that Śrīla Nārāyaṇa Gosvāmī Mahārāja first requested his followers to publish transcriptions of his morning walks, "So that in the future everyone will be able to know all the established truths we have discussed." He requested a series of books, each year of discussions becoming a book.

His new publishing team began collecting the sound-files (audio and video) for all of his walks and *darśanas* of 2008 – the first year's book. They downloaded and transcribed many files from www.purebhakti.tv, and then they wrote to devotees they knew in each country, asking for more.

They recognized most of the voices on the sound-files, but some they didn't. So they asked their spiritual brothers and sisters in each city to hear the walks or *darśanas* and fill in the missing names. In the rare instances where they were unable to get names, the page will say 'Devotee' or 'Guest.'

As more and more walks and *darśanas* were edited, some of the editors began to consider removing the names of Śrīla Mahārāja's spiritual daughters and sons, as well as the names of others, including institutional and political leaders, who were corrected or chastised by him. They were worried that these persons would be embarrassed by 'public exposure;' and worried that, imitating him, his followers might also feel free to criticize and chastise. In response to their concerns, Śrīla Mahārāja personally directed them to be transparent and not omit anything. He said there was no need for adjustment of the text; his correction or chastisement of his own disciples, or of others, would be beneficial for those individuals as well as for the world. He added that those who are not self-realized souls must not find fault with others, however, because "They have no power to do so."[1]

He agreed that the publishing team would include in the Foreword some relevant quotes from his lectures in this regard, and therefore we are happy to present them here:

> If a high-class, self-realized *guru* criticizes someone, that criticism is a blessing and a medicine. Do not oppose him, thinking, "*Guru* is now against me." Rather, understand that his chastisement is like medicine; his curse and benediction are one and the same. When a *guru* chastises, he is thinking, "I should make this person so fortunate that he can realize all the truths of pure *bhakti*."
>
> (1996. France)

[1] Please see the appendix for the transcription of this conversation.

We should try to advance. Do not waste your time in criticizing; do not try to control. *Gurudeva* can control. He is a controller, and Kṛṣṇa, Śrī Caitanya Mahāprabhu, and Śrī Nityānanda Prabhu are controllers. We should think, "I am not the controller. I should be controlled by them, and I should try to control myself." In this way we can develop our Kṛṣṇa consciousness.

If you see that a person is wretched, don't associate with him. But don't criticize, thinking you are masters to chastise, for only *guru* can criticize and chastise. Be very humble, hankering for *bhakti*, so that your hearts will melt. Try to serve Vaiṣṇavas and *guru*. If you chastise Vaiṣṇavas instead of honoring them, and at the same time you render a great deal of service to *gurudeva*, *Gurudeva* will not accept your service.

(May 21, 1997. Badger, California)

If we think of others' bad qualities, we will have to absorb those qualities in ourselves.

(September 4, 2005. Govardhana, India)

To bring a person from the clutches of the Lord's deluding material potency, *māyā*, is very, very hard. If lust or any other attachment is present in that person's heart it will go away very soon if he is chanting, remembering, and listening to *hari-kathā*. Be very careful. Don't criticize devotees – or non-devotees. First look at your own condition and try to purify yourself. Is there any lust in you? Is there any deceit in you? Be worried for that; don't worry for others. *Guru* and Kṛṣṇa are responsible for others. You cannot do anything to help them, so you have no right to criticize.

(February 7, 2005. Hilo, Hawaii)

Kṛṣṇa's devotees are more humble than trees and blades of grass. If you want to do *bhajana*, you must follow these four principles. "*Tṛṇād api sunīcena, taror api sahiṣṇunā, amāninā mānadena, kīrtanīyaḥ sadā hariḥ* – One should chant the holy name of the Lord in a humble state of mind, thinking himself lower than the straw in the street. One should be more tolerant than the tree, devoid of all

> sense of false prestige, and ready to offer all respects to others. In such a state of mind one can chant the holy name of the Lord constantly" (*Śrī Śikṣāṣṭaka* 3). Don't desire to be respected by anyone; but try to give others proper respect.
>
> (June 1, 2002. Badger, California)

Śrīla Bhaktivedānta Nārāyaṇa Gosvāmī Mahārāja is an intimate friend and spiritual successor of Śrīla Bhaktivedānta Svāmī Mahārāja, who is known throughout the world as Śrīla Prabhupāda, the renowned preacher and founder-*ācārya* of the International Society for Kṛṣṇa Consciousness. He carries on his head Śrīla Prabhupāda's order to him to spiritually nurture Śrīla Prabhupāda's disciples and followers and to continue his mission. Having been given the key that opens the various locks on the vast treasure-chest of Śrīla Prabhupāda's divine books, during Śrīla Mahārāja's walks and *darśanas* he repeatedly explains, clarifies, and sheds light on Śrīla Prabhupāda's teachings. Thus, within *Walking With A Saint*, he fulfils one of his most cherished services in this world.

Śrīla Mahārāja's native language is Hindi, and he is also proficient in Bengali and Sanskrit. Regarding his English conversations and lectures, they are full with ever-new realizations of the Supreme Lord Śrī Kṛṣṇa, as well as the Lord's associates, abode, incarnations, and energies. He impregnates seeds of pure loving devotion into the hearts of all those who sit or stand before him; and, by his watering of those seeds, those hearts automatically blossom into fragrant flowers which he offers into the lotus-like hands of that very Supreme Lord. In fact, even when he is not speaking about transcendental subject matters, his listeners are injected by his presence with the spiritual strength to overcome all the obstacles imposed by this world of birth and death.

At the same time, because English is not his first language, on occasion he uses a particular word when the meaning he intends is clearly that of another, or he uses the conventions of what students of language refer to as 'Indian English.' Therefore, for clarity of his meaning and for flow of the English language, the editors have slightly edited his words under his guidance.

The language of *Walking With A Saint* is very straightforward and easy to understand. At the same time, Śrīla Mahārāja uses many Sanskrit terms from the ancient Vedic literatures, and we have retained them in the text in order to preserve the deep mood and precision of meaning. For the benefit of the readers, these terms are always explained in English, either in the text itself or in the footnotes. When you find the explanation in the text or footnote insufficient, you are invited to turn to the glossary at the back of the book. We use standard diacritical markings to indicate the pronunciation of the Sanskrit words. Pronounce *ā* like a in father, *ī* like ea in neat, *ū* like oo in root, *ṛ* like ri in rip, *ṁ* and *ṅ* like ng in hung, *ś* and *ṣ* like sh in shy, and *c* like ch in chap.

We pray that you, our respected readers, receive from *Walking With A Saint* a new light, new paradigms, and new direction. Please excuse any errors on our part in presenting this compilation.

The Publication Team
Kārtika, October 2010

Auckland, New Zealand

January 4-9, 2008

January 4, 2008
Darśana

Śyāmarāṇī dāsī: Gurudeva, for the addendum of your *Gopī-gīta* lectures book, we are having brief biographies of the different *Bhāgavatam* commentators. One of those commentators is Śrīla Śrīdhara Svāmī. I have read that he is a devotee of Lord Nṛsiṁhadeva, and he wrote verses like:

vāg-īśā yasya vadane lakṣmīr yasya ca vakṣasi
yasyāste hṛdaye saṁvit taṁ nṛsiṁham ahaṁ bhaje

In His mouth the goddess Śuddha-Sarasvatī is always present, on His chest Lakṣmī-devī always sports, and within His heart special affection for His devotees is always manifest – I worship that Nṛsiṁhadeva.

If he is a devotee of Lord Nṛsiṁhadeva, how could he write such wonderful commentaries about the *gopīs* in *Gopī-gīta*?

Śrīla Nārāyaṇa Gosvāmī Mahārāja: I am a devotee of Kṛṣṇa, but I often discuss the glories of Rāma. What is the harm? Just as I see that Rāma is Kṛṣṇa, he knows that God is one Supreme Lord and that He is Kṛṣṇa: "I am worshiping Nṛsiṁhadeva, but Nṛsiṁhadeva is really none other than Kṛṣṇa." Vyāsadeva is a devotee of Kṛṣṇa. How did he write *Rāma-caritra* (the life history and character of Lord Rāma), *Nṛsiṁha-caritra*, and the histories of all other incarnations? How did he write in the various Purāṇas about different demigods?

Śyāmarāṇī dāsī: So he knows that Lord Nṛsiṁhadeva is not Svayam Bhagavān, but rather an expansion?

Śrīla Nārāyaṇa Gosvāmī Mahārāja: No. He knows that Nṛsiṁhadeva is Kṛṣṇa. He knows this. He knows about all the *rasas*, so he knows that *dāsya*, *sakhya*, *vātsalya*, and especially *mādhurya* are not present in Nṛsiṁhadeva. Only the *rasa* of *bhayānaka* (fear) is present.

Veṇu-gopāla dāsa: When can we sing the Nṛsiṁha prayers?

Śrīla Nārāyaṇa Gosvāmī Mahārāja: You can sing them at any time. We can pray, "O Nṛsiṁhadeva, please protect me from all *anarthas* and all kinds of problems, so that I can serve Kṛṣṇa and Rādhikā."

Anything else?

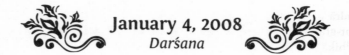

Bhadrā dāsī: Śrīla Gurudeva, how much did Vajranābha (Kṛṣṇa's great-grandson) know about Kṛṣṇa's relationship with Śrīmatī Rādhikā and the *gopīs*? Did he know anything?

Śrīla Nārāyaṇa Gosvāmī Mahārāja: He must have known everything, because he went to Vṛndāvana and discovered the sweet pastime places of Kṛṣṇa. He went to Rādhā-kuṇḍa and created two beautiful ponds.

Śrīpāda Mādhava Mahārāja: For our remembrance, he commemorated all of Kṛṣṇa's pastime places.

Śrīla Nārāyaṇa Gosvāmī Mahārāja: He associated with Bhāguri Ṛṣi, Śāṇḍilya Ṛṣi, and other great sages. These sages were present when Kṛṣṇa was here, and therefore they were very familiar with Kṛṣṇa's pastime places.

Bhāguri Ṛṣi was the *guru* of Kṛṣṇa, not Sāndīpani Muni. Sāndīpani Muni was only His school teacher. Bhāguri Ṛṣi initiated Him into the *rādhā-mantra*.

Śrīpāda Dāmodara Mahārāja: Sometimes you say that Sāndīpani Ṛṣi was not a Vaiṣṇava.

Śrīla Nārāyaṇa Gosvāmī Mahārāja: He was a Śaivite (a devotee of Lord Śiva). Kṛṣṇa saw that Sāndīpani Ṛṣi was a Śaivite, and therefore knew that He would not be recognized. That is why He chose his school.

Śrīpāda Mādhava Mahārāja: But in the end he understood.

Śyāmarāṇī dāsī: Today is Ekādaśī. In relation to Ekādaśī, you once told the history of Citrāṅga Mahārāja. You said that his first wife was willing to sacrifice the life of her son so that his new wife, Mohinī, would not leave him. What is the value of her sacrificing her own son so that a materialistic woman would stay and be happy with her husband?

Śrīla Nārāyaṇa Gosvāmī Mahārāja: She was a chaste lady (*pati-vratā*), so she wanted her husband's vow to be fulfilled. She desired that he would not be deviated from his word: "I will always follow Ekādaśī."

Śyāmarāṇī dāsī: That is clear. But Mohinī had told Citrāṅga, "If you follow Ekādaśī, I will leave you." Citrāṅga was determined to follow Ekādaśī whether Mohinī would stay or not. Still, the chaste wife did not want Mohinī to leave. Because of that, she was willing…

Śrīla Nārāyaṇa Gosvāmī Mahārāja: She knew that this new lady was favorable for him in the sense that she could fulfill his desires (*kāma-vāsanā*). She thought, "I cannot satisfy him, but she can; so it is better that she doesn't go. It is better that she stays with my husband."

Bhadrā dāsī: This is Vāsudeva Datta Prabhu. He has been in ISKCON for twenty years or more, and he has been looking forward to meeting you.

Śrīla Nārāyaṇa Gosvāmī Mahārāja: Are you happy?

Vāsudeva Datta dāsa: Yes, very happy.

Śrīla Nārāyaṇa Gosvāmī Mahārāja: ISKCON leaders cannot give you *prema-bhakti*, but we can give it to you. That is why, when I come to any city, the ISKCON leaders create festival programs so that their disciples will not come to our program.

Some ISKCON devotees preach that "Nārāyaṇa Mahārāja gives *harināma* and *dīkṣā* initiation to the disciples of Śrīla Bhaktivedānta Svāmī Mahārāja, and that is why he changed the name of Jadurāṇī to Śyāmarāṇī."

Brajanātha dāsa: They call this re-initiation.

Śrīla Nārāyaṇa Gosvāmī Mahārāja: I never do this. Out of affection, I gave her this name. I cannot address her as Jadurāṇī. I can address her as Śyāmarāṇī. Śrīla Bhaktivedānta Svāmī Mahārāja inspired me to give her this nickname. When she first came to him, he wanted her to understand Kṛṣṇa's Godhood. He therefore gave her the name Jadurāṇī, which is in relation to Kṛṣṇa in Dvārakā. Now he wants her to further her understanding of Kṛṣṇa in Vṛndāvana, so he inspired me to give her the name Śyāmarāṇī.

January 5, 2008
Morning Walk

Kamala-kānta dāsa (from Germany)**:** These days there are many *gurus* all over the world. What is the speciality of having a *sad-guru* (a bonafide, self-realized *guru*)?

Śrīla Nārāyaṇa Gosvāmī Mahārāja: You have heard the answer to this more than a thousand times. You should give the answer.

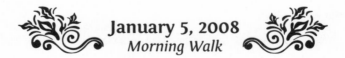

Kamala-kānta dāsa: *Sad-guru* has seen the eternal Truth. He has seen Kṛṣṇa in his heart and he has realized this knowledge. He can give a person *bhakti* and love for Śrī Kṛṣṇa because he has this love. Bogus *gurus* cannot give this.

Śrīla Nārāyaṇa Gosvāmī Mahārāja: This answer is not complete. (To Veṇu-gopāla dāsa) What are the symptoms of *sad-guru*?

Veṇu-gopāla dāsa: The Vedas are flowing in his heart like a river.

Śrīla Nārāyaṇa Gosvāmī Mahārāja: Do you know the verse from *Śrīmad-Bhāgavatam*?

Veṇu-gopāla dāsa: No, I don't.

Kamala-kānta dāsa:

tasmād guruṁ prapadyeta
jijñāsuḥ śreya uttamam
śābde pare ca niṣṇātaṁ
brahmaṇy upaśamāśrayam

(*Śrīmad-Bhāgavatam* 11.3.21)

Śrīla Nārāyaṇa Gosvāmī Mahārāja: What is the meaning?

Kamal-kānta dāsa: If you want to be happy, then you have to find a *guru*. The symptoms of that *guru*...

Śrīla Nārāyaṇa Gosvāmī Mahārāja: (to Śrīpāda Dāmodara Mahārāja) Tell them the meaning.

Śrīpāda Dāmodara Mahārāja: He is expert in the Vedic conclusions, detached from material enjoyment, and has direct realization of Kṛṣṇa.

Śrīla Nārāyaṇa Gosvāmī Mahārāja: Mādhava Mahārāja.

Śrīpāda Mādhava Mahārāja: It is mentioned in scripture:

tasmād guruṁ prapadyeta
jijñāsuḥ śreya uttamam
śābde pare ca niṣṇātaṁ
brahmaṇy upaśamāśrayam

(*Śrīmad-Bhāgavatam* 11.3.21)

Therefore any person who seriously desires real happiness must seek a bonafide spiritual master and take shelter of him by initiation. The qualification of the bonafide *guru*

> is that he has realized the conclusions of the scriptures by deliberation and is able to convince others of these conclusions. Such great personalities, who have taken shelter of the Supreme Godhead, leaving aside all material considerations, should be understood to be bonafide spiritual masters.

In this verse, the word *tasmad* means 'for this reason.' What is the reason? In this world we are slapped by the threefold miseries. If we want to attain our greatest good, then we have to approach someone who can help us. That helper is called the preceptor, expert, or *śrī guru*.

What are the symptoms of such a person? There is one primary symptom and one secondary symptom. The secondary symptom is further divided into two. The first of the secondary symptoms is *śābde niṣṇātaṁ*, realized in all the Vedic scriptures. *Śābde* means *śabde-brahma*, or 'all scriptures.' It is mentioned in our scriptures:

ṛg-yajuḥ-sāmātharvāś ca bhāratam pañcarātrakam
mūla-rāmāyaṇaṁ caiva śāstram ity abhidhīyate
yac cānukūlam etasya tac ca śāstraṁ prakīrtitam
ato'nya grantha vistaro naiva śāstraṁ kuvatma tat

(*Skanda Purāṇa*)

> The *Ṛg*, *Yajur*, *Sāma*, and *Atharva Vedas*, as well as the *Mahābhārata*, the *Nārada-pañcarātra*, and the *Rāmāyaṇa*, are certainly known as *śāstra*. Those books that favorably follow in the footsteps of these authorized scriptures are also designated as *śāstra*. All other literature simply leads one down the wrong path and can never be known as scripture.

He is expert in the Vedas, *Rāmāyaṇa*, *Mahābhārata*, *Śrīmad-Bhāgavatam*, and all the Purāṇas. If a devotee or disciple has any doubt, then, quoting from scripture, *sad-guru* can rule it out. He will not say, "I can send you an email after six months." He will immediately quote from scripture and remove the doubt.

The next secondary symptom is *upaśamāśrayam*, meaning that he must be detached from this material world. In this world, people only 'eat, drink, and be merry.' He will not be like this; he is detached from this.

Moreover, he must be a realized soul. This is the primary symptom, but this primary symptom is very difficult to detect. If we associate with Vaiṣṇavas, by their help we can understand whether a certain *guru* is real or not. The *sādhu* is seeing Śrī Kṛṣṇa and serving Him twenty-four hours a day. Although the *sādhu* is among us, he is always serving Śrī Caitanya Mahāprabhu and the Divine Couple. This is the primary symptom.

First we see the secondary symptoms, and gradually, by the association of Vaiṣṇavas, we will be able to see the primary symptom. If someone has no primary symptom and is only a great scholar, then he is not a bonafide *guru*.

It is mentioned in *śāstra* that a person wanting milk will not get it from a cow that has not had a calf. In the same way, although someone may be a learned scholar, if he is not a realized soul, then he is not a bonafide *guru*.

Veṇu-gopāla dāsa: Śrīla Gurudeva, while chanting *japa*, is it okay to chant the *pañca-tattva mantra* when we reach the end of a round?

Śrīla Nārāyaṇa Gosvāmī Mahārāja: There is no rule or regulation for this, but you can do it. Before chanting *harināma*, first offer *praṇāma* to your *guru*, your *guru-paramparā*, Vṛndāvana-dhāma, Navadvīpa-dhāma, Jagannātha Purī-dhāma, and all other *dhāmas* and personalities mentioned in the *jaya-dhvani* prayers.

Then chant *śrī-kṛṣṇa-caitanya prabhu nityānanda śrī-advaita gadādhara śrīvāsādi-gaura-bhakta-vṛnda*; and *śrī rūpa, sanātana, bhaṭṭa raghunātha, śrī jīva, gopāla-bhaṭṭa, dāsa raghunātha*; and then begin to chant *harināma*. After that, when you reach the end of a round, there is no rule or regulation regarding whether or not to utter the *pañca-tattva mantra*. If you do it, it is okay; if you don't do, it is okay.

(To Narottama dāsa, a young boy) Do you understand something of our discussions? Can you say what is the aim and object of life?

Narottama dāsa: The goal is to attain pure *bhakti*.

Śrīla Nārāyaṇa Gosvāmī Mahārāja: What is the hidden teaching in the history of the life of Hariścandra?

Kamala-kānta dāsa (of New Zealand): The teaching is that we should not identify ourselves with the body. We are soul.

Śrīla Nārāyaṇa Gosvāmī Mahārāja: The teaching is that the truths of this world are false, and that the Supersoul is the only Truth. Viśvāmitra was very, very merciful to Hariścandra by teaching him this lesson and then instructing him on spiritual topics.

January 5, 2008
Darśana
After the Walk

Madhu Paṇḍita dāsa: Śrīla Gurudeva, the devotees in the South Island (Christchurch) would like you to visit, but we know that we cannot make a big program for you like you are having here. So we are humbly asking if we can take your shoes to Christchurch.

Śrīla Nārāyaṇa Gosvāmī Mahārāja Yes. If you can procure wooden *pādukā*, sandals, you can worship them. In India they can be easily purchased in many places. I used to wear them in my boyhood.

Kamala-kānta dāsa (of New Zealand): I have a pair like that in my house. I can give it to you to offer Gurudeva.

Madhu Paṇḍita dāsa: Thank you.

January 5, 2008
Darśana

Śrīla Nārāyaṇa Gosvāmī Mahārāja (To Bhakti dāsa, a terminally-ill devotee): Don't fear death. Death simply means that you will have a new body, and by that new body you will be able to serve Śrī Kṛṣṇa and perform *bhajana* with great determination. Because of your activities until now, such as your chanting of the holy name, Kṛṣṇa will arrange to give you a pure devotee with whom to associate. We should not fear death; death is nothing. As long as you are conscious, always remember Kṛṣṇa and chant Hare Kṛṣṇa.

Those who are now babies, and also those who are now very smart and strong youths, will become old one day. No doctor or scientist, nor the combined effort of many doctors and scientists, can stop one's old age from coming. In old age we will be harassed by many diseases, and one day we will have to give up this body. No one can postpone his time of inevitable death for even a second.

What is death? The soul, which is part and parcel of Kṛṣṇa, gives up this body and enters another baby body. This is death.

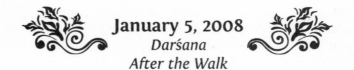

We are not this body; inside the body there is a soul, the eternal servant of Kṛṣṇa. Now, we souls have forgotten Kṛṣṇa, and that is why we are covered by so many material situations – birth, death, calamities, diseases, and problems.

Conversely, if we chant Kṛṣṇa's name, we will attain love for Kṛṣṇa and be liberated from this world. There will be no birth or death, and we will obtain a beautiful and brilliant spiritual teenage body. We will thus always serve Kṛṣṇa and be happy. In Kṛṣṇa's abode there is no need of serving anyone else but Kṛṣṇa. There is no need of money and no need of eating, as we have here. There is only nectar there – we engage only in drinking the nectar of love.

Bhadrā dāsī: Śrīla Gurudeva, this is Ann. She has been chanting Hare Kṛṣṇa for twenty-five years. Two years ago, her husband left his body. She has been missing him and grieving about this. She is a very good devotee, but she has no *guru*.

Śrīla Nārāyaṇa Gosvāmī Mahārāja: You should know that your husband has not died. He is in another body now, but you would not be able to recognize him. He has forgotten you, so you should also forget him. It is essential to know that Kṛṣṇa is your only husband. All of us are eternal servants of Kṛṣṇa, who is your only husband, son, and all other relatives.

If that man was actually your husband, why did he leave you? And what did you do with his body after his death?

Ann: I cremated it.

Śrīla Nārāyaṇa Gosvāmī Mahārāja: Ashes. If he was your husband, why did you put his body in fire? Why?

So you should not lament. Kṛṣṇa never dies, and you, the soul, never die. Do not weep or lament in vain. Weep only for Kṛṣṇa.

Ann: Thank you.

Śrīla Nārāyaṇa Gosvāmī Mahārāja: Always be happy that Kṛṣṇa, your Husband, will not die. Always know that He is eternally playing on His flute and calling you.

Madhu-paṇḍita dāsa: Śrīla Gurudeva, I would like to introduce Vāsudeva Prabhu. He has been chanting for twenty-two years and would like to give his heart to you. This is his daughter Mīna, his wife Amara, and his other daughter Nadia. He was formerly initiated by Bhavānanda.

Śrīla Nārāyaṇa Gosvāmī Mahārāja: I will help you; I must help you. Try to take a new *harināma* and *dīkṣā* initiation. It has been told in *śāstra*, in our sacred books, that if one's *guru* is fallen, one must accept another *guru* – a qualified *guru*.

Every day we perform some worship, and we must begin any devotional activity by praying to *guru* and offering him obeisances. Also, we must first offer obeisances to *guru* before chanting the holy name. If you have no *guru*, to whom will you offer obeisances?

You can attend our initiation, and in this way advance in Kṛṣṇa consciousness.

Hari-priyā dāsī: What is the best thing I can do to help my brother, Bhakti dāsa?

Śrīla Nārāyaṇa Gosvāmī Mahārāja: Pray to Kṛṣṇa, chant Kṛṣṇa's name, and remember Girirāja Govardhana. Pray to Girirāja that he will give your brother *kṛṣṇa-bhakti*, and that your brother can easily give up his body without any pain.

Bhadrā dāsī: This is Yasmin. She just met the devotees yesterday. She is already interested in initiation, but she doesn't really know what it means.

Śrīla Nārāyaṇa Gosvāmī Mahārāja: An expert professor or teacher gives lessons to his students regarding the process of studying a particular subject. A bonafide *guru*, by *dīkṣā* initiation, gives transcendental knowledge and a relationship between your soul and Kṛṣṇa. By *dīkṣā*, all your sins and all kinds of unwanted thoughts and habits disappear. Then, by this *dīkṣā* system, gradually you will realize your relationship with Kṛṣṇa.

Do you know the meaning of 'relation'? Is your father alive?

Yasmin: Yes.

Śrīla Nārāyaṇa Gosvāmī Mahārāja: Your mother?

Yasmin: Yes.

Śrīla Nārāyaṇa Gosvāmī Mahārāja: You are married?

Yasmin: Not yet.

Śrīla Nārāyaṇa Gosvāmī Mahārāja: What is your relationship with your father? He is your father. If you are sick, will your father help you or not?

Yasmin: Yes.

Śrīla Nārāyaṇa Gosvāmī Mahārāja: If you are married and have a son, you do not hesitate to spend all your money and give your whole being for that son. This is 'relation.' Similarly, when you realize your relationship with Kṛṣṇa, you will give up everything for Him, and He will give all His mercy to you.

This is the *dīkṣā* process. *Dīkṣā* is not completed in one second; it takes time. By taking *dīkṣā*, we are entering into the school in which we learn all these spiritual principles and philosophical truths.

Madhu-paṇḍita dāsa: Śrīla Gurudeva, I would like to introduce Bhakta Peter from Christchurch. He has been chanting for eighteen years. He would like to give his heart to you.

Śrīla Nārāyaṇa Gosvāmī Mahārāja: I will be happy to take your heart. Have you already given your heart, or you will give it?

Peter: I will give it.

Śrīla Nārāyaṇa Gosvāmī Mahārāja: Oh, do not say this. Rather, say, "I have just now given my heart to you – for you to keep forever." If you say 'will,' then giving it is very far away.

You may come when we perform initiations tomorrow.

Madhu-paṇḍita dāsa: Peter studied religious studies in a university. But he became discouraged by the teachers teaching impersonal Māyāvāda philosophy, so he did not complete his Ph.D.

Śrīla Nārāyaṇa Gosvāmī Mahārāja: Māyāvāda means 'influenced by a special power of Kṛṣṇa called *māyā*.' By that influence you will think, "I am God, who has no form or qualities and who is the creator of the entire world." This is Māyāvāda philosophy.

We are not the Supreme Lord. God has no problems, whereas we repeatedly suffer from the problems of birth and death and we continuously weep due to so many problems. You are fortunate to have given up that line of thought.

Peter: I read a very interesting book that you published, called *Beyond Nirvāṇa*.

Śrīla Nārāyaṇa Gosvāmī Mahārāja: You have read it? You are very lucky. This will help you.

January 6, 2008
Darśana

Śrīla Nārāyaṇa Gosvāmī Mahārāja: What is *advaya-jñāna para-tattva*?

Candramukhī dāsī: It is that this material world and all the energies of Kṛṣṇa are non-different from Him. He is simultaneously different and non-different from His manifestations.

Śrīla Nārāyaṇa Gosvāmī Mahārāja: This is somewhat okay, but not complete.

vadanti tat tattva-vidas
tattvaṁ yaj jñānam advayam
brahmeti paramātmeti
bhagavān iti śabdyate

(*Śrīmad-Bhāgavatam* 1.2.11)

> Learned transcendentalists who know the Absolute Truth call this nondual substance Brahman, Paramātmā, or Bhagavān.

Śrīla Nārāyaṇa Gosvāmī Mahārāja: Where is Ācāryajī?

(To 'Ācāryajī' Ajaya-kṛṣṇa dāsa) Yesterday I explained this *śloka*. What is *advaya-jñāna para-tattva*?

Ajaya-kṛṣṇa dāsa: According to what you said, it is Bhagavān Śrī Kṛṣṇa.

Śrīla Nārāyaṇa Gosvāmī Mahārāja: Say what you think. What I said may be right or wrong, so please say what you think.

Ajaya-kṛṣṇa dāsa: I am so much junior to you.

Śrīla Nārāyaṇa Gosvāmī Mahārāja: Go on, speak.

Ajaya-kṛṣṇa dāsa: *Advaya* means 'where there is no *dvaya*, no duality.' According to Vedānta, *advaya* is *nirvikāra* Brahman (without change, or without variety). This is what people accept. What you said last night was very beautiful.

Śrīla Nārāyaṇa Gosvāmī Mahārāja: Please say what you've understood.

Ajaya-kṛṣṇa dāsa: Those who are *tattva-vit* (knowers of the truth) see Brahman as *nirvikāra*.

Śrīla Nārāyaṇa Gosvāmī Mahārāja: First explain the meaning of *advaya-jñāna*.

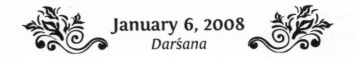

Ajaya-kṛṣṇa dāsa: *Advaya-jñāna: yato vā imāni bhūtāni jāyante.*

Śrīla Nārāyaṇa Gosvāmī Mahārāja: The heads of even big scholars spin when they try to think about what I said last night.

Dāmodara Mahārāja, what did I say?

Śrīpāda Dāmodara Mahārāja: He is the non-dual Absolute Truth. Even though the Absolute Truth is one, He is realized in different aspects by different persons.

Śrīla Nārāyaṇa Gosvāmī Mahārāja: How is He one? We see so many incarnations, like Rāma and all others; we see the transcendental world; we see so many *jīvas*; and we see so many varieties in this world, such as trees and creepers. How is He one?

Śrīpāda Dāmodara Mahārāja: The moon is always full, but sometimes we see it as a half-moon or quarter-mood. Therefore…

Śrīla Nārāyaṇa Gosvāmī Mahārāja: You could not understand my question.

Śrīpāda Dāmodara Mahārāja: Nothing is separate from Him.

Śrīla Nārāyaṇa Gosvāmī Mahārāja: That is okay, but how is He the one Absolute Truth? Śyāmarāṇī, can you tell?

Śyāmarāṇī dāsī: Last night Śrīla Gurudeva discussed the verse he just quoted here, beginning with *vadanti tat tattva-vidas tattvaṁ*. Bhagavān is one, but seen from different angles He may look like one thing or another.

Śrīla Gurudeva gave the example of a mountain. When a mountain is seen from far away, it may look like a cloud. Then, when you get close you can see that it may look like some green thing, and if you go on the mountain itself, you can see that there are so many varieties of trees, insects, plants, and shrubs.

Similarly, Bhagavān is one. If He is seen from far away, it may seem that He is the impersonal Brahman. When seen closer, it may seem that He is Paramātmā (Supersoul) in the heart of every living entity, the size of a thumb. Then, when He is seen fully, one can understand that He is Bhagavān, the Supreme Personality of Godhead, and that Paramātmā and Brahman are not independent of Him.

It is stated in the *Brahma-saṁhitā* that within the *brahma-jyoti* there are infinite universes, so one may say that these universes are separate from Him. One may say that His energies are separate from Him, one might say that the limbs of His body are separate, and one might say that His expansions are separate. But there is so much reference in *śāstra* that all of His energies and incarnations emanate from Him, are subordinate to Him, and are within Him.

It is also stated in *Brahma-saṁhitā* that each of the limbs of His body can act for any other limb. "*Aṅgāni yasya sakalendriya-vṛttimanti* – He has all the potencies of all the senses in all parts of His transcendental body." There is no difference between Kṛṣṇa's hands and legs. For example, He can see with His lotus feet and He can eat *prasādam* with His eyes. All His limbs are absolute and non-different from Him.

He has unlimited energies, but they can be divided into three – material, marginal, and spiritual – and they are all within Him. Actually, His complete, supreme energy, *parā-śakti*, is one, and is non-different from Him.

I have some energy. I can do many things with my energy, and it is non-different from me. Similarly, Kṛṣṇa has His supreme *parā-śakti,* which is also divided into *antaraṅga-śakti* (the spiritual, internal potency), *taṭasthā-śakti* (the marginal potency, or the living entities), and *bahiraṅga-śakti* (the material potency, or the material world). Regarding the spiritual potency, it is divided into the *sandhinī-śakti* (Kṛṣṇa's existence potency), *hlādinī-śakti* (Kṛṣṇa's bliss potency), and *saṁvit-śakti* (Kṛṣṇa's knowledge potency). All these energies are within Kṛṣṇa and are non-different from Him.

The *Brahma-saṁhitā* also states: "*Rāmādi-mūrtiṣu kalā-niyamena tiṣṭhan* – Kṛṣṇa is always existing with many forms simultaneously, namely Rāma, Nṛsiṁha, Varāha, and Nārāyaṇa." All incarnations emanate from Him. They are all within Him; They are not independent from Him.

In this way, one may see from different angles that there are different energies, numerous incarnations, and so many aspects of the material world; but they are all subordinate to Śrī Kṛṣṇa and are within Him. Therefore, He is the one-without-a-second Absolute Truth.

Śrīla Nārāyaṇa Gosvāmī Mahārāja: Very good.

Advaya – na dvaya – means that there are not two things. What does this mean? *Para-tattva*, that Supreme Absolute Truth, is not two. The Absolute Truth is one; there is no second.

na tasya kāryaṁ karaṇaṁ ca vidyate
na tat-samaś cābhyadhikaś ca dṛśyate

parāsya śaktir vividhaiva śrūyate
svābhāvikī jñāna-bala-kriyā ca
(*Śvetāśvatara Upaniṣad* 6.8)

The Supreme Lord has nothing to do, and no one is found to be equal to or greater than Him, for everything is done naturally and systematically by His multifarious energies.

Na tasya kāryaṁ karaṇaṁ ca vidyate. He who is known as Brahman has no mortal senses. His senses are not mortal, and therefore we cannot see them. He does not have (mortal) ears, but still He listens; He has no eyes, but still He sees; He has no legs but still He walks; He has no hands, but still He holds. His senses are transcendental.

Na tat-samaś cābhyadhikaś ca dṛśyate. No one is equal to Him or greater than Him.

Parāsya śaktir vividhaiva śrūyate. Bhagavān has one *hlādinī-parā-śakti,* which is *svābhāvikī* (natural). He performs all His activities naturally, as if automatically, without any labor. This *śakti* manifests all the transcendental worlds. Vaikuṇṭha, Goloka, and Vṛndāvana-dhāmas are the transformations of this *śakti.*

Bhagavān's form manifests from *bala-śakti,* of which Baladeva Prabhu is the predominating Deity. Kṛṣṇa's flute, crown, clothing, and ornaments, and the forms of Nanda Bābā, Kṛṣṇa, and all other associates manifest from *bala-śakti.* That same Kṛṣṇa, in the form of Baladeva Prabhu, manifests all this.

Kṛṣṇa's incarnations, like Śrī Rāma and all others, are non-different from Him. From time to time, He Himself comes in the form of Rāma, Nṛsiṁha, and other incarnations.

rāmādi-mūrtiṣu kalā-niyamena tiṣṭhan
nānāvatāram akarod bhuvaneṣu kintu
kṛṣṇaḥ svayaṁ samabhavat paramaḥ pumān yo
govindam ādi-puruṣaṁ tam ahaṁ bhajāmi
(*Brahma-saṁhitā* 5.39)

I worship the original personality, Govinda, who manifests Himself in the material world as Śrī Rāmacandra and many other incarnations who are His plenary portions and sub-portions, and who personally appears in the form of Śrī Kṛṣṇa.

In the transcendental world, the *gopas, gopīs,* cows, etc. are all manifested from Kṛṣṇa's *śakti,* and are therefore also non-different from Him.

All *jīvas* in the material world manifest from Kṛṣṇa's *taṭasthā-śakti.* They are not a transformation of Kṛṣṇa; they do not come from Him directly. When Kṛṣṇa is situated only in His *taṭasthā-śakti* and all His other *śaktis* are hidden, the *jīvas* manifest. It is for this reason that they are called *vibhinnāṁśa;* they are infinitesimal separated parts of Kṛṣṇa, and at the same time are non-different from Him.

Whatever we see in that material world, like the bodies of trees, flowers, animals, etc., are manifested from Kṛṣṇa's *māyā-śakti.* Don't think that they are separate from Kṛṣṇa. Nothing exists separately from Him. Baladeva Prabhu, Lord Rāma, the *jīvas,* and *māyā* have no separate existence from Him. This is *advaya-jñāna para-tattva.*

And what is the relationship of Kṛṣṇa with *nirviśeṣa-brahma* (Brahman), that spiritual existence which is formless and devoid of variety? *Nirviśeṣa-brahma* is the effulgence (*jyoti*) of the toenails of Kṛṣṇa's lotus feet. Do you understand? It is the effulgence of the toenails of Kṛṣṇa's lotus feet.

Let us consider the example of Sūrya, the Sun, from which comes *jyoti,* the sunshine. Sūrya has form, qualities, and activities; and although the sunshine has no form, it has activities. If there were no Sun, there would be only cold darkness. There would be no sunshine. Similarly, Kṛṣṇa is *mūla-śaktimān,* the source and Lord of all energies and all existence. If there were no Kṛṣṇa, there would be no *śakti.*

If one sees Kṛṣṇa from far away, by *jñāna,* mental speculation, he will see the effulgence (*prakāśa*) of Kṛṣṇa's toenails. Some people therefore say that He is *prakāśa-svarūpa,* made simply of effulgence. But the Vedic scriptures say, "*Satyaṁ jñānam anantaṁ brahma* – The Supreme Absolute Brahman is the embodiment of truth, knowledge, and eternity."

If one sees Kṛṣṇa from somewhat nearer, he will see Him in His form as Paramātmā, who is present in the heart of all *jīvas* as witness, and who is the size of a thumb. Impersonal Brahman has *cit,* cognizance. Paramātmā has *cit* and *sat,* cognizance and existence, but not *ānanda,* bliss. This Paramātmā is the witness of all our activities.

Śrīpāda Dāmodara Mahārāja: Does Paramātmā have activities?

Śrīla Nārāyaṇa Gosvāmī Mahārāja: Paramātmā has activities. He sees as a witness, and He gives the fruits of the *jīvas'* activities.

But *ānanda* is present only in Bhagavān. *Kṛṣṇas tu bhagavān svayam*. He is personified bliss, and He is also *ānanda mayo brahma*, full of bliss. *Ānanda-mayo'bhyāsāt* (*Vedānta-sūtra* 1.1.12). *Ānandamaya* means 'consisting of bliss,' and *abhyāsāt* means 'by nature.' By nature, the Supreme Lord is blissful. Kṛṣṇa is both *ānanda* and *ānandamaya*.

Śaṅkarācārya could not digest the understanding that Brahman is *ānandamaya*. He accepted that Brahman is *ānanda*, but he thought, "How can Brahman be *ānandamaya*? If it is *ānandamaya*, then it becomes a person with qualities. According to Śaṅkarācārya, Brahman is not a person. He reasoned that if Brahman is a person, then Brahman must transform in order to manifest variety; he did not accept that Brahman transforms. We Gauḍīya Vaiṣṇavas agree that Brahman, the Absolute Person, does not transform, but we understand from the Vedic scriptures that His energy transforms.

Because Śaṅkarācārya denied the truth of Vyāsadeva's statement, *ānanda-mayo 'bhyasat*, although he asserts that Vyāsadeva is his *guru*, Vaiṣṇavas consider it absurd to think that he accepted Vyāsadeva as such.

Only by *bhakti* can one see Bhagavān fully, along with His servitors, His *dhāma*, and His associates. This is *advaya-jñāna para-tattva*.

(To Ajaya-kṛṣṇa dāsa) It is important for you to understand these truths. I have told this especially for you, because you are a preacher.

Anurādhā dāsī: Some people say that the books written by our *ācāryas* and Gosvāmīs in disciplic succession are not *śāstras*, or Vedic scriptures; they are simply literatures. Can you say something about this? They say that Śrīla Rūpa Gosvāmī's *Bhakti-rasāmṛta-sindhu* is not called '*śāstra*;' it is simply called 'literature.'

They say that the ancient scriptures should be given preference, and if what is written by our *ācāryas* does not coincide with what was written in the ancient *śāstras*, we have to accept the ancient *śāstras*.

Śrīla Nārāyaṇa Gosvāmī Mahārāja: There is nothing wrong in this principle. If a written work is against scriptures such as *Śrīmad-Bhāgavatam*, then we cannot say it is *śāstra*; rather, it is literature. However, whatever our Gosvāmīs have written is scripture, not literature, because our Gosvāmīs have established all their writings on the basis of the ancient Vedic scriptures.

Veda is the original book of all knowledge. However, Veda is likened to a salt ocean, in the sense that practically no one can drink that water. Śrīla Vyāsadeva has taken the Veda, distilled it, and manifested the *Śrīmad-Bhāgavatam*.

From milk we get butter and from butter we get ghee (clarified butter), which is not a separate substance from milk. In the same way, the *Śrīmad-Bhāgavatam* is like the ghee taken from butter, or fresh water distilled from the salt ocean. We take the pure, filtered water; everybody can drink it and use it.

In the same way, all the books of Śrīla Rūpa Gosvāmī and the other Gosvāmīs are the essence of the *Bhāgavatam*. As the *Bhāgavatam* is like ghee churned from the butter of the Vedas, the Gosvāmīs' writings are like ghee churned from the butter of the *Bhāgavatam*. For example, the verse beginning with *anyābhilāṣitā-śūnyam* in Rūpa Gosvāmī's *Bhakti-rasāmṛta-sindhu* is not in the *Śrīmad-Bhāgavatam*, but it supports the *Bhāgavatam* and is therefore called *śāstra*.

Anurādhā dāsī: Some *brāhmaṇas* say that only a born *brāhmaṇa* can be a *brāhmaṇa*, and a person who is born as a *śūdra* cannot become a *brāhmaṇa*.

Śrīla Nārāyaṇa Gosvāmī Mahārāja: They are speaking wrongly. What was Śrī Nārada Ṛṣi? He was the son of a maidservant. Śrīla Vyāsadeva also had a very low birth – *anuloma-viloma*. [*Viloma* means the child's father is of a lower caste than the mother. *Anuloma* means that the mother's caste is lower than that of the father.] His mother was a fisherwoman. Vasiṣṭha Ṛṣi and Agastya Ṛṣi took birth from a pot, from two discharges of semen that had been kept in the pot, and Gautama Ṛṣi took birth from a rabbit.

Kṛṣṇa says in the *Bhagavad-gītā* (4.13):

cātur-varṇyaṁ mayā sṛṣṭaṁ
guṇa-karma-vibhāgaśaḥ
tasya kartāram api māṁ
viddhy akartāram avyayam

> According to the three modes of material nature and the work associated with them, the four divisions of human society are created by Me. And although I am the creator of this system, you should know that I am yet the non-doer, being unchangeable.*

The divisions of human society, namely *brāhmaṇa* (priest or teacher), *kṣatriya* (warrior or statesman), *vaiśya* (agriculturalist, merchant, or businessman), and *śūdra* (laborer), are all allotted according to one's qualities and work.

Rāvaṇa was born as a *brāhmaṇa* [His father was the powerful *brāhmaṇa* Viśravā, the son of Pulastya Ṛṣi, and his mother was a *daitya* (family of demons).] His father was a sage, but he is accepted as a *rākṣasa* demon. Prahlāda took birth in a *rākṣasa* family, but he is worshiped even by *brāhmaṇas*. What caste was Lord Rāma? He was a *kṣatriya*, so why do *brāhmaṇas* eat the remnants of His meals? Kṛṣṇa took birth in a *vaiśya* caste, and Hanumān took birth in an animal species.

Thus, we should judge one's classification according to one's qualities and activities, not by one's birth.

Śrīmad-Bhāgavatam (7.11.35) states:

yasya yal lakṣaṇaṁ proktaṁ
puṁso varṇābhivyañjakam
yad anyatrāpi dṛśyeta
tat tenaiva vinirdiśet

> If one shows the symptoms of being a *brāhmaṇa*, *kṣatriya*, *vaiśya*, or *śūdra*, as described above, even if he has appeared in a different class, he should be accepted according to those symptoms of classification.

If we see someone with the qualities of a different *varṇa* (type of work) than that of his birth, we should accept him in that *varṇa*. We should see everyone according to his or her qualities.

There was once a child named Jābāla, and that child approached Gautama Ṛṣi for initiation and learning the Vedas.

Gautama Ṛṣi asked him, "O son, what is your caste? What is your family line?"

Jābāla replied, "I don't know."

The Ṛṣi said, "Go and ask your mother."

The boy asked his mother, Jābāli, and she replied, "When I was a young girl, I had a very bad character. I was a prostitute, and therefore I cannot tell you who your father was."

Jābāla returned to his *guru* and said, "In her young age, my respectful mother was a prostitute, so she cannot say who my father is. I don't know who my father is, therefore how can I tell you?"

Gautama Ṛṣi said, "Oh, you are speaking the truth, and therefore you are actually a *brāhmaṇa*."

He then changed Jābāla's name to Satyakāma Jābāla – one who always speaks the truth – and since then, Jābāla was accepted as a *brāhmaṇa*.

January 8, 2008
Darśana

Sudevī dāsī (from New Zealand): I missed chanting some *gāyatrī-mantras* when I was giving birth to my child.

Śrīla Nārāyaṇa Gosvāmī Mahārāja: No harm. But you can chant the holy name even when giving birth to your child.

Jagannātha dāsa: How do we get the desire for *bhakti*?

Śrīla Nārāyaṇa Gosvāmī Mahārāja: Serve *parama* (great) Vaiṣṇavas fully and totally, with your entire energy. They will give you *bhakti*, because they are very merciful. There is no other way.

Is Balarāma here? Balarāma Prabhu, can you explain the meaning of *rāgānuga* and *rāgātmikā*? Is there a difference?

Balarāma dāsa: There is a difference.

Śrīla Nārāyaṇa Gosvāmī Mahārāja: A difference? They are both '*rāga*,' so how are they different?

Balarāma dāsa: *Rāgātmikā* is there in the spiritual world, and the other one is here in this world – following in that line.

Śrīla Nārāyaṇa Gosvāmī Mahārāja: Let us suppose that, by the mercy of *guru* and Gaurāṅga and Vaiṣṇavas, you are beginning to have greed to serve Śrī Śrī Rādhā and Kṛṣṇa like Śrīdāmā and Subala in *sakhya-rasa*, or like Mother Yaśodā and Nanda Bābā in *vātsalya-rasa*, or like the *gopīs* in *mādhurya-rasa*. If you are fortunate enough to have greed by their mercy – even if you are not a *sādhaka*, even if you are full of *anarthas*, and even if you have a loose character – if you begin to follow any of these associates, you are called *rāgānuga* in its very beginning stage.

Siddha devotees (those perfect in the realization of their relationship with Kṛṣṇa) need not perform any *sādhana*, because *rasa* is fully manifest in their hearts. They are called *rāgātmikā*, or eternal associates of Śrī Kṛṣṇa. A *rāgānuga* devotee is a *sādhaka*, and a *rāgātmikā* associate is *siddha*. There is a very, very big difference between them.

Kṛṣṇa-kānta dāsa: Can *rāgātmikā* associates be in this material world?

Śrīla Nārāyaṇa Gosvāmī Mahārāja: They can come with Kṛṣṇa to assist Him in enacting His sweet pastimes. They come with Him, to serve Him. Also, if Kṛṣṇa gives them an order that, "You should go to the material world as My representative," they may come at that time as well.

Śrīpāda Mādhava Mahārāja: He is asking: If one has realization of his *siddha-deha* (one's spiritual body), is he called a *rāgātmikā-bhakta*?

Śrīla Nārāyaṇa Gosvāmī Mahārāja: Not necessarily; he may still be in the practicing stage. All *anarthas* may have not yet been removed. Even if he has achieved *rati* (*bhāva-bhakti*), he is not *siddha-rāgātmikā*. In fact, even when he takes birth in Vraja (in this or any material universe) as a *gopī* or *gopa* and serves Kṛṣṇa there, still he is not *rāgātmikā*. After that, Yogamāyā will give him his birth, name, and all other spiritual designations in *aprakaṭa* (transcendental) Goloka Vṛndāvana. There he will be *rāgātmikā*.

Śrīpāda Mādhava Mahārāja: Even if a *rāgātmikā-bhakta* comes to this world and practices *bhajana*, it would be impossible for us to recognize him.

Śrīla Nārāyaṇa Gosvāmī Mahārāja: You are not able to recognize him. Only a high-class *rāgānuga* Vaiṣṇava can realize who he is.

There are some symptoms of a *rāgānuga-bhakta* who is situated even in the beginning stage of *bhāva-bhakti*:

kṣāntir avyartha-kālatvaṁ viraktir māna-śūnyatā
āśā-bandhaḥ samutkaṇṭhā nāma-gāne sadā ruciḥ

āsaktis tad-guṇākhyāne prītis tad-vasati-sthale
ity ādayo 'nubhāvāḥ syur jāta-bhāvāṅkure jane

(*Śrī Caitanya-caritāmṛta, Madhya-līlā* 23.18–19)

> When the seed of ecstatic emotion for Kṛṣṇa fructifies, the following nine symptoms manifest in one's behavior: forgiveness, concern that time should not be wasted, detachment, absence of false prestige, great hope, intense eagerness, a taste for chanting the holy name of the Lord, attachment to descriptions of the transcendental qualities of the Lord, and affection for those places where the Lord resides (that is, a temple or a holy place like Vṛndāvana). These are all called *anubhāvas*, subordinate signs of ecstatic emotion. They are visible in a person in whose heart the seed of love of God has begun to fructify.

Such a devotee can recognize the *rāgātmikā* associate of Kṛṣṇa. So many people come to me and say, "I have *prema*; I have seen Kṛṣṇa; He has given me His *darśana*." I tell these people, "You are foolish and bogus." There are symptoms. If anyone has really taken *darśana* of Kṛṣṇa, he cannot remain in a material body. His transcendental body will at once manifest and his material body will disappear.

Śrīpāda Padmanābha Mahārāja: We recognize that the *ācāryas* in our line from Śrī Caitanya Mahāprabhu's time to the present have descended from Goloka Vṛndāvana.

Śrīla Nārāyaṇa Gosvāmī Mahārāja: We can recognize them as such because Śrīla Kavi Karṇapūra Gosvāmī has given the names of the associates of Śrī Caitanya Mahāprabhu. For example, Śrī Rāya Ramānanda is Viśākhā-devī, Śrī Svarūpa Dāmodara is Lalitā-devī, and Śrīvāsa Paṇḍita is Śrī Nārada Muni. They are *rāgātmikā*, but pretending to be *sādhakas*.

Śrīpāda Padmanābha Mahārāja: Then, after Śrīman Mahāprabhu's time, coming down in our *ācārya guru-paramparā* for the past five hundred years, can we consider them as *rāgātmikā bhaktas*?

Śrīla Nārāyaṇa Gosvāmī Mahārāja: Yes, but they are not all equal. Śrīla Bhaktivinoda Ṭhākura is said to be Kamala Mañjarī, a manifestation of Śrī Gadādhara Paṇḍita. But how can we know about others? Who was Gaura-kiśora dāsa Bābājī Mahārāja? Has his name in the spiritual realm been told to us? So there are some differences.

Ajaya-kṛṣṇa dāsa: During our Janmāṣṭamī and other grand festivals, is it all right that we invite professional people to perform?

Śrīla Nārāyaṇa Gosvāmī Mahārāja: When we observe Janmāṣṭamī in Mathurā, we call all the top professional radio and television singers and musicians who can play devotional songs on *tabla* and other instruments. We also call many top learned scholars, some of whom, like Vāsudeva Caturvedī, have degrees in seven subjects.

There are seven official gradations of professor degrees – Purāṇa, *Kāvya*, Vedānta, *Chandaḥ*, *Nyāya*, *Vyākaraṇa*, and *Sāhitya* – and certain teachers have degrees in all these subjects. In Vraja, in all of Uttar Pradesh and in all of India, there are no scholars like these. In all of Vraja, no one can speak in the Sanskrit language as they do. Yet, they see me like their *guru*.

Why do we call them? We do so in order to attract more people to come to our programs. When they come, a very, very large crowd also comes. At that time I speak *hari-kathā* to inject them with Kṛṣṇa consciousness, as I am injecting you all here. I inject the audience, the scholars, and the musicians. I also give the speakers *praṇāmī* (donations) and sweets. By this process, after some time practically all of Mathurā came to me.

Ajaya-kṛṣṇa dāsa: During our Janmāṣṭamī festival we put *śālagrāma* [Kṛṣṇa'a Deity in the form of a sacred stone] in a big cucumber. Then, at the moment of Kṛṣṇa's birth, we take Him out in order to symbolize Mother Yaśodā giving birth to Kṛṣṇa. Some devotees objected to this. They said this is not bonafide.

Śrīla Nārāyaṇa Gosvāmī Mahārāja: On Janmāṣṭamī night, at midnight, not only in Mathurā but everywhere in Vraja and Uttar Pradesh and Bihar, this is followed. We also follow this. We keep a *śālagrāma* in a big cucumber.

Śrīpāda Mādhava Mahārāja: Or a big fruit, like a watermelon.

Śrīla Nārāyaṇa Gosvāmī Mahārāja: But especially we use the cucumber. Then, at the time of Śrī Kṛṣṇa's birth, considering that Mother Yaśodā is giving birth to Kṛṣṇa, we take the *śālagrāma* out of the cucumber.

So this is not *apasiddhānta*; it is not against the conclusions of Vedic scripture. Moreover this attracts many guests, and in this way we inject them with spiritual impressions.

Śrīpāda Mādhava Mahārāja: By that gathering, new devotees will come. Otherwise, the current of *bhakti* will stop.

Śrīla Nārāyaṇa Gosvāmī Mahārāja: We call everyone to the temple to hear *hari-kathā*, but why do we distribute so much delicious *prasādam* to them? This is not *hari-kathā*, so why do we do this? It is to attract them. We distribute *prasādam* to rich persons as well. By honoring that *prasādam*, they get *sukṛti* (pious credit).

Brajanātha dāsa: I have read in scripture that *rāgānuga-bhakti* begins when our intelligence is purified.

Śrīla Nārāyaṇa Gosvāmī Mahārāja: It does not depend on intelligence. It depends on the activities and impressions of one's past births. Attachment to a *rāgānuga bhakta* comes by serving and hearing. It will never come by intelligence or by purification of heart. *Bhakti* is different. It may be that one has a good character, that one is honest, or that one is very learned – like the Māyāvadis, who are learned and with no worldly ambition. Still, that person may have no *sukṛti* to be able to follow even *vaidhī-bhakti*, what to speak of *rāgānuga-bhakti*.

Brajanātha dāsa: If the first stage of *bhajana* is *guru-padāśraya*, taking shelter of the lotus feet of a bonafide *guru*...

Śrīla Nārāyaṇa Gosvāmī Mahārāja: First he will hear all *tattvas* and pastimes related to Śrī Kṛṣṇa from pure Vaiṣṇavas, then some *sukṛti* will come, and then he will have a desire to hear topics related to *rāgānuga-bhakti*.

Brajanātha dāsa: Can one be *rāgānuga* if he does not properly take shelter of *sad-guru* (a bonafide, self-realized *guru*)?

Śrīla Nārāyaṇa Gosvāmī Mahārāja: Never.

Brajanātha dāsa: If one takes shelter properly, even if one has not such good character, he can have it?

Śrīla Nārāyaṇa Gosvāmī Mahārāja: Yes, *bhakti* is like Kṛṣṇa Himself; independent. "*Bhakti svatantra avalambana ana, tahi adhīna jñāna vijñāna* – *Bhakti* is completely independent, like Kṛṣṇa Himself. *Jñāna* and *vijñāna* cannot produce any permanent results unless they are related with *bhakti*."

Brajanātha dāsa: Nowadays, some devotees are propagating a path called 'natural *bhakti*' [no need for regulative principles] in the name of *rāgānuga-bhakti*, but it is hard to understand how they are taking shelter of *guru*.

Śrīla Nārāyaṇa Gosvāmī Mahārāja: Yes, *rāgānuga-bhakti* is very rare.

muktānām api siddhānāṁ
nārāyaṇa-parāyaṇaḥ
sudurlabhaḥ praśāntātmā
koṭiṣv api mahā-mune

(*Śrīmad-Bhāgavatam* 6.14.5)

> O great sage, out of many millions of materially liberated people who are free from ignorance, and out of many millions of *siddhas* who have nearly attained perfection, there is hardly one pure devotee of Nārāyaṇa. Only such a devotee is actually completely satisfied and peaceful.

James: What are the ways by which a conditioned soul can recognize the pure Vaiṣṇava?

Śrīla Nārāyaṇa Gosvāmī Mahārāja: A conditioned soul cannot recognize a pure Vaiṣṇava. He can hear from the Vaiṣṇavas, and by regularly hearing, that pure Vaiṣṇava's mercy will come in his heart. Then, little by little by little, he will begin to realize. Otherwise, it is not possible.

Vraja-kiśorī dāsī: Śrīla Gurudeva, he's wondering: If conditioned souls can't recognize a pure *guru*, how can they accept him as their *guru*?

Śrīpāda Mādhava Mahārāja: Gurudeva just explained that an understanding comes by associating with, and hearing from, Vaiṣṇavas.

Śrīla Nārāyaṇa Gosvāmī Mahārāja: (To James) I suggest that you digest what I have told in my classes. Then there will be no question.

January 9, 2008
Morning Walk

Veṇu-gopāla dāsa: If such a great devotee as Uddhava could not pass the *gopīs*' 'entrance examination,' thus showing that he was ineligible to learn from them how to get *prema* like theirs, how can I hope to get such *prema*?

Śrīla Nārāyaṇa Gosvāmī Mahārāja: He is a *siddha-bhakta*, a devotee already at the stage of perfection (as a friend and relative), so he cannot attain a new relationship with Kṛṣṇa. But we are now independent in the sense that we are free to endeavor for that *prema*. If by serving and hearing from a *rasika tattva-jña* Vaiṣṇava one develops greed for serving the *gopīs* and Śrī Śrī Rādhā-Kṛṣṇa, then, by devotional practices one can go to Goloka Vṛndāvana. One can even attain the state of enjoying the *rāsa* dance with the *gopīs*, to serve them there.

Śrīpāda Padmanābha Mahārāja: Śrīla Gurudeva, in that connection, we hear that Śrī Nārada Muni, who is also *siddha*, situated in his eternally perfect spiritual body, performed many austerities at Nārada-kuṇḍa, and he attained the body of a *gopī*. He was already *siddha*, and yet he attained it, so why could Uddhava not get it?

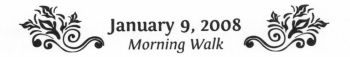

Śrīla Nārāyaṇa Gosvāmī Mahārāja: Uddhava will not attain a *gopī* body. Nārada eternally has so many forms in all the sweet pastimes of Kṛṣṇa. In one form he is Madhumaṅgala, Kṛṣṇa's cowherd boy friend; in a second form he is Nāradī Gopī; in another form, in Vaikuṇṭha, he is with Lord Nārāyaṇa; and he has another form in Svarga (heaven) with the demigods. He has so many eternal forms.

Śrīpāda Mādhava Mahārāja: Baladeva Prabhu is another example of this. He has *vātsalya* (parental mood), *sakhya* (the mood of a cowherd friend), *dāsya* (the mood of a servant), and even *mādhurya* (the mood of a *gopī*) in the form of Anaṅga Mañjarī.

Śrīla Nārāyaṇa Gosvāmī Mahārāja: But others – like Nanda Bābā and Yaśodā, Vasudeva and Devakī, Uddhava, and Akrūra – cannot add other *rasas* to their already eternally existing *rasa*.

If one has a *sthāyī-bhāva* (the foundational ecstasy of a particular relationship with Kṛṣṇa) in only one mood, he will always be in that one mood.

In the beginning of one's devotional practices, by hearing about the Lord's pastimes, one may want to serve Śrī Śrī Rādhā-Kṛṣṇa, and he may also want to serve Śrī Rāmacandra. In that case he will think about Rāma and His associates like Hanumān, Bharata, and Lakṣmaṇa, and he will also meditate on Śrī Kṛṣṇa's pastimes with His *sakhās*, or with Nanda Bābā and Yaśodā, or with the *gopīs*. In other words, in the beginning one is not situated in his permanent relationship. One will sometimes be attracted to a particular relationship when he hears about it, and at other times he may become attracted to another service relationship when he hears about it.

A devotee in our line can have two spiritual forms – one in the pastimes of Śrī Caitanya Mahāprabhu and another in the pastimes of Śrī Kṛṣṇa. These two relationships are eternal, and thus they are dormant from the beginning of such a person's devotional practices.

Dhruva dāsa: Gurudeva, does the soul somehow separate to have two forms in two pastimes?

Śrīla Nārāyaṇa Gosvāmī Mahārāja: Kṛṣṇa is *akhaṇḍa-tattva*. *Akhaṇḍa* means undivided, or whole, so how is it possible that He manifests in millions of forms?

We cannot imagine anything inconceivable, even in this world. How have the trees come? Seeds come from trees, and trees again come from seeds. Flowers come and leaves come. How does all this occur? We cannot imagine this. Everything about Śrī Kṛṣṇa is inconceivable.

Dhruva dāsa: Consciousness is always expanding, and Kṛṣṇa is always expanding. So do Kṛṣṇa's devotees also expand, even in their perfect spiritual forms?

Śrīla Nārāyaṇa Gosvāmī Mahārāja: Yes. For example, Mother Yaśodā has unlimited forms. Wherever Kṛṣṇa is, she is. This is true for Nanda Bābā also, and for Madhumaṅgala and all of Kṛṣṇa's other associates as well. But their *rasa*, their particular relationship with Kṛṣṇa, remains the same.

Veṇu-gopāla dāsa: Gurudeva, this is my friend James. This is his first time meeting with you and the Vaiṣṇavas. He is a school teacher.

Śrīla Nārāyaṇa Gosvāmī Mahārāja: (To James) Try to understand this philosophy – that you are not this body. Are you your body?

James: Hmmm

Śrīla Nārāyaṇa Gosvāmī Mahārāja: This body is a bag of stool, urine, blood, and so many other nasty things. After some time you will become old and give up this body. At that time, whatever you have been earning, you will not be able to take a single farthing with you; and your body will be placed in a burial ground. Where will you be after that?

There is soul. It is due to the presence of your soul that you are living, thinking, and going here and there. If the soul leaves the body, the body no longer functions; it will decay.

January 9, 2008
Darśana

Śrīla Nārāyaṇa Gosvāmī Mahārāja: On this visit, fifty devotees took *harināma* and *dīkṣā* initiation. The devotee congregation is gradually becoming bigger here. So I want senior devotees like Kṛṣṇa-kānta Prabhu and Balarāma Prabhu to increase their preaching; they know so much.

Also, Paṇḍitajī (Ajaya-kṛṣṇa dāsa) is very, very qualified. He has now left Māyāvāda philosophy and is hearing our classes. He is much more attracted to us now, and he has become a pure Vaiṣṇava. He was a teacher in a Sanskrit college, so he knows how to speak eloquently. He has so much speaking power, and now he is reading my books.

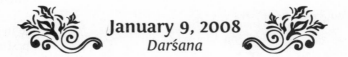

I think it is proper that on holidays like Janmāṣṭamī and Ekādaśī, and on Sundays, all of you should attend the programs at the farm, and give classes there also. Paṇḍitajī should give respect to the senior Vaiṣṇavas. Preach together, without difference of opinion, and give respect to each other. In this way so many new devotees will come.

I have created this harmonious situation in so many places. In Houston, for example, all the devotees are together, giving respect to each other and helping each other. In Mathurā, India, I used to go to homes and give programs. I used to invite those in each home to our grand-scale Janmāṣṭamī procession with horses, camels, elephants, *kīrtana* parties, big bands, and with more than 5,000 devotees performing *kīrtana*. In this way I have preached in Mathurā, Navadvīpa, and so many other places.

Try to preach like this – all together. There should be no difference of opinion. You can take turns preaching, and you can do house programs. I think that many new persons will be coming to the *āśrama*, so they should hear all the topics that I have been speaking about.

Dāmodara, are you coming to Fiji?

Dāmodara dāsa: Yes.

Śrīla Nārāyaṇa Gosvāmī Mahārāja: Very good.

Veṇu-gopāla dāsa: Śrīla Gurudeva, when will you be returning to New Zealand?

Śrīla Nārāyaṇa Gosvāmī Mahārāja: After five days.

Veṇu-gopāla dāsa: And after that?

Śrīla Nārāyaṇa Gosvāmī Mahārāja: I will come when the temple is completed. All of you please help Dāmodara Prabhu with the temple. All of you.

Śrīpāda Mādhava Mahārāja: Preaching will increase by conducting house programs. When you go to a devotee's house, he will invite others…

Śrīla Nārāyaṇa Gosvāmī Mahārāja: I want the temple to be completed so that I can come and establish Ṭhākurjī (install the Deity). Perhaps the entire construction will take two years.

(To Candramukhī and Rāgalekhā dāsīs) You and your sister can come and preach here from time to time. New Zealand is close to Australia.

Veṇu-gopāla dāsa: During the next two years, before the temple is built, should we get together at the same place every week or should we have house programs?

Śrīla Nārāyaṇa Gosvāmī Mahārāja: There should be house programs, and also programs at the *āśrama*. When there is no program at the *āśrama*, house programs may be held.

Śrīpāda Mādhava Mahārāja: By having house programs, preaching will increase. People will call their friends; so many devotees will be inspired and take initiation. House programs can be held on Saturdays, and the regular weekly program can be held on Sundays.

Vṛndā dāsī: We have Śrī Śrī Gaura-Nitāi Ṭhākurjī, and somebody told me that we should make our offering to Rādhā-Kṛṣṇa before offering to Gaura-Nitāi. Is that correct? Previously I offered straight to Gaura-Nitāi.

Śrīla Nārāyaṇa Gosvāmī Mahārāja: You can offer to both at the same time. You can utter the *mantra, śrīṁ klīṁ rādhā-kṛṣṇābhyāṁ namaḥ* and *klīṁ gaurāya svāhā.*

Śyāmarāṇī dāsī: She has Gaura-Nitāi Deities, so what about Nityānanda Prabhu?

Śrīla Nārāyaṇa Gosvāmī Mahārāja: If you can, you can offer the *bhoga* to each of Them on different plates.

Brajanātha dāsa: They don't have Rādhā-Kṛṣṇa.

Śrīla Nārāyaṇa Gosvāmī Mahārāja: Then you can offer by *gaura-mantra* and *nityānanda-mantra.* If it is given to Gauracandra, it is automatically given to Rādhā and Kṛṣṇa.

Candramukhī dāsī: What is the *mantra* for Nityānanda Prabhu?

Śrīla Nārāyaṇa Gosvāmī Mahārāja: *Oṁ nityānandaya namaḥ.*

January 9, 2008
Airport Darśana

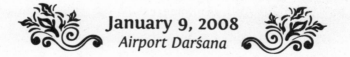

Śyāmarāṇī dāsī: Several times you have told us that when we pray to Lalitā, Viśākhā, or Girirāja Govardhana, they do not hear us because we are not *śaraṇāgata* (surrendered) devotees. When I pray to Śrīla Bhaktivinoda Ṭhākura, who is closer to us than Lalitā or Govardhana, is he hearing us? Who is hearing us when we pray to them all?

Śrīla Nārāyaṇa Gosvāmī Mahārāja: Gurudeva.

Śyāmarāṇī dāsī: Whomever we pray to, only Gurudeva is hearing us?

Śrīla Nārāyaṇa Gosvāmī Mahārāja: Gurudeva hears you and mercifully tells Śrī Kṛṣṇa. Kṛṣṇa does not hear your prayers, because He is always engaged in pastimes with the *gopīs*.

Śyāmarāṇī dāsī: But what if we pray to Śrīla Bhaktivinoda Ṭhākura or Śrīla Svarūpa Dāmodara Gosvāmī, who are nearer to us? Are they hearing?

Śrīla Nārāyaṇa Gosvāmī Mahārāja: You should pray to all of them through Gurudeva, because Gurudeva is hearing.

Śyāmarāṇī dāsī: And Gurudeva tells them to kindly listen to us?

Śrīla Nārāyaṇa Gosvāmī Mahārāja: That is why in Deity worship (*arcana*) we give the *bhoga* (un-offered foodstuffs) to Gurudeva and pray, "O Gurudeva, please offer this to Śrīmatī Rādhikā, Śrī Kṛṣṇa, and the others."

Śyāmarāṇī dāsī: So you and our Prabhupāda are very important. We can't go to anybody except through you both.

Śrīla Nārāyaṇa Gosvāmī Mahārāja: Through Śrīla Bhaktivedānta Svāmī Mahārāja. I am not qualified.

Madhu-paṇḍita dāsa: Can our *ācāryas* hear our prayers on their appearance and disappearance days? Or, is it still only through you?

Śrīla Nārāyaṇa Gosvāmī Mahārāja: First offer your prayers to Gurudeva. Offer your obeisances to him and take permission from him, and then offer your prayers and glorifications to the *ācārya* whose appearance or disappearance day it is.

Lautoka, Fiji

January 11-16, 2008

January 11, 2008
Morning Walk

Balarāma dāsa: In the *maṅgala-ārati* song, Śrīla Bhakti Prajñāna Keśava Gosvāmī Mahārāja describes how Vṛndā-devī called all the parrots to wake up Śrī Śrī Rādhā-Kṛṣṇa from Their sleep. Why did he write about the pond after that?

kusumita sarovare kamala-hillola
maṅgala saurabha bahe pavana kallola
(*Śrī Gaura-Govinda Maṅgala-āratī*, Verse 7)

In the pond, which is filled with many varieties of flowers, the lotuses sway in the center. The breezes spread their auspicious aromas in all directions, bringing pure delight and joy to all.

What is the relevance? What is the sequence?

Śrīla Nārāyaṇa Gosvāmī Mahārāja: It is all right. This scene may take place after Their awakening.

Balarāma dāsa: But They are running to go back home so that nobody discovers Them.

Śrīla Nārāyaṇa Gosvāmī Mahārāja: No, no. They are still engaged in Their loving pastimes at that time.

Balarāma dāsa: They don't have to go back home?

Śrīla Nārāyaṇa Gosvāmī Mahārāja: Vṛndā-devī will again call so many parrots and other birds, and also peacocks, to remind the Divine Couple that it is time to return to Their respective homes [the song says, *mayūra śukādi sāri kata pikarāja*]. Finally an old monkey will come, and then They will leave for Their homes.

Better to try to remove *anarthas* and all material attachments first, otherwise so many difficulties will come in our spiritual lives. So many devotees went to Rādhā-kuṇḍa *bābājīs*. The Rādhā-kuṇḍa *bābājīs* pretend to give them their *siddha-deha* (the completely spiritual body, which is fit to render service to the Transcendental Couple Rādhā and Kṛṣṇa), and tell them, "You should remember all the intimate pastimes of Rādhā and Kṛṣṇa."

And they began to do so. Then, after some time they met some ladies, they began to live with those ladies, and then they begot children.

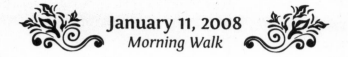

Only when you come to an advanced stage can you remember these pastimes. You should know about the Lord's pastimes, but don't try to do anything artificial. The ability to properly meditate will come automatically.

Devotee: Gurudeva, can you give an explanation of this verse:

ataḥ śrī-kṛṣṇa-nāmādi
na bhaved grāhyam indriyaiḥ
sevonmukhe hi jihvādau
svayam eva sphuraty adaḥ

(*Bhakti-rasāmṛta-sindhu* 1.2.234)

> Material senses cannot appreciate Kṛṣṇa's holy name, form, qualities, and pastimes. When a conditioned soul is awakened to Kṛṣṇa consciousness and renders service by using his tongue to chant the Lord's holy name and taste the remnants of the Lord's food, the tongue becomes purified and one gradually comes to understand who Kṛṣṇa really is.

Śrīpāda Mādhava Mahārāja: By chanting Kṛṣṇa's name and serving *guru* and Vaiṣṇavas, He will gradually manifest in our hearts.

Śrīla Nārāyaṇa Gosvāmī Mahārāja: Kṛṣṇa, His name, His form, His qualities – everything about Him – is transcendental and beyond the limit of the mind or any other sense. So try to chant the holy name. Then gradually, by chanting, when you become qualified to remember these pastimes, they will come automatically.

Jagannātha dāsa (from Russia)**:** Śrīla Gurudeva, you said that one should not remember these pastimes artificially. But *vaidhī-bhakti* is artificial. Did you mean something else by that?

Śrīla Nārāyaṇa Gosvāmī Mahārāja: *Vaidhī-bhakti* is not artificial. If you pray, "O Kṛṣṇa, please remove all my *anarthas* (bad thoughts and habits), be pleased with me and give me pure *bhakti*," that is not artificial. If a devotee engages in *śravaṇam* (hearing Kṛṣṇa's names and glories), *kīrtanam* (chanting His names and glories), *viṣṇu-smaraṇam* (remembering Him), this is not artificial.

Jagannātha dāsa: But in *vaidhī-bhakti* one has to sometimes force himself to think and act properly.

Śrīla Nārāyaṇa Gosvāmī Mahārāja: No harm; this is practice. If your mind is not fixed in one-pointed devotion, then you must bring it back from the other places. You are hearing *hari-kathā*; this is not artificial. You are performing *kīrtana*; this is not artificial. You are worshiping; this is not artificial.

Devotee: What do you mean by artificial?

Śrīla Nārāyaṇa Gosvāmī Mahārāja: If you are thinking about Rādhā and Kṛṣṇa's pastimes in a way that is beyond your qualification, this is artificial. If you are thinking, "Now I have realized my *siddha-deha*," but you have not actually realized it, this is artificial.

Balarāma dāsa: Is there a reason why we take off our shoes when we offer our obeisances?

Śrīla Nārāyaṇa Gosvāmī Mahārāja: You don't know?

Balarāma dāsa: No, I don't know; that is why I am asking.

Śrīla Nārāyaṇa Gosvāmī Mahārāja: When you take *prasādam*, what do you do? Do you take *prasādam* with shoes or without shoes?

Balarāma dāsa: Well, it depends. If somebody comes to me with your *mahā-prasādam*, I will take that straightaway.

Śrīla Nārāyaṇa Gosvāmī Mahārāja: That is a special case.

Balarāma dāsa: But normally we don't take *prasādam* while wearing shoes.

Śrīla Nārāyaṇa Gosvāmī Mahārāja: We should take off our shoes and then offer obeisances. If you are not allowed to take shoes to the altar when you are worshiping the Deity, how can you offer your *daṇḍavats* to *gurudeva* and the Vaiṣṇavas with your shoes on?

If you do not take off your shoes at the time of offering obeisances, *bhakti* will at once run away. Bhakti-devī will think, "He is neglecting me." Try to learn all these principles by seeing the activities of elevated Vaiṣṇavas. Watch their dealings.

Devotees should practice the devotional process just as Śrīla Bhaktivinoda Ṭhākura, Śrīla Rūpa Gosvāmī, Śrīla Sanātana Gosvāmī, and Śrīla Raghunātha dāsa Gosvāmī practiced. Do you know how Śrīla Raghunātha dāsa Gosvāmī practiced? What type of *prasādam* did he use to take? Did he take delicious *prasādam*?

Balarāma dāsa: He took one leaf-cup of buttermilk every three days.

Śrīla Nārāyaṇa Gosvāmī Mahārāja: When he was in Jagannātha Purī, he used to eat rotten rice that even the cows rejected. He used to wash that rice and then eat it.

First be renounced enough from material desires to be able to act like Śrīla Raghunātha dāsa Gosvāmī, and then meditate on the Lord's intimate pastimes.

January 14, 2008

Darśana

At the home of Nitin Punja

Śrīla Nārāyaṇa Gosvāmī Mahārāja: True *sādhus* do not go to other people's homes for their own needs. They do not need anything; they can easily receive a *capātī* from anywhere. They have left everything material, and some of them have been *brahmacārīs* from birth. They come to others' homes only to remind them: "Listen, you are not residents of this world. You are refugees. Old age will come soon. After that you will give up this body, and you will have to leave everything behind. You must endeavor to become free from the entanglement of this material world. Perform your work, but don't be attached."

In order to make everyone aware of these facts, *sādhus* travel here and there. Śrī Nārada Muni, Sanātana, Sanandana, Sanaka, Sanat Kumāra, Śrī Śukadeva Gosvāmī, Śrī Caitanya Mahāprabhu, and Śrī Nityānanda Prabhu went to the homes of the fallen souls. What did they do there? They gave the same instructions that I am giving you now.

They would say, "O brother, I have come to your house, asking for a donation. What is that donation? Just chant Śrī Kṛṣṇa's holy names: 'Hare Kṛṣṇa Hare Kṛṣṇa, Kṛṣṇa, Kṛṣṇa, Hare Hare, Hare Rāma Hare Rāma, Rāma, Rāma, Hare Hare.' This is all you need to do, and in this way your life will be auspicious. Simply avoid eating meat and fish, don't take alcohol and other intoxicants, and do *bhajana* of Kṛṣṇa. *Kṛṣṇa-bhajana* is the first duty of our life, and the final duty of our life. Perform your duties and do your work, but don't forget Kṛṣṇa."

This is why we have come – to remind you. In modern times, Śrīla Bhaktisiddhānta Sarasvatī Ṭhākura Prabhupāda started this preaching movement. He made *sannyāsīs*, *brahmacārīs*, and *gṛhastha bhaktas*, and told them to go house to house to tell the residents: "Meditate on the Supreme Lord. Please remember that you are not this body; you are soul. Therefore, engage in *bhajana* of the Lord."

May all the members of your family be happy, and may your lives be auspicious. Even if you don't have much time – when you first wake up and before going to sleep – chant the Lord's names.

January 14, 2008
Darśana
At the home of Jagadīśa dāsa

Śrīla Nārāyaṇa Gosvāmī Mahārāja: This human birth is very rare. Only in this human birth can one understand that this body is not the soul.

(To Jagadīśa dāsa's teenage son, Garish) You are sitting in front of me and speaking with me. But suppose that your life-air leaves your body; will you be able to speak or not? Why not? Your mouth is here, you are sitting here; simply your life-air has gone out; only your soul is not here. What is the problem?

Garish: I don't know.

Śrīla Nārāyaṇa Gosvāmī Mahārāja: What class are you in? You are in college, aren't you?

If someone cuts off your feet, you can still speak; but if your soul leaves your body, will you be able to speak with me?

Garish: No

Śrīla Nārāyaṇa Gosvāmī Mahārāja: Why not? The same body is there when it was speaking, but without the soul it can only lie down. Why can't it speak?

Who are you? Who is the 'I'? Although this body is not 'I', we think we are this body. We are not this body. In this body, there is a soul and Supersoul. We are soul, and that is 'I'. And regarding the Supersoul, He is controlling everything and He is the creator of the entire universe.

Previously you were in this world as a dog, a pig, and so many other animals. At those times you were traveling to different places, seeking happiness, but there was no happiness anywhere. There were only great suffering and problems.

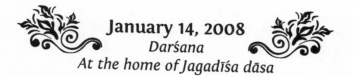

Kṛṣṇa is very merciful; He has now mercifully given you this human form of life. He did this so that somehow or other, by one reason or another, you will meet a *sādhu*. That *sādhu* is someone who has realized Kṛṣṇa and his own self, and who is detached from worldly desires. If you meet such a *sādhu*, he will convince you that you are not this body, and that only in this human form can you realize that you are a soul.

Nowhere in this world is there any happiness. One day you will have to become old – even a little boy will become old. Neither doctors nor scientists can check old age for even a moment. One day you will have to give up your body, and you will not be able to take anything in this world with you; not your house, not a penny, not a hair, not your father, mother, or anyone else. You will go alone, and where you will go, even you do not know. Therefore, the first aim and object of our life in this world should be to understand the answers to these questions: "Who am I? Why am I suffering? Why am I dying and again taking birth? How can this cycle be finished?"

Kṛṣṇa has mercifully given us this human form, which we must utilize to please Him. To please Him is not so difficult. Simply chant: "Hare Kṛṣṇa, Hare Kṛṣṇa, Kṛṣṇa Kṛṣṇa, Hare Hare, Hare Rāma, Hare Rāma, Rāma Rāma, Hare Hare." Kṛṣṇa has invested all His power, mercy, and attributes in His name; His name is very, very powerful. Don't think that chanting His name is like calling a dog's name. There is no difference between Kṛṣṇa's name and Kṛṣṇa Himself.

January 15, 2008
Excerpt of a darśana
At the home of Śrīmatī Gaurīmātā dāsī

Śrīla Nārāyaṇa Gosvāmī Mahārāja: (To Gaurīmātā dāsī) Once, when Śrīmatī Rādhikā's in-laws were away from home, Kṛṣṇa disguised Himself as a heavenly damsel and came to Her house in Yāvaṭa. He did this for the purpose of relishing Rādhikā's words and moods concerning Her love for Him.

At first the disguised Kṛṣṇa was completely silent. Seeing this beautiful 'celestial damsel,' Śrīmatī Rādhikā eagerly accepted 'Her' as Her *sakhī*. Rādhikā asked the celestial damsel-disguised Kṛṣṇa many questions, but still She did not speak at all. Rādhikā concluded that surely this attractive damsel was sick, and that is why She was not giving any answer.

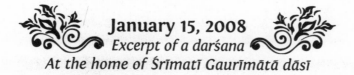

After some time, when Rādhikā had spoken to Her at length, the damsel told Rādhikā, "I have heard about Your glories, so I came here (to the Earth planet) from the heavenly planets to meet with You. When I arrived here I saw that Kṛṣṇa's *rāsa-līlā* was going on at Vaṁśīvaṭa in Vṛndāvana. When, for some reason or other You left the *rāsa* dance for the forest, Kṛṣṇa left all the other *gopīs* to follow You. But, after being together with You for some time, He also left You. I became very angry with Him when I saw Your pitiful condition. Therefore, I have come to You."

Saying this, the disguised Kṛṣṇa began to describe Kṛṣṇa's many faults. She said, "It is true that Kṛṣṇa has all good qualities, but one bad quality destroys all the good ones. You have left everything – Your father, mother, brother, friends, husband, society, shyness, and the orders of all Your elders – to love Kṛṣṇa. Yet, He is so cruel towards You that He left You and disappeared. Therefore, according to My opinion, You should not love Him. If You do, You will suffer even more in the future."

Hearing these words of Kṛṣṇa disguised as a celestial damsel, Śrīmatī Rādhikā began to explain the nature of *prema*, and Her explanation comprises the book, *Śrī Prema-sampuṭa*.

January 15, 2008
Groundbreaking Ceremony For The New Temple

Śrīla Nārāyaṇa Gosvāmī Mahārāja: (To Jagannātha dāsa and Kānti-lāl dāsa) It should not be a small temple. Build it like our Govardhana temple. It should be a splendid temple that can seat at least three-hundred people. There should be a garden with fruits and flowers, and there should be a place for people who do service in the temple. The entrance should have a beautiful archway with the name of the temple written on it, and there should be a beautiful lawn in front of the temple where people first enter the temple grounds.

[Śrīla Mahārāja then offered the first brick to inaugurate the foundation of the temple. Devotees returned the earth to the dug-out hole in the land, where the Deities' altar would be situated when the temple would be built, and which was now filled with auspicious substances to ignite the success of the future temple.]

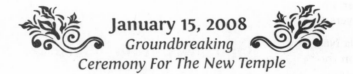

January 16, 2008
Airport Darśana

Śrīla Nārāyaṇa Gosvāmī Mahārāja: You are coming?

Sāvitrī dāsī: Yes, I will be coming after one week. I am staying here until then.

Śrīla Nārāyaṇa Gosvāmī Mahārāja: What will you do here?

Sāvitrī dāsī: I will give classes at the *āśrama* on Sunday, and also on Wednesday.

Balarāma dāsa: Śrīla Gurudeva, what is your opinion about the Indian preacher, Kṛpālu Mahārāja?

Śrīla Nārāyaṇa Gosvāmī Mahārāja: Don't hear from him; there is some poison.

Śyāmarāṇī dāsī: Your daughter Kṛṣṇa-kāminī in Vṛndāvana wants me to ask you this question: You have given us so many prayers to utter when we wake up in the morning. Are there any particular prayers that we should say before taking rest at night?

Śrīla Nārāyaṇa Gosvāmī Mahārāja: There are so many – thousands upon thousands. You can recite verses to Śrī Śrī Rādhā-Kṛṣṇa, Śrī Caitanya Mahāprabhu, Gurudeva, Vṛndāvana-dhāma, Navadvīpa-dhāma, and Śrī Harināma. To Harināma you can offer such prayers as this:

jayati jayati nāmānanda-rūpaṁ murārer
viramita-nija-dharma-dhyāna-pūjādi-yatnam
katham api sakṛd āttaṁ mukti-daṁ prāṇināṁ yat
paramamṛtam ekaṁ jīvanaṁ bhūṣaṇaṁ me

(*Śrī Bṛhad-bhāgavatāmṛta* 1.1.9)

All glories, all glories to the name of Kṛṣṇa-Murāri, the enemy of lust and the embodiment of divine bliss! It halts the cycle of birth and death and relieves one of all painful endeavors in practicing religion, meditation, charity, deity worship, and austerity. It awards liberation to one who utters it even once. *Kṛṣṇa-nāma* stands alone as the supreme nectar and sole treasure of my life.

And to Vṛndāvana-dhāma, you can offer such prayers as this:

jayati jayati vṛndāraṇyam etan murāreḥ
priyatamam ati-sādhusvānta-vaikuṇṭha-vāsāt
ramayati sa sadā gāḥ pālayan yatra gopīḥ
svarita-madhura-veṇur vardhayan prema rāse

(*Śrī Bṛhad-bhāgavatāmṛta* 1.1.5)

All glories, all glories to Śrī Vṛndāvana-dhāma; where Śrī Murāri enjoys residing more than He enjoys residing in the hearts of *sādhus* or even in Vaikuṇṭha; where He forever tends the cows, and where, by playing sweet melodies on the flute, He increases the *gopīs*' amorous love for Him.

And to Śrī Caitanya Mahāprabhu, such prayers as this:

kālaḥ kalir balina indriya-vairi-vargāḥ
śrī bhakti-mārga iha kaṇṭaka-koṭi-ruddhaḥ
hā hā kva yāmi vikalaḥ kim ahaṁ karomi
caitanya-candra yadi nādya kṛpāṁ karoṣi

(*Śrī Caitanya-candrāmṛta* 125,
by Prabodhānanda Sarasvatī)

Now it is the age of Kali. My enemies, the senses, are very strong. The beautiful path of *bhakti* is spiked with countless thorns (like *karma*, *jñāna*, and unrestricted sense enjoyment). My spirit is weak. My senses are powerful and agitated. O what shall I do? Where shall I go? O Lord Caitanya-candra, if you do not grant me Your mercy, what shall I do to save myself?

"O Śrī Caitanya Mahāprabhu, if You are not merciful to me, where else shall I go?"

Śyāmarāṇī dāsī: Nirmala Dīdī has a question. She is asking: Whenever you come, so many new people get initiated, and after you leave they don't get trained. They hardly come to any programs, and the devotees generally don't take the time to go to them. Nirmala Dīdī wants to ask for your blessings to be able to give classes and train people.

Śrīla Nārāyaṇa Gosvāmī Mahārāja: She should take the responsibility. She should train others, because she is senior now. The wife of Jagannātha Prabhu, Kṛṣṇa-līlā, is also expert, so she should also give training. And Jagannātha Prabhu is more qualified than any *brahmacārī* or *sannyāsī*.

I give *harināma* initiation, and then I leave for another place. Devotees then become somewhat weak and no longer have much enthusiasm – but the seed (*bīja*) is still there. This seed cannot be destroyed. Later the 'rains' come, at which time that seed will sprout. In other words, when I come or other preachers come, such as Tīrtha Mahārāja and Dāmodara Mahārāja, and also when Jagannātha Prabhu is here, this is like rain. When this rain comes, the seeds of devotion in the new initiates sprout and grow. If one commits offenses to *śrī gurudeva* and to Vaiṣṇavas that seed will be destroyed, otherwise it cannot be destroyed.

There is also a type of grass that burns during the summer, but the root remains. Later, when there is rain, it grows again.

A businessman checks every evening to see how much money he has made that day. He checks to see whether he has made any profit or incurred any loss. If he has made profit he is very happy, and if he has made no profit or loss, that is okay. However, if he has incurred any loss, he becomes concerned and wonders, "What did I do to bring this loss?"

Similarly before we go to sleep, we should consider whether our *bhajana* is improving, diminishing, or remaining at the same level. If it is increasing, that is good – it is unlimited, so it can be always increasing. If it has remained at the same level, we must consider how it can increase. If it is decreasing, if the mind is not attracted to *bhajana* and *hari-kathā* and is always running after material enjoyment or concerned about maintaining business, the children's education, or getting a house, car, and other things, then we must consider how to improve.

So, be careful.

Śyāmarāṇī dāsī: Some devotees say that only your small books like *The Way of Love* should go to the public, and big books like *Bhakti-rasāmṛta-sindhu-bindu* or *Brahma-saṁhitā* are only for devotees.

Śrīla Nārāyaṇa Gosvāmī Mahārāja: No. They are for all.

Śyāmarāṇī dāsī: All of your books are for all people?

Śrīpāda Mādhava Mahārāja: All books for all. Yes.

Śrīla Nārāyaṇa Gosvāmī Mahārāja: All for all. Yes.

Śyāmarāṇī dāsī: Some say that your big books, with all the Sanskrit terms and lofty concepts in them, might as well be in Chinese or any other foreign language, because no new person will understand.

Śrīla Nārāyaṇa Gosvāmī Mahārāja: Our books should go to all, whether they are *nāstika* (atheist), *āstika* (theist); irreligious or religious.

Śrīpāda Mādhava Mahārāja: Śrīla Gurudeva said this before. All the books should go everywhere.

Śrīla Nārāyaṇa Gosvāmī Mahārāja: All.

Śyāmarāṇī dāsī: So even if they don't understand the language…

Śrīla Nārāyaṇa Gosvāmī Mahārāja: No harm.

Śyāmarāṇī dāsī: They will get *sukṛti* by even trying to read the book, or by just having the book in their homes?

Śrīla Nārāyaṇa Gosvāmī Mahārāja: If they will keep the book, oh, our purpose will be served.

Brajanātha dāsa: The books will find the right persons.

Śyāmarāṇī dāsī: Also, someone will come as a guest to the house of the person who took the book but did not read it, and that guest might read it.

Śrīla Nārāyaṇa Gosvāmī Mahārāja: Yes.

Murwillumbah, Australia
February 4-7, 2008

February 4, 2008
Morning Walk

Śrīla Nārāyaṇa Gosvāmī Mahārāja: Are there any questions?

Śrīpāda Dāmodara Mahārāja: Gurudeva, I have heard that the Eleventh Canto of *Śrīmad-Bhāgavatam* is the forehead of Kṛṣṇa. What is its speciality?

Śrīla Nārāyaṇa Gosvāmī Mahārāja: Which is superior, the mind or the heart?

Śrīpāda Dāmodara Mahārāja: Isn't it the same thing?

Śrīpāda Padmanābha Mahārāja: The heart is superior to the mind.

Śrīla Nārāyaṇa Gosvāmī Mahārāja: Yes. The heart is superior. Love is in the heart and *tattva* (established philosophical truth) is in the mind. Love and affection for Kṛṣṇa is superior to knowledge of His *tattva*. Therefore, the Tenth Canto is said to be the heart and the Eleventh Canto is the mind.

Śrīpāda Dāmodara Mahārāja: I once asked you what scripture Paramagurudeva liked to preach from, and you said it was the Eleventh Canto.

Śrīla Nārāyaṇa Gosvāmī Mahārāja: He wanted to emphasize *sādhana*, the regulative practices of *bhakti*. The Eleventh Canto includes the dialogues between Vasudeva Mahārāja and Nārada Ṛṣi, and within that is the discussion between the Nine Yogendras and Nemi Mahārāja. After that, Kṛṣṇa gave instruction to Uddhava in *Uddhava-saṁvāda*, and that is the best instruction for the practice of *sādhana*. All these conversations were presented to us for the development of our *sādhana*.

Śrīpāda Dāmodara Mahārāja: Vasudeva Mahārāja told Nārada Ṛṣi, "I prayed to Bhagavān, beseeching Him to become my son. I never asked Him for liberation."

Śrīla Nārāyaṇa Gosvāmī Mahārāja: This is because he was very polite and humble, not rough like you.

Śrīpāda Dāmodara Mahārāja: I stopped being rough, from yesterday.

Śrīla Nārāyaṇa Gosvāmī Mahārāja: I know that you cannot stop.

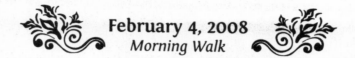

By birth and by nature he is like that; and he has associated with Śrīla Trivikrama Mahārāja, who spoke his mind to everyone. Śrīla Trivikrama Mahārāja was a very high-class Vaiṣṇava; a real Vaiṣṇava. He would reveal bluntly whatever he thought to be true, without ever caring for public opinion.

February 5, 2008
Morning Walk

Śrīpāda Padmanābha Mahārāja: This devotee has been associating with ISKCON for some years. He has not been initiated by any *guru*. He has some doubt. He is not sure whether or not he should remain in ISKCON. In ISKCON he heard that if one is not in that society, one is out of the line of Śrīla Prabhupāda Bhaktivedānta Svāmī Mahārāja.

Śrīla Nārāyaṇa Gosvāmī Mahārāja: Those who say this are bogus. Such persons cannot give *bhakti*; they can only collect money. They have so many schemes to make money, and so much money comes to them. Then, filling their pockets with that money, they run away from *bhakti* and *bhaktas*. Many of the most senior Vaiṣṇavas have left that institution and are coming to me.

Śrīpāda Dāmodara Mahārāja: Jason was collecting money for ISKCON for ten years.

Śrīla Nārāyaṇa Gosvāmī Mahārāja: I know that he can collect.

(To Jason) You can collect money for ISKCON, while associating with us for *bhakti*. I do not require money. I want only to help devotees.

Śrīpāda Padmanābha Mahārāja: Śrīla Gurudeva, sometimes, when the people in ISKCON hear such very bold and powerful statements from you, they criticize your words: They say with disdain, "Śrīla Nārāyaṇa Mahārāja says that there is no *bhakti* in ISKCON; only money." Can we say that in their society there may be some sincere devotees and that they are trying...

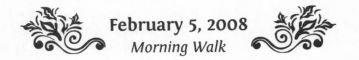

Śrīla Nārāyaṇa Gosvāmī Mahārāja: How can they be sincere? Their leaders are not sincere, so how can they be sincere? Those who are

sincere will be attracted to me. It is inevitable that they will come, because their Gurudeva, *parama-pūjyapāda* Śrīla Bhaktivedānta Svāmī Mahārāja, personally told me to help them. Whom will I help? I will help those who are sincere. Those who want to make money will never come; they will simply protest.

In general, ISKCON leaders do not chant more than sixteen rounds, and some of them do not even chant sixteen. I chant one *lākha* (sixty-four rounds) daily. If for some reason I do not complete a *lākha* one day, I complete it on the next day. If on some days I am engaged all day, then, by tongue, I constantly chant, "Hare Kṛṣṇa, Hare Kṛṣṇa." During airline flights I chant two or three *lākhas* (one-hundred twenty-eight or one-hundred ninety-two rounds).

Śrīpāda Mādhava Mahārāja: The longer the flight, the more Gurudeva chants.

Śrīpāda Padmanābha Mahārāja: Śrīla Gurudeva, hearing from Mādhava Mahārāja that when you go on long flights you chant so many rounds, I think of how impossible it would be for us to do this. I cannot even imagine chanting so many rounds.

Śrīpāda Mādhava Mahārāja: And when we arrive at the destination, he has no jetlag.

Śrīla Nārāyaṇa Gosvāmī Mahārāja: I do not sleep at all; only chanting, chanting, chanting.

Śrīpāda Padmanābha Mahārāja: Gurudeva, regarding the song written by Śrīla Bhaktivinoda Ṭhākura entitled *Gurudeva! Baḍa kṛpa kari*, in the second line he prays to his *guru*, "When will you make me qualified?"

I see that this is my dilemma. You have provided everything to us. You have given us all opportunities. You are giving us a place in the *dhāma* and instructing us to do one pointed *hari-bhajana*. Yet, I have no qualification. When will the day come that you will give me this qualification?

Śrīla Nārāyaṇa Gosvāmī Mahārāja: You have left your *gṛhastha āśrama*, your household life, and all other material situations for me. You do not collect money for yourself. If money comes to you, you try to give it to me in order to help with my book publication and other preaching projects. One day, if you are really sincere, pure *bhakti* will definitely come.

February 6, 2008
Morning Walk

Balarāma dāsa: Śrīla Gurudeva, some of your book distributors are in doubt as to whether the more philosophical books should be distributed to the general public, or if we should just concentrate on distributing simpler books.

Śrīpāda Mādhava Mahārāja: Śyāmarāṇī Dīdī asked this question in Fiji.

Śrīla Nārāyaṇa Gosvāmī Mahārāja: Give the books to those who want to take them, whether they are general persons or anyone else. Those who want the books will appreciate their value. They will think, "This is a good book." Give books to such persons.

Śrīpāda Mādhava Mahārāja: By reading the books, even general persons will become devotees.

Veṇu-gopāla dāsa: Śrīla Gurudeva, last night you discussed the Eleventh Canto of *Śrīmad-Bhāgavatam*. You explained how fear arises in the living entity when he misidentifies with the material body.

My question is this: How can I overcome fear? When I go in the ocean I am afraid of sharks, on land I am afraid of snakes; and I think that the cows I see are going to harm me in some way.

Śrīpāda Mādhava Mahārāja: He is asking about this verse:

bhayaṁ dvitīyābhiniveśataḥ syād
īśād apetasya viparyayo 'smṛtiḥ
tan-māyayāto budha ābhajet taṁ
bhaktyaikayeśaṁ guru-devatātmā

(*Śrīmad-Bhāgavatam* 11.2.37)

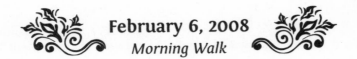

> Fear arises when a living entity misidentifies himself as the material body because of absorption in the external, illusory energy of the Lord. When the living entity thus turns away from the Supreme Lord, he also forgets his own constitutional position as His servant. This bewildering, fearful condition is induced by the potency of illusion, called *māyā*. Therefore, an intelligent person should engage unflinchingly in the unalloyed devotional service of the Lord, under the guidance of a bonafide spiritual

> master, whom he should accept as his worshipable Deity and as his very life and soul.

Śrīla Nārāyaṇa Gosvāmī Mahārāja: Fear exists when one is not performing *bhajana* of Kṛṣṇa. When you realize *kṛṣṇa-tattva*, all fear will go away automatically. One who knows that "I am a spirit soul; the soul can never be killed by anyone," will not be fearful. The wealth of the soul is Kṛṣṇa, and no one can take away that wealth. So why worry? A devotee is never fearful.

Dvitīyābhiniveśataḥ: Fear comes only when one desires *māyā*, sense gratification, in the form of wife, children, relatives, wealth, reputation, and similar things.

Why do you personally suffer when your relatives suffer? If one of your relatives dies, why would you weep?

Veṇu-gopāla dāsa: Because the body has gone…

Śrīla Nārāyaṇa Gosvāmī Mahārāja: No. It is because of your attachment.

Veṇu-gopāla dāsa: Because I'm attached to their body.

Śrīla Nārāyaṇa Gosvāmī Mahārāja: If your attachment is for Kṛṣṇa, you will have no material attachments and you will be happy.

Devotee: Gurudeva, you were saying last night that an *uttama-adhikārī* has to come down to the *madhyama* platform in order to give mercy. Can a *madhyama-adhikārī* who has come up from the *kaniṣṭhā-adhikārī* platform also give mercy?

Śrīla Nārāyaṇa Gosvāmī Mahārāja: The *madhyama-adhikārī* will give mercy to the innocent, and he will avoid those who are envious of *bhakti*, *bhakta*, and Bhagavān.

Śrīpāda Mādhava Mahārāja:

īśvare tad-adhīneṣu
bāliśeṣu dviṣatsu ca
prema-maitrī-kṛpopekṣā
yaḥ karoti sa madhyamaḥ
(*Śrīmad-Bhāgavatam* 11.2.46)

> An intermediate or second-class devotee, called *madhyama-adhikārī*, offers his love to the Supreme Personality of Godhead, is a sincere friend to all the devotees of the Lord, shows mercy to ignorant people who are innocent, and disregards those who are envious of the Supreme Personality of Godhead.

Śrīla Nārāyaṇa Gosvāmī Mahārāja: The *madhyama-adhikārī* you have described can only give mercy according to the limit of his capacity; not beyond that. He can give *hari-kathā* according to what he knows.

If Nārada Ṛṣi says to you, "*Kṛṣṇa-bhakti* will now come to you," at once you will dance and sing in *prema*. A *madhyama-adhikārī* cannot do this. He can give *hari-kathā*. In this way *bhakti* will gradually manifest, and then you will dance and sing.

How will this come about? The *madhyama-adhikārī* guides his followers in the right direction. He directs them to the pure devotee. Thus gradually, by exalted association, pure *bhakti* will manifest within their followers' hearts.

Balarāma dāsa: Śrīla Gurudeva, when you chant the verse *oṁ ajñāna-timirāndhasya*, you do not chant the word *oṁ*. Is there a reason for that? Do you chant it silently?

Śrīla Nārāyaṇa Gosvāmī Mahārāja: No *śloka* is preceded by *oṁ*.

Balarāma dāsa: It is written that way in our songbook.

Śrīla Nārāyaṇa Gosvāmī Mahārāja: I was not aware of that. I don't know who added that. *Ajñāna-timirāndhasya* is proper. Still, if one utters *oṁ* before reciting this, there is no harm in it. Let them do so.

Balarāma dāsa: I understand. I am wondering if there is any significance to chanting *oṁ*?

Śrīla Nārāyaṇa Gosvāmī Mahārāja: *Oṁ* is generally used in a *bīja-mantra* (seed *mantra*). [The seed contains all the ingredients to perfect the chanter's transcendental service-relationship with Śrī Kṛṣṇa.] For example: *oṁ nārāyaṇāya namaḥ*; *oṁ vāsudevāya namaḥ*; or *oṁ bhūr bhuvaḥ*.

Devotee: In the Eleventh Canto, when Lord Kṛṣṇa is speaking to Uddhavajī, it seems that there is a lot of emphasis on the *yoga* process. Kṛṣṇa is explaining how we have to take the subtle elements, merge them into the false ego, and then merge that into the *ātmā*. Should we very deeply study this process for meditation, or should we try simply to depend on Bhagavān?

Śrīla Nārāyaṇa Gosvāmī Mahārāja: The conclusion of Śrī Kṛṣṇa's instruction to Uddhava is that we should engage only in *bhakti-yoga* – not in *dhyāna-yoga* or any other *yoga* system. No other yoga system will suffice. The purport is that *yoga* really means *bhakti-yoga*.

The *Bhagavad-gītā* states:

sarva-dharmān parityajya
māṁ ekaṁ śaraṇaṁ vraja
ahaṁ tvāṁ sarva-pāpebhyo
mokṣayiṣyāmi mā śucaḥ

(*Bhagavad-gītā* 18.66)

> Abandon all varieties of religion and just surrender unto Me. I shall deliver you from all sinful reactions. Do not fear.

Mām ekaṁ śaraṇaṁ means "Adopt *bhakti-yoga* and give up everything else."

Are there any further questions about *bhakti*?

Kṛṣṇa-kānta dāsa: When Nṛsiṁha Bhagavān appeared to Prahlāda Mahārāja, was it His first appearance in this world?

Śrīla Nārāyaṇa Gosvāmī Mahārāja: Nṛsiṁha Bhagavān was always present in Vaikuṇṭha, but He appeared in this world for the first time to Prahlāda Mahārāja.

Kṛṣṇa-kānta dāsa: I heard that in Prahlāda Mahārāja's previous life, he had relations with a prostitute and later on slept in a Nṛsiṁhadeva *mandira* (temple) in the forest. So, was Lord Nṛsiṁhadeva's *mandira* in existence before He appeared to Prahlāda Mahārāja?

Śrīla Nārāyaṇa Gosvāmī Mahārāja: That may have been in another *kalpa*.

Kṛṣṇa-kānta dāsa: In another *kalpa*, this same pastime takes place in the same way; so how is it that Prahlāda Mahārāja appears later than Nṛsiṁha Bhagavān. How can this be?

Śrīla Nārāyaṇa Gosvāmī Mahārāja: Just as Rāmacandra comes again and again, so do Prahlāda and Nṛsiṁha. Likewise, Lord Jagannātha's temple is always present, even in Satya-yuga.

Kṛṣṇa-kānta dāsa: So, in every *kalpa* the Lord's pastimes are going on; they go on eternally. Are the same pastimes performed in every *kalpa*, or do they differ?

Śrīla Nārāyaṇa Gosvāmī Mahārāja: There may be some variety.

Jayadeva dāsa: Śrīla Gurudeva, how does a devotee know when he should increase the number of rounds he chants daily?

Śrīla Nārāyaṇa Gosvāmī Mahārāja: As your taste develops, your *bhajana* will increase automatically. There is no need to be told when to increase. Until taste has developed, *guru* and Vaiṣṇavas will remind you that you should maintain your *sādhana-bhajana*. It is essential to perform *bhajana*, and by doing so, your taste will develop.

Gokula dāsa: Some devotees told Jayadeva Prabhu that you prescribe only four rounds daily, whereas I see that you are actually telling the devotees to chant at least sixteen.

Śrīla Nārāyaṇa Gosvāmī Mahārāja: I may even say to someone, "You should chant at least one round." Why do I tell them this? The holy name is so attractive and powerful that the one round itself will foster the increase. But there should be no *aparādha* – no offenses to Vaiṣṇavas, to *nāma* (the holy name of the Lord), or to Kṛṣṇa.

Gokula dāsa: What is your expectation regarding someone who has taken *harināma* from you?

Śrīpāda Padmanābha Mahārāja: Gurudeva, in the case of our Guru Mahārāja, Śrīla Bhaktivedānta Svāmī Prabhupāda, he very strictly prescribed chanting sixteen rounds daily. Unless someone could chant that number, he would not give him *harināma* initiation. His question is connected with that.

Śrīpāda Mādhava Mahārāja: For small children, Śrīla Gurudeva may encourage them to chant one or two rounds. But for adults, he always requests them to chant a minimum of sixteen rounds. Moreover, he requests them not be stagnant there, but to gradually increase their chanting.

Śrīla Nārāyaṇa Gosvāmī Mahārāja: If someone cannot chant the required amount, he can begin from eight, ten, or twelve, and gradually try to chant sixteen, twenty, twenty-four, thirty-two, and more than that. My Gurudeva never told me how many rounds to chant. He told me to chant; that's all. We are more liberal in that regard.

Śrīla Prabhupāda Bhaktisiddhānta Sarasvatī Ṭhākura used to say that Kṛṣṇa will not accept *prasādam* from those who are not chanting one *lākha* (100,000 names, or sixty-four rounds). A *lākha* of what quality? It should be at least *nāma-abhāsa*, not *nāma-aparādha*.

Devotee: He is thinking about taking initiation, but he is uncertain.

Śrīla Nārāyaṇa Gosvāmī Mahārāja: He can decide. If he wants to be happy in this life and be situated on the transcendental platform, it is necessary to take initiation.

February 7, 2008
Morning Walk

Śrīpāda Dāmodara Mahārāja: Gurudeva, Aśvatthāmā was cursed by Kṛṣṇa.

Śrīla Nārāyaṇa Gosvāmī Mahārāja: No.

Śrīpāda Dāmodara Mahārāja: At the end of *Mahābhārata* Kṛṣṇa cursed him, saying, "You will have no friends. You will live until the end of Kali-yuga." Kṛṣṇa cursed him at the end.

Śrīla Nārāyaṇa Gosvāmī Mahārāja: Kṛṣṇa told Arjuna "Kill him," and Bhīma also told him to do so. Arjuna was deep in thought, however, and then said to Draupadī, "He has committed offenses at your lotus feet, so the decision is yours." Draupadī replied, "As I am weeping for my sons, who were killed by Aśvatthāmā, so will your Gurudeva's wife weep if you kill her son, Aśvatthāmā. I would not be able to tolerate this. Better to let him go." Kṛṣṇa then told Arjuna, "You have made a promise that you will bring to Draupadī the head of the killer of her sons, so you must fulfill it." Understanding the Lord's motive, Arjuna took up his sword and cut off Aśvatthāmā's hair, leaving him with tufts of hair all over his head. In addition, he cut out the jewel from Aśvatthāmā's forehead.

Śrīpāda Dāmodara Mahārāja: I've read in the *Mahābhārata* that Kṛṣṇa also cursed him, saying, "You will have no friends and a foul smell will emanate from your body."

Śrīla Nārāyaṇa Gosvāmī Mahārāja: I have thoroughly read the entire *Mahābhārata*, *Rāmāyaṇa*, all the Purāṇas, and all other *śāstras*. Perhaps no one has read as much as I have. I have not seen those statements.

Śrīpāda Dāmodara Mahārāja: Premānanda Prabhu was thinking very deeply last night when you cursed him…

Brajanātha dāsa: That was a blessing, not a curse.

Śrīla Nārāyaṇa Gosvāmī Mahārāja: Our Guru Mahārāja also used to 'curse.' I have learned this from him.

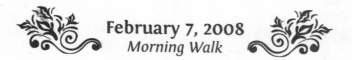

Śrīpāda Dāmodara Mahārāja: Who did he curse?

Śrīla Nārāyaṇa Gosvāmī Mahārāja: *Sannyāsīs* and senior saffron-clothed *brahmacārīs.*

Śrīpāda Dāmodara Mahārāja: Because some of them also left their *sannyāsa* or *brahmacārī āśramas?*

Śrīla Nārāyaṇa Gosvāmī Mahārāja: Some of them.

Śrīpāda Dāmodara Mahārāja: What curse did Parama-gurudeva give?

Śrīpāda Mādhava Mahārāja: He would say, "Your family life will never be happy; you will have to suffer."

Śrīla Nārāyaṇa Gosvāmī Mahārāja: He used to tell them, "You have come from your homes to do *parikramā*, and you are doing it. I cannot give you permission to return.

Gokula dāsa: How did the prostitute Piṅgalā's detachment come about? Was it from her previous life?

Śrīla Nārāyaṇa Gosvāmī Mahārāja: She met with the sage Dattātreya. Her detachment developed by his association.

Śrīpāda Dāmodara Mahārāja: He was staying at her house.

Śrīla Nārāyaṇa Gosvāmī Mahārāja: Dattātreya knew about her situation.

Gokula dāsa: So it was not from a previous life?

Śrīla Nārāyaṇa Gosvāmī Mahārāja: It might have been from that as well, but her association with that *sādhu* was prominent. *Sādhu-saṅga* was prominent.

Gokula dāsa: Although I am associating with you, and although I suffer from diseases, I am not becoming detached.

Śrīla Nārāyaṇa Gosvāmī Mahārāja: You do not understand that you are surely receiving spiritual impressions in your heart.

Do you want to serve Rāma?

Gokula dāsa: No.

Śrīla Nārāyaṇa Gosvāmī Mahārāja: Dvārakādhīśa Kṛṣṇa?

Gokula dāsa: No.

Śrīla Nārāyaṇa Gosvāmī Mahārāja: No? Do you want to be Kṛṣṇa's mother?

Gokula dāsa: No.

Śrīla Nārāyaṇa Gosvāmī Mahārāja: Do you want to be Kṛṣṇa's brother? Or His friend?

Gokula dāsa: No.

Śrīla Nārāyaṇa Gosvāmī Mahārāja: What do you want? You want to be the maidservant of Śrīmatī Rādhikā. This shows that you have received impressions in your heart. Generally people cannot decide the goal of their life, but you have decided. This comes from impressions, and such impressions are very, very rare in this world; very rare.

Gokula dāsa: I want to become detached, and to be with you always.

Śrīla Nārāyaṇa Gosvāmī Mahārāja: If a desire comes to serve Kṛṣṇa in that way, it means that you are very fortunate, and everything will follow from that – if you are sincere and do not commit any *vaiṣṇava-aparādha*. Try to be careful to avoid *vaiṣṇava-aparādha*. People generally do not commit *guru-aparādha*, but they cannot recognize a Vaiṣṇava.

Gokula dāsa: I suffer a lot from disease. Should I think, "Gurudeva is sending this so that I can give up my attachment to my body?" How should I understand this?

Śrīla Nārāyaṇa Gosvāmī Mahārāja: It comes from your past activities, and also by the mercy of Kṛṣṇa.

Gokula dāsa: *Karma?*

Śrīla Nārāyaṇa Gosvāmī Mahārāja: Yes. In the first stage, it is only *karma*. When there is no more *karma* and no more *anarthas*, then it is fully the mercy of Kṛṣṇa. Kṛṣṇa wants to show the world the humility and tolerance of His devotees.

Śrīpāda Padmanābha Mahārāja: Śrīla Gurudeva, I have heard that in the four *varṇas* – *brāhmaṇa*, *kṣatriya*, *vaiśya*, and *śūdra* – the *brāhmaṇas* and *kṣatriyas* may take *sannyāsa*, but *vaiśyas* and *śūdras* generally will not.

Śrīla Nārāyaṇa Gosvāmī Mahārāja: That is not correct. We see from the Purāṇas, Vedas, and Upaniṣads that anyone who is detached from the world and wants to fully serve Kṛṣṇa may take *sannyāsa*.

Śrīpāda Mādhava Mahārāja: If you read *Nārada-parivrājaka Upaniṣad*, you will understand everything in this regard.

Śrīla Nārāyaṇa Gosvāmī Mahārāja: The *Sannyāsopaniṣad* says that anyone who is detached and becomes established in *ātmā-tattva* can take *sannyāsa*. For such persons, there is no such consideration of *varṇāśrama-dharma*.

Veṇu-gopāla dāsa: When Śrī Kṛṣṇa's foot was shot by the hunter's arrow, did He pretend to leave His body, or did His life-air actually leave?

Śrīla Nārāyaṇa Gosvāmī Mahārāja: Yesterday I explained this very clearly.

Śrīpāda Padmanābha Mahārāja: Śrīla Gurudeva said last night that all the demigods came to the place where Kṛṣṇa was sitting. There, they praised Him and prayed to Him. At that time, right in front of them, he went to Goloka Vṛndāvana in His original body.

Veṇu-gopāla dāsa: Why did He need to be shot by the hunter?

Śrīla Nārāyaṇa Gosvāmī Mahārāja: He did this to bewilder the atheists.

Śrīpāda Dāmodara Mahārāja: Was the hunter actually Bṛghu Muni?

Śrīla Nārāyaṇa Gosvāmī Mahārāja: Why Bṛghu? I have not heard this. You may have heard this, but it is not written anywhere in *śāstra*.

Kṛṣṇa has no *karma*. How can *karma* touch Him? Neither Draupadī nor Kṛṣṇa nor any high-class *mahā-bhāgavata* is subject to the laws of *karma*. They never experience the fruits of past activities.

Śrīpāda Padmanābha Mahārāja: In the case of Lord Nityānanda Prabhu, when He was hit on the head by Mādhāi, His head started bleeding. But His body is transcendental – *sac-cid-ānanda*.

Śrīla Nārāyaṇa Gosvāmī Mahārāja: This was to bewilder others, to make them think that Nityānanda Prabhu is an ordinary human being, like them. These and similar pastimes are *naravata-līlā*. In this way one can say, "Oh! Although He was cut and blood oozed from His head, He excused his aggressors. We should follow His example."

(To Balarāma dāsa) How are you?

Balarāma dāsa: By your mercy, Śrīla Gurudeva, I am still in my body and endeavoring to make advancement in Kṛṣṇa consciousness. Please be merciful to me so that I can make some advancement.

Śrīla Nārāyaṇa Gosvāmī Mahārāja: Go and preach throughout New Zealand the topics I am now teaching you.

Devotee 1: Śrīla Gurudeva, I will be going to Haiti with Jayanta-kṛṣṇa Prabhu (now Śuddhādvaitī Mahārāja) for preaching.

Śrīla Nārāyaṇa Gosvāmī Mahārāja: Yes, do go there.

Devotee 2: Gurudeva, will you give me *harināma?*

Śrīla Nārāyaṇa Gosvāmī Mahārāja: You should decide. If you sincerely want to take *harināma,* I will give it to you.

My blessings to you all.

Mui O, Hong Kong

April 9-16, 2008

April 9, 2008
Darśana

Brajanātha dāsa: This is Seemon, the lady in whose home we are having these programs. She is doing everything for the devotees. She is giving her furniture and all her possessions for our use at the programs. She is very attracted to *kṛṣṇa-bhakti* and has been going to ISKCON for many years.

Śrīla Nārāyaṇa Gosvāmī Mahārāja: My blessings to you. You are helping us so much.

If you want to be happy in this world and the transcendental world, you must chant, "Hare Kṛṣṇa, Hare Kṛṣṇa, Kṛṣṇa Kṛṣṇa, Hare Hare, Hare Rāma, Hare Rāma, Rāma Rāma, Hare Hare." Otherwise, in future births, you may become a donkey, a dog, a cat, a pig, or any other animal. Be happy forever.

Do not be afraid to take initiation – there is no need to fear. There are hundreds of thousands of devotees in Canada, America, Europe, and elsewhere. So many beautiful young girls and boys are taking initiation. So don't fear; your life will be happy.

Wearing the three strands of *tulasī* neck-beads is very powerful. You will have no problems with blood pressure if you wear this. By wearing *tulasī*, whatever you tell will be true, and you will always be healthy and wealthy.

April 11, 2008
Darśana
after the morning walk

Śrīpāda Dāmodara Mahārāja: Mostly it is the *sādhana-siddha* (one who becomes perfect through *sādhana*, and then experiences the same spiritual bliss as that of a *nitya-siddha*) who is acting as *guru*.

Brajanātha dāsa: Mahārāja understands that in order to be *guru* and give mercy, one must be a *sādhana-siddha* devotee. A *nitya-siddha parikara*, an eternal associate of the Lord from the spiritual world who was never conditioned, cannot do so.

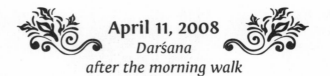

Śrīla Nārāyaṇa Gosvāmī Mahārāja: Why?

Śrīpāda Dāmodara Mahārāja: It says this in *Mādhurya-kādambinī*.

Śrīla Nārāyaṇa Gosvāmī Mahārāja: Śrīmatī Rādhikā sent Her own *nitya-siddha* associate, Jayanta, to help Gopa-kumāra. So, a *nitya-siddha* can act as *guru*.

Śrīpāda Dāmodara Mahārāja: *Nitya-siddhas* have no experience of suffering...

Śrīla Nārāyaṇa Gosvāmī Mahārāja: Generally what you say is correct. The *sādhana-siddhas* remember what they experienced in their life of *sādhana*. Even if they are now *siddha*, they can remember. It is likened to a man who was sleeping and suffering in a dream; even after he has awakened, he can remember his dream. Similarly, these self-realized persons can remember how they suffered, and their hearts melt for the suffering conditioned souls.

Śrīpāda Dāmodara Mahārāja: Whereas the *nitya-siddha* has no...

Śrīla Nārāyaṇa Gosvāmī Mahārāja: But the *nitya-siddha* can also act as *guru* – like Svarūpa in *Śrī Bṛhad-bhāgavatāmṛta*. *Nitya-siddha* devotees like Śrīla Narottama dāsa Ṭhākura, Śrīla Rūpa Gosvāmī, and Śrīla Sanātana Gosvāmī have all acted as *guru*.

Śrīpāda Dāmodara Mahārāja: They do not know what suffering is.

Śrīla Nārāyaṇa Gosvāmī Mahārāja: Who? Śrīla Sanātana Gosvāmī? If that were so, how would his heart melt, and how would he have done what he did?

Śrīpāda Mādhava Mahārāja: What to speak of Śrīla Sanātana Gosvāmī? How much suffering Śrīmatī Rādhikā experiences; how Her in-laws do not allow Her to go to Kṛṣṇa; how they create so many problems for Her.

Madhuvrata dāsa: That is not material suffering.

Śrīla Nārāyaṇa Gosvāmī Mahārāja: Generally a *sādhana-siddha* has more mercy for the conditioned souls, in the sense that he comes more often, but in a special case Kṛṣṇa may arrange that His *nitya-siddha* associate will also come to give mercy.

Śyāmarāṇī dāsī: Śrīla Gadādhara Paṇḍita, who is *nitya-siddha*, manifested as Śrīla Bhaktivinoda Ṭhākura. Śrīla Bhaktivinoda Ṭhākura showed so much mercy.

Śrīla Nārāyaṇa Gosvāmī Mahārāja: Yes. And Śrī Gadādhara Paṇḍita personally made so many disciples, like Gopāla-guru Gosvāmī, Vakreśvara Paṇḍita, and those in his line. He gave *mantras* even to Śrī Vallabhācārya.

Śrīpāda Dāmodara Mahārāja: I was thinking that *nitya-siddhas* only come along with Mahāprabhu.

Śrīla Nārāyaṇa Gosvāmī Mahārāja: No, no.

Śyāmarāṇī dāsī: Nayana Mañjarī came as Śrīla Bhaktisiddhānta Sarasvatī Ṭhākura Prabhupāda.

Śrīla Nārāyaṇa Gosvāmī Mahārāja: Whatever Śrī Kṛṣṇa and Śrī Caitanya Mahāprabhu think best to do, that is what They do. They may bring with Them Their own personal eternal associates who were never conditioned souls, and they may bring Their *sādhana-siddha* devotees with Them.

Śrīpāda Dāmodara Mahārāja: How can we know who is *sādhana-siddha* or *nitya-siddha*?

Śrīla Nārāyaṇa Gosvāmī Mahārāja: First become *siddha*, and then you can realize who is who.

Śyāmarāṇī dāsī: Gurudeva, in a few days it will be Lord Rāmacandra's appearance day. Today we are sending out your *hari-kathā* lecture from Navadvīpa at Māmagāchi, wherein you discussed the separation between Śrīmatī Sītā-devī and Lord Rāma. In that lecture you said that at the time of meeting one forgets everything internally. What does that mean? Even at the time of meeting there are so many moods, aren't there?

Śrīla Nārāyaṇa Gosvāmī Mahārāja: If I am meeting with you, and we are speaking and absorbed in some activity, we will forget what is inside.

Śyāmarāṇī dāsī: Don't we experience many internal feelings as we speak together?

Brajanātha dāsa: You forget the heart when you are externally absorbed in many things.

Śrīla Nārāyaṇa Gosvāmī Mahārāja: At the time of meeting, Śrīmatī Rādhikā forgets the internal. Externally She is speaking with Kṛṣṇa and engaging in numerous pastimes with Him, whereas separation is always internal. At that time She is always absorbed internally, oblivious to the external.

Śyāmarāṇī dāsī: In meeting, Śrīmatī Rādhikā is experiencing *mādanākhya-mahābhāva. Bhāva* means 'internal feelings', doesn't it?

Śrīla Nārāyaṇa Gosvāmī Mahārāja: *Mādanākhya-bhāva* is in meeting.

Śyāmarāṇī dāsī: It is an internal feeling, isn't it?

Śrīla Nārāyaṇa Gosvāmī Mahārāja: That is a special case, and that was only in Śrīmatī Rādhikā. She was sitting on the lap of Kṛṣṇa, but She forgot this. She was feeling only separation, totally forgetful that, "I am on the lap of Kṛṣṇa; I am with Kṛṣṇa."

Śyāmarāṇī dāsī: Also for the same Navadvīpa *hari-kathā* that we are sending out: You said that the *bhakta* (devotee) feels separation for Kṛṣṇa, and in that regard Rāma said to Sītā, "We must be separated sometimes, because this brings more joy in meeting." Why is the word 'devotee' used? Sītā is Lord Rāma's eternal consort. She is not in the category of 'devotee,' just as Kṛṣṇa's mother, Yaśodā, is not in the category of devotee.

Śrīla Nārāyaṇa Gosvāmī Mahārāja: I was using the word *bhakta* only in a general sense.

In an even more general sense, I may give the analogy of a husband and wife. If a husband has great love for his wife, who has gone for some time to her father's house, the husband thinks, "Now that she has left, I am feeling so lonely. She used to cook for me and massage me, and she always showed me so much love and affection." In this way, he remembers her.

Sāvitrī dāsī: Gurudeva, I printed these flyers to distribute in Turkey this summer, written in the Turkey language. It explains the meaning of *bhakti-yoga*, it tells something about your life, and it has a transcription of a *darśana* you gave in Fiji. Also, one book will be ready soon; I am doing the editing now.

Śrīla Nārāyaṇa Gosvāmī Mahārāja: Very good. Thank you. Thank you.

(To Śrīpāda Dāmodara Mahārāja:) You have gone with her?

Śrīpāda Dāmodara Mahārāja: We are going again.

Śrīla Nārāyaṇa Gosvāmī Mahārāja: It is a good place for preaching?

Śrīpāda Dāmodara Mahārāja: Okay. Nice.

Sāvitrī dāsī: Gurudeva, so many people in Turkey are practicing *yoga*, and also new age meditation and healing; but they know nothing about *bhakti-yoga*.

Śrīla Nārāyaṇa Gosvāmī Mahārāja: It is a Muslim country.

Śrīpāda Dāmodara Mahārāja: But they are like Europeans.

Brajanātha dāsa: We can arrange to go there.

Śrīla Nārāyaṇa Gosvāmī Mahārāja: As you like.

April 11, 2008
Darśana for the Philippine devotees in the late morning

Śrīla Nārāyaṇa Gosvāmī Mahārāja: Śyāmarāṇī will come ten times – daily.

Śyāmarāṇī dāsī: I am here because I regularly go to the Philippines.

Śrīla Nārāyaṇa Gosvāmī Mahārāja: This is the third time you have come today. I know that you will come ten times, because you are made of questions. I will not call you Śyāmarāṇī; I will call you Question-rāṇī.

Śyāmarāṇī dāsī: Good, because I have a question for Gaurāṅgi and her husband, Yadunātha Prabhu.

Śrīla Nārāyaṇa Gosvāmī Mahārāja: What question?

Śyāmarāṇī dāsī: When Yadunātha Prabhu and Gaurāṅgi were in ISKCON, they were full-time travelling preachers. They were married, but they were preaching together. Then they had two children, and from that time until now their time has been mainly spent in maintaining the family to help the children grow. Now the children are teenagers, thirteen and fourteen years old. Is now a good time for the children, who have become wonderful devotees, to assist the parents in preaching?

Śrīla Nārāyaṇa Gosvāmī Mahārāja: Very good. They should preach. Preaching is *bhakti*. They must preach. They should chant the holy name, read my books, and also preach.

Śyāmarāṇī dāsī: How can the children become free from their fear of preaching?

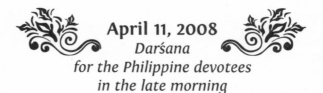

Śrīla Nārāyaṇa Gosvāmī Mahārāja: No need of shyness at all; no need.

Kṛṣṇacandra dāsa: Gurudeva, I travel all over the Philippine islands, trying to explain to people how to become Kṛṣṇa-conscious. Can you instruct me regarding the best way to do this?

Śrīla Nārāyaṇa Gosvāmī Mahārāja: Try to understand our classes. Read my books and the books of Śrīla Bhaktivedānta Svāmī Mahārāja, and preach freely without any fear. In this way the people will appreciate you, and they will come to me for initiation.

Yadunātha dāsa: We hear from *Śrīmad-Bhāgavatam* that when Kaṁsa tried to kill the female baby who was Kṛṣṇa's younger sister (Yogamāyā), that baby flew up into the sky (in the form of Durgā). So I am wondering: Subhadrā is the sister of Kṛṣṇa. How did she become Kṛṣṇa's sister?

Śrīla Nārāyaṇa Gosvāmī Mahārāja: Mādhava Mahārāja will reply.

Śrīpāda Mādhava Mahārāja: After Kaṁsa died, Vasudeva and Devakī were set free. Then, after some time, they begot Subhadrā.

Yadunātha dāsa: So she is not the same as Yogamāyā?

Śrīpāda Mādhava Mahārāja: No, she came later.

Pītāmbara dāsa: Gurudeva, how did Rādhārāṇī exit Her earthly pastimes?

Śrīla Nārāyaṇa Gosvāmī Mahārāja: Śrīmatī Rādhārāṇī left in the same way that Śrī Kṛṣṇa left – by the arrangement of Kṛṣṇa's *yogamāyā* potency. When Kṛṣṇa returned on a chariot to Vraja, Gokula, from Dvārakā, He stayed there for some time. Then, along with all His Vraja associates like Nanda Bābā, Yaśodā-maiyā, and all the *sakhīs* including Rādhikā, Lalitā, Viśākhā, and Candrāvalī, He returned to Goloka Vṛndāvana. At that time His Vraja pastimes became *aprakaṭa*, unmanifest in this world.

Nanda-nandana Kṛṣṇa's expansion Vāsudeva Kṛṣṇa, the son of Vasudeva, got back on His chariot and returned to Dvārakā alone. Later on, before the eyes of demigods like Lord Brahmā and Śaṅkara, He ascended to His abode, Goloka, in His own transcendental form.

While Śrī Kṛṣṇa was still present in Dvārakā, it seemed as though all His sons and other relatives, like Pradhyumna, Aniruddha, and so many others, fought with and killed each other. However, this was like a magic show. It was simply an external exhibition.

What actually happened was that all of Kṛṣṇa's eternal associates entered Goloka with Him. Those who had come from Svarga (the heavenly planets) to participate in His pastimes, like Indra and other demigods, returned to Svarga after His pastimes were completed, and mixed with Indra and the other demigods there. In other words, the demigods had expanded to become the members of the Yadu-dynasty (the family members of Kṛṣṇa in Dvārakā).Then, at the end of those pastimes, the portions of the demigods who were in the Yadu-dynasty mixed again into their own demigod forms. Those who had come from Ayodhyā returned there, and all those who had come from Vaikuṇṭha returned there.

Vallabha-kānti dāsa: Gurudeva, some people have asked my wife to do some preaching for children in the schools. We want to know if we can have your blessings to do that.

Śrīla Nārāyaṇa Gosvāmī Mahārāja: (To Asalata dāsī) You should go everywhere to preach – to schools, colleges, universities, and door-to-door. You are qualified, more so than your husband. You can preach. My blessings to you. Along with your husband, try to preach everywhere. It is not that you should always be writing. I also write, but I am also preaching throughout the world.

Rādhā-kānta dāsa: When Śrīmatī Rādhikā left Vṛndāvana, She entered the Yamunā, didn't she? She apparently gave up Her body in the Yamunā?

Śrīla Nārāyaṇa Gosvāmī Mahārāja: No. Śrīla Rūpa Gosvāmī has described the pastime in this way [in his book, *Śrī Lalita-mādhava*]: Rādhikā entered the Yamunā, but from there She went via the Sun planet to Dvārakā. Lalitā, Viśākhā, and all other *sakhīs* also manifested in Dvārakā, where they appeared as Kṛṣṇa's queens Rukmiṇī, Satyabhāmā, Jāmbavatī, and so on. Later on they met Kṛṣṇa; and in the end they understood that they were really from Vraja.

We also see in *Lalita-mādhava* that, due to feelings of separation from Kṛṣṇa, Śrīmatī Rādhikā jumped into a lake in Dvārakā to end Her life, but Kṛṣṇa entered the lake and embraced Her. So many pastimes are revealed in *Lalita-mādhava* and *Vidagdha-mādhava*; you can read such pastimes there.

Devotee: What are the benefits of following Cāturmāsya[1]?

---

[1] See Endnote 1 (at the end of this chapter) for more information on *cāturmāsya-vrata*.

Śrīla Nārāyaṇa Gosvāmī Mahārāja: There is so much benefit. In ancient times, the four Kumāras were performing *cāturmāsya-vrata* by always remembering Kṛṣṇa, chanting Kṛṣṇa's names, and giving classes about Kṛṣṇa. They were always remembering Kṛṣṇa in these four months.

Śrī Caitanya Mahāprabhu Himself, and all of the *ācāryas* in our *guru-paramparā* such as Śrīla Bhaktivinoda Ṭhākura, Śrīla Bhaktisiddhānta Sarasvatī Ṭhākura, Śrīla Jagannātha dāsa Bābājī Mahārāja, and my Gurudeva, Śrīla Bhakti Prajñāna Keśava Gosvāmī observed Cāturmāsya. They did not shave during these months [though they sometimes shaved after the first two months for Viśvarūpa Mahotsava].

Sāvitrī dāsī: You said last night in your class that Lord Rāma and Kṛṣṇa are the same, that they are non-different.

Śrīla Nārāyaṇa Gosvāmī Mahārāja: No. Kṛṣṇa has come as Rāma. There is no difference in *tattva* (established philosophical truth), but by *rasa-gata-vicāra* (the consideration of transcendental pastimes and relationships), Kṛṣṇa is superior. He is the Supreme Personality of Godhead who has come in the form of Rāma, the perfect example of *maryādā* (following etiquette).

April 13, 2008
Morning Walk

Śrīla Nārāyaṇa Gosvāmī Mahārāja: Some persons say, "We should not think that one falls down from *sannyāsa* because of having done something wrong." They also say that if a *brahmacārī* takes *sannyāsa* and after that becomes a *gṛhastha*, householder, he is not *vāntāśī*. They say these things, but they are wrong. That person who leaves the *sannyāsa* order is a *vāntāśī*.

Śrīpāda Mādhava Mahārāja: *Vāntāśī* means vomit-eater. If one eats something and then vomits, and then eats that vomit, he is a vomit-eater. Similarly, if one is *gṛhastha*, then rejects that householder life by taking *sannyāsa*, and then again accepts householder life, that person is a *vāntāśī*. Some say that if one who was not previously a *gṛhastha* takes *sannyāsa* and then falls from *sannyāsa* to become a *gṛhastha*, he is not *vāntāśī*.

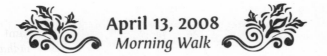

Śrīla Nārāyaṇa Gosvāmī Mahārāja: Still, he is a *vāntāśī*.

Rādhā-kānta dāsa: In Vedic culture, *brahmacārīs* would live in *gurukula* for some time, and then most of them would marry.

Śrīla Nārāyaṇa Gosvāmī Mahārāja: It has been said that a *brahmacārī* can return to *gṛhastha* life, but for *sannyāsīs* this is an offense. They have promised their Gurudeva, "I will not give up *sannyāsa*." They are giving up their promise, and therefore they are committing *guru-aparādha*.

Śrīpāda Mādhava Mahārāja: According to Vedic culture, it is not the saffron-cloth *brahmacārīs* who are allowed to marry. Some of those *brahmacārīs* who wear white-cloth maintain their *brahmacārī* life for some time, and later on they may think, "I will go to household life." *Brahmacārīs* who put on saffron cloth will not marry.

Rādhā-kānta dāsa: That is also a vow for life?

Śrīpāda Mādhava Mahārāja: Yes.

Śrīpāda Padmanābha Mahārāja: But they don't take any vow.

Śrīpāda Mādhava Mahārāja: If they put on saffron cloth, they take a vow that they will not marry for the rest of their life.

Śrīla Nārāyaṇa Gosvāmī Mahārāja: We can see that Gauḍīya Vaiṣṇava *sannyāsīs* in India, like the *sannyāsa* disciples of Śrīla Bhaktisiddhānta Sarasvatī Ṭhākura – Śrīla Bhakti Dayita Mādhava Mahārāja, my Gurudeva (Śrīla Bhakti Prajñāna Keśava Gosvāmī Mahārāja) and others – never fell down. My Indian *sannyāsīs* will not fall, as Prema-prayojana fell down, and you should also try to never fall down. There should be no example of my *sannyāsīs* falling.

Along with Bhaktisāra Mahārāja, Prema-prayojana committed some *aparādhas* to Vaiṣṇavas by criticizing them. Also, I told Prema-prayojana not to associate with ladies, but still he gave classes to them, alone.

We should also try to give up the false ego of thinking, "I am this body." Such thinking is one type of *nama-aparādha*, and it is the root of all evil. If there is no false ego, then all *anarthas* (unwanted thought and habits) will also disappear. If there is *dehātma-abhimāna* (the false ego that "I am this body"), we will think, "This is mine, this is his. I will not give my things to others. I should keep my things for my enjoyment." This thinking will come.

April 14, 2008
Morning Walk

Yadunātha dāsa: I cannot recall whether it is in a commentary, or verse, of *Śrīmad-Bhāgavatam*, but it is said that Kṛṣṇa came back to Vṛndāvana from Dvārakā and satisfied all the inhabitants of Vṛndāvana, and then He brought them all back to the spiritual world.

Śrīpāda Mādhava Mahārāja: He returned there after killing Dantavakra.

Śrīla Nārāyaṇa Gosvāmī Mahārāja: I have also told this. This history is stated in the *Śrīmad-Bhāgavatam* in a condensed form. It has also been written in other Purāṇas, such as *Hari-vaṁśa.*

(To Yadunātha dāsa:) Do people speak English in your country?

Yadunātha dāsa: They speak English, and also the local Philippino language. Ninety percent of the people speak English.

Śrīla Nārāyaṇa Gosvāmī Mahārāja: So they can read our English books.

Yadunātha dāsa: Yes, but the less educated people need to read Tagalog in order to understand the philosophy.

Vallabha-kānti dāsa: Somebody asked me whether one can take *harināma* initiation, and after that still take meat and smoke for awhile, and then slowly give it up.

Śrīla Nārāyaṇa Gosvāmī Mahārāja: Don't believe others. Believe only our *guru-paramparā*, Śrīla Bhaktivedānta Svāmī Mahārāja, and myself. And especially, you are initiated by me, so you should follow me.

Vallabha-kānti dāsa: Some persons are saying this.

Śrīla Nārāyaṇa Gosvāmī Mahārāja: They are quite wrong. It has been written in the *Śrīmad-Bhāgavatam* that Kali-yuga resides in places where the four unwanted habits are indulged in: gambling; taking meat, fish, and eggs; drinking wine; smoking and taking other intoxication, and prostitution. And there is one more place: where there is money or gold [because wherever there is gold there is also falsity, intoxication, lust, envy, and enmity]. So we should not hear from those persons.

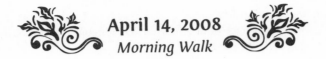

Śrīpāda Padmanābha Mahārāja: Even if someone is addicted to intoxicants, or smoking cigarettes, still we should encourage them to begin chanting the *mahā-mantra*.

Śrīla Nārāyaṇa Gosvāmī Mahārāja: Yes. We should glorify the qualities of Kṛṣṇa's holy name so that people may have some faith in it. Then, when they have faith and give up these bad habits, at that time they can take initiation. Moreover, even if they are not initiated, if they chant the holy name, then, by the power of the name, they will give up their unwanted habits. They will have *sādhu-saṅga*, and by that *sādhu-saṅga* they will be inspired.

The Chinese devotees should have a *maṭha* (preaching center). They should hear *hari-kathā* from each other, and also observe festivals like Janmāṣṭamī and Rādhāṣṭamī together.

Śrīpāda Padmanābha Mahārāja: Śrīla Gurudeva, this gentleman is a professional photographer. He is meeting us for the first time. He lives in America, in San Francisco. He is asking if he can take photos of you for CNN [a popular TV news station].

Śrīla Nārāyaṇa Gosvāmī Mahārāja: Yes, you can take photos.

Śrīpāda Padmanābha Mahārāja: He exhibited his photos in Washington DC. This is his book. He came to China and took many photos of school children. He is a very good photographer. I invited him to come to Badger when you go there.

Śrīla Nārāyaṇa Gosvāmī Mahārāja: What is your name?

P.H. Young: P.H. Young

Śrīla Nārāyaṇa Gosvāmī Mahārāja: If your soul leaves your body, will you be able to walk and talk with us?

P.H. Young: Yes, of course.

Śrīpāda Mādhava Mahārāja: If your soul leaves your body, will you be able to walk and speak?

P.H. Young: I'm sure, yes.

Śrīpāda Padmanābha Mahārāja: He does not understand.

P.H. Young: I'm sure I can communicate with you on a spiritual level.

Śrīpāda Mādhava Mahārāja: No, no. Gurudeva is asking, if your spirit soul comes out of your body, leaves your body, will you be able to speak?

P.H. Young: Not necessarily speak, but I'm sure I can communicate with you.

Śrīpāda Padmanābha Mahārāja: But what will happen with your body when your soul leaves?

P.H. Young: My body is just a vessel to contain my soul, so it is not important.

Śrīla Nārāyaṇa Gosvāmī Mahārāja: Then who are you? Are you this body or that soul?

P.H. Young: Of course I am the soul.

Śrīla Nārāyaṇa Gosvāmī Mahārāja: You should know this. And there is also a Supersoul who has created this world. Your soul cannot create this world.

P.H. Young: Probably not.

Śrīla Nārāyaṇa Gosvāmī Mahārāja: Not 'probably not.'

P.H. Young: Okay.

Śrīla Nārāyaṇa Gosvāmī Mahārāja: Suppose you accept this understanding and pray, "O Supreme Lord, I am your son. Please be merciful to me." If you accept this philosophy, you will be fully happy in this world and also in the transcendental world. You are not an inhabitant of this place, this Earth. You are an inhabitant of a transcendental place. Unfortunately you forgot the Supreme Lord and fell down.

P.H. Young: I see.

Śrīla Nārāyaṇa Gosvāmī Mahārāja: Until you remember Him and take His shelter, you cannot transcend the cycle of birth and death. This is our *siddhānta*, our philosophy. We preach everywhere in the world, and everywhere people are accepting this philosophy – the Americans, Chinese, Germans, Japanese, and all others.

April 14, 2008
Darśana

Śrīla Nārāyaṇa Gosvāmī Mahārāja: Kṛṣṇa does not interfere with their independence.

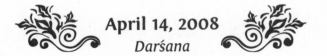

Śrīpāda Mādhava Mahārāja: Loving parents want all of their children. Kṛṣṇa is the father of the entire universe, and He wants all of His children to come to him.

P.H. Young: Of course. We see many, many religions in this world. Are there any commonalities between Kṛṣṇa and the other religions?

Śrīla Nārāyaṇa Gosvāmī Mahārāja: Among various religious beliefs, the Buddhists don't accept God or scripture. They say that we are zero – we have come from zero, and in the end we will be zero. So, there is no question of commonality for Buddhism.

Regarding Christianity, in our *sanātana-dharma* religion, God, Kṛṣṇa, is eternal and all souls are eternal dear daughters and sons of Kṛṣṇa. It has been told in the Vedic scriptures that the Supreme Lord has a form, and Christianity has also accepted this. The Bible states that God created man in His own image. However, although the Christian Bible says He has a form, Christians generally do not follow this understanding.

Similarly, in the Muslim Koran it has been said, "*Innallaha khalaqa adama ala suratihi* – Allah, or Khudā, has form, and from that form He fashioned man." God has created man after His own form. Again, in general, followers of the Koran deny this.

God, Kṛṣṇa, is eternal. The *jīva* souls are also eternal, but they have forgotten the Supreme Soul, Kṛṣṇa. All souls have a very beautiful, transcendental form, but unfortunately we are thinking that the body is the self. We are thinking, "I am this body."

P.H. Young: I understand that Buddha is a reincarnation of Kṛṣṇa.

Śrīla Nārāyaṇa Gosvāmī Mahārāja: There are two different Buddhas. Regarding the Buddha whose teachings are prominent in the present-day world, he is not an incarnation. He says that God is zero, only zero existed previously, we are now zero, the entire world is zero, and after this life everything will be zero.

On the other hand, in the Vedic literature our *sanātana-dharma* has been glorified:

oṁ pūrṇam adaḥ pūrṇam idaṁ
pūrṇāt pūrṇam udacyate
pūrṇasya pūrṇam ādāya
pūrṇam evāvaśiṣyate

(*Śrī Īśopaniṣad*, Invocation)

The Personality of Godhead is perfect and complete, and because He is completely perfect, all emanations from Him, such as this phenomenal world, are perfectly equipped as complete wholes. Whatever is produced of the Complete Whole is also complete in itself. Because He is the Complete Whole, even though so many complete units emanate from Him, He remains perfectly complete.

Kṛṣṇa, God, is infinite. Whatever emanates from that infinity is also infinite. God is infinite, His incarnations are infinite, and at the same time He remains the infinite balance.

April 14, 2008
Meeting with the Śrī Team

Śrīpāda Vaiṣṇava Mahārāja: The devotees in China want to get some advice on how to coordinate the preaching in China.

Śrīla Nārāyaṇa Gosvāmī Mahārāja: I think that in China we can preach so much more. You know better than I. You should discuss amongst yourselves how it should be, and then it will happen easily. You all discuss, and then tell me how you decided to do things.

Indirā dāsī: What is the best way to protect the preachers and devotees, especially now that the international Olympics are coming?

Śrīla Nārāyaṇa Gosvāmī Mahārāja: They should decide.

Indirā dāsī: Some devotees want to have a restaurant, some want a *yoga* studio, and some want to present Indian culture. What is the best thing to do so that we don't waste manpower?

Śrīpāda Padmanābha Mahārāja: Preaching in China is not completely open like it is in other countries. So, some devotees feel we may have to adopt some other method which is acceptable. For example, teaching *yoga* and then preaching through that. Or, opening a vegetarian restaurant and then preaching through that. They would preach sort of secretly. Would something like that be acceptable?

Śrīla Nārāyaṇa Gosvāmī Mahārāja: Somehow you should try to preach; you can decide on the best way. For example you can say, "We are preaching *yoga*."

Yamunā dāsī: I am worried about some young lady devotees – how they can maintain themselves in the future. Their families are not devotees, they are not married, and sometimes they live alone. If they work there is so much contamination, and generally they live far from each other. There is no preaching center and no training.

Śrīla Nārāyaṇa Gosvāmī Mahārāja: You should discuss this, and when you are finished discussing, come to me and tell me what you have decided.

April 15, 2008
Morning Walk

Śrīpāda Giri Mahārāja: The cause of suffering is in my mind. Are there any prominent *ślokas* that confirm this?

Śrīla Nārāyaṇa Gosvāmī Mahārāja: Yes:

tat te 'nukampāṁ su-samīkṣamāṇo
bhuñjāna evātma-kṛtaṁ vipākam
hṛd-vāg vapurbhir vidadhan namas te
jīveta yo mukti-pade sa dāya-bhāk

(*Śrīmad-Bhāgavatam* 10.14.8)

My dear Lord, one who earnestly waits for You to bestow Your causeless mercy upon him, all the while patiently suffering the reactions of his past misdeeds and offering You respectful obeisances with his heart, words, and body, is surely eligible for liberation, for it has become his rightful claim.

And:

duḥkheṣv anudvigna-manāḥ
sukheṣu vigata-spṛhaḥ
vīta-rāga-bhaya-krodhaḥ
sthita-dhīr munir ucyate

(*Bhagavad-gītā* 2.56)

One whose mind is not disturbed by the three types of miseries (*adhyātmika*, *adhibhautika*, and *adhidaivika*), who

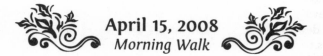

> remains free from desires in the presence of happiness, and who is free from attachment, fear, and anger, is called a steady-minded sage.

What is the program here?

Brajanātha dāsa: Yesterday they had discussions.

Śrīla Nārāyaṇa Gosvāmī Mahārāja: What did you all decide at your meeting?

Śrīpāda Vaiṣṇava Mahārāja: Yesterday we met on the top floor of your house. All the devotees agreed to form a ŚRĪ team [ŚRĪ stands for Sevā Resources Initiative]. That ŚRĪ team would help bring other devotees together who have different talents and skills and desires to perform services, like putting together books and DVDs. The ŚRĪ team would work to assist in making our *saṅga* in China more coordinated.

The *saṅga* is growing so quickly. Now we need to organize things and teach the devotees the basic things in a way that they can follow and understand. We also need to translate all the necessary things into Chinese for their training. So many devotees have come to you. Now we need to, as our Prabhupāda used to say, 'boil the milk.'

Brajanātha dāsa: You will do everything by majority vote?

Śrīpāda Vaiṣṇava Mahārāja: Yes.

Śrīla Nārāyaṇa Gosvāmī Mahārāja: Time to time they will meet and discuss.

Śrīpāda Vaiṣṇava Mahārāja: All the devotees agreed unanimously that these things should be done, and now different *sevā*-teams will come together and decide how things will be done.

Śrīla Nārāyaṇa Gosvāmī Mahārāja: Yaśodharā was at the meeting?

Śrīpāda Vaiṣṇava Mahārāja No, she had to go back to China to get a new visa.

Śrīla Nārāyaṇa Gosvāmī Mahārāja: She is translating something. She should also join.

Śrīpāda Vaiṣṇava Mahārāja: So many of the devotees are qualified.

Śrīla Nārāyaṇa Gosvāmī Mahārāja: I think that in China we can preach so much more; there is great scope. They are very polite and humble, and they have some heartly desire to serve Kṛṣṇa.

Śrīpāda Padmanābha Mahārāja: Our Guru Mahārāja, Śrī Śrīmad Bhaktivedānta Svāmī Mahārāja, said that the Chinese race would be the last ones in the world amongst all the different races to come to Kṛṣṇa consciousness, but they would be the best devotees. He said one reason why is because they are very determined people and can accept hard austerities.

Śrīla Nārāyaṇa Gosvāmī Mahārāja: We have seen some symptoms like this.

April 16, 2008
Morning Walk

Śrīpāda Dāmodara Mahārāja: In the meeting of Rāmānanda Rāya and Mahāprabhu, when Rāmānanda Rāya had *darśana* of Mahāprabhu he could remember, "Oh, I am Viśākhā." It seems amazing that he could forget his relation with Kṛṣṇa before this.

Śrīla Nārāyaṇa Gosvāmī Mahārāja: If Kṛṣṇa can forget, "I am the Supreme Lord," why can't His associates forget? Mother Yaśodā and all other associates of Vraja forget that He is the Supreme Lord; otherwise there would be no pastimes.

Yadunātha dāsa: Gurudeva, in *Śrīmad-Bhāgavatam* it is mentioned that at the end of Kali-yuga, at a proper time according to the planetary arrangements, there will be two kings who will come to external consciousness and rule the Earth.[2] Are these kings here on Earth at the present time, or are they on other planets? Also, how will they populate this Earth with people when Satya-yuga comes?

Śrīla Nārāyaṇa Gosvāmī Mahārāja: After Kali-yuga, Kalki will come and destroy all atheists. After that, Satya-yuga will again manifest, at which time two kings will be there to rule the Earth. Your statement is correct.

---

[2] "Devāpi, the brother of Mahārāja Śāntanu, and Maru, the descendant of Ikṣvāku, both possess great mystic strength and are living even now in the village of Kalāpa. At the end of the age of Kali, these two kings, having received instruction directly from the Supreme Personality of Godhead, Vāsudeva, will return to human society and re-establish the eternal religion of man, characterized by the divisions of *varṇa* and *āśrama*, just as it was before. The cycle of four ages – Satya, Tretā, Dvāpara, and Kali – continues perpetually among living beings on this Earth, repeating the same general sequence of events" (*Śrīmad-Bhāgavatam* 12.2.37–39).

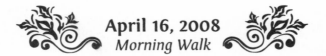

Brajanātha dāsa: He is asking if these two kings are here on Earth at present.

Śrīla Nārāyaṇa Gosvāmī Mahārāja: They are here. We were previously in Satya-yuga in another form. Similarly, they are here now in some form, and at that time they will be kings.

Yadunātha dāsa: We hear that our suffering is not caused by other living entities, but by our own *karma*. If someone is causing trouble to others, can he say, "I am not the cause of others' suffering, so don't blame me"?

Śrīla Nārāyaṇa Gosvāmī Mahārāja: (To Śrīpāda Padmanābha Mahārāja:) You should answer.

Śrīpāda Padmanābha Mahārāja: I would say that if a person does not accept responsibility for his current actions, he is creating further *karma*.

It is true that difficulty given by a certain person is arranged by the previous *karma* of those who are the victims of that difficulty. For example, if someone becomes your child, and then as your child he causes you so much difficulty, it is your *karma*. But it is also his *karma*. If that child doesn't accept responsibility for his actions, then he continues his own *karma*.

Śrīpāda Mādhava Mahārāja: Child is another thing. But suppose I am creating some chaos for you and I tell you, "It is your fault and due to your *karma*, so don't blame me." Is this correct or not?

Śrīpāda Padmanābha Mahārāja: It is true that everyone is coming together by their separate *karma* and causing each other difficulty. But I cannot say that I am not to blame if I hurt someone. Still I am to blame, because I have free will. I can choose to cause you difficulty or not.

Śrīpāda Mādhava Mahārāja: If I create chaos and beat you, I may say, "This is your *karma*." But if I tell you this, I am creating my own new *karma*.

Yadunātha dāsa: That person is making new *karma* for himself.

Śrīla Nārāyaṇa Gosvāmī Mahārāja: Suppose a bull comes and hits a person with his horns. If that person beats him to take revenge, then that person is creating new *karma* for himself. The bull is not creating new *karma* for himself. Only humans can create *karma*. Bulls and other lower species can only taste the suffering of their previous *karma*.

Śrīpāda Mādhava Mahārāja: His main question is this: Suppose one human being is hitting another human being and says, "Don't blame me, this is due to your *karma* that I am beating you."

Śrīla Nārāyaṇa Gosvāmī Mahārāja: No, this is wrong. Although the person who is being beaten is suffering his previous *karma*, the person who is doing the beating is creating his own new *karma*. He cannot blame others. Only human beings can do *karma* – not animals or birds or other species lower than that of humans.

Vallabha-kānti dāsa: What happens if a person in Kṛṣṇa consciousness thinks, "I am doing this for the benefit of others in Kṛṣṇa consciousness," but he is actually causing others distress. Can that also be considered *karma*?

Śrīpāda Mādhava Mahārāja: If an *uttama-bhakta* causes 'distress' for a *kaniṣṭha-adhikārī*, this is not *karma*; it is for the benefit of the *kaniṣṭha-adhikārī*.

Vallabha-kānti dāsa: What if the person causing distress isn't in the *uttama* stage?

Śrīpāda Mādhava Mahārāja: In that case he is on the platform of *karma*. How can he tell if what he is doing is pleasing to Kṛṣṇa? How can he say for sure that what he is doing is for Kṛṣṇa?

Kamala-kānta dāsa (from Germany): Some people think, "I do so much service. I chant and follow the process of *bhakti*, but I am still suffering."

Śrīla Nārāyaṇa Gosvāmī Mahārāja: Such persons are not really devotees. A pure devotee cannot think like this.

Kamala-kānta dāsa: What about the *madhyama* (intermediate devotee) or the *kaniṣṭha* (neophyte)?

Śrīla Nārāyaṇa Gosvāmī Mahārāja: A *kaniṣṭha* may think like this, but a pure Vaiṣṇava will not.

Kamala-kānta dāsa: I read in Śrīla Viśvanātha Cakravartī Ṭhākura's commentary on the Tenth Canto of *Śrīmad-Bhāgavatam* that there are three reasons why devotees suffer: (1) to maintain the confidentiality of devotional service; (2) to not uproot the opinions of atheists; and (3) to increase the hankering of the devotee. Is this correct?

Śrīla Nārāyaṇa Gosvāmī Mahārāja: This is okay. Devotees who chant Kṛṣṇa's name purely and practice pure devotion to Kṛṣṇa have no *karma*. Kṛṣṇa personally gives them this suffering; it is not the fruit of their *karma*. When suffering and problems come to such devotees, they consider that Kṛṣṇa wants them to be humble and tolerant. They think, "Oh, I am very wretched." Such humility will come.

Śrīpāda Giri Mahārāja: Śrīla Gurudeva, devotees think that *karma* is not punishment; it is Kṛṣṇa's mercy.

Śrīla Nārāyaṇa Gosvāmī Mahārāja: In his humility, the devotee considers such situations as both *karma* and Kṛṣṇa's mercy.

tat te 'nukampāṁ su-samīkṣamāṇo
bhuñjāna evātma-kṛtaṁ vipākam
hṛd-vāg vapurbhir vidadhan namas te
jīveta yo mukti-pade sa dāya-bhāk

(*Śrīmad-Bhāgavatam* 10.14.8)

> My dear Lord, one who earnestly waits for You to bestow Your causeless mercy upon him, all the while patiently suffering the reactions of his past misdeeds and offering You respectful obeisances with his heart, words, and body, is surely eligible for liberation, for it has become his rightful claim.

Tolerating all sufferings, he thinks, "Kṛṣṇa has given me these miseries so that I will learn tolerance." In the face of such circumstances, one who always offers obeisances to Kṛṣṇa by body, mind, and words is happy in this world and becomes an inheritor of *bhakti*.

Śrīpāda Mādhava Mahārāja: If some senior devotees are speaking with each other, and junior devotees, without any consideration, start speaking, is this good or not?

Śrīla Nārāyaṇa Gosvāmī Mahārāja: This is not right.

Śrīpāda Mādhava Mahārāja: It is an offense?

Śrīla Nārāyaṇa Gosvāmī Mahārāja: It is not an offense – it is ignorance. It simply means he was not raised in a good family and has not learned proper etiquette. He should wait.

Uttama-kṛṣṇa dāsa: Gurudeva, regarding the question of *karma*: If I beat somebody, does it mean that person previously beat me? For example, if he owed me ten dollars, now he is paying me back. Is it like this?

Śrīla Nārāyaṇa Gosvāmī Mahārāja: No. We should tolerate this, as Śrīla Haridāsa Ṭhākura was tolerant. Prahlāda Mahārāja was given poison, put in a fire, and tortured in many other ways; but he never thought, "I will take revenge against my father." This is not Vaiṣṇava etiquette.

Śrīpāda Padmanābha Mahārāja: What if that devotee is thinking, "Somebody is coming to kill me!"? But his body belongs to Gurudeva.

Śrīla Nārāyaṇa Gosvāmī Mahārāja: You are not Prahlāda or Sītā-devī. You should try to escape, to save your life.

Śrīpāda Dāmodara Mahārāja: Nityānanda Prabhu ran away when Jagāi and Mādhāi went to beat him. Śrīla Haridāsa Ṭhākura also ran away.

Śrīla Nārāyaṇa Gosvāmī Mahārāja: *Mahā-bhāgavatas* never run in fear.[3] They know that Kṛṣṇa is present with them. They know that the Lord's Sudarśana *cakra* (His disc weapon) will come and finish their aggressor.

Yadunātha dāsa: The Pāṇḍavas were insulted and they fought back. Does this mean that they are not *mahā-bhāgavatas*?

Śrīpāda Padmanābha Mahārāja: We read in *Mahābhārata* that the Pāṇḍavas were given so much trouble and insults by Duryodhana and the Kauravas. They tolerated this for many years, but in the end they fought. He is asking if this means they are not *mahā-bhāgavatas*.

Śrīla Nārāyaṇa Gosvāmī Mahārāja: While sitting on his chariot at the beginning of the Mahābhārata War and seeing all his relatives on the opposing side, Arjuna told Kṛṣṇa, "I cannot kill them. Taking the occupation of begging is better than fighting for a kingdom and opulence. Why should I fight just for the sake of winning this kingdom? I should not fight." Śrī Kṛṣṇa replied, "You should fight."

Śrīpāda Mādhava Mahārāja: Kṛṣṇa told him, "You will be the instrumental cause."

---

[3] Nityānanda Prabhu and Śrīla Haridāsa Ṭhākura were not really afraid. It is stated in Śrīla Vṛndāvana dāsa Ṭhākura's *Śrī Caitanya-bhāgavata* (*Madhya-khaṇḍa*, Chapter 13): "The two rogues were now chasing the two saints, and although they cried out, 'Catch them! Catch them!' they were still not near them. Nityānanda said, 'My dear Vaiṣṇava, Haridāsa, we have gotten ourselves into a fine mess; we can call ourselves lucky if we come out of this alive!' Ṭhākura Haridāsa replied, 'O Lord, what is the use of talking? Acting on Your advice, we now face unnatural or violent death. On account of You, we have given instructions on the holy name of Kṛṣṇa to these two faithless drunkards and now we are earning our due reaction and punishment: Death!' Speaking in this manner, Lord Nityānanda and Haridāsa continued to run, laughing gleefully while the two rogues chased after them hurling loud abuses."

Śrīla Nārāyaṇa Gosvāmī Mahārāja: He inspired Arjuna to fight, but He never inspired Duryodhana. The Pāṇḍavas did not fight for themselves. They wanted only to fulfill the desire of Śrī Kṛṣṇa. Whatever we do, we should do to please Kṛṣṇa. There should be no other reason for any of our activities.

April 16, 2008
Airport Darśana

Śyāmarāṇī dāsī: It is stated in scripture, and you also teach, that all those in the line of Śrī Caitanya Mahāprabhu have two constitutional, spiritual forms – one in the pastimes of Rādhā and Kṛṣṇa, and another in the pastimes of Śrī Caitanya Mahāprabhu.

Many scriptures describe the personal services of the servants of Śrīmatī Rādhārāṇī in Her transcendental pastimes with Kṛṣṇa. They describe the services of the followers of Rūpa Gosvāmī in his form as Śrī Rūpa Mañjarī.

So my question is this: What are the personal services of the followers of Śrīla Rūpa Gosvāmī in the pastimes of Śrī Caitanya Mahāprabhu?

Śrīla Nārāyaṇa Gosvāmī Mahārāja: Yes, they may have two constitutional forms, one in the pastimes of Kṛṣṇa and also one in the pastimes of Mahāprabhu. In his book, *Śrī Gaura-gaṇoddeśa-dīpikā*, Śrīla Kavi Karṇapūra explains that in *gaura-līlā*, Mahāprabhu's pastimes, Rādhikā is Śrī Gadādhara Paṇḍita, Lalitā-devī is Śrī Svarūpa Dāmodara, and Viśākhā-devī is Śrī Rāya Rāmānanda. Śrīla Rūpa Gosvāmī also explains this in his *Rādhā-kṛṣṇa-gaṇoddeśa-dīpikā*.

Śyāmarāṇī dāsī: With reference to the books and prayers of Śrīla Rūpa Gosvāmī, Śrīla Raghunātha dāsa Gosvāmī, Śrīla Narottama dāsa Ṭhākura, and our other *ācāryas*, you have told us many times about the personal services of the followers of Rūpa Mañjarī in Goloka Vṛndāvana.

Śrīla Nārāyaṇa Gosvāmī Mahārāja: Their services are rendered according to their group (*yūtha*). For example, Śrī Rūpa Mañjarī is in the group of Lalitā-devī. Lalitā-devī has delegated so many duties for those in her group.

Śyāmarāṇī dāsī: You have told us about their many services, like assisting Śrīmatī Rādhārāṇī in cooking for Kṛṣṇa and then serving His *prasādam*.

Śrīla Nārāyaṇa Gosvāmī Mahārāja: Some make garlands, some fan Her with a *cāmara* fan, some make powders for massaging Her, and others engage in a variety of other services.

Śyāmarāṇī dāsī: When those same maidservants are in the form of followers of Śrīla Rūpa Gosvāmī in Śrī Caitanya Mahāprabhu's pastimes, what are their services to Mahāprabhu?

Śrīla Nārāyaṇa Gosvāmī Mahārāja: You can see in *Śrī Caitanya-caritāmṛta* what Svarūpa Dāmodara, Rāya Rāmānanda, and Rūpa Gosvāmī are doing. What is Śrīla Rūpa Gosvāmī doing?

Śyāmarāṇī dāsī: Mostly *kīrtana*, offering obeisances, and writing books?

Śrīla Nārāyaṇa Gosvāmī Mahārāja:

> *śrī-caitanya-mano-'bhīṣṭaṁ sthāpitaṁ yena bhūtale*
> *svayaṁ rūpaḥ kadā mahyaṁ dadāti sva-padāntikam*
>
> (*Śrī Prema-bhakti-candrikā*,
> by Śrīla Narottama dāsa Ṭhākura)

> When will Śrī Rūpa Gosvāmī give me the shelter of his lotus feet? Because he understood the innermost desire of Śrī Caitanya Mahāprabhu, he was able to establish His mission in this world and is very dear to the Lord.

Śyāmarāṇī dāsī: Preaching and establishing His mission.

Do all the followers of Śrīla Rūpa Gosvāmī have the same kind of services?

Śrīla Nārāyaṇa Gosvāmī Mahārāja: There may be some differences, and those different duties are all according to one's particular group. Each group has various duties.

Śyāmarāṇī dāsī: Do they also render personal services?

Śrīla Nārāyaṇa Gosvāmī Mahārāja: One may write books, preach, and perform *kīrtana*. Śrīla Haridāsa Ṭhākura performed *kīrtana* and the chanting of the holy names. Śrī Svarūpa Dāmodara was always with Śrī Caitanya Mahāprabhu in the Gambhīrā. Śrīla Sanātana Gosvāmī was writing books, establishing Deities, and engaging in many other services.

Regarding their followers, they do likewise. What am I doing? I am not an eternal associate, but what am I doing? What was your Gurudeva, Śrīla Bhaktivedānta Svāmī Mahārāja, doing?

Śyāmarāṇī dāsī: Writing, preaching, and opening temples.

Śrīla Nārāyaṇa Gosvāmī Mahārāja: And inspiring everyone to perform *bhajana*. He was doing that for which Mahāprabhu appeared in this world.

Śyāmarāṇī dāsī: Do Śrīla Rūpa Gosvāmī and his followers also perform personal services for Him, like cooking and serving *prasādam*?

Śrīla Nārāyaṇa Gosvāmī Mahārāja: You can see what they do by reading *Caitanya-caritāmṛta* and other authorized books. And we should also become qualified to do this.

Jayaśrī dāsī: Śrīla Gurudeva, you say that only a pure Vaiṣṇava or *guru* can give the seed of *bhakti* to the conditioned soul. At the same time, it is said that the seed of *bhakti* is already within each soul. How can we reconcile this?

Śrīla Nārāyaṇa Gosvāmī Mahārāja: The seed of *bhakti* is present in each soul, but there is something more to be given. A seed alone will not suffice. If some water, air, soil, and sunrays are given to that seed, then it will sprout. Do you understand?

Jayaśrī dāsī: I remember you saying that *bhakti* is the sentiment for Rādhā and Kṛṣṇa – the special feeling of love and affection for Rādhā and Kṛṣṇa. Does this mean that the *guru* gives this sentiment? Is that correct?

Śrīla Nārāyaṇa Gosvāmī Mahārāja: First he gives a seed of that sentiment, meaning the desire to serve Śrī Rādhā and Kṛṣṇa. Though the seed is already in the heart of the soul, *guru* makes an environment for that seed to sprout. So he gives something.

Jayaśrī dāsī: How can the seed sprout?

Śrīla Nārāyaṇa Gosvāmī Mahārāja: By water, air, and sunrays. The bonafide spiritual master gives all these things by speaking about those topics which are favorable and inspiring for *bhakti*. He gives *hari-kathā* and *dīkṣā*, which culminate in a realized relationship with Śrī Kṛṣṇa.

Jayaśrī dāsī: *Śrīmad-Bhāgavatam* mentions that the real Buddha is an incarnation of Kṛṣṇa. Why is the real Buddha not worshiped nowadays? Why is it that a false Buddha is worshiped?

Śrīla Nārāyaṇa Gosvāmī Mahārāja: We preach about the real Buddha wherever we go. Do you know the difference between Bhagavat Buddha, meaning the incarnation of Śrī Kṛṣṇa, and the Māyāvadi Buddha?

Jayaśrī dāsī: Yes, you told us this before, many years ago in Taiwan.

Śrīla Nārāyaṇa Gosvāmī Mahārāja: Those in the line of Śrīla Bhaktisiddhānta Sarasvatī Ṭhākura teach this truth. Therefore some people know – but where we do not go, they do not know. Now it is the duty of all of you to preach this mission.

Dīnanātha dāsa: Your Gurudeva's book, *Māyāvādakī Jīvana* (*Beyond Nirvāṇa*), mentions that Śrī Śaṅkarācārya was defeated by the Buddhists in Tibet, and then he gave up his life by plunging into a vat of boiling oil.

Śrīla Nārāyaṇa Gosvāmī Mahārāja: Yes.

Dīnanātha dāsa: It is true?

Śrīla Nārāyaṇa Gosvāmī Mahārāja: What my Gurudeva has written is true. He has evidence.

Jayaśrī dāsī: How can this be true? Was Śaṅkarācārya not a scholar like the Tibetan Lama (Buddhist) *guru*?

Śrīla Nārāyaṇa Gosvāmī Mahārāja: Śaṅkarācārya defeated all kinds of religious persons in India, but he could not defeat any devotee. He never defeated any devotee of Kṛṣṇa, or Rāma, or any incarnation of Viṣṇu. He only defeated *jñānīs* (mental speculators) and *karmīs* (materialistic philosophers).

Dīnanātha dāsa: Just some *jñānīs* and *karmīs*.

Jayaśrī dāsī: Isn't Śaṅkarācārya more advanced than any Buddhist? How could he be defeated by them?

Śrīla Nārāyaṇa Gosvāmī Mahārāja: He could be defeated by them because he accepted Buddhism. He accepted and preached 'covered Buddhism,' a hidden form of Buddhism. The root of Śaṅkarācārya's teaching is Buddhism. His *guru* was Govindapāda, whose *guru* was Gauḍapāda. They knew more about Buddhism more than he knew.

Jayaśrī dāsī: So, the *guru* of Śaṅkarācārya is more powerful than Śaṅkarācārya.

Śrīla Nārāyaṇa Gosvāmī Mahārāja: Yes, more powerful.

Nanda-nandana dāsa: Since both of them are not bonafide, what is the significance of one unbonafide teaching or teacher defeating another unbonafide teaching?

Śrīla Nārāyaṇa Gosvāmī Mahārāja: Śaṅkarācārya taught a special thing: He accepted the Vedas, and also the Supreme Lord as the Creator. He taught that the Supreme Lord exists, but has no form. He taught that the Supreme is impersonal. This is the only difference. Buddhism does not accept the existence of God.

Gauḍapāda was the *guru* of Śaṅkarācārya's *guru*. The disciple of Gauḍapāda wrote commentaries called *Sāṅkhya-kārika*, from which Śaṅkarācārya based his own commentary and preached his Māyāvāda (impersonal) philosophy. They knew more than Śaṅkarācārya in the matter of their own teachings, no doubt.

On the other hand, Śaṅkarācārya was actually Śaṅkara, Mahadeva (Lord Śiva). No one can defeat Śaṅkara, so it was only by the wish of Kṛṣṇa that he appeared to be defeated. Now his duty was completed. There was no need of his staying any longer in this world.

Jayaśrī dāsī: But the way he died was quite horrible – to die in boiling oil! Why didn't Kṛṣṇa arrange for a better way?

Śrīla Nārāyaṇa Gosvāmī Mahārāja: There was a ruling by the Buddhists that no one should deviate from Buddhism and no one should follow Śaṅkarācārya. To this end, they determined that everyone should see how he received that painful death. It was declared before the debate that he who loses will enter boiling oil.

This may be likened to the Muslim Kazi who declared that Śrīla Haridāsa Ṭhākura should not be beaten inside a house, but in twenty-two marketplaces. In this way all would know, and no one would dare to give up being Muslim to accept Hinduism.

Dīnanātha dāsa: Yes. It was to create fear.

But, at least the Māyāvāda philosophy accepted the Lord, although they said He is impersonal, without form. This is more favorable than Buddhism. If Śaṅkarācārya had defeated that Buddhist, wouldn't that have been more favorable for Caitanya Mahāprabhu's mission?

Śrīla Nārāyaṇa Gosvāmī Mahārāja: Somehow this was the will of Kṛṣṇa. No one can challenge Kṛṣṇa. Without Kṛṣṇa's will, nothing can be done. Even a blade of grass cannot move and leaves cannot fall without His will. So, there was some reason why Śaṅkarācārya was defeated.

Why did Duryodhana want to disrobe Draupadī and make her naked? Was she meant to suffer for some past *karma*?

Jayaśrī dāsī: He was envious.

Śrīla Nārāyaṇa Gosvāmī Mahārāja: No, no, no. Kṛṣṇa personally inspired Duryodhana to do this. From within Duryodhana's heart, Kṛṣṇa told him: "You should do this." Kṛṣṇa thought, "In this way the Mahābhārata battle will take place and I will have the opportunity to kill all the Kauravas."

Śrīpāda Mādhava Mahārāja: Kṛṣṇa considered, "I will take away the burden from the Earth."

Śrīla Nārāyaṇa Gosvāmī Mahārāja: There are so many reasons.

Śrīpāda Mādhava Mahārāja: Kṛṣṇa also wanted to show the world Draupadī's full surrender to Him. She called Him, and He was bound to come.

Śrīla Nārāyaṇa Gosvāmī Mahārāja: This may also be the reason.

During the attempted disrobing of Draupadī, Bhīma declared, "Because Duryodhana said, 'Naked Draupadī will sit on my lap,' I will break his leg. And I will break the arm of Duḥśāsana because he pulled her cloth with that arm."

Śyāmarāṇī dāsī: Śrīla Gurudeva, a couple of days ago you were speaking about the pastimes of Lord Rāma. You said that Rāma placed the real Sītā in the care of Agni-deva, the fire-god, and a false Sītā was kidnapped. Then Rāma wept in the forest, "Alas Sītā, alas Sītā!"

Śrīla Nārāyaṇa Gosvāmī Mahārāja: This was Rāma's sweet human-like pastime.

Śyāmarāṇī dāsī: But He already knew that She was with Agni-deva. Why would He weep?

Śrīla Nārāyaṇa Gosvāmī Mahārāja: At that time Rāma forgot all of this.

Śyāmarāṇī dāsī: Oh, very interesting.

Śrīla Nārāyaṇa Gosvāmī Mahārāja: (leaving for his gate to board his plane, calling out to the devotees present) Come to India in October–November for Vraja-maṇḍala *parikramā*. I am inviting you all.

Endnotes

[1] "The Cāturmāsya period begins in the month of Āṣāḍha (June–July) from the full-moon day of Āṣāḍha until the full-moon day of Kārtika. That is also a period of four months. This period, calculated by the lunar months, is called Cāturmāsya, The whole period takes place during the rainy season. Cāturmāsya should be observed by all sections of the population. It does not matter whether one is a *gṛhastha* or a *sannyāsī*. The observance is obligatory for all *āśramas*. The real purpose behind the vow taken during these four months is to minimize the quantity of sense gratification. This is not very difficult. In the month of Śrāvaṇa one should not eat spinach, in the month of Bhādra one should not eat yogurt, and in the month of Āśvina one should not drink milk... On the whole, during the four-month period of Cāturmāsya one should practice giving up all food intended for sense enjoyment" (*Śrī Caitanya-caritāmṛta, Madhya-līlā* 4.169, purport).

"The Cāturmāsya ceremony is observed during the four months of the rainy season in India (approximately July, August, September, and October), beginning from Śrāvaṇa. During these four months, saintly persons who are accustomed to travel from one place to another to propagate Kṛṣṇa consciousness remain at one place, usually a holy place of pilgrimage. During these times, there are certain special rules and regulations which are strictly followed. It is stated in the *Skanda Purāṇa* that during this period, if someone circumambulates the temple of Viṣṇu at least four times, it is understood that he has traveled all over the universe. By such circumambulation, one is understood to have seen all the holy places where the Ganges water is flowing, and by following the regulative principles of Cāturmāsya one can very quickly be raised to the platform of devotional service" (*Nectar of Devotion*, Chapter Nine).

Vancouver, Canada

April 17-21, 2008

April 17, 2008
Evening darśana at the home of Śrīman Ragbhir dāsa

Śrīla Nārāyaṇa Gosvāmī Mahārāja: I am very happy to see so many devotees. I did not think I would be meeting with so many Canadians.

Do you know why I have come here from so far away, from India? I have come to remind you that you are refugees in this world. You have come to this world because you have forgotten Kṛṣṇa. Kṛṣṇa has mercifully given us this human form only so that we can remember Him and perform His devotional services; not for any other reason. Always remember that death is on our head, death is below us, in front of us, and behind us – waiting.

One day soon you will become old; you must become old. At that time no doctor or scientist will be able to save you, for they will also become old. Neither your mother, nor your father, nor your friends, nor anyone else will be able to go with you when you have to leave this world, and you will not be able to take with you a single farthing. Therefore, what you are doing at present may be likened to the activities of the donkeys – laboring all day with no result. Always remember this.

Do not worry about being happy in this world, and do not try to remove your suffering artificially. As suffering comes without invitation, happiness will also come automatically; there is no need to endeavor for this.

Kṛṣṇa has invested all His power and mercy in His names. All His qualities are endowed in His holy names: Hare Kṛṣṇa, Hare Kṛṣṇa, Kṛṣṇa Kṛṣṇa, Hare Hare, Hare Rāma, Hare Rāma, Rāma Rāma, Hare Hare.

Time is very short; no one knows when death will come. Even an old person may remain alive after his or her children die. Nothing is certain, so do not endeavor for anything material. Go on chanting, and certainly everything for your maintenance will be automatically provided. Always chant and remember Kṛṣṇa, and be happy forever. This is the essence of our entire Indian literature, including the Vedas, Upaniṣads, *Bhagavad-gītā*, and *Śrīmad-Bhāgavatam*. If you want to be happy, chant and serve Kṛṣṇa, and then happily return to your original place, Goloka Vṛndāvana – back to Godhead, back to home.

Devotee: Will we know you there?

Śrīla Nārāyaṇa Gosvāmī Mahārāja: I will keep a place for you there.

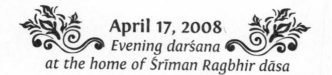

April 19, 2008
Morning darśana
at the home of Hemanta dāsa Adhikārī

Śrīla Nārāyaṇa Gosvāmī Mahārāja: Please consider that you are not your body. If your soul leaves your body, your body will become inert and lifeless. It will not able to walk or do anything. When the soul leaves, your body will die; it will have no soul. At that time, because it will begin to rot, your relatives will bring it to a crematorium, set fire to it, and it will burn.

What is this body? It is a bag of urine, blood, stool, and so many other foul substances. Actually, you are not this body; you are the soul within the body. The soul has a very beautiful form with all good qualities, but it is now covered by this gross and subtle body.

Actually, you are an eternal servant of Kṛṣṇa, but due to the influence of *māyā*, the deluding potency of the Lord, you have forgotten this. You wanted to taste the pleasure of *māyā*.

Whatever wealth and possessions you are collecting in this world cannot give you happiness. Now you are thinking, "I am very strong. My health is so good." But one day you will all become old. Those who have taken birth must become old. At that time you will be overwhelmed with diseases and you will be forced to give up this body. Kindly do not waste your time with this false conviction: "By worldly things I will be happy."

In this world we should try to maintain our body only to realize our eternal identity. Then we can attain real happiness. Śrī Kṛṣṇa, the Supreme Lord, has mercifully given us this human form of life only to facilitate the realization of who we truly are, who Kṛṣṇa is, and what is our eternal, transcendental relationship with Him. When we realize these truths, we will be forever free from the cycle of birth and death, and we will be happy.

If you are drinking and smoking, and eating meat, fish, and eggs, you will not be able to take *harināma*. Do you know what meat is? M-e-a-t: ME-EAT. Those whom you are eating will take revenge and eat you, life after life. Kṛṣṇa has given us all freedom, or independence, so it is not for us to disturb anyone else's independence. Kṛṣṇa has given it, so how can we disturb it? In my opinion, as a well-wisher and seeing you as my dear daughters and sons, I am suggesting that you give up these addictions at once, and at once try to do *bhajana*. Then you will be happy.

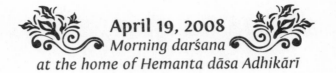

As I travel throughout the world, hundreds of thousands of people, including wealthy and educated people, college professors, deans, doctors, engineers, and many others, are giving up these bad habits and chanting the holy name; and their lives are now full of joy. This is my request to you all: Give up these bad habits, be qualified to chant Hare Kṛṣṇa, and thus be happy forever.

In truth we are the eternal servants of the Supreme Lord. The Lord is one without a second, and that one Lord is Kṛṣṇa. In the Christian religion we see Christ. Who is Christ? In Jesus' youth he traveled to India, where he visited Vṛndāvana, Jagannātha Purī, Ayodhyā, and many other holy places. He saw the Deities of Kṛṣṇa in Vṛndāvana and heard everyone chanting His name, 'Kṛṣṇa.' In Jagannātha Purī he heard the devotees pronouncing Kṛṣṇa as 'Kroosna.' From Kroosna came 'Christa,' and the pronunciation later became 'Christ.' So Christ is actually none other than Kṛṣṇa Himself.

We are eternal servants of the Supreme Lord, whether we know this or not. Not only humans, but all living entities are His eternal servants. Unfortunately we have forgotten this, and as a result, for countless births we have been experiencing the endless pain and sorrow of birth and death. In past lives we could not be happy, but we are still seeking it.

Śrī Kṛṣṇa has mercifully given us this human life, and for the purpose of attaining the ultimate goal of life, He has given us the opportunity to realize "Who am I," and who is He, our Holy Master.

Very unhappy that His sons and daughters have been greatly suffering since time immemorial, He sends some of His associates, who descend to this world in a disciplic line and teach how the people of the world can attain pure devotion to Him. He requests them, "Tell everyone: 'You are not inhabitants of this world. You are like refugees from Goloka Vṛndāvana. You are an eternal resident of Goloka Vṛndāvana. You cannot find any real happiness in this world.' Help them to return back to Godhead."

By his mercy, Śrīla Bhaktivedānta Svāmī Mahārāja, your Śrīla Prabhupāda, came from India before me and traveled throughout the world to convey this message. His *guru* had told him to come, and in a few years he established so many preaching centers – in the mountains, on islands in the midst of oceans, and throughout the world. He translated and wrote commentaries on many transcendental literatures such as *Śrīmad-Bhāgavatam* and *Bhagavad-gītā As It Is*. He also made hundreds of thousands of disciples.

My *dīkṣā-gurudeva*, Śrīla Bhakti Prajñāna Keśava Gosvāmī Mahārāja, and *śikṣā-gurudeva*, Śrīla Bhaktivedānta Svāmī Mahārāja, have sent me to help with this same purpose. I am 88 years old and I have traveled throughout the world about twenty-six times. Why? Not for money. In India I can easily acquire *dahl* and *capātīs*, as they are available everywhere. So why have I come here? I came only to fulfill the desire of my Gurudeva and *guru-paramparā*. Very few can realize our message.

Nowadays, true *gurus* are very rare. So many false *gurus* come to Western countries from India, perhaps for money, or for name and fame. They collect a great deal of money from America, England, and Europe, but what will they do with this money? In the end they will have to give it all up. They will not be able to take a farthing with them when they die.

No one in our bonafide *guru-paramparā* line was motivated to make money. Their only concern was to selflessly help the conditioned souls. This is our aim and objective. At the same time, if I am traveling, some money is needed for my airfare and that of my associates. Who will give this? Therefore, wherever I go, the devotees donate something so that I can travel. This comes easily, without my asking them.

If in my travels I can inspire one person to become a devotee of Kṛṣṇa, my tour will be successful.

April 21, 2008
Airport Darśana

Lola dāsī: You told the pastime in which the milk in the pot at the home of Mother Yaśodā was lamenting, "I am not able to serve Kṛṣṇa." So now we understand that the milk in Goloka Vṛndāvana is conscious. My question is this: when the milk becomes *rasagullās* (Indian sweets) and each cowherd boy eats one *rasagullā*, how is it that the milk is eternal?

Śrīla Nārāyaṇa Gosvāmī Mahārāja: When Kṛṣṇa ate the *rasagullā*, it entered His mouth and into His stomach. There it became eternally situated in His stomach; at the same time it was already eternal, for everything related to Kṛṣṇa is eternal. Whatever Kṛṣṇa eats – all those things are eternal. Do you understand?

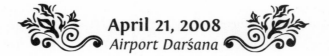

Śyāmarāṇī dāsī: No.

Śrīla Nārāyaṇa Gosvāmī Mahārāja: Kṛṣṇa is eternal, and in Vṛndāvana everything is eternal. So Kṛṣṇa ate the *rasagullā* and kept it in His stomach. If He can keep the entire world in His stomach, why can't He keep a *rasagullā* in His stomach?

Śyāmarāṇī dāsī: Does that *rasagullā* remain eternally conscious?

Śrīla Nārāyaṇa Gosvāmī Mahārāja: Everything in Kṛṣṇa is conscious.

Śyāmarāṇī dāsī: It is inconceivable.

Śrīla Nārāyaṇa Gosvāmī Mahārāja: Yes.

cintāmaṇi-prakara-sadmasu kalpa-vṛkṣa-
lakṣāvṛteṣu surabhīr abhipālayantam
lakṣmī-sahasra-śata-sambhrama-sevyamānaṁ
govindam ādi-puruṣaṁ tam ahaṁ bhajāmi
(*Brahma-saṁhitā* 5.29)

The transcendental realm is eternally adorned by millions of wish-fulfilling trees, by pavilions made of desire-fulfilling jewels, and by innumerable wish-fulfilling cows. There, thousands upon thousands of Lakṣmīs, or *gopīs*, are rendering services to the Supreme Personality with great affection. I worship that original Supreme Personality, Śrī Govinda.

Śyāmarāṇī dāsī: I think this is one of those things we can only understand when we are there in Goloka Vṛndāvana.

Śrīla Nārāyaṇa Gosvāmī Mahārāja: When you go there, then you will be able to understand.

Rāmacandra dāsa: Then also, we will not understand. Then we will understand only Kṛṣṇa; we will not think about how all this is happening.

Śrīla Nārāyaṇa Gosvāmī Mahārāja: The entire world is present in Kṛṣṇa's stomach. All persons and all living beings reside there, and they are also eternal. So the *rasagullā* is also eternal there.

Śyāmarāṇī dāsī: The *rasagullā* was previously milk. Does it become another living being when it becomes a *rasagullā*?

Śrīla Nārāyaṇa Gosvāmī Mahārāja: Kṛṣṇa can take many forms, His abode can take many forms, and His associates may also take many forms. So why can the milk not take many forms?

Śyāmarāṇī dāsī: Gurudeva, just before your flight at the Hong Kong airport you were explaining the types of services performed by the pure Gauḍīya Vaiṣṇavas when they are with Caitanya Mahāprabhu in Navadvīpa. You said that when we become perfect, we will go there to meet with Mahāprabhu and serve Him under the direction of His associates.

Regarding Śvetadvīpa (Mahāprabhu's eternal abode of Navadvīpa as it is manifest in the transcendental world within the realm of Goloka Vṛndāvana), is there a difference in what the devotees do there? I am asking because there is no need to write books in Śvetadvīpa Goloka. There is no need to preach to others there.

Śrīla Nārāyaṇa Gosvāmī Mahārāja: You will be an associate of Śrī Caitanya Mahāprabhu there. You will serve there, as Śrī Gadādhara Paṇḍita, Śrī Svarūpa Dāmodara, and Śrīla Rāya Rāmānanda serve Him. You will serve under their guidance.

What is Gadādhara Paṇḍita doing in the Navadvīpa pastimes of Caitanya Mahāprabhu? He is always with Mahāprabhu. So under him, and under those like him, you will do something. There are so many things to do.

Śyāmarāṇī dāsī: Like what? We have never heard.

Śrīla Nārāyaṇa Gosvāmī Mahārāja: It is endless.

Śyāmarāṇī dāsī: Can you give us a few examples of the endless things that they do in Śvetadvīpa (Navadvīpa in Goloka)?

Śrīla Nārāyaṇa Gosvāmī Mahārāja: Gadādhara Paṇḍita is like a friend. He is with Mahāprabhu and serving Him in so many ways.

Śyāmarāṇī dāsī: Sometimes cooking? Sometimes feeding?

Śrīla Nārāyaṇa Gosvāmī Mahārāja: No cooking. He would joke, sometimes asking questions with double meanings, and with very deep meanings. What is Śrī Rāya Rāmānanda doing?

Śyāmarāṇī dāsī: In Gambhīrā, he is singing songs and inspiring the Lord's moods. In Godāvarī he is…

Śrīla Nārāyaṇa Gosvāmī Mahārāja: What is Śrīvāsa Paṇḍita doing?

Śyāmarāṇī dāsī: He is doing *kīrtana* and hosting Him…

Rāmacandra dāsa: Śrīvāsa Paṇḍita is glorifying Lakṣmī, and Svarūpa Dāmodara is mock-arguing with him. This kind of pastime is going on.

Śrīla Nārāyaṇa Gosvāmī Mahārāja: You will have so many endless services to do there.

Śyāmarāṇī dāsī: What does Rūpa Gosvāmī do there in Śvetadvīpa?

Śrīla Nārāyaṇa Gosvāmī Mahārāja: He will glorify Mahāprabhu there, and play with Him.

Śyāmarāṇī dāsī: Playing? Doesn't he consider himself a disciple?

Śrīla Nārāyaṇa Gosvāmī Mahārāja: All His associates play with Him there.

Śyāmarāṇī dāsī: What do you mean by playing? Joking and talking and singing and dancing? In Indradyumna-sarovara lake in Jagannātha Purī, they were all joking. Advaita Ācārya and Nityānanda Prabhu and others were all joking and splashing each other. Like that?

Śrīla Nārāyaṇa Gosvāmī Mahārāja: How does a friend serve his friend? How are the cowherd boys serving Kṛṣṇa?

Śyāmarāṇī dāsī: By playing games, joking, challenging, mock-fighting.

Śrīla Nārāyaṇa Gosvāmī Mahārāja: There are so many things in Caitanya Mahāprabhu's pastimes that they can do.

Rāmacandra dāsa: Once you told me that Navadvīpa is the *mādhurya-dhāma* (the abode of sweet, human-like pastimes). I asked you what is the position of Rūpa Gosvāmī, because we have not heard that he is in Navadvīpa. We have seen that he is in Purī…

Śrīla Nārāyaṇa Gosvāmī Mahārāja: In Śvetadvīpa, all the places where Mahāprabhu performed His pastimes throughout the day (*aṣṭa-kālīya-līlā*) are present.

Rāmacandra dāsa: One time you said that Mahāprabhu is enjoying Rādhārāṇī's mood, and at that time Rūpa Gosvāmī and other associates are supporting that activity.

Śrīla Nārāyaṇa Gosvāmī Mahārāja: Do you understand?

Śyāmarāṇī dāsī: What do they do to support Lord Caitanya's mood?

Śrīla Nārāyaṇa Gosvāmī Mahārāja: As Mahāprabhu is doing *kīrtana*, they will join…

Rāmacandra dāsa: They may recite *Bhāgavatam ślokas* according to His mood.

Śrīla Nārāyaṇa Gosvāmī Mahārāja: So many things.

[Time to board the plane]

Toronto, Canada

April 22-23, 2008

April 22, 2008
Morning Walk

Trilokanātha dāsa: Śrīla Gurudeva, I have a question about my name. Śrīla Prabhupāda gave me the name Trilokanātha. I have heard that this means 'Lord of the three worlds,' which is not a very *rasika* understanding. Do you have a more *rasika* understanding of this name?

Śrīla Nārāyaṇa Gosvāmī Mahārāja: With reference to your name, it is different from the Trilokanātha who is Indra. Indra is the king of the three worlds, *bhūr*, *bhuvaḥ*, and *svaḥ*, but your name does not refer to Indra.

In this connection, the three worlds are the material world (*jaḍa-jagat*), the realm of the living entities (*jīva-jagat*), and the transcendental world (*cit-jagat*), Goloka Vṛndāvana. Therefore, Trilokanātha is one of the names of Śrī Kṛṣṇa Himself.

When Indra's false ego was shattered, he performed Kṛṣṇa's bathing ceremony (*abhiṣeka*). At that time Surabhī cow prayed to Kṛṣṇa, "Indra may be Trilokanātha, but You are the soul of the complete universe, and from You only all this cosmic world has manifested. Therefore, although Indra tried his best to kill my descendant cows in Vṛndāvana, they remained under Your shelter and You have protected them all so well. We do not know anyone else as the Supreme, nor do we go to any other god or demigod for protection. You are our Indra, You are the Supreme Father of the entire cosmic creation, and You are the protector and elevator of all the cows, *brāhmaṇas*, demigods, and all the pure devotees of Your Lordship."

Jagadīśa dāsa: When you first gave me *harināma* initiation, I started reading *Śrī Caitanya-caritāmṛta*. But then I was told by others to read *Śrīmad-Bhāgavatam*. They said that *Caitanya-caritāmṛta* is too high for me. Does it matter which book I read?

Śrīla Nārāyaṇa Gosvāmī Mahārāja: You can read *Śrī Caitanya-caritāmṛta*, and by reading it, you will be able to understand *Śrīmad-Bhāgavatam*. *Caitanya-caritāmṛta* will help you greatly in understanding *Śrīmad-Bhāgavatam*. All other scriptures are included and clarified there, and the explanations of all the verses of *Śrīmad-Bhāgavatam* are present there.

Jagadīśa dāsa: Thank you.

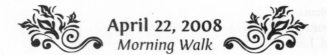

Trilokanātha dāsa: Śrīla Gurudeva, I am being encouraged by some of your senior disciples to do some public speaking, but I feel unprepared. I am wondering when I will know that I am ready.

Śrīla Nārāyaṇa Gosvāmī Mahārāja: If you start speaking, a flow of thoughts will automatically come to you. In order to speak you will study, and gradually you will develop.

Trilokanātha dāsa: May I have your blessings to do this?

Śrīla Nārāyaṇa Gosvāmī Mahārāja: Yes, my blessings are upon you. When I joined the *maṭha*[4], I knew nothing about all these topics. Gradually, by the mercy of Gurudeva, by hearing from him and by reading and writing and memorizing *ślokas*, I became knowledgeable.

April 23, 2008
Morning Walk Excerpt

Trilokanātha dāsa: Śrīla Gurudeva, I have one other question about a devotee's name. My wife's name is Mahojjvala. When Śrīla Prabhupāda gave her this name, the devotees told her that it means 'great light.' She was not satisfied with this explanation. Now she is wondering about the true meaning of her name.

Śrīla Nārāyaṇa Gosvāmī Mahārāja: Did your Gurudeva personally explain the meaning?

Trilokanātha dāsa: No. She didn't get the explanation directly from Śrīla Prabhupāda. She received the name in a letter from him.

Śrīpāda Mādhava Mahārāja: *Rādhikā ujjvala-rasera ācārya.* [Śrīmatī Rādhikā is the *ācārya* of the mellows of amorous love (*ujjvala-rasa*).]

Śrīla Nārāyaṇa Gosvāmī Mahārāja: There are two types of *mādhurya-rasa*; one is *svakīya*, the mood of wedded love, and one is *parakīya*, the mood of paramour love. Rādhikā is the embodiment of that *parakīya* mood in its highest stage. *Unnata-ujjvala-rasāṁ sva-bhakti-śriyam.*

---

4 *Maṭha* – a monastery; a temple of the Lord with an attached *āśrama* for *brahmacārīs* and *sannyāsīs*.

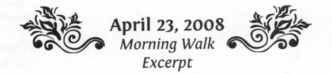

This highest *unnata-ujjvala rasa* is only in Rādhikā, and therefore She Herself is Mahojjvala.

Mahojjvala does not simply mean 'light.' Rather, so much light emanates from the nails of Śrīmatī Rādhikā.

Trilokanātha dāsa: Thank you.

Śrīla Gurudeva, you said that the *guru* is 'brooming' the disciples' hearts. He sweeps the dirty things out of the heart.

Śrīla Nārāyaṇa Gosvāmī Mahārāja: He does not broom; he clears by his words. He is not a sweeper.

Trilokanātha dāsa: I am asking you for the strength to keep my heart clean after you clean it out, so that the dirty things will not come back in.

Śrīla Nārāyaṇa Gosvāmī Mahārāja: My blessings are upon you so that you will become strong, with your *bhakti* gradually increasing, and so that unwanted things should not come in your heart. This blessing is for all.

Śyāmasundara dāsa: My younger brother was here yesterday. He is six years younger than me. He has been having a very difficult time over the past few years, struggling with an alcohol addiction. He told me that due to the alcohol addiction he was in the hospital, at death's door, and at that time he came to some understanding of God. He turned to God and asked for help, and now he understands that it is only by God's grace that he is alive today. He told me that he is now looking for a relationship with God. So I told him to come and meet you, thinking that perhaps he would take to Kṛṣṇa consciousness.

Śrīla Nārāyaṇa Gosvāmī Mahārāja: Very good. Then he will be happy forever.

Brajanātha dāsa: He still smokes?

Śyāmasundara dāsa:. Yes, he does. He said that he is working on one addiction at a time.

Śrīla Nārāyaṇa Gosvāmī Mahārāja: There are so many histories like this. There is a verse in the song, *Bhajahū Re Māna*: *rāmacandra-saṅga māge narottama dāsa*. Rāmacandra Kavirāja, the disciple of Śrīnivāsa Ācārya, had a younger brother, Durgadha, who was always worshiping Kali. He often told Durgadha that he should do *bhajana* of Kṛṣṇa, but his younger brother didn't care to listen.

Once, Durgadha became very sick. Although several people tried to save his life by administering medicines and by worshiping the demigoddess Durgā, still, day by day his health was decreasing and he was about to die. Rāmacandra Kavirāja came to him and asked, "Why are you worshiping Durgā? Why aren't you worshiping Kṛṣṇa, Govinda? Take responsibility for yourself and chant 'Govinda' one-pointedly. In this way you'll be cured, your life will be saved, and you'll be happy forever." Durgadha finally agreed, thinking, "Durgā couldn't help me," and he took initiation from Rāmacandra. Then gradually, in three or four days, as if by some magical effect his illness was cured, his health was restored, and he began to do *bhajana* under the guidance of his *guru*.

From then on he became known as Govinda dāsa Kavirāja. He was an excellent writer and poet, and after he wrote "*Bhajahū re māna,*" he sent it to Śrīla Jīva Gosvāmī. When Jīva Gosvāmī heard the *bhajana* of Govinda dāsa, he appreciated it so much that he told him, "Continue to compose *kīrtanas* like these. You are very qualified, so you should compose more and send them to me in Vṛndāvana." Śrīla Govinda dāsa Kavirāja then composed many poems glorifying Śrī Caitanya Mahāprabhu and Śrī Śrī Rādhā-Kṛṣṇa.

Trilokanātha dāsa: Yesterday we received an e-mail from a devotee who is making carrot cakes and distributing them as *prasādam* She is wondering if it is just the Indian carrots that we cannot eat. The North American carrot is orange, rather than red. She is wondering whether this should not be eaten as well, or it is okay to eat.

Śrīla Nārāyaṇa Gosvāmī Mahārāja: There are two kinds of carrots. One is very dark red and one is orange. Though I don't take either of these two types of carrots, I have allowed the Western devotees to take the orange type because it is not red like blood. The red one is like blood, so they should not eat it.[5] I have also allowed the Delhi devotees to eat carrots, but I don't eat either one.

[Next day]

Trilokanātha dāsa: Gurudeva, yesterday morning you said that it is okay for us to eat the orange carrots, but that you don't eat them. So the question is, since you personally don't eat them, how can we? We offer *bhoga* to Rādhā and Kṛṣṇa through you. Then, after you have eaten Their remnants, you distribute those remnants to us.

---

[5] Endnote 1 (at the end of this chapter) gives more information on why not to eat carrots, onions, garlic, etc.

So the question is, if you are not eating those carrots, how can we eat them? How will it be true *prasādam*?

Śrīla Nārāyaṇa Gosvāmī Mahārāja: Yes, that is the question.

April 23, 2008
Darśana

Śrīla Nārāyaṇa Gosvāmī Mahārāja: Chanting the holy name will help you millions of times more than wealth.

Ratna: More than wealth?

Śrīla Nārāyaṇa Gosvāmī Mahārāja: Neither your relatives, nor your sons nor daughters nor anyone else can help you in your old age or at the time of death. Only the holy name will help you. In my opinion, you should chant the holy name. If you cannot chant sixteen rounds, then you can gradually increase your chanting.

Ratna: I am very good at *karma-yoga*, but I am not good at practicing the devotional principles.

Śrīla Nārāyaṇa Gosvāmī Mahārāja: *Karma-yoga* cannot save you. Never, never. You will have to return to this world again and again.

Ratna: So, chanting is number one.

Śrīla Nārāyaṇa Gosvāmī Mahārāja *Karma*: Reading, writing, eating, and all other activities should be favorable for *kṛṣṇa-bhakti*. If any activity is not favorable for our advancement in *bhakti*, we should not perform that activity. Do you understand? Activities which are not favorable for *bhakti* will make you suffer, whereas *karma* that is favorable for *bhakti* can help you.

I therefore request you to chant Hare Kṛṣṇa in a pure way.

Brajanātha dāsa: Do you understand?

Ratna: No.

Brajanātha dāsa: Let's say you have a job and earn money, and you don't worry about earning more money than you need to maintain your body. Then, you take the balance of your time to chant Kṛṣṇa's name and associate with devotees. That work is favorable. On the other hand, if you work only for money and have no time for chanting or associating with devotees, then…

Ratna: I am also helping to edit your manuscripts.

Śrīla Nārāyaṇa Gosvāmī Mahārāja: Very good, this is *bhakti*.

Ratna: But I would also need to chant?

Śrīla Nārāyaṇa Gosvāmī Mahārāja: All activities that are performed to please Kṛṣṇa are in the category of *bhakti*. You are editing to please the Supreme Lord, Kṛṣṇa, and that is *bhakti*. Whatever you do to please Kṛṣṇa is *bhakti*.

Brajanātha dāsa: She said that whenever she received a chapter of your *Gopī-gīta* manuscript to edit, she could not sleep. She would read it again and again before trying to do the editing.

Śrīla Nārāyaṇa Gosvāmī Mahārāja: Very good.

Ratna: Do you think I should take initiation now, or wait until I feel I can really chant the rounds?

Śrīla Nārāyaṇa Gosvāmī Mahārāja: There is no certainty when death will come. You should take initiation at once; no delay.

Ratna: Okay.

Śrīla Nārāyaṇa Gosvāmī Mahārāja: Now you will be able to edit more and more.

Endnotes

[1] Excerpt from a conversation with Śrīla Nārāyaṇa Gosvāmī Mahārāja in Paxton, Australia, on February 25, 2002:

Sañjaya dāsa: There's a story about a *brāhmaṇa's* wife. She ate a piece of a cow, and some of it turned into carrot, some of it turned into garlic, some of it turned into onion, and the blood turned into red lentils. Is that story true?

Śrīla Nārāyaṇa Gosvāmī Mahārāja: It is quite true; so we should not eat those things. What Vyāsadeva has written is true. Vyāsadeva knows everything – past, present, and future – and he is able to see what qualities are present in each entity. For example, *Bhagavad-gītā* describes the *sāttvika* (mode of goodness), *tāmasika* (mode of ignorance), *rājasika* (mode of passion), and *nirguṇa* (transcendental) natures of various persons, plants, foodstuffs, activities, knowledge, and so on.

Śrīpāda Mādhava Mahārāja: American scientists have discovered in their laboratories that there are twenty-one different types of slow-acting poisons in both onions and garlic; they are not innocent foods.

In Satya-yuga, the sages performed *gomedha* (cow) and *aśvamedha* (horse) sacrifices for the welfare of the universe. [This was done to give evidence of the efficacy of the recitation of the Vedic *mantras* uttered during the sacrifice.] A very old cow or horse would be sacrificed by being cut into pieces and placed in the sacrificial fire. Afterwards the *ṛṣis* would utter *mantras*, and the same animal would come to life in a beautiful young body.

Once, the pregnant wife of a sage who was about to perform a *gomedha* sacrifice had a very strong desire to eat. She had heard that if, during pregnancy, one has a desire to eat and does not fulfill that desire, the newly born child will continually salivate. This would be troublesome for both the mother and the child.

She had a strong desire to eat meat, and thus she stealthily took one piece of meat from the body of the cow that had been offered in the sacrifice. She hid it and was planning to eat it later on. In the meantime, the sage was finishing the sacrifice and uttering all the *mantras* for the cow to come to life. When he saw the new cow, he noticed that there was a small part missing from her left side. He was surprised because this had never happened before. He went into meditation and realized that his wife had taken away a piece of meat during the sacrifice.

Due to the effect of the *mantras* uttered by the sage, there was now life in this small piece of meat. Therefore, the wife now also understood what had happened, and she quickly threw the meat far away. Shortly afterwards, red lentils sprouted from the blood of this meat, garlic sprouted from the bones (garlic and the bones of a cow are both white), and onions and carrots sprouted from the flesh. Thus, these foods are never eaten by any Vaiṣṇava. They are foods in the mode of ignorance

Alachua, Florida

April 28 - May 5, 2008

April 28, 2008
Darśana with Gurukula Alumni

Śrīla Nārāyaṇa Gosvāmī Mahārāja: You are all *gurukulis*. You have studied in the school of *guru*, in *gurukula*, and you know about Śrīla Bhaktivedānta Svāmī Prabhupāda.

Do you know him?

Rukmiṇī Chacon: Yes.

Śrīla Nārāyaṇa Gosvāmī Mahārāja: Why did he come, and why did he establish the *gurukula*? He did this only to teach you all that after studying you should preach this mission.

What is the mission? It is the teaching that you are not the physical body. If the soul is gone, your body can neither walk, nor speak, nor realize anything. Your body will die, after which either insects will come to eat it, or it will be thrown in a fire. You must therefore know, "I am not this physical body."

The Supreme Lord Kṛṣṇa has very mercifully given us this body because we are His parts and parcels and we have forgotten Him. It is because we have forgotten Him that we are rotating in the endless cycle of birth, death, old age, and suffering; sometimes in a human body, sometimes as animals such as dogs, cats, pigs, hogs, fish, and birds, and sometimes as demigods.

You want happiness. Now you are thinking, "I am happy;" but when old age comes you will realize that you are not at all happy. So many diseases will come, you will no longer be able to walk, and after that you will have to give up your body altogether.

No doctors or scientists can check old age. You should know that you must become old, and that death is unavoidable. You cannot take with you even a single farthing, or any of the things that you are collecting in this world. Your father, mother, relatives, sons, daughters – no one will come with you.

Kṛṣṇa has given you this human form of life. Only in this form of a human being can you realize your true spiritual identity. I have told you that you are not this body, but who are you? And who is the Supersoul, the Creator of the world? The Supreme Lord is the root-cause of all souls, and He has given you a human body so that you can realize this: "I am an eternal servant of Kṛṣṇa, and Kṛṣṇa is the Supreme Personality of Godhead."

In order to realize this, you must accept a very qualified *guru*. He will tell you how to realize your relationship with Kṛṣṇa and how to receive *kṛṣṇa-prema*. That bonafide *guru's* symptoms have been written in the Vedic scriptures. He is very expert in all varieties of *śāstra*, and he can thus remove the doubts of all his disciples. He has personal experience of the Supreme Lord, and he is detached from worldly desires. You can take initiation from him, and thus you can begin chanting the name of Kṛṣṇa and performing devotional service. By this, you will be happy in this world and the next.

Wealth cannot save you. Where there is wealth, there are so many unwanted things. Possessing much wealth is an obstacle in *kṛṣṇa-bhakti*, so do not endeavor for it. As suffering comes without any effort, in the same way happiness will come, whether you endeavor for it or not. Therefore, simply try to do *bhajana*.

śravaṇaṁ kīrtanaṁ viṣṇoḥ
smaraṇaṁ pāda-sevanam
arcanaṁ vandanaṁ dāsyaṁ
sakhyam ātma-nivedanam

(*Śrīmad-Bhāgavatam* 7.5.23)

> Hearing and chanting about the transcendental holy name, form, qualities, paraphernalia, and pastimes of Lord Viṣṇu; remembering them; serving the lotus feet of the Lord; offering the Lord respectful worship with sixteen types of paraphernalia; offering prayers to the Lord; becoming His servant; considering the Lord one's best friend; and surrendering everything unto Him (in other words, serving Him with the body, mind, and words) – these nine processes are accepted as pure devotional service.

In this way your life will be successful. Many of you were *brahmacārīs*. '*Brahmacārī*' means to know the Supreme Lord. Your teachers were not able to teach you that you are *brahmacārī* to realize Kṛṣṇa. So now, try to take shelter of a very bonafide *guru*, begin to chant, and everything auspicious will come to you. If you do not already have a bonafide *guru*, it is essential to find one very soon, and thus practice *bhakti-yoga*.

In brief, this is the sum and substance of the purpose of Śrīla Bhaktivedānta Svāmī Mahārāja's establishing *gurukula*.

Śrīpāda Mādhava Mahārāja: If anyone has questions, you can ask.

Rukmiṇī Chacon: I have always wondered why you re-initiate Śrīla Prabhupāda's disciples.

Śrīla Nārāyaṇa Gosvāmī Mahārāja: I have never done that. Some persons make propaganda that this is a fact, but can they show any example of this? I only initiate those who have left ISKCON, who have nothing to do with ISKCON, whose *gurus* have fallen down. There is no example of what you have said.

Rukmiṇī Chacon: But you have changed their names.

Śrīla Nārāyaṇa Gosvāmī Mahārāja: I do not change names. Out of affection I sometimes give them nicknames. For example, I call Jadurāṇī 'Śyāmarāṇī,' as a nickname.

Rukmiṇī Chacon: Oh, okay.

Śrīla Nārāyaṇa Gosvāmī Mahārāja: You may know that on the eve of his departure from this world, he sent for me, and I immediately went to see him. He took my hands in his hands and began to weep. He told me, "I have collected so many monkeys from around the world. I could not train them fully due to their lack of qualification to be fully trained. Please help them by continuing their training." I promised him that I would do so.

He also told me to give him his *samādhi*. His god-brothers like Bon Mahārāja and others were present there, as were Tamāla-kṛṣṇa and his other disciples, so why did he request me to give him *samādhi*? You should know the reason. He wrote to me, "Your relation with me is transcendental, just as my relationship with my Gurudeva is transcendental."[6] He did not write this to any of his other disciples.

I rendered him many services. I sent him a lot of paraphernalia – *karatālas*, *mṛdaṅgas*, Deities, *pera* (a sweet) from Mathurā, his Sanskrit scriptures, and other things. Some years after his departure (1982–83), in order to give evidence in a court case to prove that he had taken *sannyāsa*, I went to Bombay several times.[7]

So why are the ISKCON leaders now avoiding me and not allowing me to enter their temples? And why do they say that if any of my

6 "Our relationship is certainly based on spontaneous love. That is why there is no chance of us forgetting one another. By the mercy of *guru* and Gaurāṅga may everything be auspicious for you. This is my constant prayer. From the first time I saw you I have been your constant well-wisher. At his first sight of me, Śrīla Prabhupāda also saw me with such love. It was in my very first *darśana* of Śrīla Prabhupāda that I learned how to love" (Excerpt from Śrīla Bhaktivedānta Svāmī Mahārāja's letter, to Śrīla Bhaktivedānta Nārāyaṇa Gosvāmī Mahārāja – 28 September, 1966).

7 See Endnote 1 (at the end of this chapter) for more information on this court case.

disciples go to their temples, they will kick them out from ISKCON? They are *guru-drohīs*; they are neglecting the order of their Gurudeva, Śrīla Bhaktivedānta Svāmī Mahārāja. You should know this.

Still, even though they are committing offenses, I want to help them. For the purpose of helping *parama-pūjyapāda* Śrī Śrīmad Bhaktivedānta Svāmī Mahārāja's senior disciples, I am traveling around the world. So many of his senior disciples are coming to me and I am helping them as a *śikṣā-guru*.

Govinda Syer: Many of the younger generation of devotees are very hesitant to take a *guru* and fully apply themselves to Kṛṣṇa consciousness. Although most of the people I know are aware in their hearts that this is where they are supposed to be, they kind of took a break for awhile. They are perhaps burned-out about what happened in *gurukula*, and perhaps there are other reasons.

What advice can you give to the young generation for the next twenty years, in terms of their confusion about *guru* issues and institutions? We just want to follow Kṛṣṇa consciousness and what we were raised to know from the books of Śrīla Prabhupāda.

Śrīla Nārāyaṇa Gosvāmī Mahārāja: I have come also to inspire them.

Earnestly, from the core of your heart, first pray to Kṛṣṇa. He is *caitya-guru*, the *guru* in your heart; He will guide you to follow the right path. Secondly, if an elevated Vaiṣṇava comes in your midst, continually hear *hari-kathā* from him.

satāṁ prasaṅgān mama vīrya-saṁvido
bhavanti hṛt-karṇa-rasāyanāḥ kathāḥ
taj-joṣaṇād āśv apavarga-vartmani
śraddhā ratir bhaktir anukramiṣyati

(*Śrīmad-Bhāgavatam* 3.25.25)

> In the association of pure devotees, discussion of the pastimes and activities of the Supreme Personality of Godhead is very pleasing and satisfying to the ear and the heart. By cultivating such knowledge one gradually becomes advanced on the path of liberation, thereafter he is freed, and his attraction becomes fixed. Then, real devotion and devotional service begin.

This is most essential: do not neglect *hari-kathā*. By hearing *hari-kathā*, all of your doubts will disappear and you will be able to embark on the direct path to serve Kṛṣṇa. Kṛṣṇa is very merciful. He wants us to pray to Him and He wants to help us, but we are not interested.

You also have some lack of *sukṛti* (spiritual pious credits from past *bhakti*-related activities). It is for this reason that although you were in *gurukula*, you found no exalted, qualified *guru* after Śrīla Bhaktivedānta Svāmī Mahārāja. This is due to *sukṛti*. So pray to Kṛṣṇa, and if you attend our classes, you will definitely be inspired to once again engage in the process of *bhakti*.

At the same time there are some persons who, although they were *brahmacārīs* with a high-class Vaiṣṇava *guru*, still fell into *māyā*. Be careful about this. It is alright that *gṛhasthas* remain *gṛhasthas*, but *sannyāsīs* and *brahmacārīs* wearing saffron cloth should have no other desire than the service of Kṛṣṇa. They deviated because they were not careful.

Do you understand my view?

Govinda Syer: Yes. Thank you very much.

Govinda Mādhava (Govi) Allin: I feel, and correct me if I am wrong, but I feel that initiation is a big step. My brother is a good role model for me. I consider him to be a good devotee, and he still hasn't taken initiation.

You recommend us to take initiation soon, but I don't feel that I am ready. I have heard that you have given initiation to young people of my age. I wonder if you can clarify that.

Śrīla Nārāyaṇa Gosvāmī Mahārāja: Good question; a very good question. Please try to understand my mood. The reason you cannot reconcile this is that you are not at my stage of *bhakti*.

Have you read *Śrī Caitanya-caritāmṛta*?

Govinda Mādhava (Govi) Allin: Well, I have looked….

Śrīla Nārāyaṇa Gosvāmī Mahārāja: I know that you have not read it. It is best for you to come in this line – reading *Caitanya-bhāgavata*, *Śrīmad-Bhāgavatam*, *Bhagavad-gītā*, *Śrī Caitanya-caritāmṛta*, and all the books of Śrīla Bhaktivedānta Svāmī Mahārāja. It is not beneficial to think, "I will do nothing. My *guru* and Kṛṣṇa will do everything for me."

Śrī Caitanya Mahāprabhu went to South India and told those who desired to follow Him:

yāre dekha, tāre kaha 'kṛṣṇa'-upadeśa
āmāra ājñāya guru hañā tāra' ei deśa

(*Śrī Caitanya-caritāmṛta, Madhya-līlā* 7.128)

Instruct everyone to follow the orders of Lord Śrī Kṛṣṇa as they are given in the *Bhagavad-gītā* and *Śrīmad-*

> *Bhāgavatam*. In this way become a spiritual master and try to liberate everyone in this land.

Śrī Caitanya Mahāprabhu requested those whom He met, "I am telling you, 'Hare Kṛṣṇa, Hare Kṛṣṇa, Kṛṣṇa Kṛṣṇa, Hare Hare, Hare Rāma, Hare Rāma, Rāma Rāma, Hare Hare,' and I am asking you to tell this to those whom you will meet." In this way all of South India became Vaiṣṇavas.

Similarly, I give initiation to aspiring devotees very soon after I meet them, even to small boys, telling them that if they will chant even one round with *mālā* in hand, or even one time, "Hare Kṛṣṇa, Hare Kṛṣṇa, Kṛṣṇa Kṛṣṇa, Hare Hare, Hare Rāma, Hare Rāma, Rāma Rāma, Hare Hare," or even "Hare Kṛṣṇa," or if someone cannot do that but only says, "Hare," they will enter the path of true *bhakti* and become liberated. If those boys do not commit any *guru-* or Vaiṣṇava- or *nāma-aparādha*, if they have said "Kṛṣṇa" one time, they will surely become liberated.

For example, Ajāmila was very wretched. He was a drunkard, a gambler, and a murderer, and he lived with a prostitute. But he named his son Nārāyaṇa. He was always calling his son, "Oh Nārāyaṇa, Oh Nārāyaṇa, come here," and taking him on his lap.

Unknowingly he was practicing *nāma-ābhāsa*. Therefore, at the time of death, when the Yamadūtas (the constables of the god of death) came to take his soul, Lord Nārāyaṇa's four messengers (the Viṣṇudūtas) appeared at that spot. The reason that four messengers came is that the name Nārāyaṇa has four syllables: *nā-rā-ya-ṇa*. Ajāmila had chanted those four syllables again and again, and therefore four Viṣṇudūtas appeared. Those Viṣṇudūtas told the Yamadūtas, "Go away from here. You cannot touch this person. He has uttered the name Nārāyaṇa at least one time, and now he is absolved of his past sins."

In this way, even if one chants one holy name, such as Hare, Kṛṣṇa or Rāma, he is surely receiving *sukṛti* and will gradually develop *śraddhā* (faith), *niṣṭhā* (steadiness), *ruci* (taste), *āsakti* (attachment), *bhāva* (spiritual emotions), and *prema* (pure love for Kṛṣṇa).

I give *harināma* initiation easily. But for *dīkṣā* I see if the candidates are chanting at least sixteen rounds and strictly following the four regulative principles, and I look at other things as well.

Śrīpāda Mādhava Mahārāja: Not only that; Śrīla Gurudeva has been coming here since 2003. So it is not that he gives initiation 'soon.' Besides that, any bonafide *guru* can see the entire life of a disciple in a moment.

Śrīpāda Dāmodara Mahārāja: It says in scripture that the *guru* and disciple have to examine each other for one year.

Śrīla Nārāyaṇa Gosvāmī Mahārāja: This injunction was for ancient times. We cannot apply this in present times, because life is short, and there are many other reasons. Śrī Caitanya Mahāprabhu and his followers were very generous.

Purandara dāsa: One point you just made was very important to me. You said, "Try to understand my mood." Can you go a little bit deeper into that explanation of your mood?

Śrīla Nārāyaṇa Gosvāmī Mahārāja: I want people to chant "Hare Kṛṣṇa" or even "Hare," even once. This brings them to the path of *bhakti*. This is my mood. I understand this, but you cannot understand. Why did Śrī Caitanya Mahāprabhu come to this world? You must come to His level in order to truly understand.

Brajanātha dāsa: Many devotees in ISKCON who have been chanting sixteen rounds for ten or fifteen years, and following every rule and regulation, come to Śrīla Gurudeva for more inspiration. Only from a bonafide *guru* can one receive inspiration. In that way they also get very strong *sukṛti*.

Rukmiṇī Chacon: A lot of my friends from *gurukula* have been initiated by you. Before you came here, they said to me, "Take initiation. Take initiation."

Śrīla Nārāyaṇa Gosvāmī Mahārāja: They are very, very compassionate. They have said this out of compassion.

Rukmiṇī Chacon: I am asking this because, just like when Śrīla Prabhupāda left the planet – not left; he is always here – many of his disciples left *bhakti*. Everyone is urging me to take initiation from you, but what will happen when you are no longer here with us?

Śrīla Nārāyaṇa Gosvāmī Mahārāja: No harm. Even if you have chanted one day, or one moment, from the core of your heart, you will definitely come in the line of *bhakti*. There will be no loss, only ever-increasing gain.

My Guru Mahārāja gave me *harināma*, *dīkṣā*, and *sannyāsa*. No one thought at that time that I would be preaching all over the world, but I am doing so. My Gurudeva and *guru-paramparā* have given me the power to do so.

Kṛṣṇa is very merciful. He wants everyone to enter the path of *bhakti*. He repeatedly comes to this world, either personally, or as His incarnation, or by sending His representative. A real, bonafide *guru* is His representative. A *madhyama-adhikārī* Vaiṣṇava can help you more, not an *uttama* (he sees everyone as already engaged in the Lord's service) or *kaniṣṭha-adhikārī*. The *uttama* Vaiṣṇava therefore acts in the role of a devotee on the *madhyama* platform and thus give his mercy.

Bhakti-latā dāsī: I feel very inspired by many ISKCON *gurus*, and personally I am aspiring to receive initiation from Rādhānātha Svāmī. That is where I receive my inspiration. I have received some feedback from people about my even casually wanting to come to this festival.

People were asking, "Why are you going? Don't go." A Mahārāja asked me out of concern and compassion, "What is going on?" He said you have re-initiated thirty of his disciples without asking him. I was wondering if you can ease my concern in that regard. What is the etiquette involved with that? It seems like what you are doing is offending other *gurus*, and I feel a little bit offended because I am inspired by them. Maybe you can clarify this to ease my concern?

Śrīla Nārāyaṇa Gosvāmī Mahārāja: Devotees come to me and tell me, "I have rejected my *guru* and ISKCON. I have nothing to do with them, because I realize that they are not practically following the footsteps of Śrīla Bhaktivedānta Svāmī Mahārāja. They are disobeying him and committing so many offenses. I have rejected them and have come to you." When they come to me in this way, I try to help them as a *śikṣā-guru*. I also explain the meaning of the *mantras* so that they may become more inspired in *bhakti*.

Brajanātha dāsa: ISKCON policy is that anyone who comes to Śrīla Gurudeva cannot go back to them, so he is bound to give them shelter.

Śrīla Nārāyaṇa Gosvāmī Mahārāja: They have said, "If any of you go to Nārāyaṇa Mahārāja, we will ban you from ISKCON." When they come to me after having been banned, how can I give them up? I must give them shelter.

Bhakti-latā dāsī: Can you give some illumination as to why someone who comes to take shelter of you would not be allowed to return to ISKCON?

Śrīla Nārāyaṇa Gosvāmī Mahārāja: You can determine this yourself, because you have some relation with them. Why do they do this?

Bhakti-latā dāsī: I am not sure.

Śrīla Nārāyaṇa Gosvāmī Mahārāja: (To Prema-prayojana dāsa) You can explain.

Prema-prayojana dāsa: I attended a meeting with Śrīla Gurudeva and Hṛdayānanda Mahārāja in Three Rivers. At that time there was a ban, declaring that if any devotees would go to Śrīla Nārāyaṇa Mahārāja, they would not be allowed to return to ISKCON. They were also not allowed to hear from him.

Śrīla Gurudeva told Hṛdayānanda Mahārāja, "If you will lift the ban to stop them from hearing from me, I will stop initiating. I will not initiate anyone if you allow them to hear from me. I just want to help." They did not agree with this. The devotees were still banned after this discussion, so Gurudeva was bound to give them shelter.

Śrīla Nārāyaṇa Gosvāmī Mahārāja: You may also know that Tamāla-kṛṣṇa Svāmī, Girirāja Svāmī, and many other ISKCON *gurus* who had previously (since 1990) been receiving my help, came to me in 1995 and said, "ISKCON leaders have now decided to ban you. You will not be invited to any ISKCON temples or preaching centers." I replied, "If you ban me, I will begin to give initiation to whomever you reject, and I will 'jump over' the entire world to preach. You will not bc able to check me." I was like a sleeping lion. Then, when they banned me, I 'jumped up' at once, like a lion, to preach around the world.

Now I have so many disciples in Australia, Europe, America, and elsewhere. I never thought that I would initiate anyone in India or anywhere else; but due to the inspiration of my Gurudeva, Śrīla Bhaktivedānta Svāmī Mahārāja, and Kṛṣṇa, I am doing so. I am not qualified, but due to the power of my Gurudeva and *guru-paramparā*, I am preaching and giving shelter to aspiring devotees throughout the world.

Mādhavī dāsī: I have a comment. I was living in the Miami ISKCON temple before I took initiation from Śrīla Gurudeva. I was serving there and was fully engaged in preaching and bringing new people into the temple. I went to see Gurudeva and was very inspired in my Kṛṣṇa consciousness, so I took initiation. When I came back to the Miami temple a few days later, the vice-president told me that I could no longer live there. I went to the temple president and said, "Now I can do more service, so please engage me." He said, "You can't live here." At that time the temple was practically empty, and I was more than willing to continue serving there. I was not glorifying Śrīla Gurudeva or saying, "Everyone should take initiation from him." I was studying Śrīla Prabhupāda's books and learning, but I was pushed away.

It is not because Gurudeva's disciples don't want to serve and be inspired by Śrīla Prabhupāda. We have been inspired by him since the beginning of our lives. Some GBC men or some people decided that we are banned. It is not from this circle at all.

Govinda Mādhava (Govi) Allin: I personally feel that – I don't know why – this is a touchy subject for Śrīla Prabhupāda's disciples who are in charge of ISKCON. I do think about the future though. In twenty years or so, the *gurukulis* will be in charge. That is why we are here and asking for guidance.

Śrīla Nārāyaṇa Gosvāmī Mahārāja: I will give you everything. I assure you that if you come to me, I will give you many topics to preach. Can any of you come? I want to give you leadership responsibility, but first come and learn what to preach. I know that you do not know what is the aim and object of *bhakti*. You do not know what is the goal of your life. First you must know this, and then take responsibility and preach everywhere. I desire that hundreds of thousands of devotees will come.

Purandara dāsa: I want to share something. For many years I was not inspired by any *guru*. After some time I became inspired by Rādhānātha Mahārāja. I spent time in India, in his *āśrama*, and with his devotees traveling throughout India. Over the years I had seen Śrīla Gurudeva now and then, and was very inspired by him. I returned to Rādhānātha Mahārāja and told him, "I want to go and see Śrīla Nārāyaṇa Mahārāja. Can I go?" He said, "Yes, go."

I did not take initiation from Gurudeva for three or four years; but one day I said "Yes."

Śrīla Nārāyaṇa GosvāmīMahārāja: Rādhānātha Mahārāja is a pure Vaiṣṇava. He is very humble. I like him.

Rūpa-kiśora dāsa: Can you please illuminate a little more about the meaning of initiation? We have a concept that it is sort of regimented – like we are entering into something akin to a business contract.

Śrīla Nārāyaṇa Gosvāmī Mahārāja: I have explained this many times. I gave you initiation, but you refused to accept its significance. You have no *śikhā*, and now you are wearing a tie. You have heard so much *hari-kathā*, but everything is now spoiled. You have entered *gṛhastha* life from the life of a *brahmacārī*; all right. But you must follow the Kṛṣṇa conscious principles such as waking up early in the morning, performing *āhnika* (utterance of the *gāyatrī-mantras*), reading, chanting, and also preaching. Then you are a disciple.

Please take off this tie in my presence.

Rūpa-kiśora dāsa: You want me to take it off now?

Śrīla Nārāyaṇa Gosvāmī Mahārāja: Yes, take it off, and be my sincere disciple. Otherwise, I will tell my daughter, your wife, to reject you. (To his wife) If he does not follow, you should reject him.

(To all) Thank you all. Try to come to our classes, where you will hear so much *hari-kathā* and surely be inspired.

Rūpa-kiśora dāsa: One last point regarding understanding Kṛṣṇa and *guru*: We are always told that we should have unconditional love for *guru* and Kṛṣṇa. My question is this: Does *guru* and Kṛṣṇa have unconditional love for us?

Śrīla Nārāyaṇa Gosvāmī Mahārāja: (To Prema-prayojana dāsa) You explain first.

Prema-prayojana dāsa: We have heard from Śrīla Gurudeva and from *Bhagavad-gītā* and other texts that Kṛṣṇa is very humble, merciful, and kind. At the same time, He does not interfere with the independence of the living entity. Kṛṣṇa says in *Bhagavad-gītā* (4.11):

ye yathā māṁ prapadyante
tāṁs tathaiva bhajāmy aham
mama vartmānuvartante
manuṣyāḥ pārtha sarvaśaḥ

O Pārtha, in whichever way a person renders service to Me I reciprocate accordingly. Everyone follows My path in all respects.

He says there, "As you offer your love to Me, I will reciprocate with you." And at the end of the *Gītā* He says:

iti te jñānam ākhyātaṁ
guhyād guhyataraṁ mayā
vimṛśyaitad aśeṣeṇa
yathecchasi tathā kuru

(*Bhagavad-gītā* 18.63)

Thus I have explained to you still more confidential knowledge. Deliberate on this fully and then do what you wish to do.*

He never said, "You have to do it." Love can never be by force. It can only be by free will, given voluntarily. *Guru* and Kṛṣṇa have unconditional love for the living entities, but this does not mean that they will reveal the transcendental spiritual world to a person whose heart really doesn't want it.

Śrīla Nārāyaṇa Gosvāmī Mahārāja: The sun shines in the sky. Does it make any condition before giving its nourishing light and heat?

Rūpa-kiśora dāsa: No.

Śrīla Nārāyaṇa Gosvāmī Mahārāja: But if one does not come in front of the sun and instead remains in the shade, how can the sun give that person its heat and light? You may think that this is conditional, but really it is not. Kṛṣṇa, *guru*, and Vaiṣṇavas give their mercy in this way.

April 29, 2008
Morning Walk

Śrīla Nārāyaṇa Gosvāmī Mahārāja: We have discussed *Śrīmad-Bhāgavatam*, Tenth Canto, and many topics in our various *hari-kathā* festivals, but we have not yet discussed Śrī Caitanya Mahāprabhu. I have decided that here in Alachua, from the beginning of the festival, we will talk about Śrī Nityānanda Prabhu, Śrīla Haridāsa Ṭhākura, Śrīla Raghunātha dāsa Gosvāmī, Ratha-yātrā – which is very beautiful – *Rāya Rāmānanda Saṁvāda*, *Rūpa-śikṣā*, *Sanātana-śikṣā*, and all related topics.

(To Śrīpāda Āśrama Mahārāja) I request that you perform a drama about the pastimes of Jagāi and Mādhāi. Prema-prayojana once performed a very marvelous drama on the life of Śrīla Raghunātha dāsa Gosvāmī. I think it will be very good if he performs that drama here. Perform both dramas; first Jagāi and Mādhāi, and then Śrīla Raghunātha dāsa Gosvāmī.

Śrīpāda Padmanābha Mahārāja: Śrīla Gurudeva, you are saying that this week we are going to cover so many topics about Śrī Caitanya Mahāprabhu.

Śrīla Nārāyaṇa Gosvāmī Mahārāja: If I do not complete this here, I will finish in Badger.

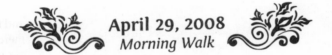

Śrīpāda Padmanābha Mahārāja: But these topics are so vast; it can take one week just to cover one of them.

Śrīla Nārāyaṇa Gosvāmī Mahārāja: If done properly, it will take at least one month to cover each topic; but it will be to everyone's great gain even if they are discussed in brief.

Śrīpāda Bhāgavata Mahārāja: Will we begin from Mahāprabhu's childhood pastimes, or from *Sanātana-śikṣā*, or from *Rūpa-śikṣā*?

Śrīla Nārāyaṇa Gosvāmī Mahārāja: We will gradually cover everything. This evening we can discuss *guru-tattva*, tomorrow the reasons for Śrī Caitanya Mahāprabhu's appearance in this world, and in this evening's class I will announce what we will discuss after that. This evening you should all be prepared to speak about *guru-tattva* from *Śrī Caitanya-caritāmṛta* and other books. You will be asked to explain the qualities of a bonafide *guru* and disciple, the responsibilities of a disciple whose *guru* falls, the identity of the *śikṣā-* and *dīkṣā-gurus*, and similar topics.

Śrīpāda Āśrama Mahārāja: Śrīla Gurudeva, in *Śrī Caitanya-caritāmṛta* there is this verse:

prema-rasa-niryāsa karite āsvādana
rāga-mārga-bhakti loke karite pracāraṇa
rasika-śekhara kṛṣṇa parama-karuṇa
ei dui hetu haite icchāra udgama

(*Śrī Caitanya-caritāmṛta, Ādi-līlā* 4.15–16)

> The Lord's desire to appear was born from two reasons: The Lord wanted to taste the sweet essence of the mellows of love of God, and He wanted to propagate devotional service in the world on the platform of spontaneous attraction. Thus He is known as supremely jubilant and as the most merciful of all.

It is in Goloka that Kṛṣṇa tries to understand Śrīmatī Rādhārāṇī's love. Why does He need to come here and perform pastimes in order to understand it, when He can do so in Goloka?

Śrīla Nārāyaṇa Gosvāmī Mahārāja: Kṛṣṇa is very merciful. He did not want this *rasa* to be limited to Goloka Vṛndāvana. He thought, "Why not give it to the entire world? It should be to everyone's benefit." He therefore gave *rāga-mārga*, the path of spontaneous love for Kṛṣṇa, so that the people of this world would be able to attain that highest stage of devotion. This is why.

If He tastes Her love only in Goloka Vṛndāvana, how would we be able to attain *rāgānuga-bhakti* and ultimately *rūpātmika-bhakti*? He came and gave this secret thing. Especially, Advaita Ācārya (who is a manifestation of Sadāśiva Viṣṇu) had prayed to Kṛṣṇa, "Come at once. If You do not come, I will destroy the entire universe. You must come. Only You can give that *prema*. I can give *yuga-dharma*, the religious practice for the age, and I can preach the glories of the *mahā-mantra*, but I cannot give the highest *kṛṣṇa-prema – gopī-prema*. You will have to give that."

Prāṇa-govinda dāsa: Śrīla Gurudeva, if someone does not come in contact with a *sādhu*, he may read about the Lord's activities and then commit offenses by thinking that these activities – cows licking His body and His bones separating at the joints – are not God's activities. What is that person's situation?

Śrīla Nārāyaṇa Gosvāmī Mahārāja: Śrī Caitanya Mahāprabhu's associates like Śrīla Rāya Rāmānanda, Śrīla Svarūpa Dāmodara, and Śrīla Rūpa Gosvāmī descended from Goloka Vṛndāvana to explain the moods of Śrī Caitanya Mahāprabhu. This is why they came. Just as Kṛṣṇa does not come to this world alone, Mahāprabhu also does not come alone.

Śrīpāda Padmanābha Mahārāja: Śrīla Gurudeva, many years ago, when we were in Fiji on Śrī Advaita Ācārya's appearance day, you were asking each of us to speak about the *pañca-tattva*. You asked, "Can Advaita Ācārya give *vraja-prema*? Can Gadādhara Paṇḍita or Nityānanda Prabhu give it? You then explained that all of them can give *prema* because they are all there in Goloka Vraja; Nityānanda Prabhu is there as Anaṅga Mañjarī and Balarāma, and Advaita Ācārya is there as Gopīśvara Mahādeva and Sadāśiva.

Śrīla Nārāyaṇa Gosvāmī Mahārāja: Only Gadādhara Paṇḍita can give *prema* as Śrī Caitanya Mahāprabhu gave it. While the others can also give it, Mahāprabhu and Gadādhara Paṇḍita give it better.

Sugata dāsa: Why is that so?

Śrīla Nārāyaṇa Gosvāmī Mahārāja: Śrī Kṛṣṇa is *viṣaya-vigraha* (the object of *bhakti*) and Gadādhara is *āśraya-vigraha* (the reservoir, or container, of *bhakti*). Gadādhara, who is Rādhikā Herself, can therefore give it better than Śrī Caitanya Mahāprabhu. With

Gadādhara Paṇḍita's help, Mahāprabhu is able to give it better than the others, because He is Kṛṣṇa who is now realizing the love of Śrīmatī Rādhikā. He has taken Her beauty and intrinsic mood.

Sugata dāsa: But first we approach *guru* and Nityānanda Prabhu?

Śrīla Nārāyaṇa Gosvāmī Mahārāja: Yes, that is right.

A *madhyama-adhikārī guru* knows everything about our conditioning in this world and our suffering due to being absorbed in worldly conceptions. His mercy comes first,[8] then the mercy of Śrī Nityānanda Prabhu and the *uttama-adhikārīs*' mercy, and then Śrīman Mahāprabhu's and Śrī Kṛṣṇa's mercy.

Śrīpāda Āśrama Mahārāja: Kṛṣṇa is *rasika-śekhara*, the topmost relisher, and He is *raso vai saḥ*, the embodiment of *rasa*. I have heard it said that Rādhārāṇī does not have *rasa*, but She is Mahābhāva Ṭhākurāṇī. She has *bhāva*, but Kṛṣṇa does not have *bhāva*.

I am wondering; is this idea okay?

Śrīla Nārāyaṇa Gosvāmī Mahārāja: It is correct to say that Kṛṣṇa is the embodiment of *rasa*; but *rasa* cannot taste itself. It cannot know how tasteful it is. Rather, one who is drinking that *rasa* can taste it. Śrīmatī Rādhikā is drinking that nectar.

Śrīpāda Mādhava Mahārāja: *Śyāma-rasa*.

Śrīla Nārāyaṇa Gosvāmī Mahārāja: Therefore She knows the extent of the beauty, taste, and qualities of that *rasa*. Śrī Kṛṣṇa, who is Rasa Himself, cannot fully taste, tell, or explain about Himself.

Abhirāma dāsa: You said that one must first take shelter of a *madhyama-adhikārī guru*. If an *uttama-adhikārī guru* has not come down to the stage of *madhyama* to preach, can he still give shelter?

Śrīla Nārāyaṇa Gosvāmī Mahārāja: *Uttama-adhikārīs* do not have disciples, because they consider that everyone is already serving Kṛṣṇa and is therefore already liberated. They do not preach or give initiation. Śukadeva Gosvāmī is an example.

Śrīpāda Mādhava Mahārāja: And what about Nārada Ṛṣi?

Śrīla Nārāyaṇa Gosvāmī Mahārāja: *Uttama-adhikārīs* like Nārada Ṛṣi sometimes come to the platform of *madhyama-adhikārī*, and then they make disciples.

---

8 A *madhyama-adhikārī guru* can only give the highest mercy when he is an *uttama-adhikārī* in the role of a *madhyama* – ed.

Śrīpāda Mādhava Mahārāja: In the same way, all the *ācāryas* in our *guru-paramparā* are *uttama-adhikārīs* who have come down to the *madhyama* platform to bestow mercy upon us. Don't think that those in our *guru-varga* are *madhyama-adhikārīs*.

April 29, 2008
Darśana

[Dear Reader, Please excuse us; our sound file didn't include the first question.]

Śrīla Nārāyaṇa Gosvāmī Mahārāja: Is he really *guru*, or not? Is he always chanting and remembering Kṛṣṇa, or not? Does he have some realization of his relationship with Kṛṣṇa, or not? He must know all the Vedic scriptures so that he can remove all his disciples' doubts, and he must be detached from worldly desires.

One should try and take initiation from such a *guru*. Unfortunately, if a devotee has not tested the *guru*, he may accept a person who will fall down – as so many ISKCON leaders are falling down. As soon as a devotee discovers that his *guru* has fallen, he must give him up, no longer maintaining any connection with him.

Śrīla Jīva Gosvāmī quotes, "*Punaś ca vidhinā samyag grāhayed vaiṣṇavād guroḥ* (*Hari-bhakti-vilāsa* 4.144).[9] It is best to take shelter of a *guru* who has the qualifications I mentioned, and again take initiation; one need not delay. Then, according to the bonafide *guru's* advice, one can engage in the practice of *bhakti*.

Devotee: Thank you.

Śrīla Nārāyaṇa Gosvāmī Mahārāja: You received the same answer to your two questions. Are you satisfied?

Devotee: Absolutely. Thank you.

Śrīla Nārāyaṇa Gosvāmī Mahārāja: If one has the type of *guru* you just described, that *guru* should be given up at once, forever. Otherwise, if you associate with him, you will also follow him in his fall from *bhakti*. Rather, seek a high-class *guru* at once, and take shelter of him. Now you are old; you don't know when you will die. You will do well to take shelter of a bonafide *guru* very soon.

---

9 See Endnote 2 (at the end of this chapter) for more quotes from *śāstra* on this topic.

Mukunda dāsa: Śrīla Gurudeva, this is Lakṣmī-Nṛsiṁha Prabhu. He has rendered very, very faithful service to our Śrīla Prabhupāda for many years. He traveled and preached a lot with the Rādhā-Dāmodara bus party in the early days of Śrīla Prabhupāda's mission. After that he served as temple president and temple commander in New York City and many other places, and many devotees have received inspiration from him.

And this is Bādarāyaṇa Prabhu, a very accomplished musician.

Śrīla Nārāyaṇa Gosvāmī Mahārāja: Very good. I will give him a chance to participate during the program.

(To Bādarāyaṇa dāsa) You must attend.

Śrīpāda Bhāgavata Mahārāja: Also, Lakṣmī-Nṛsiṁha Prabhu plays *mṛdaṅga* very nicely, and he sings very nice *kīrtana*.

Śrīla Nārāyaṇa Gosvāmī Mahārāja: Very good. Please remind me about this during the evening program.

Lakṣmī-Nṛsiṁha dāsa: Mahārāja, I have been reading *Manaḥ-śikṣā* by Śrīla Raghunātha dāsa Gosvāmī, the first verse of which is about pride and surrender. I've noticed that throughout *śāstra* there are many Sanskrit synonyms for pride, but the one that seems to be most prominent is *dambha*. Kṛṣṇa says in *Bhagavad-gītā* (13.8): *amānitvam adambhitvam* – humility and pridelessness.

Also, Raghunātha dāsa Gosvāmī and Śrī Caitanya Mahāprabhu mention the word *dambha*. What I've gleaned from my reading is that there are three basic types of pride – *darpa*, *dambha*, and I believe another synonym is *māyā*.

I've read various translations of Śrīla Bhaktivinoda Ṭhākura's *Bhajana-darpaṇa ṭīkā* on *Manaḥ-śikṣā*. One translation says that six aspects of pride are illusion, ignorance, pretense, deceit, deviousness, and *aparādha*. Another translation says that these six aspects are not exactly part of pride; it is something else. So I am a little confused...

Śrīla Nārāyaṇa Gosvāmī Mahārāja: Don't be confused. What Śrīla Bhaktivinoda Ṭhākura has written has been written by Śrī Kṛṣṇa Himself. He is the authority on *bhakti*. If the word meanings make it appear that Bhaktivinoda Ṭhākura's translation is incorrect...

Śrīpāda Mādhava Mahārāja: What he is saying is that in different books there are different translations.

Śrīla Nārāyaṇa Gosvāmī Mahārāja: We accept whatever Śrīla Bhaktivinoda Ṭhākura has told, and if explanations are given that support his commentary, we follow that.

Examples of *dambha* are someone thinking, "I am very beautiful," "I am a very rich person," "I am a very good artist," "Oh, I am a very learned scholar," or "I am from an aristocratic family." Especially, the greatest pride of all is pride related to one's wealth. With the appearance of pride, meat, eggs, drinking, smoking, and other bad habits follow.

The purport of Bhaktivinoda Ṭhākura's commentary includes all these truths. Do not be in confusion.

Lakṣmī-Nṛsiṁha dāsa: From my reading and understanding, It seems that *dambha* specifically relates to pride of one's religion – when a practicing devotee thinks he is *bara* (a great) Vaiṣṇava.

Śrīla Nārāyaṇa Gosvāmī Mahārāja: That is what I meant by 'learned' – the thinking that "No one is my equal." This is the same symptom.

Raj: We want to let Śrīla Gurudeva know that we have been doing a television program in Orlando. We generally feature Gurudeva's *bhajanas* and the teachings from his books, and Sudarśana gives explanations. We would like to do some short interviews with Gurudeva directly, talking about his mission. We can show this; not only in Orlando, but also in New York.

Śrīla Nārāyaṇa Gosvāmī Mahārāja: Yes, you may do an interview.

Raj: I have the camera and everything ready. Just tell me when I can come.

Śrīpāda Mādhava Mahārāja: I will tell you this afternoon.

Bādarāyaṇa dāsa: Mahārāja, in *Jaiva-dharma* Śrīla Bhaktivinoda Ṭhākura speaks about the *jīva* being situated in *taṭasthā-śakti*, but he doesn't seem to speak about the fall of the *jīva*. I know there is some difference of opinion among Vaiṣṇavas, so I'm wondering if you would make the subject more clear.

Śrīla Nārāyaṇa Gosvāmī Mahārāja: It is also important to read *Brahma-saṁhitā*. What Śrīla Bhaktivinoda Ṭhākura has written is correct, and further clarification will come from *Brahma-saṁhitā*. A *jīva* who is serving in Goloka cannot fall down. Why not? Because there is no illusory *māyā* there. Only Yogamāyā, who helps us to serve Kṛṣṇa, is present there. It is for this reason that *Bhagavad-gītā* (15.6) states:

na tad bhāsayate sūryo
na śaśāṅko na pāvakaḥ
yad gatvā na nivartante
tad dhāma paramaṁ mama

> That supreme abode of Mine is not illumined by the sun or moon, nor by fire or electricity. Those who reach it never return to this material world.*

Those whose *anarthas* have gone away by the practice of *bhakti-yoga*, who have advanced to the stage of *prema* – not only *prema*, but *prema* like that of the *gopīs* and other Vrajavāsīs – if they have gone to Goloka Vṛndāvana, how can they possibly fall down? There is no illusory *māyā* in Goloka Vṛndāvana. Even someone who has reached the stage of *bhāva*, or *rati* (the stage attained just prior to *prema*), cannot fall down, so how can such a devotee fall? He is always serving Kṛṣṇa there. In this way, it should be known that the *jīva* comes from *taṭasthā-śakti*.

What is *taṭasthā-śakti?* [*Sthā* means 'place.'] *Taṭa* is the marginal line, the line between land and water, and it is actually an imaginary line. Today the water is here and the *taṭasthā* is there, and on the next day you will see that the water is there and the land is here. During high and low tide you can observe this, so this has been told as an example.

Kāraṇodakaśāyī Viṣṇu is lying in the Causal Ocean; the *taṭasthā-śakti jīvas* come from Him, from His glance. Kṛṣṇa always possesses all types of *śakti*, but when He is present with only His *taṭasthā-śakti* and all other *śaktis* are hidden, His *aṁśa* (part) is called *vibhinnāṁśa* (His separated, infinitesimal part and parcel expansion known as the *jīva*), not *svaṁśa* (His direct, plenary expansion). The *taṭasthā-śakti jīva* of this world, who is a manifestation of *taṭasthā-śakti*, emanates from Kāraṇodakaśāyī Mahā-Viṣṇu's glance upon His *māyā-śakti*. Do you understand? The *taṭasthā-śakti* is neither in Vaikuṇṭha nor the material world. It is between the two.

> Kṛṣṇa establishes Himself [as the predominating Deity] in each of His *śaktis*, and manifests His *svarūpa* according to the nature of that *śakti*. When He is situated in the *cit-svarūpa*, He manifests His essential *svarūpa*, both as Śrī Kṛṣṇa Himself, and also as Nārāyaṇa, the Lord of Vaikuṇṭha; when He is situated in the *jīva-śakti*,

He manifests His *svarūpa* as His *vilāsa-mūrti* (pastime expansion) of Vraja, Baladeva; and when He situates Himself in the *māyā-śakti*, He manifests the three Viṣṇu forms: Kāraṇodakaśāyī, Garbhodakaśāyī, and Kṣīrodakaśāyī.

(*Jaiva-dharma*, Chapter 15)

Innumerable *nitya-pārṣada* (eternally liberated) *jīvas* manifest from Śrī Baladeva Prabhu to serve Vṛndāvana-vihārī Śrī Kṛṣṇa as His eternal associates in Goloka Vṛndāvana, and others manifest from Śrī Saṅkarṣaṇa to serve the Lord of Vaikuṇṭha, Śrī Nārāyaṇa, in the spiritual world. Forever relishing *rasa*, engaged in the service of their worshipable Lord, they always remain fixed in their constitutional position. They always strive to please the Lord and are always attentive to Him.

(*Jaiva-dharma*, Chapter 16)

There are also innumerable atomic conscious *jīvas* who emanate from Kāraṇodakaśāyī Mahā-Viṣṇu's glance upon His *māyā-śakti*. Since these *jīvas* are situated next to *māyā*, they perceive her wonderful workings. Although they have all the qualities of the *jīvas* I have already described, because of their minute and marginal nature, they sometimes look to the spiritual world and sometimes to the material world.

In this marginal condition, the *jīva* is very weak because up to this point in time he has not attained spiritual strength by the mercy of his worshipful Lord. Among these unlimited *jīvas*, those who want to enjoy *māyā* become engrossed in mundane sense gratification and enter a state of perpetual slavery to her.

(*Jaiva-dharma*, Chapter 16)

Bādarāyaṇa dāsa: From what I understand from you, when Śrīla Prabhupāda Bhaktivedānta Svāmī Mahārāja says that we are all originally Kṛṣṇa conscious entities, he means that we are coming from Kāraṇodakaśāyī Viṣṇu, not from Goloka Vṛndāvana.

Śrīla Nārāyaṇa Gosvāmī Mahārāja: Yes.

Śrīpāda Mādhava Mahārāja: If you want to know the details, you can study the second part of *Jaiva-dharma*, Chapters 15 and 16.

Śrīla Nārāyaṇa Gosvāmī Mahārāja: Tamāla-kṛṣṇa Mahārāja, Girirāja Mahārāja, and others used to come to learn *śāstra* from me. They told me, "We want to take you to the Western countries, but there is one condition: You cannot say that the *jīva* has come from the marginal point – *taṭasthā-śakti.*" And they had some other conditions as well. I told them, "I am not going to be controlled by you, and I do not want to take bribes from you. I will not agree to change the correct philosophical conclusions.

Śrīpāda Mādhava Mahārāja: Soon we will publish a book about *jīva-tattva*, from the teachings of the Gosvāmīs and of your Gurudeva.

Śrīla Nārāyaṇa Gosvāmī Mahārāja: Your Gurudeva has never taught that the *jīva* came from Goloka Vṛndāvana. He has been misunderstood.

Śrīpāda Mādhava Mahārāja: All explanations will be in that book.

Bādarāyaṇa dāsa: One more question, if it is alright. This is regarding my own personal spiritual life, or lack of it. I would like some advice regarding my chanting. Sometimes I find that worldly duties take more prominence in my life than my chanting. I want my chanting to become a more prominent thing in my life. I want to commit to chanting more deeply. Can you help me with some advice in that regard?

Śrīla Nārāyaṇa Gosvāmī Mahārāja: As you know, your Gurudeva was a householder. Why did he leave household life? Why did he leave his sons, his wife, his wealth, his position, and his big factories?

Bādarāyaṇa dāsa: So that he could focus more on his preaching.

Śrīla Nārāyaṇa Gosvāmī Mahārāja: You can try to follow this.

You must know that you are the eternal servant of Kṛṣṇa. By your constitutional form, you are His eternal servant. Your first duty is to serve Him, and in fact you have no other duty. You have forgotten this and come to this world. When you came to this world, *Māyā* gave you a gross and subtle body, and covered you; so now you think, "My duty is to support my wife, my children, and others." This is wrong. We should think that our primary duty is to serve Kṛṣṇa.

Therefore, take shelter of a transcendental, very high-class *guru*, take his advice, and take initiation from him. Then, when he gives you second initiation, or *dīkṣā*, you will develop a relationship with Kṛṣṇa in which you have the mood that "Kṛṣṇa is my most beloved," or "Kṛṣṇa is my son," or "Kṛṣṇa is my friend." You will develop your relationship in any of four *rasas*.

Give up all false relations and come at once. This is your first and only duty.

labdhvā su-durlabham idaṁ bahu-sambhavānte
mānuṣyam artha-dam anityam apīha dhīraḥ
tūrṇaṁ yateta na pated anu-mṛtyu yāvan
niḥśreyasāya viṣayaḥ khalu sarvataḥ syāt
(*Śrīmad-Bhāgavatam* 11.9.29)

> After many, many births and deaths one achieves the rare human form of life, which, although temporary, affords one the opportunity to attain the highest perfection. Thus a sober human being should quickly endeavor for the ultimate perfection of life as long as his body, which is always subject to death, has not fallen down and died. After all, sense gratification is available even in the most abominable species of life, whereas Kṛṣṇa consciousness is possible only for a human being.

At once return to your spiritual home. It is for this reason that your Gurudeva came to this world, and I have also come to remind you all. Do not delay.

Mohinī dāsī: Śrīla Gurudeva, I want to give you something.

Śrīla Nārāyaṇa Gosvāmī Mahārāja: How are you?

Mohinī dāsī: I'm fine.

Śrīla Nārāyaṇa Gosvāmī Mahārāja: Such a large donation?

Mohinī dāsī: You ordered me to practice my profession, so I am doing that. You gave me mercy, so I am giving this to you.

Śrīla Nārāyaṇa Gosvāmī Mahārāja: Mukunda Prabhu approves?

Mohinī dāsī: I work. It is all for you.

Śrīla Nārāyaṇa Gosvāmī Mahārāja: It is too much.

Mohinī dāsī: No.

Śrīla Nārāyaṇa Gosvāmī Mahārāja: Thank you.

Sugata dāsa: We are instructed by our *guru* to serve the Vaiṣṇavas. Our parents and children are Vaiṣṇavas, but still, parents are elderly and children are growing up. We must maintain them, and this keeps us from chanting full-time. How do we reconcile this?

Śrīla Nārāyaṇa Gosvāmī Mahārāja: Let us take the example of Śrī Caitanya Mahāprabhu. What did He do? His mother was old. Did she believe in God, or not?

Sugata dāsa: She was a Vaiṣṇavī.

Śrīla Nārāyaṇa Gosvāmī Mahārāja: She was not just a Vaiṣṇavī; she was a *parama* (topmost) Vaiṣṇavī. She came from Goloka Vṛndāvana; She is Mother Yaśodā herself, and Kauśalyā (the mother of Lord Śrī Rāmacandra) is her manifestation. As far as Mahāprabhu's wife, Viṣṇupriyā-devī, is concerned, she was not at all against *bhakti*. Rather, she is the embodiment of *bhakti*.

So why did Mahāprabhu leave His mother and wife? Why did He go to Kaṭvā to take *sannyāsa*? It was not for Himself. He did it to teach all *jīvas*, "Your first duty is to serve Kṛṣṇa." And, even more prominent than Kṛṣṇa's service is Rādhā's service. This is what Mahāprabhu's associate, Śrīla Rūpa Gosvāmī, came to tell you.

Mahā-vegavatī dāsī: Gurudeva, this is an individual question. I know the verse:

tat te 'nukampāṁ su-samīkṣamāṇo
bhuñjāna evātma-kṛtaṁ vipākam
hṛd-vāg vapurbhir vidadhan namas te
jīveta yo mukti-pade sa dāya-bhāk

(*Śrīmad-Bhāgavatam* 10.14.8)

My dear Lord, one who earnestly waits for You to bestow Your causeless mercy upon him, all the while patiently suffering the reactions of his past misdeeds and offering You respectful obeisances with his heart, words and body, is surely eligible for liberation, for it has become his rightful claim.

I must accept everything that is coming to me as my *karma*, due to my past misdeeds of so many lifetimes. But when that *karma* comes to the extent that it affects my ability to serve my Guru Mahārāja and Kṛṣṇa, the pain is so severe that I become angry.

For instance, I've had many head injuries as a devotee which I sustained in my service. I was beaten many times in the head. I have not been able to read a book since 1978. I have been beaten in the spine and am in severe pain. I was put into a motor wheelchair, which I cannot even read the instructions to use. The pain is so severe that I don't sleep at night unless I take a very strong pill. The pain is so severe that I develop uncontrollable anger against Kṛṣṇa and call Him all kinds of names. This is very serious, because I came to my Guru Mahārāja's lotus feet to develop love for Kṛṣṇa.

Because of not being able to do what I want to do in service, I have become angry. I feel very, very guilty that I am not able to practice Kṛṣṇa consciousness to the extent I was before. I was one of those very materially intelligent devotees, and I was physically very strong. If I had any pride, I was not aware of it.

I understand that this is my *karma* and it is for my purification, but at the same time, it is very, very difficult for me to bear the strength of this *karma*. I'm asking you to please help me.

Śrīla Nārāyaṇa Gosvāmī Mahārāja: I have heard everything you said. You said that you believe in *karma*. In that regard it is also important for you to know the meaning of *tat te 'nukampām*. *Karma* applies to general people, yet we see that those who have accepted a pure, bonafide *guru* and chant the holy name also have some suffering.

Śrīla Haridāsa Ṭhākura was beaten in twenty-two market places, although he had no *karma*. Draupadī had no *karma*, but she was attempted to be made naked in public. Sītā-devī and Rāmacandra had no *karma* to cause them to have to be banished to the forest for fourteen years. Although Prahlāda Mahārāja committed no offenses and had no *karma*, his father gave him poison and tried to kill him by fire and so many other means. This was not Prahlāda's *karma*, rather it was the mercy of Kṛṣṇa. Through His personal example and the examples of His personal associates, Śrī Kṛṣṇa wants to teach the world that in order to do *bhajana* one must be as tolerant as they are.

You may try to reconcile in this way. Understand that it is the mercy of Kṛṣṇa that someone has beaten you or that you have been put into any difficulty. Knowing this, you can return to Kṛṣṇa consciousness. Peacefully chant Kṛṣṇa's name, read books…

Śrīpāda Mādhava Mahārāja: She wants to, but because of her injuries she cannot read anymore.

Śrīla Nārāyaṇa Gosvāmī Mahārāja: Then don't read, but chant and hear *hari-kathā*, and attend my classes. Wherever you go, this will be the best thing for you. What we are teaching is the same message taught in all the *śāstras*. Kṛṣṇa says in *Bhagavad-gītā*:

kāma eṣa krodha eṣa
rajo-guṇa-samudbhavaḥ

mahāśano mahā-pāpmā
viddhy enam iha vairiṇam

(*Bhagavad-gītā* 3.37)

> It is lust only, Arjuna, which is born of contact with the material mode of passion and later transformed into wrath, and which is the all-devouring sinful enemy of this world.*

If you become angry, all your intelligence will disappear. You will become mad and go to hell.

Mahā-vegavatī dāsī: I know this.

Śrīla Nārāyaṇa Gosvāmī Mahārāja: Then follow it; no need for questions. Best to simply follow it.

April 30, 2008
Morning Walk

Śrīpāda Bhāgavata Mahārāja: Śrīla Gurudeva, this is Janārdana. He has been living with us in Houston for one year, and chanting every day. He took *harināma* from you last year in Badger and now wants to take *dīkṣā*. He wrote a very nice paper on the meaning of *dīkṣā*.

Śrīla Nārāyaṇa Gosvāmī Mahārāja: Can he preach?

Śrīpāda Bhāgavata Mahārāja: Yes, he is doing well.

Śrīla Nārāyaṇa Gosvāmī Mahārāja: How many rounds does he chant?

Śrīpāda Bhāgavata Mahārāja: Sixteen rounds every day.

Śrīla Nārāyaṇa Gosvāmī Mahārāja: Not more than that? Don't make a promise that, "I will never chant more than sixteen rounds." Try to increase your rounds, read our books, and become still more qualified. When you develop a real taste for reading, hearing, chanting, remembering, and all other services, then you will be a first-class (*pukka*) *brahmacārī*.

Prāṇa-govinda dāsa: It was very good to hear what you said yesterday regarding surrender. I was very happy to hear it, but it is very scary to surrender completely. I know it is necessary, but I am still very scared. I don't know why.

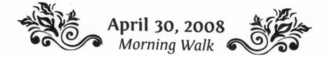

Śrīla Nārāyaṇa Gosvāmī Mahārāja: There is a *śloka* (Sanskrit verse) in *Śrīmad-Bhāgavatam* regarding fear dispelled by hearing:

tasmin mahan-mukharitā madhubhic-caritra-
pīyūṣa-śeṣa-saritaḥ paritaḥ sravanti
tā ye pibanty avitṛṣo nṛpa gāḍha-karṇais
tān na spṛśanty aśana-tṛḍ-bhaya-śoka-mohāḥ
(*Śrīmad-Bhāgavatam* 4.29.40)

My dear King, in the place where pure devotees live, following the rules and regulations and thus purely conscious and engaged with great eagerness in hearing and chanting the glories of the Supreme Personality of Godhead, in that place if one gets a chance to hear their constant flow of nectar which is exactly like the waves of a river, one will forget the necessities of life – namely hunger and thirst – and become immune to all kinds of fear, lamentation, and illusion.

What is the meaning?

Śrīpāda Padmanābha Mahārāja: I do not know the meaning of this *śloka*.

Śrīla Nārāyaṇa Gosvāmī Mahārāja: If you cannot explain it, I will think that you are not a *sannyāsī*.

Where is Prema-prayojana? Please explain this verse.

Prema-prayojana dāsa: This verse was spoken by Śrī Nārada Ṛṣi to King Prācīnabarhi after he described the pastimes of King Purañjana. At the conclusion of that *kathā* Nārada Ṛṣi said, "*Tasmin mahan-mukharitā madhubhic-caritra.*" When we come in the association of a *mahat*, a pure Vaiṣṇava, we come in contact with a river of *hari-kathā* that flows from his lotus lips. That river flows, just as the Ganges flows from the mountains down to the ocean, in an uninterrupted stream. A powerful river of *hari-kathā* flows from a very high place, which is the heart of the Vaiṣṇava, and then from his mouth into the ears of those who are listening.

If those listeners have a very strong thirst, they will drink again and again. Their thirst to hear never goes away; rather they want to hear more. As they become more and more absorbed in that *kathā*, then, *bhaya-śoka-mohāḥ* – all their fear goes away, all illusion goes away, and all lamentation goes away. Śrīla Gurudeva recommends this as the process to become free from fear.

Śrīla Nārāyaṇa Gosvāmī Mahārāja: Do you understand?

Prāṇa-govinda dāsa: Yes, but...

Śrīla Nārāyaṇa Gosvāmī Mahārāja: You understand, but not fully.

Prāṇa-govinda dāsa: Yes, surrendering is the scary part.

Śrīla Nārāyaṇa Gosvāmī Mahārāja: All Vaiṣṇavas are *guru*. From the highest *guru*, the *rasika tattva-jña* Vaiṣṇava *guru*, flows a river of *hari-kathā*. For those who hear this *hari-kathā*, which flows like a fountain, nothing remains to be done. For those who hear with great interest, all fear, illusion, and unhappiness automatically disappear, and *bhakti* manifests in their hearts.

This is the *śloka* I was originally thinking of:

yasyāṁ vai śrūyamāṇāyāṁ
kṛṣṇe parama-pūruṣe
bhaktir utpadyate puṁsaḥ
śoka-moha-bhayāpahā

(*Śrīmad-Bhāgavatam* 1.7.7)

Simply by giving aural reception to this Vedic literature, the feeling for loving devotional service to Lord Kṛṣṇa, the Supreme Personality of Godhead, sprouts up at once to extinguish the fire of lamentation, illusion, and fearfulness.

Śrīpāda Mādhava Mahārāja: In his commentary on the other verse, *tasmin mahan-mukharitā*, Śrīla Viśvanātha Cakravartī Ṭhākura explained why Śrīla Vyāsadeva wrote *madhu-bhit*. It is because Nārāyaṇa killed the Madhu demon, who is a symbol of *anarthas*. Thus, if you hear the pastimes of Kṛṣṇa from great Vaiṣṇavas, the Lord will cut out all *anarthas*.

Śrīla Nārāyaṇa Gosvāmī Mahārāja: *Madhubhic-caritra* also means that Kṛṣṇa has appeared in the Madhu dynasty, and that His sweet pastimes are like honey (*madhu*); they are very tasteful. Therefore, if you hear narrations of His pastimes, *bhakti* will come and all kinds of fear will gradually disappear. This is the purpose for which Śrīla Vyāsadeva manifested *Śrīmad-Bhāgavatam* – all varieties of lamentation, illusion, and fear will disappear from the heart of those who hear its narrations.

Prāṇa-govinda dāsa: Thank you.

Gaṅgā-prasāda dāsa: Kṛṣṇa and the living entity are qualitatively equal.

Śrīla Nārāyaṇa Gosvāmī Mahārāja: First of all, your *tilaka* should be like ours; *gauḍīya-tilaka*. Yours looks like the *tilaka* of the Śrī *sampradāya*.

Śrīpāda Padmanābha Mahārāja: Gurudeva means that it is too wide. If you put a red line in the middle, it will be just like the Śrī *sampradāya tilaka*.

Gaṅgā-prasāda dāsa: Kṛṣṇa is *rasika-śekhara*, the supreme taster of *rasa*, so how is it that He cannot taste His own self? In other words, why can't He taste what the devotees experience in their love for Him?

Śrīla Nārāyaṇa Gosvāmī Mahārāja: Can the honey in the beehive taste itself, or not? Who will taste it?

Gaṅgā-prasāda dāsa: The bee.

Śrīla Nārāyaṇa Gosvāmī Mahārāja: Yes. Similarly, Śrī Kṛṣṇa is an ocean of *rasa*. Śrīmatī Rādhikā, all the *gopīs*, and all Vrajavāsīs are tasting that *rasa*.

Śrīpāda Mādhava Mahārāja: And vice versa. They are reservoirs of *rasa*, and Kṛṣṇa is the connoisseur.

Gaṅgā-prasāda dāsa: But if Kṛṣṇa and the living entities are qualitatively equal, then…

Śrīla Nārāyaṇa Gosvāmī Mahārāja: *Prema* is reciprocal. Kṛṣṇa loves the *gopīs* and the *gopīs* love Kṛṣṇa.

When Kṛṣṇa loves the *gopīs*, He becomes very happy because He realizes the happiness of His love for them. However, when the *gopīs* see Kṛṣṇa and they become happy because of their love for Him, He does not know what their happiness is like. He wonders, "What is the greatness of Rādhikā's happiness when She sees Me and tastes all the varieties of My sweetness (*mādhurī*)?" It is with this greed that He came as Śacīnandana.

Gaṅgā-prasāda dāsa: Thank you.

Mādhava dāsa: In the spiritual world there is no jealousy. How is it, then, that pastimes like that of Jaya and Vijaya took place there? Or, did the pastime of Jaya and Vijaya take place only in the material world?

Śrīpāda Mādhava Mahārāja: When the four Kumāras went to the Vaikuṇṭha planet, there where two guards, Jaya and Vijaya, who checked their entry. The four Kumāras told the gate-keepers, "There is no fear or envy here. Why are you preventing us from entering?" The gate-keepers replied, "You are not qualified to enter Vaikuṇṭha." The four Kumāras then cursed them to fall down to the material world.

Śrīla Viśvanātha Cakravartī Ṭhākura wrote, and it is also mentioned in the *Bhāgavatam*, that Lakṣmī-devī had once gone out of Vaikuṇṭha to do some work, and when she returned, she was stopped by Jaya and Vijaya.

Why did all this happen? It is because Nārāyaṇa wanted to perform some pastimes in this material world. Jaya and Vijaya checked Lakṣmī-devī, she became very angry, and it was due to her anger that Jaya and Vijaya were later cursed by the four Kumāra brothers.

After the four Kumāras went away, Nārāyaṇa told this fact to Jaya and Vijaya. He said, "Do you remember that you also checked Lakṣmī-devī?"

> This departure from Vaikuṇṭha was foretold by Lakṣmī, the goddess of fortune. She was very angry because when she left My abode and then returned, you stopped her at the gate while I was sleeping.
>
> (*Śrīmad-Bhāgavatam* 3.16.30)

All of this happened in the spiritual world, not in this material world.

Śrīla Nārāyaṇa Gosvāmī Mahārāja: The root cause of Jaya and Vijaya's descent to the material world is that Nārāyaṇa wanted to enjoy *vīra-rasa*, chivalrous sports. Jaya and Vijaya knew this, and therefore they were waiting for an opportunity to fight with their Lord and fulfill His desire. They wanted to satisfy Him; this was why they first stopped Lakṣmī-devī, and later the four Kumāra brothers.

The four Kumāras had never before cursed anyone. Therefore, after they had cursed Jaya and Vijaya, they began thinking, "How did this curse come in our heart? Without the desire of our Lord, it could not have come."

Lord Nārāyaṇa confirmed this by telling them, "The offense by Jaya and Vijaya is My offense. The offense of the servant is the offense of the master." Why did He say this? Because it was He who had inspired them to curse Jaya and Vijaya.

Padmanābha dāsa (from India): Śyāmarāṇī Dīdī was saying that the seed of the *bhakti-latā* is already present in the heart of the *jīva*.

Śrīla Gurudeva only waters it and gives it sunshine and does the gardening. But the verse in *Śrī Caitanya-caritāmṛta* says that the *bīja*, or seed, is separately given by *guru.*

brahmāṇḍa bhramite kona bhāgyavān jīva
guru-kṛṣṇa-prasāde pāya bhakti-latā-bīja
(*Śrī Caitanya-caritāmṛta, Madhya-līlā* 19.151)

According to their *karma*, all living entities are wandering throughout the entire universe. Some of them are being elevated to the upper planetary systems, and some are going down into the lower planetary systems. Out of many millions of wandering living entities, one who is very fortunate gets an opportunity to associate with a bonafide spiritual master by the grace of Kṛṣṇa. By the mercy of both Kṛṣṇa and the spiritual master, such a person receives the seed of the creeper of devotional service.

Śrīla Nārāyaṇa Gosvāmī Mahārāja: "*Jīvera 'svarūpa' haya, kṛṣṇera 'nitya-dāsa'* – by constitution, the living entity is the eternal servant of Kṛṣṇa."

When we are conditioned souls (*baddha-jīvas*) covered by *māyā*, is the mood to serve Kṛṣṇa present, or not? Is the conception of one's relationship with Kṛṣṇa and the manner in which to serve Him present, or not?

Padmanābha dāsa: I think the *svarūpa* is there, but it is covered.

Śrīla Nārāyaṇa Gosvāmī Mahārāja: That seed was in a latent stage. When *śāstra* says that at a particular time Kṛṣṇa arranges a *guru* to give the *bīja* (seed) it means that the water, sunrays, and fertilization of the seed take place by the work of the *guru* and *sādhus*. Then, when all of these paraphernalia mix together, the sprout manifests.

Śivānanda Sena dāsa: Śrīla Gurudeva, three days ago Rāmacandra Prabhu (of Badger) and his wife Mahā-Lakṣmī went to a car race, where the local people race cars. In that one day he distributed over 500 books.

Śrīla Nārāyaṇa Gosvāmī Mahārāja: I know that he is a very good book distributor.

Śivānanda Sena dāsa: He has been a good distributor for many years.

Śrīla Nārāyaṇa Gosvāmī Mahārāja: He is number one in book distribution. We should give him some reward.

Rāmacandra dāsa: Only a swift kick.

Brajanātha dāsa: He wants a kick from your lotus feet.

Śrīla Nārāyaṇa Gosvāmī Mahārāja: No, I will give you some reward.

(To Brajanātha dāsa) Please count how many books people are distributing in England and elsewhere. Then calculate the first, second, and third largest book distributors.

Brajanātha dāsa: Viśvambhara is already doing this.

Śrīla Nārāyaṇa Gosvāmī Mahārāja: (To Mukunda dāsa, one of the festival's organizers) Is everything being managed well?

Mukunda dāsa: Yes, Śrīla Gurudeva; so far. It is difficult to organize everything for so many devotees, but it is very sweet.

Śrīla Nārāyaṇa Gosvāmī Mahārāja: Is everyone happy?

Mukunda dāsa: Yes, Gurudeva.

Śrīla Nārāyaṇa Gosvāmī Mahārāja: And the *prasādam*?

All devotees: Very good.

Śrīla Nārāyaṇa Gosvāmī Mahārāja: I am very happy that you organizers are managing so well. And our classes are very inspiring. So many devotees and others will benefit.

Brajanātha dāsa: Gurudeva, on the first night you did not come. The devotees in the audience told me how impressed they were by how well your *sannyāsīs* spoke.

Śrīla Nārāyaṇa Gosvāmī Mahārāja: In general, ISKCON *sannyāsīs* and leaders are not able to speak like them. They should first of all hear my *sannyāsīs' hari-kathā*, and that of our *gṛhastha bhaktas* as well. There are so many *gṛhasthas* who know and speak the philosophy very well.

Aniruddha dāsa: Śrī Caitanya Mahāprabhu is Kṛṣṇa Himself. Kṛṣṇa came as Mahāprabhu to experience Śrīmatī Rādhārāṇī's feelings. In order to experience the feelings of a woman, why did He not come as a woman?

Śrīla Nārāyaṇa Gosvāmī Mahārāja: Kṛṣṇa did not desire to come in the form of a lady. He was thinking, "I should be a *sannyāsī*, and therefore all of My associates, such as Rādhārāṇī, Viśākhā, and Lalitā, should come as males."

Prema-prayojana, are you prepared to perform the dram Raghunātha dāsa Gosvāmī? Try to do it.

Śrīpāda Āśrama Mahārāja: We will do our drama on Saturday he can do his on Sunday.

Devotee: You were saying in your *iṣṭagoṣṭhī* on Tuesday morning that if one's *guru* falls, that disciple should immediately give him up and take shelter of *śrī guru*, a real *guru*. My question is this: In *Śrī Kṛṣṇa-bhajanāmṛta*, Śrī Narahari Śarkarā Ṭhākura says that the disciple should wait one year. If the *guru* does not give up his non-Vaiṣṇava activities, then reject him; but if he does, then:

api cet su-durācāro
bhajate mām ananya-bhāk
sādhur eva sa mantavyaḥ
samyag vyavasito hi saḥ

(*Bhagavad-gītā* 9.30)

> Even if one commits the most abominable action, if he is engaged in devotional service he is to be considered saintly because he is properly situated in his determination.*

This means we should still consider him to be saintly. You also said to have no relation with such a fallen *guru*. So, what relation should we have with a *guru* who reinstates himself in devotional service?

Śrīla Nārāyaṇa Gosvāmī Mahārāja: Nowhere is that written that a bonafide *guru* will fall down and then re-instate himself, or that the disciple should wait [meaning that the devotee's translation of the *Śrī Kṛṣṇa-bhajanāmṛta* is incorrect]. Can you show me where this is written?

Devotee: I have the book, but I don't have it here.

Śrīpāda Mādhava Mahārāja: In his *Bhakti-sandharba*, Śrīla Jīva Gosvāmī quotes:

avaiṣṇavopadiṣṭena mantreṇa nirayaṁ vrajet
punaś ca vidhinā samyag grāhayed vaiṣṇavād guroḥ

(*Hari-bhakti-vilāsa* 4.144)

> One goes to hell if he accepts *mantras* from an *avaiṣṇava-guru*, that is, one who is associating with women, and

who is devoid of *kṛṣṇa-bhakti*. Therefore, according to the rules of *śāstra*, one should take *mantras* again from a Vaiṣṇava *guru*.

He also writes:

A *guru* who is envious of pure devotees, who blasphemes them, or behaves maliciously towards them should certainly be abandoned, remembering the verse *guror api avaliptasya*. Such an envious *guru* lacks the mood and character of a Vaiṣṇava. The *śāstras* enjoin that one should not accept initiation from a non-devotee (*avaiṣṇavopadiṣṭena…*). Knowing these injuctions of the scriptures, a sincere devotee abandons a false *guru* who is envious of devotees. After leaving one who lacks the true qualities of a *guru*, if a devotee is without a spiritual guide, his only hope is to seek out a *mahā-bhāgavata* Vaiṣṇava and serve him. By constantly rendering service to such a pure devotee, one will certainly attain the highest goal of life

(*Bhakti-sandarbha, Anuccheda* 238)

Śrīla Nārāyaṇa Gosvāmī Mahārāja: Śrīla Jīva Gosvāmī has clearly explained all these truths.

May 1, 2008
Morning Walk

Śrīla Nārāyaṇa Gosvāmī Mahārāja: With reference to this verse, what were Śrī Kṛṣṇa's three desires?

śrī-rādhāyāḥ praṇaya-mahimā kīdṛśo vānayaivā-
svādyo yenādbhuta-madhurimā kīdṛśo vā madīyaḥ
saukhyaṁ cāsyā mad-anubhavataḥ kīdṛśaṁ veti lobhāt
tad-bhāvāḍhyaḥ samajani śacī-garbha-sindhau harīnduḥ

(*Śrī Caitanya-caritāmṛta, Ādi-līlā* 1.6)

Desiring to understand the glory of Rādhārāṇī's love, the wonderful qualities in Him that She alone relishes through Her love, and the happiness She feels when

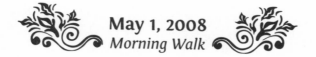

> She realizes the sweetness of His love, the Supreme Lord Hari, richly endowed with Her emotions, appeared from the womb of Śrīmatī Śacī-devī, as the moon appeared from the ocean.

Śrīpāda Bhāgavata Mahārāja: He wanted to understand the *prema* tasted by Śrīmatī Rādhārāṇī.

Śrīla Nārāyaṇa Gosvāmī Mahārāja: What *prema*?

Śrīpāda Bhāgavata Mahārāja: The greatness of the *prema*.

Śrīla Nārāyaṇa Gosvāmī Mahārāja: What *prema*?

Śrīpāda Bhāgavata Mahārāja: He wanted to understand His own *rūpa-mādhurī*, the sweetness of His form …

Śrīla Nārāyaṇa Gosvāmī Mahārāja: You have not presented this correctly.

Śrīpāda Bhāgavata Mahārāja: Śrīmatī Rādhārāṇī was seeing something in Him and He wanted to understand what She was seeing.

Śrīla Nārāyaṇa Gosvāmī Mahārāja: No, no, no. Your presentation is totally wrong. First properly explain the first desire, and then the second desire.

Śrīpāda Bhāgavata Mahārāja: First was the *prema*. Kṛṣṇa wanted to know the nature of the love She was experiencing.

Śrīla Nārāyaṇa Gosvāmī Mahārāja: It is true that *prema* means 'love,' but in this verse the word *praṇaya*[10] is used, not *prema*. Is there something special in *praṇaya* that differentiates it from *prema*?

Śrīpāda Bhāgavata Mahārāja: There is a special thing in *praṇaya*.

Śrīla Nārāyaṇa Gosvāmī Mahārāja: What is it?

---

10 *Praṇaya*: "When *prema* is imbued with an exceptional feeling of intimacy known as *viśrambha*, it is called *praṇaya*. When *praṇaya* is present, there is a complete absence of awe and reverence towards the beloved even in the midst of a circumstance that would normally evoke such feelings… *Viśrambha* is defined as the feeling of being identical with the beloved. Such a feeling causes one to consider one's mind, life, intelligence, body, and possessions to be one with the mind, life, intelligence, body, and possessions of the beloved. The feeling of oneness being referred to means that out of great love one feels equally at ease with the beloved as one does with oneself, and this feeling is mutually experienced" (*Śrī Śikṣāṣṭaka*, Verse Seven, *Śrī Sanmodana-bhāṣya* by Śrīla Bhaktivinoda Ṭhākura).

Śrīpāda Bhāgavata Mahārāja: There are stages of *prema* up to *mādanākhya-mahābhāva*, like *rāga*, *anurāga*, *praṇaya*, and so on.[11]

Śrīla Nārāyaṇa Gosvāmī Mahārāja: Yes, not merely *prema*. *Prema* develops further to *sneha* and *māna*,[12] and then to *praṇaya*. *Praṇaya* is Śrīmatī Rādhikā's exalted mood. It is this mood that Kṛṣṇa wanted to experience.

Then, what was His second desire?

Śrīpāda Bhāgavata Mahārāja: Secondly, Kṛṣṇa thought, "Śrīmatī Rādhikā is seeing something in Me. She sees My *rūpa-mādhurī* (the sweetness of My extraordinarily beautiful form), *veṇu-mādhurī* (the sweet, mellow sound of My flute), and My *līlā-mādhurī* (the sweetness of My supremely captivating pastimes). What is She seeing in Me?"

Śrīla Nārāyaṇa Gosvāmī Mahārāja: You do not understand. Try to understand from those who know. Do not think that you know everything. This is not a topic that can be learned in one day. Try to hear again, and to know.

(To Śrīpāda Āśrama Mahārāja) Please explain this to him.

Śrīpāda Āśrama Mahārāja: *Śrī-rādhāyāḥ praṇaya-mahimā kīdṛśo vānayaivā*. First, Kṛṣṇa wants to understand the *mahimā*, meaning the glory, of Śrīmatī Rādhikā's *praṇaya*. For instance, He sees that in Her mood of separation from Him, She sometimes runs to a *tamāla* tree and embraces it, thinking it to be Him. Sometimes She chastises a rain-cloud, thinking it to be Him.

Kṛṣṇa was thinking, "What is the glory of Her love? I do not embrace the *kadamba* tree when I feel separation from Her. My love is not so high." In this way He develops greed to understand the greatness of Śrīmatī Rādhārāṇī's love.

Secondly, *svādyo yenādbhuta-madhurimā kīdṛśo vā madīyaḥ*. Śrī Kṛṣṇa is full with four *mādhurīs*, or four qualities of sweetness, the first of which is *rūpa-mādhurī*, the sweetness of His form. It is stated in *Śrīmad-Bhāgavatam*:

barhāpīḍaṁ naṭa-vara-vapuḥ karṇayoḥ karṇikāraṁ
bibhrad vāsaḥ kanaka-kapiśaṁ vaijayantīṁ ca mālām
randhrān veṇor adhara-sudhayāpūrayan gopa-vṛndair
vṛndāraṇyaṁ sva-pada ramaṇaṁ prāviśad gīta-kīrtiḥ

(*Śrīmad-Bhāgavatam* 10.21.5)

---

[11] The words *mādanākhya-mahābhāva*, *rāga*, and *anurāga* are explained in the glossary.

[12] The words *sneha* and *māna* are explained in the glossary.

> Wearing a peacock-feather ornament upon His head, blue *karṇikāra* flowers on His ears, a yellow garment as brilliant as gold, and the *vaijayantī* garland, Lord Kṛṣṇa exhibited His transcendental form as the greatest of dancers as He entered the forest of Vṛndāvana, beautifying it with the marks of His footprints. He filled the holes of His flute with the nectar of His lips, and the cowherd boys sang His glories.

This sweet form is not possessed by any of His incarnations. Only Kṛṣṇa has this *rūpa-mādhurī*.

Then, *veṇu-mādhurī*:

iti veṇu-ravaṁ rājan
sarva-bhūta-manoharam
śrutvā vraja-striyah sarvā
varṇayantyo 'bhirebhire
(*Śrīmad-Bhāgavatam* 10.21.6)

> O King, the sound of Kṛṣṇa's flute steals the minds of all living beings, both animate and inanimate. When the young *gopīs* of Vraja heard that sound, they began to describe it. As they went on describing the sound of the flute, they entered a state of ecstatic trance and became completely absorbed in thoughts of Śrī Kṛṣṇa. Within their hearts, they began to embrace Śrī Kṛṣṇa, who is the embodiment of all *rasa* and the reservoir of supreme spiritual bliss.

All living entities in Vṛndāvana become charmed and enchanted when they hear the song of Kṛṣṇa's flute. Kṛṣṇa cannot understand this from the position of being the object of love (*viṣaya*). In order to understand, He must take the position of the abode of love (*āśraya*). Śrīla Gurudeva has explained...

Śrīla Nārāyaṇa Gosvāmī Mahārāja: This explanation is not exactly correct. *Asvādyo yenādbhuta* means 'the wonderful sweetness that is relished by Śrīmatī Rādhikā.' Only Śrīmatī Rādhikā can enjoy this. These four *mādhurīs* are *kīdṛśaḥ*. [*Kīdṛśaḥ* means 'of what kind?'] Śrī Kṛṣṇa does not know how glorious His four *mādhurīs* are; only Śrīmatī Rādhikā knows.

What is Śrī Kṛṣṇa's third desire?

Śrīpāda Āśrama Mahārāja: *Saukhyaṁ cāsyā mad-anubhavataḥ kīdṛśaṁ veti lobhāt*. Only Śrīmatī Rādhikā is able to taste the *mādhurīs* of

Kṛṣṇa in a most super-excellent way; no one else can do so. *Hṛdaya-prema-darpaṇa* – according to the love within one's heart, one will be able to perceive the sweetness of the object of one's love. Therefore, although Śrīmatī Rādhikā does not desire any happiness for Herself, when She tastes the sweetness of Śrī Kṛṣṇa, She feels a happiness which is unsurpassed. Seeing this, Śrī Kṛṣṇa becomes very greedy to experience Her happiness.

Śrīla Nārāyaṇa Gosvāmī Mahārāja: Śrīmatī Rādhikā enjoys the four *mādhurīs* of Kṛṣṇa and becomes so happy; and Kṛṣṇa wants to know what kind of happiness She is feeling.

(To Bhāgavata Mahārāja) You should know the details very clearly. It is not so easy to understand and express this with precision. It is not like eating a *rasagullā* (an Indian sweet).

Are there any questions?

Raghunātha Bhaṭṭa dāsa: I have a question, Gurudeva. Why were these three internal desires considered to be a reason for Kṛṣṇa to come to this material world? Why could He not simply fulfill them in the spiritual world?

Śrīla Nārāyaṇa Gosvāmī Mahārāja: I gave the answer to this question yesterday, but you were not here.

(To Śrīpāda Āśrama Mahārāja) What did I say yesterday?

Śrīpāda Āśrama Mahārāja: You said that Śrī Kṛṣṇa is *parama-karuṇa*, most merciful. He comes here so that those within this material world would be able to understand this very deep, confidential topic.

Śrīla Nārāyaṇa Gosvāmī Mahārāja: If Śrī Kṛṣṇa had tasted this only in Goloka, we would never have known about it. He descended with all of His associates to give us knowledge of all these truths.

Mukunda dāsa: Śrīla Gurudeva, in *Śrīmad-Bhāgavatam* Canto Ten there is a verse that explains this point:

anugrahāya bhaktānāṁ
mānuṣaṁ deham āsthitaḥ
bhajate tādṛśīḥ krīḍā
yāḥ śrutvā tat-paro bhavet

(*Śrīmad-Bhāgavatam* 10.33.36)

When the Lord assumes a human-like body to show mercy to His devotees, He engages in such pastimes as will attract those who hear about them to become dedicated to Him.

Śrīla Nārāyaṇa Gosvāmī Mahārāja: Yes, certainly. Kṛṣṇa descends only to distribute His mercy.

Are there any questions from anyone?

Śrīpāda Āśrama Mahārāja: Śrīla Gurudeva, Sthāyī-bhāva Prabhu has a question: We understand that the prayers to Śrī Śrī Rādhā-Kṛṣṇa by a conditioned soul who has not yet achieved an advanced stage of *bhakti* are not heard directly by Them. Such prayers are heard only by Paramātmā. Is this the case when a conditioned soul prays to Śrī Nityānanda Prabhu and Śrī Caitanya Mahāprabhu?

Śrīla Nārāyaṇa Gosvāmī Mahārāja: Śrī Nityānanda Prabhu is *gurudeva*. In other words, He is the personification of the principle of *guru-tattva*. Although Śrī Caitanya Mahāprabhu may not hear, Nityānanda Prabhu will hear.

Devotee: How do I always remain humble?

Śrīla Nārāyaṇa Gosvāmī Mahārāja: We remain humble by remembering the instructions of Śrī Caitanya Mahāprabhu:

tṛṇād api sunīcena
taror api sahiṣṇunā
amāninā mānadena
kīrtanīyaḥ sadā hariḥ

(*Śrī Śikṣāṣṭaka*, Verse 3)

> One should chant the holy name of the Lord in a humble state of mind, thinking oneself lower than the straw in the street; one should be more tolerant than a tree, devoid of all sense of false prestige, and ready to offer all respect to others. In such a state of mind one can chant the holy name of the Lord constantly.

You can remember the history and character of Śrī Prahlāda Mahārāja; remember how tolerant he was. Also remember Haridāsa Ṭhākura, who remained humble although beaten in twenty-two marketplaces.

Aniruddha dāsa: Śrīla Gurudeva, when you order disciples to preach, is this instruction to be followed immediately, or in the future?

Śrīla Nārāyaṇa Gosvāmī Mahārāja: If I ask you to bring me a glass of water, when do I want you to bring it? Do I mean that you should do this for your whole life? I am requesting you to do it now. When

I say, "Always be meek and humble," am I requesting you to only be humble for today or for right now? It is not that I want you to be like this only for the moment. If I say, "Kṛṣṇa is the Supreme Personality of Godhead; therefore, you should perform *bhakti*," is this instruction only meant for the immediate moment? No, it is for this life and all lives to follow.

Devotee: You said earlier that one should be more tolerant than a tree. How can someone be more tolerant than a tree? If no one gives water to the tree, the tree will not ask for water. If someone cuts the tree, it will not resist. I think we can be *taror iva*, or as tolerant as a tree, but not more tolerant than a tree.

Śrīla Nārāyaṇa Gosvāmī Mahārāja: *Taror api*, meaning 'more so than a tree,' is correct. The trees and blades of grass are material (*jaḍa*). We are superior to the trees and grass because we are conscious (*cetana*). In other words, the consciousness of the human being is more developed than that of the tree and grass. If you put your foot on grass, the grass will bend down; but when you remove your foot, the grass will stand up again. A Vaiṣṇava should be more humble than that.

Devotee: I had always been confused about this. Now I understand.

Giridhārī dāsa: There is a verse:

bhakti-anukūla-mātra kāryera svīkāra
bhakti-pratikūla-bhāva-varjanāṅgīkāra

(*Ṣad-aṅga śaraṇāgati*,
by Śrīla Bhaktivinoda Ṭhākura)

Accepting things favorable for devotional service, and rejecting the unfavorable.

This verse states that we should give up moods that are unfavorable for devotional service, not necessarily the sense objects themselves. I think that we do not have to fear bad association; rather we should develop our hearts. These are my thoughts, but I can't find them confirmed in any *śāstra*. I want to know if this is the correct understanding.

Śrīla Nārāyaṇa Gosvāmī Mahārāja: If there is a prostitute, will you associate with her?

Giridhārī dāsa: I should not.

Śrīla Nārāyaṇa Gosvāmī Mahārāja: Why not? Is it that you should associate with that prostitute and enjoy her – but try to have the right mood? Do you understand the difference between mood and actual activity? Here in this verse, the word *bhāva* refers to the activity. Can you drink wine? We must know which activities to accept, and which to reject. There is no deeper meaning here. It is very easy to understand.

Prema-prayojana dāsa: We practice *sādhana* in order to attain *rati*. In our line, as followers of Śrīla Rūpa Gosvāmī, do we want to attain *rati* for Kṛṣṇa, or Rādhā, or Rādhā-Kṛṣṇa?

Śrīla Nārāyaṇa Gosvāmī Mahārāja: There is some difference in reply for people in general and for special devotees. A person acts according to his qualification.

First *bhāva*, *śuddha-sattva*, should come. Then one will actually have the qualification to decide which associate he wants to follow. When his consciousness is free from all material covering and he becomes completely pure, the pure mood of *śuddha-sattva* will enter his heart. He will then know his own spiritual identity and what service he wants to perform.

Prema-prayojana dāsa: What is the speciality of those devotees in the line of Śrīla Rūpa Gosvāmī, the *rūpānugas*?

Śrīla Nārāyaṇa Gosvāmī Mahārāja: In the form of Śrī Rūpa Mañjarī in *kṛṣṇa-līlā*, Śrīla Rūpa Gosvāmī personally performs activities such as these:

tāmbūlārpaṇa-pāda-mardana-payo-dānābhisārādibhir
vṛndāraṇya-maheśvarī priyatayā yās toṣayanti priyāḥ
prāṇa-preṣṭha-sakhī-kulād api kilāsaṅkocitā bhūmikāḥ
keli-bhūmiṣu rūpa-mañjarī-mukhās tā dāsikāḥ saṁśraye

(*Vraja-vilāsa-stava*, Verse 38)

I take shelter of Śrī Rūpa Mañjarī and the other maidservants of Śrīmatī Rādhārāṇī, the great Queen of Vṛndāvana. Those maidservants perpetually satisfy Her by their loving services, such as offering Her betel nuts, massaging Her feet, bringing Her water, and arranging for Her meetings with Lord Kṛṣṇa. The *prāṇa-preṣṭha-sakhīs* are dearer to Śrīmatī Rādhikā than Her very life, but these maidservants are still more dear, because without feeling shy they can enter the area where the Divine Couple enjoy Their most confidential pastimes.

Rūpa Gosvāmī is an eternal associate of Caitanya Mahāprabhu in *gaura-līlā*, and he is Rūpa Mañjarī in Kṛṣṇa's pastimes. Rūpa Mañjarī's service is *rādhā-dāsya*, the service of Śrīmatī Rādhārāṇī. *Rūpānuga* devotees are followers of Rūpa Gosvāmī in his form as the personal associate of Śrī Caitanya Mahāprabhu and in his form as Rūpa Mañjarī, the leader of the maidservants of Śrīmatī Rādhikā.

Prema-prayojana dāsa: Is it that Rūpa Mañjarī's *rati* for Rādhikā is her *sthāyī-bhāva* and her *rati* for Kṛṣṇa is a *sañcārī-bhāva*, or is it that her *rati* for Kṛṣṇa is her *sthāyī-bhāva* and her *rati* for Rādhikā is a *sañcārī-bhāva*?

Śrīla Nārāyaṇa Gosvāmī Mahārāja: Śrī Rūpa Mañjarī's entire existence is dedicated to Śrīmatī Rādhikā, and she sees Kṛṣṇa as Rādhikā's most beloved. Thus, when at any time Kṛṣṇa comes to Rādhikā and performs some loving pastime with Her, a *sañcārī-bhāva* comes in Rūpa Mañjarī's heart. For example, if Kṛṣṇa is embracing Rādhikā, Rūpa Mañjarī thinks, "That embrace is coming to me." Her *rati* for Rādhā and Kṛṣṇa accords with this understanding.

Prāṇa-govinda dāsa: Śrīla Gurudeva, you said that when *śuddha-sattva* comes in one's heart by serving under the guidance of *śrī guru*, that person will realize his *svarūpa*. If the *svarūpa* of the disciple is in *sakhya-rasa* (the mood of a cowherd friend of Kṛṣṇa) and the *guru* reveals to him the *guru's* own *svarūpa* in *dāsya-rasa* (the mood of a servant)...

Śrīla Nārāyaṇa Gosvāmī Mahārāja: This cannot occur. If the disciple is in a certain *rasa*, it is absurd to think that a real *guru* does not know this and is in another, lower, *rasa*. If a *guru* does not know the *svarūpa* of his disciple, he is not *guru*. It means that he himself is not situated in *śuddha-sattva*. How can he help his disciple?

May 2, 2008

Darśana
After the walk

Śyāmarāṇī dāsī: Śrīla Gurudeva, this is Mañjarī's painting for *Śrī Navadvīpa-dhāma-māhātmya*. It shows Śrī Nityānanda Prabhu and Śrīla Jīva Gosvāmī.

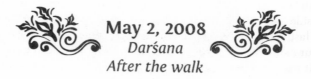

Mañjarī dāsī: What is the age of Śrīla Jīva Gosvāmī?

Śrīla Nārāyaṇa Gosvāmī Mahārāja: He should be somewhat smaller.

Śyāmarāṇī dāsī: She will make him smaller in the computer.

Śrīla Nārāyaṇa Gosvāmī Mahārāja: Śrī Nityānanda Prabhu should be like his grandfather. Śrīla Jīva Gosvāmī should be like a boy.

Śyāmarāṇī dāsī: How old should he be?

Śrīla Nārāyaṇa Gosvāmī Mahārāja: Ten or twelve years old.

Mañjarī dāsī: Should Nityānanda Prabhu have gray hair?

Śrīla Nārāyaṇa Gosvāmī Mahārāja: No.

Śrīpāda Mādhava Mahārāja: He is Bhagavān, so He never becomes old.

Śyāmarāṇī dāsī: Is everything else okay in the painting besides the height?

Śrīla Nārāyaṇa Gosvāmī Mahārāja: Everything is okay. Śrīla Jīva Gosvāmī should not have a garland – only a *brāhmaṇa* thread.

Śyāmarāṇī dāsī: Mañjarī wants me to ask you a question. She says that you often tell her and other young ladies to preach. She is asking if they should combine together as a travelling *kīrtana* party, or stay in small groups.

Śrīla Nārāyaṇa Gosvāmī Mahārāja: It is not that you should only preach. You must also do *bhajana* properly.

First teach those who are not yet trained, and then two or three ladies in each group can preach together.

Śyāmarāṇī dāsī: I was also asked to ask you about the paintings of Rūpa Mañjarī and Rati Mañjarī. In the beginning, in 1993, when they were first completed, you installed them on the Sevā-kuñja altar in Vṛndāvana. At that time, Rūpa Mañjarī was on Kṛṣṇa's right side and Rati Mañjarī was on Rādhikā's left side. Then, in Delhi last year, when we showed you the posters of Sevā-kuñja and the four *mañjarīs* that we were printing, you switched them around. Does it matter which side they are on?

Śrīla Nārāyaṇa Gosvāmī Mahārāja: It matters. This side is wrong. She looks to the other side. Where is she looking? Rūpa Mañjarī's eyes are looking towards Kṛṣṇa, so she must be on Rādhikā's side, and Rati Mañjarī must come here on Kṛṣṇa's side.

Śyāmarāṇī dāsī: Should we switch their places in Rūpa-Sanātana Gauḍīya Maṭha also? From the beginning, for the past fifteen years, she has been on this side at the Rūpa-Sanātana Gauḍīya Math. Should we switch them?

Śrīla Nārāyaṇa Gosvāmī Mahārāja: Yes. In fact, with my own hand, I had originally placed them the correct way.

May 3, 2008
Morning Walk

Raghunātha Bhaṭṭa dāsa: Śrīla Gurudeva, I have one question: Yesterday, Brajanātha Prabhu mentioned in his speech that when Śrī Kṛṣṇa leaves Vraja and goes to Mathurā, He becomes Mathureśa-Kṛṣṇa, and when He goes to Dvārakā He becomes Dvārakādhīśa-Kṛṣṇa. So when Śrīman Mahāprabhu leaves Navadvīpa and goes to South India or other places, is it a similar situation for Him?

Śrīpāda Mādhava Mahārāja: He is asking if Mahāprabhu would become 'Nīlācala-Mahāprabhu' or 'Gambhīrā-Mahāprabhu.'

Śrīla Nārāyaṇa Gosvāmī Mahārāja: No. In the form of Śrī Caitanya Mahāprabhu, Kṛṣṇa took the beauty and intrinsic mood of Śrīmatī Rādhikā so that He would be able to taste the fulfillment of His three desires.[13] That is why He became Śrī Śacīnandana Gaurahari[14]. One may say that He is comparable to Dvārakādhīśa-Kṛṣṇa when He goes to Purī, but that is not the fact. Rather, Mahāprabhu was relishing Kṛṣṇa of Vṛndāvana.

Moreover, this question is not proper. There is something wrong in the question itself. Śrī Caitanya Mahāprabhu is Kṛṣṇa, but He

---

13 "Desiring to understand the glory of Rādhārāṇī's love, the wonderful qualities in Him that She alone relishes through Her love, and the happiness She feels when She realizes the sweetness of His love, the Supreme Lord Hari, richly endowed with Her emotions, appeared from the womb of Śrīmatī Śacī-devī, as the moon appeared from the ocean" (*Śrī Caitanya-caritāmṛta, Ādi-līlā* 1.6).

This topic is elaborately discussed in the previous morning walk.

14 The name Śacīnandana literally means, 'the son of Śacī-devī.' The name Gaurahari means that Kṛṣṇa, Hari, has covered Himself with the golden (*gaura*) complexion of Śrīmatī Rādhikā. In Navadvīpa He is known as Śrī Śacīnandana Gaurahari, Gaurasundara, and Nimāi Paṇḍita. After taking *sannyāsa* and travelling to Purī and other holy places., He became known as Śrī Caitanya Mahāprabhu.

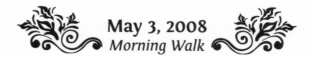

is Kṛṣṇa who has taken the beauty of Śrīmatī Rādhikā and who is tasting the glory of Her love. We should therefore think about Mahāprabhu's moods in relation to Rādhikā. He cannot be addressed as 'Purī-Mahāprabhu' or any similar name.

Śrīpāda Mādhava Mahārāja: He is understood according to Rādhikā's moods, not Kṛṣṇa's moods.

Śrīla Nārāyaṇa Gosvāmī Mahārāja: In the pastimes of Mahāprabhu, Śrī Kṛṣṇa is not Kṛṣṇa. He is totally absorbed in Śrīmatī Rādhikā, thinking, "I am Rādhikā." No need to think about Him in relation to Kṛṣṇa's moods.

Śrīmatī Rādhikā does not go out of Vṛndāvana for even one moment; and Śrī Kṛṣṇa, in His original, complete feature, also does not leave. Her original feature, always residing in Vṛndāvana, is Vṛṣabhānu-nandinī Rādhā.

When Rādhikā is in Nandagrāma and lamenting in separation from Kṛṣṇa when He [His manifestation] has gone to Dvārakā, She is Viyoginī-Rādhā. Therefore, when Mahāprabhu is in Jagannātha Purī [which represents Dvārakā], He is in the mood of Viyoginī-Rādhā. When Rādhikā meets Kṛṣṇa at Kurukṣetra She is Saṁyoginī-Rādhā, and when Mahāprabhu is on the bank of Godāvarī with Rāmānanda Rāya, He is in the mood of that Saṁyoginī-Rādhā. In Navadvīpa, which is hidden Vṛndāvana, He is in the mood of Vṛṣabhānu-nandinī Rādhā.

Mahāprabhu actually never leaves Navadvīpa, where the twelve forests of Vṛndāvana are situated in a hidden way. Jagannātha Purī or Godāvarī have not been told to be the same as Vṛndāvana.

Sugata dāsa: What is the internal reason that Śrī Caitanya Mahāprabhu did not stay long in Vṛndāvana?

Śrīla Nārāyaṇa Gosvāmī Mahārāja: When He was in Vṛndāvana, He would see Govardhana and Yamunā and other stimulus for His thinking, "I am Kṛṣṇa," and "I performed so many sweet pastimes here." He did not want this mood to envelop Him. He did not want His mood as Mahāprabhu (in *rādhā-bhāva*) to disappear. He therefore quickly returned to Purī.

Where is 'Bengali' Prāṇa-govinda dāsa? Last night you told the wrong thing in class; you did not properly explain Kṛṣṇa's three desires. And why were you so nervous when you spoke?

Prāṇa-govinda dāsa: Although I am accustomed to speak in front of audiences, before this I had never spoken in your presence. I need your mercy.

Śrīla Nārāyaṇa Gosvāmī Mahārāja: But you have not understood Kṛṣṇa's three desires.

Prāṇa-govinda dāsa: I will listen to you again.

Śrīla Nārāyaṇa Gosvāmī Mahārāja: Yes, listen very carefully.

Last night, Giridhārī spoke best [in the contest at the end of Śrīla Mahārāja's class, to determine which contestant could speak best about the reasons for Mahāprabhu's advent], but I declared that Mahā-Lakṣmī was the winner. Why? Because Mahā-Lakṣmī quoted a *śloka*, and in three minutes explained everything. Giridhārī was simply reading – for more then five minutes.

(To Giridhārī dāsa) Did you hear what I just told them? You simply read. You should be able to speak without looking so much at the paper. Also, you took more than five minutes; so I gave you second position.

Śrīpāda Bhāgavata Mahārāja: Yesterday we were speaking about the Pāṇḍavas and Draupadī becoming the *pāṇḍava-vṛkṣa* trees next to Śyāma-kuṇḍa, and we also discussed Uddhava's becoming grass at Kusuma-sarovara. I am hoping to get some clarification in this regard. I would like to know if the *jīva* can change his *svarūpa* (intrinsic, constitutional nature) by changing from one *rasa* to another? Can the conditioned souls change their *svarūpa*?

Śrīla Nārāyaṇa Gosvāmī Mahārāja: Conditioned souls have no realization of their *svarūpa*, so where is the question of changing it?

Śrīpāda Bhāgavata Mahārāja: Is the *svarūpa* of the conditioned soul eternal?

Śrīla Nārāyaṇa Gosvāmī Mahārāja: Yes.

Śrīpāda Bhāgavata Mahārāja: If a *jīva* comes in contact with a high-caliber self-realized devotee...

Śrīla Nārāyaṇa Gosvāmī Mahārāja: If one first comes in association with a *dāsya-rasa* Vaiṣṇava (the elevated devotee who is situated in his eternal relationship with Kṛṣṇa in the mellow of servant), that Vaiṣṇava will illuminate *dāsya-rasa*. After one comes in contact with a *mādhurya-rasa* Vaiṣṇava, then, if he is qualified for that *rasa* (if his *svarūpa* is in that *rasa*), *mādhurya-rasa* will manifest in his heart. If someone is not in *mādhurya-rasa*, but at the time of *sādhana* is thinking of himself as a *gopī* and performing the *sādhana* for that, his practice will not fructify into any *rasa*.

When a person enters the stage of *rati*, he will realize his *svarūpa*; not before that.

Lakṣmīpati dāsa: I heard from Viśvambhara that you are having big problems with your Spanish publications. Five books are ready to be published, but there is no money. In Mexico the devotees have a big debt to the book fund; they are not paying for the books they received on credit.

There is so much potential for book distribution, not only in Mexico, but in Houston and other places in the United States, but there is lack of organization. So I am willing to help 200%.

Śrīla Nārāyaṇa Gosvāmī Mahārāja: Oh yes, please help. I will be happy if many books are published.

Lakṣmīpati dāsa: I don't see any good reason why all your Spanish books should not be published.

Śrīla Nārāyaṇa Gosvāmī Mahārāja: Thank you. Yes, try to publish all my books.

Lakṣmīpati dāsa: The problem is in management.

Śrīla Nārāyaṇa Gosvāmī Mahārāja: If you desire we can give something, but you will have to return the funds. There are so many rich persons in Spain, Brazil, South America, Alachua, and Venezuela.

Brajanātha dāsa: We are ready to fund, but there must be proper coordination.

Vrajendra-nandana dāsa: If Śrī Caitanya Mahāprabhu was in the mood of Śrīmatī Rādhikā, why was He chanting, "*Gopī, gopī*," after returning from Gaya?

Śrīla Nārāyaṇa Gosvāmī Mahārāja: He was not always in the mood of Śrīmatī Rādhikā. When He was in internal consciousness, He was sometimes in the mood of a *sakhī* or *mañjarī*. He was especially in the mood of Śrīmatī Rādhikā, but sometimes He was in the mood of a *sakhī*. He would sometimes become angry, because the *sakhīs* cannot tolerate when Kṛṣṇa cheats Śrīmatī Rādhikā and makes Her 'suffer.' It is for this reason that He would sometimes chant "*Gopī, gopī*" rather than Kṛṣṇa's name.

Prema-prayojana dāsa: Should we consider that Mahāprabhu was in a *sakhī*-mood at the time that student said, "Chant Kṛṣṇa," and Mahāprabhu took a stick to beat him?

Śrīla Nārāyaṇa Gosvāmī Mahārāja: Yes, that is right. Sometimes He feels like a *mañjarī* or *sakhī*, but that is rare.

Vrajendra-nandana dāsa: You said that Mahāprabhu was teaching us that in order to make progress in *bhajana*, we must give up our dearest object of love, just as He gave up the association of Viṣṇupriyā-devī. My question is this: If He was so attached to Viṣṇupriyā, why did He not show her very much affection until their last night together?

Śrīla Nārāyaṇa Gosvāmī Mahārāja: He did not have the same kind of love and affection as Kṛṣṇa, because He was in Rādhikā's mood. When Kṛṣṇa was in the form of Śacīnandana Gaurahari, at that time His queen, Satyabhāmā, was in the form of Viṣṇupriyā-devī. In Dvārakā, Satyabhāmā was most beloved to Kṛṣṇa because she greatly resembled Rādhikā; that is why Kṛṣṇa married her. Rukmiṇī was His principal queen, but Satyabhāmā was dearer to Him than Rukmiṇī because, like Rādhikā, she had a leftist, or contrary, mood (*vāmya-bhāva*).

Aniruddha dāsa: A devotee asked me why we call ourselves Vaiṣṇavas, which means 'devotees of Viṣṇu.' We are devotees of Kṛṣṇa.

Śrīla Nārāyaṇa Gosvāmī Mahārāja: Kṛṣṇa and His incarnations – from Kṛṣṇa Himself to the Viṣṇu incarnation who is His smallest fraction, Kṣīrodakaśāyī Viṣṇu as Paramātmā – are all Viṣṇu-tattva. So as a whole, in general language, we are known as Vaiṣṇavas.

Prema-prayojana dāsa:

vikrīḍitaṁ vraja-vadhūbhir idaṁ ca viṣṇoḥ
śraddhānvito 'nuśṛṇuyād atha varṇayed yaḥ
bhaktiṁ parāṁ bhagavati pratilabhya kāmaṁ
hṛd-rogam āśv apahinoty acireṇa dhīraḥ

(*Śrīmad-Bhāgavatam* 10.33.39)

Anyone who faithfully hears or describes the Lord's [addressed here as Viṣṇu] playful affairs with the young *gopīs* of Vṛndāvana will attain the Lord's pure devotional service. Thus he will quickly become sober and conquer lust, the disease of the heart.

Śrīla Nārāyaṇa Gosvāmī Mahārāja: Kṛṣṇa is actually the Supreme Viṣṇu. That is why we are Vaiṣṇavas.

Devotee: In his introduction to *Śrīmad-Bhāgavatam*, Śrīla A.C. Bhaktivedānta Svāmī Prabhupāda writes, "We shall eagerly wait for the happy days of *bhagavat-dharma*, or *prema-dharma*, inaugurated by Lord Śrī Caitanya Mahāprabhu." Does that mean that we have not yet entered the Golden Age within Kali-yuga? Has the Golden Age of *bhagavat-dharma* arrived already, or is it yet to come?

Śrīla Nārāyaṇa Gosvāmī Mahārāja: When Śrī Caitanya Mahāprabhu appeared, that was the Golden Age. In addition, it will be a Golden Age for those who realize it; not for all.

Kamala-kānta dāsa: Śrīla Gurudeva, I heard in a lecture that Jagāi and Mādhāi are incarnations of Jaya and Vijaya. Is it true?

Śrīla Nārāyaṇa Gosvāmī Mahārāja: Yes. In their first incarnation they were Hiraṇyākṣa and Hiraṇyakaśipu; in the second, Rāvaṇa and Kumbhakarṇa; in the third, Śiśupāla and Dantavakra; and in the fourth, they were Jagāi and Mādhāi.

Devotee: You have often said that we must 'serve' *hari-kathā*. How do we 'serve' *hari-kathā*? We 'hear' *hari-kathā* and we have to 'understand' *hari-kathā*, but how do we 'serve' *hari-kathā*?

Śrīla Nārāyaṇa Gosvāmī Mahārāja: By serving *śrī guru* intimately (*viśrambheṇa guroḥ sevā*), like a bosom friend. Do you understand? Then, when you will hear *hari-kathā* in that situation, you will be able to understand it. Hearing alone will not suffice.

In the *Bhagavad-gītā* this process has been given:

tad viddhi praṇipātena
paripraśnena sevayā
upadekṣyanti te jñānaṁ
jñāninas tattva-darśinaḥ

(*Bhagavad-gītā* 4.34)

> Just try to learn the truth by approaching a spiritual master. Inquire from him submissively and render service unto him. The self-realized souls can impart knowledge unto you because they have seen the truth.*

Sugata dāsa: Śrīla Gurudeva, many people are beginning to chant. Chanting is becoming very popular in the outer *yoga*-world, in *yoga* studios throughout America and the world. Sometimes they chant "Hare Kṛṣṇa," and sometimes "*Oṁ namaḥ śivāya*," or they chant to Durgā.

Because *kīrtana* is becoming very popular, some *kīrtana* leaders are also becoming famous and popular. Is this the influence of

Lord Caitanya and also your grace? Or is this *māyā*? Will you say something about this?

Śrīla Nārāyaṇa Gosvāmī Mahārāja: This is occurring because Śrīla Bhaktivedānta Svāmī Mahārāja preached all over the world. I am also coming, and gradually the number of the people performing *kīrtana* is increasing. People are seeing that we give great honor to *kīrtana*, and therefore they are inspired to give honor as well. But they don't know what is true *saṅkīrtana*. Therefore they sometimes perform *kīrtana* for Śiva or Durgā, and sometimes they chant "Jaya Gaṇeśa, Jaya Gaṇeśa."

Vṛndāvana dāsa: Śrīla Gurudeva, should we see the oneness and not the difference in our *kīrtana* groups? Should we see all this as the mercy of Lord Caitanya – that we are the same, although different – and then go to those *kīrtana* groups in the mood that we are the same?

Śrīpāda Padmanābha Mahārāja: What do you mean by 'the oneness'?

Vṛndāvana dāsa: The oneness of the principle of chanting the holy name.

Śrīla Nārāyaṇa Gosvāmī Mahārāja: Better to serve the Vaiṣṇavas and follow the Vaiṣṇava-etiquette; then you can ask a question. Otherwise, you will not be able to ask a proper question.

Prema-prayojana dāsa: Gurudeva, I have a difficult question. He asked an easy question; I have a difficult one.

In *Bhakti-rasāmṛta-sindu*, Śrīla Rūpa Gosvāmī says that if a devotee has got some *rati*, but he commits some offense, then he may receive one of two reactions: His *rati* may become *rati-ābhāsa*, or his *rati* may go down to a lower *rasa*. If he is in a higher *rasa*, his *rati* will go to a lower *rasa*. My question is: Will that *rati* go down to a lower *rasa* forever, or only until the effect of the offense wears off, and then maybe go back?

Śrīla Nārāyaṇa Gosvāmī Mahārāja: If that devotee commits an offense, he comes down. If his offense is very, very grave, his *rati* will disappear forever. If His offense is not so great, then, by good association, it may return.

Prema-prayojana dāsa: If, for example, the devotee is in *sakhya-rasa*, he can go down to *dāsya-rasa*, and then when the reaction to his offense is gone, he can still go back to *sākhya-rasa*?

Śrīla Nārāyaṇa Gosvāmī Mahārāja: When *rati*, or *śuddha-sattva* comes, it is very rare for a devotee to commit any offense. We see this only in the life of Bharata and Citraketu Mahārāja, but even in those two examples, they did not really fall down. What they did was due to the wish of Kṛṣṇa.

Śrīpāda Mādhava Mahārāja: It was only to give some instruction to the world.

Śrīla Nārāyaṇa Gosvāmī Mahārāja: In class this evening, we will discuss Sarvabhauma Bhaṭṭācārya, and then *Rāya Rāmānanda-saṁvāda*. Then, if time allows, we will begin to discuss *sanātana-śikṣā* or *rūpa-śikṣā*.

May 3, 2008
Darśana
After the walk

Kṛṣṇa-mayī dāsī: Śrīla Gurudeva, the young students in the non-devotee school where I work drew these pictures of you. They are hoping you will come to Los Angeles so that they can meet you.

Śrīla Nārāyaṇa Gosvāmī Mahārāja: Tell them that I am offering my heartly blessings, and that I love them.

Brajanātha dāsa: Śrīla Gurudeva, some devotees have made a new website for your services.

Vasanti dāsī: At the Advisory Board meetings there was a discussion about a communication network. Śrīpāda Nemi Mahārāja, Śrīpāda Vaikhānas Mahārāja, Śilpa-kāriṇī Dīdī, Jaya-gopāla Prabhu in America, and Śyāma Prabhu and I have created this Sevā-Teams website.

Brajanātha dāsa: So many devotees are serving all around the world, and they want proper coordination and communication. For this, the Sevā-Team group has developed a tool, by computer, so that everybody can easily discover how to communicate with each other and take advantage of already achieved results, like book publishing.

Vasanti dāsī: For example, those devotees who want to do *sevā* can write in and say, "I am a web designer" or "I am an accountant." If there are existing teams that need help, we can coordinate and engage people in *sevā*.

Śrīla Nārāyaṇa Gosvāmī Mahārāja: Very good. Continue to develop this.

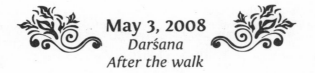

Vasanti dāsī: And the existing teams, like Bhakti Trust, Bhakti Projects, and the Webcast team, will be all listed.

Brajanātha dāsa: Śrīla Gurudeva's other projects, like Navadvīpa and Purī, should also be listed, with a list of the various ways devotees may help.

Śrīpāda Padmanābha Mahārāja: This is a way in which any devotee in any part of the world can find out how he can engage in opportunities to serve in different departments.

Śrīla Nārāyaṇa Gosvāmī Mahārāja: You should do this. Very good.

Brajanātha dāsa: In the devotees' specific countries, there will be proper possibilities to communicate.

Śyāma dāsa: Can I take *dīkṣā* tomorrow?

Brajanātha dāsa: He did all this Sevā-Teams service on computer. He is very expert. He is asking for *dīkṣā*.

Are you chanting sixteen rounds daily?

Śyāma dāsa: Yes.

Śrīla Nārāyaṇa Gosvāmī Mahārāja: You can enlist your name.

Thank you.

May 4, 2008
Morning Walk

Mukunda dāsa: Śrīla Gurudeva, I have one question. You spoke about *guru-tattva* on the first night. You said that when the *guru* gives the disciple a relationship with Kṛṣṇa at the time of *dīkṣā*, brahminical initiation, it means he is giving it 'in seed form.' Some people are thinking that this means *siddha-praṇālī*, so they are confused.

Śrīla Nārāyaṇa Gosvāmī Mahārāja: No. Until one performs pure *bhajana* to the extent that all kinds of *anarthas* have left his heart, one's *siddha-deha* (one's spiritual body, which is fit for serving Rādhā and Kṛṣṇa) cannot manifest. It may come at the stage of *rati* (*bhāva-bhakti*).

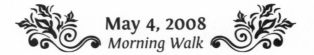

One must first attain the stages of *śraddhā*, *bhajana-kriyā*, *niṣṭhā*, *ruci*, *āsakti*, and after that *rati* manifests. At this stage *śuddha-sattva*

will come, and then the devotee will be *siddha* (perfectly self-realized). Those who try to imagine their *siddha-deha* will be like the *sahajiyā bābājīs* at Rādhā-kuṇḍa, all of whom partake in immoral relationships with widows and perhaps even have sons from these relationships.

Śrīpāda Āśrama Mahārāja: Can you say something about *kṛṣṇa-sevā-vāsanā*, the desire to serve Śrī Kṛṣṇa?

Śrīla Nārāyaṇa Gosvāmī Mahārāja: It may come even before initiation. One attains the seed of the desire to serve Kṛṣṇa by associating with an elevated devotee; that pure devotee, *śrī guru*, gives the seed of this desire. It is for this reason that a person comes to *śrī guru* and *guru* accepts him. The disciple first receives *laukika-śraddhā*, meaning that he will offer his obeisances in a general way. Then, when he gets more association, he becomes fixed in actual transcendental *śraddhā*.

The seed is already present in the heart, but it is latent. *Guru* gives the water, heat, and light, after which a sprout develops and gradually grows.

Laksmī-pati dāsa: Gurudeva, let me introduce Ekā-bhoktā from Mexico.

Śrīla Nārāyaṇa Gosvāmī Mahārāja: Ekā-bhoktā???

Śrīpāda Mādhava Mahārāja: The lone enjoyer.

Śrīla Nārāyaṇa Gosvāmī Mahārāja: Who gave you that name?

Ekā-bhoktā dāsa: Hṛdayānanda Mahārāja gave me that name twenty-seven years ago, and then you gave me *dīkṣā* in 2001.

Laksmī-pati dāsa: He has many skills for publication in Spanish. He wants to help us.

Śrīla Nārāyaṇa Gosvāmī Mahārāja: We want this. They can make a board for my Spanish publications and produce all my books.

Ekā-bhoktā dāsa: I worked with the BBT in Mexico for twelve years. I want to say that just by your presence, all sins are banished. You have kindly given the seed of *bhakti* in my heart, so I want to thank you very much for that.

Śrīla Nārāyaṇa Gosvāmī Mahārāja: Very good. The seed has come and it may sprout; don't worry. But always remain in the association of Vaiṣṇavas.

Ekā-bhoktā dāsa: I want to go back to Mexico to preach. Will you kindly give me your blessings and empowerment?

Śrīla Nārāyaṇa Gosvāmī Mahārāja: Very good. If you read my *Jaiva-dharma*, it will help you so much.

Śrīpāda Mādhava Mahārāja: Puṣkara is a painter, like Śyāmarāṇī Dīdī. Śrīla Bhaktivedānta Svāmī Mahārāja used to guide them in painting.

Śrīpāda Bhāgavata Mahārāja: He knows many Sanskrit verses. He is very learned.

Śrīla Nārāyaṇa Gosvāmī Mahārāja: What is the meaning of this verse?

kṛṣṇa-bhakti-rasa-bhāvitā matiḥ
krīyatāṁ yadi kuto 'pi labhyate
tatra laulyam api mūlyam ekalaṁ
janma-koṭi-sukṛtair na labhyate
(*Śrī Caitanya-caritāmṛta, Madhya-līlā* 8.70)

> Pure devotional service in Kṛṣṇa consciousness cannot be had even by pious activity in hundreds upon thousands of lives. It can be attained only by paying one price – that is, the intense greed to obtain it. If it is available somewhere, one must purchase it without delay.

Puṣkara dāsa: One will not get *kṛṣṇa-bhakti* even after millions of years, unless one has greed (*laulyam*).

Śrīla Nārāyaṇa Gosvāmī Mahārāja: But what is *kṛṣṇa-bhakti-rasa-bhāvitā matiḥ*? This is the question.

Puṣkara dāsa: Our Śrīla Prabhupāda defined it as Kṛṣṇa consciousness, thinking of Kṛṣṇa.

Śrīpāda Padmanābha Mahārāja: When our Guru Mahārāja named his International Society for Kṛṣṇa Consciousness, he named it after this phrase.

Śrīla Nārāyaṇa Gosvāmī Mahārāja: I know this, but what is *kṛṣṇa-bhakti-rasa-bhāvitā matiḥ*?

Puṣkara dāsa: I do not know. I do not have it.

Śrīla Nārāyaṇa Gosvāmī Mahārāja: You should understand that there is some difference between *bhakti* and *bhakti-rasa*. *Bhakti* is one thing and *bhakti-rasa* is another. *Bhakti* was present in this world before Śrī Caitanya Mahāprabhu and Śrīla Rūpa Gosvāmī came. Mādhavācārya, Rāmānujācārya, Viṣṇusvāmī, Nimbāditya, and others followed the principals of *bhakti* – but not *bhakti-rasa*.

It is essential to know what is *rasa*, which is present only in *rāgātmikā-bhaktas*. When one is firmly situated in *rāgātmikā-bhakti*, ones' service to Kṛṣṇa is called *rasa*: *dāsya-rasa*, *sakhya-rasa*, *vātsalya-rasa*, and *mādhurya-rasa*. At that time, *mamatā*, a sense of 'mine-ness' for Kṛṣṇa, manifests in a very thick way in the devotees' heart. This is true for Kṛṣṇa's *sakhās*, more so for Mother Yaśodā, more so for the *gopīs*, more for Lalitā and Viśākhā, and still more so for Śrīmatī Rādhikā.

When a person hears about this topic from a *rasika tattva-jña* Vaiṣṇava in the line of Śrīla Rūpa Gosvāmī, Śrī Svarūpa Dāmodara, and Śrīla Raghunātha dāsa Gosvāmī, greed to serve like Kṛṣṇa's intimate associates may enter his heart; it is not possible otherwise.

What is the nature of such greed? One will think, "I want the same *rasa* as Mother Yaśodā," or "I want the same *rasa* as Subala and Śrīdhāma." Or, one may think, "I would like to be like the *gopīs* in their *parakīya* mood of *unnata-ujjvala-rasa*. They left everything for Kṛṣṇa's service. And among these *gopīs* I want to serve Śrīmatī Rādhikā and Her mood of service."

Such greed comes from that association. *Koṭi koṭi janma sukṛtair* (hundreds upon thousands of lifetimes of spiritual pious merit) cannot bring it. It comes only by hearing very attentively from a *rasika-bhakta* in the line of Śrīla Rūpa Gosvāmī and Svarūpa Dāmodara Gosvāmī – and keeping their words in one's heart.

Śrīpāda Padmanābha Mahārāja: You are saying that *bhakti-rasa* resides in the hearts of *rāgātmikā-bhaktas*?

Śrīla Nārāyaṇa Gosvāmī Mahārāja: Yes, and Mahāprabhu and Śrīla Rūpa Gosvāmī also brought that *bhakti-rasa* to this world. There was no *bhakti-rasa* before their appearance; there was only *bhakti*.

Śrīpāda Mādhava Mahārāja: *Bhaktas* like Śrī Rāmacandra's Hanumān and others are also *rāgātmikā-bhaktas*. Do they have *bhakti-rasa* or not?

Śrīla Nārāyaṇa Gosvāmī Mahārāja: Yes, Hanumān is in *dāsya-rasa*. Yudhiṣṭhira Mahārāja has a mixture of *dāsya-*, *sakhya-*, and *vātsalya-rasa*, and Arjuna is situated in *dāsya* and *sakhya-rasa*.

Śrīpāda Dāmodara Mahārāja: If that is the case, how can it be said that before Śrī Caitanya Mahāprabhu there was no *bhakti-rasa*?

Śrīpāda Mādhava Mahārāja: It was not preached in this world before Mahāprabhu came.

Śrīpāda Dāmodara Mahārāja: It was preached.

Śrīpāda Mādhava Mahārāja: Before Caitanya Mahāprabhu, preaching about *bhakti-rasa* was done only in relation to *dāsya-bhāva* (servitorship) in the mood of *aiśvarya* (awe and reverence). Only at that point in history when Śrī Caitanya Mahāprabhu came did the preaching of *bhakti-rasa* manifest in its full blown form in Vraja, up to *pārakīya bhakti-rasa*.

Śrīpāda Padmanābha Mahārāja: The potential for tasting *bhakti-rasa* begins at this stage?

śuddha-sattva-viśeṣātmā
prema-sūryāṁśu-sāmyabhāk
rucibhiś citta-māsṛṇya-
kṛd asau bhāva ucyate

(*Bhakti-rasāmṛta-sindhu* 1.3.1)

When devotional service is situated on the transcendental platform of pure goodness, it is like the first rays of sunlight of love of Kṛṣṇa. At such a time, devotional service causes the heart to be softened by various tastes and is called *bhāva* (transcendental emotions).

Śrīla Nārāyaṇa Gosvāmī Mahārāja: *Śuddha-sattva*, also known as *viśuddha-sattva*, refers to the moods in the heart of the *gopīs*, Yaśodā-maiyā, Nanda Bābā, and Subala and Śrī Kṛṣṇa's other friends. When the devotee meditates on Śrī Kṛṣṇa with a longing for the moods of these associates, their moods enter his heart.

kṛṣṇaṁ smaran janaṁ cāsya
preṣṭhaṁ nija-samīhitam
tat-tat-kathā-rataś cāsau
kuryād vāsaṁ vraje sadā

(*Bhakti-rasāmṛta-sindhu* 1.2.294)

One should always think of Kṛṣṇa within oneself and should choose a very dear devotee who is a servitor of Kṛṣṇa in Vṛndāvana. One should constantly engage in topics about that servitor and his or her loving relationship with Kṛṣṇa, and one should live in Vṛndāvana. If one is physically unable to go to Vṛndāvana, he should live there mentally.

Gajahanta dāsa: Śrīla Gurudeva, we sing the song, "*Kṛpā bindu diyā* – Please give me a drop of your mercy." Does receiving this *laulyam* (greed) depend on *śrī guru*?

Śrīla Nārāyaṇa Gosvāmī Mahārāja: The *guru* must be able to give it. He must be an elevated *rasika* and *tattva-jña* Vaiṣṇava. That type of *guru* may give that transcendental greed.

Gajahanta dāsa: Our disciplic succession of *gurus* from Śrīla Bhaktivinoda Ṭhākura are all high-class *rasika*. So should we be praying to them for us to get *laulyam*?

Śrīla Nārāyaṇa Gosvāmī Mahārāja: Certainly.

Gajahanta dāsa: We feel that Śrīla Prabhupāda Bhaktivedānta Svāmī Mahārāja was the first wave of *bhakti* in our life, and you are coming as the second wave.

Śrīla Nārāyaṇa Gosvāmī Mahārāja: He declared everywhere that Kṛṣṇa is the Supreme Personality of Godhead, and now he has told me to preach that you should forget this. In that regard it seems like there is something different in our preaching, but it is important to know that both conceptions are in one line with one purport. The first stage calls out to the conditioned souls: "Come, you must know that Kṛṣṇa is the Supreme Personality of Godhead." Then, after this conception is fixed, <u>then</u> try to forget it; otherwise you will not attain *vraja-bhakti*.

Gajahanta dāsa: Will there be many more waves in the future?

Śrīla Nārāyaṇa Gosvāmī Mahārāja: Yes, so many waves. No one is able to count them.

Aniruddha dāsa: It seems that the *dhotī*, *śikhā*, and *kaṇṭhī-mālā* are all external. What is the relationship of these things to *bhakti*? Are they actually necessary?

Śrīla Nārāyaṇa Gosvāmī Mahārāja: Try to realize that Śrī Caitanya Mahāprabhu has told us to do this, as did Śrīla Rūpa Gosvāmī; and Śrīla Sanātana Gosvāmī has written about this in his *Hari-bhakti-vilāsa*. Why did Śrī Caitanya Mahāprabhu follow these principles? Why did Śrīla Bhaktivinoda Ṭhākura and Śrīla Rūpa Gosvāmī follow this? It is external?

May 5, 2008
Morning walk

Śrīla Nārāyaṇa Gosvāmī Mahārāja:

smara-garala-khaṇḍana mamaṁ śirasi maṇḍanaṁ
dehi pada-pallavam udāram

(*Gīta-govinda* 10.8)

O Śrīmatī Rādhikā, I am burning in the fire of separation. Please be merciful to Me and decorate My head with the footdust of Your lotus feet, to relieve Me from this burning poison of Cupid.

In this verse, Kṛṣṇa is begging Śrīmatī Rādhikā to place Her lotus feet on His head. Actually, She would not allow this. Indian ladies maintain certain rules and regulations regarding relationships with their husbands or beloveds. Therefore, Kṛṣṇa may try to place Her feet on His head, but She does not allow it.

Prema-prayojana dāsa: Gurudeva, you said that Śrīmatī Rādhikā will not keep Her feet there?

Śrīla Nārāyaṇa Gosvāmī Mahārāja: *Vraja-prema* also has *maryādā* (etiquette). *Prema* is not without *maryādā*. In *prema*, the dearmost beloved may say, "I want to keep Your feet on My head," and He will try to put Her foot there, but She will not allow it.

Śrīpāda Mādhava Mahārāja: Because *prema* has some etiquette, the *gopīs* did not embrace Uddhava, although he looks like Kṛṣṇa. Due to the *tamāla* trees' slight resemblance to Kṛṣṇa they embraced the *tamāla* trees, but not Uddhava.

Śrīla Nārāyaṇa Gosvāmī Mahārāja: Śrīmatī Rādhikā can embrace a *tamāla* tree, thinking it to be Kṛṣṇa. On the other hand, although Uddhava's form and clothing greatly resembled Kṛṣṇa's, She never embraced him.

Prema-prayojana dāsa: Śrīla Gurudeva, Śrīla Raghunātha dāsa Gosvāmī wrote this verse in *Vilāpa-kusumāñjali*:

yasyāṅka-rañjita-śiras tava-māna-bhaṅge
goṣṭhendra-sūnur adhikaṁ suṣamam upaiti

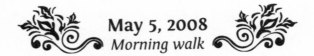

lakṣā-rasaḥ sa ca kadā padayor adhas te
nyasto mayāpy atitarāṁ chavim āpsyatīha

(*Vilāpa-kusumāñjali*, Verse 43)

Just to soothe Your proud pique, the prince of Vraja places Your feet on His head, thus making it even more beautiful with the mark of Your footlac! When will I make Your feet most splendid with this nectarean footlac?

This verse says that when Śrī Kṛṣṇa has the *lac* (red dye) from Śrīmatī Rādhikā's feet on His head, He looks more beautiful. There seems to be some *līlā* describing how the *lac* from Her feet came on Kṛṣṇa's head.

Śrīla Nārāyaṇa Gosvāmī Mahārāja: Rādhikā will not knowingly allow this. If She is sleeping, or if She has fainted and is devoid of external consciousness – at that time Kṛṣṇa can place Her lotus feet there. But if She is conscious, She will not allow it.

Prema-prayojana dāsa: It says in *śāstra* that when Kṛṣṇa is decorating Rādhikā and He is doing it too slow or making mistakes, She will push Him.

Śrīla Nārāyaṇa Gosvāmī Mahārāja: He may paint Her feet. This is okay, but She will not place Her feet on His head.

Brajanātha dāsa: This morning, Ramā Dīdī gave a donation and wrote you a letter.

Śrīla Nārāyaṇa Gosvāmī Mahārāja: (To Ramā dāsī) You are somewhat restless; you are Cañcalā- (restless) devī. And your daughter has no taste in hearing *hari-hathā*. When we discuss *hari-kathā*, she goes outside and plays on a swing.

Aniruddha dāsa: I want to take *sannyāsa*. I want to live closer to *sannyāsīs* and *brahmacārīs*.

Śrīla Nārāyaṇa Gosvāmī Mahārāja: *Sannyāsa* is not so easy. He (Prema-prayojana dāsa) knows so much. He knows all *śāstras* better than anyone, and he can remember all verses.

But I think that he has never actually read or heard anything. Why do I say this? If one is truly hearing *Śrīmad-Bhāgavatam* and understanding its meaning, he will at once become detached. How worldly attachment has pulled him!

I want him to return to *sannyāsa*, I tell him to return, and I am also giving him scope to return.

(To Prema-prayojana dāsa) I give you time to speak in class, and you are speaking. But I want you to understand that you have already enjoyed what is to be enjoyed. I want you to take *sannyāsa* again, very soon. Don't delay.

I become very unhappy when I see you as a *gṛhastha*, because I gave you the highest *āśrama* of life, the *sannyāsa āśrama*, and you left it without my permission. Do not delay, otherwise this life and your next lives will be destroyed. You preach this to others, but you should do it yourself. Try to be very strong.

(To all) I am not saying this only to him; I am telling this for everyone. But I want him to return; I am waiting and waiting for this. When a man wants to catch a fish from a pond or any body of water, he puts some bait on a hook and then throws that hook in the water.

Prema-prayojana dāsa: Śrīla Gurudeva, during your morning walk the other day, we were discussing Śrīla Rūpa Gosvāmī's internal mood. You said that if Kṛṣṇa has met with a *gopī* of another group, the love of Śrī Rūpa Mañjarī and Rādhikā's other *dāsīs* for Him may go down because He did something against Rādhikā.

Śrīla Nārāyaṇa Gosvāmī Mahārāja: They will become somewhat angry, but it is not that their love will reduce. *Prema* is like a serpent; it is not without some anger. If Kṛṣṇa is with a rival *gopī*, the *mañjarīs* will trick Him into coming with them to meet with Śrīmatī Rādhikā. They will create some excuse to take Him with them.

For example, one day Śrī Kṛṣṇa was with Candrāvalī in Gaurī-kuṇḍa. Rūpa Mañjarī went there and told Him, "Oh, a very big demon has come. If You do not come with me now, all of the calves will die." Kṛṣṇa replied, "I am coming." He then told Candrāvalī, "Wait for a little while; I am coming right back."

Sthāyī-bhāva dāsa: I am preaching to ISKCON devotees whose *gurus* are finished or who have committed offenses to you. I want to give those devotees the proper philosophical understanding about you. I definitely cannot glorify their *gurus*. What should I do?

Śrīla Nārāyaṇa Gosvāmī Mahārāja: You are right. You should not glorify those *gurus*, even if their disciples desire that you do so. They may glorify their *gurus* if they like, but they are wrong in doing so. They should give up that *guru* who is fallen, and take a new initiation from any bonafide *guru*.

We cannot glorify that *guru*. For example, Satsvarūpa was very good and Jagadīśa was very good. Many were so good; but they are now fallen, so I cannot glorify them. I may say that "They were very good Vaiṣṇavas, but how strange it is – *māyā* is so strong that it pulls down even such *sannyāsīs*. So we should be alert." I would say only that.

Mukunda dāsa: In your Introduction to the *Bhagavad-gītā*, you explain the six things necessary to analyze any *śāstra* in order to ascertain its importance. You talk about *upakrama* and *upasaṁhāra* (the book's opening and closing statements); *abhyāsa* (its repetition of a subject); *apūrvatā* (its extra-ordinary claims); *phala* (its result or fruit); *artha-vāda* (its praise of a subject); and *upapatti* (its logical arguments that establish a conclusion).

In that regard, the first verse of *Śrīmad-Bhāgavatam* contains the commentary of the *gāyatrī-mantra*. Then, the last verse of *Śrīmad-Bhāgavatam* glorifies *nāma-saṅkīrtana*.

nāma-saṅkīrtanaṁ yasya
sarva-pāpa-praṇāśanam
praṇāmo duḥkha-śamanas
taṁ namāmi hariṁ param

(*Śrīmad-Bhāgavatam* 12.13.23)

> I offer my respectful obeisances unto the Supreme Lord, Hari, the congregational chanting of whose holy names destroys all sinful reactions, and the offering of obeisances unto whom relieves all material suffering.

Śrīla Nārāyaṇa Gosvāmī Mahārāja: The first verse is the meaning of *gāyatrī*.

Mukunda dāsa: Yes, the first.

I am shy to say, but I was thinking that, like the first verse, this last verse is saying that Mahāprabhu is coming.

Śrīla Nārāyaṇa Gosvāmī Mahārāja: Yes, it is about Mahāprabhu, but not in reference to His coming. In Śrīla Viśvanātha Cakravartī Ṭhākura's commentary on the first verse of *Śrīmad-Bhāgavatam*, he reveals that the most general explanation refers to Kṛṣṇa as the Creator; a deeper explanation further manifests the author's intention and refers to Vrajendra-nandana Śrī Kṛṣṇa; a still deeper explanation refers to both Rādhā and Kṛṣṇa; after that it refers only to Rādhikā; and after that, the deepest explanation refers to Caitanya Mahāprabhu.[15]

Śrīpāda Mādhava Mahārāja: His question is this: Regarding *upakrama* and *upasaṁhāra* (the book's opening and closing statements), he is suggesting that there is a link between the first *śloka* of the *Bhāgavatam*, beginning *janmādy asya yato*, and the last *śloka*, beginning with *nāma-saṅkīrtanaṁ yasya*.

Śrīla Nārāyaṇa Gosvāmī Mahārāja: No. The link to the first is a few *ślokas* before that last one. The first *śloka* ends with *satyaṁ paraṁ dhīmahi*, and this *śloka* does as well:

kasmai yena vibhāsito 'yam atulo jñāna-pradīpaḥ purā
tad-rūpeṇa ca nāradāya munaye kṛṣṇāya tad-rūpiṇā
yogīndrāya tad-ātmanātha bhagavad-rātāya kāruṇyatas
tac chuddhaṁ vimalaṁ viśokam amṛtaṁ satyaṁ paraṁ dhīmahi
(*Śrīmad-Bhāgavatam* 12.13.19)

> I meditate upon that pure and spotless Supreme Absolute Truth, who is free from suffering and death and who in the beginning personally revealed this incomparable torchlight of knowledge to Brahmā. Brahmā then spoke it to the sage Nārada, who narrated it to Kṛṣṇa-dvaipāyana Vyāsa. Śrīla Vyāsa revealed this *Bhāgavatam* to the greatest of sages, Śukadeva Gosvāmī, and Śukadeva mercifully spoke it to Mahārāja Parīkṣit.

These are *upakrama* and *upasaṁhāra*, *Śrīmad-Bhāgavatam's* opening and closing statements, which both reveal Śrīla Vyāsadeva's true import and intent. Then, in the 'middle,' in the Second Canto, that same Absolute Truth, Śrī Kṛṣṇa, reveals Himself to Brahmā in *Catuḥ-ślokī Bhāgavatam*. Śrīla Jīva Gosvāmī has given much evidence in his explanations of these principles.

Prema-prayojana dāsa: In *Śrīmad-Bhāgavatam*, Śrī Kṛṣṇa says:

gacchoddhava vrajaṁ saumya
pitror nau prītim āvaha
gopīnāṁ mad-viyogādhiṁ
mat-sandeśair vimocaya
(*Śrīmad-Bhāgavatam* 10.46.3)

---

15 See Endnote 3 (at the end of this chapter) for more of Śrīla Bhaktivedānta Nārāyaṇa Gosvāmī Mahārāja's explanations of the first verse of *Śrīmad-Bhāgavatam*.

> Lord Kṛṣṇa said: "Dear gentle Uddhava, go to Vraja and give pleasure to our parents. And also relieve the *gopīs*, suffering in separation from Me, by giving them My message."

Did Kṛṣṇa speak that message and Uddhava remembered it, or was it written down? How should we understand this?

Śrīla Nārāyaṇa Gosvāmī Mahārāja: It was verbal. Kṛṣṇa spoke it to Uddhava and requested him to tell the *gopīs*.

At first, at the beginning of the creation of the world, nothing was written down. There were no books at that time. There was only *śruti*, meaning 'hearing, and remembering.' All *gurus* used to give their audiences verbal instructions. The hearers remembered everything, and in turn verbally passed on the message.

Advaita dāsa: Śrīla Gurudeva, we have read that Śrī Caitanya Mahāprabhu went to Godāvarī to learn from Śrīla Rāmānanda Rāya. But it seems that Śrīman Mahāprabhu was in the position of a teacher testing the student, not as the student Himself, because He was saying, "This is not very good. This is good. This is excellent." So what exactly did Śrīman Mahāprabhu learn from him?

Śrīla Nārāyaṇa Gosvāmī Mahārāja: It is when Mahāprabhu said, "*Eho uttama*, this is the best. Now please tell something even more *uttama*." He asked Rāya Rāmānanda to speak about still further best topics, and then He finally told him to stop. These are the confidential topics He learned.

Prema-prayojana dāsa: He is asking this: Caitanya Mahāprabhu is giving judgment that "This is good," or "...better," or "...best." So it seems like Mahāprabhu already knows.

Śrīla Nārāyaṇa Gosvāmī Mahārāja: Rāmānanda Rāya had told Mahāprabhu in the beginning, "You know all of these topics. You are like an ocean of all these truths, and I am a puppet whose strings are pulled by You. You have inspired all of these truths in my heart, and it is You who are making me speak."

Prema-prayojana dāsa: He wants to know if Mahāprabhu learned and realized anything new.

Śrīla Nārāyaṇa Gosvāmī Mahārāja: All knowledge was already present in Mahāprabhu. However, in the same way that a new pearl forms when water enters an oyster shell during the Svāti-nakṣatra constellation, something new was revealed to Him.

Prema-prayojana dāsa: He is asking what is that pearl.

Śrīla Nārāyaṇa Gosvāmī Mahārāja: I will tell you; it is Śrīmatī Rādhikā's highest love:

pahilehi rāga nayana-bhaṅge bhela
anudina bāḍhala, avadhi nā gela
nā so ramaṇa, nā hāma ramaṇī
duṅhu-mana manobhava peṣala jāni'
e sakhi, se-saba prema-kāhinī
kānu-ṭhāme kahabi vichurala jāni'
nā khoṅjaluṅ dūtī, nā khoṅjaluṅ ān
duṅhukeri milane madhya ta pānca-bāṇa
ab sohi virāga, tuṅhu bheli dūtī
su-purukha-premaki aichana rīti

(*Śrī Caitanya-caritāmṛta, Madhya-līlā* 8.194)

> Alas, before We met there was an initial attachment between Us brought about by an exchange of glances. In this way attachment evolved. That attachment has gradually grown, and there is no limit to it. Now that attachment has become a natural sequence between Ourselves. It is not that it is due to Kṛṣṇa, the enjoyer, nor is it due to Me, for I am the enjoyed. It is not like that. This attachment was made possible by mutual meeting. This mutual exchange of attraction is known as *manobhāva*, or Cupid. Kṛṣṇa's mind and My mind have merged together. Now, during this time of separation, it is very difficult to explain these loving affairs. My dear friend, though Kṛṣṇa might have forgotten all these things, you can understand and bring this message to Him. But during Our first meeting there was no messenger between Us, nor did I request anyone to see Him. Indeed, Cupid's five arrows were Our via media. Now, during this separation, that attraction has increased to another ecstatic state. My dear friend, please act as a messenger on My behalf, because if one is in love with a beautiful person, this is the consequence.

These moods are great jewels; more than jewels. The most valuable jewels are Śrī Rāmānanda Rāya's explanations of Śrīmatī Rādhikā's moods. The jewels begin from *sakhya-rasa*, then go to *vātsalya-rasa*, and then especially to *mādhurya-rasa*. Within *mādhurya-rasa*, the greatest jewel is the mood of Rādhikā; within this, Śrīmatī Rādhikā's feeling of separation; and still greater is Her special mood of *mādanākhya-bhāva*.

In *mādanākhya-bhāva*, although Śrīmatī Rādhikā is meeting with Kṛṣṇa, still She may feel separation from Him. For example at Prema-sarovara, while sitting on Śrī Kṛṣṇa's lap, She forgot that She was with Him. She cried out, "Where has Madhusūdana gone?" and then She fainted. These moods are jewels.

Śrīpāda Mādhava Mahārāja: Rāmānanda Rāya had personally seen both Rādhikā and Kṛṣṇa in Kṛṣṇa's pastimes because he is Viśākhā-devī in those pastimes. But now, after uttering the verse beginning *pahilehi rāga nayana-bhaṅge bhela*, He witnessed Mahāprabhu in His combined form of Rasarāja-Mahābhāva, Rādhā and Kṛṣṇa combined. Rāmānanda Rāya saw that each and every limb of Rādhikā was covered by each limb of Kṛṣṇa, and the body of Kṛṣṇa was covered with the golden complexion of Śrīmatī Rādhikā. Rāya Rāmānanda had never before seen this form, and he fainted.

Abhirāma dāsa: Śrīla Bhaktivinoda Ṭhākura prays, *rādhe rādhe boli muralī ḍakibe madīyā īśvarī nāma*. When a *mañjarī* hears the sound of Kṛṣṇa's flute, does she hear her own name, or the name of Śrīmatī Rādhikā?

Śrīla Nārāyaṇa Gosvāmī Mahārāja: All the *gopīs* thought, "Kṛṣṇa is calling me." That is why they all came to the *rāsa-maṇḍala* (the place where the *rāsa* dance was held) after hearing the sound of Kṛṣṇa's flute song (*klīṁ*[16]).

Yes, it is also possible for the *mañjarīs* to hear their own names. Without the *sakhīs* there can be no *līlā*.

Devotee: Śrīla Gurudeva, you have been showering us with the pearls of *gaura-līlā*. What do you recommend for us to do in order to come closer to Śrīmatī Rādhikā?

Śrīla Nārāyaṇa Gosvāmī Mahārāja:

tan-nāma-rūpa-caritādi-sukīrtanānu-
smṛtyoḥ krameṇa rasanā-manasī niyojya
tiṣṭhan vraje tad-anurāgi-janānugāmī
kālaṁ nayed akhilam ity upadeśa-sāram

(*Śrī Upadeśāmṛta*, Verse 8)

16 See Endnote 4 (at the end of this chapter) for an additional explanation by Śrīla Bhaktivedānta Nārāyaṇa Gosvāmī Mahārāja on the word *klīṁ*.

> While living in Vraja as a follower of the eternal residents of Vraja, who possess inherent spontaneous love for Śrī Kṛṣṇa, one should utilize all his time by sequentially engaging the tongue and the mind in meticulous chanting and remembrance of Kṛṣṇa's names, form, qualities, and pastimes. This is the essence of all instruction.

Also:

gurau goṣṭhe goṣṭhālayiṣu sujane bhūsura-gaṇe
sva-mantre śrī-nāmni vraja-nava-yuva-dvandva-śaraṇe
sadā dambhaṁ hitvā kuru ratim apūrvam atitarām
aye svāntarbhrātaś-caṭubhir abhiyāce dhṛta-padaḥ

(*Śrī Manaḥ-śikṣā*, Verse 1)

> O my dear brother, my foolish mind! Taking hold of your feet, I humbly pray to you with sweet words. Please give up all pride and quickly develop sublime and incessant *rati* for *śrī gurudeva*, Śrī Vraja-dhāma, the residents of Vraja, the Vaiṣṇavas, the *brāhmaṇas*, your *dīkṣā-mantras*, the holy names of the Supreme Lord, and the shelter of Kiśora-Kiśorī Śrī Śrī Rādhā-Kṛṣṇa, the eternally youthful Divine Couple of Vraja.

If anyone adopts this process, he will surely attain this most exalted *prema*.

Śrīpāda Padmanābha Mahārāja: Śrīla Gurudeva, you have often instructed us to follow *Upadeśāmṛta* first.

Śrīla Nārāyaṇa Gosvāmī Mahārāja: Yes.

Śrīpāda Padmanābha Mahārāja: And you have said that when we become more qualified, we should follow the *Manaḥ-śikṣā* of Śrīla Raghunātha dāsa Gosvāmī.

Śrīla Nārāyaṇa Gosvāmī Mahārāja: You will never be able to advance without following the instructions of *Śrī Upadeśāmṛta*. This is the first step. Because these steps are very high, you cannot gallop or jump over them.

I wanted to speak about this at the end of the class last night, but I was only able to touch on it briefly because I wanted to leave time for the drama.

Vṛndāvana dāsa: This is your son Baladeva Prabhu from New York. He wanted to meet you and have your personal *darśana*.

Brajanātha dāsa: He is Ujjvala's brother.

Śrīla Nārāyaṇa Gosvāmī Mahārāja: You attended our classes and heard something?

Baladeva dāsa: Yes.

Śrīla Nārāyaṇa Gosvāmī Mahārāja: Very good. Keep it in your heart.

Endnotes

1 **The following is an excerpt from an interview with** Śrīla Nārāyaṇa Gosvāmī Mahārāja **in 1996, which was later quoted in the book,** *Their Lasting Relation***:**

"Some years ago [in the early 1980s] Śrīla Bhaktivedānta Svāmī Mahārāja's son told the Bombay court that Śrīla Svāmī Mahārāja was a *vaiśya*, a businessman – that he was not a *sannyāsī*. Śrīla Svāmī Mahārāja's son said that only a *brāhmaṇa* can take *sannyāsa*, and that because Śrīla Svāmī Mahārāja was a businessman, he went to the West for business and that ISKCON is a family business. The son's conclusion was that he himself is the master of all of ISKCON's property.

"An ISKCON leader came and told me, 'If you don't give evidence, this son will take all of ISKCON, all over the world.' He told me that I must go immediately. I told him that I want only to serve Śrīla Svāmī Mahārāja, and that I would surely go. After that I went to Bombay several times and sat in court the entire day. Every day I would take *prasādam* early in the morning, at about 7 am, and then immediately go to the court."

Śrīla Nārāyaṇa Gosvāmī Mahārāja was the priest at Śrīla Prabhupāda's *sannyāsa* ceremony in 1959. It was he who had made his *daṇḍa*, presented his *sannyāsa* cloth to him and marked his body with *tilaka* in twelve places. He was thus able to prove the authenticity of Prabhupāda's *sannyāsa āśrama*, and won the case on behalf of ISKCON.

2 "A *guru* addicted to sensual pleasure and polluted by vice, who is ignorant and has no power to discriminate between right and wrong, or who is not on the path of *suddha-bhakti* must be abandoned" (*Mahābhārata, Udyoga-parva* 179.25).

"A *guru* who is envious of pure devotees, who blasphemes them or behaves maliciously towards them should certainly be abandoned, remembering the verse *guror api avaliptasya*. Such an envious *guru* lacks the mood and character of a Vaiṣṇava. The *śāstras* enjoin that one should not accept initiation from a non-devotee (*avaiṣṇavopadiṣṭena*...). Knowing these injuctions of the scriptures, a sincere devotee abandons a false *guru* who is envious of devotees. After leaving one who lacks the true qualities of a *guru*, if a devotee is without a spiritual guide, his only hope is to seek out a *mahā-bhāgavata* Vaiṣṇava and serve him. By constantly rendering service to such a pure devotee, one will certainly attain the highest goal of life" (*Bhakti-sandarbha, Anuccheda* 238).

"One should not accept a spiritual master based on hereditary, social, or ecclesiastical convention. Such a professional *guru* should be rejected. One must accept a qualified spiritual master who can help one advance towards the ultimate goal of life, *kṛṣṇa-prema*" (*Bhakti-sandarbha, Anuccheda* 210).

[3] In *Secret Truths of the Bhāgavatam*, Chapter 1, Śrīla Nārāyaṇa Gosvāmī Mahārāja gives further explanations of the first verse of *Śrīmad-Bhāgavatam*. Here are some excerpts:

"The first meaning refers to Kṛṣṇa and to this creation. The second refers to *mādhurya-rasa* in relation to Vrajendra-nandana Kṛṣṇa. The third is in relation to conjugal Rādhā and Kṛṣṇa. The fourth is only in relation to Rādhikā. This is because without power Kṛṣṇa cannot do anything. Finally, the fifth meaning is in relation to Śrī Caitanya Mahāprabhu. All the meanings of all the words will then refer to Him. *Satyaṁ paraṁ dhīmahi*. Śrī Caitanya Mahāprabhu is *parama-satya* because He is conjugal – both Rādhā and Kṛṣṇa. He has come to distribute all these truths, to sprinkle His mercy by preaching *rāga-mārga*, and also to taste the beauty of the moods of Rādhikā. Therefore *satyaṁ paraṁ dhīmahi* means, "This Śrī Caitanya Mahāprabhu should kindly be manifest in our hearts.

"The second line of this first *śloka* is *tene brahma hṛdā ya ādi-kavaye*. Kṛṣṇa Himself gave inspiration in the heart of Brahmā, the *ādi-kavi* (first poet). He inspired Brahmā by *śabda-brahma*, transcendental sound vibration, thus giving him all knowledge of Himself, of the *jīvas*, *māyā*, etc.

"When *satyaṁ paraṁ* refers to Kṛṣṇa of Vṛndāvana, *ādi-kavaye* means Śrī Śukadeva Gosvāmī. 'Kṛṣṇa' means Kṛṣṇa who is the ocean of *rasa*, from whom *mādhurya-rasa* comes. Therefore the word is *ādi*. All *rasas* are included in Kṛṣṇa. He is *rasa-brahma*, and He inspired the heart of Śukadeva Gosvāmī, the first *kavi*. *Muhyanti yat sūrayaḥ*. Brahmā, Śaṅkara, and all other demigods are in confusion. They cannot understand this deeper meaning.

"When *satyaṁ paraṁ* refers to Śrī Caitanya Mahāprabhu, the word *ādi-kavi* means Śrīla Rūpa Gosvāmī. Śrī Caitanya Mahāprabhu inspired all truths in him at Prayāga, and thus he wrote *Bhakti-rasāmṛta-sindhu*, *Ujjvala-nīlamaṇi*, *Vidagdha-mādhava*, and so many other books. He then manifested this over the whole world. Now we are in this line. You should know how fortunate you are to have come in the line of Śrī Caitanya Mahāprabhu. Always think in this way."

[4] "The definition of *klīṁ* is understood by this verse in *Śrīmad-Bhāgavatam* (10.29.3): '*vanaṁ ca tat-komala-gobhī rañjitaṁ, jagau kalaṁ vāma-dṛśāṁ manoharam* – Lord Śrī Kṛṣṇa saw the unbroken disk of the full moon glowing with the red effulgence of newly applied vermilion, as if it were the face of the goddess of fortune. He also saw the *kumuda* lotuses opening in response to the moon's presence, and the forest gently illuminated by its rays. Thus the Lord began to play sweetly on His flute, attracting the mind of the beautiful-eyed *gopīs*.'

"It was evening time. The moon was golden and full, and rising on the very reddish eastern horizon. The eastern direction is like the moon's beloved. It was as though by his rays, which are like his hands, the moon had taken a large quantity of red color and was decorating the face of the eastern horizon. Seeing this, Kṛṣṇa at once placed His flute upon His lips and played a very sweet tune (*jagau kalaṁ*). That tune is included in the seed *mantra*, *klīṁ*. Upon hearing it, Rādhā, Lalitā, and all other *gopīs* thought, 'He is calling me alone; no one else.'

"The essence of the *gopāla-mantra* is the seed *klīṁ*. *Kalaṁ* (translated in this verse as 'sweetly') is a combination of two Sanskrit letters *ka* + *la*. The fourth letter of the Sanskrit alphabet is called *vāma-dṛśāṁ* (translated in this verse as 'the girls who have charming eyes'). As the English alphabet begins with 'a, b, c, d,' the Sanskrit alphabet begins with '*a*, *ā*, *i*, *ī*.' The fourth Sanskrit letter, 'ī,' is called *vāma-dṛśāṁ*.

So even grammar, the essence of grammar, is in this sound. *Ka* and *la*, combined with *ī*, becomes *klī*.

"And what is the meaning of the word *manoharam* in this verse? Ultimately *manohara* is Kṛṣṇa, He who attracts the mind. That same Kṛṣṇa gave a portion of His quality of attracting the mind to Candra, the moon-god. The predominating Deity of the mind is Candra, and that moon has now taken the shape of *candra-bindu*, a dot. In Sanskrit this dot is called *anusvāra*, and thus the word *klīṁ* is completed. By *klīṁ*, each and every *gopī* thought that Kṛṣṇa was calling her alone, and therefore they all came to Him" (*Secret Truths of the Bhāgavatam*, Chapter 4).

Miami, Florida

May 13 - 28, 2008

May 13, 2008
Morning Walk

Līlānātha dāsa: There are different kinds of *yoga* teachers, the highest of which is the Vaiṣṇava. At the same time, there are many persons claiming to be Vaiṣṇavas on the basis of their wearing *tilaka*, *dhotī*, and *mālā*. How does one recognize the authentic Vaiṣṇava?

Śrīla Nārāyaṇa Gosvāmī Mahārāja: You must know the meaning of *yoga*. It comes from the ancient Indian culture. It is a Sanskrit word meaning 'to add two components or elements.' One plus one equals two, three plus four equals seven.

You are the transcendental soul present in your body, and also residing there is the transcendental Supersoul, who is Śrī Kṛṣṇa, the Supreme Lord. When these two come together in love and affection, this is true *yoga*.

If one wants to link himself to, or join, the Supreme Lord, he cannot do so on his own. He must first hear about the process, called *bhakti-yoga*, from a qualified teacher, who will inform him how to do so.

One then takes initiation from that bonafide *guru*. At that time he begins to follow all the principles of *bhakti-yoga*, such as chanting Kṛṣṇa's holy names and remembering Him. Then, through the mercy of that *guru*, one gradually advances in *bhakti-yoga* and becomes liberated from material entanglement. He then begins to engage in the direct service of Lord Śrī Kṛṣṇa, the Supreme Lord. This is real *yoga*.

Those who are initiated by a bonafide *guru* and, wearing *tilaka*, *tulasī-mālā*, and *śikhā* chant and remember Kṛṣṇa, are truly God conscious. Only they are to be recognized as true *yogīs*, or *bhaktas*.

Brajanātha dāsa: Gurudeva, in Kali-yuga there are many people who pose as Vaiṣṇavas, but are not Vaiṣṇavas.

Śrīla Nārāyaṇa Gosvāmī Mahārāja: Yes, there are many. However, true Vaiṣṇavas are those who chant Hare Kṛṣṇa and follow our *guru-paramparā*. They are the real *yoga* teachers.

Līlānātha dāsa: There are many ancient cultures, like the Roman Empire and the Ottoman Empire, which have physical proof of their existence. Is there any physical proof that our ancient Vedic culture existed?

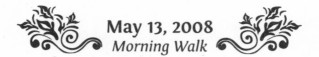

Śrīla Nārāyaṇa Gosvāmī Mahārāja: Actually, the empires and ancient cultures you mentioned have no evidence of their existence at all. On the other hand, we Indians have evidence that our culture existed millions of years ago, even from the beginning of creation.

For example, it may be said that we are in the Kaśyapa *gotra* (the Kaśyapa dynasty). There was a saintly person named Kaśyapa Ṛṣi, who was a self-realized soul and devotee of Kṛṣṇa. We are his descendents, and there are other saints, like Vasiṣṭha and Gautama Ṛṣis, who also have dynasties and descendents. There have been innumerable saintly persons since the beginning of creation, whose Vedic knowledge and culture we are following.

There are also many scriptural evidences of our culture, such as the *Rāmāyaṇa*, *Mahābhārata*, Purāṇas, and Vedas. As of yet, the empires which you mention have no evidence of literatures dating from such ancient times. The scriptural literature of the Western culture is very new in comparison to that of the Indian culture. For instance, the Bible has only existed for about two thousand years, and the Koran, the scriptural text of the Mohammedans, is fairly new as well.

With regards to physical evidence, the Roman buildings are not more than five hundred to one thousand years old, whereas the bridge from India to Śrī Laṅkā, which is millions of years old, still exists as its own evidence of our civilization.

Līlānātha dāsa: From Treta-yuga.

Śrīla Nārāyaṇa Gosvāmī Mahārāja: Yes.

Even science has shown that remnants of the city of Dvārakā, where Kṛṣṇa personally lived in His palaces 5,000 years ago, are still present under the ocean. Present day archeologists have seen remnants of Dvārakā's great opulence.

Śrīpāda Mādhava Mahārāja: Do you know the meaning of the word *gotra*? *Gotra* means 'family.' Lord Brahmā [the first living being in the universe, and the great-grandfather of all other beings] had so many sons, like Gautama, Atri, Pulastya, to name a few. All of these sons were *ṛṣis* who were performing *bhajana*. The descendants of those *ṛṣis* are still alive, and they trace their origin to Lord Brahmā's dynasty.

Śrīla Nārāyaṇa Gosvāmī Mahārāja: The Vedas have been manifest in this world from time immemorial. What is Vedic knowledge? "We are spirit souls; we are not this physical body." In no other scriptures of the world other than the Vedas is this knowledge revealed with such depth and clarity: we are soul, not this body, and there is a Supreme Lord who has a form and who has created this world.

Devotee: Right now we are living in Kali-yuga, the degraded age of quarrel and hypocrisy, so why is there a rumor in the world that human civilization is escalating to new heights of consciousness? For example, there are more vegetarians than ever before and human rights have improved. *Śrīmad-Bhāgavatam* states that at the end of Kali-yuga men will be very small, but we see that our kids are bigger than us. Why is this so? How do we reconcile this?

Śrīla Nārāyaṇa Gosvāmī Mahārāja: All Kali-yugas except for this particular Kali-yuga are full of innumerable sinful activities. Although this Kali-yuga is also full of sinful activities, they are less in comparison to previous Kali-yugas.

In this Kali-yuga Śrī Caitanya Mahāprabhu, who is Śrī Kṛṣṇa Himself, came and preached "Hare Kṛṣṇa, Hare Kṛṣṇa." He taught us that all beings are spirit souls and that they must have love and affection for Kṛṣṇa. We are also preaching this message in every country, and that is why this Kali-yuga is special.

Śrīpāda Mādhava Mahārāja: This Kali-yuga is called *dhanya-kali*, meaning 'blessed Kali-yuga.'

Śrīla Nārāyaṇa Gosvāmī Mahārāja: At the end of the other Kali-yugas, the Kalki incarnation descends and cuts off the heads of the demons, ushering in Satya-yuga again. In this Kali-yuga, Kalki will not appear.

Līlānātha dāsa: Yesterday I was reading a book by Śrīla Gour Govinda Mahārāja, which stated that *guru* is *nitya-siddha* (an eternally perfect associate of the Lord).

My question is this: How does a *guru* who is not a *nitya-siddha*, meaning that he was not naturally inclined from birth to serve Śrī Gaurāṅga and Nityānanda, compare with a *guru* who is *nitya-siddha*?

Brajanātha dāsa: Prabhu is saying that there are spiritual masters who have been practicing Kṛṣṇa consciousness since birth, without any inclination towards anything other than *kṛṣṇa-bhajana*. And there are others, who were born in Western countries and who were addicted since birth to eating meat and engaging in other sinful activities. What is their position as *gurus*?

Śrīla Nārāyaṇa Gosvāmī Mahārāja: The *nitya-siddha guru* comes from the transcendental world, and therefore he cannot help us unless he plays the role of a *madhyama-adhikārī*. The *madhyama-adhikārī* Vaiṣṇava can help us:

īśvare tad-adhīneṣu
bāliśeṣu dviṣatsu ca
prema-maitrī-kṛpopekṣā
yaḥ karoti sa madhyamaḥ
(*Śrīmad-Bhāgavatam* 11.2.46)

An intermediate or second-class devotee, called *madhyama-adhikārī*, offers his love to the Supreme Personality of Godhead, is a sincere friend to all the devotees of the Lord, shows mercy to ignorant people who are innocent, and disregards those who are envious of the Supreme Personality of Godhead.

Madhyama-adhikārīs know how to differentiate between all types of persons. They understand everyone's qualification and disqualification.

On the other hand *nitya-siddhas*, having come from the transcendental world, cannot know who is happy and who is suffering. Rather, with their topmost vision, they consider that everyone is already serving Kṛṣṇa.

Śrīpāda Mādhava Mahārāja: What about Śrī Nārada Ṛṣi and Śrīla Rūpa Gosvāmī?

Śrīla Nārāyaṇa Gosvāmī Mahārāja: Nārada Ṛṣi is *nitya-siddha*, but he came to this world in the role of a *madhyama-adhikārī*, and in that way he initiated many disciples. Devotees like Śukadeva Gosvāmī, Nārada Ṛṣi, and Vyāsadeva are very rare.

May 14, 2008
Morning Walk

Śrīla Nārāyaṇa Gosvāmī Mahārāja: Are there any questions?

Raghunātha dāsa: By your mercy, we will open a preaching center in Miami very soon. The devotees want to make an arrangement for my Rādhā-Govinda Deities to go to the preaching center. I am attached to my Deities, but if it is your desire that They go to the center, I will allow Them to go.

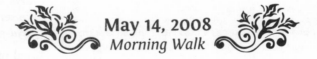

Śrīla Nārāyaṇa Gosvāmī Mahārāja: You are alone, and you are traveling with me here and there. How can you personally manage Their worship? I think it is better that you accept the advice of the devotees. If there is a preaching center there must be Deities, so it will be good if you can donate your Deities. The devotees will perform *arcana* and make many other nice arrangements for the Deities there, and from time to time you will also go there and serve Them.

Raghunātha dāsa: Okay, Gurudeva. If this is your desire, then it is no problem.

Mahābuddhi dāsa: The devotees in South Florida have been discussing the possibility of renting a preaching center. We have been having programs in devotees' homes for the past four or five years, and now we want to have a place to accommodate more guests. Many guests are already coming, and many devotees are also coming. At the time of Śrīla Bhaktivedānta Svāmī Prabhupāda, he ordered us to open preaching centers. Is it also your desire to have a center here?

Śrīla Nārāyaṇa Gosvāmī Mahārāja: You can begin. At the time of Śrīla Bhaktisiddhānta Sarasvatī Ṭhākura Prabhupāda, the devotees also used to rent preaching centers. In this way, with the devotees continually preaching, worldly people would come and join.

Mahābuddhi dāsa: There is a local Indian priest who recites *Bhagavad-gītā* and *Śrīmad-Bhāgavatam*, and he knows Bengali and Hindi. He wants to take initiation from you.

Śrīla Nārāyaṇa Gosvāmī Mahārāja: See if he will follow the four regulative principles. He will have to follow Ekādaśī, and he cannot take meat, wine, eggs, etcetera.

Mahābuddhi dāsa: If he hears this personally from you, it will make a strong impression on him and he will be able to follow.

Śrīla Nārāyaṇa Gosvāmī Mahārāja: Please bring him; I will tell him.

Devotee: Gurudeva, what can my wife and I do as new parents to ensure that our new baby will be a good devotee?

Śrīla Nārāyaṇa Gosvāmī Mahārāja: You can chant Hare Kṛṣṇa more loudly while the baby is in the womb. If your wife practices *bhakti*, some good *sukṛti* (spiritual pious credits) will come to the baby. Then, when the baby is born, you can give him or her a good name of Kṛṣṇa or Rādhā. You can also tell the baby *hari-kathā*, the sweet pastimes of Kṛṣṇa.

Devotee: Śrīla Bhaktisiddhānta Sarasvatī Ṭhākura says that the true disciple should seek internal and external *darśana* (audience) of *śrī guru*. Can you explain this further?

Śrīla Nārāyaṇa Gosvāmī Mahārāja: Following *śrī guru's* words of instruction is internal *darśana*. Watching his behavior and the way in which he performs his activities is external *darśana*. If your *guru* is still physically present in the world, you can also personally serve him.

Mahābuddhi dāsa: How do we become serious about this process?

Śrīla Nārāyaṇa Gosvāmī Mahārāja: By engaging in pure *bhakti* as described in this verse:

anyābhilāṣitā-śūnyaṁ
jñāna-karmādy-anāvṛtam
ānukūlyena kṛṣṇānuśīlanam
bhaktir uttamā

(*Bhakti-rasāmṛta-sindhu* 1.1.11)

> The cultivation of activities that are meant exclusively for the pleasure of Śrī Kṛṣṇa, or in other words the uninterrupted flow of service to Śrī Kṛṣṇa, performed through all endeavors of the body, mind, and speech, and through the expression of various spiritual sentiments (*bhāvas*), which is not covered by *jñāna* (knowledge aimed at impersonal liberation) and *karma* (reward-seeking activity), which is performed under the guidance of Śrī Kṛṣṇa's *uttama-bhaktas*, and which is devoid of all desires other than the aspiration to bring happiness to Śrī Kṛṣṇa, is called *uttama-bhakti*, or pure devotional service.

Try to follow *uttama-bhakti*, the principles of topmost pure devotion. When, under the guidance of *śrī guru* and the Vaiṣṇavas, all your energy and all the activities of your mind, body, and words are engaged continuously like the flow of honey and aimed at the goal of pure *bhakti*, your activities will then be called *bhakti*. Worldly desires, such as *jñāna* (mental speculation with the desire to merge in an impersonal God), *karma* (the desire to personally enjoy the fruits of action), *yoga* (exercises), and *tapasya* (austerity performed for a worldly end) have no place in the heart of the devotee.

Begin from *śraddhā* (initial faith) and try to progress to *niṣṭhā* (steadiness), *ruci* (taste for devotional activities), *āsakti* (natural attachment for Kṛṣṇa), and then to *śuddha-sattva*, *rati* (the stage of spiritual emotions).

May 15, 2008
Morning Walk

Mahābuddhi dāsa: (Introducing a guest) Gurudeva, he was the *pūjārī* at one of the local temples in Miami, and now he teaches *yoga* in San Francisco. He knows *Bhagavad-gītā* by heart and is also teaching it; and he is reading *Śrī Caitanya-caritāmṛta*. He saw you the last time you were here. Since then, he has developed some faith and he has been coming to our programs. He has the desire to accept a real *guru* and follow instructions. He wants to ask for initiation.

Śrīla Nārāyaṇa Gosvāmī Mahārāja: You are a priest?

Nityānanda dāsa: Yes, this is my job. I chant *gāyatrī* in the morning.

Śrīla Nārāyaṇa Gosvāmī Mahārāja: The generally-accepted meaning of *gāyatrī* is not the actual meaning. The deep meaning is hidden within. Who is Gāyatrī? We will have to know this. Kṛṣṇa is the Supreme Personality of Godhead, and Gāyatrī is His power. *Gāyatrī-mantra* is also known as *brahma-gāyatrī*. Who is the Absolute Truth, *brahma*? The Sun-god Sūrya is not *brahma*.

aho bhāgyam aho bhāgyaṁ
nanda-gopa-vrajaukasām
yan-mitraṁ paramānandaṁ
pūrṇaṁ brahma sanātanam

(*Śrīmad-Bhāgavatam* 10.14.32)

> How greatly fortunate are Nanda Mahārāja, the cowherd men, and all the other inhabitants of Vrajabhūmi! There is no limit to their good fortune, because the Absolute Truth, the source of transcendental bliss, the eternal Supreme Brahman, has become their friend.

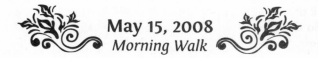

Kṛṣṇa is the Supreme Personality of Godhead (*parama-brahma*), the one-without-a-second Absolute Truth. His personal power, *hlādinī-śakti*, is Śrīmatī Rādhikā, and Gāyatrī-devī is Rādhikā's manifestation. *Savitur vareṇyaṁ* means that the Sun gives light, heat, and life to all the fourteen worlds in each universe. But who gives life to the Sun? Kṛṣṇa's power, Gāyatrī, gives it life and light. We meditate on this and utter *dhīmahi*, which means "May She come in my heart." This is the real meaning of the *gāyatrī-mantra*. Generally people think this is the *mantra* of Sūrya, but it is not so.

So this is the only difficulty; your job requires you to worship Gaṇeśa, Durgā, and Kali.

Mahābuddhi dāsa: That is his job. But he was telling me that first he worships Rādhā-Kṛṣṇa, and then he worships the other *pañcopāsanā* deities (Durgā, Śiva, Gaṇeśa, Sūrya, and an impersonal idea of Viṣṇu).

Śrīla Nārāyaṇa Gosvāmī Mahārāja: There is something you can do in this regard. You can first worship Śrī Śrī Rādhā-Kṛṣṇa, and then offer Their *caraṇāmṛta* and the *prasādam* of Their foodstuffs and flowers to the demigods. In this way the demigods' *pūjā* can be done. If you do this, I can give you initiation.

Your job is to offer *pūjā* to these deities; so you can do this *pūjā*, although we never do it. We only offer the demigods *praṇāma*.

Mahābuddhi dāsa: If someone has a job, not as a priest but also not so favorable for *bhakti*, it is almost the same. He still worships Kṛṣṇa first, but in that person's job he may be…

Śrīla Nārāyaṇa Gosvāmī Mahārāja: Kṛṣṇa will personally be merciful to him. Kṛṣṇa will sprinkle His mercy upon him.

Mahābuddhi dāsa: Now we have about seventy-five to one hundred devotees who are, more or less, active in this Miami *saṅga*.

Is your writing going well? We are very hopeful for that.

Śrīla Nārāyaṇa Gosvāmī Mahārāja: Yes; very interesting. If these books are published, devotees will be very happy. Your Gurudeva, *parama-pūjyapāda* Śrīla Bhaktivedānta Svāmī Mahārāja, has hidden something, and I am opening his hidden meanings.[17] I am taking his remnants.

Mahābuddhi dāsa: I think the whole world will be benefitted by getting the Eleventh and Twelfth Cantos from your Divine Grace.

Śrīla Nārāyaṇa Gosvāmī Mahārāja: I will do it.

---

17 It is the service of the *ācāryas* to reveal further deep meanings in the literary works of the previous *ācāryas*.

Mahābuddhi dāsa: But you have to complete it.

Śrīla Nārāyaṇa Gosvāmī Mahārāja: Then you will have to pray to Kṛṣṇa that He will give me long life and health.

Mahābuddhi dāsa: My prayers have no value.

Śrīla Nārāyaṇa Gosvāmī Mahārāja: If everyone prays, then Kṛṣṇa is bound to hear.

Go on preaching in your university. Many Ph.D scholars will come from that program, and they will preach.

Mahābuddhi dāsa: We are happy to see that it is now growing. Many devotees are coming and participating.

We are all waiting for the English translation of *Śrī Ujjvala-nīlamaṇi*. We are not qualified to read some of the books you are publishing, so we are putting them on the altar and worshiping them. Unless you give us the qualification, how can we read them?

Śrīla Nārāyaṇa Gosvāmī Mahārāja: When you read these books, Śrīla Rūpa Gosvāmī will personally give you the power and qualification to understand them. The process is that while reading we should pray to Śrīla Rūpa Gosvāmī to make us qualified to understand and realize the deep secrets given in his books.

May 17, 2008
Morning Walk

Raghunātha dāsa: Śrīla Gurudeva, when we have the good fortune of your physical association, by your causeless mercy we feel great strength. But when you travel all around the world, preaching, making new disciples, and giving mercy in other places, we feel weak again. When you are far away, how can we maintain the strength we feel in your personal association?

Śrīla Nārāyaṇa Gosvāmī Mahārāja: You should think that I am always with you in the form of my books and classes; know that I am always guiding you. If you do this you will not be weak, and you will also be able to make others very strong.

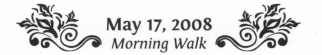

Sāvitrī dāsī: When we preach, we tell people that God, Kṛṣṇa, has a personal form. We tell them He is a person with a beautiful, attractive form. When we tell this to people, especially impersonalists, they argue that to say God has a form is limiting Him. How do we explain the truth to them?

Śrīla Nārāyaṇa Gosvāmī Mahārāja: I explain this wherever I go.

Śrīpāda Mādhava Mahārāja: Gurudeva has explained that the Bible says that God created man after His own image. In the Koran, Mohammedan says, "*Innallaha khalaqa adama ala suratihi* – Allah has form, and from that likeness He fashioned man."

Sāvitrī dāsī: Even when I tell people that His form is not material, that it is a transcendental form, still they...

Śrīla Nārāyaṇa Gosvāmī Mahārāja: Try to catch my arguments; try to satisfy them as I do. For example, I say, "There is fire everywhere; there is no place where fire is not present. Generally we cannot see fire, but we can see it by following the process to do so. When we use matches and apply a small flame to any dry substance, this can take the form of a great fire that will not be extinguished even by large amounts of water. It will only be extinguished by the arrangement of Kṛṣṇa; by heavy rain. In America we sometimes see forest fires that cannot be extinguished by any machines or human endeavor. They can be extinguished only by rain.

"Similarly, by following a certain process we can see the very beautiful form of Kṛṣṇa, and we can also see His Universal Form. He is everywhere, whether or not we are seeing Him, but we can see Him by the practice of *bhakti-yoga*."

Raghunātha dāsa: Śrīla Gurudeva, I am asking about my personal experience. I have been chanting Hare Kṛṣṇa for many years and I am also getting the mercy and association of Vaiṣṇavas, especially your mercy; but I still have material desires in my heart. Is this because I am committing offenses to the Vaiṣṇavas? Does it mean that my *bhakti* is 'leaking out,' as you sometimes mention in your classes? What do you think may be the reason I still have material desires in my heart?

Śrīla Nārāyaṇa Gosvāmī Mahārāja: Now you are somewhat realizing, "There is some defect in me, and that is why I have no taste in hearing from Vaiṣṇavas. It may be that I am offending a Vaiṣṇava."

Those in this world who are always totally engaged, one hundred percent or even more than one hundred percent, in sense gratification, don't realize this. They take wine, they gamble, smoke, and eat meat, beef, and other abominable things. Now you understand something, and by chanting the holy name in the association of elevated

Vaiṣṇavas, you will gradually improve further. All unwanted things will disappear and you will be always happy.

You are on the right path. You are inviting me with my traveling group, bearing our expenses, and moreover you are helping my projects. You should know that by this process you will very soon be able to give up all your unwanted habits and mentalities (*anarthas*). The reactions to any offenses to Vaiṣṇavas will go away, as will all kinds of problems. So be strong by chanting and remembering.

May 18, 2008
Morning Walk

Ramā dāsī: Śrīla Gurudeva, I want to chant in such a way that my restless mind can take rest. Please help me to chant.

Śrīla Nārāyaṇa Gosvāmī Mahārāja: You are a teacher, so you should teach children.

Ramā dāsī: You are the real teacher, Gurudeva.

Śrīla Nārāyaṇa Gosvāmī Mahārāja: Kindly preach my mission in the school.

Aniruddha dāsa: She cannot do that.

Śrīla Nārāyaṇa Gosvāmī Mahārāja: She can teach *Bhagavad-gītā*. There is no ban on *Gītā* anywhere.

Aniruddha dāsa: The school administrators do not like anyone to speak about devotion during class.

Śrīla Nārāyaṇa Gosvāmī Mahārāja: Sometimes she can inject devotional topics. She can say, "We are not the body; we are souls. We should try to realize this. One day you will be old and forced to give up this body. We should try to believe in God."

Today is Nṛsiṁha-caturdaśī. Be tolerant and humble, just like Prahlāda Mahārāja – especially when suffering comes. Be like Prahlāda. Although his father tried to kill him, he never opposed him in retaliation.

Devotee: When will I get a taste for *harināma*?

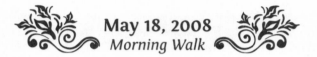

Śrīla Nārāyaṇa Gosvāmī Mahārāja: You will have taste when you are free from worldly desires – when you no longer think about worldly desires, and when you give up the idea that, 'I am this body.' At that time, you will be able to continuously cry like Mahāprabhu.

Rasika-prīya dāsī: Śrī Caitanya Mahāprabhu is Kṛṣṇa feeling the separation moods of Śrīmatī Rādhikā in this world only, because in Goloka Vṛndāvana there is no separation. In Goloka They are always happily meeting.

Śrīla Nārāyaṇa Gosvāmī Mahārāja: No. There are also separation feelings in Goloka Vṛndāvana. If there are no separation feelings there, they cannot be present here. Whether the separation is practical or by mood, there is separation. For example, although there is no Kaṁsa Mahārāja in Goloka Vṛndāvana, the Vrajavāsīs think that Kṛṣṇa has gone to Mathurā and killed him. Kṛṣṇa does not take birth from the womb of Mother Yaśodā there, but she always considers that she has given birth to Him. Thus, there are certain pastimes which in Goloka Vṛndāvana are only conceptions, but which in Kṛṣṇa's pastimes in the myriad material universes actually take place.

Brajanātha dāsa: Śrīman Mahāprabhu came here when Śrī Kṛṣṇa contemplated, "How much does Śrīmatī Rādhikā love Me? How great is Her love? How great is Her happiness? And what qualities in Me does She relish?" Is this also happening in Goloka Vṛndāvana, or only when Kṛṣṇa's pastimes manifest in this world?

Śrīla Nārāyaṇa Gosvāmī Mahārāja: After Śrī Kṛṣṇa's pastimes in this world were completed – in Vṛndāvana, Mathurā, and everywhere else – He disappeared and went to Goloka Vṛndāvana. It is there in Goloka Vṛndāvana that He experienced these three desires.

Śrīpāda Padmanābha Mahārāja: Śrī Caitanya Mahāprabhu is eternally in His abode of Śvetadvīpa in Goloka Vṛndāvana (*nitya-dhāma*), and there He tastes *unnata-ujjvala-rasa* eternally. Is this not true?

Śrīla Nārāyaṇa Gosvāmī Mahārāja: Yes. He manifested this here as well, because this is also *nitya-dhāma*, but conditioned souls are not qualified to witness the pastimes in this *nitya-dhāma*. They will be able to see these divine pastimes only when their eyes are no longer covered by *māyā*.

Śrīpāda Mādhava Mahārāja:

adyāpi kare līlāya gaura-rāya,
kona kona bhāgyavān dekhibāre pāya

(*Bhakti-ratnākara* 1.57)

> Even today Śrī Gaurasundara performs pastimes here with His associates, but only an exceedingly fortunate living entity can behold them.

This means that Śrī Kṛṣṇa's pastimes are eternally going on, but only those who are very fortunate are able to witness them.

Śrīpāda Padmanābha Mahārāja: Śrīman Mahāprabhu is the personification of the moods of separation (*vipralambha-bhāva*). Even in *prakaṭa* Navadvīpa-dhāma, in His *kīrtanas* He experiences these moods in places like Śrīvāsa-aṅgana. He is experiencing all of Śrīmatī Rādhikā's moods there. Is this correct?

Śrīla Nārāyaṇa Gosvāmī Mahārāja: Yes. Not vividly, but in a covered way. For example, a student of Navadvīpa challenged Mahāprabhu: "Why are You chanting the names 'Gopī! Gopī!' instead of the holy name of Kṛṣṇa?"

At that time Mahāprabhu was totally absorbed in the moods of the *gopīs* and Śrīmatī Rādhikā. He was especially absorbed in the moods of the *gopīs*, and He had been thinking that Kṛṣṇa was giving suffering to Śrīmatī Rādhikā.

May 19, 2008
Morning Walk

Raghunātha dāsa: Śrīla Gurudeva, we learn from your lectures and books, and also from the books of Śrīla Bhaktivedānta Svāmī Mahārāja, that we must be patient in order to achieve our goals. How can we develop intense eagerness to surrender completely to the spiritual master and advance more rapidly, rather than having to wait for many lifetimes?

Śrīla Nārāyaṇa Gosvāmī Mahārāja: You will have to wait. But at the same time, with great eagerness and following all the practices prescribed in Śrīla Rūpa Gosvāmī's books, you must have this greed: "How can I achieve *kṛṣṇa-prema*? When will Śrī Kṛṣṇa sprinkle His mercy upon me?"

The first stage is to follow *Śrī Upadeśāmṛta* (*Nectar of Instruction*), and the second stage is to follow Śrīla Raghunātha dāsa Gosvāmī's *Śrī Manaḥ-śikṣā*. In this way you can develop in your *bhakti*.

May 20, 2008
Morning Walk

Śrīla Nārāyaṇa Gosvāmī Mahārāja: Does your son chant?

Mahābuddhi dāsa: Yes, every day. He has taken *harināma* initiation from you, but he is weak in his practices. As his father, I can't push him too much. He is devotional, but he needs more association, as I do.

Śrīla Nārāyaṇa Gosvāmī Mahārāja: If he attends our classes, he will change. Our classes in Alachua were very good. Try to come to Badger.

Mahābuddhi dāsa: I have never been to Badger even though there have been so many programs there. I am very fallen.

Śrīla Nārāyaṇa Gosvāmī Mahārāja: No, no. You arranged very good classes in Florida.

Brajanātha dāsa: Under the guidance of Śrīla Bhaktivedānta Svāmī Mahārāja, he developed New Vṛndāvana from practically nothing. He did everything. ISKCON Bombay, also.

Padmanābha Mahārāja: And Dallas ISKCON as well.

Mahābuddhi dāsa: At that time I was engaged in many responsible services, and now I do hardly any service.

Śrīpāda Padmanābha Mahārāja: Our Guru Mahārāja, Śrīla Prabhupāda, used to call on him to go to different places and solve problems.

Mahābuddhi dāsa: I used to solve problems, and now I am the problem.

I used to have the same responsibility for Śrīla Prabhupāda that Brajanātha Prabhu has for you now. I would coordinate his *darśanas* in Vṛndāvana and Māyāpura. I remember you came to see him when I was his guard there. He told me that you can come and see him at any time. I had to stop some people, as Brajanātha Prabhu has to stop me. On the other hand, when some of his god-brothers came to see him, like Kṛṣṇadāsa Bābājī Mahārāja, he told me they can speak with him at any time.

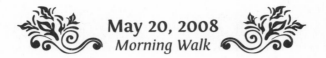

We used to get editorials from professors for his books, and he was very pleased that the professors appreciated his books. He told me to continue with our education services, wherein I was often visiting professors, colleges, and universities, and distributing his books to the educated class.

Śrīla Nārāyaṇa Gosvāmī Mahārāja: You were *brahmacārī* then?

Mahābuddhi dāsa: I was *brahmacārī* for nine years. Then they gave me the position of temple president, and I became *gṛhastha*.

Śrīla Nārāyaṇa Gosvāmī Mahārāja: How is it that you became attracted to a lady?

Mahābuddhi dāsa: I was influenced by *rajaḥ-guṇa* (the mode of passion). I am only influenced by *rajaḥ-guṇa* and *tamaḥ-guṇa* (the mode of ignorance). I don't think I am influenced by any *sattva-guṇa* (the mode of material goodness).

Śrīla Nārāyaṇa Gosvāmī Mahārāja: Then how did your Gurudeva accept you?

Mahābuddhi dāsa: Only by his mercy. And I don't know how you are accepting me.

Śrīla Nārāyaṇa Gosvāmī Mahārāja: I see something in you. He saw something and I also see something. But I don't know how you have accepted me.

Mahābuddhi dāsa: Śrīla Prabhupāda told me to meditate on this verse every day:

teṣāṁ satata-yuktānāṁ
bhajatāṁ prīti-pūrvakam
dadāmi buddhi-yogaṁ taṁ
yena mām upayānti te

(*Bhagavad-gītā* 10.10)

> To those who are constantly devoted to serving Me with love, I give the understanding by which they can come to Me.*

He said, "Kṛṣṇa will give you the intelligence how to serve." So I thought this way and prayed. Then, when I came to Alachua, you had me sit next to you when you were talking to Śrīpāda Bhāgavata Mahārāja's son, telling him the dangers of meat-eating. My eyes began to water. Then you put your hand on my heart and said, *teṣāṁ satata-yuktānāṁ bhajatāṁ prīti-pūrvakam*.

So, how can I serve you best?

Śrīla Nārāyaṇa Gosvāmī Mahārāja: You are trying to serve me.

Mahābuddhi dāsa: Trying, but not doing very well.

Śrīla Nārāyaṇa Gosvāmī Mahārāja: I am desirous that the *gaura-vāṇī*, the instructions of Śrī Caitanya Mahāprabhu which our *paramparā* preached and which Caitanya Mahāprabhu personally followed, should not stop after I leave this world. It should continue.

Everyone should be united. Try to preach everywhere and publish my books; there are so many books. The temples should not be divided into separate *maṭhas* with separate interests. All the temples and devotees should be united. You will have to try for that.

(To Rādhikā dāsī) It is very good that you have an interest in hearing *hari-kathā*. Only *hari-kathā* can help anyone; nothing else can help.

satāṁ prasaṅgān mama vīrya-saṁvido
bhavanti hṛt-karṇa-rasāyanāḥ kathāḥ
taj-joṣaṇād āśv apavarga-vartmani
śraddhā ratir bhaktir anukramiṣyati
(*Śrīmad-Bhāgavatam* 3.25.25)

In the association of pure devotees, discussion of the pastimes and activities of the Supreme Personality of Godhead is very pleasing and satisfying to the ear and the heart. By cultivating such knowledge one gradually becomes advanced on the path of liberation, and thereafter he is freed and his attraction becomes fixed. Then real devotion and devotional service begin.

And also:

jñāne prayāsam udapāsya namanta eva
jīvanti san-mukharitāṁ bhavadīya-vārtām
sthāne sthitāḥ śruti-gatāṁ tanu-vāṅ-manobhir
ye prāyaśo 'jita jito 'py asi tais tri-lokyām
(*Śrīmad-Bhāgavatam* 10.14.3)

Lord Brahmā said, "My dear Lord, those devotees who have thrown away the impersonal conception of the Absolute Truth and have therefore abandoned discussing empiric philosophical truths should hear from self-realized devotees about Your holy name, form, pastimes, and qualities. They should completely follow the principles of devotional service and remain free from illicit sex, gambling, intoxication, and animal slaughter.

> Surrendering themselves fully with body, words, and mind, they can live in any *āśrama* or social status. Indeed, You are conquered by such persons, although You are always unconquerable.

These two verses glorify the association with pure devotees (*sādhu-saṅga*). If you want *kṛṣṇa-bhakti*, it is essential to attend the *hari-kathā* of a pure devotee (*satāṁ*). Śrī Kṛṣṇa is *parama-satya*, the Absolute Truth.

satya-vrataṁ satya-paraṁ tri-satyaṁ
satyasya yoniṁ nihitaṁ ca satye
satyasya satyam ṛta-satya-netraṁ
satyātmakaṁ tvāṁ śaraṇaṁ prapannāḥ

(*Śrīmad-Bhāgavatam* 10.2.26)

> The demigods prayed: O Lord, You never deviate from Your vow, which is always perfect because whatever You decide is perfectly correct and cannot be stopped by anyone. Being present in the three phases of cosmic manifestation – creation, maintenance, and annihilation – You are the Supreme Truth. Indeed, unless one is completely truthful, one cannot achieve Your favor, which therefore cannot be achieved by hypocrites. You are the active principle, the real Truth in all the ingredients of creation, and therefore you are known as *antaryāmī*, the inner force. You are equal to everyone, and Your instructions apply for everyone, for all time. You are the beginning of all truth. Therefore, offering our obeisances, we surrender unto You. Kindly give us protection.

He who serves Kṛṣṇa is the true *sādhu* (*satāṁ*). *Hari-kathā* automatically flows from that *sādhu's* mouth like a flowing stream, and those who take bath in that stream will very soon be able to control Kṛṣṇa. Although Kṛṣṇa is not conquerable, He is conquered by those devotees.

The Vedic scriptures have stated:

nāyaṁ sukhāpo bhagavān
dehināṁ gopikā-sutaḥ
jñānināṁ cātma-bhūtānāṁ
yathā bhaktimatām iha

(*Śrīmad-Bhāgavatam* 10.9.21)

> The Supreme Personality of Godhead, Kṛṣṇa, the son of Mother Yaśodā, is accessible to devotees engaged in spontaneous loving service, but He is not as easily accessible to mental speculators, to those striving for self-realization by severe austerities and penances, or to those who consider the body the same as the self.

This verse means that those who have *bhakti* will very easily attain the direct service of Śrī Kṛṣṇa. He is not attained by *jñānīs* or *yogīs*, or by any means other than *bhakti*.

Devotee: Gurudeva, Prema dāsa and I took initiation from you last week. We are moving next month to the Houston area, to be close to your temple there, and we want to do some very substantial service to you there.

Śrīla Nārāyaṇa Gosvāmī Mahārāja: You can be there. You have no wife?

Devotee: Neither of us have any obligations whatsoever.

Śrīla Nārāyaṇa Gosvāmī Mahārāja: So you can both stay in our temple in Houston and help the devotees there. You can do so many services. Do you have a house?

Devotee: No.

Śrīla Nārāyaṇa Gosvāmī Mahārāja: Very good. Then it is easy.

Mahābuddhi dāsa: You said that you don't want the *gaura-vāṇī* of Lord Caitanya to diminish when you are gone. I understand the mood you are expressing, but if our advancement and understanding of what you are teaching is small, how will we perform substantial service to you, to make sure it doesn't disappear?

Śrīla Nārāyaṇa Gosvāmī Mahārāja: If all the *sannyāsīs* and other preachers give up their false pride, self-interest, and desire for their own prestige, then all endeavors will easily yield positive fruits. If they give up these contaminations for the service of *guru* and Kṛṣṇa, all devotees can be united.

Mahābuddhi dāsa: What about us fallen householders?

Śrīla Nārāyaṇa Gosvāmī Mahārāja: This instruction is true for *gṛhasthas* (householders) as well. A Vaiṣṇava *gṛhastha* lives in his home, but his heart is given totally to *guru* and Kṛṣṇa.

Actually there is no difference between *gṛhasthas* and *sannyāsīs*. In fact, sincere *gṛhasthas* are superior to those *sannyāsīs* who have worldly desires and selfish motives, and who are not properly following the principles of *bhakti*:

tṛṇād api sunīcena
taror api sahiṣṇunā
amāninā mānadena
kīrtanīyaḥ sadā hariḥ

(*Śrī Śikṣāṣṭaka* 3)

> Considering oneself to be more insignificant than a blade of grass, being more tolerant than a tree, free from all desire for personal prestige, and offering all respect to others, one should constantly be absorbed in *hari-kīrtana*.

Our Guru Mahārāja has said that if a *gṛhastha* follows that verse, he is superior.

yei bhaje sei baḍa—abhakta hīna chāra
kṛṣṇa-bhajane nāhi jāti-kulādi-vicāra

(*Śrī Caitanya-caritāmṛta, Antya-līlā* 4.67)

> Therefore, in the discharge of devotional service to the Lord there is no consideration of the status of one's family.

Mahābuddhi dāsa: In order to keep this *gaura-vāṇī* alive, your books are most important because of the realizations you have illuminated there.

Śrīla Nārāyaṇa Gosvāmī Mahārāja: If anyone reads my books, he will surely become attracted to *bhakti*.

Brajanātha dāsa: A Buddhist leader in China somehow received the *mahā-mantra* and became interested in chanting. He has 46,000 followers.

Śrīla Nārāyaṇa Gosvāmī Mahārāja: He also received my book somewhere.

Brajanātha dāsa: Then he met our devotees and received Gurudeva's book and picture. He started to read the book and then accepted Gurudeva within his heart. Since that time, six years ago, he started to chant sixty-four rounds every day, and yesterday he took initiation by phone.

Śrīla Nārāyaṇa Gosvāmī Mahārāja: Giri Mahārāja arranged this.

Brajanātha dāsa: Giri Mahārāja calls almost every day. He is travelling, moving around every few days, and he always brings new people – doctors and Buddhist leaders...

Śrīla Nārāyaṇa Gosvāmī Mahārāja: He is doing well.

Mahābuddhi dāsa: How can we receive the impression of *rādhā-dāsyam* which you are preaching?

Śrīla Nārāyaṇa Gosvāmī Mahārāja: The impression is received only by hearing from a *rasika tattva-jña* Vaiṣṇava (the pure devotee who is well-versed in all established truths and tasting all *rasas*, or transcendental mellows).

Mahābuddhi dāsa: But my *sukṛti* is very small. I am not as advanced as others who can come and hear you regularly.

Śrīla Nārāyaṇa Gosvāmī Mahārāja: If your resolve is this: "My aim and object of life is to somehow receive pure *bhakti*," then you will give up your house, wife, son, prestige, and everything that is unfavorable for your advancement.

Mahābuddhi dāsa: So, that is coming?

Śrīla Nārāyaṇa Gosvāmī Mahārāja: It must come. As stated in *Śrīmad-Bhāgavatam* (1.2.7):

> *vāsudeve bhagavati*
> *bhakti-yogaḥ prayojitaḥ*
> *janayaty āśu vairāgyaṁ*
> *jñānaṁ ca yad ahaitukam*

> By rendering devotional service unto the Personality of Godhead, Śrī Kṛṣṇa, one immediately acquires causeless knowledge and detachment from the world.

Surely this will develop. Both transcendental knowledge and renunciation are bound to make their appearance.

But there are so many people who are like *jñānīs*, like Prema-prayojana. They know all of the topics concerning *rādhā-dāsyam*, and were giving classes only on this topic. But I saw how they 'went to hell.'

Śrīla Bhaktivinoda Ṭhākura has written this verse:

āmnāyaḥ prāha tattvaṁ harim iha paramaṁ sarva-śaktiṁ rasābdhiṁ
tad-bhinnāṁśāṁś ca jīvān prakṛti-kavalitān tad-vimuktāṁś ca bhāvād
bhedābheda-prakāśaṁ sakalam api hareḥ sādhanaṁ śuddha-bhaktiṁ
sādhyaṁ tat-prītim evety upadiśati janān gauracandraḥ svayaṁ saḥ

Pramāṇa (evidence):
(1) The teachings of the Vedas received through *guru-paramparā* are known as *āmnāya*. The infallible evidence of the Vedas, of the *smṛti-śāstras* headed by the *Śrīmad-Bhāgavatam*, as well as evidence such as direct sense perception (*pradhāna*) that concur with the guidance of the Vedas, are all accepted as *pramāṇa* (evidence). This *pramāṇa* establishes the following *prameyas* (fundamental truths):

Sambandha (relationship):
(2) *parama-tattva* – Śrī Hari alone is the Supreme Absolute Truth.
(3) *sarva-śaktimān* – He is the possessor of all potencies (omnipotent).
(4) *akhila-rasāmṛta-sindhu* – He is the ocean of all nectarean mellows and divine sweetness.
(5) *vibhinnāṁśa-tattva* – both the *mukta* (liberated) and *baddha* (conditioned) *jīvas* are His eternally separated parts and parcels.
(6) *baddha-jīvas* – conditioned souls are subject to the control and covering of *māyā*.
(7) *mukta-jīvas* – liberated souls are forever free from *māyā*.
(8) *acintya-bhedābheda-tattva* – the entire universe, consisting of the conscious (*cit*) and unconscious (*acit*), is Śrī Hari's *acintya-bhedābheda-prakāśa*; that is to say, it is His manifestation which is inconceivably both different and non-different from Him.

Abhidheya (activities in relationship):
(9) *śuddha-bhakti* – pure devotional service is the only practice (*sādhana*) to attain spiritual perfection (*sādhya*).

Prayojana (the goal of life):
(10) *kṛṣṇa-prīti* – transcendental love and affection for

Śrī Kṛṣṇa is the one and only final object of attainment (*sādhya-vastu*).

The Supreme Personality of Godhead, Śrī Gaurāṅgadeva, has herein instructed ten distinct *tattvas* (fundamental truths) to the faithful *jīvas*.

Also, Śrīla Rūpa Gosvāmī has written these two verses:

tan-nāma-rūpa-caritādi-sukīrtanānu-
smṛtyoḥ krameṇa rasanā-manasī niyojya
tiṣṭhan vraje tad-anurāgi-janānugāmī
kālaṁ nayed akhilam ity upadeśa-sāram

(*Śrī Upadeśāmṛta* 8)

While living in Vraja as a follower of the eternal residents of Vraja, who possess inherent spontaneous love for Śrī Kṛṣṇa, one should utilize all his time by sequentially engaging the tongue and the mind in meticulous chanting and remembrance of Kṛṣṇa's names, form, qualities, and pastimes. This is the essence of all instruction.

anyābhilāṣitā-śūnyaṁ
jñāna-karmādy-anāvṛtam
ānukūlyena kṛṣṇānuśīlanaṁ
bhaktir uttamā

(*Bhakti-rasāmṛta-sindhu* 1.1.11)

Uttama-bhakti means the cultivation of activities which are meant exclusively for the pleasure of Śrī Kṛṣṇa, or in other words, the uninterrupted flow of service to Śrī Kṛṣṇa performed by all endeavors of the body, mind, speech, and through the expression of various spiritual sentiments (*bhāvas*), which is not covered by *jñāna*, knowledge of oneness with *brahma*, or *nitya-* and *naimittika-karma*, *yoga*, *tapasya*, and so forth, which is performed under the guidance of Śrī Kṛṣṇa's *uttama-bhaktas*, and which is devoid of all desires other than the aspiration to bring happiness to Śrī Kṛṣṇa.

By sincerely preaching these verses, you will conquer the entire world.

May 21, 2008
Morning Walk

Līlānātha dāsa: Śrīla Gurudeva, in some classes you say that we should be like Śrī Prahlāda Mahārāja, and in other classes you say that Prahlāda Mahārāja cannot even touch the lotus feet of Śrīla Mādhavendra Purī. How do we harmonize this?

Śrīla Nārāyaṇa Gosvāmī Mahārāja: You must know all established philosophical truths, and then reconcile. This is very easy to understand, but you are not able to reconcile.

What is the aim and object of your life? What kind of *bhakti* do you aspire for?

Līlānātha dāsa: We should have no material desires.

Śrīla Nārāyaṇa Gosvāmī Mahārāja: Can you answer the specific question?

Līlānātha dāsa: My goal is to attain *prema-bhakti.*

Śrīla Nārāyaṇa Gosvāmī Mahārāja: What kind of *prema*?

Līlānātha dāsa: I want *rādhā-dāsya prema.*

Śrīla Nārāyaṇa Gosvāmī Mahārāja: What is the meaning of *rādhā-dāsya*?

Līlānātha dāsa: *Rādhā-dāsya* means following the moods of Śrīla Rūpa Gosvāmī and what you are preaching to us.

Śrīla Nārāyaṇa Gosvāmī Mahārāja: A clear way to express this is that your goal is the service of Śrīmatī Rādhikā under the guidance of Śrīla Rūpa Gosvāmī. Śrī Prahlāda Mahārāja cannot give this type of *bhakti* because he does not have it.

Śrīpāda Mādhava Mahārāja: He is a *jñānī-bhakta.*

Śrīla Nārāyaṇa Gosvāmī Mahārāja: He teaches us tolerance, and how to properly honor others. For example:

tṛṇād api sunīcena
taror api sahiṣṇunā
amāninā mānadena
kīrtanīyaḥ sadā hariḥ

(*Śrī Śikṣāṣṭakam*, Verse 3)

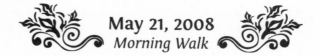

> One who thinks himself lower than the grass, who is more tolerant than a tree, and who does not expect personal honor, yet is always prepared to give all respect to others, can very easily always chant the holy name of the Lord.*

We can follow him in this way, but regarding *upāsanā-tattva*, the established truths regarding our worshipable Deity, we must look to the most elevated example of worship, namely Śrīla Rūpa Gosvāmī.

Brajanātha dāsa: We cannot progress unless we become like Prahlāda Mahārāja.

Śrīla Nārāyaṇa Gosvāmī Mahārāja: Yes. In the preliminary stage of advancement one must follow the example of Prahlāda Mahārāja.

Mahābuddhi dāsa: Śrīla Gurudeva, yesterday you said that it is your mission to protect *gaura-vāṇī*, but we may not be qualified to assist in that mission.

Śrīla Nārāyaṇa Gosvāmī Mahārāja: I was not referring to everyone. I told this for those who are preachers, like Padmanābha Mahārāja, Vana Mahārāja, Mādhava Mahārāja, Nemi Mahārāja, Śuddhādvaitī Mahārāja, and all other preachers. Try to help them stay together and preach. How can you help them? You can beg them, "Oh, Prabhu, please do not be influenced by prestige and self-interest. Please remain together and preach."

Mahābuddhi dāsa: Even though you are translating and writing so many wonderful literatures, we are still so unqualified. If we are trying for *rādhā-dāsyam*, the personal service of Śrīmatī Rādhikā, we must have some real taste.

Śrīla Nārāyaṇa Gosvāmī Mahārāja: *Bhakti* is like the stream of a river. One who is actually practicing *bhakti-yoga* will not remain in the same stage of spiritual development. You will gradually progress, and one day you will have that qualification to enter.

Mahābuddhi dāsa: You also emphasized the importance of *sādhu-saṅga*. Without the blessings and mercy of *rasika* Vaiṣṇavas...

Śrīla Nārāyaṇa Gosvāmī Mahārāja: Are you not associating with me and hearing all this *hari-kathā*?

Mahābuddhi dāsa: I am trying, but my *buddhi*, my intelligence, is very little.

Śrīla Nārāyaṇa Gosvāmī Mahārāja: Do you want to serve Lord Rāmacandra like Sītā, or Dvārakādīśa like Rukmiṇī?

Mahābuddhi dāsa: No.

Śrīla Nārāyaṇa Gosvāmī Mahārāja: Why not?

Mahābuddhi dāsa: Because you have given us some taste for the service of Śrī Śrī Rādhā and Kṛṣṇa.

Śrīla Nārāyaṇa Gosvāmī Mahārāja: By your saying this, it is evidence that your *bhakti* is developing. If anyone is practicing *bhakti-yoga*, he will not remain at the same stage.

Mahābuddhi dāsa: You have given us the clarity to know that specific goal. Otherwise we would not have known it.

Śrīla Nārāyaṇa Gosvāmī Mahārāja: Can you repay me for this? Even if you give all of your wealth, can you repay me?

Mahābuddhi dāsa: Even though we cannot repay you, being unqualified, we still have to try. We are indebted. It is painful to know that we are not qualified.

Śrīla Nārāyaṇa Gosvāmī Mahārāja: Yes. Śrīla Rūpa Gosvāmī has written that the first limb of *bhakti* is *viśrambheṇa guroḥ sevā*, meaning that one should render intimate service to *śrī guru*. This is because *śrī guru* gives such an incomparable gift that even the wealth of the entire world does not equal it. Those who realize this will totally surrender themselves to him.

Raghunātha dāsa: Śrīla Gurudeva, I was listening to a recorded class that you gave in Badger. You said that if someone chants Hare Kṛṣṇa with material desires and *anarthas* (unfavorable behaviors and mentalities) and he is not working to free himself from them, this is like trying to blow up one's cheeks and laugh at the same time; it is impossible to simultaneously do both. I think there is no hope for me because I am full of *anarthas*.

Śrīla Nārāyaṇa Gosvāmī Mahārāja: We must try to remove our *anarthas*, and at the same time continuously perform *bhajana*. Both at the same time. Do not commit any offenses or covet worldly desires, and avoid attachment to any worldly objects, situations, or ladies. Chant and remember Kṛṣṇa, and dwell in Vṛndāvana. If you cannot physically reside there, then under the guidance of a *rasika tattva-jñā* Vaiṣṇava, always consider, "I am in Vṛndāvana."

Raghunātha dāsa: In the case of a neophyte like myself, when I chant *japa*, should I try to remember the sweet pastimes of Śrī Śrī Rādhā and Kṛṣṇa, or should I try to pray to Nāma Prabhu (the holy name) to deliver me?

Śrīla Nārāyaṇa Gosvāmī Mahārāja: It is not that there is one instruction for everyone. Practice chanting according to your qualification. You can pray, and while praying you can mentally perform *parikramā* of Vraja-maṇḍala, Govardhana, and Vṛndāvana.

Śrīpāda Mādhava Mahārāja: You can remember the pastimes of Śrī Kṛṣṇa, like how He delivered Pūtanā. And while remembering this, you can pray, "She was a witch and so fallen, and still You delivered her. Please bestow Your mercy upon me so that I can also progress and be delivered."

Tulasī dāsī: I have been initiated into the *mahā-mantra* by you. I teach *yoga* and I have a lot of *yoga* students. Many of my students ask me for a practice. We do *kīrtanas* and *bhajanas*, but can I also give the *mahā-mantra* to someone as a meditation?

Śrīla Nārāyaṇa Gosvāmī Mahārāja: If the students are eating meat, fish, and eggs, drinking wine, gambling, and smoking, they can chant without *japa-mālā* (chanting beads). As you glorify the holy name to them and they develop some belief in *nāma*, they will give up their sinful habits; then you can teach them how to chant with *japa-mālā*. You can also invite preachers to give classes to your students.

Mahābuddhi dāsa: She can also have her students come to our programs.

Tulasī dāsī: Yes, we have been coming.

Madhuvrata dāsa: I gave class there two times.

Śrīla Nārāyaṇa Gosvāmī Mahārāja: Very good. He can speak well; better than me. All of my students can speak better than me. Śrīla Bhaktisiddhānta Sarasvatī Ṭhākura used to say, "I do not make disciples; I make *gurus*."

So go on teaching them *yoga*, and inject Hare Kṛṣṇa in their hearts. Teach them about the Supreme Lord Kṛṣṇa, and about His qualities and pastimes. Teach them, little by little.

Brajanāth dāsa: A Buddhist teacher took *harināma* initiation from Gurudeva two days ago. He has been chanting for many years and reading Śrīla Gurudeva's books. He has 46,000 students and tells them all to chant Hare Kṛṣṇa. He is very inspired because he has discovered that this is better than any Buddhist teaching. At the time of initiation, Śrīla Gurudeva named him Kṛṣṇa dāsa.

Śrīla Nārāyaṇa Gosvāmī Mahārāja: I am happy about this.

May 22, 2008
Morning Walk

Śrīla Nārāyaṇa Gosvāmī Mahārāja: Do you have any questions?

Mahābuddhi dāsa: You have so many centers in India. But here in the West, although there are so many devotees, there are not many institutions. You have said that we should set up centers and temples. How do you wish to see this done?

Śrīla Nārāyaṇa Gosvāmī Mahārāja: You know, perhaps, that *pūjyapāda* Śrīla Bhaktivedānta Svāmī Mahārāja, your Gurudeva, was engaged in preaching and encouraging his disciples to preach Kṛṣṇa consciousness. At the same time, he encouraged his disciples to collect funds. He told them, "Go and approach some wealthy persons, and any donations you collect from them should either be given to me or used to establish centers." The preachers brought a lot of money to him for his projects, and they also used the donations to open many preaching centers.

Nowadays, however, I see that I am practically the only one collecting money and establishing centers here and there. For the most part, when my preachers and other disciples receive money, they keep it for themselves and give me only a hundred dollars or a thousand dollars; not more than that.

I do not want the money for myself. I want them to use these funds for setting up preaching centers and cultivating people in Kṛṣṇa consciousness, just as the ISKCON leaders have done. Not many of my disciples are following this practice in the Western countries.

Here in the West I am not personally very involved in creating centers. However, for our projects in India I have been collecting funds from various countries like USA, Europe, England, Russia, Hong Kong, China, Brazil, Australia, Fiji, and New Zealand. In this way we have been able to establish first-class centers in Navadvīpa, Vraja-maṇḍala, Delhi, Kolkata, and other places.

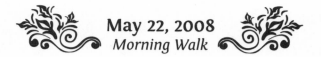

Brajanātha dāsa: You are also doing this in New Zealand and Fiji.

Śrīla Nārāyaṇa Gosvāmī Mahārāja: Yes, New Zealand and Fiji.

Śrīpāda Mādhava Mahārāja: You gave funds for the school in Badger and for the temple in Los Angeles.

Śrīla Nārāyaṇa Gosvāmī Mahārāja: Hardly any of my disciples in India are collecting anything for the projects there. Vana Mahārāja is giving something, but not enough to establish any centers. Whatever people have given to me as donations (*praṇāmī*), I accepted and used to complete these projects.

Brajanātha dāsa: Your daughters in London are establishing centers.

Śrīla Nārāyaṇa Gosvāmī Mahārāja: Yes, they have created some centers.

Brajanātha dāsa: Then, when they outgrow these centers they search for bigger premises.

Śrīla Nārāyaṇa Gosvāmī Mahārāja: Āśrama Mahārāja and others have been trying for a long time to establish some large centers, but this has not yet manifest.

Mahābuddhi dāsa: Nowadays your preachers follow you from one *hari-kathā* festival to another. Instead of circling continuously in the United States, they are accompanying you around the world. As you travel with the sun, they follow you.

Śrīla Nārāyaṇa Gosvāmī Mahārāja: Anyway, I am satisfied. The preaching must continue, with or without preaching centers, and I see that it is going on.

Śrīpāda Mādhava Mahārāja: But if the devotees have no preaching centers, how will people be able to come together for congregational chanting and hearing *hari-kathā* in the association of devotees? Preaching centers are needed.

Śrīla Nārāyaṇa Gosvāmī Mahārāja: They can meet in any person's house. That is the same as having a preaching center.

Mahābuddhi dāsa: *Nāma-haṭṭa*; we are already doing this.

Śrīpāda Mādhava Mahārāja: But new people don't like to go to someone else's house. There should be a neutral place for them to visit, otherwise they may not come.

Śrīla Nārāyaṇa Gosvāmī Mahārāja: At the time of Śrīla Prabhupāda Bhaktisiddhānta Sarasvatī Ṭhākura, the devotees used to rent places and use them as bases for carrying on their preaching work. This is how he was able to preach in so many places. He would tell his followers, "We are not construction workers; construction is not our mission." Then, after Prabhupāda left, his disciples began to make their own preaching centers.

Mahābuddhi dāsa: I have heard from some devotees that you don't want any centers in the West; only in India.

Śrīla Nārāyaṇa Gosvāmī Mahārāja: This is not true; I have never said this. Why are the devotees not opening centers? Rādhā-kānta from California wrote to me asking why so many preaching centers are being developed in India, but so few in Western and other countries.

I replied to him, "We actually do have many centers in the West; in London, Birmingham, Bali, Kuala Lumpur, Hong Kong, and many more places. But the problem is how to manage them. We cannot manage the Los Angeles temple; we talk about selling it. Best is to do what you all can do easily, and thus carry on the preaching work between yourselves with a proper combined effort."

Our *brahmacārīs* in India are managing everything smoothly. I do not give them a single penny. They are personally collecting and managing everything. Many Western devotees want to stay with Premānanda, Rasānanda, and others like them. But here in America, even three devotees or *brahmacārīs* cannot stay together in one place. They quarrel and then split up.

I sent Jīva, and so many others, to San Francisco, but they quarreled, and now he is preaching elsewhere.

Mahābuddhi dāsa: What can we do to become more qualified?

Śrīla Nārāyaṇa Gosvāmī Mahārāja: What can we do? We cannot change their habits and natures so easily. We Indians can stay in a room with twenty to forty devotees living alongside each other, whereas the Western devotees prefer to have separate rooms. Each Western devotee likes to be alone; no one else should live with him.

Mahābuddhi dāsa: That is our fault. It's because of the way in which we have been brought up. Still, though we are not qualified, how can we better serve?

Śrīla Nārāyaṇa Gosvāmī Mahārāja: They should learn from the Indians how to be together.

Śrīpāda Padmanābha Mahārāja: Śrīla Gurudeva, when we were young *brahmacārīs*, we also lived like that, next to each other.

Śrīla Nārāyaṇa Gosvāmī Mahārāja: I am still living like that. Even though I am in this advanced age, during the Vraja-maṇḍala and Navadvīpa *parikramās* so many *brahmacārīs* and *sannyāsīs* live with me. Tīrtha Mahārāja and others live together.

Brajanātha dāsa: Śrīla Bhaktivedānta Svāmī Mahārāja said that he wanted to come to the West with a group of Indian devotees to teach proper *sadācāra* (principles of behavior) to the Westerners.

Śrīla Nārāyaṇa Gosvāmī Mahārāja: That is why he was inviting me.

Mahābuddhi dāsa: Now we're here, not qualified, so what to do?

Śrīla Nārāyaṇa Gosvāmī Mahārāja: How can you change your nature, which is due to the influence of money? From birth you have been nourished and supported in a country where there is plenty of money; that is why your nature is like this. This is from birth. Indians are somewhat poor, but now that their wealth is increasing, they are becoming more and more habituated to living like Westerners.

I am creating large centers in Navadvīpa and Vraja-maṇḍala – only for Western devotees. For Indians, there is no need of these facilities. Many thousands of them can stay together in a single camp. They have no need of even a bathroom; they will go outside somewhere.

Mahābuddhi dāsa: We must be very far from spiritual life.

Śrīla Nārāyaṇa Gosvāmī Mahārāja: In Navadvīpa, we see 15,000 people coming together from villages for the *parikramā*. We do not have to bother for them. We know that somehow they will manage. They are content to stay in any spot under the roof of the sky, and they live there together. They are helpless only at the time of rain, and they never complain.

Śrīpāda Mādhava Mahārāja: Many of these people have nice houses; but when they come to Navadvīpa they live like this. Some of these Indians are also wealthy, respected persons.

Somebody came to Gurudeva and told him about a lady and her sons who attend Navadvīpa *parikramā* every year in spite of the conditions. She and her family live in a comfortable house equipped with all facilities. Someone had asked her "Why do you go there every year when there is so much difficulty for you?" She replied, "You take your meals every day. Why don't you stop doing this? This *parikramā* is the food for my soul. I have to go." After Gurudeva heard this story, he repeated it in his class.

Sāvitrī dāsī: Śrīla Gurudeva, it is difficult to establish a place in the West because of the great expense. The preachers need cars and they have to pay the rent.

Śrīla Nārāyaṇa Gosvāmī Mahārāja: There are many wealthy persons there who can easily help with these costs. At the time of Śrīla Bhaktivedānta Svāmī Mahārāja, there were so many preaching centers around the world.

Mahābuddhi dāsa: Śrīla Prabhupāda sent his householder disciples to open centers. He would send them to far-off places. They would open little preaching centers there, and gradually those centers would grow.

Śrīla Nārāyaṇa Gosvāmī Mahārāja: Some of them collected money even by foul means. I do not want my disciples to do this. This is one of the reasons why, after the divine departure of Śrīla Bhaktivedānta Svāmī Mahārāja, they left their devotional practices.

Mahābuddhi dāsa: What would you like to see us do here?

Śrīla Nārāyaṇa Gosvāmī Mahārāja: I am satisfied that the devotees are preaching. If any center can be opened easily, then it should be done. The devotees are doing this in different places, like New Zealand, Fiji, and Birmingham.

Brajanātha dāsa: There is a center in Holland and also in Stuttgart.

Raghunātha dāsa: Gurudeva, you mention in *Bhakti-rasāyana* that when narrations of Kṛṣṇa's pastimes (*līlā-kathā*) enter the ears and heart of the *sādhaka*, it snatches away all of the *anarthas* and contamination of millions of lifetimes. At that time there is no need even to perform separate renunciation.

My question is: How can someone get the proper attitude to listen to *līlā-kathā* in order to get *vraja-prema*, and within *vraja-prema*, the supreme goal, *rādhā-dāsyam*?

Śrīla Nārāyaṇa Gosvāmī Mahārāja: Why do you go to India at the time of Vraja-maṇḍala *parikramā*?

Raghunātha dāsa: To get the association of Vaiṣṇavas.

Śrīla Nārāyaṇa Gosvāmī Mahārāja: That opportunity has already come to you, so why have you invited me here to Miami? It is because some interest has awakened in your heart, surely. So the process you are already following is sufficient.

We are sending our *sannyāsīs* and others to preach in different places. So many parties are preaching around the world; about thirty different parties. Whether or not we have preaching centers, I want my disciples to continue their preaching. If need be, they can rent a building and use it as a preaching center.

Śrīpāda Mādhava Mahārāja: When you visit any place, so many people come to see you. But later on, if there is no preaching center, no neutral place for them to visit, they will go away. Our preaching will not expand.

Mahābuddhi dāsa: Would it be possible to pool our resources and have at least one national center in the United States, wherever you would want, by which people can identify your preaching mission? All the *yoga* groups have something like that here.

Śrīla Nārāyaṇa Gosvāmī Mahārāja: You can do this in any important city.

Mahābuddhi dāsa: How can we become better qualified to serve you?

Śrīla Nārāyaṇa Gosvāmī Mahārāja: Hare Kṛṣṇa. By remembering the sweet pastimes of Kṛṣṇa. This is the only reason we are engaged in so many activities. This is our main object, not making money or establishing centers or anything else. This is why we print and distribute books. If in the course of your preaching work what you are suggesting can be easily accomplished, that is good. But do not over-endeavor for it.

In this connection Śrīla Rūpa Gosvāmī has instructed: *bahu-ārambha-tyāgaḥ*. This means that to start many things at the same time is not advisable and is unfavorable for *bhakti*. Do not struggle to do too much. For myself, for Prabhupāda, your Gurudeva, it was easy to organize large festivals in Navadvīpa and Vraja-maṇḍala. Besides these festivals, we may accept whatever else can be accomplished without much difficulty.

Simply concentrate on increasing your chanting and remembering, and then preach as far as you are able. If you become too involved in establishing very big centers, you will have to give all of your energy for maintaining them. Your focus and enthusiasm for performing *sādhana-bhakti* will diminish, and after some time may disappear altogether.

Śrīpāda Mādhava Mahārāja: Not big places; just small preaching centers, so that the devotees can come together.

Mahābuddhi dāsa: Śrīla Gurudeva's point is correct. We've experienced having to manage big, big centers. As a result, we became more like managers and less like devotees.

Śrīla Nārāyaṇa Gosvāmī Mahārāja: I don't like this.

Mahābuddhi dāsa: Then what is the best way that we can serve you?

Śrīla Nārāyaṇa Gosvāmī Mahārāja: You are already serving. Moreover, if your chanting and remembering increases, I will be served automatically, because this is the exact purpose for my coming to this country. I was thinking, "How can I plant a seed in their desert-like hearts?" It is very difficult to do, but that is what we are doing through the process of our *guru-paramparā*.

Mahābuddhi dāsa: Yesterday you asked how we can repay you. We can't, but we must somehow try to do something.

Śrīla Nārāyaṇa Gosvāmī Mahārāja: Try to follow me and know my will.

śrī-caitanya-mano-'bhīṣṭaṁ
sthāpitaṁ yena bhūtale
svayaṁ rūpaḥ kadā mahyaṁ
dadāti sva-padāntikam

(*Śrī Prema-bhakti-candrikā*,
by Śrīla Narottama dāsa Ṭhākura)

> When will Śrī Rūpa Gosvāmī give me the shelter of his lotus feet? Because he understood the innermost desire of Śrī Caitanya Mahāprabhu, he was able to establish His mission in this world and is very dear to the Lord.

Mahābuddhi dāsa: Thank you.

Līlāvatī dāsī: I am working as an airline stewardess. This job sometimes involves serving meat and also giving out alcohol. I don't feel happy about this, but at the same time it is a good opportunity for me as I am earning a good salary. I am travelling a lot, and this has given me the opportunity for me and my mom to see you more often, whereas I would normally have very little money or opportunity for traveling. Still, I would like to improve myself in this other area.

Śrīla Nārāyaṇa Gosvāmī Mahārāja: Try to change this situation.

May 22, 2008
Darśana
After the Walk

Mahābuddhi dāsa: Śrīla Gurudeva, Senator Obama, who is running for President of the United States, is coming here today. We called him yesterday. If he meets you and becomes a Vaiṣṇava, it will be so beneficial for the world.

Brajanātha dāsa: He will be holding a meeting in the same room in which you gave class.

Śrīla Nārāyaṇa Gosvāmī Mahārāja: Oh.

Mahābuddhi dāsa: So I called his office and tried to make an appointment. I got to his finance minister. He said he would call me back today to see if there's an opportunity for the two of you to meet.

Śrīla Nārāyaṇa Gosvāmī Mahārāja: Why are you calling him?

Mahābuddhi dāsa: The devotees asked me to call him.

Śrīla Nārāyaṇa Gosvāmī Mahārāja: What is the need?

Brajanātha dāsa: It is good for him to have your *darśana*.

Mahābuddhi dāsa: It is difficult, though, because he is surrounded by so many persons. We'll try.

Śrīla Nārāyaṇa Gosvāmī Mahārāja: Persons in the renounced order should not see any politicians.

Śrīpāda Padmanābha Mahārāja: In India you meet many politicians.

Śrīla Nārāyaṇa Gosvāmī Mahārāja: I only do so if they come to me. I never invite them. If they come by their own desire, then it is all right. In this way he may come to me. But don't make invitations and so many other arrangements; there is no need. What can he do for us?

Brajanātha dāsa: You can help him, Gurudeva. If he becomes President, it will be good if he has a blessing from you for improving the American nation.

Raghunātha dāsa: Just imagine, Gurudeva, if the President of the United States becomes a Vaiṣṇava, by your mercy, how the world would change.

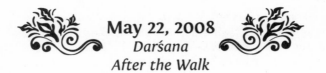

Śrīla Nārāyaṇa Gosvāmī Mahārāja: Kali Mahārāja (the personification of Kali-yuga) will not allow this. Rather, he will make them oppose us. They can only disturb us. In India, the government likes Buddhists but not Vaiṣṇavas. They are doing so much for the Buddhists and Christians, but they have no sympathy at all for the Vaiṣṇavas.

They are against us. If we would not show them that we are doing public welfare work, they would close down our centers. Therefore we have to show them externally that we have charitable dispensaries and schools and food distribution.

In India, in Mathurā, and elsewhere, some of the politicians are now chanting.

May 23, 2008
Morning Walk

Nitāi-Caitanya dāsa: Regarding the distribution of mercy: What is the position of a disciple who does not feel a strong *guru*-disciple relationship and who is afraid to approach the *guru*, but does service in the background?

Śrīla Nārāyaṇa Gosvāmī Mahārāja: As all qualifications are not the same in this world, so they are also not the same in devotees. According to the devotees' qualifications, some are coming close, some are more distant, and there are those who are even more distant.

Gradually they will come nearer to me. (Pointing to a devotee standing nearby:) Can you come and serve me like him?

Nitāi-caitanya dāsa: No, not right now.

Śrīla Nārāyaṇa Gosvāmī Mahārāja: Why not? If a disciple has faith, then one day he will come close to me. Are you serving like those who are near? How is it possible for those who do not give their energy to me to come closer to me? As much as my disciples give their energy to me, that is how much they will receive inspiration and a sense of closeness.

Suppose a man is in a room and wants to see the sun; he wants the sunrays to come to him. But how will the sun come to him if he does not leave his room?

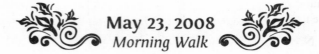

Mahābuddhi dāsa: We Western devotees have a lot of trouble in trying to give up sex desire. How can we be successful in doing that, so that we can give our full energy to your service?

Śrīla Nārāyaṇa Gosvāmī Mahārāja: *Gṛhasthas* can remain with their family members and at the same time perform *bhajana*. Remaining with only one family has been equated to *brahmacarya*. But those who look here and there, who divorce and remarry, are not pure *gṛhasthas*.

Mahābuddhi dāsa: But if one desires to advance further – to not always remain in *gṛhastha* life – how does one give up the desire for it?

Śrīla Nārāyaṇa Gosvāmī Mahārāja: Such devotees should give up householder life at once. They need not delay.

Raghunātha dāsa: What if one is not married but still has a strong desire for the opposite sex? How can one adjust?

Śrīla Nārāyaṇa Gosvāmī Mahārāja: How can this be adjusted? He should try to give up that desire. If he does not give it up, then he can do as he likes. No one can stop him; not even *guru* or Kṛṣṇa can stop him. If someone wants to go to hell, what can I do?

Sāvitrī dāsī: I have been sending out some information about our programs in Turkey. I just received an email saying that peace is found only in Islam. What do I say in reply to this?

Śrīla Nārāyaṇa Gosvāmī Mahārāja: You know the answer. No need to ask me.

Sāvitrī dāsī: In Islam, in the Koran, it says that no one can come between Allah and the servant – as in Kṛṣṇa consciousness, no one can come between Kṛṣṇa and His servant.

Śrīla Nārāyaṇa Gosvāmī Mahārāja: Why did Chānd Kāzī and Śrīla Haridāsa Ṭhākura give up Islam and come to Kṛṣṇa consciousness?

Do the Muslims eat meat?

Sāvitrī dāsī: Yes.

Śrīla Nārāyaṇa Gosvāmī Mahārāja: This is not Islam. Muslim kings used to fight with and kill their fathers, mothers, and sisters, only for the purpose of controlling a kingdom. Is this Islam? Even now, Muslim countries fight with each other, and many terrorists are Muslims.

Sāvitrī dāsī: In Islam it says that one cannot use force in religion. That is the written rule in the Koran, but people do not follow it. They are creating…

Śrīla Nārāyaṇa Gosvāmī Mahārāja: So try to do what you want to do there. Actually, no one can solve this. In ancient times there were so many Muslims who used to come to fight with Kṛṣṇa, as did Kālayavana.

Śyāmalā dāsī: Gurudeva, now that you have several thousand devotees, many devotees ask how they can come closer to you.

Śrīla Nārāyaṇa Gosvāmī Mahārāja: I just answered that. They should give their energy, mind, intelligence, money, and all they possess to *śrī guru*. To the proportion they give to *guru*, to that proportion they will be near to him.

guru-śuśrūṣayā bhaktyā
sarva-labdhārpaṇena ca
saṅgena sādhu-bhaktānām
īśvarārādhanena ca

śraddhayā tat-kathāyāṁ ca
kīrtanair guṇa-karmaṇām
tat-pādāmburuha-dhyānāt
tal-liṅgekṣārhaṇādibhiḥ

(*Śrīmad-Bhāgavatam* 7.7.30–31)

> One must accept the bonafide spiritual master and render service unto him with great devotion and faith. Whatever one has in one's possession should be offered to the spiritual master, and in the association of saintly persons and devotees one should worship the Lord, hear the glories of the Lord with faith, glorify the transcendental qualities and activities of the Lord, always meditate on the Lord's lotus feet, and worship the Deity of the Lord strictly according to the injunctions of the *śāstra* and *guru*.

Prahlāda Mahārāja has said, "*Sarva labdhārpaṇena ca* – Whatever is mine is actually Gurudeva's." The disciple not only thinks in this way, but acts practically on this understanding.

Raghunātha dāsa: For many years we have been hearing instructions on how to be strong in spiritual life and abandon material desires.

Still, we do not apply these instructions in our lives. Is this because of lack of sincerity or lack of *saṁskāras* and *sukṛti*? What is the reason that although we understand the philosophy theoretically, we do not apply it?

Śrīla Nārāyaṇa Gosvāmī Mahārāja: It is both.

Mahābuddhi dāsa: How do we increase our sincerity and *sukṛti*?

Śrīla Nārāyaṇa Gosvāmī Mahārāja: To the proportion you give your energy, to that same proportion your *sukṛti* and sincerity will increase.

Mahābuddhi dāsa: It is very discouraging that although I am an 'older devotee,' I am still a *prākṛta-bhakta*, a materialistic devotee, serving my senses. When will the opportunity come to me that I can cut this madness and give all my energy to serving *guru* and Kṛṣṇa? It is like looking up to a huge mountain. It makes me feel helpless.

Śrīla Nārāyaṇa Gosvāmī Mahārāja: Energy is one, and mind is one. They cannot be in two places, in the same way that two swords cannot live in the same sheath. If you give your mind to sense gratification, you will lose the opportunity to advance in *bhakti*. When you fully give your energy and mind to transcendental topics and personalities, you will then progress in spiritual life.

You can check to see how much of your energy you are giving to transcendental life. You give about 25% to spiritual things and 75% or more to worldly things, so how can you advance?

These questions do not come in my mind, because I have no energy, not even 0.0001%, for worldly things. Not even one moment of my time goes in vain. Even during my sleep I am sometimes chanting, sometimes offering prayers, sometimes remembering, and engaged in so many other services.

May 24, 2008
Morning Walk

Śrīla Nārāyaṇa Gosvāmī Mahārāja: Today, I am asking a question. Do you know why and how Brahmājī stole the friends and calves of Śrī Kṛṣṇa? Who will answer? Do you know?

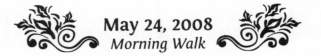

Nitāi-Caitanya dāsa: I just know it is *līlā*. Maybe he was testing Kṛṣṇa?

Śrīla Nārāyaṇa Gosvāmī Mahārāja: You can hear from Padmanābha Mahārāja.

Śrīpāda Padmanābha Mahārāja: Śrī Kṛṣṇa performs His pastimes for many purposes. By performing one pastime, He accomplishes many things. Ordinarily Lord Brahmā would not have done such a thing, because he understands Kṛṣṇa's position. He is the *ādi-guru*, the first *guru*, in our *sampradāya*. By Yogamāyā's potency, some questions came to his mind, "Who is this small cowherd boy? How can He be the Supreme?"

Śrīla Nārāyaṇa Gosvāmī Mahārāja: This is wrong. Mādhava Mahārāja will explain.

Śrīpāda Mādhava Mahārāja: In Vraja, when Kṛṣṇa used to return from cow-grazing, all of the motherly *gopīs* would embrace Him with more affection than they would their own sons. They thought, "Mother Yaśodā is always taking Kṛṣṇa in her arms and sleeping with Him. If He were our son, we would be able to show Him our love in the way she does."

When Kṛṣṇa milked the cows, those cows would think, "If Kṛṣṇa becomes our baby, we would be able to feed Him as much milk as He desires, directly from our udders." Also, the young *gopīs* thought, "If Kṛṣṇa becomes our beloved, our lives will be successful."

As the Supreme Personality of Godhead and thus knowing everyone's mind, Kṛṣṇa considered, "I must fulfill their desires."

Śrīla Nārāyaṇa Gosvāmī Mahārāja: You left something out.

Śrīpāda Mādhava Mahārāja: I was going to mention it.

Śrīla Nārāyaṇa Gosvāmī Mahārāja: Why didn't you tell it before?

Śrīpāda Mādhava Mahārāja: While playing with His friends like an ordinary boy, He performed the pastime of killing Aghāsura. Lord Brahmā was passing by and thought, "Is Kṛṣṇa the Supreme Personality of Godhead or just an ordinary boy?"

Śrīla Nārāyaṇa Gosvāmī Mahārāja: No. You still did not come to the point. He knew Kṛṣṇa as the Supreme Lord. When Kṛṣṇa killed Aghāsura, Lord Brahmā saw Aghāsura's soul enter into Kṛṣṇa's lotus feet. He thought, "How wonderful this is! I want to see more sweet pastimes." That is why he thought of stealing the calves and boys.

In the meantime, Kṛṣṇa was thinking how to fulfill four wishes: (1) the desire of all of the teenage *gopīs*; (2) the desires of the cows and mothers; (3) the desire of Lord Brahmā; and (4) His own desire to taste the affection of these associates.

When Kṛṣṇa was contemplating in this way, Yogamāyā at once appeared to Him and said, "Prabhu, you are thinking about tasting these relationships, so I will arrange for this right away." This is why she caught hold of Brahmā and brought him under her influence. She made this thought arise in him: "I am Brahmā. I should steal away the cowherd boys and calves. Then I will see what He will do. Maybe He will come to me and ask where they are."

Brahmā saw all the cowherd boys sitting together, with Kṛṣṇa in the center, absorbed in laughing and joking and enjoying *prasādam*. By the influence of Yogamāyā, Brahmā thought, "This is the perfect time to steal the boys and calves." He created very green grass far away, and the calves became allured to go there and graze. At that time Brahmā stole them and put them in a cave.

Kṛṣṇa told His friends, "Just wait here and take *prasādam* while I personally go to look for the calves." Then, as soon as Kṛṣṇa left the cowherd boys, Brahmā took them and put them in the cave, and then he returned to Brahma-loka.

Who were the calves and cowherd boys stolen by him? The real cowherd boys and calves are *nitya-parikaras* (eternal associates) of Kṛṣṇa. Lord Brahmā is not qualified to even touch the dust of their feet, what to speak of kidnap them.

Actually, there were three sets of boys: The first set was the original cowherd boys and calves. Yogamāyā created the second set, which Lord Brahmā stole, and Kṛṣṇa personally expanded as the third set.

Brajanātha dāsa: Where did the first set stay when the illusory set was stolen?

Śrīla Nārāyaṇa Gosvāmī Mahārāja: Kṛṣṇa told Yogamāyā, "Please cover them in such a way that they will sit and take their meal, and the calves will graze as usual. No one, not even Baladeva Prabhu or any Vrajavāsī, should see them."

Yogamāyā thus covered the original cowherd boy associates of Kṛṣṇa for one year. No Vrajavāsī could see them, and even Baladeva could not see them. When Kṛṣṇa was with them, they had been eating yogurt and rice just as He was doing. Now that Kṛṣṇa had left just as they were about to put their next morsel of *prasādam*[18]

[18] Their mothers had offered the *prasādam* to the Deity of Śālagrāma in their homes.

in their mouths, they began thinking, "We will not eat anything until our *sakhā*, Kṛṣṇa, returns to us. Being worried that we are not eating without Him, He will surely return very soon." In this way, for one year Yogamāyā influenced their minds in thinking that Kṛṣṇa would return in the very next moment, and this year passed for them like a moment.

Śrīpāda Padmanābha Mahārāja: Was this something like the *rāsa-līlā* in relation to time? Kṛṣṇa's *yogamāyā* potency expanded the *rāsa-līlā* to last for the duration of a night of Brahmā, but the *gopīs* experienced it to be less than a moment.

Brajanātha dāsa: When Lord Brahmā went to his own planet, his guards questioned him, "Who are you?"

Śrīla Nārāyaṇa Gosvāmī Mahārāja: Lord Brahmā said, "You are my guards. You do not recognize me?"

The guards replied, "You are not Brahmā. Our Prabhu is on His throne and managing everything. He told us that if an imposter tries to come in, we should not allow him entrance."

Lord Brahmā wondered, "Why is this happening?" Then, in his trance of meditation he realized, "I have made a mistake."

There is so much deep *siddhānta* in this pastime.

Śrīpāda Padmanābha Mahārāja: This brings a question: There is a similar occurrence in Rāma's pastimes. The demon Rāvaṇa could not take the real Sītā-devī; he could only take an illusory Sītā. We were discussing this in Alachua the other day. It was the illusory Sītā who was taken by Rāvaṇa. The whole pastime of her residing in Rāvaṇa's kingdom took place with this illusory Sītā. It was this Sītā who was in the Aśoka garden, feeling great separation from Lord Rāma.

So the question is, how can an illusory Sītā feel such separation?

Śrīla Nārāyaṇa Gosvāmī Mahārāja: Because she was created by Yogamāyā, she had such power and mood. The illusory material *māyā*, Mahāmāyā, would not have been able to do something like this, but Yogamāyā can do so.

Brajanātha dāsa: And the real Sītā was protected by Agni all that time.

Śrīla Nārāyaṇa Gosvāmī Mahārāja: Later, when Lord Rāmacandra finally met the real Sītā, it seemed like only one second had passed.

Śrīpāda Padmanābha Mahārāja: Going back to *brahma-vimohana-līlā*, this brings a question. You mentioned that there were four reasons why Kṛṣṇa performed this pastime. Of these, which is the main reason? Śrī Caitanya Mahāprabhu had external and internal reasons for appearing, so is there any order in the reasons regarding this pastime with Brahmā? The internal reason for Mahāprabhu's appearance was to taste *rasa*. Can we say there is a main reason for Kṛṣṇa manifesting this pastime with Brahmā?

Śrīla Nārāyaṇa Gosvāmī Mahārāja: Mahāprabhu's second reason was to give *rāgānuga-mārga*, the third was because of Advaita Ācārya's prayer, and the fourth was this:

yadā yadā hi dharmasya
glānir bhavati bhārata
abhyutthānam adharmasya
tadātmānaṁ sṛjāmy aham

(*Bhagavad-gītā* 4.7)

> O Bhārata, whenever there is a decline of *dharma* (religion) and an increase in *adharma* (irreligion), at that time I manifest My eternally perfect form in this mundane world.

And there are so many other reasons.

Śrīpāda Padmanābha Mahārāja: Can we say that the main reason for *brahma-vimohana-līlā* was for Śrī Kṛṣṇa to taste the *vātsalya-prema* of all the cows and *gopīs*?

Śrīla Nārāyaṇa Gosvāmī Mahārāja: Kṛṣṇa externally performed this pastime to satisfy the desire of Lord Brahmā, and internally to fulfill the desires of the young *gopīs*, the mothers, and the cows.

This is very mysterious. What can you pay me for this? Only *daṇḍavat-praṇāma*?

Brajanātha dāsa: Śrīla Gurudeva, Vṛndā has a question. Navadvīpa is like Vṛndāvana. It is *gupta*, or hidden, Vṛndāvana. All *rasas*, namely, *dāsya* (servitorship), *sakhya* (friendship), *vātsalya* (parenthood), and *mādhurya* (amorous love) are present in Vṛndāvana. Regarding Śrīman Mahāprabhu's pastimes, all *rasas* must also be present. How is *mādhurya-rasa* present in Mahāprabhu's *līlā*?

Śrīla Nārāyaṇa Gosvāmī Mahārāja: Mahāprabhu is the *gupta-avatāra*, the hidden incarnation. Everything is present within Him and His abode, but it is hidden. Vṛndāvana, Rādhā-kuṇḍa, Śyāma-kuṇḍa, Girirāja Govardhana, Nandagrāma, Varṣāṇā, and all other pastime places are situated in Navadvīpa, but in a hidden way. Only those who take shelter of an elevated Vaiṣṇava and Śrī Kṛṣṇa can see this.

Vṛndā-devī dāsī: How did Mahāprabhu experience *mādhurya-rasa* if outwardly the *sakhīs* and *mañjarīs* are not present there?

Śrīla Nārāyaṇa Gosvāmī Mahārāja: He does so by mind. Everything is eternally present there, although it is not manifest externally.

Śrīpāda Padmanābha Mahārāja: Śrīla Gurudeva, the other day you said that Kṛṣṇa, in the form of Mahāprabhu, was fulfilling His three desires[19] in a hidden way in Navadvīpa; and when He took *sannyāsa* and went to Purī with Rāmānanda Rāya and Svarūpa Dāmodara, He outwardly fulfilled these desires. So were His desires fulfilled, or not fulfilled, in Navadvīpa? Did He have to take *sannyāsa* to fulfill His desires?

Śrīla Nārāyaṇa Gosvāmī Mahārāja: Everything is already fulfilled in Mahāprabhu. He took *sannyāsa* for the benefit of the *jīvas* of the world. "*Rāga-mārga bhakti loke karite pracāraṇa* – He wanted to propagate devotional service in the world on the platform of spontaneous attraction."

Śrīpāda Mādhava Mahārāja:

anugrahāya bhaktānāṁ
mānuṣaṁ deham āsthitaḥ
bhajate tādṛśīḥ krīḍā
yāḥ śrutvā tat-paro bhavet

(*Śrīmad-Bhāgavatam* 10.33.36)

When the Lord assumes a human-like body to show mercy to His devotees, He engages in such pastimes as will attract those who hear about them to become dedicated to Him.

[19] "Desiring to understand the glory of Rādhārāṇī's love, the wonderful qualities in Him that She alone relishes through Her love, and the happiness She feels when She realizes the sweetness of His love, the Supreme Lord Hari, richly endowed with Her emotions, appeared from the womb of Śrīmatī Śacī-devī, as the moon appeared from the ocean" (*Śrī Caitanya-caritāmṛta*, *Ādi-līlā* 1.6).

May 25, 2008
Darśana

Mahābuddhi dāsa: Is your translation going well?

Śrīla Nārāyaṇa Gosvāmī Mahārāja: Yes,

Śrīpāda Padmanābha Mahārāja: Śrīla Gurudeva, what are you translating now?

Śrīla Nārāyaṇa Gosvāmī Mahārāja: I am not translating. Tīrtha Mahārāja is translating and sending me his work. I am correcting and rewriting, changing almost all of his work. His language is not Hindi, so there are some mistakes. There are only very small mistakes in the *bhāva* of his translation, but there is quite a defect in his Hindi grammar. He is able to translate because he knows so much and he can explain everything so well.

Brajanātha dāsa: Śrīla Gurudeva, was everything you said yesterday about *brahma-vimohana-līlā* taken exactly from the commentary of Śrīla Viśvanātha Cakravartī Ṭhākura?

Śrīla Nārāyaṇa Gosvāmī Mahārāja: Yes. Without Śrīla Viśvanātha Cakravartī Ṭhākura's commentary, how can we know *Śrīmad-Bhāgavatam*? Śrīla Sanātana Gosvāmī wrote his commentary on *Śrīmad-Bhāgavatam*, and then Śrīla Jīva Gosvāmī took the essential parts of that commentary and wrote his own. Śrīla Viśvanātha Cakravartī Ṭhākura took their remnants, meaning that he took all of their conclusions into his heart and then added something special so that the import would be filled with still more nectar. He took the commentaries of all our previous *ācāryas*, including Śrīla Śrīdhara Svāmī and Śrīla Vallabhācārya, and added his own contribution.

Śrīla Sanātana Gosvāmī has written the largest commentary on *Śrīmad-Bhāgavatam* and Śrīla Jīva Gosvāmī has commented briefly. Śrīla Viśvanātha Cakravartī Ṭhākura later took the essential parts of their work, not the entirety, and illuminated them further.

He explained their commentaries in a *rasika* mood. There is no commentary anywhere in the world which is as full of *rasa* as that written by Śrīla Viśvanātha Cakravartī Ṭhākura.

He was both a manifestation and follower of Śrīla Rūpa Gosvāmī. Just as Śrīla Rūpa Gosvāmī is *rasika* (expert in relishing transcendental mellows), he is also *rasika*. I like all of his commentaries and books. I have translated almost all of them.

Brajanātha dāsa: You also wanted to translate his Sanskrit commentary on *Śrī Caitanya-caritāmṛta*.

Śrīla Nārāyaṇa Gosvāmī Mahārāja: It may be that after completing my translation of *Śrīmad-Bhāgavatam* and *Vedānta-sūtra*, I will be able to complete this as well.

May 26, 2008
Darśana

Ānanda dāsa: Gurudeva, this is my mother, Bhadra, and this is my aunt, Ophelia. My aunt only chants once in a while, but my mother chants four, five, or six rounds a day.

Śrīpāda Mādhava Mahārāja: Without a devotee's chanting sixteen rounds, Śrīla Gurudeva will not give second initiation.

Ānanda dāsa: Okay.

Śrīla Nārāyaṇa Gosvāmī Mahārāja: America is like heaven on Earth. In heaven there are beautiful flower gardens, as there are beautiful gardens here in America. Many people are wealthy here, with all their desires for enjoyment fulfilled. It is therefore very difficult for them to do *bhajana*.

India is not like America. Although there are some rich persons in India, it is mostly poor, so there is a good chance for the people to do *bhajana*. In India there is Vraja-maṇḍala, Navadvīpa-maṇḍala, Jagannātha Purī, Girirāja Govardhana, Yamunā River, Gaṅgā, the birthplaces of Lord Rāmacandra, Lord Nṛsiṁhadeva, and Śrī Kṛṣṇa; and Śyāma-kuṇḍa and Rādhā-kuṇḍa are present there. It is therefore very easy to do *bhajana*.

In America, being heaven, wherever I go I meet someone and think, "That person is very wealthy." But then I meet another person and see that he is wealthier than the first, and then another still wealthier. I see that people's houses are like palaces, with rivers inside their compounds and with mango trees that are like the *pārijāta* trees of heaven. There are large roads, cars, and parks – and thus it is very hard to do *bhajana*. Everyone here is sinking in the ocean of material sense enjoyment. They cannot give up those objects of enjoyment, so how can they do *bhajana*?

This is why I have come here, and *parama-pūjyapāda* Śrīla Bhaktivedānta Svāmī Mahārāja also preached in this barren land bereft of *bhakti*.

If you want to be happy you must chant at least eight rounds, but better to chant sixteen rounds. I see that you are always thinking of wealth. Please remember that wealth cannot give you happiness. It simply absorbs you in maintaining your houses and property and in doing business day and night.

We have come to remind you that you cannot be happy by such absorption. Even the demigods are not happy, and in fact they are even more miserable than us. Try to realize this, and do *bhajana*.

Old age is bound to come, at which time you will not be able to walk without a stick, and finally you will be forced to give up your body. Remember that you will die, at which time you will not be able to carry even one penny with you.

Tulasī-mālā saves us from bad influences; it controls blood pressure, protects us from evil elements entering our hearts, and helps us in our *kṛṣṇa-bhajana*.

Devotee: This is my mother, Śrīla Gurudeva. She is a Christian.

Śrīla Nārāyaṇa Gosvāmī Mahārāja: Very good. We are refined Christians, because we follow the orders of God. Not only all people, but all animals and birds are sons and daughters of God. If you kill and eat them, God will not be pleased; He will punish you. We do not eat beef, or any meat, or any fish, and we do not smoke or gamble. We are therefore pure Christians.

Try to be a pure Christian. You should know that Jesus went to India in his youth. He went to Vṛndāvana and saw that everyone there was worshiping Śrī Kṛṣṇa. Then, when he went to Jagannātha Purī, he saw that everyone was addressing Kṛṣṇa as Kroosna. Krista came from Kroosna, and thus the name Christ comes originally from the name Kṛṣṇa.

Devotee: One last question, Śrīla Gurudeva. Why did Śrī Caitanya Mahāprabhu take *sannyāsa*? Was it just to gain respect, or did He want to teach us something?

Śrīla Nārāyaṇa Gosvāmī Mahārāja: He took *sannyāsa* in order to perform sweet, heart-wrenching pastimes, so that by hearing about them at present or in the future one will at once become a devotee. Everyone will follow the Lord's instructions and character, thinking, "We should be ideal like Śrī Caitanya Mahāprabhu. We should give up material enjoyment and perform *bhajana*."

Ānanda dāsa: My aunt came only to see you, and when she saw you she said she wants to get initiated. Can you please do something to help her?

Śrīla Nārāyaṇa Gosvāmī Mahārāja: I have come only for this purpose, to give everyone *kṛṣṇa-bhakti*. Therefore, if she is not smoking or drinking alcohol or eating meat, I will definitely give her initiation.

(To the aunt) You will have to promise not to eat meat, beef, or eggs, and you will have to give up wine and smoking. Then I will give you initiation.

By chance you have been thrown into this world from Goloka Vṛndāvana. The guard of that Goloka planet, Yogamāyā-devī, threw us into this world.[20] You are actually a male or female servant of Śrī Śrī Rādhā-Kṛṣṇa, but you wanted to enjoy sense gratification and have forgotten your true heritage.

You will not be able to remain in this material body. At present you are enveloped in the deluding *māyā* potency, thinking, "I am this body," but you are not this body. Śrī Kṛṣṇa has mercifully given you this human form of life, and it is only in this form that you can remember Him and return to your eternal home.

This is not your first birth here in this material world. You have experienced millions upon millions of births and deaths here. You have had so many problems, not only in the human form, but as a dog, pig, donkey, monkey, cat, hog, and so on. Moreover, if you do not remember Kṛṣṇa and do *bhajana*, you will have to take birth again. You might come as a fish, and at that time someone will catch and eat you. It is therefore essential to do something for your spiritual welfare before your next death. In that way you can have *sādhu-saṅga*, although such an auspicious opportunity is very, very rare.

How is *sādhu-saṅga* attained? Best to serve a pure Vaiṣṇava and give your energy to anything related to Śrī Kṛṣṇa, such as His

---

20 Śrīla Nārāyaṇa Gosvāmi Mahārāja has explained that our *ācāryas* sometimes give 'baby-food to babies.' In other words, they give explanations that are easy for aspiring devotees to accept and understand according to those devotees' level of advancement. On very rare occasions he personally gives this 'baby-food' to his new audiences.

Śrīla Prabhupāda writes in his *Madhya-līlā* 21.31 purport of *Śrī Caitanya-caritāmṛta*: "First a child is shown the branches of a tree, and then he is shown the moon through the branches. This is called *śākhā-candra-nyāya*. The idea is that first one must be given a simpler example. Then the more difficult background is explained."

Śrīla Mahārāja's teachings, and our *ācārya's* teachings, is that the souls of this world fell here from a region in between the material and spiritual worlds.

Vṛndāvana-dhāma or Navadvīpa-dhāma. Spending your energy, money, and everything you possess for this, or even offering some water and flowers, you will attain *sukṛti* (spiritual pious activities, which create impressions on the heart). It is by this *sukṛti* that you will be able to have the association of exalted Vaiṣṇavas, and then you will be granted remembrance of Śrī Kṛṣṇa and entrance into your original abode. There are no problems at all in that spiritual abode; no suffering, sorrows, old age, or death.

May 27, 2008
Morning Walk

Devotee: In one of your *Bhakti-rasāyana* lectures you said that *smaraṇa* (remembrance, meditation) is more important than *śravaṇa* (hearing) and *kīrtana* (chanting).

Śrīla Nārāyaṇa Gosvāmī Mahārāja: As long as the mind is not fully controlled, we must continue to chant Hare Kṛṣṇa. When the mind is totally controlled, we will be able to remember *aṣṭa-kālīya-līlā* (the daily pastimes of Śrī Śrī Rādhā-Kṛṣṇa and Their associates) and forget the external world.

Śrīpāda Mādhava Mahārāja: When the mind is controlled, which is more important: *śravaṇa*, *kīrtana*, or *smaraṇa*?

Śrīla Nārāyaṇa Gosvāmī Mahārāja: By performing *kīrtana*, *smaraṇa* will automatically come; it will be natural. Moreover, it is possible that *kīrtana* may stop when you are serving by your mind and engaged only in *aṣṭa-kālīya-līlā*.

Mahābuddhi dāsa: So until then, you are doing *kīrtana*, and afterward the mind…

Śrīla Nārāyaṇa Gosvāmī Mahārāja: By *kīrtana*, *smaraṇa* will come.

Mahābuddhi dāsa: Automatically?

Śrīla Nārāyaṇa Gosvāmī Mahārāja: Automatically.

Śrīpāda Mādhava Mahārāja: Without *kīrtana*, *smaraṇa* will not be possible.

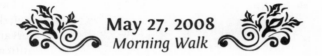

Śrīla Nārāyaṇa Gosvāmī Mahārāja: For example:

yaśomatī-nandana, vraja-vara-nāgara,
gokula-rañjana kāna
gopī-parāṇa-dhana, madana-manohara,
kālīya-damana-vidhāna

> Kṛṣṇa is Yaśodā-maiyā's beloved son, and the topmost lover in Vrajabhūmi. As Kāna (an affectionate name for Him) He delights Gokula and is the wealth of the life of the *gopīs*. He is an inveterate thief, stealing the hearts of all, and He crushed the Kāliya serpent.

When we are advanced in *bhakti*, all the pastimes of Śrī Kṛṣṇa that are present in these *kīrtanas* will manifest in our heart. When we are fully absorbed in these pastimes and there is no longer external consciousness, at that time *kīrtana* will stop.

Śrīla Śukadeva Gosvāmī is the example of this. He was giving class on *Śrīmad-Bhāgavatam* to Parīkṣit Mahārāja, and when he uttered the verse *anayārādhito nūnaṁ bhagavān harir īśvaraḥ*, he at once became silent.

anayārādhito nūnaṁ
bhagavān harir īśvaraḥ
yan no vihāya govindaḥ
prīto yām anayad rahaḥ

(*Śrīmad-Bhāgavatam* 10.30.28)

> The *vraja-gopīs* said: O my friend, leaving us aside, Kṛṣṇa has gone off to a secluded place with a particular *gopī*. She must truly be expert in worshiping (*anayārādhito*) Him, for He was so pleased with Her service that He has left us all behind.

Absorbed in that pastime, Śrīla Śukadeva Gosvāmī went there internally. Most of the sages present in his assembly could not understand his silence, but Nārada Ṛṣi and Śrī Vyāsadeva knew the reason.

Generally, in the material world, when a person faints he has neither external nor internal consciousness. On the other hand, although a devotee may look as though he has fainted, actually he has entered a state of *samādhi* (trance) and all of his internal senses are active.

Devotee: Does this mean that *kīrtana* is not our *sādhya* (goal)?

Śrīla Nārāyaṇa Gosvāmī Mahārāja: *Kīrtana* is the *sādhya*, because by the help of *kīrtana*, *smaraṇa* (remembrance) comes.

Śrīpāda Mādhava Mahārāja: *Kīrtana* is both the *sādhana* (process) and the *sādhya* (goal). Śrī Caitanya Mahāprabhu has therefore said, "*param vijāyate śrī-kṛṣṇa-saṅkīrtanam* – Let there be supreme victory for the chanting of the holy names of Śrī Kṛṣṇa."

Mahābuddhi dāsa: You gave the example that when one is chanting *kīrtana* and remembering the pastimes, one gradually enters into those pastimes.

Śrīla Nārāyaṇa Gosvāmī Mahārāja: Śrīla Rūpa Gosvāmī has written:

tan-nāma-rūpa-caritādi-sukīrtanānu-
smṛtyoḥ krameṇa rasanā-manasī niyojya
tiṣṭhan vraje tad-anurāgi-janānugāmī
kālaṁ nayed akhilam ity upadeśa-sāram

(*Śrī Upadeśāmṛta*, Verse 8)

While living in Vraja as a follower of the eternal residents of Vraja, who possess inherent spontaneous love for Śrī Kṛṣṇa, one should utilize all his time by sequentially engaging the tongue and the mind in meticulous chanting and remembrance of Kṛṣṇa's names, form, qualities, and pastimes. This is the essence of all instruction.

Raghunātha dāsa: Śrīla Gurudeva, when one achieves perfection and gets the opportunity to serve Śrī Śrī Rādhā-Kṛṣṇa...

Śrīla Nārāyaṇa Gosvāmī Mahārāja: If Śrī Kṛṣṇa or Śrīmatī Rādhikā will order you to serve, then you will serve. The pure devotee is totally dependent on Them.

Kamala-kānta dāsa: Śrīla Gurudeva, we understand that *Śrīmad-Bhāgavatam* is the highest evidence. So how should we think of *Śrī Caitanya-caritāmṛta*? Is it the same, less, or higher than *Śrīmad-Bhāgavatam*? It seems to me that it is higher.

Śrīla Nārāyaṇa Gosvāmī Mahārāja: *Śrī Caitanya-caritāmṛta* is important for our *sampradāya*, not for other *sampradāyas*. On the other hand, our *sampradāya* and all others accept as evidence the *Śrīmad-Bhāgavatam*.

Śrīpāda Mādhava Mahārāja: *Śrīmad-Bhāgavatam*, *Ujjvala-nīlamaṇi*, *Bhakti-rasāmṛta-sindhu*, *Lalita-mādhava*, *Vidagdha-mādhava*, and other such scriptures are present in *Śrī Caitanya-caritāmṛta*.

Śrīla Nārāyaṇa Gosvāmī Mahārāja: *Śrī Bhakti-rasāmṛta-sindhu* depends on *Śrīmad-Bhāgavatam* in the sense that *Śrīmad-Bhāgavatam* is its basis. The essence of *Śrīmad-Bhāgavatam* is *Bhakti-rasāmṛta-sindhu*, *Ujjvala-nīlamaṇi*, and the other afore-mentioned scriptures.

Mahābuddhi dāsa: When preaching in the West, is our aim to cultivate new devotees but encourage them to stay in their homes and remain in their present position? Or, is it to try to bring them to the temples and train them in Kṛṣṇa consciousness? I am trying to understand Śrīla Bhaktivinoda Ṭhākura; that is why I am asking.

Śrīla Nārāyaṇa Gosvāmī Mahārāja: You can understand what to do by the preaching of your Gurudeva Śrīla Bhaktivedānta Svāmī Mahārāja, Śrīla Bhaktisiddhānta Sarasvatī Ṭhākura, and Śrīla Bhakti Prajñāna Keśava Gosvāmī Mahārāja. They never told anyone, "You should become a *gṛhastha* (householder)." Rather, if a person desires to marry, they would say, "Oh, yes, you can marry." Marriage is a deep dark well. Why would the spiritual master say, "You should fall down in that dark well?"

Mahābuddhi dāsa: Most of the people we preach to are already in the well.

Śrīla Nārāyaṇa Gosvāmī Mahārāja: I know that, but we are in Śrī Nārada Ṛṣi's *paramparā*. What did he do everywhere he went? He told everyone that they should give up their married life.

Do you know Priyavrata, the son of Svāyambhuva Manu? He was very intelligent and qualified. Svāyambhuva Manu wanted him to marry and take over the rule of his kingdom, which was the entire universe, so that he himself could retire to a life of renunciation in the forest.

Having been trained by Nārada Ṛṣi in the principles of celibacy and renunciation, Priyavrata denied his request and said, "I cannot take the kingdom. I have decided to take the renounced order of life and perform *bhajana*." At that time Nārada Ṛṣi came to inspire him in his resolve, saying, "You must take the renounced order at once."

In the meantime Lord Brahmā, the father of both Nārada and Svāyambhuva Manu, came and told Priyavrata, "I am not happy with your decision. You are the only one qualified to take charge of the universal affairs. You must take charge. If a man has controlled his senses, it does not matter whether he remains at home or enters in the renounced order of life; there is no difference. On the other hand, if a man who has not controlled his senses goes to the forest, he will eventually leave it and return to household life due to remembrance of the objects of his sensual enjoyment. Therefore, I think it will be better for you to marry, rule the kingdom for some time, and then take the renounced order."

King Priyavrata wanted to fulfill the order of both of his spiritual authorities, Nārada and Brahmā. He replied to Brahmā, "I will obey your order." He then ruled the kingdom of the universe, at the same time remaining detached and fixed in self realization.

Although Nārada Ṛṣi was not satisfied with the idea of King Priyavrata being engaged in household life, he considered, "If I interfere, Brahmājī will be angry." He therefore remained silent, but internally he was unhappy.

Lord Brahmā returned to his abode, but he regretted his actions: "What a mistake I have made! I know that household life is a dark well in which one's life is ruined. I ordered King Priyavrata to enter married life for the purpose of creation, but I am not happy." Lord Brahmā knew the truth, but because Śrī Kṛṣṇa ordered him to create the universe and universal population, he had given those instructions to the king.

On the other hand, Nārada Ṛṣi tells everyone to be renounced.

Raghunātha dāsa: Śrīla Gurudeva, you said that when one becomes advanced, one will control the mind and remembrance will automatically come. But for me, controlling the mind is the most difficult thing to do.

Śrīla Nārāyaṇa Gosvāmī Mahārāja: Yes, this is confirmed in scripture:

cañcalaṁ hi manaḥ kṛṣṇa
pramāthi balavad dṛḍham
tasyāhaṁ nigrahaṁ manye
vāyor iva suduṣkaram

(*Bhagavad-gītā* 6.34)

> O Kṛṣṇa, because the mind is by nature restless, powerful, obstinate, and capable of completely overpowering the intelligence, body, and senses, it seems as difficult to control as the wind.

However, by *abhyāsa-yoga* (continual practice), the mind can be controlled.

abhyāsa-yoga-yuktena
cetasā nānya-gāminā
paramaṁ puruṣaṁ divyaṁ
yāti pārthānucintayan

(*Bhagavad-gītā* 8.8)

He who meditates on Me as the Supreme Personality of Godhead, his mind constantly engaged in remembering Me, undeviated from the path, he, O Pārtha, is sure to reach Me.*

If you give a boy something more tasteful than what he was already eating, he will give up what he was eating.

Śrīpāda Mādhava Mahārāja:

viṣayā vinivartante
nirāhārasya dehinaḥ
rasa-varjaṁ raso 'py asya
paraṁ dṛṣṭvā nivartate

(*Bhagavad-gītā* 2.59)

He who identifies himself with his body may restrict his enjoyment by withdrawing the senses from their objects, yet his taste for sense-pleasure still remains. One whose intelligence is fixed, however, has realized Paramātmā; therefore, his taste for sense objects automatically ceases.

Śrīla Nārāyaṇa Gosvāmī Mahārāja: Similarly, your mind is very restless with the subject matters of this world. However, when you give the mind a better food, like a *rasagullā* (a tasty sweet) in the form of the sweet pastimes of Kṛṣṇa, it will gradually give up thinking of this world.

To a 'jaundiced' person the *rasagullā* may taste bitter at first, but it is the only medicine. By continuing to eat that *rasagullā*, the sense of bitterness gradually disappears and the sweetness becomes evident.

Raghunātha dāsa: But especially in my case, which is that I am a neophyte...

Śrīla Nārāyaṇa Gosvāmī Mahārāja: In the beginning you will have to force your mind, with a whip, to focus on Kṛṣṇa. If the mind refuses to be controlled and continues to run wildly, you should 'take a whip to the horse.' If there is no running horse, there is no need of a whip.

Mahābuddhi dāsa: Can you please use that whip on us?

Śrīla Nārāyaṇa Gosvāmī Mahārāja: If you marry, you will have to make money to support your wife. If you have two or three sons or daughters, you will have to give all your energy to support and nourish them.

Then you will need a beautiful house and a car. In fact, you will need not only one car, for that will not fulfill all your desires. You will need a car for your sons and daughters, and you will all have to travel to so many places in order to see what is going on in the world. You will purchase many beautiful chairs, and a bed that costs two thousand dollars.

You will want to obtain wonderful expensive items to decorate your house, so that you can be proud when people come and marvel at it and exclaim, "Ohhh, very beautiful, very beautiful!" When your guest says, "Very good! It looks just like a palace!" you will be quite puffed up and think, "Aahhh!"

Mahābuddhi dāsa: You are describing our lives.

Śrīla Nārāyaṇa Gosvāmī Mahārāja: This is *gṛhastha* life.

Mahābuddhi dāsa: How will we get out of this?

Śrīla Nārāyaṇa Gosvāmī Mahārāja: Take my hand and come with me.

Very interesting?

Mahābuddhi dāsa: Very truthful. You have not been there, but you describe very well what it is like.

[The walk is now over, and Śrīla Nārāyaṇa Gosvāmī Mahārāja enters his quarters with a few devotees.]

Śrīla Nārāyaṇa Gosvāmī Mahārāja: Tomorrow is our last day here.

Mahābuddhi dāsa: We are sad that you are leaving here.

Śrīla Nārāyaṇa Gosvāmī Mahārāja: You are very selfish. I am going to help them as I have helped you. You are not happy about that?

Mahābuddhi dāsa: I am happy that you are going to help them, but sad that you are leaving. It is true that I am selfish. It is true, but we don't often get this opportunity.

Raghunātha dāsa: You go, Gurudeva, but at the same time you stay in our hearts.

Śrīla Nārāyaṇa Gosvāmī Mahārāja: The devotees of Mathurā and Vṛndāvana are overwhelmed by feelings of separation from me.

I have about ten thousand disciples in Mathurā, where I used to preach most of the time. Now I do not live there; I spend almost zero time there. Whenever I come to India I usually stay in Govardhana or Vṛndāvana, not so much in Mathurā. Whenever I finally go there, they weep with happiness.

Śrīla Bhaktivinoda Ṭhākura has written in his commentary on *Śrī Upadeśāmṛta* that the first three verses are not for renounced people. They are for householders.

vāco vegaṁ manasaḥ krodha-vegaṁ
jihvā-vegam udaropastha-vegam
etān vegān yo viṣaheta dhīraḥ
sarvām apīmāṁ pṛthivīṁ sa śiṣyāt

(*Śrī Upadeśāmṛta*, Verse 1)

A wise and self-composed person who can subdue the impetus to speak, the agitation of the mind, the onset of anger, the vehemence of the tongue, the urge of the belly, and the agitation of the genitals can instruct the entire world. In other words, all persons may become disciples of such a self-controlled person.

atyāhāraḥ prayāsaś ca
prajalpo niyamāgrahaḥ
jana-saṅgaś ca laulyaṁ ca
ṣaḍbhir bhaktir vinaśyati

(*Śrī Upadeśāmṛta*, Verse 2)

Bhakti is destroyed by the following six kinds of faults: (1) eating too much or collecting more than necessary, (2) endeavors that are opposed to *bhakti*, (3) useless mundane talks, (4) failure to adopt essential regulations or fanatical adherence to regulations, (5) association with persons who are opposed to *bhakti*, and (6) greed, or the restlessness of the mind to adopt worthless opinions.

utsāhān niścayād dhairyāt
tat-tat-karma-pravartanāt
saṅga-tyāgāt sato vṛtteḥ
ṣaḍbhir bhaktiḥ prasidhyati

(*Śrī Upadeśāmṛta*, Verse 3)

Progress in *bhakti* may be obtained by the following six practices: (1) enthusiasm to carry out the rules that enhance *bhakti*; (2) firm faith in the statements of *śāstra* and the *guru*, whose words are fully in line with *śāstra*; (3) fortitude in the practice of *bhakti* even in the midst of obstacles, or patience during the practice stage of *bhakti* even when there is delay in attaining one's desired goal; (4) following the limbs of *bhakti* such as hearing (*śravaṇa*) and chanting (*kīrtana*), and giving up one's material sense enjoyment for the pleasure of Śrī Kṛṣṇa; (5) giving up illicit connection with women, the association of those who are overly attached to women, and the association of Māyāvādīs, atheists, and pseudo-religionists; and (6) adopting the good behavior and character of pure devotees.

It is essential that householders learn all these principles and practice them. Then, when they become qualified, they can leave their homes. Leaving householder life prematurely will not produce a good result.

You were all *brahmacārīs* at the time of the manifest presence of your Gurudeva, Śrīla Bhaktivedānta Svāmī Mahārāja. But you did not follow all the teachings in these three verses, and that is why you fell again in the well.

Mahābuddhi dāsa: Our Gurudeva has sent you to pull us out.

Śrīla Nārāyaṇa Gosvāmī Mahārāja: Yes. "*Guru-kṛṣṇa-kṛpāya pāya bhakti-latā-bīja* – By the mercy of *guru* and Kṛṣṇa, one gets the seed of *bhakti*."

Devotee: How can I conquer pride and become humble?

Śrīla Nārāyaṇa Gosvāmī Mahārāja: You can become humble by considering that if you do not perform *bhajana* with this body, then you life is useless. You can become prideless by forgetting, "I am so wealthy, beautiful, and qualified." Always remember that you will soon become old, at which time all of your beauty will disappear. After that, when you die, if your body is buried rather than cremated, so many insects will feast on it as it rots. You can be humble by thinking in this way.

Whether or not you have good material qualities, if you are humble, *bhakti* will come to you. It is for this reason that Śrī Caitanya Mahāprabhu has uttered the verse:

tṛṇād api sunīcena
taror api sahiṣṇunā

amāninā mānadena
kīrtanīyaḥ sadā hariḥ

(*Śrī Śikṣāṣṭakam*, Verse 3)

Thinking oneself to be even lower and more worthless than insignificant grass that has been trampled beneath everyone's feet, being more tolerant than a tree, being prideless and offering respect to all others according to their respective positions, one should continuously chant the holy name of Śrī Hari.

May 28, 2008
Morning Walk

Śrīla Nārāyaṇa Gosvāmī Mahārāja: Are there any questions?

Devotee: Is it possible for you to speak something about your spiritual master, Śrīla Bhakti Prajñāna Keśava Gosvāmī Mahārāja?

Śrīla Nārāyaṇa Gosvāmī Mahārāja: Once, after taking the permission of his Gurudeva, Śrīla Bhaktisiddhānta Sarasvatī Ṭhākura, my Gurudeva went to visit Śrīla Gaura-kiśora dāsa Bābājī Mahārāja. At that time Bābājī Mahārāja had closed the door of his *bhajana-kuṭīra*, which was a municipal outhouse. He had locked himself inside and refused to meet with anyone.

The police superintendent and district magistrate had previously come there and told him, "Bābājī Mahārāja, why are you sitting in this impure place? We will make you a very beautiful place where you can do *bhajana*."

Bābājī Mahārāja had replied, "Oh, I am very weak. I cannot open the door." Why did he say this? He used to tell his devotees, "The smell of this outhouse is nothing in comparison to the stench of the sense enjoyers who come and disturb me, saying, 'Bābājī Mahārāja, give me a son, a very qualified wife, and much wealth.' They used to harass me in this way. I cannot tolerate this. Staying in an outhouse is preferable to dealing with those people. No one will disturb me while I am here."

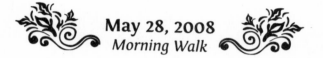

Gurudeva, along with his paternal aunt, Śrīmatī Saroja-vāsinī, and a *brahmacārī* who later became a very good speaker by the name of Śrīpāda Nemi Mahārāja, all went to see Bābājī Mahārāja. They saw that the door was closed and called to him, "Bābājī Mahārāja, please be merciful and open your door. We want to take your *darśana*.[21]"

At first, Bābājī Mahārāja gave the same answer he had given the superintendent: "I am very weak. I cannot open the door."

My Gurudeva, who was at that time eighteen-year-old Vinoda-bihārī Brahmacārī, replied, "Bābājī Mahārāja, we are disciples of Śrīla Sarasvatī Ṭhākura. He has sent us to see you."

Bābājī Mahārāja then said, "Oh, you are disciples of Śrīla Sarasvatī Ṭhākura? Okay, okay. I will open the door." He thus allowed the three devotees to enter. They went into the municipal latrine and offered their obeisances.

Bābājī Mahārāja told my Gurudeva, "You should boldly preach the mission and instructions of Śrī Caitanya Mahāprabhu. Do not fear; I will save you from all problems and dangers."

Guru Mahārāja used to tell us this story with tears in his eyes, saying, "This is how I am now able to boldly preach in Bengal and Assam and so many other places." He told us that later on this actually took place – Śrīla Gaura-kiśora dāsa Bābājī Mahārāja protected him whenever obstacles came.

For example, Śrīla Guru Mahārāja was once preaching boldly in Assam, where his audience consisted of many persons opposed to Gauḍīya Vaiṣṇavism. This group did not accept the worship of Śrīmatī Rādhikā with Śrī Kṛṣṇa; they worshiped Śrī Kṛṣṇa alone. Guru Mahārāja told them, "*Kṛṣṇa-bhakti* alone is not perfect. It is like an offense. Also, those who do *bhajana* but at the same time eat meat, eggs, and fish, and also drink alcohol, are not pure *bhaktas*. In fact their mouths are like drains, because their mouths are the containers of all kinds of stool, urine, and other wastes."

Hearing this, some of the members of the very large opposition crowd became enraged and shouted, "Caitanya Mahāprabhu is not the Supreme Lord. Do you have any proof that He is?"

In response, our Guru Mahārāja requested Śrīla Vāmana Mahārāja to stand up and provide sastric evidence that Mahāprabhu is the Supreme Lord, at which time Śrīla Vāmana Mahārāja quoted one-hundred-one Sanskrit verses.

The crowd then began to throw stones and many other things, trying to kill both Guru Mahārāja and Śrīla Vāmana Mahārāja. However, there were also some favorable persons present in the audience who began to throw stones back at the aggressors, and somehow the conflict subsided.

---

21 Meaning, "We humbly request your audience."

In this way, he used to preach boldly. If anyone said anything against Śrīla Prabhupāda Bhaktisiddhānta Sarasvatī Ṭhākura or our *sampradāya*, he would become furious. He would at once attack them, like a lion, with so many sastric arguments that no one could defeat him.

Some time in 1956, Śrīla Gurudeva came to Mathurā to visit Śrī Keśavajī Gauḍīya Maṭha. At that time some followers of the Nimbārka *sampradāya* in Vṛndāvana used to publish a spiritual journal called *Śrī Sudarśana*. In one issue they made false accusations against Śrī Caitanya Mahāprabhu, saying that He was a disciple of Keśava Kaśmīrī. They said that Keśava Kaśmīrī was not actually defeated by Śrī Caitanya Mahāprabhu. Rather, he defeated Mahāprabhu and initiated Him into the *gopāla-mantra*.[22]

When I showed this to Śrīla Gurudeva, he became extremely angry. He told me, "Bring a paper and pen," and began to dictate. He then immediately published this dictation as a short essay in our *Śrī Bhāgavata Patrikā*. The headline was 'Śrī Nimbāditya and Nimbārka are not the same person.' In the essay he said that nowhere in the scriptures is there any mention of a Nimbārka *sampradāya*. The Purāṇas mention a Vaiṣṇava *ācārya* named Śrī Nimbāditya, and the four Kumāras have accepted Nimbāditya Ācārya as their *sampradāya-ācārya*.

Nimbārka Svāmī is a completely different person. Nimbāditya was a disciple of Nāradajī at the end of Dvāpara-yuga, but Nimbārka Ācārya appeared much more recently. Great and eminent authors of scriptures, such as Śrīla Jīva Gosvāmī, have mentioned the names of the prominent *ācāryas* of all the other *sampradāyas*, but they have not mentioned the name of Nimbārka Ācārya anywhere.

The scriptures of the Six Gosvāmīs mention the names of *ācāryas* such as Śrī Rāmānuja, Śrī Mādhva, Śrī Viṣṇusvāmī, Śrī Nimbāditya, and Śrī Vallabha Ācārya. If the Nimbārka *sampradāya* had existed even to a slight extent at that time, then they would most certainly have mentioned the name of Nimbārka Ācārya as well. None of the other *sampradāya ācāryas*, such as Śrī Rāmānuja, Śrī Mādhva, Śrī Viṣṇusvāmī, and so on have mentioned Nimbārka Ācārya's name in any of the scriptures they have written."

The Nimbārka *sampradāya* currently uses the *Pārijāta-bhāṣya*, which was written, not by Nimbāditya Ācārya but rather by Śrīnivāsa

22 "The next morning the poet came to Lord Caitanya and surrendered unto His lotus feet. The Lord bestowed His mercy upon him and cut off all his bondage to material attachment" (*Śrī Caitanya-caritāmṛta, Ādi-līlā*, 16.107).

Ācārya [different from the Śrīnivāsa Ācārya in the Gauḍīya *sampradāya*] and Keśava Kaśmīrī. These two wrote this scripture and then preached that it had been written by their *guru*.[23]

When Gurudeva's essay was published in *Śrī Bhāgavata Patrikā*, the office directors of the *Sudarśana* journal announced that they were making arrangements to prosecute for slander. Śrīla Gurudeva replied firmly, "We will prove each and every word that we have written on the basis of evidence supported by *śāstra*."

The scholars filed a court case demanding one hundred thousand rupees for defamation. They went to an advocate (lawyer) who told them, "You do not know Śrīpāda Keśava Mahārāja. He is a very dangerous person. He knows the law better than we advocates do. Do not put your hands in a snake's hole, otherwise that snake will come and bite you. Better to leave this alone; better to be silent."

When the prosecution party heard about Śrīla Gurudeva's immense scriptural knowledge and profound personality, they became absolutely silent, and from that day onwards they did not dare to write any more nonsense.

Devotee: In the past you have described how affectionate your Guru Mahārāja was. Can you speak something now in this regard?

Śrīla Nārāyaṇa Gosvāmī Mahārāja: Once, while *pūjyapāda* Vāmana Gosvāmī Mahārāja was doing service at a printing press in Chuṅchuṛā, his fingers were severely injured. Our Guru Mahārāja began to weep and at once took him to a medical hospital in Kolkata, where he arranged treatment for him. Although Śrīla Vāmana Mahārāja's fingers had been crushed under the printing press, after some time they were completely healed with only a scar remaining.

There was a disciple of our Guru Mahārāja who joined before me, whose name was Anaṅga-mohana. He used to play very sweetly on *mṛdaṅga*, and he engaged in many personal services for our Guru Mahārāja, such as cooking, washing clothes, and so on.

He contracted tuberculosis, at which time he was vomiting blood, even on the body of our Guru Mahārāja. Guru Mahārāja served him with his own hand, cleaning away his stool, feeding him, and nourishing him in every way.

I told Guru Mahārāja, "Please feel free to go and preach. I will look after him. Do not worry." Kindly giving me this 'love-burden' of caring for Anaṅga-mohana, he then went to preach.

---

23 On Śrīla Nārāyaṇa Gosvāmī's request, we have added some sentences from his biography of his Guru Mahārāja to his discussion of Nimbāditya Ācārya.

I would clean Anaṅga-mohana's vomit and stool, burying it in the earth. Guru Mahārāja also sent me with him and Triguṇātīta Brahmacārī to Tambaram Hospital in Madras, which was a hospital for tuberculosis patients, and he was there for about three or four months.

Because this hospital was very expensive, Guru Mahārāja's god-brothers became upset and told him, "We cannot give you any of the money we have collected. These are such heavy expenses! Why are you doing all of this for your disciple?!" In this regard he did not care for the opinion of his opposing god-brothers, who finally gave up his association. How loving he was!

Although Guru Mahārāja spent a great deal of money to save Anaṅga-mohana, Anaṅga-mohana left his body in Tambaram Hospital. At the time of his departure Guru Mahārāja was performing *parikramā* in Navadvīpa with thousands of pilgrims. I wrote him a letter saying, "Although you gave me so much wealth to save and protect Anaṅga-mohana, I could not save him. Triguṇātīta Prabhu and I are returning to Sidhāvāḍī. Please excuse me." He read my letter and began to weep loudly.

He loved me so much for this. I had also developed slight symptoms of tuberculosis, and Guru Mahārāja took me to a hospital in Kolkata, where I was treated and recovered.

Guru Mahārāja gave *sannyāsa* first to Śrīla Vāmana Gosvāmī Mahārāja, Śrīla Trivikrama Gosvāmī Mahārāja, and me. We three then began to increase our preaching fields and we performed many other services.

Previously, Guru Mahārāja's respectful relationships with his god-brothers obliged him to be controlled by their opinions and ideas, but now he was independent. He would go to various places with thirty or forty *brahmacārīs* and *sannyāsīs*, and preach. Once he had an audience of 15,000 people. At that time there were no microphones, so his audience heard him by his loud speaking.

I was also present with him, and at those times I would cook for him, massage him, and wash his clothes. When he gave classes, I would take notes. On his order I learned Bengali and read the *Jaiva-dharma*, and then I became a very good speaker. Also, at that time I was known as the best singer in the Gauḍīya Maṭha.

ISKCON leaders know that Guru Mahārāja also gave *sannyāsa* to *parama-pūjyapāda* Śrīla Bhaktivedānta Svāmī Mahārāja. At first they wrote this in their books, but later they deleted his name. The two were bosom friends.

Mahābhuddi dāsa: How could our Śrīla Prabhupāda have been one of the co-founders of the Gauḍīya Vedānta Samiti if they were not friends? How would he have taken *sannyāsa* from him if they were not friends?

Śrīla Nārāyaṇa Gosvāmī Mahārāja: In fact, Śrīla Bhaktivedānta Svāmī Mahārāja wrote to me: "Our relationship is certainly based on spontaneous love. That is why there is no chance of us forgetting one another. By the mercy of Guru and Gaurāṅga may everything be auspicious for you. This is my constant prayer. From the first time I saw you I have been your constant well-wisher. At his first sight of me Śrīla Prabhupāda also saw me with such love. It was in my very first *darśana* of Śrīla Prabhupāda that I learned how to love."

Brajanātha dāsa: Remembering your Guru Mahārāja, you spoke for such a long time.

Śrīla Nārāyaṇa Gosvāmī Mahārāja: I became unaware of the time.

Houston Texas

May 30 - June 5, 2008

May 30, 2008
Morning Walk

Śrīla Nārāyaṇa Gosvāmī Mahārāja: Are there any questions?

Aniruddha dāsa: There is no *mādhurya-rasa* in Vaikuṇṭha. Can someone from Vaikuṇṭha attain *mādhurya-rasa*?

Śayarsi dāsa: Do they ever have an inkling of a desire to one day attain that *rasa*?

Śrīla Nārāyaṇa Gosvāmī Mahārāja: They will always have the desire to serve Śrī Śrī Lakṣmī-Nārāyaṇa.

Śrī Nārada Ṛṣi is the exception. He can reside in this world, in heaven, in Brahma-loka, in Vaikuṇṭha, in Ayodhyā with Lord Rāmacandra, and in Dvārakā, Mathurā, and Vṛndāvana. He is independent; he is not controlled by anyone. But this is not so for others; Garuḍa and Viṣvaksena cannot be situated in other *rasas*.

Śrīpāda Bhāgavata Mahārāja: So, is it good to become like Nārada, to taste everything?

Śrīla Nārāyaṇa Gosvāmī Mahārāja: You cannot be like him, in any life.

Prāṇa-govinda dāsa: Śrīla Gurudeva, can *baddha-jīvas*, conditioned souls, enter Goloka Vṛndāvana in *dāsya-rasa*?

Śrīla Nārāyaṇa Gosvāmī Mahārāja: They can enter in any *rasa*, according to their constitutional position.

Śayarsi dāsa: One of my god-brothers, named Mahā-mantra, took *sannyāsa* within the ISKCON society and is now living in New Vṛndāvana. He talks about and follows the path of *sakhya-rasa*. He says that Śrīla Prabhupāda is a *priya-narma-sakhā*.

Is it possible for Śrīla Prabhupāda to be a *mañjarī* and at the same time train his disciples who are in *sakhya-rasa*?

Śrīla Nārāyaṇa Gosvāmī Mahārāja: All *rasas* – *śānta*, *dāsya*, *sakhya*, *vātsalya*, and *mādhurya* – are present in the *gopīs' mādhurya* mood. The *gopīs* can manifest *śānta*, *dāsya*, *sakhya*, *vātsalya*, and *mādhurya*.

Śayarsi dāsa: It is okay for a particular disciple whose *sthāyī-bhāva* may be in *sakhya-rasa* to see Śrīla Prabhupāda as a *priya-narma* cowherd boy?

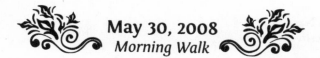

Śrīla Nārāyaṇa Gosvāmī Mahārāja: Someone can think like that if he desires, but he is quite wrong – wrong, and wrong, and wrong.

Brajanātha dāsa: That *sannyāsī* quotes from *Jaiva-dharma*, where Vijaya Kumāra and Vrajanātha see their *guru* in two different ways. One sees him as a manifestation of Subala, as a *priya-narma-sakhā*, and the other sees him as an intimate *sakhī* of Śrīmatī Rādhikā.

Śrīla Nārāyaṇa Gosvāmī Mahārāja: Actually, *pūjyapāda* Śrīla Bhaktivedānta Svāmī Mahārāja has come in the line of Śrī Caitanya Mahāprabhu and Śrīla Rūpa Gosvāmī, so he must be like them. He has written this in his books.[24]

Śrīpāda Bhāgavata Mahārāja: He has written that, "I am a servant of Śrīmatī Rādhikā."[25]

May 30, 2008
Darśana

Śrīla Nārāyaṇa Gosvāmī Mahārāja: After some days you will become old, at which time all your beauty and power will disappear. After that you will have to pass on from this world, and at that time you will not be able to take a single farthing with you. Moreover, your relatives, sons, daughters, wives, and husbands will not be able to go with you.

Śrī Kṛṣṇa has mercifully given you this human body for the sole purpose of chanting His names and remembering Him. It is only in this form that you can know, by the association of a special Vaiṣṇava *guru*, that you are transcendental *jīvas*, His maidservants (*nitya-sakhīs*). Being refugees in this world, you will have to give up these human bodies, taking nothing with you. You will be penniless. Neither your wealth, nor your reputation, nor anything else will be of any use when you pass from this world. Therefore, chant and remember Kṛṣṇa.

24 See Endnote 1 (at the end of this chapter) for quotes in this regard from the books of Śrīla Bhaktivedānta Svāmī Mahārāja.

25 "There is no harm in taking birth again and again. Our only desire should be to take birth under the care of a Vaiṣṇava. Fortunately we had the opportunity to be born of a Vaiṣṇava father who took care of us very nicely. He prayed to Śrīmatī Rādhārāṇī that in the future we would become a servant of the eternal consort of Śrī Kṛṣṇa. Thus somehow or other we are now engaged in that service" (*Śrī Caitanya-caritāmṛta, Madhya-līlā* 1.24, purport).

Viṣṇu dāsa: Can you give him blessings? His health is not good.

Śrīla Nārāyaṇa Gosvāmī Mahārāja: He should take proper medicine; especially Indian Ayurvedic medicine will help him. I went to see a very highly qualified Ayurvedic doctor in India. He gave me medicine, and now I am feeling much better. Indian Ayurvedic doctors are expert, especially South Indian doctors. There are so many such doctors in Bombay, Puna, and elsewhere.

(To Sachin) How many rounds are you chanting?

Sachin: I chant one round daily.

Śrīla Nārāyaṇa Gosvāmī Mahārāja: Within the twenty-four hours of a day you cannot find the time to chant more rounds? The holy name alone can save you. Your knowledge, wealth, mother, and father cannot save you. So, chant more. Now you are intelligent; you are going to college.

Viṣṇu dāsa: He goes to Rice University. I also attended school there.

Śrīla Nārāyaṇa Gosvāmī Mahārāja: Oh, a top university.

Viṣṇu dāsa: So Gurudeva, how do we ourselves increase our taste for chanting so that we will want to chant more and more?

Śrīla Nārāyaṇa Gosvāmī Mahārāja: We have only one energy; energy means money or any service. If we use that energy to please Kṛṣṇa and His dear devotees, doing something for them – even giving them a glass of water – *sukṛti* will come and then a taste for chanting will come. *Sādhu-saṅga, sādhu-saṅga, sādhu-saṅga.* Only by the association of elevated, *rasika-tattva-jña* Vaiṣṇavas can we develop taste (*ruci*).

Vimalā dāsī: Śrīla Gurudeva, does transcendental greed come from *sukṛti* or by the mercy of *guru*?

Śrīla Nārāyaṇa Gosvāmī Mahārāja: *Sukṛti* and the mercy of *guru* are the same, in the sense that by *sukṛti* one attains the mercy of devotees and by the mercy of devotees one develops greed.

Viṣṇu dāsa: *Śrī guru's* physical association and his instructions are the same. At the same time, when we are sitting in front of you, our minds are completely focused and peaceful and spiritualized; whereas when we are reading, our minds wander here and there.

Śrīla Nārāyaṇa Gosvāmī Mahārāja: *Vāṇī* (instructions) and *vapu* (physical presence) are the same. However, if you follow *śrī guru's* instructions, you will be attracted to Kṛṣṇa very quickly. So try to follow his words. Association means 'to follow him,' not 'to physically be with him.' It does not matter whether or not you are physically with him. If you follow his instructions, there will be an effect.

Cāru-candrikā dāsī: In *Jaiva-dharma*, Śrīla Bhaktivinoda Ṭhākura says that the *sandhinī-śakti* manifests the bodies of Rādhā, Kṛṣṇa, the *gopīs*, *gopas*, etc. How is it possible for the *sandhinī-śakti* to manifest the bodies of Śrīmatī Rādhārāṇī and the *gopīs*?

Śrīla Nārāyaṇa Gosvāmī Mahārāja: As you know, although Yogamāyā is the power of Kṛṣṇa, she controls Kṛṣṇa. How is this possible? Śrī Kṛṣṇa has made her in such a way that she can cover His own knowledge regarding His godhood and *aiśvarya* (opulence). She is the power of Kṛṣṇa, and He has empowered her to do this.

Cāru-candrikā dāsī: So Śrī Kṛṣṇa has empowered the *sandhinī-śakti* to manifest the bodies of all these personalities?

Śrīla Nārāyaṇa Gosvāmī Mahārāja: Yes.

May 31, 2008
Morning Walk

Śrīla Nārāyaṇa Gosvāmī Mahārāja: (To Śrīpāda Bhāgavata Mahārāja) I heard that you, Arun Prabhu, Viṣṇu Prabhu, and others have made a good plan for preaching and making a very good temple.

Śrīpāda Bhāgavata Mahārāja: Yes. We have a board, and we have been discussing how to develop the different stages of the plan so that we can get the temple built here.

Śrīla Nārāyaṇa Gosvāmī Mahārāja: Very good. You can all come at ten o'clock tomorrow to discuss with me how you are doing and what the plans are. I will also inspire them. All other groups have temples and preaching centers, like the Sikhs and Svāmī Nārāyaṇa, but we do not.

Jaya Ṛṣi dāsa: This devotee has been chanting on and off for five years. He is asking if you can help him to increase his chanting, both in quality and quantity.

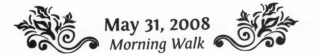

Śrīla Nārāyaṇa Gosvāmī Mahārāja: Is he following the four regulative principles?

(To the guest) You should be totally finished with meat, fish, eggs, wine, gambling, and smoking.

Jaya Ṛṣi: He is Christian.

Śrīpāda Mādhava Mahārāja: No problem.

Jaya Ṛṣi: (To the guest) You don't have to change your religion to come to Gurudeva.

Śrīla Gurudeva, Bhakta Mathew was asked to leave the ISKCON temple. He is a sincere young man and he wants to ask if you can help clarify the situation.

Śrīla Nārāyaṇa Gosvāmī Mahārāja: You can happily come to me. I will help you. I am the abode of love for all, without consideration of caste and creed. My door is open for all. All those who are being rejected can come to me. Those leaders who reject others for coming to me are unknowingly cutting off their own feet.

Mathew: How do we associate with those who are creating this division? How is it possible to associate while this division is going on?

Śrīla Nārāyaṇa Gosvāmī Mahārāja: At the time of their *gurudeva*, Śrīla Bhaktivedānta Svāmī Mahārāja, who is renowned throughout the world as Prabhupāda, everything was okay. Everyone was following his instructions. However, after his disappearance many persons gave up that submission to him, and now they want to control everyone. Simply desiring money, such persons think, "If devotees go to Nārāyaṇa Mahārāja, all money will go to him as well, and he will enjoy."

In reality, I do not want anyone for money or facilities. I am satisfied with whatever devotees easily offer as *praṇāmī* [any monetary contribution given to *sādhus* or Deities]. Without any self-interest, I want to give my wealth for the benefit of the entire world.

Śrīpāda Bhāgavata Mahārāja: If they do not allow Śrīla Gurudeva to come to their temples, then we ourselves should not go there.

Śrīla Nārāyaṇa Gosvāmī Mahārāja: It is better not to discuss this topic. It is better to discuss only *kṛṣṇa-bhakti*. If there is any question about *bhakti* or anything transcendental, you can inquire about that from me. Try to forget this other topic.

They should do what they want to do. I always think of them as my children. I know that they are doing these things out of ignorance. I excuse them. I have been helping them since the early 1980s, and I want to continue helping them.

Abhirāma dāsa: Śrīla Gurudeva, in the *Śrī Upadeśāmṛta* Śrīla Rūpa Gosvāmī says:

tan-nāma-rūpa-caritādi-sukīrtanānu-
smṛtyoḥ krameṇa rasanā-manasī niyojya
tiṣṭhan vraje tad-anurāgi-janānugāmī
kālaṁ nayed akhilam ity upadeśa-sāram

(*Śrī Upadeśāmṛta*, Verse 8)

While living in Vraja as a follower of the eternal residents of Vraja, who possess inherent spontaneous love for Śrī Kṛṣṇa, one should utilize all his time by sequentially engaging the tongue and the mind in meticulous chanting and remembrance of Kṛṣṇa's names, form, qualities, and pastimes. This is the essence of all instruction.

This is the essence of *Upadeśāmṛta*. Is there one particular verse in Śrīla Raghunātha dāsa Gosvāmī's *Manaḥ-śikṣā* that is the essence of the entire *Manaḥ-śikṣā*?

Śrīla Nārāyaṇa Gosvāmī Mahārāja: Yes:

gurau goṣṭhe goṣṭālayiṣu sujane bhūsura-gaṇe
sva-mantre śrī-nāmni vraja-nava-yuva-dvandva-śaraṇe
sadā dambhaṁ hitvā kuru ratim apūrvām atitarā-
maye svāntar bhrātaś caṭubhir abhiyāce dhṛta-padaḥ

(*Śrī Manaḥ-śikṣā*, Verse 1)

O my dear brother, my foolish mind! Taking hold of your feet, I humbly pray to you with sweet words. Please give up all pride and quickly develop sublime and incessant *rati* for *śrī gurudeva*, Śrī Vraja-dhāma, the residents of Vraja, the Vaiṣṇavas, the *brāhmaṇas*, your *dīkṣā-mantras*, the holy names of the Supreme Lord, and the shelter of Kiśora-Kiśorī Śrī Śrī Rādhā-Kṛṣṇa, the eternally youthful Divine Couple of Vraja.

Bhāgavata Mahārāja, do you know the meaning of this verse?

Śrīpāda Bhāgavata Mahārāja: No, I cannot remember the verse.

Śrīla Nārāyaṇa Gosvāmī Mahārāja: Now you are a *sannyāsī*. This is a very, very important verse, and essential for you to know. Try to read *Manaḥ-śikṣā* from beginning to end. I know you have not read it. Actually, it is important for you to read both *Manaḥ-śikṣā* and *Upadeśāmṛta*.

Mādhava Mahārāja will explain this verse.

Śrīpāda Mādhava Mahārāja: Śrīla Raghunātha dāsa Gosvāmī is praying to his mind. He is an eternal associate of Śrī Caitanya Mahāprabhu and the Divine Couple, and therefore he does not need to pray in this way. He is simply setting an example for us. Our minds are uncontrolled, whereas his mind is more than one hundred percent fixed in his *bhajana*.

Our mind is the cause of both liberation and bondage. Here, liberation means Kṛṣṇa consciousness – to go back to home, back to Godhead – and attain the service of the Divine Couple in Goloka Vṛndāvana. If the mind is favorable, then everything will be favorable. However, if the mind is uncontrolled, it creates chaos.

In this verse Śrīla Raghunātha dāsa Gosvāmī tells his mind, "O mind, I am catching hold of your feet. Please help me. I pray to you, please develop transcendental *rati* (love) for *śrī guru*. Why *guru*? Without love for *guru*, the Supreme Lord will not be satisfied. The Lord has personally said:

prathamaṁ tu guruṁ pūjya
tataś caiva mamārcanam
kurvan siddhim avāpnoti
hy anyathā niṣphalaṁ bhavet

(*Hari-bhakti-vilāsa* 4.344)

In this verse the Lord is saying, "If you want to execute *bhakti* to Me, then first worship and please your *guru*. Then, taking his permission and guidance, you can worship Me. If you do this, your activity will be *bhagavad-bhakti*; otherwise your worship will be in vain."

Thus, Śrīla Raghunātha dāsa Gosvāmī is instructing his mind to first of all develop *rati* for the lotus feet of *śrī guru*. The word *gurau* in this verse refers to both the *dīkṣā-guru* and *śikṣā-guru*.

The word *goṣṭhe* refers to the places where the Vrajavāsīs reside, like Nandagrāma, Varsāna, Madhuvana, Bhāṇḍīravana, Tālavana, Kumudvana, Bahulāvana, Kāmyavana, Khadīravana, Vṛndāvana, Baelvana, Bhadravana, Mahāvana, and Lohavana. It also refers to Navadvīpa, Gaura-maṇḍala, and Kṣetra-maṇḍala.

The word *goṣṭālayiṣu* refers to the residents of those places, like Śrīdhāma, Subala, Vasudāma, Madhumaṅgala, Nanda, Yaśodā,

Rohiṇī, Lalitā, Viśākhā, Campakalatā, Tuṅgavidyā, Raṅgadevī, Citrā, Sudevī, and moreover Śrīmatī Rādhā Ṭhākurāṇī. We must have *rati* for them.

Sujane refers to saintly persons who are not in the Gauḍīya *sampradāya*. We must respect Vaiṣṇavas in other *sampradāyas* as well.

Bhūsura-gaṇe refers to the *brāhmaṇas* living in Vraja. We must respect them also.

Śrīla Nārāyaṇa Gosvāmī Mahārāja: This especially refers to those who are established in *bhakti*.

Śrīpāda Mādhava Mahārāja: Especially those who have *bhakti* and are following the path of Kṛṣṇa consciousness.

Śrīla Nārāyaṇa Gosvāmī Mahārāja: This refers also to those devotees who are worshiping Lord Rāmacandra and Lord Nṛsiṁhadeva.

Śrīpāda Mādhava Mahārāja: All incarnations. If devotees are worshiping any incarnation of Kṛṣṇa, they are worthy of our respect.

The word *sva-mantre* indicates that after we have begged mercy from all of our worshipful personalities, we chant our own *mantras* that were given to us by our *guru*. *Sva-mantre* especially refers to the *gāyatrī mantras*.

After that, Raghunātha dāsa Gosvāmī said *śrī-nāmni*, which means *śrī harināma*. Why has he said *śrī-nāmni* instead of just *nāmni*? This is because *śrī* means Lakṣmī, the goddess of fortune, who presides over all the Vaikuṇṭha planets in the spiritual world. Śrīmatī Rādhikā is *sarva-lakṣmī-mayi* and *para-devatā*. She is the abode of all Lakṣmīs. In this way, *śrī harināma* means Hare Kṛṣṇa, or in other words, the holy names of Śrīmatī Rādhikā and Śrī Kṛṣṇa. Śrīla Raghunātha dāsa Gosvāmī is especially asking us to accept those names that are related to Śrīmatī Rādhikā.

Vraja-nava-yuva-dvandva-śaraṇe: We must give our *rati* (*prema*, or love) to the Divine Couple of Vraja, who are eternally performing Their unlimited pastimes.

Sadā dambhaṁ: we must give up the false ego by which we think, "I am a great man; I am so qualified; I am a learned scholar; I can speak very nicely and attract other people."

Whatever we are able to accomplish successfully is only by the causeless mercy of *śrī guru* and Śrī Kṛṣṇa. Śrīla Bhaktivinoda Ṭhākura has said that if we think that we are the doers and it is by our own effort that name and fame are coming to us, we will go to hell without fail. If any name and fame is coming to us, it is coming by the causeless mercy of the lotus feet of *śrī guru*. Therefore we should think, "I am not the enjoyer of this name and fame and profit. I must offer everything to the lotus feet of *śrī guru*."

Hitvā kuru ratim apūrvām atitarām: Raghunātha dāsa Gosvāmī is saying, "O my dear brother mind, you must immediately attain *rati* for these transcendental personalities. I am holding your feet and begging you to do this."

This is the essence of *Manaḥ-śikṣā*. If we remember and follow this teaching, our life will be successful and we will be able to quickly advance in our Kṛṣṇa consciousness. There is no other way.

Śrīla Nārāyaṇa Gosvāmī Mahārāja: Do you understand?

Abhirāma dāsa: Yes. Thank you.

Śrīla Nārāyaṇa Gosvāmī Mahārāja: Caitanya Mahāprabhu has said that if you want to chant "Hare Kṛṣṇa," this mood is important to imbibe:

tṛṇād api sunīcena
taror api sahiṣṇunā
amāninā mānadena
kīrtanīyaḥ sadā hariḥ

(*Śrī Śikṣāṣṭaka*, Verse 3)

> Thinking oneself to be even lower and more worthless than insignificant grass which is trampled beneath everyone's feet, being more tolerant than a tree, being prideless, and offering respect to all others according to their respective positions, one should continuously chant the holy name of Śrī Hari.

It is essential for us to meditate in this way: "I am more wretched than a blade of grass. I should be more tolerant than the trees, whose wood, leaves, bark, fruits, and flowers are for others." Even if a tree is about to die without water, he will not say, "Oh, give me water." Although someone may cut that tree, he does not protest and say, "Why are you cutting me?" He allows us to make our bed, table, and chairs with his bark and wood.

In this way, if you desire to progress on the path of pure *bhakti*, give proper respect, not only to devotees but to all living entities, because Śrī Kṛṣṇa is present with them in their hearts.

Also, do not hanker for self-interest and praise. If you follow the principles of this verse, your *bhakti* will develop without obstruction.

Brajanātha dāsa: Prabhu is asking this question: You were discussing how we must respect all living entities. In that regard, what should we do if we see cockroaches or mosquitoes in our house?

Śrīla Nārāyaṇa Gosvāmī Mahārāja: Do not kill them. Merely catch them and take them out of your house. If an ant is in your way as you are walking, try to save it. Avoid eating meat, fish, and eggs – and even walking on the grass, unless there is a good reason to walk there.

Be kind to all, otherwise Kṛṣṇa, God, will not be kind to you. Christians, Buddhists, and Muslims mostly do not follow this. They eat meat, fish, and all other abominable things.

They profess to be religious and not promote cruelty or violence, and therefore some amongst them avoid traveling by train, airplane, boat, and car so as to avoid killing other living entities; but they eat meat, fish, and eggs.

Devotee: Śrīla Gurudeva, in Alachua you told me to read your books. What book should I start with?

Śrīla Nārāyaṇa Gosvāmī Mahārāja: First read *Jaiva-dharma*, and then *Bhagavad-gītā* with the commentary of Śrīla Viśvanātha Cakravartī Ṭhākura. Then you can gradually read the *Śrīmad-Bhāgavatam* and *Śrī Caitanya-caritāmṛta*. There are also other foundational books, like Śrīla Bhaktivinoda Ṭhākura's *Bhakti-tattva-viveka*, *Śrī Śikṣāṣṭaka*, and Śrīla Viśvanātha Cakravartī Ṭhākura's *Rāga-vartma-candrikā* and *Mādhurya-kādambinī*.

Rāya-kṛṣṇa dāsa: Śrīla Gurudeva, I have the transcriptions of all of your lectures that are your commentaries on the *Vilāpa-kusumāñjali* of Śrīla Raghunātha dāsa Gosvāmī. I would like to read these transcriptions to the devotees while they honor breakfast *prasādam*. Can I read these lectures to them?

Śrīla Nārāyaṇa Gosvāmī Mahārāja: Only those who have greed, true eagerness, to read or hear these topics should do so; not others.

June 1, 2008
Morning Walk

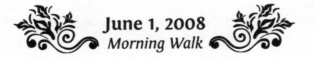

Abhirāma dāsa: Is it the correct understanding that when one accepts a *śikṣā-guru*, he is still serving his *dīkṣā-guru* in his heart and mind through the instructions of the *śikṣā-guru*? My question is this: Does one receive from the *śikṣā-guru* instructions on how to preach, where to preach, and with whom to preach? Or does he always follow those instructions he received from the *dīkṣā-guru*?

Śrīla Nārāyaṇa Gosvāmī Mahārāja: Both. If the *śikṣā-guru* is present and the *dīkṣā-guru* is not, you can take the *śikṣā-guru*'s advice.

Brajanātha dāsa: You always say that the *śikṣā-guru* should not be less than the *dīkṣā-guru*.

Śrīla Nārāyaṇa Gosvāmī Mahārāja: No, no. He will be in the same mood as your *dīkṣā-guru*, and favorable to your *dīkṣā-guru*. If he has an opposing idea, he cannot be your *śikṣā-guru*. If he criticizes your *dīkṣā-guru* and does not have affection for him, he cannot be your *śikṣā-guru*.

Indubhūṣaṇa dāsa: Śrī Kṛṣṇa performs miraculous pastimes in Vṛndāvana. Why doesn't anybody there know that He is God?

Śrīla Nārāyaṇa Gosvāmī Mahārāja: This is due to Kṛṣṇa's *yogamāyā-śakti*. Kṛṣṇa has a very powerful potency, known as *yogamāyā*. We cannot even imagine in what ways and to what extent she is inconceivable. Even Kṛṣṇa forgets His supremacy under her influence, and so do Mother Yaśodā and all other residents of Vṛndāvana. But sometimes, for instance when Kṛṣṇa lifted Girirāja Govardhana, some of the Vrajavāsīs may have thought, "Oh, who is He? No ordinary person can do this. He must be a demigod, or something like that."

June 4, 2008
Morning Walk

Aniruddha dāsa: Śrīla Gurudeva, how do we get *sukṛti*?

Śrīla Nārāyaṇa Gosvāmī Mahārāja: I will give you an example to help you understand. For example, you earn money to maintain your wife, your children, and yourself.

Aniruddha dāsa: Actually Kṛṣṇa maintains everything. I do not do anything.

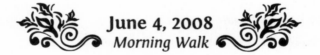

Śrīpāda Mādhava Mahārāja: In that case, Kṛṣṇa will ask your question. You don't have to ask your question.

Śrīla Nārāyaṇa Gosvāmī Mahārāja: In that case, come to stay with me – at once – and Kṛṣṇa will maintain you. Put on saffron cloth. Since you don't do anything at your home, don't return there. I will not let you go; I will keep you with me.

You say you don't maintain your family. Even if that were true, other people have to maintain their families. So, for people who have to maintain their families…

Aniruddha dāsa: They think they maintain…

Śrīla Nārāyaṇa Gosvāmī Mahārāja: Whether you accept it or deny it, they maintain their families.

In the same way, if they serve a high-class Vaiṣṇava, if they go to a holy *dhāma* like Vṛndāvana, Navadvīpa, or Jagannātha Purī, or if they spend some money for *vaiṣṇava-sevā* and *tulasī-sevā*, they will get *sukṛti*.

This *sukṛti* will help us. *Sādhu-saṅga* will come as a result of it, and then a taste in *hari-kathā* will come. This is the process.

> *bhaktis tu bhagavad-bhakta-saṅgena parijāyate*
> *sat-saṅga-prāpyate pumbhiḥ sukṛtaiḥ pūrva-sañcitaiḥ*
>
> (*Bṛhan-nāradīya Purāṇa* 4.33)

> *Bhakti* becomes manifested by the association of the Lord's devotees. The association of devotees is obtained by previously accumulated piety (*sukṛti*).

Aniruddha dāsa: When Śrīla Prabhupāda came to the Western countries, he said that he was creating the devotees' *sukṛti*.

Śrīla Nārāyaṇa Gosvāmī Mahārāja: This is correct.

Aniruddha dāsa: How did he do it?

Śrīla Nārāyaṇa Gosvāmī Mahārāja: For example, he approached the devotees and said, "I will take *prasādam* here today." Then, when the devotees served him *prasādam*, they received *sukṛti*. He also told them, "I want some cloth. Can you please give me some cloth?" The devotees who served him in that connection also received *sukṛti*. He did not personally require anything. He requested services only to give *sukṛti*.

Do you know why I just told you to renounce your family life and come to stay with me? I was not actually telling you that Kṛṣṇa is doing everything to maintain your family and you are doing nothing. It is you who have said this. You implied that you do not have any freedom; Kṛṣṇa does everything and you do nothing; only Kṛṣṇa acts; you do only what He inspires you to do.

This idea is incorrect. The *jīva* has independence, and when he misuses that independence and does something wrong, Kṛṣṇa punishes him.

Prāṇa-govinda dāsa: Śrīla Gurudeva, Śrīla Bhaktisiddhānta Sarasvatī Ṭhākura says in his *Upadeśāvalī*, "Serving the Vrajavāsīs who felt great separation from Kṛṣṇa when He left Vraja to reside in Mathurā is our supreme constitutional occupation." Can you please explain this?

Śrīla Nārāyaṇa Gosvāmī Mahārāja: He has explained this himself; what is the need to explain further?

Do you know the meaning of *mathurā-viraha*? When Śrī Kṛṣṇa leaves Vṛndāvana and goes to Mathurā and Dvārakā, the Vrajavāsīs feel great separation. They weep bitterly, they faint, and they manifest ecstatic symptoms such as *divyonmāda* and *pralāpa*. In the *gopīs'* divine madness, they experienced the extreme manifestations of the eight kinds of *sāttvika-bhāvas*. Uddhavajī saw this and was struck with wonder.

In this life, you will have to experience the nature of their separation mood. If you somehow become qualified to serve them in their feelings of separation, you have attained the aim and object of life.

June 5, 2008
Morning Walk

Aniruddha dāsa: It seems that this verse is related to *acintya-bhedābheda-tattva*:

sākṣād-dharitvena samasta-śāstrair
uktas tathā bhāvyata eva sadbhiḥ
kintu prabhor yaḥ priya eva tasya
vande guroḥ śrī-caraṇāravindam

(*Śrī Gurvaṣṭaka*, Verse 7)

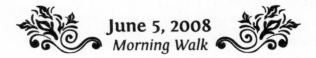

> All the scriptures proclaim *śrī gurudeva* to be *sākṣāt-hari-tva*, endowed with the potency of Śrī Hari, and he is also considered by all the great saints to be His direct representative. Indeed, *śrī gurudeva* is very dear to the Lord, being His confidential servitor (*acintya-bhedābheda prakāśa-vigraha*, the inconceivable different and non-different worshipable manifestation of the Lord). I offer prayers unto his lotus feet.

How can I understand that *guru* is a manifestation of Kṛṣṇa, simultaneously one with and different from Him?

Śrīla Nārāyaṇa Gosvāmī Mahārāja: There are many kinds of *gurus*, including *dīkṣā-guru*, *śikṣā-guru*, *vartma-pradarśaka guru*, and *caitya-guru*. Do you know about all these types of *guru*?

Kṛṣṇa is *caitya-guru* in the heart of every living being. Any Vaiṣṇava can be a *vartma-pradarśaka guru*, meaning 'he who takes one to a real *guru*.' Then, there is *śikṣā-guru* and *dīkṣā-guru*. The *dīkṣā-guru* and Kṛṣṇa are simultaneously one and different. What does this mean? Kṛṣṇa has two features, namely *viṣaya-kṛṣṇa* and *āśraya-kṛṣṇa*. *Viṣaya-kṛṣṇa* is Kṛṣṇa Himself, and *āśraya-kṛṣṇa* is that personality who perfectly teaches Kṛṣṇa's identity. Because *guru* takes the disciple to the Supreme Lord, he is known as *āśraya-bhagavān*. Try to understand this.

Kṛṣṇa Himself is *viṣaya-tattva* (the object of worship) and *guru* is *āśraya-tattva* (the perfect worshiper). *Śrī guru* takes us to Kṛṣṇa Bhagavān, so He is Bhagavān in the form of *guru*; he is as good as Bhagavān. At the same time, he is most near and dear to Kṛṣṇa; he is the devotee (*bhakta*), not the Supreme Lord Himself. Both are the same from the perspective of being *guru*, but from the perspective of the worshipable Deity, they are not the same.

ENDNOTES

1 "Without the *gopīs*, these pastimes between Rādhā and Kṛṣṇa cannot be nourished. Only by their cooperation are such pastimes broadcast. It is their business to taste these mellows" (*Śrī Caitanya-caritāmṛta, Madhya-līlā* 8.203).

"The Vedānta says that God is *ānandamaya*, full of bliss and pleasure, and we are part and parcel of God, we are also of the same quality. *Ānandamayo 'bhyāsāt*. So our whole process is to join the supreme *ānandamaya*, Kṛṣṇa, in His dance party. That will make us actually happy" (Lecture on *Bhagavad-gītā* 6.1 Los Angeles, February 13, 1969).

"Unless you take shelter under the shade of the lotus feet of Nityānanda, *rādhā-kṛṣṇa pāite nāi*, it will be very difficult to approach Rādhā-Kṛṣṇa. This Kṛṣṇa consciousness movement is for approaching Rādhā-Kṛṣṇa, to be associated with the Supreme Lord in His sublime pleasure dance. That is the aim of Kṛṣṇa consciousness. So Narottama dāsa Ṭhākura's advice is, 'If you actually want to enter into the dancing party of Rādhā-Kṛṣṇa, then you must take shelter of the lotus feet of Nityānanda'" (Purport to *Nitāi-Pada-Kamala*, Los Angeles, December 21, 1968).

"Without the help of the *gopīs*, one cannot enter into these pastimes. Only one who worships the Lord in the ecstasy of the *gopīs*, following in their footsteps, can engage in the service of Śrī Śrī Rādhā-Kṛṣṇa in the bushes of Vṛndāvana. Only then can one understand the conjugal love between Rādhā and Kṛṣṇa. There is no other procedure for understanding" (*Śrī Caitanya-caritāmṛta, Madhya-līlā* 8.204–205).

"The means for returning home, for going back to Godhead, is devotional service, but everyone has a different taste in the Lord's service. One may be inclined to serve the Lord in servitude (*dāsya-rasa*), fraternity (*sakhya-rasa*), or parental love (*vātsalya-rasa*), but none of these can enable one to enter into the service of the Lord in conjugal love. To attain such service, one has to follow in the footsteps of the *gopīs* in the ecstasy of *sakhī-bhāva*. Then only can one understand the transcendental mellow of conjugal love" (*Śrī Caitanya-caritāmṛta, Madhya-līlā* 8.204–205, purport).

San Francisco, California
June 7-20, 2008

June 7, 2008
Darśana

[Śrīla Nārāyaṇa Gosvāmī Mahārāja requested the devotees to sing this kīrtana:]

hari hari kabe mora ha'be hena dina
vimala vaiṣṇave, rati upajibe, vāsanā haibe kṣīṇa

O Hari! O Mahāprabhu! When will the fortunate day come when *rati*, deep love and attachment, will come in my heart for the lotus feet of the pure-hearted Vaiṣṇavas? [At that time I will honor and serve them, and thus all my material desires and *anarthas*, especially lust and anger, will disappear.]

antara-bāhire, sama vyavahāra, amānī mānada ha'ba
kṛṣṇa-saṅkīrtane, śrī-kṛṣṇa-smaraṇe, satata majiyā ra'ba

With a heart free from duplicity, my outer behavior will correspond to my inner feelings and thoughts. [Seeing myself as completely insignificant] I will give all respect to others, seeking no honor in return. Always dancing and singing the holy names, I will remain constantly absorbed in remembering Śrī Kṛṣṇa's beautiful pastimes.

e dehera kriyā, abhyāse koriba, jīvana jāpana lāgi'
śrī-kṛṣṇa-bhajane, anukūla jāhā, tāhe ha'ba anurāgī

My bodily maintenance should simply go on by habit so that my mind can be fully given to *harināma*. I will become attached only to that which is favorable for serving Śrī Kṛṣṇa.

bhajanera jāhā, pratikūla tāhā, dṛḍha-bhāve teyāgiba
bhajite bhajite, samaya āsile, e deha chāḍiyā diba

I will firmly reject whatever is unfavorable for His service. Continuing to do *bhajana*, in time I will give up this body [happily and peacefully].

bhakativinoda, ei āśā kari', basiyā godruma-vane
prabhu-kṛpā lāgi', vyākula antare, sadā kānde saṅgopane

> Residing alone in the forest of Godruma and continuously weeping, Bhaktivinoda anxiously prays, "I am living only with the hope that Mahāprabhu will bestow His mercy upon me."

Śrīla Nārāyaṇa Gosvāmī Mahārāja: When one remembers Kṛṣṇa, his bodily hairs stand on end, tears come in his eyes, and many *sāttvika-bhāvas* manifest in his heart.

Rādhā-kānta dāsa: *Vimala vaiṣṇave, rati upajibe, vāsanā haibe kṣīṇa* means "By attachment to a *rasika tattva-jñā* Vaiṣṇava, my material desires will be destroyed."

Antara-bāhire, sama vyavahāra, amānī mānada ha'ba. Antara means 'internal' and *bāhire* means 'external.' Śrīla Bhaktivinoda Ṭhākura is praying, "Oh, when will that fortunate day come when my external activities – my speaking, thoughts, and actions – will be one with my internal aspirations to serve Rādhā and Kṛṣṇa? I will then be able to offer all respects to others, without expecting any respect in return."

Kṛṣṇa-saṅkīrtane, śrī-kṛṣṇa-smaraṇe, satata majiyā ra'ba. This means "Thus, while performing *śrī kṛṣṇa-saṅkīrtana*, I will be absorbed in remembering the name, form, qualities and pastimes of Śrī Kṛṣṇa at all times."

E dehera kriyā, abhyāse koriba, jīvana jāpana lāgi'. This means that I should try to mould my life in such a way that I can live very simply, not spending much time, energy, and effort on my bodily maintenance.

Śrīla Nārāyaṇa Gosvāmī Mahārāja: *Abhyāse kori.* This phrase means that Śrīman Mahāprabhu never put any effort or thought into eating or maintaining the body. *Abhyāse* means "I am eating, but my mind is with Kṛṣṇa."

Rādhā-kānta dāsa: *Śrī-kṛṣṇa-bhajane, anukūla jāhā, tāhe ha'ba anurāgī.* This means "When will that day come that I will be greatly attached to performing only those activities which are favorable to *kṛṣṇa-bhajana?*"

Śrīla Nārāyaṇa Gosvāmī Mahārāja: What is the meaning of *anurāga*?

Rādhā-kānta dāsa: With attachment.

Śrīla Nārāyaṇa Gosvāmī Mahārāja: Only 'attachment'?

Rādhā-kānta dāsa: *Anurāga* means 'great intense feeling.'

Śrīla Nārāyaṇa Gosvāmī Mahārāja: The stage after *bhāva-bhakti* is *prema*. As *prema* develops it becomes *sneha*, *māna*, *praṇaya*, *rāga*, and then *anurāga*.[26] *Anurāga* is a most elevated mood. One in *anurāga* is totally colored, or saturated, in love and affection for Śrī Kṛṣṇa. *Anurāga* means *nitya-navīnā rāga*, or continuous ever-fresh, ever-new feelings of love for Śrī Kṛṣṇa.

Rādhā-kānta dāsa: *Bhajite bhajite, samaya āsile, e deha chāḍiyā diba.* This means "If I constantly do *bhajana* like this, then one day, when my body will be given up, I will very easily…

Śrīla Nārāyaṇa Gosvāmī Mahārāja: No, no, no. This is not the meaning. *E deha chāḍiyā diba* means "I will give up my body. I will not be controlled by death; I will control death."

This state is very, very hard to achieve: The devotee gives up his body by his own will, without any problems. It is likened to taking off cloth from the body.

Rādhā-kānta dāsa: *Bhakativinoda, ei āśā kari', basiyā godruma-vane.* This means that Śrīla Bhaktivinoda Ṭhākura is residing in Godruma forest at the end of his life. He has given up everything. He is doing *bhajana* and bitterly weeping. He has one hope: *ei āśā kari' prabhu-kṛpā lāgi', vyākula antare.*

Śrīla Nārāyaṇa Gosvāmī Mahārāja: What is the meaning here? Śrīla Bhaktivinoda Ṭhākura is thinking, "I am continually waiting for the mercy of Kṛṣṇa. When will the day come that I will attain these devotional qualities? I do not have these qualities now, but when His mercy comes, I will be successful."

All of Śrīla Bhaktivinda Ṭhākura's prayers are very high-class like this one. If one follows even one line…

Rāmacandra dāsa: He was living in Godrumadvīpa, but he wrote *ei āśā kari*, which means that he is praying to live in Godruma. How is it that he desires to live there when he is already living there?

Śrīla Nārāyaṇa Gosvāmī Mahārāja: No, no. He is not praying for residence in Godrumadvīpa. Living there, he is waiting for the mercy of Śrī Kṛṣṇa, and praying, "When will I attain all these devotional qualities?"

Now we will sing *Yaśomatī-nandana*, which also contains very deep meanings.

---

[26] See Endnote 1 (at the end of this chapter) for the definitions of the stages of *prema*, as explained in *Jaiva-dharma*, Chapter 36.

[All devotees then sing Yaśomatī-nandana:]

yaśomatī-nandana vraja-vara-nāgara,
gokula-rañjana kāna
gopī-parāṇa-dhana madana-manohara,
kālīya-damana-vidhāna

Kṛṣṇa is Yaśodā-maiyā's beloved son, and the topmost lover in Vrajabhūmi. As Kāna (an affectionate name for Him) He delights Gokula and is the wealth of the life of the *gopīs*. He is an inveterate thief, stealing the hearts of all, and He crushed the Kāliya serpent.

amala harināma amiya-vilāsā
vipina-purandara navīna-nāgara-vara,
vaṁśī-vadana, suvāsā

These spotless holy names are filled with all of Kṛṣṇa's sweet pastimes. He is the king of all the forests of Vraja. He is the ever-fresh and ever-youthful lover, always wearing very beautiful garments, attracting the *gopīs* with His bodily fragrance, and holding the flute to His mouth.

vraja-jana-pālana asura-kula-nāśana,
nanda-godhana-rākhowālā
govinda, mādhava navanīta-taskara,
sundara nanda-gopālā

He always protects the Vrajavāsīs, destroys the demons, and tends Nanda Bābā's cows. As Govinda, He gives pleasure to the cows, land, *gopas*, *gopīs*, and the senses. As Mādhava, He is the husband of the topmost Lakṣmī – Śrīmatī Rādhikā. He is always stealing butter (the *prema* of the Vrajavāsīs) to increase the Vrajavāsīs' love for Him, and He is the beautiful son of Nanda Bābā.

yamunā-taṭa-cara gopī-vasanahara,
rāsa-rasika kṛpāmaya
śrī rādhā-vallabha vṛndāvana-naṭavara,
bhakativinoda-āśraya

Roaming along the banks of Yamunā, He stole the clothes of the very young *gopīs*. He is the enjoyer of the *rāsa* dance and is full of mercy. He is most beloved to Śrīmatī

Rādhārāṇī and is the most expert dancer in Vṛndāvana. Bhaktivinoda wants to take shelter of this Kṛṣṇa.

[Training the devotees in the correct way to sing this song with all its nuances of melody, Śrīla Nārāyaṇa Gosvāmī Mahārāja then requests the devotees to sing the entire song again, this time personally leading the singing.]

Śrīla Nārāyaṇa Gosvāmī Mahārāja: What is the meaning?

Rādhā-kānta dāsa: These are names of Śrī Kṛṣṇa which describe His pastimes. The son of Yaśodā-devī is the hero of all of the residents of Vraja.

Śrīla Nārāyaṇa Gosvāmī Mahārāja: *Nāgara* means 'the most beloved of all the *gopīs*.' He is the life and soul of all the Vrajavāsīs, but He is the *nāgara* only of the *gopīs*. He is especially *rādhā-nāgara*, the most beloved of Śrīmatī Rādhikā.

Gokula-rañjana kāna: He performs sweet pastimes that make all of the Vrajavāsīs extremely happy and which cause them to sink in an ocean of love and affection.

This is also written in *Śrī Dāmodarāṣṭakam* (Verse 3):

itīdṛk-sva-līlābhir ānanda-kuṇḍe
sva-ghoṣaṁ nimajjantam ākhyāpayantam
tadīyeśita-jñeṣu bhaktair jitatvaṁ
punaḥ prematas taṁ śatāvṛtti vande

By childhood pastimes such as this, He perpetually immerses the inhabitants of Gokula in pools of pure bliss, and through them He informs the devotees desirous of knowing His aspect of supreme opulence and majesty that He is conquered only by those who are free from knowledge of His *aiśvarya*. With great love, I again and again worship that Dāmodara Śrī Kṛṣṇa.

Śrī Kṛṣṇa plays with all of His *sakhās*, giving them an abundance of love. He performs innumerable sweet pastimes in the house of Nanda and Yaśodā, and He is always playing, singing, and dancing with the *gopīs*.

Gopī-parāṇa-dhana, madana-manohara: He is the wealth of the life of the *gopīs*. He bewilders even Cupid himself, because His beauty defeats that of millions of Cupids. How? On the full moon night, during the *rāsa* dance, in a very secluded place on the bank of the river, cuckoos were singing, bees were humming, gentle breezes were blowing, and flowers were in bloom. No one besides Kṛṣṇa and the *gopīs* were present there, where, touching the *gopīs*, Śrī Kṛṣṇa danced and played with them. Moreover Kāmadeva (Cupid) was also not present there, meaning that neither Kṛṣṇa nor the *gopīs* were influenced by lusty desires.

Kālīya-damana-vidhāna: Yaśodā-nandana is very soft, and simultaneously He is like a thunderbolt. He controlled the Kāliya serpent like a thunderbolt, saying, "Go away from here." He was rhythmically dancing on Kāliya's hoods and crushing his hoods. As blood gushed from Kāliya's mouths, Kāliya began to think, "Who is He? I fought with Garuḍa, who is extremely powerful, but this person is so much more powerful!" Thus, Kāliya surrendered.

Amala harināma amiya-vilāsā: Kṛṣṇa's names are non-different from Him. The holy names are non-different from the possessor of those names. Thus, by the performance of *saṅkīrtana* of the holy names, all of Kṛṣṇa's pastimes are present. When you sing this *kīrtana*, all the pastimes manifest.

Vipina-purandara: *Vipina* indicates Vṛndāvana. *Purandara* consists of *pura* (complete, or full) plus *indra* (master). Kṛṣṇa is Purandara, the full master, of Vṛndāvana. His footprints, marked with the club, lotus, disk, and conch shell – nineteen auspicious signs – are found everywhere in Vṛndāvana. There is no place in Vṛndāvana where Śrī Kṛṣṇa has not performed pastimes. By each tree, on the bank of Yamunā River, on the bank of Mānasī-gaṅgā, in Kāmyavana, here and there and everywhere, He is performing His sweet pastimes and playing His flute.

Navīna-nāgara-vara: The *gopīs* see Kṛṣṇa as 'newer and newer' at every moment. Moment by moment, He is ever-increasingly ever-new and ever-fresh. In fact, even while dancing and singing with Him, Rādhikā thinks, "Who is He? I have never seen Him before."

Vaṁśī-vadana: Kṛṣṇa is always playing on the flute, and by His expert flute-playing He controls everyone. However, He personally declares, "If Rādhikā very sweetly says anything, I forget to play My flute." All of Kṛṣṇa's sweet pastimes reside in His names.

Yamunā-taṭa-cara: He is present on the bank of the Yamunā. Why does He go there? What is it there that attracts Him?

Rādhā-kānta dāsa: There is very beautiful sand, and the moon is rising.

Śrīla Nārāyaṇa Gosvāmī Mahārāja: No, nothing of the sort. The *gopīs* go there to take water, and that is why Kṛṣṇa goes there. *Gopī-vasanahara* means "Kṛṣṇa took all of the clothes of the *gopīs*."

Rāsa-rasika kṛpāmaya: He is very fond of *rāsa* – dancing and singing. When He sings in the fifth note (*sa, re, ga, ma, pa, da, ni*), Lalitā and Viśākhā sing higher than Him. Śrīmatī Rādhikā sings the highest, enlivening Kṛṣṇa to clap and call out, "*Sādhu, sādhu,*" meaning "Bravo, bravo!"

Śrīpāda Mādhava Mahārāja: He could not reach that high note.

Śrīla Nārāyaṇa Gosvāmī Mahārāja: Śrīla Bhaktivinoda Ṭhākura is not less than Śrīla Narottama Ṭhākura; he is the Seventh Gosvāmī. All of these hidden meanings reside in his *kīrtanas*.

I have come here only to give the gift of these deep meanings.

(To Rādhā-kānta dāsa) I have given you the management to oversee, and I will simply give these deep truths. I have not come to make temples and manage the Society's affairs. *Praṇāmī* (donations) are coming, and with these donations I am serving Vraja, Navadvīpa, and Jagannātha Purī dhāma, the dearmost pastime places of Śrī Caitanya Mahāprabhu. But my real purpose is to give what I have realized. Sometimes people do not understand me or what I am doing.

June 20, 2008
Morning Walk

Śrīla Nārāyaṇa Gosvāmī Mahārāja: *Parama-pūjyapāda* Śrī Śrīmad Bhaktivedānta Svāmī Mahārāja called for me just before he departed from this world, and I came to his bedside. At that time he told his disciples "Be always under Nārāyaṇa Mahārāja's guidance; learn something from him. I brought you all, but I could not complete your training." Perhaps you were there?

Bhagavān dāsa: I have heard this many times. That's why I was saying in Badger, "It's about love and it's about the heart. All you have to do is see with your heart.

Śrīla Nārāyaṇa Gosvāmī Mahārāja: Many of the ISKCON leaders are doing nonsense, but I don't mind. I still have so much affection for them. I think of them as my children.

Śrīpāda Mādhava Mahārāja: When children are small, they can pull their father's and mother's hair, no problem. But when they are big…

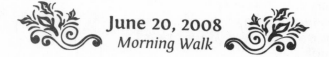

Bhagavān dāsa: The problem is that they are not small.

Śrīla Nārāyaṇa Gosvāmī Mahārāja: They fear that "If devotees mix with Nārāyaṇa Mahārāja, they will be attracted to him and we will be nothing." This is their only fear. I wanted to visit all the places where he stayed or visited, but the ISKCON leaders banned me, saying, "You cannot go there."

Bhagavān dāsa: In Vedic culture even the enemy is supposed to be welcome, what to speak of *sādhus*.

Śrīla Nārāyaṇa Gosvāmī Mahārāja: Yes. They welcome Māyāvādīs, so many cinema actors, so many bogus people. I have told them, "If you are favorable, I will not initiate your disciples or anyone who has a connection with you." But they are not interested.

They think that their disciples are their property. I do not think that way. If any of my disciples want to be with them and learn from them, they are free to do so.

Śrīpāda Mādhava Mahārāja: Some of Śrīla Gurudeva's disciples are serving in ISKCON. Śrīla Gurudeva has no problem with that; they are serving God, Kṛṣṇa, so what harm is there?

Advaita dāsa: Śrīla Gurudeva, I have a question. To be born where Kṛṣṇa is performing His pastimes in *bhauma-līlā*, Kṛṣṇa's pastimes in the material world, a person needs to achieve *vastu-siddhi* (one's spiritual body, which is fit to serve Rādhā and Kṛṣṇa). Is it easier to be born in the place where Lord Caitanya is having His pastimes?

Śrīla Nārāyaṇa Gosvāmī Mahārāja: Do not think about these things right now. At this time in your development of *bhakti*, it is better to think, "How can I give up my *anarthas*, lust, and worldly desires?" After that, what is to be will come automatically. You need not bother about this. Kṛṣṇa and His Yogamāyā will think about what to do for you.

Our only problem now is our *anarthas*. If *anarthas* are present in our heart, we cannot advance, and that is why I spoke in class on the topic in Śrīla Jagadānanda Paṇḍita's *Prema-vivarta*. Jagadānanda Paṇḍita has told everything we need to know regarding how to become free from *anarthas*. He has left nothing unsaid.

Śrīla Rūpa Gosvāmī has explained the same principles in *Śrī Upadeśāmṛta*. Therefore, I tell everyone to first read *Upadeśāmṛta*, and then *Śrī Manaḥ-śikṣā*. However, many want to jump from the root to the top of the tree, where the fruit is situated, and they are falling down. They think, "Now I am the master of all these confidential topics." But they are not; they cannot give up their unfavorable desires.

Rādhā-kānta dāsa: Gurudeva, you have also said that we should meditate on the positive – Kṛṣṇa's *līlā* – then automatically, through the potency of *bhakti*, *anarthas* will go away. So, to what extent should we think about our *anarthas*?

Śrīla Nārāyaṇa Gosvāmī Mahārāja: One first meditates on the pastimes of Śrī Caitanya Mahāprabhu, and when that meditation matures, automatically it will be transferred to Kṛṣṇa. Jagadānanda Paṇḍita Prabhu has explained this.

Rādhā-kānta dāsa: Should we simultaneously study and meditate on *mahāprabhu-līlā* and *kṛṣṇa-līlā* or in the beginning primarily on Mahāprabhu's *līlā*?

Śrīla Nārāyaṇa Gosvāmī Mahārāja: We should meditate on Śrīman Mahāprabhu, and also on what He has told about Kṛṣṇa. Both. Then, when our service mood towards Mahāprabhu matures, it will automatically go to Kṛṣṇa.

Some devotees don't read *Śrī Sanātana-śikṣā*[27]. They only read the topics of *rāsa*, and they will not 'come down' from those topics.

Rādhā-kānta dāsa: If we accept a path of a higher qualification than our current qualification, is that *niyamāgraha*[28]?

Śrīla Nārāyaṇa Gosvāmī Mahārāja: Yes, yes.

Rādhā-kānta dāsa: This is a criticism of our *saṅga* from those outside our *saṅga*. They say that because we have association with such a high-class *rasika* Vaiṣṇava, many devotees may fall victim to this.

Śrīla Nārāyaṇa Gosvāmī Mahārāja: I always give classes on *Śrī Sanātana-śikṣā*, *Rāya Rāmānanda Saṁvāda*, the subjects of *Śrīmad-Bhāgavatam* like Prahlāda Mahārāja, *Bharata-caritra* (the life history

---

27 The teachings of Śrī Caitanya Mahāprabhu to Śrīla Sanātana Gosvāmī.

28 *Niyamāgraha* is one of the six impediments to *bhakti*, as described by Śrīla Rūpa Gosvāmī in the second verse of *Śrī Upadeśāmṛta*. The word *niyamāgraha*, when broken into its constituent parts, has two meanings: (1) *niyama* + *āgraha* means over-zealousness in following rules; and (2) *niyama* + *agraha* means failure to accept rules. When the first meaning is applied, it refers to enthusiasm for those rules that yield an inferior result, such as promotion to the heavenly planets, leaving aside the endeavor for the superior attainment of the service of the Lord. When the second meaning is applied, it refers to indifference towards those rules that nourish *bhakti*.

and character of Bharata Mahārāja), and Ajāmila. Although I don't speak about the topics of *rāsa*, as an example I sometimes quote Sanskrit verses on the subject.[29]

Bhagavān dāsa: Śrīla Prabhupāda wrote about *rāsa-līlā* in the *Kṛṣṇa Book*. Then he had all the devotees in every country go and distribute it on the streets – to people who didn't know anything about Kṛṣṇa consciousness. He also had the devotees distribute other, similar books, like *Teachings of Lord Caitanya*.

ENDNOTES

1 Definitions of the stages of *prema* from *Jaiva-dharma*, Chapter 36:

Śrī Gopāla Guru Gosvāmī: ...*Madhura-rati* is made unshakable by the presence of antagonistic elements. Then it is called *prema*. This *prema* gradually manifests its own sweetness as it develops into *sneha*, *māna*, *praṇaya*, *rāga*, *anurāga*, and *bhāva*... Just as the seed of sugar cane grows and progressively develops into cane juice, *guḍa*, *khaṇḍa*, *śarkarā*, *sitā*, and *sitotpala*, similarly *rati*, *prema*, *sneha*, *māna*, *praṇaya*, *rāga*, *anurāga*, and *bhāva* are all one substance in progressive stages of development. In this context, the word *bhāva* refers to *mahābhāva*.

Vijaya Kumāra: Why have you referred to all these *bhāvas* as *prema* when they all have different names?

Śrī Gopāla Guru Gosvāmī: *Paṇḍitas* have used the word *prema* to denote all the stages beginning with *sneha* because they are six progressive stages in the development of the unmitigated pleasure sports (*vilāsa*) of *prema* itself. As *prema* for Śrī Kṛṣṇa appears in His *bhaktas*, the corresponding type of *prema* also arises in Kṛṣṇa for His *bhaktas*.

Vijaya Kumāra: What is the primary characteristic of *prema*?

Śrī Gopāla Guru Gosvāmī: In *madhura-rasa*, the bond of emotion between the Youthful Couple never breaks despite there being cause for the destruction of the relationship. That indestructible emotional bond is called *prema*...

When *prema* attains its ultimate limit and illuminates the lamp of the *citta* (mind) and melts the heart, it is called *sneha*. Here the word *citta* denotes the attainment of the object (*viṣaya*) of *prema*. The marginal characteristic of *sneha* is that one is never satiated, despite repeatedly looking at the object of one's affection... *Māna* is *sneha* that has attained the pinnacle of its excellence and has externally assumed a guileful or crooked mood to cause the *nāyaka* and *nāyikā* to realize a new sweetness...

Vijaya Kumāra: What is *praṇaya*?

---

29 Śrīla Mahārāja spoke on these topics, but only in special places with a special audience. Some of these *darśanas* have since been transcribed and published as books, such as *Veṇu-gīta* and *Gopī-gīta*.

Regarding the publishing of these and other books of similar topics, if he had not done this, we would be in complete darkness, swallowed by the speculations of third- and fourth-class persons in the garb of Vaiṣṇavas. We would have no other option but to read their concoctions. By Śrīla Mahārāja's causeless mercy, authentic Gauḍīya Vaiṣṇava literatures have been published for the benefit of all present, as well as future, sincere spiritual aspirants – ed.

Śrī Gopāla Guru Gosvāmī: When *māna* is imbued with *viśrambha* so that one considers oneself non-different from one's beloved, it is called *praṇaya*...

Vijaya Kumāra: Now please describe the symptoms of *rāga*.

Śrī Gopāla Guru Gosvāmī: *Praṇaya* is called *rāga* in its highest state, when even extreme distress seems like happiness.

Vijaya Kumāra: *Rāga* is now clear to me. Kindly describe *anurāga*.

Śrī Gopāla Guru Gosvāmī: When *rāga* soars to heights of new, ever-fresh *bhāva* – that allows the *nāyikā* to perceive the *nāyaka* at every moment as novel and perennially unique – then *rāga* has been transformed into *anurāga*.

Badger, California
June 13-18, 2008

June 13, 2008
Morning Walk

Śrīla Nārāyaṇa Gosvāmī Mahārāja: (To Śrīpāda Tridaṇḍi Mahārāja) Thank you for your good preaching. Everywhere I go I hear that your preaching is very good. Everyone is happy.

Brajanātha dāsa: Yesterday was Sahadeva's birthday.

Śrīla Nārāyaṇa Gosvāmī Mahārāja: Oh, yesterday? *Maṅgalaṁ bhāvatu* (all auspiciousness to you). *Kalyāṇaṁ bhāvatu* (may your true welfare manifest). *Sukhī bhāvatu* (may you be happy). May you be happy in this world and in the transcendental world.

But where is my *dakṣiṇā*?

Sahadeva dāsa: I give my heart to you.

Śrīla Nārāyaṇa Gosvāmī Mahārāja: My blessings to you.

Haridāsa dāsa: Gurudeva, my birthday was a month ago.

Śrīla Nārāyaṇa Gosvāmī Mahārāja: *Maṅgalaṁ bhāvatu. Kalyāṇaṁ bhāvatu. Bhaktir bhāvatu.*

But, *śikhā bhāvatu* also ['may you wear a *śikhā*, the tuft of hair on the back of the head, signifying that one is a Vaiṣṇava']. Without a *śikhā* there can be no blessings.

Haridāsa dāsa: The barber took it off. I don't know how that happened.

Śrīla Nārāyaṇa Gosvāmī Mahārāja: I wish to see you wearing a *śikhā*.

(To Īśa dāsa) Thank you for my website. So many people throughout the world are hearing my classes through our website and praising your work. All are very happy.

Īśa dāsa: I am just your machine, Śrīla Gurudeva.

Śrīla Nārāyaṇa Gosvāmī Mahārāja: But you are doing well. Devotees are sitting in their houses and hearing my *hari-kathā* on the internet.

Brajanātha dāsa: Śacīnandana Prabhu is also doing a lot of service. He has a website called 'Saṅga-Space.' He has a very nice computer program wherein all the devotees can communicate with each other and also hear your lectures.

Śrīla Nārāyaṇa Gosvāmī Mahārāja: (To Śacīnandana dāsa) But what are you doing now?

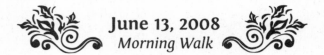

Śacīnandana dāsa: I have a job in a computer store.

Śrīla Nārāyaṇa Gosvāmī Mahārāja: Where?

Śacīnandana dāsa: In Fresno, where your plane landed yesterday.

Śrīla Nārāyaṇa Gosvāmī Mahārāja: Are you with your wife, or not?

Śacīnandana dāsa: No.

Śrīla Nārāyaṇa Gosvāmī Mahārāja: Divorced?

Śacīnandana dāsa: She wants that.

Śrīla Nārāyaṇa Gosvāmī Mahārāja: I think that you committed some mistakes. Whenever I marry a couple, I tell them, "Don't divorce." Try to follow your duty towards her, and she should also follow her duty. I think it would be better if you compromise and remain with her. Try to satisfy her, and support her and the children.

(To all the devotees) Are there any questions?

Aniruddha dāsa: Śrīla Gurudeva, which is more important: *vapu*, the physical presence of *guru*, or *vāṇī*, the instructions of *guru*?

Śrīla Nārāyaṇa Gosvāmī Mahārāja: When we compare *vapu* and *vāṇī*, *vāṇī* is better. It is better to serve. The disciple must follow *gurudeva's* instructions. However, if *vāṇī* is with *vapu*, then *vapu* is so exalted.

Śrīpāda Sajjana Mahārāja: The *svarūpa* (constitutional position) of the *jīva* is *nitya-siddha kṛṣṇa-prema*, meaning that pure love for Kṛṣṇa is eternally established in the hearts of all living entities. This means that the seed of *kṛṣṇa-prema* is already within us. At the same time, we hear that *guru* gives the seed of *bhakti*. How do we reconcile these two apparently contradictory statements?

Śrīla Nārāyaṇa Gosvāmī Mahārāja: The seed is already present. The spiritual master gives nourishment to that seed in the form of spiritual water, sun, rain, and good soil. If one does not give good water to a seed, it will not sprout. The seed is in a latent stage, and the bonafide *guru* causes it to sprout.

Śrīpāda Mādhava Mahārāja: Without *gurudeva's* mercy it will not sprout.

Śrīla Nārāyaṇa Gosvāmī Mahārāja: Are there any other questions?

(To Śrīpāda Viṣṇu Mahārāja) How are you doing? Is your preaching successful?

Śrīpāda Viṣṇu Mahārāja: Yes, very good, Gurudeva.

Śrīla Nārāyaṇa Gosvāmī Mahārāja: You should preach.

Rādhānātha dāsa: Śrīla Gurudeva, I have a question. You often quote this verse:

anarpita-carīṁ cirāt karuṇayāvatīrṇaḥ kalau
samarpayitum unnatojjvala-rasāṁ sva-bhakti-śriyam
hariḥ puraṭa-sundara-dyuti-kadamba-sandīpitaḥ
sadā hṛdaya-kandare sphuratu vaḥ śacī-nandanaḥ
(*Śrī Caitanya-caritāmṛta, Ādi-līlā* 1.4)

May the Supreme Lord who is known as the son of Śrīmatī Śacī-devī be transcendentally situated in the innermost chambers of your heart. Resplendent with the radiance of molten gold, He has appeared in the age of Kali by His causeless mercy to bestow what no incarnation has ever offered before; the most sublime and radiant mellow of devotional service, the mellow of conjugal love.

This verse says that Śrī Caitanya Mahāprabhu has not given *unnatojjvala-rasāṁ sva-bhakti-śriyam* (*mañjarī-bhāva*, the mood of a maidservant of Śrīmatī Rādhikā) for a very long time. I was wondering, how did He give this? Did He give it only through the Gosvāmīs' teachings, or has He personally, through His own life's activities, shown how He is giving it?

Śrīla Nārāyaṇa Gosvāmī Mahārāja: He gave this in both ways. He especially inspired all of His teachings in the heart of Śrīla Rūpa Gosvāmī, and sometimes He personally displayed *mañjarī-bhāva* in His own activities. He especially inspired Śrīla Rūpa Gosvāmī, who later wrote that one should remember Kṛṣṇa, and at the same time also remember those who are absorbed in the service for which one has greed.

kṛṣṇaṁ smaran janaṁ cāsya
preṣṭhaṁ nija-samīhitam
tat-tat-kathā-rataś cāsau
kuryād vāsaṁ vraje sadā
(*Bhakti-rasāmṛta-sindhu* 1.2.294)

One should constantly remember one's dearest *nava-kiśora* Śrī Nanda-nandana, and the beloved associates of Kṛṣṇa who are possessed of *sajātīya-bhāva*, or the

> identical mood for which one aspires. One should always reside in Śrī Vraja-dhāma with great attachment for hearing topics regarding Kṛṣṇa and His devotees. (If one is physically unable to live in Vraja, one should do so mentally). This is the method of *rāgānuga-bhakti-sādhana*.

If you have greed to serve Kṛṣṇa like His cowherd friends Śrīdāmā and Subala, remember them. If you have greed to serve like Mother Yaśodā and Nanda Bābā, remember them. And, if you have greed to serve like the *gopīs*, then remember them. There are so many *gopīs*, so remember that *gopī* whose service is appropriate for you. In this way you can practice remembering (*smaraṇa*).

But first follow *Upadeśāmṛta*, and then you can ask these types of questions. If you are engaged in worldly intoxication with a desire for married life and wealth, and at the same time you aspire to be like the *gopīs*, you will not be successful in *bhakti*. Material and spiritual desires cannot simultaneously occupy the same heart.

Śrīpāda Mādhava Mahārāja: It is not possible for two swords to fit in one sheath.

Śrīla Nārāyaṇa Gosvāmī Mahārāja: Try to first realize this: Two opposite desires cannot mix; worldly desires and transcendental desires cannot mix. If a person has both of these desires, how can he ask this type of question?

One should first realize, "I have no qualification for that type of *bhāva*." First realize your level of qualification, and then totally give up all your material desires. Completely give up these desires, one-hundred per cent; no, not one-hundred percent but two-hundred percent. Ninety-nine per cent will not suffice.

You must give up all desires, but to whom? First give yourself to *guru*, for *guru-niṣṭhā* is the backbone of *bhakti*. If we have *niṣṭhā* (strong, steady faith) for Kṛṣṇa, for Rādhikā, for the *mañjarīs*, or for anyone else, but we have no *niṣṭhā* for *gurudeva*, how will our *niṣṭhā* be pure? If we cannot give our whole self to *gurudeva*, how can we develop real attachment to Kṛṣṇa? Who will give us to Kṛṣṇa? *Guru* is so powerful that he can take away the results of our past sinful activities and give us as an offering to the lotus feet of Śrī Śrī Rādhā-Kṛṣṇa.

Ānandī-kṛṣṇa dāsa: Gurudeva, will you give me *dīkṣā*?

Śrīpāda Mādhava Mahārāja: How many rounds are you chanting daily?

Ānandī-kṛṣṇa dāsa: I'm not chanting regularly.

Śrīla Nārāyaṇa Gosvāmī Mahārāja: Are you chanting at least two rounds a day? I have already given you *harināma*. If you chant sixteen rounds daily, then I will give you *dīkṣā*. First practice.

Ānandī-kṛṣṇa dāsa: If I pass away before I get initiation, then wouldn't it have been better that I took *dīkṣā* now?

Śrīla Nārāyaṇa Gosvāmī Mahārāja: There is no harm in waiting. You will come back in the next life, and again I will come, and I will give you *dīkṣā* then. The soul never dies.

Śrīpāda Mādhava Mahārāja: If you have so much interest in *dīkṣā*, then you must chant sixteen rounds every day. Now your chanting is inconsistent.

Dhruva dāsa: Śrīla Gurudeva, what should be my regard for senior devotees who are taking so many good things from your books, yet they are not taking guidance from you personally and simultaneously they are not allowing other devotees to come to see you?

Brajanātha dāsa: His question is: How should we respect senior devotees who are reading your books yet do not allow other devotees to come to you?

Śrīla Nārāyaṇa Gosvāmī Mahārāja: Why don't they allow others to see me? Oh, they are very cruel; very, very cruel.

Dhruva dāsa: Is there any value in trying to preach with them?

Śrīla Nārāyaṇa Gosvāmī Mahārāja: If they don't want to hear from my disciples, why go there to preach with them? The entire world is available for preaching; you can preach anywhere in this world. If they are unfavorable, then better not to preach with them.

Dhruva dāsa: What is the consequence of their taking so many good things from your teachings and your books, and at the same time disrespecting you by not letting others come to you and not coming to you for guidance themselves?

Śrīpāda Sajjana Mahārāja: And although they speak to others and give classes from your books, they do not acknowledge that the knowledge in your books is coming from you.

Śrīla Nārāyaṇa Gosvāmī Mahārāja: Their disciples should not obey them. They should kick out such so-called *gurus*.

Śivānanda Sena dāsa: Śrīla Gurudeva, how do you do this? You are traveling all over the world, being so strong. I stay with you for one week in Badger and I am so tired for a month after that, whereas you are traveling all over the world with so much strength. This is a most amazing thing.

Śrīla Nārāyaṇa Gosvāmī Mahārāja: I have good doctors everywhere. Actually, the doctors tell me not to travel so much, so I want to reduce my travels.

Śivānanda Sena dāsa: You say this every year, but still you increase your travels.

Śrīla Nārāyaṇa Gosvāmī Mahārāja: (To all the devotees present) I know you have no more questions. You have finished all your questions, so now I am asking a question:

Kṛṣṇa is the embodiment of love and affection. Everyone likes to be in that place where they will be surrounded by affection. In Vraja, all the *sakhās* serve Kṛṣṇa from their hearts and please Him. This is especially true for Mother Yaśodā, Nanda Bābā, and all the other elder *gopas* and *gopīs*, who are like fathers and mothers to Kṛṣṇa; they give Him abundant love, and in fact He is always sinking in the ocean of their love. Moreover, when He is with the young *gopīs*, He even forgets Himself. He tells them, "I cannot repay you." This is especially true when He is with the *aṣṭa-sakhī gopīs*, and still more so when He is with Śrīmatī Rādhikā.

Feeling this deep love and affection, why did Śrī Kṛṣṇa leave Vṛndāvana and go to Mathurā? And after that, why did He go so far away to Dvārakā? Why did He leave without Rādhikā, without any *gopas*, and without Nanda and Yaśodā? Why did He go alone? When He was in Mathurā and Dvārakā, He knew that the Vrajavāsīs were lamenting, weeping, and fainting; in fact no one could say whether or not they were still alive. Why was He so cruel?

Padmanābha Mahārāja will explain this.

Śrīpāda Padmanābha Mahārāja: First of all, it is told in *śāstra* that Kṛṣṇa never leaves Vṛndāvana: *Vṛndāvanaṁ parityajya padam ekaṁ na gacchati.* He remains there in a concealed way, tasting all of the moods of the *vraja-gopīs* and observing their feelings of intense separation. In truth, it was not cruel of Kṛṣṇa to cause the *vraja-gopīs* and all the Vrajavāsīs to sink in the ocean of the mood of separation, because truly this is the highest ecstasy. It may appear that they were suffering externally, but internally they tasted the highest nectar.

In fact, in their mood of separation they were internally meeting with Kṛṣṇa and relishing their meeting with Him.

Once, Kṛṣṇa was sitting in Vraja at Prema-sarovara, and Śrīmatī Rādhikā was sitting on His lap. At that time a bumblebee flew around Śrīmatī Rādhikā's beautiful lotus face, thinking it to be a lotus flower, and She was trying to make the bumblebee go away.

Madhumaṅgala was watching this. He came and began to chase away the bumblebee. He chased it far away, and when he returned he told Śrīmatī Rādhikā, "I have chased Madhusūdana far away, and he will never return."

When Rādhikā heard this, She began to think that Kṛṣṇa Himself had gone far away. Whereas one of Kṛṣṇa's names is Madhusūdana because He always drinks the honey (*madhu*) of the *gopīs'* love for Him, the bumblebee is named Madhusūdana because it takes honey from the flowers. Thus, when Śrīmatī Rādhikā heard the name Madhusūdana, She took this to mean that Kṛṣṇa had left forever and She became completely overwhelmed in the mood of separation. She suddenly began to weep and call out, "Oh, where is the dearmost beloved of my life? He has gone! He has gone so far away!" She then fainted on His lap.

Kṛṣṇa tried to tell Her, "Here I am, right in front of You." But Rādhikā was so absorbed in Her mood of separation from Kṛṣṇa that She could not hear Him. Seeing this, Kṛṣṇa began to consider, "Her feeling of separation has risen so high that even though I am with Her personally I cannot console Her."

He then began to contemplate, "She is happier when I am away than when I am with Her. When I am separated from Her She remembers Me so intensely that everything reminds Her of Me. She becomes completely absorbed in Me, and in that mood She thinks that She is embracing Me. She becomes very happy, whereas actually She is embracing the *tamāla* tree. Everything She sees that is blackish in color reminds Her of Me."

At that time Kṛṣṇa considered that by leaving Vraja and causing Śrīmatī Rādhikā to be separated from Him, She would become most happy. Ultimately, He wanted the entire world to know and realize Her glories. By hearing the descriptions of Her separation moods in *Śrīmad-Bhāgavatam*, especially when She speaks to the bumblebee in *Brahmara-gīta*, devotees would realize that no other personality can compare to Her, either in Her moods of separation or in the depth of Her love.

Śrīla Nārāyaṇa Gosvāmī Mahārāja: Very good.

Śrīpāda Mādhava Mahārāja: And that Kṛṣṇa who went to Mathurā and Dvārakā is the manifestation of Vrajendra-nandana Śyāmasundara, who is always in Vraja.

Śrīpāda Padmanābha Mahārāja: Yes.

And there are also some external reasons why Kṛṣṇa left Vṛndāvana. For example Kṛṣṇa says in *Bhagavad-gītā*:

ye yathā māṁ prapadyante
tāṁs tathaiva bhajāmy aham
mama vartmānuvartante
manuṣyāḥ pārtha sarvaśaḥ

(*Bhagavad-gītā* 4.11)

O Pārtha, in whichever way a person renders service to Me I reciprocate accordingly. Everyone follows My path in all respects.

Kṛṣṇa has to reciprocate with every devotee according to their worship and mood towards Him. There were so many devotees in Mathurā and Dvārakā, and for this reason He had to leave Vraja. He had to go to Mathurā to protect His mother and father, and He also had to rescue and marry 16,000 princesses.

In addition, His purpose for coming to this world was to remove the burden of the Earth. At the time of Kṛṣṇa's appearance, the Earth was overburdened with many demonic kings and their very powerful military forces, and therefore He had to take away that burden.

As He says in the *Bhagavad-gītā*:

paritrāṇāya sādhūnāṁ
vināśāya ca duṣkṛtām
dharma-saṁsthāpanārthāya
sambhavāmi yuge yuge

(*Bhagavad-gītā* 4.8)

To deliver the pious and to annihilate the miscreants, as well as to reestablish the principles of religion, I Myself appear, millennium after millennium.*

In conclusion, there are external and internal reasons why Kṛṣṇa left Vraja, but the main reason was to glorify Śrīmatī Rādhikā's supreme *prema* and to make it known to the world that no one else can compare with Her.

Śrīla Nārāyaṇa Gosvāmī Mahārāja: These points are all right, but here is one more thing to know.

Kṛṣṇa thinks, "I will have to remove the burden from the Earth, and I will have to fulfill the desires of Vasudeva, Devakī, and others, like the Pāṇḍavas." In Mathurā, He and Baladeva killed Kaṁsa and all his brothers and associates, and then He gave the kingdom to Ugrasena.

Meanwhile, Nanda Bābā was waiting for Kṛṣṇa and Baladeva to return to their camp, thinking, "Still They have not come? Perhaps Devakī and Vasudeva and all the Mathurāvāsīs are telling Them, 'You are the son of Devakī and Vasudeva, not the son of Yaśodā and Nanda Bābā. They have no issue of their own. They have merely brought You up and taken care of You, so do not return to Vṛndāvana.'"

Baladeva and Kṛṣṇa returned to Nanda Bābā in the evening, without mentioning this to Vasudeva and Devakī. They came to the place where he had been waiting with a bullock-cart for Them to return. Seeing Them approach, Nanda Bābā began to weep. Kṛṣṇa and Baladeva both sat on His lap, one on the left side and one on the right. Nanda Bābā asked Them, "Why have You delayed for so long?"

Baladeva replied, "Father, a very strange thing is happening! Many people are saying that We are actually the sons of Vasudeva, but I don't accept this. Even if We are the sons of Vasudeva, We don't know any father besides you! If for any reason a mother and father renounce a son, then those who raise him are his real mother and father. There are many different kinds of fathers – the one who begets the child, the one who raises him, the king, the spiritual master, the father-in-law, and the family priest. Among them, the best is the father who raises and protects him.

"I am your son only. I don't know any father other than you. I don't want to remain here in Mathurā for even one more second. I want to immediately accompany you and Kṛṣṇa back to Vraja! Bābā, I cannot live without you and Kṛṣṇa. If you take Kṛṣṇa with you and leave Me here alone, I will die. I cannot live without Kṛṣṇa."

Nanda Bābā was thinking, "What should I do?" and said, "My son, don't speak like this! If my younger brother Vasudeva hears this he will die, and Devakī will also die!" Nanda Bābā said this because he knew they really would die. He was more magnanimous than Vasudeva and Devakī, who didn't consider the Vrajavāsīs' feelings while Kṛṣṇa stayed with them in Mathurā. He continued, "Oh Baladeva, six of their sons were killed. If You hadn't been brought to Gokula, You would have also been slain. Therefore we are forever indebted to Vasudeva. If both You and Kṛṣṇa come with me to Vraja, they will think, 'Oh, Nanda Bābā is my enemy. We have only one son, Baladeva, and Nanda has taken Him away from us.' What should I do?"

Kṛṣṇa said, "Bābā, I can tell you one thing. Baladeva cannot remain here alone, and at the same time He must satisfy His father. Since He cannot live without Me, why shouldn't We both remain in Mathurā for two or three days? We will satisfy His father, and then We will both return to Vraja."

Weeping bitterly in this dilemna, thinking, "What should I do?" Nanda Bābā then considered, "Somehow I will have to accept this, but how can I return to Vraja without Kṛṣṇa? I have promised the Vrajavāsīs to bring Him back."

Kṛṣṇa had also promised the *gopīs*, "I will return tomorrow, or the day after tomorrow; certainly, certainly, certainly." He vowed three times to return, so He certainly should have returned, but we see that He did not return. What is the fact?

This is what I wanted to tell you: Śrīla Viśvanātha Cakravartī Ṭhākura has explained that Kṛṣṇa became two, Baladeva Prabhu became two, and Nanda Bābā became two. In one *prakoṣṭha* (section of Their pastime), or in one manifestation, Kṛṣṇa and Baladeva happily returned to Vraja with Nanda Bābā, and they all entered Nandagrāma together. In addition, all the associates of Vṛndāvana became two – in one *prakoṣṭha* they were feeling separation and in the other they were enjoying Kṛṣṇa's presence. In one *prakoṣṭha* Kṛṣṇa is always performing *rāsa* with the *gopīs*, and in another, Nanda Bābā returned to Vraja alone, weeping.

What proof is there to substantiate that Kṛṣṇa was present with the *gopīs* and Nanda Bābā in Vṛndāvana? When Uddhava went to Vṛndāvana, he remembered, "Kṛṣṇa told me, 'I am only partly in Dvārakā, and I am completely in Vraja.'" He thought, "I see that Kṛṣṇa is here, cow-herding, and -all the *gopīs* and Vrajavāsīs are very happy to be with Him." He saw this scene for some time, and afterwards it disappeared.

So in one *prakoṣṭha* Kṛṣṇa is present there, hidden, and in one *prakoṣṭha* He is not present. This is because there are so many devotees, and each devotee wants to serve Kṛṣṇa. He must fulfill all their desires.

Mahābuddhi dāsa: Does this mean that you also have to manifest in many places to satisfy all the devotees?

Śrīla Nārāyaṇa Gosvāmī Mahārāja: Yes.

Vinaya dāsa: Also, when Akrūra was taking…

Śrīla Nārāyaṇa Gosvāmī Mahārāja: Yes, I was also going to tell this.

Akrūra saw this phenomenon of Kṛṣṇa and Balarāma simultaneously in more than one place when he was bathing within the Yamunā. He saw Them simultaneously sitting on his chariot and also within the water. The manifestations of Kṛṣṇa and Balarāma then went with him to Mathurā on the chariot, and Kṛṣṇa and Balarāma of Vṛndāvana returned to Vṛndāvana.

June 13, 2008
Darśana

Śrīla Nārāyaṇa Gosvāmī Mahārāja: I cannot say what you should do. As you like, you can do. You are intelligent. You should see what you want to do.

Raghunātha Bhaṭṭa dāsa: I am discouraged, Gurudeva. I can't go on like this.

Śrīla Nārāyaṇa Gosvāmī Mahārāja: What can I do if you cannot do anything? So you should do what you want to do.

Śrīpāda Mādhava Mahārāja: These devotees are from Montreal.

Nandinī dasī: I want to arrange my life so that I can please you, but I am so weak.

Śrīla Nārāyaṇa Gosvāmī Mahārāja: My blessings are for you, that you will become very strong.

Nandinī dasī: I have so many attachments, but I only want to be attached to you.

Śrīla Nārāyaṇa Gosvāmī Mahārāja: It is best to give your attachment to Kṛṣṇa and Rādhikā. You can give all your attachments to Them through me.

(To Phula-kiśorī dasī) Are you from Montreal?

Phula-kiśorī dasī: No, from Russia. Whenever I come into the *saṅga* of you and your devotees, I feel inspired. When I go back home I work in order to take care of my family, and at that time I get covered by *māyā*.

Śrīla Nārāyaṇa Gosvāmī Mahārāja: Try to accept my very strong words. Live in the world, but do not be entangled. Live with your mother, son, daughter, and husband as a duty and responsibility, but try to give all your attachment to Kṛṣṇa.

Do you have any job in America?

Phula-kiśorī dasī: Yes, I am a baby-sitter here. My husband also works. But the problem is that he eats meat. He doesn't eat beef, but…

Śrīla Nārāyaṇa Gosvāmī Mahārāja: Tell him to choose between meat and you. Tell him this frankly; otherwise your life will be spoiled.

(To Gītā dāsī) How are you?

Gītā dāsī: I am far better than last year.

Śrīla Nārāyaṇa Gosvāmī Mahārāja: You were worshiping the Deities in Los Angeles. What are you doing now?

Gītā dāsī: Now I go to school to cultivate my interest. My question is how can I learn something without it being for sense gratification? I think it is sense gratification because I want to learn for my own interest.

Śrīpāda Mādhava Mahārāja: What are you learning?

Gītā dāsī: Gemstone and jewelry making.

Śrīla Nārāyaṇa Gosvāmī Mahārāja: Better not to do these things. Better to somehow maintain your life, chant, and read my books. Now you are old, so you need only chant and remember Rādhā and Kṛṣṇa – and somehow or other maintain your life.

Śrīpāda Tridaṇḍi Mahārāja: I was in New Zealand for one month.

Śrīla Nārāyaṇa Gosvāmī Mahārāja: You went to New Zealand? Where?

Śrīpāda Tridaṇḍi Mahārāja: I went everywhere in the South Island. I was going to do some *Jaiva-dharma* work, but it didn't happen.

Śrīla Nārāyaṇa Gosvāmī Mahārāja: I am very, very happy that you are preaching everywhere, and that all are happy.

Stavyadeva dāsa: Sometimes, some of my children do bad things. As a father, what should be my disposition towards them?

Śrīla Nārāyaṇa Gosvāmī Mahārāja: What can you do? Now they are quite independent; they can hear neither me nor you. How can we help them? They ruin their own lives and also the lives of my *brahmacārīs*. Sometimes I become worried about how I will save my devotees, my *brahmacārīs* and *sannyāsīs*. Let them do what they are doing, and when they have problems and realize their mistakes, they will automatically return to the proper path.

Jagadiśa dāsa: Gurudeva, Dhutidhara Mahārāja is sending his obeisances to your lotus feet.

Śrīla Nārāyaṇa Gosvāmī Mahārāja: Please give my blessings to him.

Jagadiśa dāsa: He cannot come here because of legal reasons.

Śrīla Nārāyaṇa Gosvāmī Mahārāja: I know there are some…

Jagadiśa dāsa: We are coming to Kārtika in the fall.

Śrīla Nārāyaṇa Gosvāmī Mahārāja: Yes, tell him he must come.

Devotee: Gurudeva, please forgive my offenses.

Śrīla Nārāyaṇa Gosvāmī Mahārāja: You have enjoyed sense gratification so much in your young age. Now you are entering old age, and you do not know when you will die. Still you desire a boyfriend or girlfriend? Why are you involving yourself with these things? Give up such relationships totally, and give your entire energy and attention to Kṛṣṇa consciousness.

Lola dāsī: I am not able to go deeply into *bhajana*. Can you bless me so that I can properly engage in *bhajana*?

Śrīla Nārāyaṇa Gosvāmī Mahārāja: I want that for you, but you must hear and read more. Engage your time in deeply going through the books we have published. The books themselves will be merciful and help you to understand them. When you read Śrīla Rūpa Gosvāmī's books, you can pray to Śrīla Rūpa Gosvāmī in this way: "Please be merciful so that I can understand you."

Trilokanātha dāsa: My wife and I would like some instruction from you as to how we can best serve you.

Śrīla Nārāyaṇa Gosvāmī Mahārāja: You can preach; you are both qualified to preach. Speak what you have heard from me, and thus help others to come in this line.

Veṇu-gopāla dāsa: Śrīla Gurudeva, some devotees in Canada would like to preach and perhaps open a center, in either Kelowna or Vancouver. Please give us your blessings and advice.

Śrīla Nārāyaṇa Gosvāmī Mahārāja: Yes, you must try for this. But the *brahmacārīs* should follow the etiquette of shaving both their head and beard only on Pūrṇimā. [Meaning that they should not shave their beard at other, additional times – ed.]

Veṇu-gopāla dāsa: Even in the West? Even when we are going out to the public and distributing books?

Śrīla Nārāyaṇa Gosvāmī Mahārāja: No harm.

June 14, 2008
Morning Walk

Kamala-kānta dāsa: Śrīla Gurudeva, in the last two years a few devotees committed suicide. What is their destination? What is the future of souls who take their own lives?

Śrīla Nārāyaṇa Gosvāmī Mahārāja: Committing suicide is a sign that one has no belief in God. Such persons are like *karmīs*, materialists, who must enjoy or suffer the fruits of their material activities. One who believes in Kṛṣṇa would never commit suicide. Kṛṣṇa has given us this life for performing devotional activities in a mood of devotion (*bhajana*). If a person somehow gets a bonafide *guru* and good association but then neglects this opportunity by killing himself, he will be punished more than a person who commits suicide without having had such contact.

Śrīpāda Sajjana Mahārāja: What about the case of Mahāprabhu's associate, Choṭa Haridāsa, who also took his own life?

Śrīla Nārāyaṇa Gosvāmī Mahārāja: This fact does not apply in his case, because he is an associate of Śrī Caitanya Mahāprabhu.[30]

30 "Mahāprabhu only pretended to reject Choṭa Haridāsa, who was His eternal associate. Choṭa Haridāsa was a liberated soul. There was actually no offense on his part, but Mahāprabhu wanted to teach everyone by the example of this pastime. Mahāprabhu wanted to show that He cannot tolerate hypocritical behavior" (Śrīla Nārāyaṇa Gosvāmī Mahārāja. Lecture in Italy, June 15, 2001).

Thus, Choṭa Haridāsa did not actually feel so dejected by being rejected by the Lord that he committed suicide. His so-called suicide was a magical arrangement by the Lord. Therefore he did not get a sinful reaction, as an ordinary person would have gotten for committing suicide – ed.

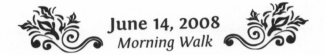

Śrīpāda Mādhava Mahārāja: Madhuvrata Prabhu has a question. When the *jīvas* first come into this world from the glance of Kāraṇodakaśāyī Viṣṇu, they receive either a human body or a non-human body. In the human species the *jīva* performs materialistic activities (*karma*) and consequently suffers or enjoys the fruits of his work. Humans perform karmic (fruitive) activities, but other species do not. Other species only suffer the results of the karmic actions which they performed when they were previously humans.

Does this mean that all *jīvas* first come into this world from the *taṭasthā* region as human beings, and then, due to their *karma*, they enter into other species?

Śrīla Nārāyaṇa Gosvāmī Mahārāja: No, this is not the process. The species in which the *jīva* takes birth depends on Kṛṣṇa. The *jīva* gets a body according to the degree of his desire to enjoy this world. If he has a strong desire to enjoy independently from Kṛṣṇa, he takes birth in the animal species. If his desire to be independent is moderate, he takes a human birth. So, the *jīva's* appearance in different species depends on the will of Kṛṣṇa, and it also depends on the degree of his desire to enjoy separately from Kṛṣṇa.

Madhuvrata dāsa: The *jīva* has no *karma* when he first decides to come to this world.

Śrīla Nārāyaṇa Gosvāmī Mahārāja: He has no *karma* at that time, but he has independence in the sense of free will. And it is not that all independence is the same; there is gradation. Some *jīvas* desire a little independence, or a small sense of autonomy, while others desire total independence.

Raghunātha Bhaṭṭa dāsa: In your class yesterday, you described how the living entities in the *taṭasthā-śakti* region fall to this material world. You gave the analogy of mustard seeds landing on the sharp blade of a knife and then falling on one side of the knife or the other. You said that, like those mustard seeds, the *jīva* can go either to the material world or the spiritual world. I am trying to understand if this happens because of our minute independence, or by chance, that we come here.

Śrīla Nārāyaṇa Gosvāmī Mahārāja: Independence was first, and chance was second. Without independence, how can the *jīva* look toward either Yogamāyā or Mahāmāyā?

Vṛndāvana dāsa: So it is a choice, Gurudeva? The *jīva* is responsible?

Śrīla Nārāyaṇa Gosvāmī Mahārāja: Yes; the *jīva* has independence, and Kṛṣṇa never interferes with that.

Here is an analogy to help explain this principle. In the government, there is a magistrate for each district. If a person does something for the benefit of the public he will be rewarded by that magistrate, and if he commits a crime he will be punished.

There are some people who know that if they commit a crime they will be punished or even put to death; yet they commit the crime. There are numerous culprits who go to jail, and when they are released they commit the crime again, because they like to be in jail. Some *jīvas* are like that; even though they suffer repeatedly in this material world, they are ignorantly attached to remaining here.

Govinda dāsa: Śrīla Gurudeva, in yesterday's morning walk you quoted Śrīla Rūpa Gosvāmī saying that one should remember and meditate on Rādhā and Kṛṣṇa. On the other hand, when Lord Nityānanda is preaching He says, "*Bhaja gaurāṅga kaha gaurāṅga laha gaurāṅgera nāma re* – Worship Gaurāṅga, glorify Gaurāṅga, and chant the name of Gaurāṅga." How can we reconcile this?

Śrīla Nārāyaṇa Gosvāmī Mahārāja: We must follow Nityānanda Prabhu, because He has come to help us. He is *akhaṇḍa guru-tattva*, the undivided principle of *guru*.

Whatever we know is due to the mercy of Śrī Caitanya Mahāprabhu. Whatever Rūpa Gosvāmī knew is also coming from Caitanya Mahāprabhu's instructions. One should first meditate on Gauracandra (Caitanya Mahāprabhu) as one's *guru*, as Śrīla Raghunātha dāsa Gosvāmī has stated in his *Manaḥ-śikṣā* (Verse 2):

> *na dharmaṁ nādharmaṁ śruti-gaṇa-niruktaṁ kila kuru*
> *vraje rādhā-kṛṣṇa-pracura-paricaryām iha tanu*
> *śaci-sūnuṁ nandīśvara-pati-sutatve guru-varaṁ*
> *mukunda-preṣṭhatve smara param ajasraṁ nanu manaḥ*

> My dear mind, please do not perform the religious activities prescribed in the Vedas, nor the irreligious works forbidden by these scriptures. The ultimate conclusion of the entire Vedic literature is that the Divine Couple, Śrī Śrī Rādhā-Kṛṣṇa, is the Supreme object of worship, and that loving service to Them is the most relishable experience of all. Therefore, O mind, engage yourself fully in serving Them with love and devotion. Always meditate upon Śrī Caitanya Mahāprabhu, the son of Śrī

> Śacī-mātā, with the understanding that He is absolutely non-different from Śrī Kṛṣṇa, the son of Mahārāja Nanda. Dear mind, also meditate upon *śrī guru*, who is a dearmost devotee of Śrī Mukunda Kṛṣṇa.

We should consider that Śrī Caitanya Mahāprabhu is *jagad-guru* (the *guru* of the entire universe) and that He has come to distribute a very costly thing that has never been distributed before. As *guru*, he taught Śrīla Rūpa Gosvāmī, Śrīla Sanātana Gosvāmī, Śrī Tapana Miśra, Śrī Sārvabhauma Bhaṭṭācārya, Śrī Rāya Rāmānanda, and so many others. We should follow the same instructions He gave to them. He told them to chant "Hare Kṛṣṇa, Hare Kṛṣṇa," and always remember Kṛṣṇa. By following His orders, both sides will be reconciled.

Mahī-bharata dāsa: Śrīla Gurudeva, it says in *Navadvīpa-dhāma Māhātmya* that before Mahāprabhu's appearance five-hundred years ago, He manifested His form to many devotees, like Śrī Rāmānuja and Śrī Viṣṇusvāmī. At those times, did He appear as a *sannyāsī* or as He was in Navadvīpa?

Śrīla Nārāyaṇa Gosvāmī Mahārāja: He appeared in His Navadvīpa-form. This is His eternal form, just as Śrī Kṛṣṇa's eternal form is His human-like cowherd form of Śrī Vrajendra-nandana, the son of Nanda Mahārāja in Vṛndāvana. In that form Kṛṣṇa plays a flute and carries a stick. In this eternal form, and in His other forms, He comes to this world and manifests various sweet pastimes.

Śrī Caitanya Mahāprabhu's form in Navadvīpa is eternal; it is eternally situated in Goloka Śvetadvīpa. His *sannyāsa* form is His *naimittika-līlā* (meaning that those pastimes take place only in this world; they do not take place in the spiritual world). Various personalities, like Śrī Rāmānuja, Brahmā, Indra, Mārkaṇḍeya Ṛṣi, the *surabhī* cow in Godruma, and Suvarṇa Sena Mahārāja saw that very Caitanya Mahāprabhu of Navadvīpa performing Hare Kṛṣṇa *kīrtana*.

Veṇu-gopāla dāsa: In *Jaiva-dharma* it is said that when Kṛṣṇa situates Himself in the *taṭasthā-śakti*, He manifests the *jīva*. What does this mean?

Śrīla Nārāyaṇa Gosvāmī Mahārāja: At this time, Kṛṣṇa is only with His *taṭasthā-śakti*. He has somehow hidden His *cit-śakti* (transcendental potency), *hlādinī-śakti* (spiritual pleasure potency), and all other potencies. When all other potencies are hidden, the *jīva* manifests.

jīvera 'svarūpa' haya—kṛṣṇera 'nitya-dāsa'
kṛṣṇera 'taṭasthā-śakti' 'bhedābheda-prakāśa
(*Śrī Caitanya-caritāmṛta, Madhya-līlā* 20.108)

It is the living entity's constitutional position to be an eternal servant of Kṛṣṇa, because he is the marginal energy of Kṛṣṇa and a manifestation simultaneously one with and different from Him.

The head of *taṭasthā-śakti* is Baladeva Prabhu. Kāraṇodakaśāyī Viṣṇu, who manifests the innumerable *taṭasthā-jīvas* in the region between the material and spiritual worlds, is an expansion of Mahā-Saṅkarṣaṇa (in Vaikuṇṭha), and Mahā-Saṅkarṣaṇa is an expansion of Baladeva.

So, your question was, "What is the meaning of the statement, 'When Kṛṣṇa situates Himself in the *taṭasthā-śakti*, He manifests the *jīva*?'" The answer is that Kṛṣṇa manifests His form as Baladeva, and Baladeva manifests the *jīva*.

Mahābuddhi dāsa: Are the *jīvas* who manifest from Kāraṇodakaśāyī Viṣṇu significantly different from those who directly manifest from Mahā-Saṅkarṣaṇa (Lord Nārāyaṇa) in Vaikuṇṭha or Baladeva in Vraja?

Śrīla Nārāyaṇa Gosvāmī Mahārāja: Their qualities are the same, except that those who emanate from Baladeva and Mahā-Saṅkarṣaṇa in the spiritual world possess the eternal shelter of *cit-śakti*.

Śrīpāda Dāmodara Mahārāja: Śrīla Gurudeva, Vedic culture was previously practiced throughout the world. It was practiced before Mohammed. What is the position of the Mohammedans?

Śrīla Nārāyaṇa Gosvāmī Mahārāja: Do you know the story of Sagara Mahārāja? He had many sons, and one son was named Asamañjasa. From his boyhood, Asamañjasa was very wicked, so much so that he used to kill other boys by drowning them. Sagara Mahārāja exiled him and told him, "You are no longer in our family line. Go from here." Asamañjasa then went to the forest, where he began to grow a mustache and beard, and engage in all activities that were opposed to Indian culture. It is from him that the Yavana race manifested.

When we follow Ekādaśī, the Yavanas refuse to follow Ekādaśī. The only similarity between us and them is that we walk on our feet and they do as well. If they could walk on their hands, they would.

Śrīpāda Dāmodara Mahārāja: Śrīla Ṭhākura Bhaktivinoda and Śrīla Bhaktivedānta Svāmī Mahārāja have said that Mohammed was a good devotee, but that he did not tell everything because of time, place, and circumstance. Is this true?

Śrīla Nārāyaṇa Gosvāmī Mahārāja: The words of Śrīla Bhaktivinoda Ṭhākura and Śrīla Bhaktivedānta Svāmī Mahārāja are authentic.

Śrīpāda Dāmodara Mahārāja: Isn't this just to catch people and bring them in?

Śrīla Nārāyaṇa Gosvāmī Mahārāja: We should follow what they have told us. Jesus was also empowered to preach to a certain section of the world population in order to help them develop their faith in God.

We should respect all of them.

Śrīpāda Padmanābha Mahārāja: Śrīla Gurudeva, in your class yesterday you said that our *sampradāya*, the disciplic line of Śrī Caitanya Mahāprabhu, has a speciality that is not present in the other Vaiṣṇava *sampradāyas*.

Śrīla Nārāyaṇa Gosvāmī Mahārāja: Yes.

Śrīpāda Padmanābha Mahārāja: You were saying that the teaching in the other Vaiṣṇava *sampradāyas* is that the *jīva* is actually part and parcel of Kṛṣṇa, but that in our *sampradāya* the teaching is that the *jīva* is coming from Kṛṣṇa's spiritual potency (*śakti*), not directly from Kṛṣṇa.

Śrīla Nārāyaṇa Gosvāmī Mahārāja: Yes, this is called *śakti-pariṇāma*.

Śrīpāda Padmanābha Mahārāja: I had thought that all four Vaiṣṇava *sampradāyas* accepted the fact that the Supreme Lord has potencies, and that the *jīva* is one of His potencies.

Śrīla Nārāyaṇa Gosvāmī Mahārāja: Proponents of the other *sampradāyas* know that the *jīva* is one of the Lord's potencies, and they have written this; but their understanding is that the marginal potency, the living entity, is directly coming from Kṛṣṇa's body. They do not accept that the *jīva* is a manifestation of Kṛṣṇa's potency called *jīva-śakti*, which in turn is a partial manifestation of the spiritual potency called *cit-śakti*.

They do not accept the philosophy of *śakti-pariṇāma-vāda*, which is the understanding that all manifestations are transformations of the Supreme Lord's potencies. Only Śrī Caitanya Mahāprabhu and His *sampradāya* have accepted this.

Śrīla Madhvācārya accepted the theory of *vastu-pariṇāma-vāda*. He wrote that the *jīva* and this material world are compared to two separate adjectives qualifying a noun, the noun in this analogy being Brahman (the Absolute Truth). He wrote that the material world is the external body of Brahman and the *jīva* is Brahman's subtle body, as the mind, intelligence, and false ego comprise our subtle body.

Madhvācārya gave this analogy to create the understanding that Reality is one, but with specialities. It is clear that although he accepts the philosophy that Kṛṣṇa and Viṣṇu have *śakti*, he has not accepted *śakti-pariṇāma-vāda*. In other words, he accepted the false idea that Kṛṣṇa Himself is transformed (*vikāri*), whereas it is His divine potency that is transformed.

The philosophies of Śrī Viṣṇusvāmī, Śrī Nimbāditya (Nimbārka), and Rāmānujācārya are similar to that of Śrī Madhvācārya in the sense that they have also accepted the philosophy of *vastu-pariṇāma-vāda*. Śrī Caitanya Mahāprabhu did not approve of this philosophy. He preached *śakti-pariṇāma-vāda*.

Who is managing the festival?

Brajanātha dāsa: Nanda-gopāla.

Śrīla Nārāyaṇa Gosvāmī Mahārāja: (To Nanda-gopāla dāsa) Rādhā-kānta should also give class.

Nanda-gopāla dāsa: Yes, Gurudeva, I have Rādhā-kānta on the list.

Śrīla Nārāyaṇa Gosvāmī Mahārāja: And also Jīva (now Śrīpāda Viṣṇu Mahārāja).

Śrīpāda Mādhava Mahārāja: And Brajanātha Prabhu.

Śrīla Nārāyaṇa Gosvāmī Mahārāja: Brajanātha Prabhu and others.

Brajanātha dāsa: And Nanda-gopāla.

Śrīla Nārāyaṇa Gosvāmī Mahārāja: Nanda-gopāla afterwards.

Dhīra-kṛṣṇa dāsa: If the *jīva* is conscious and transcendental (*cit*), how is it that he manifests via the *taṭasthā-śakti* and not the *cit-śakti*, since the *taṭasthā-śakti* is inferior to the *cit-śakti*?

Śrīla Nārāyaṇa Gosvāmī Mahārāja: The *jīva* is actually *cit-śakti*. The philosophy of the *taṭasthā-śakti* has been given only as an indication.

In actuality there is no specific geographic area between the spiritual and material worlds called *taṭasthā*. *Taṭasthā* as a line between the two worlds is imaginary. There is certainly *jīva-śakti* and *taṭasthā-śakti*, but the concept of *taṭasthā* as a geographical place is provisional. *Taṭasthā-śakti* is ultimately also *cit-śakti*, in the sense that the *jīva* is conscious (*cit*), not inert (*acit*).

Candraśekhara dāsa: In regards to those *jīvas* who look towards Kṛṣṇa and the spiritual world from the *taṭasthā-śakti*, from where does their eligibility come to make such a choice? One's choices in one's present life are generally made according to one's *sukṛtis* (past and present spiritual pious activities) and *saṁskāras* (impressions on the heart, coming from past pious or impious acts, or from reformatory procedures).

Śrīla Nārāyaṇa Gosvāmī Mahārāja: At that time (when the *jīvas* make the choice from the *taṭasthā* region) there are neither *sukṛtis* nor *saṁskāras*.

Candraśekhara dāsa: Nothing at all?

Śrīla Nārāyaṇa Gosvāmī Mahārāja: Nothing, nothing.

Śrīpāda Mādhava Mahārāja: This question was asked before, and Śrīla Gurudeva replied that the very act of their looking toward the Vaikuṇṭha planets was their *sādhana* (spiritual practices), *sukṛti*, and *saṁskāra*.

Candraśekhara dāsa: How can the *jīva* look toward Kṛṣṇa or be attracted to Kṛṣṇa without *sukṛti* and *saṁskāra*?

Śrīla Nārāyaṇa Gosvāmī Mahārāja: Oh, this is chance. [There is a chance that he may do so – ed.]

Śrīpāda Mādhava Mahārāja: Gurudeva replied before that there was no other *sukṛti* or *saṁskāra* required. Those *jīvas* used their independence properly, and that is sufficient.

Śrīpāda Viṣṇu Mahārāja: Gurudeva, how is chance possible, since everything is the desire of Kṛṣṇa?

Śrīpāda Sajjana Mahārāja: Kṛṣṇa desires this pastime with the *jīvas*, to rectify them and to bring them back to Him?

Śrīla Nārāyaṇa Gosvāmī Mahārāja: You should read thoroughly Śrīla Bhaktivinoda Ṭhākura's *Jaiva-dharma*, and try to follow its teachings. At this stage you cannot reconcile all these things. Do *bhajana*, and when you become advanced in *bhakti*, at that time all doubts and questions will be solved automatically. Try to increase your *bhajana*.

Vidura dāsa: Śrīla Gurudeva, is there any resemblance or similarity between the personality of someone in this material world and that person's soul and personality in the spiritual world?

Dhīra-kṛṣṇa dāsa: (speaking in Hindi) Is there any difference between the body and soul of the *jīva* in the spiritual world?

Śrīla Nārāyaṇa Gosvāmī Mahārāja: They are one. There is no difference. As Kṛṣṇa's body, mind, senses, and soul are all soul, it is the same with the *jīva*. Kṛṣṇa can hear with His feet, He can walk with His eyes; He can perform any activity with any sense. The *jīva* is also like that.

Brajanātha dāsa: Vidura Prabhu is actually asking this question: Is there any similarity between our material conditioned personality and our spiritual personality?

Śrīla Nārāyaṇa Gosvāmī Mahārāja: No. We now have a different soul, mind, body, and senses. In this world there are twenty-eight categories, including the eleven senses, the sense objects, and other elements, and they are all different with respect to one another. On the other hand, in the spiritual world all the aspects of a person are one. The *jīva* in the spiritual world has senses, mind, body, and soul, and they are all one spiritual substance.

Devotee: Gurudeva, don't all the *gopīs* in Vṛndāvana possess different characteristics and different personalities?

Śrīla Nārāyaṇa Gosvāmī Mahārāja: There are many millions of varieties of moods there. Each *gopī* represents one mood, and Kṛṣṇa enjoys each of those moods. Without all the varieties of *sakhīs*, *rāsa* could not be performed and the specialty of Rādhikā would not be shown.

rādhāra svarūpa—kṛṣṇa-prema-kalpalatā
sakhī-gaṇa haya tāra pallava-puṣpa-pātā

(*Śrī Caitanya-caritāmṛta*, *Madhya-līlā* 8.209)

By nature, Śrīmatī Rādhārāṇī is just like a creeper of love of Godhead, and the *gopīs* are the twigs, flowers, and leaves of that creeper.

Where is Padmanābha Mahārāja?

Śrīpāda Padmanābha Mahārāja: Here, Gurudeva.

Śrīla Nārāyaṇa Gosvāmī Mahārāja: And others?

In the *Bhagavad-gītā*, Śrī Kṛṣṇa has spoken of four kinds of knowledge: *guhya* (confidential), *guhyataram* (more confidential), *guhyatamam* (still more confidential), and *sarva-guhyatamam* (most confidential). Can you explain these four kinds of knowledge?

(To Dāmodara Mahārāja) Do you know?

Śrīpāda Dāmodara Mahārāja: *Guhya* is knowledge of the *ātmā*.

Śrīla Nārāyaṇa Gosvāmī Mahārāja: Can you quote any *ślokas* (Sanskrit verses) to explain this?

Śrīpāda Dāmodara Mahārāja: There are so many.

Śrīla Nārāyaṇa Gosvāmī Mahārāja: Can you quote one of them?

Śrīpāda Dāmodara Mahārāja:

dehino 'smin yathā dehe
kaumāraṁ yauvanaṁ jarā
tathā dehāntara-prāptir
dhīras tatra na muhyati

(*Bhagavad-gītā* 2.13)

As the embodied soul continuously passes, in this body, from boyhood to youth to old age, the soul similarly passes into another body at death. A sober person is not bewildered by such a change.*

Śrīpāda Mādhava Mahārāja:

nainaṁ chindanti śastrāṇi
nainaṁ dahati pāvakaḥ
na cainaṁ kledayanty āpo
na śoṣayati mārutaḥ

(*Bhagavad-gītā* 2.23)

The soul can never be cut to pieces by any weapon, nor burned by fire, nor moistened by water, nor withered by the wind.*

Śrīla Nārāyaṇa Gosvāmī Mahārāja: Also:

vāsāṁsi jīrṇāni yathā vihāya
navāni gṛhṇāti naro 'parāṇi
tathā śarīrāṇi vihāya jīrṇāny
anyāni saṁyāti navāni dehī

(*Bhagavad-gītā* 2.22)

> As a person puts on new garments, giving up the old ones, the soul similarly accepts new material bodies, giving up the old and useless ones.*

So the body is not the soul. This is *guhya*. And what is general knowledge? In the *Bhagavad-gītā*, Arjuna lamented, "I will kill them. They will die."

Śrīpāda Mādhava Mahārāja: "I am the doer."

Śrīla Nārāyaṇa Gosvāmī Mahārāja: "We are this body. I cannot fight for this kingdom." This is general knowledge. Greater than this general knowledge is the understanding that no one can kill the soul. This is *guhya*, confidential knowledge.

And second? Who will answer? Jīva, can you answer?

Śrīpāda Dāmodara Mahārāja: *Paramātmā-tattva.*

Śrīla Nārāyaṇa Gosvāmī Mahārāja: What is the *śloka*? Where is Prema?

Śrīpāda Padmanābha Mahārāja: *Guhyataram* is more confidential knowledge; the knowledge that Śrī Kṛṣṇa is the Supreme Personality of Godhead.

Śrīla Nārāyaṇa Gosvāmī Mahārāja: Prema? What is it?

Prema-prayojana dāsa: Kṛṣṇa said in *Gītā*:

īśvaraḥ sarva-bhūtānāṁ
hṛd-deśe 'rjuna tiṣṭhati
bhrāmayan sarva-bhūtāni
yantrārūḍhāni māyayā

(*Bhagavad-gītā* 18.61)

> The Supreme Lord is situated in everyone's heart, O Arjuna, and is directing the wanderings of all living entities, who are seated as on a machine, made of the material energy.*

Guhyataram is the knowledge that Īśvara, the Supreme Lord, is situated in the hearts of all living entities who are as if situated on a machine made of material energy, and is causing them to wander in this material world. Kṛṣṇa is telling Arjuna, "Arjuna, you should surrender unto Him." Śrī Kṛṣṇa said, "*Tam eva śaraṇaṁ gaccha* – Surrender unto Him," because He wants to separate the knowledge of Paramātmā from knowledge of His form as Bhagavān (the Supreme Personality of Godhead).

Śrīla Nārāyaṇa Gosvāmī Mahārāja: Knowledge of Paramātmā is *guhyataram*. And third?

Śrīpāda Mādhava Mahārāja: *Guhyatamam.*

ahaṁ sarvasya prabhavo
mattaḥ sarvaṁ pravartate
iti matvā bhajante māṁ
budhā bhāva-samanvitāḥ

(*Bhagavad-gītā* 10.8)

> I am the source of all spiritual and material worlds. Everything emanates from Me. The wise who perfectly know this engage in My devotional service and worship Me with all their hearts.*

Śrīla Nārāyaṇa Gosvāmī Mahārāja: Kṛṣṇa says, "I am superior to the *jīvas* and also superior to Brahman (the impersonal aspect of the Absolute Truth)." In the eleventh and thirtheenth chapters it is therefore said that He is Puruṣottama (the Supreme Personality of Godhead). This is the third, *puruṣottama-jñāna* (*guhyatamam*).

And fourth?

Śrīpāda Padmanābha Mahārāja: *Sarva-guhyatamam*, the most confidential knowledge – all living entities should surrender to Him fully.

man-manā bhāva mad-bhakto
mad-yājī māṁ namaskuru
mām evaiṣyasi yuktvaivam
ātmānaṁ mat-parāyaṇaḥ

(*Bhagavad-gītā* 18.65)

> Always think of Me, become My devotee, worship Me and offer your homage unto Me. Thus you will come to Me without fail. I promise you this because you are My very dear friend.*

Śrīla Nārāyaṇa Gosvāmī Mahārāja: What is the real *tattva* (deep truth) in this verse? Puruṣottama cannot perform such sweet pastimes as Kṛṣṇa performs. By the words *man-mana bhāva*, Kṛṣṇa refers to Himself as that personality who performs sweet pastimes in Vṛndāvana, Mathurā, and in Dvārakā. He reminds Arjuna, "I am that Kṛṣṇa." He is indicating, "You should remember those sweet pastimes of My boyhood in Vraja." This is the most confidential knowledge.

Regarding this verse, I previously explained the pastime of a *gopī* who had recently moved to Nandagrāma. She had heard about Kṛṣṇa and wanted to see Him. One day, as Kṛṣṇa was playing His flute and returning home with millions of cows and calves and cowherd friends, He considered, "A new girl has come and she wants to see Me. Her mother-in-law did not allow her to leave the house." Her mother-in-law had told her, "Don't go, otherwise a black snake will bite you." That *gopī* had replied, "Then why are you going? I must go, even if you expel me from your house." She went out, Kṛṣṇa touched her chin with His flute, and she became maddened.

Śrīpāda Mādhava Mahārāja: General knowledge is that we are this body; confidential knowledge (*guhya*) is that we are the soul; more confidential knowledge (*guhyataram*) is *paramātmā-tattva*; the most confidential knowledge (*guhyatamam*) is *puruṣottama-tattva*; and the supermost confidential knowledge (*sarva-guhyatamam*) is *aprākṛta-tattva*, Śrī Kṛṣṇa in Vraja.

Śrīpāda Dāmodara Mahārāja: Puruṣottama means Nārāyaṇa?

Śrīla Nārāyaṇa Gosvāmī Mahārāja: Yes, Nārāyaṇa in Vaikuṇṭha.

I have explained all these *tattvas* in the introduction to the *Gītā*. This is the idea of Śrīla Bhaktivinoda Ṭhākura. Śrī Kṛṣṇa has told everything in *Gītā*, but in a brief and a hidden way. Therefore it is said that the primary book is *Gītā* and the post-graduate study is *Śrīmad-Bhāgavatam*.

Dhruva dāsa: Śrīla Gurudeva, you said that when the *jīva* first falls from the *taṭasthā* region his birth is not determined by *karma*; it is determined by the degree of his desire for independence. If he has taken birth as an animal at that time, what determines his movement from that animal body up to his next body? He has no *karma* at that point.

Śrīla Nārāyaṇa Gosvāmī Mahārāja: Best not to bother about these things. Rather try to chant more and increase your *bhakti*; then all truths will be revealed automatically. These are subjects beyond your limit, and therefore it has not been discussed in *śāstra*. Try to ask proper questions. This is not a proper question, and that is why *śāstra* has not explained it. If you want to know all these things in detail, try to do more *bhajana*. By your *bhajana* you will realize all truths.

Śrīpāda Sajjana Mahārāja: Our Śrīla Prabhupāda said that "If your house is on fire, don't try to inquire how the fire began."

Śrīla Nārāyaṇa Gosvāmī Mahārāja: If there is a fire in your house and everything is burning, there is no time to ask, "How has this fire begun?" Run away from the house, save your life, and then try to extinguish the fire. After that you can think about how the fire started.

Vṛndāvana dāsa: Gurudeva, is the *sthāyī-bhāva* of Rūpa Gosvāmī towards Rādhikā, or towards Kṛṣṇa?

Śrīla Nārāyaṇa Gosvāmī Mahārāja: Towards Rādhikā.

Mahābuddhi dāsa: I am not so intelligent like these other devotees. I want to know how can we lower devotees become empowered to serve the preaching mission of you and Śrīla Prabhupāda. How do we attain the *śakti* to please you both?

Śrīla Nārāyaṇa Gosvāmī Mahārāja: If you are sincere, extremely sincere, topmost sincere, all spiritual power and all spiritual truths will manifest in your heart. As our sincerity increases, Kṛṣṇa and *gurudeva* give all these in reciprocation.

Try to take your life and soul in your hands (be prepared to give your life) to serve *gurudeva*, thinking, "I am not my mind. I belong to Kṛṣṇa and *gurudeva*." Then, automatically, everything will come.

We know all these truths and we want to serve, but *māyā* is very powerful. She always seeks to find a loophole in our devotion. Even if a loophole is as small as a hair, she will enter. In *Śrī Caitanya-caritāmṛta* it has been said that *bhakti* is like a creeper. If you give water to the creeper of *bhakti*, it will grow up to Goloka Vṛndāvana. However, if there are weeds, those weeds will also get the water. The weeds will take the water and the main creeper will be choked.

What does this mean? If there is any ambition for recognition or desire for fame, or any slight desire to enjoy this world while you are performing *bhakti*, your *bhakti* will be stopped and your material desire will bear fruit: "I will enjoy this and that with a wife and children."

Even if, in the eyes of others, someone is performing *bhajana* and telling *hari-kathā* more beautifully than Kṛṣṇa and *gurudeva* – even if he is very learned and all devotees are praising him and giving him high esteem – still, it may actually be that his *bhakti* is drying up. That is why these desires come. Even knowing everything theoretically, he is powerless, because he is unable to overcome his material desires.

Śrīpāda Padmanābha Mahārāja: Because of desire for recognition?

Śrīla Nārāyaṇa Gosvāmī Mahārāja: It is due to the desire for recognition, and also the desire to enjoy in this world with ladies. By performing the activities of *bhakti*, such as hearing Kṛṣṇa's glories (*śravaṇam*), chanting Kṛṣṇa's names and glories (*kīrtanam*), and remembering Kṛṣṇa (*smaraṇam*) – and at the same time thinking proudly, "I am doing *bhakti*" – that desire to enjoy increases, not *bhakti*.

Śrīpāda Padmanābha Mahārāja: Regarding this point about sincerity, you said that sincerity is the main factor. Can we say that if any devotee is still maintaining any attachment in this world, his sincerity is not complete?

Śrīla Nārāyaṇa Gosvāmī Mahārāja: Yes, it can be said in this way.

Śivānanda Sena dāsa: But Śrīla Gurudeva, you have also instructed that if, within our hearts, we confess our disqualification to *guru*, *guru* can reverse this situation.

Śrīla Nārāyaṇa Gosvāmī Mahārāja: But he should be sincere and obey *guru*. Without obeying *guru*, this is not possible. Even if *guru* tells him to jump in fire, he should be ready to jump. In this way he should be sincere.

Vinaya dāsa: Yesterday you told the history of Rāmacandra Kavirāja. You said that he left his newly married wife. You said we should follow this example, but at other times you said that once one is married he should not divorce. How do we reconcile this?

Śrīla Nārāyaṇa Gosvāmī Mahārāja: I speak according to one's qualification. Therefore, for those who cannot follow my order to be renounced from family life, I say, "You can marry, but you cannot divorce."

June 14, 2008
Darśana
After the Walk

[The morning walk is now over. Śrīla Nārāyaṇa Gosvāmī Mahārāja and the disciples who have been walking with him arrive at his residence, where some of his other disciples are waiting:]

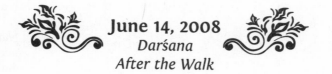

Cāru-candrikā dāsī: In *Jaiva-dharma*, Śrīla Bhaktivinoda Ṭhākura says that the *jīva's* going through material existence is Kṛṣṇa's pastime. I don't understand this. Even though suffering takes place in the mind, nevertheless, the *jīva* is suffering. It seems that this is very cruel of Kṛṣṇa.

Śrīla Nārāyaṇa Gosvāmī Mahārāja: If you read *Jaiva-dharma* thoroughly, you will see that this is one of Kṛṣṇa's sweet pastimes.[31]

Cāru-candrikā dāsī: But the *jīva* does not think, "This is a sweet pastime." He thinks, "This is suffering." And this suffering is not by his choice. You said yesterday that the *jīva's* misuse of independence is compared to mustard seeds falling on the blade of a knife and then falling on one side of the blade or the other. It seems like chance, not choice, that the *jīva* is suffering here in this material world. How can we reconcile this? How is 'chance' Kṛṣṇa's pastime?

Śrīla Nārāyaṇa Gosvāmī Mahārāja: Kṛṣṇa has given independence to all *jīvas*, and He does not want to take that away. The *jīva* looks here and there; because he has eyes, he must look somewhere. If it happens that he looks towards the transcendental world he is attracted to Yogamāyā, and if he looks toward Mahāmāyā he is attracted to this world.

Cāru-candrikā dāsī: This cannot be the *jīva's* conscious choice, because he does not have experience of Kṛṣṇa and the spiritual world.

Śrīla Nārāyaṇa Gosvāmī Mahārāja: He has no experience, but Kṛṣṇa has given him independence, and by that independence he looks where he wants to go.

June 14, 2008
Darśana

Raghunātha Bhaṭṭa dāsa: You have asked me to come (to the West Coast) and preach. I have been absorbed in material business for so many years. My Guru Mahārāja said that if one cannot quote *śāstra*, he is not a Vaiṣṇava. So, I am not really a Vaiṣṇava. I am wondering

31 See Endnote 1 (at the end of this chapter) for an excerpt from *Jaiva-dharma* that discusses this matter.

what system I can adopt to learn *śāstra*, and in this way be able to preach nicely.

Śrīla Nārāyaṇa Gosvāmī Mahārāja: Continue to preach whatever you know. There is no need for you to study *śāstra* separately, and thus waste time. When you begin to preach, you will automatically see *Śrī Caitanya-caritāmṛta*, *Śrīmad-Bhāgavatam*, and other books, and their truths will automatically manifest in your heart.

Raghunātha Bhaṭṭa dāsa:

mūkaṁ karoti vācālaṁ paṅguṁ laṅghayate girim
yat-kṛpā tam ahaṁ vande śrī-guruṁ dīna-tāraṇam

(Adapted from *Bhavārtha-dipikā*, *Maṅgala Stotram* 1)

I offer my respectful obeisances unto *śrī guru*, the deliverer of all fallen souls, whose mercy turns the dumb into eloquent speakers, and enables the lame to cross mountains.

Śrīla Nārāyaṇa Gosvāmī Mahārāja: This ability will come. Regarding my material education, I have not studied in college, but *guru-kṛpā hi kevalam*; simply by the mercy of *śrī guru*, I am now an eloquent speaker and giving discourses throughout the world.

Do you know our Tīrtha Mahārāja? He was educated only in primary school, because he joined the mission when he was very young. But he is very intelligent. By serving me, he is preaching all over the world.

You can also do this. You are very learned. You have heard *hari-kathā* from your Gurudeva and me and others. Don't be fickle-minded. Try to be steady, and preach.

Raghunātha Bhaṭṭa dāsa: I am feeling so empty. I hope you will fill me up.

Śrīla Nārāyaṇa Gosvāmī Mahārāja: Why are you feeling empty? You are hearing so much *hari-kathā*. Don't feel like that.

Raghunātha Bhaṭṭa dāsa: I have many holes; in other words I can't seem to retain anything I hear. Sound comes in one ear and then goes out the other.

Śrīla Nārāyaṇa Gosvāmī Mahārāja: You are thinking in that way, but when you follow the instructions of your Gurudeva, everything will be complete. Don't worry.

You know Śyāmarāṇī? And there are others as well. Do you know Sītā Ṭhākurāṇī and Kamala of the Gaṅgāmātās in England? They are not more qualified than you, and they are preaching all over England and many other places. They are very bold, preaching everywhere, so why can't you? Kiśorī-mohana and Sudevī did not know anything at first, but they began preaching and now everyone praises them. You are not less than them. You can preach.

Nṛhari dāsa: Does that come by faith in Kṛṣṇa and *guru*?

Śrīla Nārāyaṇa Gosvāmī Mahārāja: First have faith in *guru*, and he will give you faith in Kṛṣṇa.

Any questions?

Jayadeva dāsa: I can't seem to memorize any verses. I want to learn.

Śrīla Nārāyaṇa Gosvāmī Mahārāja: Do you remember Hare Kṛṣṇa?

Jayadeva dāsa: I remember Hare Kṛṣṇa. I know that one.

Śrīla Nārāyaṇa Gosvāmī Mahārāja: Do you remember your name?

Jayadeva dāsa: Yes.

Śrīla Nārāyaṇa Gosvāmī Mahārāja: What is your name?

Jayadeva dāsa: Jayadeva dāsa.

Śrīla Nārāyaṇa Gosvāmī Mahārāja: So, you have remembered.

There is no need to remember verses. You can very easily speak about what you have heard from your Gurudeva; that will suffice. Can you say this? "We are not this body. The body is a bag of urine, stool, blood, and other unwanted things. The soul is present in the body, as is the Supersoul, the Supreme Lord. So we should chant His name. When you die, you will not be able to take anything with you." Can you speak about these things?

Jayadeva dāsa: Yes.

Mahābuddhi dāsa: Śrīla Gurudeva, what is your vision for the *gurukula* here in Badger?

Śrīla Nārāyaṇa Gosvāmī Mahārāja: You can consider what is best. The students are taking general courses, memorizing verses and their meanings, learning how to chant *harināma* and *gāyatrī mantras*, and so on. This is good; and if you want more, you can advise the teachers and management.

I want the children to receive impressions (*saṁskāras*) in their hearts, so that in the future they will be pure devotees. They should know Vaiṣṇava behavior right from childhood, they should chant the holy name, and they should know the teachings of Śrīman Mahāprabhu.

Will there be any drama plays performed this week?

Devotee: Sunday, Monday, Tuesday, and Wednesday.

Śrīla Nārāyaṇa Gosvāmī Mahārāja: Very good, very good.

Bhāva-tāriṇī dāsī: Gurudeva, when I asked Śrīla Prabhupāda, "How may I serve you best?" he said, "The best service is to chant Hare Kṛṣṇa always, and to spread the chanting to every town and village." Do you have any instructions for me?

Śrīla Nārāyaṇa Gosvāmī Mahārāja: What he told you is right. There is no higher instruction than chanting the holy name and preaching the glories of chanting.

Yaśasvinī dāsī: Is it more important to chant, or to study *śāstra*?

Śrīla Nārāyaṇa Gosvāmī Mahārāja: Actually, serving *gurudeva* is first. Among the sixty-four limbs of *bhakti* given to us by Śrīla Rūpa Gosvāmī, first is *viśrambheṇa-guroḥ sevā* (intimate service to *śrī guru*), and then following the process given by him.

Raghunātha Bhaṭṭa dāsa: You made it very clear that *guru-sevā* is of primary importance. Her question was this: Of the two, chanting or studying *śāstra*, which is more important?

Śrīla Nārāyaṇa Gosvāmī Mahārāja: I know of many pure devotees who were unable to read at all. Śrīla Gaura-kiśora dāsa Bābājī Mahārāja and Śrīla Haridāsa Ṭhākura were both illiterate, but all literate persons bowed down to their lotus feet. How learned they were!

Śrīla Gaura-kiśora dāsa Bābājī Mahārāja was blind, and was therefore not able to study anything. However, by the mercy of his *guru-paramparā* and the influence of his *bhajana*, He was able to tell a very learned scholar of *Śrīmad-Bhāgavatam*, "Your explanation is quite wrong." That scholar then replied, "Bābā, please explain and I will hear." Śrīla Gaura-kiśora dāsa Bābājī Mahārāja then explained *Śrīmad-Bhāgavatam* in such a way that the entire audience was moved. Thus, chanting, remembering, and service to Kṛṣṇa are so exalted.

mūkaṁ karoti vācālaṁ paṅguṁ laṅghayate girim
yat-kṛpā tam ahaṁ vande śrī-guruṁ dīna-tāraṇam

(Adapted from *Bhavārtha-dipikā*, *Maṅgala Stotram* 1)

I offer my respectful obeisances unto *śrī guru*, the deliverer of all fallen souls, whose mercy turns the dumb into eloquent speakers and enables the lame to cross mountains.

Indulekhā dāsī's niece: This is my first time here. I would like to know how I go about honoring you and honoring Kṛṣṇa. I had a car accident and I know that God saved me so that I can do something good, to serve Him better. But, I don't know even the first step to take.

Śrīla Nārāyaṇa Gosvāmī Mahārāja: The best way is to serve *guru* and follow his instructions. By chanting the holy name, all of your wishes will be fulfilled, and all your miseries and problems will disappear. In this way, after some time, you will serve Rādhā and Kṛṣṇa in your transcendental form and be happy forever. This is the highest aim and object of our life. I want everyone to be happy.

Indulekhā dāsī's niece: Yesterday was the first time that I observed Ekādaśī. I did it for my mother, though, because she is dying of liver cancer.

Śrīla Nārāyaṇa Gosvāmī Mahārāja: This is good. There was once a cow lying on the street, dying. Her body was flapping about, but her life was not leaving her body. One of my lady disciples saw her and said, "O Mother cow, I am giving you the fruit of one of my Ekādaśīs. You should now be able to very easily give up your life." Then at once, without delay, the cow left her body.

Last year, one of Nanda-gopāla's horses was dying, and at the same time not dying. I said, "Hare Kṛṣṇa" in his ear, and he easily left. This chanting is miraculous and very powerful.

Indulekhā dāsī: It is painful for us to see our mother or father die. I am attached to them.

Śrīla Nārāyaṇa Gosvāmī Mahārāja: You should know who your real father is. Who is your father?

Indulekhā dāsī: You are my father, Gurudeva.

Śrīla Nārāyaṇa Gosvāmī Mahārāja: Kṛṣṇa is everyone's father. He is father of father of fathers. We should not worry for our material father and mother. If you can give some inspiration to them to do *bhajana*; this is good, but don't be attached to them. Our entire attachment should be given first to *guru* and then to Kṛṣṇa.

Rāmānanda Rāya dāsa: I need some new neck beads. My beads broke.

Śrīpāda Mādhava Mahārāja: I will give you neck beads.

Śrīla Nārāyaṇa Gosvāmī Mahārāja: (After putting the beads around his neck) Everyone should wear three separate strands: One for *guru*, one for Kṛṣṇa and Rādhikā, and one for Śrī Caitanya Mahāprabhu; or, one for service to Kṛṣṇa by mind, one for service by body, and one for service by words; or, one for Brahmā, one for Viṣṇu, and one for Maheśa (Śiva); or, one for *bhakta*, one for *bhakti*, and one for Bhagavān.

June 15, 2008
Morning Walk

Raghunātha Bhaṭṭa dāsa: Yesterday you were speaking about our Śrīpāda Tīrtha Mahārāja. You described how he became a good devotee.

Śrīla Nārāyaṇa Gosvāmī Mahārāja: He was not learned in the beginning.[32]

Śrīpāda Mādhava Mahārāja: He could not remember any verse, so everyone in the *maṭha* would tease him.

Śrīla Nārāyaṇa Gosvāmī Mahārāja: He was from a lower class, poor family. Actually he was born in a poor family of *kṣatriya* origin, which is referred to in Bengal as a lower class, poor family.

Raghunātha Bhaṭṭa dāsa: I am worse than lower class.

Śrīla Nārāyaṇa Gosvāmī Mahārāja: But you have finished high-school and perhaps university.

Raghunātha Bhaṭṭa dāsa: I did not finish university.

---

32 At present he knows several thousand verses – ed.

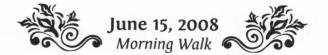

Śrīla Nārāyaṇa Gosvāmī Mahārāja: You did not finish, but you studied there. I did not study in any university. Moreover, Śrīla Gaura-kiśora dāsa Bābājī was totally illiterate and Śrīla Haridāsa Ṭhākura was as well.

Raghunātha Bhaṭṭa dāsa: My position is that I am a very fallen soul. I am asking you to please bless me and make me a *sādhu.*

Śrīla Nārāyaṇa Gosvāmī Mahārāja: If you are sincere and pray to God, Kṛṣṇa, who is very merciful, He will at once make you a *sādhu.* It is for this reason that He has given you such elevated *sādhu-saṅga* without your praying for it. That is why you are hearing so many beautiful subject matters.

Śrī Kṛṣṇa is very merciful. You are fortunate to have this association, so try to take it in your heart.

Devotee: Śrīla Gurudeva, Śrīla Prabhupāda used the term 'Back to Godhead' for more than thirty years. I have also heard you use the term sometimes. I would like to know what this phrase means.

Śrīla Nārāyaṇa Gosvāmī Mahārāja: I explained this in my class yesterday – Śrī Kṛṣṇa is beautiful, Śrīmatī Rādhikā is more beautiful, and together they perform so many sweet pastimes. Our home is with Them.

Brajanātha dāsa: Śrīla Gurudeva, in English, the phrase 'Back to Godhead' means that one has been there before and that one will be returning there.

Śrīla Nārāyaṇa Gosvāmī Mahārāja: According to our Vaisnava philosophy, this is not the correct meaning. By your permanent, natural constitution, your home is in Goloka Vṛndāvana; but unfortunately you fell from the *taṭasthā* region to this world. Now you should try to go home.

Now, I have a question: Why did Brahmā test Kṛṣṇa? What was the reason?

Tīrthapāda dāsa: The basic answer is that this is part of a pastime.

Śrīla Nārāyaṇa Gosvāmī Mahārāja: This is part of a pastime, of course; but why was this pastime performed?

Govinda dāsa: Brahmā did this because Kṛṣṇa wanted to accomplish many other pastimes by this one.

Śrīla Nārāyaṇa Gosvāmī Mahārāja: What were those pastimes?

Śrīpāda Padmanābha Mahārāja: When Śrī Kṛṣṇa killed the demon Aghāsura, Lord Brahmā saw Aghāsura's soul come out of his body and enter Kṛṣṇa's lotus feet. Seeing this, Brahmā wanted to witness more sweet pastimes of Śrī Kṛṣṇa.

Śrīla Nārāyaṇa Gosvāmī Mahārāja: This is all right. Can you explain further?

Śrīpāda Padmanābha Mahārāja: There are many reasons why this pastime had to take place.

Śrīla Nārāyaṇa Gosvāmī Mahārāja: Why?

Śrīpāda Padmanābha Mahārāja: The cows and elderly *gopīs* of Vṛndāvana had a desire to have Kṛṣṇa as their own son. They wanted to breastfeed Him, to give Him their milk.

Śrīpāda Mādhava Mahārāja: And the teenage *gopīs* wanted Kṛṣṇa as their beloved.

Śrīpāda Padmanābha Mahārāja: Therefore, during that pastime, those teenage *gopīs* were betrothed to Kṛṣṇa, who was then in the form of the innumerable cowherd boys.

Śrīpāda Mādhava Mahārāja: Knowing the desire of Kṛṣṇa, Yogamāyā attracted Brahmājī to steal the cowherd boys and calves.

Śrīpāda Padmanābha Mahārāja: In *Brahma-vimohana-līlā*, Lord Brahmā began to think, "I just saw that Kṛṣṇa killed the demon Aghāsura, and the demon's soul entered into Kṛṣṇa's body. Yet, I also see Him sitting among His friends. He looks almost like an ordinary cowherd boy." In this way, the question came into his mind, "How can He be the Supreme Lord of all?"

Śrīla Nārāyaṇa Gosvāmī Mahārāja: No. He only thought, "I want to see some more sweet pastimes." To fulfill Kṛṣṇa's desire, Yogamāyā came and made that thought enter his mind.

Śrīpāda Padmanābha Mahārāja: At that time he questioned Kṛṣṇa's supremacy and power.

Śrīpāda Mādhava Mahārāja: No. He thought, "What will Kṛṣṇa do if I steal His cowherd boys and calves?"

Śrīpāda Padmanābha Mahārāja: Yogamāyā then made the calves wander some distance away from the place where Kṛṣṇa was taking breakfast with His cowherd friends. Kṛṣṇa told His friends, "Don't be disturbed. I will go and find the calves."

He then went to search for the calves. In the meantime Lord Brahmā came, stole the cowherd boys by his mystic power, and put them to sleep in a cave.

Śrīla Nārāyaṇa Gosvāmī Mahārāja: Is he speaking correctly?

Brajanātha dāsa: No.

Prema-prayojana dāsa: In the same way that Rāvaṇa cannot steal Sītā, Lord Brahmā cannot steal the cowherd boys. Lord Brahmā merely thought that he had stolen them.

Śrīla Nārāyaṇa Gosvāmī Mahārāja: Try to hear this with attention.

Prema-prayojana dāsa: The cowherd boys are eternal associates of Śrī Kṛṣṇa. How can any person who is insignificant in comparison to them steal them away and exert his influence over them? This is quite impossible. Actually, Yogamāyā gave him the impression that he had stolen the boys and put them in a cave. He then returned to Brahma-loka, but when he reached there he was not allowed entrance to his palace.

Śrīpāda Mādhava Mahārāja: Yogamāyā made the second set of boys.

Prema-prayojana dāsa: And Śrī Kṛṣṇa made a third set. The original boys were still on the bank of the Yamunā, and Yogamāyā made the second set.

Śrīla Nārāyaṇa Gosvāmī Mahārāja: There were three sets: One set consisted of the original boys and calves, and they were covered by Yogamāyā. Mahāmāyā made the second set…

Śrīpāda Mādhava Mahārāja: Yogamāyā made the second set.

Śrīla Nārāyaṇa Gosvāmī Mahārāja: No, it was Mahāmāyā.[33] Mahāmāyā made a replica of those same cowherd boys and calves, and this was the second set, the set that Brahmājī stole.

Regarding the third set, Kṛṣṇa personally expanded as that third set. This is the thing I wanted to tell you. This is very mysterious, very mysterious.

Balarāma dāsa: What happened to the original set of cowherd boys?

Śrīla Nārāyaṇa Gosvāmī Mahārāja: Yogamāyā covered them so that no one would be able to see them. Neither Lord Brahmā nor the Vrajavāsīs, nor even Baladeva Prabhu, could see them. Being covered

---

33 See Endnote 2 (at the end of this chapter) for further explanation.

by Yogamāyā and under her influence, the year passed in a flash for them.

Śrīpāda Viṣṇu Mahārāja: Śrīla Gurudeva, what is the need of Mahāmāyā creating the other cowherd boys? Why not Yogamāyā?

Śrīla Nārāyaṇa Gosvāmī Mahārāja: If Yogamāyā had created them, how would Brahmā have been able to steal them?

Śrīpāda Viṣṇu Mahārāja: Even though Brahmā is the head of our *sampradāya* and he is able to watch this *līlā*?

Śrīla Nārāyaṇa Gosvāmī Mahārāja: Still. Being influenced by Yogamāyā, even Balarāma did not understand what was actually taking place, so what to speak of Brahmā.

Nṛhari dāsa: I read that Śrīla Madhvācārya omitted this chapter about Lord Brahmā in his commentary.

Śrīla Nārāyaṇa Gosvāmī Mahārāja: Yes, but Śrī Caitanya Mahāprabhu and His followers have accepted it. Śrīla Madhvācārya considered, "Brahmājī is my Gurudeva. He cannot be bewildered by illusion." Śrī Caitanya Mahāprabhu reconciled this. He explained that this is one of the very sweet pastimes of Kṛṣṇa. By performing this pastime, Kṛṣṇa fulfilled the desires of the cows, mothers, and young *gopīs*.

Śrīpāda Mādhava Mahārāja: Madhvācārya did not write commentaries on the fourteenth and fifteenth chapters of the Tenth Canto (the chapters describing Brahmā stealing the cows and cowherd boys). It is not that he took out those chapters; rather he did not write commentaries on them.

Śrīpāda Sajjana Mahārāja: Śrīla Śukadeva Gosvāmī did not mention in the *Śrīmad-Bhāgavatam* that Śrī Kṛṣṇa went to Brahma-loka and took the form of Lord Brahmā.

Śrīla Nārāyaṇa Gosvāmī Mahārāja: It has been told in other Purāṇas and in the commentary of Śrīla Viśvanātha Cakravartī Ṭhākura. What happened when Brahmājī went to Brahma-loka?

Śrīpāda Sajjana Mahārāja: When Brahmājī reached there, the guards blocked the door and told him, "Get out! Get out! You are an impostor!"

Śrīla Nārāyaṇa Gosvāmī Mahārāja: "Our Brahmājī is already here."

Śrīpāda Sajjana Mahārāja: "And He told us to keep the impostor from entering here."

Śrīla Nārāyaṇa Gosvāmī Mahārāja: Then what did Brahmā do?

Śrīpāda Mādhava Mahārāja: Brahmājī then returned to Earth and meditated on the possible reasons why his servants had treated him in that way. During his trance of meditation, he realized that Śrī Kṛṣṇa was behind the whole incident. Kṛṣṇa had ordered them to do so; He had bewildered them.

Śrīla Nārāyaṇa Gosvāmī Mahārāja: There he realized.

Śrīpāda Sajjana Mahārāja: Brahmā returned to Earth after one year of Earth-time. He saw that so many wonderful pastimes had taken place in Vraja during that year, like the betrothal of the young *gopīs*. He looked in the cave where he had put the cowherd boys and calves created by Yogamāyā, and saw that they were still there. Then he looked further and saw that all of the calves and cowherd boys were continuing to play with Kṛṣṇa as before. He then saw those cowherd boys transforming into the four-armed forms of Śrī Kṛṣṇa known as Lord Nārāyaṇa. Seeing this, he understood that Śrī Kṛṣṇa had personally taken the form of all of His cowherd boyfriends and calves.

Rohiṇī-nandana dāsa: Gurudeva, today we are celebrating the Annakūṭa ceremony of Śrī Govardhana. What should we be meditating on and trying to feel in our hearts while performing our devotional service and making preparations for Śrī Govardhana?

Śrīla Nārāyaṇa Gosvāmī Mahārāja: Girirāja Govardhana can give what Śrī Kṛṣṇa Himself cannot give, because Govardhana is *āśraya-vigraha*, meaning, 'the abode of love for Kṛṣṇa.' We pray to him in this way: "*Govardhano me diśatām abhīṣṭam* – May Govardhana Hill fulfill my deepest desire" (*Śrī Govardhanāṣṭakam*, by Śrīla Viśvanātha Cakravartī Ṭhākura).

pramada-madana-līlāḥ kandare kandare te
racayati nava-yūnor dvandvam asminn amandam
iti kila kalanārthaṁ lagnakas tad-dvayor me
nija-nikaṭa-nivāsaṁ dehi govardhana! tvam

(*Śrī Govardhana-vasa-prarthana-dāsakam*, Verse 2.
By Śrīla Raghunātha dāsa Gosvāmī)

O Govardhana, please grant me a dwelling near your side so that I can easily witness and serve the youthful lovers, Śrī Rādhā-Kṛṣṇa, as They perform newer and newer secret, amorous *līlās* within your many caves, and where They become completely maddened from drinking *prema*. You are present and making everything possible.

Śrīla Nārāyaṇa Gosvāmī Mahārāja: "You can enable me to see the sweet pastimes of Śrī Kṛṣṇa – even the intimate *kuñja* pastimes. You can also give me the service of Śrī Śrī Rādhā and Kṛṣṇa." Śrī Govardhana, Yamunā devī, and Lalitā Sakhī can grant the fulfillment of these desires.

Śrīpāda Sajjana Mahārāja: Gurudeva, today is Father's Day. We wish you a Happy Father's Day.

Śrīla Nārāyaṇa Gosvāmī Mahārāja: Do not merely speak it. This sentiment should manifest by your actions.

Anupama dāsa: Yesterday you mercifully gave me *harināma*. I want to know how I can serve you better and get your blessings.

Śrīla Nārāyaṇa Gosvāmī Mahārāja: You can think, "I must try to serve in any way that I can, by all means." In what ways can you serve? What qualifications do you have?

Anupama dāsa: I am very fallen. I have no qualification.

Śrīla Nārāyaṇa Gosvāmī Mahārāja: Then chant "Hare Kṛṣṇa." I will be happy by that.

Anupama dāsa: Can you please explain the meaning of my name – Anupama?

Śrīla Nārāyaṇa Gosvāmī Mahārāja: This is a name of Kṛṣṇa. It means that no one in this world or the transcendental world is equal to Him.

Śrīpāda Mādhava Mahārāja: Incomparable; matchless.

Devotee: *Śrī Caitanya-caritāmṛta* explains that Śrīla Rāmānanda Rāya is a manifestation of Śrīmatī Viśākhā-devī, and that he is Arjuna of the five Pāṇḍavas. Can you please explain how this is possible? Is it not *rasābhāsa* to think like that?

Śrīla Nārāyaṇa Gosvāmī Mahārāja: In Caitanya Mahāprabhu's pastimes, Śrīla Haridāsa Ṭhākura is a combination of Śrī Prahlāda Mahārāja and Brahmā. In the same way, Śrīla Rāmānanda Rāya is a combination of Śrīmatī Viśākhā Sakhī and Arjuna. But which Arjuna?

Śrīpāda Mādhava Mahārāja: He is not Pāṇḍava Arjuna. He is Arjuna, the *priya-narma-sakhā* (intimate cowherd friend) in the sweet pastimes of Kṛṣṇa in Vraja.

Nṛhari dāsa: Śrīla Gurudeva, is the Arjuna of the Pāṇḍavas an expansion of Arjuna of Vraja?

Śrīla Nārāyaṇa Gosvāmī Mahārāja: Yes. Śrī Kṛṣṇa loved Arjuna of the Pāṇḍavas because he had the same name as His dear friend Arjuna in Vraja.

Gaurasundara dāsa: In your book *The Origin of Ratha-yātrā* there is a pastime in which Mother Kuntī asked Vasudeva Mahārāja, "After we were in trouble in the house of shellac and it burned down, why did you not ask about our welfare or help us in any way?" Vasudeva Mahārāja replied, "I was in prison, being kicked by the soldiers of Kaṁsa. When I was released, I immediately sent a message to you."

My question is this: Didn't the pastimes of the Pāṇḍavas begin after Vasudeva Mahārāja was already freed from prison?

Śrīla Nārāyaṇa Gosvāmī Mahārāja: Kṛṣṇa was still young when Vasudeva Mahārāja was in prison. It was during this time that the Kauravas tried to burn the Pāṇḍavas in the fire.

Śrīpāda Mādhava Mahārāja: Arjuna and Kṛṣṇa are the same age, and Bhīma is a little older; so the pastimes of the Pāṇḍavas were taking place even before Kṛṣṇa killed Kaṁsa.

Śrīpāda Dāmodara Mahārāja: Gurudeva, Śrīla dāsa is here.

Śrīla Nārāyaṇa Gosvāmī Mahārāja: (To Śrīla dāsa) My dear friend. You have no wife, nor any children, nor any related responsibilities; but you do not come with us to preach around the world. You are not merciful to me, or even to Kṛṣṇa.

Śrīla dāsa: I have no mercy on myself.

Śrīla Nārāyaṇa Gosvāmī Mahārāja: You are very cruel. Kṛṣṇa wants to take you with Him, but you refuse to go.

Viśvambhara dāsa (from Hawaii)**:** Śrīla Gurudeva, you have often quoted this verse:

barhāpīḍaṁ naṭa-vara-vapuḥ karṇayoḥ karṇikāraṁ
bibhrad vāsaḥ kanaka-kapiśaṁ vaijayantīṁ ca mālām
randhrān veṇor adhara-sudhayāpūrayan gopa-vṛndair
vṛndāraṇyaṁ sva-pada ramaṇaṁ prāviśad gīta-kīrtiḥ

(*Śrīmad-Bhāgavatam* 10.21.5)

> Wearing a peacock-feather ornament upon His head, blue *karṇikāra* flowers on His ears, a yellow garment as brilliant as gold, and the *vaijayantī* garland, Lord Kṛṣṇa exhibited His transcendental form as the greatest of dancers as He entered the forest of Vṛndāvana, beautifying it with the marks of His footprints. He filled the holes of His flute with the nectar of His lips, and the cowherd boys sang His glories.

I would like to know if there is a special potency in this verse. Every time I think of it or read it, I begin to cry. I don't know why. There must be some magic in it.

Śrīla Nārāyaṇa Gosvāmī Mahārāja: Śrīla Śukadeva Gosvāmī has filled this verse with all of the sweetness of Śrī Kṛṣṇa's form (*rūpa-mādhurī*). The *gopīs* experience the truth of this verse, and you are fortunate to realize it.

Trilokanātha dāsa: Some years ago in Hilo, Hawaii, you said that Kṛṣṇa's pastimes of *sambhoga* (meeting) are superior to those of *vipralambha* (separation). You cited the example of the *gopīs* cursing Lord Brahmā for creating eyelids that cover their eyes. However, a few days ago, we heard that Śrīmatī Rādhikā feels separation from Śrī Kṛṣṇa even while sitting on His lap, and Kṛṣṇa very much appreciates Her love in these moods of separation. Śrīla Prabhupāda has also stressed the superiority of feelings of separation.

Śrīla Nārāyaṇa Gosvāmī Mahārāja: It has been told in scripture that the mood of separation dances on the head of the happiness of meeting. But do you think that the *gopīs* will be happy in separation from Śrī Kṛṣṇa? Do you want Śrīmatī Rādhikā and Śrī Kṛṣṇa to be separated?

Devotees: No.

Śrīla Nārāyaṇa Gosvāmī Mahārāja: It is in this regard that I have said that meeting is the highest situation; it is in accordance with this line of thought (that is, from their associates' point of view).

Śrīpāda Mādhava Mahārāja: Śrīla Sanātana Gosvāmī has written that feelings of separation dance on the head of the happiness of meeting. However, in the next verse he says that Kṛṣṇa cannot tolerate His devotees' feelings of separation and immediately appears before them.

Rohiṇī-nandana dāsa: It is said that the most dangerous thing for us is to commit *vaiṣṇava-aparādha*. In that connection, I fear that I am not making advancement because I have offended you. I'm hoping that you will forgive me so that I can make some advancement.

Śrīla Nārāyaṇa Gosvāmī Mahārāja: I have forgiven you, but you should know that in your past lives you committed many offenses. This is the reason why, when you chant *harināma*, tears do not fall from your eyes and the hairs of your body do not stand on end.

hena kṛṣṇa-nāma yadi laya bahu-bāra
tabu yadi prema nahe, nahe aśrudhāra

tabe jāni, aparādha tāhāte pracura
kṛṣṇa-nāma-bīja tāhe nā kare aṅkura

(*Śrī Caitanya-caritāmṛta, Ādi-līlā* 8.29–30)

If one chants the exalted holy name of the Lord again and again and yet his love for the Supreme Lord does not develop and tears do not appear in his eyes, it is evident that because of his offenses in chanting, the seed of the holy name of Kṛṣṇa does not sprout.

June 16, 2008
Morning Walk

Raghunātha Bhaṭṭa dāsa: Śrīla Gurudeva, I want to express something to you. For many years I have been asleep in *māyā*, like an owl hiding from the light. Now you are bringing light to me; you are waking me up, and I feel grateful for this. Now I feel that, due to my ignorance, I have committed many offenses to you. I beg you to please forgive me.

Śrīla Nārāyaṇa Gosvāmī Mahārāja: Certainly I will. Don't worry about that. Ignorance is not so bad if one is sincere, but lack of sincerity is very bad.

Rāsapriya dāsi: Śrīla Gurudeva, you said in Vancouver that Kṛṣṇa was thinking in Goloka Vṛndāvana: "Rādhikā's mood of devotion and love are so incredibly great, and Her beauty is incomparable. If I take Her mood and beauty, I can then deliver the conditioned souls." My question is this: we usually hear that Kṛṣṇa is simply enjoying with the *gopīs*, *gopas*, and other residents of the spiritual world. We do not really hear of Him thinking of the conditioned souls.

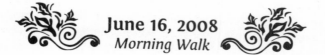

Śrīla Nārāyaṇa Gosvāmī Mahārāja: (To Śrīpāda Padmanābha Mahārāja) You can answer.

Śrīpāda Padmanābha Mahārāja: Kṛṣṇa is both *sarvajña*, all-knowing, and *mugdha*, like an ignorant child, at the same time. When He is on the lap of Mother Yaśodā, He is not all-knowing. He can be *sarvajña* or *mugdha* at any moment.

Śrīla Nārāyaṇa Gosvāmī Mahārāja: He can be both at the same time. He is always in Vṛndāvana, enjoying. At the same time, His all-knowing potency called *aiśvarya-śakti* (or *sarvajña-śakti*) is thinking, "When will I serve my Prabhu?" She is always waiting for this opportunity. When she sees any opportunity to serve, she serves at once.

Dhīra-kṛṣṇa dāsa: Śrīpāda Padmanābha Mahārāja said yesterday that since the *jīva* has come from *taṭasthā-śakti*, his constitutional right is up to the *taṭasthā* region, which is Brahma-loka or Brahma-kānti. He said that the *jīva* cannot go above this unless He has the mercy of Hari, Guru, and Vaiṣṇavas.

Śrīpāda Padmanābha Mahārāja: He is speaking of a conversation I had with him. I had heard that the *taṭasthā-jīva* coming to this world has the constitutional right to again attain the stage of Brahman realization. That is why even Māyāvādīs, by their austerities, can reach up to the limit of Brahman realization.

Śrīla Nārāyaṇa Gosvāmī Mahārāja: No. *Jīvera 'svarūpa' haya, kṛṣṇera 'nitya-dāsa.* The *jīva* has this constitutional right. However, he can only realize this constitutional right by the help of *guru* and Vaiṣṇava.

Śrīpāda Tridaṇḍi Mahārāja: Śrīla Gurudeva, can you explain the difference between *śuddha-sattva* and *viśuddha-sattva*? *Śuddha-sattva* is pure existence, and *viśuddha-sattva* is more than that?

Śrīla Nārāyaṇa Gosvāmī Mahārāja: Kṛṣṇa and His incarnations, and also His eternal associates like the *gopīs*, Nanda Bābā, and Yaśodā-maiyā are *viśuddha-sattva*. When the *jīva* becomes pure, he becomes *śuddha-sattva*.

sattvaṁ viśuddhaṁ vasudeva-śabditaṁ
yad īyate tatra pumān apāvṛtaḥ
sattve ca tasmin bhagavān vāsudevo
hy adhokṣajo me namasā vidhīyate

(*Śrīmad-Bhāgavatam* 4.3.23)

> I am always engaged in offering obeisances to Lord Vāsudeva in pure Kṛṣṇa consciousness. Kṛṣṇa consciousness is always pure consciousness, in which the Supreme Personality of Godhead, known as Vāsudeva, is revealed without any covering.[34]

Śrīpāda Mādhava Mahārāja: Śrīla Gurudeva explained in Mathurā that *sattva* means 'existence;' *miśra-sattva* refers to existence mixed with the three modes of material nature, which is the state of the conditioned souls; *śuddha-sattva* refers to liberated souls, those who have attained perfection; and finally *viśuddha-sattva* refers to Kṛṣṇa and His eternal associates.

Śrīpāda Tridaṇḍi Mahārāja: What about Hanumānjī?

Śrīla Nārāyaṇa Gosvāmī Mahārāja: He is *viśuddha-sattva*, because he is an eternal associate of Lord Rāmacandra. He is not a *jīva*; he is a manifestation of Sadāśiva (a form of Lord Viṣṇu).

Brajanātha dāsa: Śrīla Gurudeva, when the *jīva* attains perfection, does he also become *viśuddha-sattva*?

Śrīla Nārāyaṇa Gosvāmī Mahārāja: No, never.

Śrīpāda Tridaṇḍi Mahārāja: We can only come to *śuddha-sattva*?

Śrīpāda Padmanābha Mahārāja: Like a particle of a ray of *prema*, *śuddha-sattva viśeṣātmā* (the transcendental platform of pure goodness) descends into the *sādhaka's* heart from the hearts of the *viśuddha-sattva* eternal associates of the Lord. So when that *jīva* enters Goloka, he does not become *viśuddha-sattva*?[35]

---

34 "In the mode of pure goodness (*viśuddha-sattva*) the Vāsudeva form of the Lord is manifest. Lord Śiva describes this in the Fourth Canto, Chapter Three (*Śrīmad-Bhāgavatam* 4.3.23):

"An explanation of this verse follows. The word *viśuddha* here means 'because it is the Lord's internal potency it is free from even the slightest touch of matter,' and that is why the adjective *śuddha* (pure) is used here. This *viśuddha-sattva* is here called '*vāsudeva-sattva*.' Why is it called *vāsudeva-sattva*? Because the Supreme Personality of Godhead (*pumān*) Lord Vāsudeva is manifest (*īyate*) because of it (*yat*).

"Firstly, the word *sattva* is used here because this potency manifests the Supreme Truth and is thus like the *sattva* (goodness) that enables the unseen to be seen in this world. Secondly, the word *vāsudeva* is used because this potency enables one to understand the Supreme Personality of Godhead, Lord Vāsudeva. These two words are then put together into *vāsudeva-sattva*, which is the same as *viśuddha-sattva* (pure goodness)" (*Bhagavat-sandarbha, Anuccheda* 103).

35 See Endnote 3 (at the end of this chapter) for more explanations by Śrīla Nārāyaṇa Gosvāmī Mahārāja of the verse beginning with *śuddha-sattva viśeṣātmā*.

Śrīla Nārāyaṇa Gosvāmī Mahārāja: No, never. Whether they have come from Baladeva Prabhu, Saṅkarṣaṇa, or Kāraṇodakaśāyī, they are always *śuddha-sattva*.[36]

Abhirāma dāsa: Gurudeva, sometimes in our preaching we speak about the *Śikṣāṣṭakam* verses. In the last verse, the word *lampaṭa* is translated as 'debauchee.' I am concerned that new people, who have never heard about Kṛṣṇa, may be confused.

Śrīla Nārāyaṇa Gosvāmī Mahārāja: In that case you can avoid using this word. Best to use it only when speaking with devotees. Otherwise, if you do wish to use it, then simply explain it.

You can explain to people that Kṛṣṇa's so-called immorality is transcendental; it is not worldly. The word debauchee has been told only for comparison's sake, in order to give us an example. We say, "It is like this, but not this." Kṛṣṇa is like a *lampaṭa*, but He is not a *lampaṭa*. Rather, His divine pastimes are indications of a very high class of extreme love and affection. This is the true meaning of *lampaṭa* in this connection. Otherwise, if Kṛṣṇa actually has bad qualities, why would Śrīmatī Rādhikā love Him?

Raghunātha Bhaṭṭa dāsa: Śrīla Gurudeva, I have a practical question. Śrīla Gour Govinda Mahārāja used to give us very strict instructions. He would say that men should not hear from women when women are singing in *kīrtana* or giving class. In the Gauḍīya Maṭha in India it is like this. Women do not give class in the *maṭha*. Should we also follow this in the West?

Śrīla Nārāyaṇa Gosvāmī Mahārāja: You see what I am doing. I have women leading *kīrtanas* and *bhajanas*, and giving class.

Raghunātha Bhaṭṭa dāsa: When you are present, it is all right. But when you are not present, if many women give class, the *brahmacārīs* may get disturbed.

Śrīla Nārāyaṇa Gosvāmī Mahārāja: When Jāhnavā Ṭhākurāṇī would give classes, all the *brahmacārīs* and *sannyāsīs*, including Śrīla Rūpa Gosvāmī, Śrīla Sanātana Gosvāmī, and others like them would offer her respect as Nityānanda-śakti (the eternal consort and potency of Nityānanda Prabhu).

Raghunātha Bhaṭṭa dāsa: Should we make a distinction between those who are advanced and those who are not? What is the standard?

---

36 See Endnote 4 (at the end of this chapter) for still more explanations of the verse beginning with *śuddha-sattva viśeṣātmā*, and a discussion of the matter by the editors.

Śrīla Nārāyaṇa Gosvāmī Mahārāja: The main thing is that men should not be attached to ladies.

Śrīpāda Mādhava Mahārāja: Those who are disturbed should not listen.

Śrīla Nārāyaṇa Gosvāmī Mahārāja: Ladies are generally not allowed to give class in the Gauḍīya Maṭha, but if they are qualified they can do so. For example, there was a disciple of Śrīla Prabhupāda Bhaktisiddhānta Sarasvatī Ṭhākura named Saroja-vāsinī. She was very bold; she would even question Śrīla Prabhupāda. Once she asked him, "If you are not giving *guru-mantra* or *dīkṣā* to ladies, should we go to another *guru* to receive this?"

Śrīpāda Mādhava Mahārāja: She asked, "Have you taken a vow to deliver only those in a male form and not in a female form?"

Śrīla Nārāyaṇa Gosvāmī Mahārāja: And thus she became Śrīla Prabhupāda's first lady disciple.

Śrīpāda Mādhava Mahārāja: He was saying that if ladies give class, then the *brahmacārīs* will be disturbed by them.

Śrīla Nārāyaṇa Gosvāmī Mahārāja: Why? If Śyāmarāṇī or Umā give classes, why would any male be disturbed? Some ladies will give class; it is not that all will give.

Guest: Śrīla Gurudeva, at what stage does one attain a spiritual body? When does one realize this?

Śrīla Nārāyaṇa Gosvāmī Mahārāja: One attains a spiritual body when one is liberated from material bondage and achieves *prema*. When *rati* (*bhāva-bhakti*) manifests, at that time a person can have a glimpse of his own reality; he will see a shadow of his spiritual form.

Gopa-vṛndapāla dāsa: Gurudeva, in the *paramparā* system, the *guru* is giving not only *tattva* (established philosophical truths) but also transcendental moods, *bhāva*. In our *paramparā*, the mood of Rādhā-Kṛṣṇa conjugal *rasa* is given from *guru* to disciple, *guru* to disciple, in the chain of disciplic succession. This goes back all the way to Śrī Caitanya Mahāprabhu, Śrī Īśvara Purī Prabhu, and Śrīla Mādhavendra Purīpāda. Where did this conjugal mood come from before Śrīla Mādhavendra Purīpāda?

Śrīpāda Sajjana Mahārāja: The worshipable Deities of Lakṣmīpati Purī, the *guru* of Mādhavendra Purī, were Kṛṣṇa and Balarāma.

Śrīla Nārāyaṇa Gosvāmī Mahārāja: From where did Mādhavendra

Purī's mood come? It came from the special mercy of Kṛṣṇa. Nothing else can be said.

Śrīpāda Mādhava Mahārāja: Someone asked this question a few months ago, and you said that it was because of the special mercy of Śrīman Mahāprabhu.

Prema-prayojana dāsa: Mādhavendra Purīpāda came from Goloka Vṛndāvana, so he can bring it with him.

Śrīla Nārāyaṇa Gosvāmī Mahārāja: Śrīla Rūpa and Sanātana were associates; they are Rūpa and Rati Mañjarīs. But it is not said in *śāstra* who Mādhavendra Purī was.

Śrīpāda Dāmodara Mahārāja: *Gaura-gaṇoddeśa-dīpikā* says he is a *kalpa-vṛkṣa* (desire tree).

Śrīla Nārāyaṇa Gosvāmī Mahārāja: It has only been told that he was compared to the sprout of *prema* (*premāṅkura*). He was compared with the sprout of the creeper on the desire tree of *prema*.

jaya śrī mādhavapurī kṛṣṇa-prema-pūra
bhakti-kalpatarura teṅho prathama aṅkura
(*Śrī Caitanya-caritāmṛta, Ādi-līlā* 9.10)

> All glories to Śrī Mādhavendra Purī, the storehouse of all devotional service unto Kṛṣṇa! He is a desire tree of devotional service, and it is in him that the seed of devotional service first fructified.

He was not the whole *kalpa-vṛkṣa* of devotional service. The whole *kalpa-vṛkṣa* tree is Caitanya Mahāprabhu Himself, and Mahāprabhu has so many roots. Mādhavendra Purī is the sprouted seed, or the fructification of the seed, of devotional service. Nityānanda Prabhu and Advaita Ācārya are main branches.

Śrīpāda Mādhava Mahārāja: And Paramānanda Purī and others are the nine main roots.

Prema-prayojana dāsa: Śrīla Kṛṣṇadāsa Kavirāja Gosvāmī said that only three people tasted the verse beginning with *ayi dīna-dayārdra nātha he*: Rādhārāṇī, Mahāprabhu, and Mādhavendra Purī. The mood within this verse is *mohanakhya-mahābhāva*. No *jīva* in this world could have such *mahābhāva*.

Śrīla Nārāyaṇa Gosvāmī Mahārāja: Only they can understand something. Mādhavendra Purī is an eternal associate, but he never revealed this. He acted as though he became an associate after achieving perfection. Rādhārāṇī came from Goloka Vṛndāvana as a *nitya-parikara*, eternal associate, of Kṛṣṇa. Śrī Caitanya Mahāprabhu is Kṛṣṇa Himself. And who is Mādhavendra Purī?

Śrīpāda Mādhava Mahārāja: It is not mentioned anywhere, but there is no forth person to understand this verse.

Śrīla Nārāyaṇa Gosvāmī Mahārāja:

ahaṁ vedmi śuko vetti
vyāso vetti na vetti vā
bhaktyā bhāgavataṁ grāhyaṁ
na buddhyā na ca ṭīkayā
(*Śrī Caitanya-caritāmṛta, Madhya-līlā* 24.313)

(Lord Śiva said) "I may know; Śukadeva Gosvāmī, the son of Vyāsadeva, may know; and Vyāsadeva may know or may not know *Śrīmad-Bhāgavatam*. On the whole, *Śrīmad-Bhāgavatam*, the spotless Purāṇa, can be learned only through devotional service, not by material intelligence, speculative methods, or imaginary commentaries."

Śaṅkara (Lord Śiva) is telling this. Why has he uttered this?

Śrīpāda Mādhava Mahārāja: It is because Vyāsadeva is not *āśraya-vigraha*; (the devotee, or the abode of love) He is *śaktyāveśa-avatāra* (an incarnation of Kṛṣṇa, who is *vīśaya-tattva*, the object of love). That is why He may or may not know. But Śivajī and others are *āśraya-ṭattva*, so they know the mood of the *āśraya* (devotees).

Devotee: Śrīla Gurudeva, I want to know if I can get your blessings. I am translating your books into Farsi, the language of Iran.

Śrīla Nārāyaṇa Gosvāmī Mahārāja: Oh, very good. Good idea. You can translate *Jaiva-dharma* and *Bhagavad-gītā* first.

Jayanta-kṛṣṇa dāsa: A few years ago, to ease the minds of the devotees who are suffering in this material world, you taught us this verse:

tat te 'nukampāṁ su-samīkṣamāṇo
bhuñjāna evātma-kṛtaṁ vipākam
hṛd-vāg vapurbhir vidadhan namas te
jīveta yo mukti-pade sa dāya-bhāk
(*Śrīmad-Bhāgavatam* 10.14.8)

> My dear Lord, one who earnestly waits for You to bestow Your causeless mercy upon him, all the while patiently suffering the reactions of his past misdeeds and offering You respectful obeisances with his heart, words and body, is surely eligible for liberation, for it has become his rightful claim.

Why did Lord Caitanya Mahāprabhu chastise Sārvabhauma Bhaṭṭācārya for changing the word '*mukti*' to '*bhakti*' in the last line of the verse?

Śrīla Nārāyaṇa Gosvāmī Mahārāja: *Mukti* is situated at the lotus feet (*mukti-pade*) of *bhakti*, so there is no harm in using the word *mukti*.

Raghunātha Bhaṭṭa dāsa: Some devotees are saying that when the *jīvas* become *sādhana-siddha* (self-realized by the performance of *sādhana-bhakti*) or *kṛpā-siddha* (self-realized by the mercy of *guru* and Kṛṣṇa), they become equal to the *nitya-siddhas* (the eternally perfect associates of the Lord) in all respects. But I heard that *anugatya* (service under proper guidance) is required for *sādhana-siddha* and *kṛpā-siddha*, and now you just mentioned that the *sādhana-siddha jīvas* can only reach *śuddha-sattva*, not *viśuddha-sattva*.

Śrīla Nārāyaṇa Gosvāmī Mahārāja: When *jīvas* become *siddha* (perfect), they will have a body like that of the *gopīs* or the other Vrajavāsīs. They have equal opportunity to serve, but still they are *śuddha-sattva*.

Śrīpāda Padmanābha Mahārāja: One last question remains about *śuddha-sattva* and *viśuddha-sattva*. You said that *śuddha-sattva* manifests when the *taṭasthā-jīva* attains perfection in the spiritual world. When someone becomes liberated (*mukta*) but attains only Brahman (the impersonal aspect of the Lord), is that *miśra-sattva* or *śuddha-sattva*?

Śrīla Nārāyaṇa Gosvāmī Mahārāja: There is neither *śuddha-sattva* nor *viśuddha-sattva*, nor any *sattva*. In Brahman there is no differentiation.

Vṛndāvana dāsa: I have heard that Śrīla Bhaktivedānta Svāmī Mahārāja sometimes said that those who attain the *brahma-jyoti* would again come down into the material world; that they would fall from that position.

Śrīla Nārāyaṇa Gosvāmī Mahārāja: It has been told in *Śrīmad-Bhāgavatam*:

ye 'nye 'ravindākṣa vimukta-māninas
tvayy asta-bhāvād aviśuddha-buddhayaḥ
āruhya kṛcchreṇa paraṁ padaṁ tataḥ
patanty adho 'nādṛta-yuṣmad-aṅghrayaḥ
(*Śrīmad-Bhāgavatam* 10.2.32)

O lotus-eyed Lord, although non-devotees who accept severe austerities and penances to achieve the highest position may think themselves liberated, their intelligence is impure. They fall down from their position of imagined superiority because they have no regard for Your lotus feet.

They imagine that they are liberated, but actually they are not. They fall down from their imagined position.

Vṛndāvana dāsa: If they attain *sāyujya-mukti*, is it not like annihilation of any relationship?

Śrīla Nārāyaṇa Gosvāmī Mahārāja: The soul exists, but there is no activity in his being. He is completely unconscious. His existence is not fully gone. Existence is there, but he cannot realize anything.

Vṛndāvana dāsa: Can they come again to the material world?

Śrīla Nārāyaṇa Gosvāmī Mahārāja: They will not come. Moreover, they have no chance to do *bhakti*. That is why it has been told in *śāstra* that *mukti* is like a tigress. *Mukti-vyāghryāḥ*. Like a tigress, *mukti* swallows us. If a tiger eats someone, that person does not remain alive. It is explained in *Śrī Bṛhad-bhāgavatāmṛta* that if a great soul's glance lands upon the living entity stuck in the *brahma-jyoti* while that great soul is travelling through it, that particular living entity may be released. This is the only way for such release.

June 17, 2008
Morning Walk

Śrīpāda Tridaṇḍi Mahārāja: Śrīla Gurudeva, will you be teaching us *Prema-vivarta* here in Badger?

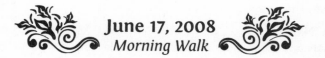

Śrīla Nārāyaṇa Gosvāmī Mahārāja: I wanted to speak about this subject in the previous nights' classes, but I had no time because I had to complete the other topics first. Today and tomorrow I will discuss *Prema-vivarta* along with a discussion on Śrīla Rūpa Gosvāmī.

Nityānanda dāsa: Śrīla Gurudeva, it is said that Kṛṣṇa can see with any part of His body and perform any activity with any part of His body. Is this also true of Śrīmatī Rādhikā and the *gopīs*, or only for Kṛṣṇa?

Śrīla Nārāyaṇa Gosvāmī Mahārāja: Yes, it is also true for the *gopīs*, because they are Kṛṣṇa's power (*śakti*). Kṛṣṇa performs all of His activities with their help. All of Kṛṣṇa's incarnations such as Śrī Rāmacandra can do so as well, because they are all transcendental (*cinmaya*), composed of eternal existence, unfathomable knowledge, and unlimited spiritual bliss (*sat-cit-ānanda*).

Nityānanda dāsa: I have a related question. It is said that Kṛṣṇa and His name are non-different. Are Rādhā and the *gopīs*' names non-different from themselves?

Śrīla Nārāyaṇa Gosvāmī Mahārāja: This is true for all associates of the Lord, even for Śrī Nārada Ṛṣi.

Nṛhari dāsa: Śrīla Gurudeva, yesterday you mentioned that the disciples of our Śrīla Prabhupāda were cheated. Does that refer to only some of his disciples?

Śrīla Nārāyaṇa Gosvāmī Mahārāja: Some of them were cheated, not everyone. They were cheated by *māyā*, and therefore they left the *sannyāsa* and *brahmacārī āśramas* to marry. They could not maintain steadiness in their *bhakti*. They had not come to the stage of *ruci* (a natural taste for chanting and remembering Kṛṣṇa), and therefore they fell down. If they had attained *ruci*, they would not have fallen unless they committed *vaiṣṇava-aparādha*; but it is very rare for one to commit an offense at the stage of *ruci*.

Brajanātha dāsa: You said that some persons think that Ekalavya was a great devotee. They misunderstood the message of their spiritual master, and that is how they have been cheated.

Śrīla Nārāyaṇa Gosvāmī Mahārāja: Śrīla Bhaktivedānta Svāmī Mahārāja would never have glorified Ekalavya. No *rūpānuga-vaiṣṇava* in our line of Śrīman Mahāprabhu would glorify him. Only those who are unaware of proper *siddhānta* would say that Ekalavya is a great devotee.

Govinda dāsa: Śrīla Gurudeva, some people use the example of Gopa-kumāra in an attempt to establish that the *jīva* can fall from Goloka. On the other hand, the way Śrīla Bhakti Rakṣaka Śrīdhara Mahārāja and Śrīla Bhakti Pramoda Purī Mahārāja tell the story is that when Gopa-kumāra reached Goloka Vṛndāvana, the other cowherd boys asked, "Who is he? Why is Kṛṣṇa embracing him like this?" This was because they had never seen him before. This proves that Gopa-kumāra had never previously been in Goloka Vṛndāvana.

Śrīla Nārāyaṇa Gosvāmī Mahārāja: Those who say that the *jīva* fell from Goloka Vṛndāvana are foolish.

Jayanta-kṛṣṇa dāsa: Śrīla Gurudeva, last night Dāmodara Mahārāja said that those who commit an offense to a pure devotee (*mahā-aparādha*) still have *bhakti* but their *bhakti* becomes covered. But I heard in one of your classes that when someone commits such an offense, Kṛṣṇa will have to make a separate new hell for him.

Śrīla Nārāyaṇa Gosvāmī Mahārāja: I have told this. If the *bhakti-latā* (creeper of devotion) is uprooted, there is no root; so how can the creeper grow again?

yadi vaiṣṇava-aparādha uṭhe hātī mātā
upāḍe vā chiṇḍe, tāra śukhi' yāya pātā
(*Śrī Caitanya-caritāmṛta, Madhya-līlā* 19.156)

> If the devotee commits an offense at the feet of a Vaiṣṇava while cultivating the creeper of devotional service in the material world, his offense is compared to a mad elephant that uproots the creeper and breaks it. In this way the leaves of the creeper are dried up.

The leaves will dry up and the creeper will be totally destroyed. So what I have told is all right. While I was hearing Dāmodara Mahārāja speak, I was thinking, "What is he telling?"

Brajanātha dāsa: He was speaking very fast.

Śrīla Nārāyaṇa Gosvāmī Mahārāja: Yes, very, very fast.

Īśa dāsa: Śrīla Gurudeva, you said that the names of Rādhā and the *gopīs* are non-different from themselves. Is this the same for our Śrīla Prabhupāda and yourself?

Śrīpāda Mādhava Mahārāja: Yes, surely.

Devotee: Śrīla Gurudeva, I have a question. In previous *yugas*, there were great *bhaktas* such as Prahlāda Mahārāja, who never knew of Kṛṣṇa in Vraja. Can they, or do they, receive *kṛṣṇa-prema*?

Śrīla Nārāyaṇa Gosvāmī Mahārāja: Prahlāda Mahārāja said:

matir na kṛṣṇe parataḥ svato vā
mitho 'bhipadyeta gṛha-vratānām
adānta-gobhir viśatāṁ tamisraṁ
punaḥ punaś carvita-carvaṇānām
(*Śrīmad-Bhāgavatam* 7.5.30)

> Materialistic persons are simply mulling over that which has already been mulled and chewing that which has already been chewed. Because their senses are not controlled they are proceeding towards the dreadful hell of this material existence, repeatedly trying to enjoy that which has already been consumed. The intelligence of such materially attached persons can neither be turned towards Bhagavān Śrī Kṛṣṇa by their own endeavor, by the instruction of others, or by the association of similar materialistic persons.

These are the words of Śrī Prahlāda Mahārāja, which he had heard from Nārada Muni while still in the womb of his mother. It may be said that he is a worshiper of Nṛsiṁhadeva, but we can know that in a deeper sense he is a worshiper of Kṛṣṇa. It was Kṛṣṇa who came to save him, in the form of Lord Nṛsiṁhadeva. If any problem comes to us, although we are worshipers of Śrī Śrī Kṛṣṇa and Rādhikā, He may come in the form of Lord Nṛsiṁhadeva when He wants to save us.

Īśa dāsa: I asked you this question in Houston, and you explained that Prahlāda knew about Vrajendra-nandana Kṛṣṇa, but his worshipable Deity was Viṣṇu.

Brajanātha dāsa: This is because a promise made by Brahmā must come true. In order to keep Brahmā's promise, Kṛṣṇa had to appear in His half-man–half-lion form.

Śrīla Nārāyaṇa Gosvāmī Mahārāja: Yes, He had to come in that form. He came in that form for a special reason.

Devotee: What about the *ṛṣis* and other mystics in previous *yugas* who never knew of Kṛṣṇa?

Śrīla Nārāyaṇa Gosvāmī Mahārāja: They will not attain *kṛṣṇa-prema*. They will perform *tapasya* (austerities) and *yajñas* (fire sacrifices), and they will go to heaven. But *ṛṣis* like Nārada attain *kṛṣṇa-prema*.

Prema dāsa: Śrīla Gurudeva, you were speaking about the *bhakti* practice, and you mentioned that astrology is one of the dangers that we should protect ourselves from. Before surrendering to you I was a professional astrologer. I am wondering if astrology is only a material science, and how we can use it to assist the conditioned *jīva* and be of service to you.

Śrīla Nārāyaṇa Gosvāmī Mahārāja: *Yoga* (practice for attainment of mystic perfections), *jñāna* (speculations to achieve impersonal Brahman), and *karma* (fruitive activities) are not favorable for *bhakti*. Astrology is *karma*. I see that most astrologers are very poor. I have seen that many of them beg on the streets in India and cheat people. Elevated astrologers like Gargācārya actually knew past, present, and future. Their practice was okay, and they were not professional. Nowadays, professional astrologers (those who practice only to earn a livelihood) cheat others. They are not sufficiently proficient in the complex mathematics required for accuracy.

Prema dāsa: So if it is pure, if it is from the heart, how can it be of service to the conditioned *jīva*?

Śrīla Nārāyaṇa Gosvāmī Mahārāja: You can consider how it may help them.

Śrīpāda Mādhava Mahārāja: You can help calculate dates for our *Śrī Caitanya Pañjikā* (Vaiṣṇava calendar). I will introduce you to Pādābja Prabhu, the devotee who makes our calendar.

Īśa dāsa: Gurudeva, two disciples of our Śrīla Prabhupāda wrote to him and asked, "Can we do our charts?" Śrīla Prabhupāda said, "No. Regarding my disciples, they have nothing to do with astrology."

Śrīla Nārāyaṇa Gosvāmī Mahārāja: I say the same.

Brajanātha dāsa: Śrīla Bhaktivedānta Svāmī Mahārāja used to say that if you clap your hands in front of Ṭhākurajī, then all of the lines on the palms of your hands will be changed.

Śrīla Nārāyaṇa Gosvāmī Mahārāja: Yes.

Balarāma dāsa: Śrīla Gurudeva, is it possible for a *jīva* in a Western body to achieve the stage of *bhāva*? Are there any examples?

Śrīla Nārāyaṇa Gosvāmī Mahārāja: I have not seen that statement written, but it can happen anywhere in the world. If one has very high-class devotee association and he is practicing *bhakti* in the proper manner, he may achieve *bhāva* – but it is very rare.

Western countries are like *svarga-bhūmi* (heaven). Why do we live in Vṛndāvana? Because Vṛndāvana-dhāma and Navadvīpa-dhāma are *siddha-bhūmi*, the land of spiritual perfection; they have wonderful power and they can change everything. The *dhāmas* are like Kṛṣṇa, so it is very easy to perform *bhajana* there.

Nanda-gopāla dāsa: Śrīla Gurudeva, I have heard you and our Śrīla Prabhupāda describe the process of alchemy. By an alchemical process, one can turn bell metal into gold. Our Prabhupāda gave the example that one who achieves perfection through the performance of *sādhana* becomes like gold.

Śrīla Nārāyaṇa Gosvāmī Mahārāja: Such persons become *parikaras*, associates of Kṛṣṇa, and serve Him as His eternal associates.

Nanda-gopāla dāsa: You were saying that there is a difference between *śuddha-bhaktas* and the *viśuddha-bhaktas*. When one goes to the spiritual world, is there still a difference even though one will have achieved perfection through his *sādhana*?

Śrīla Nārāyaṇa Gosvāmī Mahārāja: There is always a difference. A *jīva* cannot be exactly like Kṛṣṇa, can he?

Nanda-gopāla dāsa: No.

Śrīla Nārāyaṇa Gosvāmī Mahārāja: Then why are you asking this? Rādhā is not *jīva-tattva* and She is not *sādhana-siddha*. Subala and Śrīdāmā are not *sādhana-siddha*; they are eternal associates (*nitya-parikara*) of Kṛṣṇa. These eternal associates are *viśuddha-sattva*.

Śrīpāda Mādhava Mahārāja: In this example, Gurudeva explained that although one substance was mined and one came from the alchemic process, both substances are gold. In the same way, although one has become perfect through the process of *bhajana* and *sādhana*, now both are associates.

Śrīla Nārāyaṇa Gosvāmī Mahārāja: Yes, but they will not be *viśuddha-sattva* like Śrī Kṛṣṇa, Śrīmatī Rādhikā, or Mother Yaśodā. Even the *jīvas* who have emanated from Baladeva Prabhu in Vṛndāvana, or from Saṅkarṣaṇa in Vaikuṇṭha are *jīva-tattva*, not *viśuddha-sattva*.[37]

---

[37] See Endnote 3 and 4 (at the end of this chapter) for more information.

Devotee: Śrīla Gurudeva, this community (Badger) is called New Vraja. Would you like to see it develop along the lines of Vraja in India?

Śrīla Nārāyaṇa Gosvāmī Mahārāja: I have no desire at all, but I like it here. The resident devotees here are making it like Vraja, with the river like Yamunā and mountains like Govardhana. A devotee thinks like that – that New Vraja is Vṛndāvana – but actually only Vṛndāvana is Vṛndāvana.

Cirañjīva dāsa: I have always had problems in my life because every time I make any endeavor to enjoy, I over-indulge. Is there any fear of over-indulging in chanting *harināma*?

Śrīla Nārāyaṇa Gosvāmī Mahārāja: Not only can you 'over-indulge,' but you can endeavor in excess of 'over-indulgence.' You can indulge to the super-most extent. In this world and that world, nothing can be compared to chanting *harināma*. Be totally absorbed in that, more than in anything else.

Devotee: When we *jīvas* eventually go back to Godhead, is there a chance in the future that some *sādhu* will write a pastime of Śrī Śrī Rādhā and Kṛṣṇa and also write about us in that pastime?

Śrīla Nārāyaṇa Gosvāmī Mahārāja: Why does he want his name to be in a scripture?

Śrīpāda Padmanābha Mahārāja: That is a good answer to his question. His question is, "Will the *jīva* who attains Goloka Vṛndāvana again come here?"

Śrīla Nārāyaṇa Gosvāmī Mahārāja: The devotee may come with Kṛṣṇa, or Kṛṣṇa may send His devotee somewhere. But besides that, he is asking if someone will write about him. Who will write it?

Śrīpāda Mādhava Mahārāja: Śrīla Viśvanātha Cakravartī Ṭhākura writes that when Śrī Kṛṣṇa came to this world, over one billion *gopīs* were present in the *rāsa* dance, but he did not mention their names.

Kamala-kānta dāsa: Śrīla Gurudeva, who is the worshipable Deity of Prahlāda Mahārāja?

Śrīla Nārāyaṇa Gosvāmī Mahārāja: We have already discussed that.

Kamala-kānta dāsa: Yes, but some say it is Paramātmā, some say Kṛṣṇa…

Śrīla Nārāyaṇa Gosvāmī Mahārāja: If you believe what they are telling you and not my words, that is all right. I have said that Kṛṣṇa is his worshipful Deity. I quoted his verse from *Śrīmad-Bhāgavatam*.

Śrīpāda Mādhava Mahārāja: Prahlāda Mahārāja did not mention Lord Nṛsiṁhadeva in that verse.

Dhruva dāsa: Then why did Prahlāda not get *vraja-bhakti*?

Śrīla Nārāyaṇa Gosvāmī Mahārāja: *Vraja-bhakti* is very rare. Whoever follows Śrī Caitanya Mahāprabhu will have *vraja-bhakti*, otherwise it is not possible.

Dhruva dāsa: But Prahlāda Mahārāja heard from Nārada Muni.

Śrīla Nārāyaṇa Gosvāmī Mahārāja: I think that Nārada Muni may have heard from Śrī Caitanya Mahāprabhu.

Without the mercy of Śrī Caitanya Mahāprabhu and Śrīla Rūpa Gosvāmī, it is very difficult to attain the highest goal.

Mahābuddhi dāsa: Śrīla Gurudeva, last night you said that the disciple should pray to his *guru* to remove all the unwanted weeds from his heart if he is not strong enough to take them out himself. How do we attain strong faith in *guru*?

Śrīla Nārāyaṇa Gosvāmī Mahārāja: We have been discussing this in our classes. You must certainly give up, forever, whatever is not favorable for *bhakti*, and you must adopt whatever is favorable for *bhakti*. Follow Śrīla Rūpa Gosvāmī's *Śrī Upadeśāmṛta* and Śrīla Raghunātha dāsa Gosvāmī's *Śrī Manaḥ-śikṣā*. This is the process. Our Gosvāmīs have explained this process in their books.

Rāmānanda Rāya dāsa: Śrīla Gurudeva, in your class yesterday you spoke about not harming any animals. I have noticed that many of the Prabhus here are very good about not wearing leather shoes, and others see the example we set in our community. Is there some specific instruction you can give, especially for the Prabhus here who are very good about this, to share with the rest of the community about not purchasing leather or even supporting any industry like the white sugar industry which processes the sugar with cow bones?

Śrīla Nārāyaṇa Gosvāmī Mahārāja: Yes, devotees must certainly avoid all these unfavorable practices. They should not wear leather; they should not harm any cow or calf, or any other animal. We should not kill even insects, including ants.

Śrīpāda Padmanābha Mahārāja: Here in America there is a law that milk manufacturers have to add vitamin D to the milk, but that is coming from fish.

Devotee: Not all of it; some use synthetic vitamin D.

Śrīla Nārāyaṇa Gosvāmī Mahārāja: If you know that a product contains animal substances, you should reject it. For example if you know that the milk contains these unwanted products, it is best to avoid it.

Padmanābha dāsa (of India)**:** If anyone will call the milk producer, the milk producer will tell him what is in the milk.

Rāmānanda Rāya dāsa: Śrīla Gurudeva, I am your servant, and I beg for your forgiveness for any offenses I have committed to any animals or bugs; first to you and then to any animals.

Śrīla Nārāyaṇa Gosvāmī Mahārāja: By chanting *harināma* continuously, all these sins will go away.

Padmanābha dāsa: Śrīla Gurudeva, yesterday you said that we should not criticize or praise anybody, but sometimes we criticize or praise people in our minds.

Śrīla Nārāyaṇa Gosvāmī Mahārāja: I know that you criticize people. This is a very bad thing. We should not do this.

Padmanābha dāsa: By tongue we may not criticize, but criticism starts from the mind.

Śrīla Nārāyaṇa Gosvāmī Mahārāja: We should also try to take it out of our mind. Do not criticize. Try to see an individual's good qualifications.

uttama hañā vaiṣṇava habe nirabhimāna
jīve sammāna dibe jāni' 'kṛṣṇa'-adhiṣṭhāna

(*Śrī Caitanya-caritāmṛta, Antya-līlā* 20.25)

> Although a Vaiṣṇava is the most exalted person, he is prideless and gives all respect to everyone, knowing everyone to be the resting place of Kṛṣṇa.

Śrīpāda Padmanābha Mahārāja: A question came into my mind yesterday, when you quoted this verse:

para-svabhāva-karmāṇi
na praśaṁsen na garhayet

viśvam ekāmakaṁ paśyan
prakṛtyā puruṣeṇa ca
(*Śrīmad-Bhāgavatam* 11.28.1)

> The Supreme Personality of Godhead said: "One should neither praise nor criticize the conditioned nature and activities of other persons. Rather, one should see this world as simply the combination of material nature and the enjoying souls, all based on the one Absolute Truth.

Here it is said, "Do not criticize or praise." You have also said that by criticizing, one builds a bridge to the other person's bad qualities, which then come into the body of the one who is criticizing. But if we praise someone and build a bridge, and their good qualities come into us, what is the problem?

Śrīla Nārāyaṇa Gosvāmī Mahārāja: This injunction applies to sense enjoyers. Do not criticize or praise any sense enjoyer. But it is essential to always glorify devotees.

Śrīpāda Mādhava Mahārāja: Śrīla Rāmānujācārya said that when we wake up from taking rest every day, we should glorify our *guru* and *guru-paramparā*.

Śrīla Nārāyaṇa Gosvāmī Mahārāja: One more thing: A *guru* or elevated Vaiṣṇava may give an instruction to his disciples or to general people by saying, "Do not be like that, otherwise you will be ruined;" or "Do not follow them;" or "He is not a good man." For the bonafide *guru* and pure Vaiṣṇava, this does not fall in the category of criticism.

Śrīpāda Padmanābha Mahārāja: Many devotees have deviated from the proper path of *bhakti*, and some have committed *vaiṣṇava-aparādha*. Is it considered criticism to discuss that they have done wrong?

Śrīla Nārāyaṇa Gosvāmī Mahārāja: Only in a special case, to save ourselves. In special cases we can do so, but do not criticize anyone without this good reason. "Oh, he was this or that;" do not do this at all.

There was once a *sādhu* and a prostitute. They used to live nearby each other. That *sādhu* always criticized the prostitute, saying, "Oh, she is a prostitute, a very degraded person. She is selling her body and doing many nonsense activities. She will surely go to hell." In contrast, the prostitute used to say, "Oh, fie on me, fie on me. How saintly that *sādhu* is! So many people go to him for good instructions on *bhakti*. His life is successful."

After some time passed, one day the Yamadūtas, the constables of Yamarāja, the god of death, went to that *sādhu* and began to take him away. The *sādhu* objected, "No, don't take me. I am not a sinful person. You've made a mistake. It is that prostitute you must take." The Yamadūtas replied, "No, no, we are right. You always criticized that prostitute. You've never thought anything good." They forcibly took that man to hell.

The Viṣṇudūtas, the messengers of Lord Nārāyaṇa in Vaikuṇṭha, went to the prostitute, and she told them, "Oh, I am not the right person. Go to that *sādhu*." The Viṣṇudūtas said, "We know that we have come for the right person. You have always thought about the good qualities of the *sādhu*, so we are knowingly coming to you to take you to Vaikuṇṭha."

It is important to know this history. Do not criticize anyone, even if he is doing nonsense.

Īśa dāsa: Can Paṅkaja (Padmanābha dāsa) drop out of school and help me in Alachua with my *sevā*?

Śrīla Nārāyaṇa Gosvāmī Mahārāja: I know that he will not do anything. Don't believe him.

Śrīpāda Sajjana Mahārāja: Śrīla Gurudeva, devotees feel spiritually strong when you travel to different places and spend time with them. They are wondering how they can remain strong when you go away. What instructions can you give them so that they can all keep their strength even when they are bereft of *sādhu-saṅga*?

Śrīla Nārāyaṇa Gosvāmī Mahārāja: They should always follow the instructions of Śrīla Rūpa Gosvāmī, Śrīla Raghunātha dāsa Gosvāmī, and Śrīman Mahāprabhu. They should follow the instructions given by Kṛṣṇa to Uddhava.

Śrīpāda Sajjana Mahārāja: You are always in our hearts. Even though we turn away from you, you are always with us. How can we keep the understanding and feeling that *guru* is always present with us?

Śrīla Nārāyaṇa Gosvāmī Mahārāja: If you turn away, you are in a very hopeless condition.

Devotee: Śrīla Gurudeva, our Śrīla Prabhupāda has written in his books that the world leaders are *rākṣasa* demons (who eat meat and the like) who exploit the citizens of the world. In addition to chanting *harināma*, how should we deal with this problem?

Śrīla Nārāyaṇa Gosvāmī Mahārāja: Why think about that? Why not concentrate on all the good instructions that your Prabhupāda gave, like, "Always chant and remember Kṛṣṇa"? Why be absorbed in such negativity? Why does your mind attach itself to such topics? Why not absorb it in remembering Kṛṣṇa? Always remember Prahlāda Mahārāja, Śrīla Rūpa Gosvāmī, and Śrīla Sanātana Gosvāmī.

Aniruddha dāsa: If, due to my ignorance or false ego, I have committed any offense to you, or to your disciples, or to any Vaiṣṇava, or to any living entity, please forgive me.

Nirguṇa dāsa: Do those who reach the *brahma-jyoti* (impersonal Brahman effulgence of the Lord) lose their existence, or do they come back?

Śrīla Nārāyaṇa Gosvāmī Mahārāja: They will not come back; they will remain there forever. That is why it has been said:

asad-vārtā-veśyā visṛja mati-sarvasva-haraṇīḥ
kathā mukti-vyāghryā na śṛṇu kila sarvātma-gilanīḥ
api tyaktvā lakṣmī-pati-ratim ito vyoma-nayanīm
vraje rādhā-kṛṣṇau sva-rati-maṇi-dau tvaṁ bhaja manaḥ

(*Śrī Manaḥ-śikṣā*, Verse 4)

O my dear brother mind, please abandon altogether the prostitute of contemptible mundane talk, which plunders the entire treasure of pure wisdom. You must unequivocally give up hearing all talk of impersonal liberation which, like a tigress, devours your very soul. Furthermore, please abandon even the attachment to Lakṣmīpati Śrī Nārāyaṇa, which leads to Vaikuṇṭha. You should live in Vraja and worship Śrī Śrī Rādhā-Kṛṣṇa, who bestow upon devotees the precious jewel of love for Them.

Mukti is like a tigress; she swallows them forever.
But the Brahmavādīs may be saved:

brahma-bhūtaḥ prasannātmā
na śocati na kāṅkṣati
samaḥ sarveṣu bhūteṣu
mad-bhaktiṁ labhate parām

(*Bhagavad-gītā* 18.54)

> One who is thus transcendentally situated at once realizes the Supreme Brahman and becomes fully joyful. He never laments or desires to have anything. He is equally disposed toward every living entity. In that state he attains pure devotional service unto Me.*

In the case of a Brahmavādī, if such a person associates with an exalted devotee he can attain *para-bhakti* (*vraja-bhakti*); otherwise it is not possible.

Brajanātha dāsa: Śrīla Gurudeva, Māyāvādīs are different from Brahmavādīs, correct?

Śrīla Nārāyaṇa Gosvāmī Mahārāja: Brahmavādīs and Māyāvādīs are not the same. Do you understand?

Nirguṇa dāsa: What is the difference?

Śrīla Nārāyaṇa Gosvāmī Mahārāja: Sanaka, Sānandana, Sanātana, Sanat Kumāra, and Śukadeva Gosvāmī were not Māyāvādīs. At first they were Brahmavādīs, and after that they became pure *bhaktas*.

Nirguṇa dāsa: What was their goal when they were Brahmavādīs?

Śrīla Nārāyaṇa Gosvāmī Mahārāja: The Brahmavādīs accept the existence of Brahman, but they think that He is without form. They do not criticize or deny the glories of Kṛṣṇa when He comes to this world, but due to lack of association they do not understand Him. The Māyāvādīs are offensive, but the Brahmavādīs are not.

June 17, 2008
Darśana
After the Walk

Vicitrī dāsī: Śrīla Gurudeva, I have a question. When we were in Houston you explained to me the meaning of *guṇa-mayi-deha*, the body made of the three modes of material nature [in relation to the *gopīs* leaving their households to meet with Kṛṣṇa at night]. You said it does not mean 'body;' it means 'mood.'

Śrīla Nārāyaṇa Gosvāmī Mahārāja: This refers to the *gopīs*.

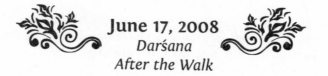

Vicitrī dāsī: Yes, for those *gopīs*. So why is it that when you translated this into Hindi, you did not explain it like that?

Śrīla Nārāyaṇa Gosvāmī Mahārāja: Why should I explain it?

Vicitrī dāsī: Otherwise no one will be able to understand.

Śrīla Nārāyaṇa Gosvāmī Mahārāja: It has not been explained in the commentaries of the previous *ācāryas*, so why should I explain it? Simply hear. Do not explain it, otherwise you will write something wrong.

Rādhā-kānti dāsī: Śrīla Gurudeva, in Vṛndāvana you explained that in *rāgānuga-bhakti*, as the *bhakti-latā-bīja* grows, certain weeds are pulled out. You said that one of these weeds represents *vaidhī-bhakti*.

Śrīla Nārāyaṇa Gosvāmī Mahārāja: I did not say that. I said that if we want to attain *bhakti* like that of the *gopīs*, it is necessary for us to give up the moods of *vātsalya* (parental love), *sakhya* (fraternal love), and *dāsya* (servitorship). We must give up even the desire for the moods of Lalitā Sakhī, Viśākhā Sakhī, and all the other *gopīs* in their category, in the sense that they have a direct relationship with Kṛṣṇa. We should only take guidance from Śrīla Rūpa Gosvāmī, or Rūpa Mañjarī.

Brajanātha dāsa: The reference here is to 'trimming,' not 'taking out the weeds.'

Umā Dīdī: Without the foundation of *vaidhī-bhakti*, no one can attain *rāgānuga-bhakti*.

vidhi-mārga-rata-jane, svādhīnatā ratna-dāne
rāga-mārge karāna praveśa

(*Kalyāṇa-kalpataru*,
by Śrīla Bhaktivinoda Ṭhākura)

> Kṛṣṇa eventually bestows the jewel of independence unto those persons who are attached to the path of rules and regulations, thereby allowing them entrance into the path of spontaneous loving service.

Śrīla Nārāyaṇa Gosvāmī Mahārāja: You should always follow the regulations of *vaidhī-bhakti*; by that you will be able to attain the mood of the *gopīs*. If you do not follow *vaidhī-bhakti*, you will go to hell.

June 18, 2008
Morning Walk

Śrīla Nārāyaṇa Gosvāmī Mahārāja: (To Nanda-gopāla dāsa) Tonight, after my class, you should make an announcement thanking all the devotees who helped and participated in the festival in any way.

Nanda-gopāla dāsa: Yes, Gurudeva.

Govinda dāsa: I was thinking of a song by Śrīla Narahari Ṭhākura, *yadi gaurāṅga nahito, tabe ki haito*. In that song he says, "I chant Gaurāṅga's name and glories every day, but still my heart is not melting. How can I tolerate the burden of this body? Kṛṣṇa has created the body of Narahari, but instead of giving a heart he has given a stone." If such a *mahā-bhāgavata* as Narahari prayed in this way, where is my hope?

Śrīla Nārāyaṇa Gosvāmī Mahārāja: Narahari Ṭhākura was imbued with pure devotion, but still he lamented. Śrīmatī Rādhikā also lamented, although all the loving sentiments of pure devotion reside in Her heart. She is *pūrṇa*, complete, and *pūrṇatama*, most complete. She is always sitting beside Kṛṣṇa, so why is She lamenting?

Śrīpāda Mādhava Mahārāja: She even says, "I have no *prema* for Kṛṣṇa."

Śrīla Nārāyaṇa Gosvāmī Mahārāja: Similarly, Śrīla Narottama dāsa Ṭhākura, Śrīla Narahari Ṭhākura, Śrī Premānanda Ṭhākura, Śrīla Bhaktivinoda Ṭhākura, and all other great *ācāryas* sincerely lament in this way.

Govinda dāsa: So these moods should come in our hearts?

Śrīla Nārāyaṇa Gosvāmī Mahārāja: They should come.

Śrīpāda Mādhava Mahārāja: When you gave *Bṛhad-bhāgavatāmṛta* classes in Mathurā, you quoted Śrīla Sanātana Gosvāmī saying that *prema* and humility are the same. To the proportion one possesses *prema*, to that same proportion one possesses humility.

Brajanātha dāsa: And you also said that anyone who says, "I love you so much, I love you so much, I love you so much"...

Śrīla Nārāyaṇa Gosvāmī Mahārāja: ...they have no love at all.

(To Govinda dāsa) This evening, can you sing this song before class: "*Yadi gaurāṅga nahito, tabe ki haito, kemane dharita de?*"

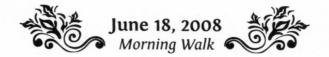

Vṛndāvana dāsa: Gurudeva, yesterday, in the beginning of your class, you discussed the difference between a Brahmavādī and a Māyāvādī. The Brahmavādīs reside in Siddha-loka?

Śrīla Nārāyaṇa Gosvāmī Mahārāja: An example of the Brahmavādīs is the four Kumāras: Sanaka, Sānandana, Sanātana and Sanat Kumāra. They reside in Tapa-loka. They are always meditating upon Kṛṣṇa in His four-armed form as Nārāyaṇa. They can also manifest a form similar to His. They have such power. At first they were Brahmavādīs, and after that they became *bhaktas*.

Vṛndāvana dāsa: What about Śrīla Śukadeva Gosvāmī?

Śrīla Nārāyaṇa Gosvāmī Mahārāja: He was previously a Brahmavādī; in the beginning stage.

The four Kumāras can also go to Vaikuṇṭha; they have that power. When they went to Vaikuṇṭha, Jaya and Vijaya made a 'mistake' by the influence of Yogamāyā. They could not understand the actual identity of the four boys.

Vṛndāvana dāsa: Do they again come into the material world?

Śrīla Nārāyaṇa Gosvāmī Mahārāja: Yes. Their permanent abode in this material creation is Tapa-loka. From there they can go anywhere in the material world and also up to Vaikuṇṭha.

Śacīnandana dāsa: Śrīla Gurudeva, who or what do the Brahmavādīs meditate on, if they do not meditate on a form?

Śrīla Nārāyaṇa Gosvāmī Mahārāja: They try to meditate on *nirguṇa-brahma* – God who has no shape and no qualities.

Gopī-jana-vallabha dāsa: Śrīla Gurudeva, what would happen to a person who does not worship his bonafide *guru* before worshiping the Deity?

Śrīla Nārāyaṇa Gosvāmī Mahārāja: That *pūjā* will not bear any fruit.

Gopī-jana-vallabha dāsa: Is this an offense?

Śrīla Nārāyaṇa Gosvāmī Mahārāja: If that person knowingly neglects *guru* and worships the Deity directly, then it is an offense; otherwise not.

Balarāma dāsa: Śrīla Gurudeva, regarding the cows that we pass by on the morning walk; having had *darśana* of a pure devotee, what is their destination in their next life?

Śrīla Nārāyaṇa Gosvāmī Mahārāja: They will receive a human form and some *sukṛti* (spiritual pious credits) by which they can advance in *bhakti*. They will also be able to attain the association of pure devotees.

It is for this reason that *sādhus* like Nārada travel here and there in forests and continually chant the names of Śrī Śrī Rādhā-Kṛṣṇa, "Rādhikā-Ramaṇa." Everyone who hears this will come in the line of *bhakti*.

Devotee: Gurudeva, your book, *The Essence of All Advice*, states that one must first come to *jñāna-bhakti* before he can have *śuddha-bhakti*. Can you please explain this?

Śrīla Nārāyaṇa Gosvāmī Mahārāja: *Jñāna-bhakti* does not refer to the cultivation of the impersonal knowledge of the Māyāvādī. That statement refers to *jñānī-bhaktas* like Prahlāda. Śrī Prahlāda sees Kṛṣṇa everywhere, and he sees all living beings in Kṛṣṇa. He was a pure devotee, in a much higher stage than those at the stage of *śaraṇāgati*.

Rādhā-kānta dāsa: We were studying in *Rūpa-śikṣā* that generally the worshipful Deity of the devotee in *śānta-rasa* is either Paramātmā or the impersonal feature of God. But yesterday, when you were speaking about Prahlāda Mahārāja, you said that his worshipful Deity is Kṛṣṇa. But Prahlāda Mahārāja is a *jñānī-bhakta* situated in *śānta-rati*.

Śrīla Nārāyaṇa Gosvāmī Mahārāja: He is situated in *dāsya-rasa*, not *śānta-rasa*. *Śānta-bhaktas* are exemplified by the four Kumāras.

Rādhā-kānta dāsa: But sometimes we say that *jñānī-bhaktas* do not engage in service.

Śrīla Nārāyaṇa Gosvāmī Mahārāja: He offers prayers. He also tells *hari-kathā* to his classmates. For example, he told them:

kaumāra ācaret prājño
dharmān bhāgavatān iha
durlabhaṁ mānuṣaṁ janma
tad apy adhruvam arthadam

(*Śrīmad-Bhāgavatam* 7.6.1)

> One who is sufficiently intelligent should use the human form of body from the very beginning of life – in other words, from the tender age of childhood – to

> practice the activities of devotional service, giving up all other engagements. The human body is most rarely achieved, and although temporary like other bodies, it is meaningful because in human life one can perform devotional service. Even a slight amount of sincere devotional service can give one complete perfection.

He engages in *śravaṇam* (hearing about the Lord), *kīrtanam* (chanting the Lord's glories), and also *smaraṇam* (remembering the Lord). In this way he is *dāsa*, a servant.

Śrīpāda Mādhava Mahārāja: He is in the category of *aiśvarya-dāsya*. Hanumān is in *śuddha-dāsya* (pure servitorship), and Prahlāda is in *aiśvarya-miśra-dāsya* (servitorship mixed with awe and reverence).

Rādhā-kānta dāsa: His eternal position in the spiritual world is serving in Vaikuṇṭha?

Śrīla Nārāyaṇa Gosvāmī Mahārāja: It has not been written, but we can say that. When he was in the womb of his mother, Nārada Muni told him so much *hari-kathā* and trained him in Kṛṣṇa consciousness. So we can also say that he is *sādhana-siddha*.

Śrīpāda Dāmodara Mahārāja: Śrīla Gurudeva, can you tell us the meaning of the word *vivarta* in Jagadānanda Paṇḍita's *Prema-vivarta*?

Śrīla Nārāyaṇa Gosvāmī Mahārāja: I have explained that it is like a whirlpool.

Śrīpāda Dāmodara Mahārāja: In *vivarta-vada* philosophy they give the example of the rope and the snake…

Śrīla Nārāyaṇa Gosvāmī Mahārāja: No, no; it is not the same word. When *vivarta* is used in relation to *prema-vivarta*, it means 'crooked and very deep whirlpool of love.' For example, after his love-quarrel with Mahāprabhu, Śrī Jagadānanda Paṇḍita enters into *māna* (a sulky mood), Mahāprabhu comes to him and pacifies him, and again he begins quarreling. On one occasion, after their quarrel Jagadānanda Prabhu fasted and wept throughout the night, and the next day Mahāprabhu brought him to His house where Mother Śacī gave him food and a bath.

They had been quarreling and mock-fighting since their boyhood.

Śrīpāda Dāmodara Mahārāja: Does Bhagavān not display *māna*?

Śrīla Nārāyaṇa Gosvāmī Mahārāja: Sometimes He may have *māna*, just to show Rādhikā.

Śrīpāda Mādhava Mahārāja: Once, Kṛṣṇa asked Śrīmatī Rādhikā, "How do You do so much *māna*? I try My level-best to break it, and even My flute sometimes fails."

Rādhikā said, "All right, I can teach You."

Kṛṣṇa asked, "How?"

"You can sit here," Rādhikā said. "Now, turn Your face away from Me for as long as I ask You, 'O My dear beloved, look towards Me.' I will try My level-best to pacify You, but do not look towards Me; turn away when I come close to Your face."

Kṛṣṇa did this, and then Rādhikā said, "I am simply teaching You, and now You have become really sulky."

Śrīpāda Dāmodara Mahārāja: Once you said that *prema-vivarta* is like a fan that is moving so fast in one direction that it looks like it is going backwards.

Śrīla Nārāyaṇa Gosvāmī Mahārāja: Yes.

Nṛhari dāsa: Śrīla Gurudeva, you mentioned that Jagadānanda Paṇḍita's behavior is like that of Satyabhāmā.

Śrīla Nārāyaṇa Gosvāmī Mahārāja: When Rādhikā expanded as Satyabhāmā in *dvārakā-līlā*, Her nature did not change. She kept the same nature in the sense that Satyabhāmā also entered into sulky moods.

But there was a difference in the *māna* of Satyabhāmā. She had some fear. Kṛṣṇa once said, "Where is the daughter of Satrājit (Satyabhāmā)? She is very naughty. I will expel her from My palace because she could not tolerate hearing Me glorify the *gopīs*." Trembling, Satyabhāmā then returned to Kṛṣṇa.

Śrīmatī Rādhikā would not tolerate such words, and Kṛṣṇa would never speak to Her in that way. Satyabhāmā was His wife, so He can say such words to her, but how would He be able to say this to Śrīmatī Rādhikā? Rādhikā would reply, "Get out of My palace."

Brajanātha dāsa: Prabhu is asking who is Jagadānanda Paṇḍita in Kṛṣṇa's pastimes?

Śrīla Nārāyaṇa Gosvāmī Mahārāja: He is an exalted *sakhī* of Rādhikā.

Mahā-mantra dāsa: In the pastime between Jagadānanda Paṇḍita and Caitanya Mahāprabhu, after Mahāprabhu broke the pot of oil...

Śrīla Nārāyaṇa Gosvāmī Mahārāja: Śrīman Mahāprabhu ordered that Jagadānanda Paṇḍita's gift of the pot of oil be given to Lord Jagannātha rather than be used for Himself. So Jagadānanda Paṇḍita became sulky and broke the pot.

Mahā-mantra dāsa: After he stayed for three days in his room, he came out and cooked a wonderful feast. Then, when Mahāprabhu tasted his *prasādam*, He said something like, "Even when you cook in an angry mood, the food tastes wonderful." It was not mentioned last night, but I think I read this in *Caitanya-caritāmṛta*. After that He sent Jagadānanda Paṇḍita far away, to Mother Śacī's house in Navadvīpa. Why did He send him so far away?

Śrīla Nārāyaṇa Gosvāmī Mahārāja: Śrīla Jagadānanda Paṇḍita personally recounted this in his *Prema-vivarta*. Śrīman Mahāprabhu skillfully sent him to see the residents of Navadvīpa, and to feel separation from Himself as well.

Mahā-mantra dāsa: How long was he separated?

Śrīla Nārāyaṇa Gosvāmī Mahārāja: He cannot live without Śrī Caitanya Mahāprabhu. When Caitanya Mahāprabhu disappeared from this world, he also disappeared, and all of Mahāprabhu's eternal associates also gradually left. Then, when Śrī Svarūpa Dāmodara, Śrī Rāya Rāmānanda, and Śrī Gadādhara Paṇḍita left, Śrīla Raghunātha dāsa Gosvāmī was unable to tolerate his situation. He felt so bereft of the association of his guardians that he saw the entire world as zero.

He determined, "I should not remain here." He went to Vṛndāvana with the intention of giving up his life by jumping from the top of Girirāja Govardhana or drowning in the river Yamunā; but Śrīla Rūpa Gosvāmī and Sanātana Gosvāmī saved him. It was a very pathetic scene.

Raghunātha Bhaṭṭa dāsa: This is a practical question. We are in the Bay Area, and we plan to get another place in a good location, somewhere in Berkeley perhaps. We want to create an atmosphere where good quality people can join.

Śrīla Nārāyaṇa Gosvāmī Mahārāja: The thing is that you always change your idea. By focusing on one point, you can do so many things; but you don't focus. Whatever you decide to do, be fixed in that. In the future I want to know that you are preaching with all the devotees there.

Raghunātha Bhaṭṭa dāsa: Śrīla Gurudeva, for attracting good quality devotees who want to stay at the temple, what standards should we set?

Śrīla Nārāyaṇa Gosvāmī Mahārāja: You can see what we do in our *maṭhas*, like Mathurā Maṭha, Vṛndāvana, and other *maṭhas*. Your *maṭha* should be like that. You were in Śrīla Gour Govinda Mahārāja's *maṭha*, so maintain the same standards at present.

Rūpa-raghunātha dāsa: Śrīla Gurudeva, Śrīla Prabhupāda told his disciples many times that they should all become *gurus*. Some have tried to be *guru*, and there have been so many problems as a result. Do you have any instructions on this matter?

Brajanātha dāsa: He is asking what is your mood in relation to your own disciples? Should they become *guru*?

Śrīla Nārāyaṇa Gosvāmī Mahārāja: Śrīla Prabhupāda Bhaktisiddhānta Sarasvatī Gosvāmī said, "I have never made any disciples; I have made *gurus*." He made them qualified. Similarly, I want my disciples, *sannyāsīs*, and *brahmacārīs* to become very qualified; never to fall down. Although one or two have fallen down, my real disciples will not fall.

Rūpa-raghunātha dāsa: So should they become *gurus*?

Śrīla Nārāyaṇa Gosvāmī Mahārāja: They are *guru* if they are preaching. Śrīla Prabhupāda Bhaktisiddhānta Sarasvatī Ṭhākura did not tell Śrīla Bhaktivedānta Svāmī Mahārāja, "You should be *guru*." He did not say this to anyone. Neither to my *guru*, Śrīla Bhakti Prajñāna Keśava Mahārāja, nor to Śrīla Śrīdhara Mahārāja did he say, "You should become *ācārya*." But they became *guru*. Actually one is not made *guru* or *ācārya* by an order to become *guru* or *ācārya*. By one's own qualities and services to his *guru*, one automatically becomes *ācārya*.

Brajanātha dāsa: Śrīla Bhaktivedānta Svāmī Mahārāja quoted his Guru Mahārāja saying that among his disciples, the *ācārya* would automatically manifest.

Śrīpāda Sajjana Mahārāja: So many of my god-brothers were eager to accept the position of *guru*, and because they received so much honor and respect, *pratiṣṭhā* (a sense of false prestige) came, and then they fell down. And they also fell down because of disrespecting pure devotees. This is a very great lesson for me and for many of my god-brothers and god-sisters – that we should not be so anxious to imitate the position of *guru*.

Śrīla Nārāyaṇa Gosvāmī Mahārāja: Śrīla Bhaktivedānta Svāmī Mahārāja knew that they were not qualified. If a thorn is stuck in a person's foot, he will have to take it out with another 'thorn,' and then throw both thorns away. Similarly, Śrīla Svāmī Mahārāja wanted this Hare Kṛṣṇa *mahā-mantra* to go everywhere, even if the chanters chanted *nāma-aparādha* or *nāma-ābhāsa*.

He considered that the hearers, the people in general, would not be committing *aparādhas*, because they did not know *siddhānta*. If a mistake is made knowingly it is an *aparādha*. If it is made in ignorance there is no offense; it may be *nāma-ābhāsa*. He knew that if the people of the world would begin chanting somehow or other, they would all be gradually liberated from their sins and would come to this line of pure *bhakti*. You see that now, by his preaching, everywhere people are chanting and developing an interest in Kṛṣṇa consciousness.

He knew that many of those he engaged to spread the chanting would fall down after his departure, and they fell down.

Aniruddha dāsa: You and Mahāprabhu have said that the only means to perfection in Kali-yuga is *harināma*. *Harer nāma eva kevalam*. Some of your disciples don't have faith in this, because they do not see the immediate results. They do not see that Kṛṣṇa consciousness is spread all over the world by this. They think that it is not important to wear devotional clothing and *tilaka*.

Śrīla Nārāyaṇa Gosvāmī Mahārāja: This is not the idea of others; it is your special idea. So change this idea. It has been told in scripture that all other devotional processes – *śravaṇam* (hearing), *smaraṇam* (remembering), *pāda-sevanam* (serving the Lord's lotus feet), *arcanam* (Deity worship), *vandanam* (offering prayers), *dāsyam* (becoming a servant), *sakhyam* (becoming a friend), *ātma-nivedanam* (self-surrender) – will only give their fruit if they are accompanied by *harināma-saṅkīrtana*. If one is doing *śravaṇam*, it must be accompanied by *kīrtana*, if one is doing *smaraṇam*, he must do *kīrtana*.

kīrtana-prabhāve, smaraṇa svabhāve

(*Vaisnava Ke?* Verse 19,
by Śrīla Bhaktisiddhānta Sarasvatī Thākura)

> The transcendental power of congregational chanting automatically awakens remembrance of the Lord and His divine pastimes in relation to one's own eternal spiritual form.

I know that this doubt is your personal problem, and you have so many problems like this. You should try to reform yourself.

Jayanta-kṛṣṇa dāsa: Gurudeva, I have a question. In this material world there are millions upon billions of universes. In each of these universes there are innumerable conditioned living entities. Do the members of our *guru-varga*, after entering *nitya-līlā*, also go to those other universes to save those conditioned souls, or do they only appear here on this planet Earth?

Śrīla Nārāyaṇa Gosvāmī Mahārāja: Yes, certainly. Vṛndāvana and Navadvīpa-dhāma are present in all universes.

Balarāma dāsa: Gurudeva, I have a question. Every morning after the sun has risen, devotees are very conscious about not stepping on your shadow. Is there an injunction about this?

Śrīla Nārāyaṇa Gosvāmī Mahārāja: It is an injunction, but when you cannot avoid it, there is no offense. How can you avoid that here? It is not possible here, so I will not take any offense and Kṛṣṇa will not take any offense. You are eager to hear something from me, and that is why you are coming to walk with me.

Śrīpāda Padmanābha Mahārāja: Śrīla Gurudeva, your lectures in Badger are coming to an end. Now you will be going to a very big festival in Italy where there will be about one thousand devotees. Have you decided upon the subject matter yet?

Śrīla Nārāyaṇa Gosvāmī Mahārāja: I don't know. When I go there, I will decide.

Śrīpāda Padmanābha Mahārāja: The lectures you have been giving here on *Prema-vivarta* were very short. The book is very large and contains so much instruction and philosophy. If you think it appropriate, can you continue speaking on the book in Italy?

Prema-prayojana dāsa: It will be Ratha-yātrā time in Italy.

Śrīla Nārāyaṇa Gosvāmī Mahārāja: The observance of Ratha-yātrā will take place at that time, but we can also continue *Prema-vivarta*.

Śrīpāda Padmanābha Mahārāja: Yesterday your *kathā* was so sweet, Śrīla Gurudeva. You brought a big flood of nectar upon all the devotees.

Brajanātha dāsa: Not a flood, a whirlpool.

Mahābuddhi dāsa: Śrīla Gurudeva, now your visit here in North America is finished this year. Is there any special instruction regarding how you would like to see the preaching carried out here?

Śrīla Nārāyaṇa Gosvāmī Mahārāja: You should all preach my mission, which is the mission of Mahāprabhu and our *guru-paramparā*. Whether or not I am in this world, try to preach everywhere. By this, the entire world will benefit.

Śrīpāda Padmanābha Mahārāja: Many times in previous festivals you have told all the devotees, "The next time I come, I would like each of you to bring five new people.

Śrīla Nārāyaṇa Gosvāmī Mahārāja: Oh, yes.

All *brahmacārīs* and *sannyāsīs* must follow my example. On Pūrṇimā days, they should shave both their beard and hair. They should not try to be stylish by shaving only their beard.

ENDNOTES

1 Excerpt from *Jaiva-dharma*, Chapter Sixteen:

Vrajanātha: Master, I understand that this marginal position is situated in the junction of the spiritual and material worlds. Why is it that some *jīvas* go from there to the material world, while others go to the spiritual world?

Raghunātha dāsa Bābājī: Kṛṣṇa's qualities are also present in the *jīvas*, but only in a minute quantity. Kṛṣṇa is supremely independent, so the desire to be independent is eternally present in the *jīvas* as well. When the *jīva* uses his independence correctly, he remains disposed towards Kṛṣṇa, but when he misuses it, he becomes indifferent to Him. It is just this indifference that gives rise to the desire in the *jīva's* heart to enjoy *māyā*.

Because of the desire to enjoy *māyā*, he develops the false ego that he can enjoy material sense gratification, and then the five types of ignorance – *tamah* (not knowing anything about the spirit soul), *moha* (the illusion of the bodily concept of life), *maha-moha* (madness for material enjoyment), *tamisra* (forgetfulness of one's constitutional position due to anger or envy), and *andha-tamisra* (considering death to be the ultimate end) – cover his pure, atomic nature. Our liberation or subjugation simply depends on whether we use our minute independence properly or misuse it.

Vrajanātha: Lord Kṛṣṇa is overflowing with mercy, so why did He make the *jīva* so weak that he became entangled in *māyā*?

Raghunātha dāsa Bābājī: It is true that He is overflowing with mercy, but He is also overflowing with desire to perform pastimes. Desiring various pastimes to be enacted in different situations, Śrī Kṛṣṇa made the *jīvas* eligible for all conditions, from the marginal state to the highest state of the *gopī's* love for Kṛṣṇa, called *mahābhāva*. To facilitate the *jīva's* progressing practically and steadfastly towards becoming qualified for His service, He has also created the lower levels of material existence – beginning from the lowest inert matter up to false ego – which is the cause of unlimited obstruction in attaining supreme bliss.

Having fallen from their constitutional position, the *jīvas* who are entangled in *māyā* are indifferent to Kṛṣṇa and engrossed in personal sense gratification. However, Śrī Kṛṣṇa is the reservoir of mercy. The more the *jīva* becomes fallen, the more Kṛṣṇa provides him with opportunities to attain the highest spiritual perfection. He brings this about by appearing before him along with His spiritual abode and eternal associates. Those *jīvas* who take advantage of this merciful opportunity and sincerely endeavor to attain the higher position gradually reach the spiritual world and attain a state similar to that of Śrī Hari's eternal associates.

Vrajanātha: Why must the *jīvas* suffer for the sake of the Lord's pastimes?

Śrī Raghunātha dāsa Bābājī: The *jīvas* possess some independence. This is actually a sign of God's special mercy upon them. Inert objects are very insignificant and worthless, because they have no such independent desire. The *jīva* has attained sovereignty of the inert world only because of this independent desire.

Misery and happiness are conditions of the mind. Thus, what we may consider misery is happiness for one engrossed in it. Since all varieties of material sense gratification finally result in nothing but misery, a materialistic person only achieves suffering.

When that suffering becomes excessive, it gives rise to a search for happiness. From that desire discrimination arises, and from discrimination, the tendency for inquiry is born. As a result of this, one attains *sat-saṅga*, the association of saintly devotees, whereupon *śraddhā* (faith in serving Kṛṣṇa) develops. When *śraddhā* is born, the *jīva* ascends to a higher stage, namely the path of devotional service to the Lord.

Gold is purified by heating and hammering. Being indifferent to Kṛṣṇa, the *jīva* has become impure through engaging in mundane sense gratification. Therefore, he must be purified by being beaten with the hammers of misery on the anvil of this material world. By this process, the misery of the *jīvas* averse to Kṛṣṇa finally culminates in happiness. Suffering is therefore just a sign of God's mercy. That is why far-sighted people see the suffering of *jīvas* in Lord Kṛṣṇa's pastimes as auspicious, though the near-sighted can only see it as an inauspicious source of misery.

Vrajanātha: The *jīva's* suffering in his conditioned state is ultimately auspicious, but at the same time it is very painful. Since Kṛṣṇa is omnipotent, couldn't He think of a less troublesome path?

Raghunātha dāsa Bābājī: Lord Kṛṣṇa's pastimes are extremely wonderful and of many varieties; and this is also one of them. If He is independent and almighty, and performs all kinds of pastimes, why should this be the only pastime that He neglects? No pastime can be rejected if there is to be full variety. Besides, the participants in other types of pastimes also must accept some sort of suffering.

Śrī Kṛṣṇa is the Supreme Enjoyer and the active agent. All ingredients and paraphernalia are controlled by His desire and subject to His activities. It is natural to experience some suffering when one is controlled by the desire of the agent. However, if that suffering brings pleasure in the end, it is not true suffering. How can you call it suffering? The so-called suffering one undergoes in order to nourish and support Kṛṣṇa's pastimes is actually a source of delight.

The *jīva's* independent desire has caused him to abandon the pleasure of serving Kṛṣṇa, and instead accept suffering in *māyā*. This is the *jīva's* fault, not Kṛṣṇa's.

2 The following is an excerpt of a *darśana* with Śrīla Nārāyaṇa Gosvāmī Mahārāja in Johannesburg, South Africa, on January 29, 2010:

Śyāmarāṇī dāsī: Was it Yogamāyā or Mahāmāyā who created the set of cowherd boys stolen by Brahmā?

Śrīla Nārāyaṇa Gosvāmī Mahārāja: It was actually Yogamāyā, but she acted through the agency of her shadow, Mahāmāyā. It was the action of Yogamāyā, but through Mahāmāyā. Do you understand?

Śyāmarāṇī dāsī: Are you referring to the same Mahāmāyā who controls the material world?

Śrīla Nārāyaṇa Gosvāmī Mahārāja: Yes. She who was Yogamāyā with Yaśodā, and who came with Vasudeva Mahārāja to Mathurā, at once became Mahāmāyā for Kaṁsa. They are the same *māyā*, but by action, or function, they are known as Yogamāyā or Mahāmāyā.

Brajanātha dāsa: Mādhava Mahārāja said that the *gopīs* worshiped Kātyāyanī, Mahāmāyā, and it was that same Mahāmāyā who bewildered Brahmā.

Śrīla Nārāyaṇa Gosvāmī Mahārāja: For the *gopīs*, that *māyā* was Yogamāyā. *Māyā* is one, and by her function she is two. When she acts upon Kṛṣṇa and His associates, she is Yogamāyā. When she acts to bewilder the conditioned living entity, then she is Mahāmāyā.

Someone may say, "Nārāyaṇa Mahārāja is a most angry person." Another person may say, "No, he is very loving." The first person saw me chastising someone, and therefore his idea is that I am an angry person. The second person saw my very sweet behavior and thinks, "Oh, he loves everyone."

3 An explanation of the verse beginning with *śuddha-sattva viśeṣātmā* is given in the following books of Śrīla Nārāyaṇa Gosvāmī Mahārāja:

"In *Bhakti-rasāmṛta-sindhu* (1.3.1) it is stated, *śuddha-sattva viśeṣātmā prema-sūryāṁśu-sāmyabhāk rucibhiś citta-māsṛṇya-kṛd asau bhāva ucyate*. When the heart becomes melted by *ruci*, or in other words, an intense longing to attain the Lord, then what was previously *sādhana-bhakti* is now called *bhāva-bhakti*. The primary characteristic of *bhāva* is that it is a phenomena constituted entirely of *viśuddha-sattva* (unalloyed goodness), and as such it is compared to a ray of the sun of *prema-bhakti*. The conclusion established by this verse is that *bhāva-bhakti* or *rati* is the sprout of *prema* and an atom of *prema*.

"In its initial stage, *prema* is called *bhāva*. In that stage, various transformations of ecstacy arising from *viśuddha-sattva* (*sattvika-bhāvas*) such as tears, standing of the hairs of the body on end, etc., are observed to a very slight extent" (*Śrī Śikṣāṣṭaka*, Verse 6, *Sanmodana-bhāṣya*).

The above-mentioned definition of *bhāva-bhakti* is also given in *Jaiva-dharma*, Chapter 22. Here, *śuddha-sattva* and *viśuddha-sattva* have been used interchangeably:

"The characteristic feature of *bhāva* is that it is situated in unalloyed goodness (*śuddha-sattva-viśeṣa-rūpa-tattva*). It can be compared to a tiny ray of the *prema*-sun.

"The constitutional characteristic (*svarūpa-lakṣaṇa*) of *bhāva* is that it is situated in unalloyed goodness (*viśuddha-sattva*). *Bhāva* is also known by the name *rati*, and is sometimes called a sprout of *prema* (*premāṅkura*). The propensity for divine knowledge (*saṁvit-vṛtti*) is an aspect of the all-enlightening internal potency (*svarūpa-śakti*), and is the state of unalloyed goodness (*śuddha-sattva*), having no connection with *māyā*. When this *saṁvit-vṛtti* combines with the propensity for unalloyed bliss (*hlādinī-vṛtti*), the essential aspect of that combination is called *bhāva*."

"*Sattva* can also mean that everything in the spiritual world is *viśuddha-sattva*, comprised of pure spiritual energy. There is not a touch of mundane qualities of goodness (*sattva*), passion (*rajas*), or ignorance (*tamas*) in that realm. There are so many objects in Vaikuṇṭha, and they are all *viśuddha-sattva*. Especially it is known as the essence of the *hlādinī* and *saṁvit* potencies combined, which is found in the hearts of the eternal *rāgātmikā* devotees there. If greed arises in the heart of a living entity for the sentiment of those devotees, and he performs *bhajana* following in their footsteps, then, when even one molecule of their devotion reflects into his heart, it can be called *sattva*. There are three kinds of *sattva*: *viśuddha-sattva*, *sattva*, and *miśra-sattva* (*miśra* means 'mixed'). *Miśra-sattva* exists within the conditioned souls, *sattva* within the liberated souls who have not yet developed *bhakti*, and *viśuddha-sattva* within the *dhāma* and Bhagavān's eternal associates" (*Bhakti-rasāyana*, Chapter 2).

"Only after the *jīva* attains *svarūpa-siddhi* and will imminently enter into *vastu-siddhi* can it be said that he is in *viśuddha-sattva*. Bhagavān and all of His devotees in Vaikuṇṭha, whether they are peacocks or monkeys or whatever, are situated in *viśuddha-sattva*" (*Bhakti-rasāyana*, Chapter 2).

"By the essence of the *hlādinī* and *saṁvit* potencies together, this sentiment arises in the heart of a *jīva*. This is called *viśuddha-sattva*, and this is the activity of Yogamāyā. She performs unlimited types of service in Vaikuṇṭha, Dvārakā, Mathurā, and finally in Vṛndāvana" (*Going Beyond Vaikuntha*, Chapter 8).

"The *saṁvit* function of the self-manifesting *svarūpa-śakti* is called *śuddha-sattva*. *Bhāva* imbued with very thick *mamatā* (possessiveness) for Kṛṣṇa is the special function of the *hlādinī* aspect of *cit-śakti*. That supremely astonishing *bhāva* which arises when these two mix together in the heart of the pure *jīva* is called *viśuddha-prema*" (*Bhakti-tattva-viveka*, Part 5).

"*Karya-rūpa* refers to endeavors that manifest as effects upon attainment of the stage of *bhāva*, or in other words the *anubhāvas* of *bhāva-bhakti*. Included within this category are the eight *sāttvika-bhāvas*, such as crying and standing of the hairs on end, and the *anubhāvas* such as singing and dancing. All these effects (*anubhāvas*) are expressions arising from the mind that is constituted of *viśuddha-sattva*" (*Bhakti-rasāmṛta-sindhu-bindu*, Verse 1, *Śrī Bindu-vikāśinī-vṛtti*).

[4] The statements from the above-mentioned endnote, taken from Śrīla Nārāyaṇa Gosvāmī Mahārāja's books, are examples of *śuddha-sattva* and *viśuddha-sattva* being used interchangeably. These statements reveal that even a *jīva* at the stage of *bhāva-bhakti* is situated in *viśuddha-sattva*, what to speak of a *jīva* who has attained *prema* and becomes a resident of Goloka Vṛndāvana. How, then, do we understand Śrīla Nārāyaṇa Gosvāmī Mahārāja's words in this June 16, 2008 morning walk? How is this reconciled? The answer is that there is actually no contradiction.

In his *Harināmāmṛta-vyākaraṇa*, Śrīla Jīva Gosvāmī shares with us the following logic: "*Pūrva-parayor madhye para-vidhir balavān* – When there are so many statements supporting an accepted *siddhānta*, and also statements which are less in number and seemingly different from the accepted *siddhānta*, those statements which are large in number and which accord with *siddhānta* have higher value."

What, then, does Śrīla Nārāyaṇa Gosvāmī Mahārāja mean when he says that the *jīva* cannot be *viśuddha-sattva*?

As quoted in the above sastric statements, *viśuddha-sattva* is the essence of *saṁvit* and *hlādinī* (which is called *bhakti*). This is manifest to the fullest extent in Śrīmatī Rādhārāṇī and Her *nitya-siddha kāya-vyūha* associates, and to a lesser extent in Kṛṣṇa. This same principle can be applied to Nanda Bābā and Śrī Yaśodā-maiyā. In other words, Śrīla Nārāyaṇa Gosvāmī Mahārāja's beautiful statements may be understood by taking the meaning of the word *viśuddha-sattva* to be 'pure, unalloyed *bhakti*.' With this consideration, we can understand that Śrī Kṛṣṇa is *viśuddha-sattva*, Śrī Nanda Bābā and Mother Yaśodā are *viśuddha-viśuddha-sattva*, and Śrīmatī Rādhārāṇī and Her *kāya-vyūha gopīs* are *viśuddha-viśuddha-viśuddha-sattva*.

The *jīva* can never attain the greatness of Śrīmatī Lalitā-devī's position, or Rūpa Mañjarī's position, or Mother Yaśodā's position, or the positions of any such eternal associates of Kṛṣṇa – these positions are already taken.

In that sense, the *jīva* is always *śuddha-sattva* and never *viśuddha-sattva*. This is also true for Śrī Hanumān. He is *viśuddha-sattva*, as Śrīla Nārāyaṇa Gosvāmī Mahārāja mentions above, because he the topmost among all *dāsya-bhaktas* as well as an expansion of Lord Viṣṇu's form known as Sadāśiva. No *jīva* can become an expansion of Sadāśiva; in that sense the *jīva* can only be *śuddha-sattva*, or in a position lower than Him.

The pinnacle of a *jīva's* attainment is that he can be *tadātmā* with these associates. [Please see Alachua, May 4, 2008 – Morning Walk.] Taking a look at the following conversation with this perspective, we may get a glimpse of Śrīla Nārāyaṇa Gosvāmī Mahārāja's mood in this regard:

Question: What is the ingredient that makes the difference between *śuddha-sattva* and *viśuddha-sattva*?

Śrīla Nārāyaṇa Gosvāmī Mahārāja: The *jīva* can go up to *śuddha-sattva*; he cannot be *viśuddha-sattva*. Vāsudeva (Kṛṣṇa) is *viśuddha-sattva*, and Nanda Bābā is *viśuddha-viśuddha-sattva* [i.e. Kṛṣṇa is God, so He is superior to us, and Nanda Bābā is superior to Kṛṣṇa in *bhakti*].

Savitā dāsī: And the *gopīs* are *viśuddha-viśuddha-viśuddha sattva* [i.e. the *gopīs* are superior to Nanda Bābā in *bhakti*].

Śrīla Nārāyaṇa Gosvāmī Mahārāja: Yes.

Question: Even when the *jīva* goes to Goloka Vṛndāvana, does he still stay as *śuddha-sattva*?

Śrīla Nārāyaṇa Gosvāmī Mahārāja: The *jīva* is always *śuddha-sattva*, but he can be *tadātmā* (one in quality) with *viśuddha-sattva*. By the power of *svarūpa-śakti* – *saṁvit*, and *hlādinī* – he can work as *viśuddha-sattva*, but he is *śuddha-sattva*. This existence in pure goodness fully blooms at the stage of *prema*. It first manifests at the stage of *bhāva*, then further in *prema*, and then still further in *sneha*, *māna*, *praṇaya*, and so on.

Śrīla Prabhupāda Bhaktivedānta Svāmī Mahārāja confirms this understanding in his Tenth Canto *Śrīmad-Bhāgavatam* purport (10.8.49). There he writes, "In other words, it is not possible for a *sādhana-siddha* living being to become the father or mother of Kṛṣṇa, for Kṛṣṇa's father and mother are already designated. But by following the principles exhibited by Nanda Mahārāja and Yaśodā and their associates, the inhabitants of Vṛndāvana, ordinary living beings may attain such affection as exhibited by Nanda and Yaśodā."

[Please also see Badger, June 17, 2008 – Morning Walk.]

Verbania, Italy

June 29, 2008

June 29, 2008
Darśana

Jayadeva dāsa: In *Śrīmad-Bhāgavatam* there is a statement that whatever the living entity desires, Kṛṣṇa fulfills. Is this true, or not true?

Śrīla Nārāyaṇa Gosvāmī Mahārāja: It is true in one sense, and not true in another. Kṛṣṇa thinks, "I am very wise. I know what will benefit him, better than he knows. If he prays for worldly attainments, such as wealth, sons, daughters, wife, or position, it will not be good for him. These things are like poison, so, why should I give them to him? Because I am wise, I must give him *bhakti*." In this way, Kṛṣṇa sometimes does not fulfill their desires; He gives them *bhakti* instead.

If you desire *vraja-bhakti*, thinking, "I want to have the same service mood as very elevated devotees like Śrīdāmā and Subala," or "...Mother Yaśodā and Nanda Bābā," or "...the *gopīs*," He will very easily fulfill this desire.

Devotee: Yesterday, I heard you say that we *jīvas* were originally in the spiritual world and, somehow or other, because we forgot Kṛṣṇa, we fell down to this world.

Śrīla Nārāyaṇa Gosvāmī Mahārāja: I have never said this. Rather, I have said that the *jīvas* came from the *taṭasthā-śakti*, the marginal point. The conditioned souls of this world have come from the marginal point. Those who manifested from Śrī Baladeva Prabhu in Vṛndāvana are always serving there; they cannot fall down. However, by the wish of Kṛṣṇa they may come here to help others.

Rāsa-līlā dāsī: How can I sing *kīrtana* in such a way that I feel Kṛṣṇa is with me? How, by my *kīrtana*, can I come closer to Kṛṣṇa and develop *kṛṣṇa-prema*?

Śrīla Nārāyaṇa Gosvāmī Mahārāja: It depends on the quality of the *kīrtana*. It depends on whether or not the *kīrtana* is sung in a mood of surrender (*śaraṇāgati*). When you sing the prayers of Śrīla Narottama dāsa Ṭhākura, Śrīla Bhaktivinoda Ṭhākura, and other *ācāryas*, it is essential to sincerely feel those prayers: "I am very, very fallen, so please help me. I want to give myself to Your lotus feet, but I cannot."

Greed to serve Kṛṣṇa like the residents of Vṛndāvana is called in Sanskrit *lālasāmayī*. You are new to this *saṅga*, so it is important for you to hear from my preachers and others who are close to me. They will speak this elevated *hari-kathā* to you, and then you will know how to develop that greed: "I want to serve Kṛṣṇa like Mother Yaśodā and the *gopīs*." When you perform *kīrtana* at that time, you will be in the mood: "I want to serve You."

Gītā dāsī: In *yuga* cycles other than the present one, who comes in Dvāpara-yuga? Is it Vāsudeva Kṛṣṇa or a Viṣṇu incarnation?

Śrīla Nārāyaṇa Gosvāmī Mahārāja: Śrī Kṛṣṇa only comes once in one day of Brahmā.[38] This is also true for Śrī Caitanya Mahāprabhu and Śrī Rāmacandra. In other Dvāpara-yugas, it is the manifestations of Kāraṇodakaśāyī Viṣṇu or Garbhodakaśāyī Viṣṇu who come, and they establish *yuga-dharma* (the religious process for the age). For example, the *yuga-dharma* of Dvāpara-yuga is *arcana* (temple worship), and the *yuga-dharma* of Kali-yuga is *harināma-saṅkīrtana.*

Śrīpāda Padmanābha Mahārāja: This devotee lives in Europe. She has a devotee friend who is translating books in the Finnish language but cannot sell the books due to living alone. What should she do?

Śrīla Nārāyaṇa Gosvāmī Mahārāja: She can take help of other devotees.

Mahā-kratu dāsa: Does the attainment of *rāgānuga-bhakti* depend on the quality of our *vaidhī-bhakti sādhana?*

Śrīla Nārāyaṇa Gosvāmī Mahārāja: It depends on whether one is hearing *Śrīmad-Bhāgavatam* and *Śrī Caitanya-caritāmṛta.* All the moods of the Vrajavāsīs have been explained there. If one reads these books, he will develop transcendental greed.

If you desire the mood of the *gopīs* but that mood is not in your constitutional form, you will not be able to perform *rāgānuga-bhakti.* You can obtain only that mood which is in seed in your constitutional form. When you perform *bhajana* in the correct way, following the correct process, you will cross *niṣṭhā* (the stage of steadiness in *bhakti)* and *ruci* (genuine taste for the practices of *bhakti*). Then *āsakti* (natural attachment for Bhagavān and *bhakti*) will come, and

---

[38] "Now, let us try to calculate the life span of Brahmā by calculating his one day. Kṛṣṇa says, '*sahasra-yuga-paryantam ahar yad brahmaṇo viduḥ* – Brahmā's day lasts for a thousand *yuga* cycles.' In each cycle there are four *yugas*, or ages – Satya, Tretā, Dvāpara, and Kali – which last a total of 4,320,000 years. So one of Brahmā's days (a day is morning to evening) lasts 4,320,000,000 of our years, and Brahmā lives one hundred years composed of these days and equally long nights" (*Transcendental Teachings of Prahlada Maharaja*, Chapter 2).

then you will enter the stage of *rati* (the sprouting of pure love for Kṛṣṇa). At that time you can realize your transcendental form and mood. Before then, your constitutional mood is not fixed.

I think it is better for you all not to ask these high-level questions, but to ask how to remove your *anarthas* – lust, anger, greed, illusion, envy, and the intoxication of pride. You can ask, "O Gurudeva, how can I become free from my *anarthas?*" When these are gone, you can control your mind and progress in *bhajana*; otherwise not.

Devotee: You said yesterday that *sannyāsīs* should not speak to women. How, then, can they travel and teach Kṛṣṇa consciousness?

Śrīla Nārāyaṇa Gosvāmī Mahārāja: Yes, I have said this.

(To Śuddhādvaitī Mahārāja) Can you explain the meaning of my statement?

Śrīpāda Śuddhādvaitī Mahārāja: Gurudeva said that *sannyāsīs* should not speak to ladies, even in their dreams. This means that they should not indulge with ladies in frivolous talk, talks in relation to sense gratification.

Śrīpāda Mādhava Mahārāja: This question was raised before. Śrīla Gurudeva replied that we must consider elderly ladies as mothers, younger ladies as daughters, and ladies of equal age as sisters. We have to treat them like mothers, sisters, or daughters; not looking at them or talking with them in a mood of sense gratification.

Śrīla Nārāyaṇa Gosvāmī Mahārāja: Do you understand? Your mother is a lady, your sister is a lady, and your daughter is also a lady. You cannot avoid their association. Rather, keep this mood: "All elders are my mothers, those equal in age are my sisters, and those younger than me are my daughters." There should be no illicit relationship or attachment.

Rāma-kānta dāsa: What is the best method for the devotees in Holland to preach and to bring one hundred devotees to you at Kārtika?

Śrīla Nārāyaṇa Gosvāmī Mahārāja: Do as I am doing. Follow me, as well as Padmanābha Mahārāja, Śuddhādvaitī Mahārāja, Nemi Mahārāja, Āśrama Mahārāja, and all those who are preaching on my behalf. Perform *nagara-saṅkīrtana*, chanting in the streets, parks, and other public venues; give classes like the classes we are conducting here; go on book distribution; go from door-to-door and tell *hari-kathā*. This is the process.

My book table is here. I have been requesting all of you again and again to empty my book table. Take books and distribute them to your friends and others – and also take my posters. We distributed all the books and posters from the book table in Badger. But alas, here they remain on the table.

Perhaps the devotees here are not qualified to take my books, and that is why they are not taking them all. I want to see that my table is empty, knowing that when you leave here you will be distributing the books in your countries and cities. I want to see this today. Otherwise, I will think, "They are not pure devotees. They are not fulfilling my desires."

Istanbul, Turkey

September 14–16, 2008

September 14, 2008
Darśana

Śrīla Nārāyaṇa Gosvāmī Mahārāja: Whatever the Supreme Lord can do, His names can do. The holy names will take away all of the pain of life – birth, death, and all problems – and thus you will be happy. This process of chanting the holy names is called *bhakti-yoga*.

Would you like to ask any questions?

Guest: Do you think it is better for spiritual life to be single? Or, is it better to be married – living with a family and practicing spiritual life together with family?

Śrīla Nārāyaṇa Gosvāmī Mahārāja: If the husband and wife have love and affection for each other, then it is alright to be married. They should not quarrel and after some time divorce. If marriage is favorable for spiritual life, then it is alright to marry; if not, it is better to be renounced like us, and be happy.

This instruction is for both husbands and wives, for males and females. Ladies should try to have husbands who are very humble and polite; otherwise they should remain single and renounced like us.

Why is it best to remain single and renounced? In married life we give birth to daughters and sons, and all of our attention goes towards them. If you can be single and renounced, you will possess nothing material to give your energy to. You will be able to meditate on Kṛṣṇa.

(To Sāvitrī dāsī:) Because you have preached so well, many guests have come here. Very good, very good. Thank you for bringing all these guests.

Śrīpāda Dāmodara Mahārāja: This gentleman is doing Ramadan, meaning that for one month he is fasting all day and eating only at night.

Śrīla Nārāyaṇa Gosvāmī Mahārāja: Very good.

Śrīpāda Dāmodara Mahārāja: But at night he eats fish.

Śrīla Nārāyaṇa Gosvāmī Mahārāja: God is one without a second. Our God, your God, others' God – the Muslims' God, the Christians' God, and the Indians' God – are not separate. The only difference is in the names.

Allah has so many names. The names Allah and Khudā are the same as Kṛṣṇa, Rāma, Bhagavān, and Paramātmā. You are Muslim, but your soul is not Muslim. Your soul, my soul, and everyone's soul is part and parcel of the one Supreme Lord; so we are all brothers and sisters.

Most Muslims do not accept the existence of the transcendental body of the Supreme Lord, but it is stated in the Koran, "Inallah kalaqa mein suratih." This means that Allah, or Khudā, has created humans in His image. It is also said in the Bible that "God created man after His own image." Every soul has a transcendental body; by that body he serves the Supreme Lord and remains happy forever.

One more thing: There is nothing written in the Koran saying that you may kill and eat animals. The cow is the mother of everyone. Without any consideration she gives milk to Christians, Muslims, Hindus, Buddhists, and everyone else, and therefore she is like a mother. We cannot kill our mothers and eat their meat. So do not eat meat.

If you eat meat, the result will be m-e-a-t, me-eat. This means that the animal or fish you are eating will take revenge on you. They will eat your flesh and meat in your future life.

Do not eat meat; otherwise those animals will kill you. They are standing in line, waiting for you to die and take birth again so that they can kill you. One animal will kill you in your next life, and the next animal is ready to kill you in the life after that; and then the next and then the next, each one waiting for his turn to come. It is an endless line. For endless births they will kill and eat you.

In addition you should not eat garlic, because it contains twenty-one kinds of slow poisons. Although it has some good properties, it also contains slow poisons. If you take a particular medicine for a sickness, you discontinue its use when you are cured; and if you do not stop, you will be overwhelmed by so many problems. Similarly, if you absolutely must take garlic as a medicine for some disease, then stop it as soon as the disease passes. Don't touch it after that.

Yasodānandana dāsa: Śrīla Gurudeva, you said that if a person eats cows, then those cows come back and eat him. How is eating meat bad for spiritual growth?

Śrīla Nārāyaṇa Gosvāmī Mahārāja: If it is not bad, then kill your mother and eat her meat. If you do that, you will not only get many diseases, but you will become mad. Similarly, do not eat eggs, because a soul is present there. If you eat eggs, that unborn animal in the egg will take revenge in your next life. At that time, when you enter your mother's womb as an egg, you will in turn be eaten. All activities in the world have a reaction – a good or bad reaction.

Devotee: Can you please say something about *karma*?

Śrīla Nārāyaṇa Gosvāmī Mahārāja: Not all actions performed with your hands, feet, head, and eyes are *karma*. Some actions are *karma* (action for fruitive gain) some are *bhakti-yoga*, (action in devotion), and some are *jñāna-yoga*, (action performed to obtain impersonal, transcendental knowledge).

Here is an example: If you go to the market and purchase many tasteful fruits and sweets for your husband, sons, daughters, and yourself, this is *karma*. *Karma* includes all the activities performed for yourself and your family. On the other hand, if you go to the market and purchase the same very tasteful fruits and sweets for the purpose of offering them to the Lord, Allah, Khudā, and then you partake of the *prasādam* (remnants), this is not *karma*; it is *bhakti-yoga*. Whatever you bring and offer to Śrī Kṛṣṇa is *bhakti-yoga*. If you know that you are not the body, and you think, "The body is eating something; I am not eating; I am soul," this is *jñāna-yoga*.

If you are engaged in *karma*, you will have to come again in this world, in the rotation of birth and death. However, if you offer everything to the Supreme Lord and partake of His remnants, you will not return here.

Śrīpāda Dāmodara Mahārāja: Can you please invite our guests to Vraja-maṇḍala *parikramā*?

Śrīla Nārāyaṇa Gosvāmī Mahārāja: In India, there is a very sacred place called Vṛndāvana (Vraja-maṇḍala). We do *parikramā*, or pilgrimage, of this holy land, wherein we circumambulate it.

In one of Vṛndāvana's holy pastime places, the Supreme Lord Śrī Kṛṣṇa lifted on His finger a very high mountain. This mountain is still there.

In another place, He performed the *rāsa* dance. He danced with hundreds of thousands of *gopīs* (cowherd girls), expanding Himself into as many manifestations of Himself as there were *gopīs*, and holding each of their hands as they all sang and danced. That place is still there.

Another time He jumped into a very poisonous river filled with ferocious waves, and within that river He controlled the poisonous thousand-hooded snake who had created the danger.

Once, there was an ugly demoness who assumed the form of a beautiful lady. She wanted to kill Kṛṣṇa, who at the time was a transcendental baby boy of only six days old. She had no milk in her breasts; rather, her breasts were smeared with poison. She picked up that boy, saying, "Oh, my dear son," and then she pumped her breast to inject Him with the poison. Baby Kṛṣṇa then sucked out all the poison, along with her life-air, and she died. While she was dying, she expanded into a six mile-long form and fell upon all the trees, creepers, and plants in that area.

We will go to all of these pastime places, so I invite you all to this very beautiful, holy land. Please come and perform *parikramā* with us.

Sāvitrī: Thirteen Turkish people have already booked their tickets to come.

Śrīla Nārāyaṇa Gosvāmī Mahārāja: Why not one-hundred thirty?

September 16, 2008
Darśana

Śrīla Nārāyaṇa Gosvāmī Mahārāja: Do you have any questions?

Sercan: I have so many questions; a whole list. I stayed in India, where I made many plans. All those plans were frustrated, but eventually everything worked out well. Then I realized that there must be a controller apart from myself, and that that controller is looking after all of us, arranging everything.

Śrīla Nārāyaṇa Gosvāmī Mahārāja: He is the Supreme Lord, Kṛṣṇa. He knows what you are doing at each and every moment, and He knows everything about the entire creation as well. He is very strict, and also very kind.

Sercan: How does the spiritual journey start, and what happens to affect this journey?

Śrīla Nārāyaṇa Gosvāmī Mahārāja: If you want to go to school, you first agree to follow the rules and regulations of the school, which only the teacher can explain to you. Then you are admitted in the school, and then the teacher trains you.

In the same way, you come to this transcendental school, this *bhakti-yoga* school, and ask a very expert teacher, "How can I enter the transcendental world?" That teacher will first say, "Surrender totally to me," and then he will instruct you in the process. He will tell you, "In this world everyone performs activities with the goal of becoming happy, but we see that no one has become happy nor is anyone becoming happy. People may say, 'We are happy,' but very soon old age runs after them along with so many diseases, and then at last they become hopeless."

So go to such a teacher, take shelter of him, and he will tell you the process.

Sercan: Some people say that as the spiritual energy of the planet increases, everyone will become their own *guru*. They say that others are simply mirrors of us, so that we can understand our own self. What do you think of this idea?

Śrīla Nārāyaṇa Gosvāmī Mahārāja: This is quite absurd. Since the beginning of the creation, there is no one who has received any knowledge from himself. From the time a child takes birth, his parents, brothers, and sisters teach him everything. They teach him to say 'papa,' 'aunty,' 'water,' 'father,' 'mother,' and so on. They teach him, "This is fire. Don't put your hand in fire." In the same way, your *guru* will teach you how to enter into the transcendental world.

Without the help of others, how can a man obtain knowledge? Is there even one example of someone who became wise without taking knowledge from others? Is there any example in this world? Are you an example?

Sercan: Oh, no. This is not my theory; I am simply presenting the opinions of others. I am neutral in this regard.

Śrīla Nārāyaṇa Gosvāmī Mahārāja: They are quite wrong. Don't believe them. What they say is totally false. They cannot teach you that you are not this physical body, that you will soon grow old and die, and that you will not be able to take even a farthing with you to your next life.

We can teach you all of this, and so much more. We will teach you *bhakti-yoga*, devotion to Kṛṣṇa, by practicing which your life will be successful. We can teach you that the Supreme Lord is very, very kind, beautiful, and causelessly merciful. He has created this entire material existence, and it is He who supports it. He is like a father, a mother, and any other loving relative. So abandon all of your worldly desires and practice *bhakti-yoga*.

Sercan: Thank you.

Śrīla Nārāyaṇa Gosvāmī Mahārāja: (To Gunamāla dāsi) Do you have any questions?

Gunamāla dāsi: Every day I have so many problems in my life, and because of this I cannot focus on my devotional practices.

Śrīla Nārāyaṇa Gosvāmī Mahārāja: This means that you are not practicing *bhakti-yoga*. Every day millions upon millions of people are dying, and even more than that are taking birth. Some people are feeling miseries and some experience material happiness, and this is all due to their past activities. Why bother about all this? Come to *bhakti-yoga* and don't worry about this. You can think in this way: "If I am like the materialists, I will have to suffer."

Gunamāla dāsi: Are you saying that every day we have to chant *japa*?

Śrīla Nārāyaṇa Gosvāmī Mahārāja: Chanting, and also reading and remembering the sweet transcendental pastimes of Śrī Kṛṣṇa. Then you will be happy in this world.

Devotee: Many people here are practicing meditation.

Śrīla Nārāyaṇa Gosvāmī Mahārāja: To them I ask, "Can you meditate on my father? Do you know what he was like? No? If you cannot meditate on my father because you have not seen him and you do not know him, how can you meditate on God? Have you seen God so that you can meditate on him? Do you know what He looks like? Is He ugly or beautiful? Is He strong? If you have seen someone or something, then you can meditate upon that person or that thing.

It is better if you can chant His name: "Hare Kṛṣṇa, Hare Kṛṣṇa, Kṛṣṇa Kṛṣṇa, Hare Hare, Hare Rama, Hare Rama, Rama Rama, Hare Hare." Sing, and you can also dance. Do you know how to dance? Do this, and be happy forever.

Devotee: How is this meditation?

Śrīla Nārāyaṇa Gosvāmī Mahārāja: Oh, it gives great happiness – great pleasure. By chanting, you will realize the Supreme Lord. You will forget your material body and you will be able to realize your spiritual body.

Sercan: There are so many ways to obtain liberation.

Śrīla Nārāyaṇa Gosvāmī Mahārāja: No, this is not true. There are not many ways to liberation. Can you become liberated by smoking cigarettes or by drinking wine?

Sercan: Rather I should say that there are so many different philosophies and types of *yoga*.

Śrīla Nārāyaṇa Gosvāmī Mahārāja: Other philosophies fail. They all fail to give perfection. Only the philosophy of *bhakti-yoga* is perfect. Only by this can you achieve perfection and liberation.

Sercan: How can we believe that what you say is true?

Śrīla Nārāyaṇa Gosvāmī Mahārāja: If you are a new student in a school and you do not know even A, B, C, D, can you understand whether or not a teacher is expert?

Sercan: No.

Śrīla Nārāyaṇa Gosvāmī Mahārāja: Yes, you can. There is one way by which you can understand if a teacher is qualified. If you see that each year so many students are passing their exams with the help of that teacher, then you can know that he is okay. This is the only way to know.

You will see that so many devotees are coming to me from all over the world. They desired to be happy, and by coming to me they have become happy. If you will come with us to Odessa, even for a single day, you will see that over 1,000 devotees are there from throughout Europe, and all of them are very happy. They want to continually hear sweet classes about Kṛṣṇa consciousness.

I have toured the world twenty-nine times, and throughout the world a variety of high-class businessmen, doctors, lawyers, engineers, and others have come to me and have taken my shelter.

These young men here have left their very wealthy families and come to me, and they are now preaching this Kṛṣṇa consciousness mission. This is the proof.

You can ask him, "Are you happy or not?"

Guest: (To Śrīpāda Dāmodara Mahārāja) Are you happy?

Śrīpāda Damodara Mahārāja: Yes.

Śrīla Nārāyaṇa Gosvāmī Mahārāja: (To Śrīpāda Dāmodara Mahārāja) Why did you leave your father, mother, and wealth?

Śrīpāda Damodara Mahārāja: I could see that my father was very rich, but he was not happy.

Śrīla Nārāyaṇa Gosvāmī Mahārāja: He came to me. I gave nothing to him, but he is serving me day and night.

Sāvitrī was a very high-class lawyer, and in a moment she gave it up. Her mother came to me in a very humble and sweet way; very happy that my daughter, Sāvitrī, is my daughter. If you want to be happy, follow them and come to me. I will give you happiness.

Guest: But how do we know if someone is liberated?

Śrīla Nārāyaṇa Gosvāmī Mahārāja: That person will be always happy. He will not want anything from anyone. He is detached from the world and he is always joyful.

Ishil: Our minds are always disturbed. We are not peaceful.

Śrīla Nārāyaṇa Gosvāmī Mahārāja: You have so many desires, and they are not being fulfilled; that is why you are unhappy and disturbed. Is it true that you have many desires to be happy?

Ishil: Yes, it is true.

Śrīla Nārāyaṇa Gosvāmī Mahārāja: That is why you are not happy; so give them all up. I will solve all of your problems in a moment.

Odessa, Ukraine
September 20-25, 2008

September 20, 2008
Morning Walk

Śrīla Nārāyaṇa Gosvāmī Mahārāja: I had thought that Turkey was a Muslim country, and I was wondering how we would be able to preach there. But when I went there, I saw that there was no discrimination between Hindus, Christians, and Muslims. Just as people in European countries like Indians, so do the Turkish people like Indians. Many devotees came when I was preaching there. It is a very good place for preaching.

(To Śrīpāda Padmanābha Mahārāja) Do you know what *bhavāṭavī* is?

Śrīpāda Padmanābha Mahārāja: Which?

Śrīpāda Madhava Mahārāja It is discussed in the Fifth Canto of *Śrīmad-Bhāgavatam*.

Śrīpāda Padmanābha Mahārāja: What does *ṭavī* mean?

Śrīla Nārāyaṇa Gosvāmī Mahārāja: If you do not know this, it means that you have not read *Śrīmad-Bhāgavatam* at all. What have you been reading? You have been simply reading that "Rādhā is dancing with Kṛṣṇa," and thinking, "Oh, very sweet!"?

We should know what is necessary for us to read and hear at our present stage of development in *bhakti*.

Śrīpāda Padmanābha Mahārāja: Oh, I remember. It is the forest of material enjoyment. Our Guru Mahārāja, Śrīla Prabhupāda, translated that chapter.

Śrīpāda Nemi Mahārāja: We know all about the forest of material enjoyment. In fact, we have a Ph.D. in material enjoyment.

Śrīla Nārāyaṇa Gosvāmī Mahārāja: Yesterday I spoke about Lord Rāmacandra and told you that Hanumān prayed to Him, "You are the Supreme Lord. It is not possible for you to weep in a fire of separation from Sītā."

What is the hidden meaning behind this pastime?

Śrīpāda Padmanābha Mahārāja: Lord Rāma came as a king in order to be an ideal example of a perfect human being – a perfect ruler, brother, and husband. He is *maryādā-puruṣottama*, the Supreme Lord who exemplifies righteousness and proper etiquette.

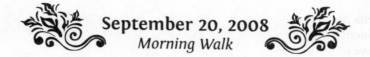

Śrīla Nārāyaṇa Gosvāmī Mahārāja: Why did He weep when Sītā was stolen? The teaching is that if one is too attached to his wife, he will have to weep.

Lord Rāmacandra is teaching us not to be attached to any lady, and not to marry. One should give this life to Śrī Kṛṣṇa. Why should a person marry? In Bhārata-varṣa, India, so many saints, including both Māyāvādīs and devotees, have taught that the form of a lady is the embodiment of *māyā*. Even Lord Brahmā, Śaṅkara, and Nārada were cheated by the form of a woman, what to speak of others.

So always be careful of ladies. They want to enter into a man's life – like a needle ('in like a needle, out like a plow.') They tell men, "I have so much affection for you. I will serve you." And later they become like she-elephants and tigresses.

If I say this among the ladies, they will think that I am criticizing ladies; but this is the fact. Ladies speak very sweetly, and in this way their voices and mood enter a man's heart. They attract even *sannyāsīs*.

Śrīpāda Padmanābha Mahārāja: Some of your *sannyāsīs* do not carry their *daṇḍas* anymore. They are traveling and preaching, but they do not carry their *daṇḍas*. Is this correct?

Śrīla Nārāyaṇa Gosvāmī Mahārāja: My Guru Mahārāja and I always carried our *daṇḍas*. I carried my *daṇḍa* for over sixty years; I stopped only in the last few years. Now I see that only some of you are carrying your *daṇḍas*, not all. Giri Mahārāja never takes his *daṇḍa* with him. Where is Giri Mahārāja? (To Giri Mahārāja) Where is your *daṇḍa*? Now you have become the *paramahaṁsa* of *paramahaṁsas*?

Śrīpāda Giri Mahārāja: My *daṇḍa* is in Vṛndāvana, Śrīla Gurudeva.

Śrīla Nārāyaṇa Gosvāmī Mahārāja: You are now like me, and Śrīla Bhaktivedānta Svāmī Mahārāja in his last days? You can carry very large bags, but you cannot carry your *daṇḍa*? You carry not less than forty kilos, so why can't you carry a *daṇḍa*? Do you understand? I want you all to carry your *daṇḍas*, and I am happy if you do. Vana Mahārāja and Tīrtha Mahārāja carry theirs. Mādhava Mahārāja would carry his, but because of me, he is not doing so. He can only take one or the other – me or his *daṇḍa*. When you become old like me, unable to walk without help, at that time you will not have to carry it.

September 20, 2008

Darśana

Śrīla Nārāyaṇa Gosvāmī Mahārāja: Do you have any questions?

Śrīpāda Sādhu Mahārāja (translating and speaking for the Russian devotees): He is a new devotee from South Russia. He wants to take *harināma* initiation from you.

Śrīla Nārāyaṇa Gosvāmī Mahārāja: Are you following the four regulative principles? Have you given up meat, fish, eggs, wine, and even onions?

Śrīpāda Sādhu Mahārāja: He was previously trying to maintain these principles, and since the beginning of this festival he has become determined to follow them until the end of his life.

This is Āsīt-kṛṣṇa Prabhu from Moscow. He has been helping so much. He is asking how we can fight against, and subdue, our *hṛdaya-daurbalya*, our weakness of heart.

Śrīla Nārāyaṇa Gosvāmī Mahārāja: Follow my instructions and chant the holy name. Read my books and the books of *parama-pūjyapāda* Śrīla Bhaktivedānta Svāmī Mahārāja, and try to follow the instructions therein. If your mind is always engaged in this way, it will be automatically controlled. It is better not to give the mind any time to think of bogus things.

If you want to control a horse, you need to firmly hold onto the reins. That horse will keep on running, and when he is tired, he will be controlled.

Śrīpāda Sādhu Mahārāja: This is Kiśorī-mohana Prabhu from South Russia. He has a question about *śaraṇāgati*, the six limbs of surrender. How do we determine what is favorable for *bhakti*, and what is not favorable?

Śrīla Nārāyaṇa Gosvāmī Mahārāja: All the truths regarding what is favorable and what is unfavorable for *bhakti* are written in the Vedic literatures. For example, it is written that gambling is unfavorable.

Kiśorī-mohana dāsa: We know that this is unfavorable. Gambling is prohibited; it breaks one of the four regulative principles.

Śrīla Nārāyaṇa Gosvāmī Mahārāja: How do you know this?

Kiśorī-mohana dāsa: We learned it from you. But there are so many different things to remember.

Śrīla Nārāyaṇa Gosvāmī Mahārāja: Do you remember your wife, your son, and your business? How do you remember and maintain them all?

Kiśorī-mohana dāsa: I only have a wife.

Śrīla Nārāyaṇa Gosvāmī Mahārāja: How do you remember the name of this place? If you can remember this, and all other things of the world, you can remember what things are favorable and unfavorable for *bhakti*.

Śrīpāda Sādhu Mahārāja: Śrīla Gurudeva, Śrīnidhi Prabhu is from Moscow, where, unlike India, there are not many of your devotees. He is asking if it is okay to have programs together with devotees of ISKCON, because we are all in the family of Caitanya Mahāprabhu. Is it possible to co-operate with them in some respects?

Śrīla Nārāyaṇa Gosvāmī Mahārāja: There is no possibility of co-operation; the leaders are continuously against me.

Śrīpāda Sādhu Mahārāja: I am referring to the general ISKCON devotees; the 'ordinary' *bhaktas*.

Śrīla Nārāyaṇa Gosvāmī Mahārāja: It is all right to cooperate with them, but it is better not to associate with those who are inimical.

Śrīpāda Sādhu Mahārāja: This is your new disciple, Taruṇī dāsī. She met you in India. She says that she felt spontaneous attraction towards you at that time and received *harināma* initiation. She does not have much experience in spiritual life, so she is asking you what to do. She does not know if she should get married or remain a *brahmacāriṇī*. Will you kindly advise her?

Śrīla Nārāyaṇa Gosvāmī Mahārāja: If there is a pure devotee available for marriage, then she can marry. I do not want the men to reject their wives, and I do not want divorce.

Śrīpāda Sādhu Mahārāja: She would also like to take *dīkṣā* initiation from you.

Śrīla Nārāyaṇa Gosvāmī Mahārāja: I will give her *dīkṣā* if she is chanting sixteen rounds daily.

Śrīpāda Sādhu Mahārāja: She also wants to know if she should remain in Russia or go to Vṛndāvana.

Śrīla Nārāyaṇa Gosvāmī Mahārāja: If she can maintain herself in Vṛndāvana, she can go there.

Śrīpāda Sādhu Mahārāja: This is Kamala Dīdī from St. Petersburg. You were saying in your classes that Kṛṣṇa performs His *rāsa-līlā* in many places, such as Govardhana, Rādhā-kuṇḍa, and at the *rāsa-sthalī* of Vṛndāvana. Is the *rāsa-līlā* occurring simultaneously in all these places; or consecutively, one after another?

Śrīla Nārāyaṇa Gosvāmī Mahārāja: You may consider that these pastimes are occurring consecutively, because it is beyond your capacity to imagine Kṛṣṇa doing everything, everywhere, simultaneously, while also creating this world.

He can perform all of His sweet pastimes, including those of Rāma, Nṛsiṁha, Kalki, and Vāmana, simultaneously, because He is all-powerful and almighty. We cannot grasp this reality; therefore, we can think of His pastimes as manifesting one after another. We can think that first He created this world, then He performed pastimes as Matsya *avatāra* (the fish incarnation), then as Kūrma (the tortoise incarnation), then as Nṛsiṁha (the half-man–half-lion incarnation), then as Paraśurāma (the warrior incarnation), then as Rāma, and then as Kṛṣṇa.

Śrīpāda Sādhu Mahārāja: This devotee is from ISKCON. She is asking if it is possible to have a *śikṣā-guru* in her life who is more qualified than her *dīkṣā-guru* in ISKCON?

Śrīla Nārāyaṇa Gosvāmī Mahārāja: Certainly. Sometimes the *śikṣā-guru* is more qualified than the *dīkṣā-guru*. There are instances where the *dīkṣā-guru* will personally send his disciples to receive instruction from the more qualified *guru*. For example, the *gurus* of Śrīla Śyāmānanda Prabhu, Śrīla Narottama dāsa Ṭhākura, and Śrīnivāsa Ācārya did this. Their *gurus* sent them to Śrīla Jīva Gosvāmī, saying, "Śrīla Jīva Gosvāmī is the authority on *bhakti*; go and take *śikṣā* from him." They went to Śrīla Jīva Gosvāmī for instruction, but they did not reject their *dīkṣā-gurus*. They considered Śrīla Jīva Gosvāmī to be their *śikṣā-guru* and the others their *dīkṣā-gurus*. There is no fault in this; it is certainly authentic and proper.

Śrīpāda Sādhu Mahārāja: Sītā-devī is asking about the same topic: Many devotees come to you from ISKCON, where they received their first initiation, and then take shelter of you and receive *dīkṣā*. It is with their *gurus'* blessings that they have come to you for this. What is their relationship with their *gurus* in ISKCON after they obtain your shelter?

Śrīla Nārāyaṇa Gosvāmī Mahārāja: If the *guru* is happy that you have come to me, then you should respect him as *guru*. If that *guru* says, "You can go and take *dīkṣā*," he must be respected.

Regarding how you should think of me, you can think of me as you like. I have no objection regarding anyone who wants to receive my help. My doors are open for everyone, regardless of caste or creed, and regardless of whether they are in ISKCON or anywhere else.

Śrīpāda Sādhu Mahārāja: This lady is from a small town near Moscow. It is very difficult for her to travel to Moscow, and there is no association in her town. However, she is eager to receive *dīkṣā* from you, as she is very inspired.

Śrīpāda Mādhava Mahārāja: How many rounds is she chanting?

Śrīpāda Sādhu Mahārāja: She is chanting thirty-two rounds per day.

Śrīla Nārāyaṇa Gosvāmī Mahārāja: (To the lady) I will give you *dīkṣā* tomorrow.

(To all devotees) You can consider what I am about to say either as a request or as an order. I want each devotee to bring me ten new disciples. Each of you must bring at least ten devotees to be initiated. I do not require money; I want people to love God and be happy. No one can be happy without chanting the holy names and taking shelter of a bonafide *guru*.

Śrīpāda Sādhu Mahārāja: Śrīla Gurudeva, this lady also has two sons in ISKCON.

Śrīla Nārāyaṇa Gosvāmī Mahārāja: (To the lady) Very good, but you should be with me.

Śrīpāda Sādhu Mahārāja: Both sons are reading your books.

Śrīla Nārāyaṇa Gosvāmī Mahārāja: Please tell them that they can meet me if they like.

Śrīpāda Sādhu Mahārāja: She is worried, because her younger son is a disciple of an ISKCON *guru*. He is afraid that he will disobey his *guru* by coming to you, and in that way commit an offense to him.

Śrīla Nārāyaṇa Gosvāmī Mahārāja: If a *guru* tells his disciples not to meet with a higher class Vaiṣṇava, that '*guru*' should be rejected.[39]

Śrīpāda Sādhu Mahārāja: Here is a lady with a question. She is asking how it is possible to serve you, since she is in a female body, and to also satisfy her husband. Her husband is a devotee, your disciple, from Siberia.

Śrīla Nārāyaṇa Gosvāmī Mahārāja: Do you know Śyāmarāṇī? She is standing over there. She is serving me in so many ways; more so than many male persons. She uses all of her intelligence for me.

You should serve me like that: chanting, reading, and preaching, and also by publishing and distributing books.

September 22, 2008
Morning Walk

Śrīpāda Nemi Mahārāja: During the morning walk of the day before yesterday, we talked about Śrī Caitanya Mahāprabhu experiencing *madanākhya-mahābhāva* in the Gambhīrā. We spoke about His body sometimes becoming very long, and sometimes becoming like a pumpkin.[40]

---

39 *guror apy avaliptasya kāryākāryam ajānataḥ*
utpatha-pratipannasya parityāgo vidhīyate
(*Mahābhārata, Udyoga Parva 179.25*)

It is one's duty to give up a *guru* who is attached to sense gratification rather than the practices of *bhakti*, who does not know what he should or should not do, and who deviates from the path of pure *bhakti*, either because of bad association or because he is opposed to Vaiṣṇavas.

Śrīla Jīva Gosvāmī's Commentary: "A *guru* who is envious of pure devotees, who blasphemes them or behaves maliciously towards them should certainly be abandoned, remembering the verse *guror api avaliptasya*. Such an envious *guru* lacks the mood and qualities of a Vaiṣṇava *guru*. The *śāstras* enjoin that one should not accept initiation from a non-Vaiṣṇava. Knowing these injunctions of the scriptures, a sincere devotee should abandon a false *guru*, who is envious of the pure devotee. After leaving a false *guru*, if a devotee is without a spiritual guide, his only hope is to seek out a *mahā-bhāgavata* Vaiṣṇava and serve him. By constantly rendering service to such a pure devotee, one will certainly attain the highest goal of life" (*Bhakti-Sandarbha, Anuccheda* 238).

40 For more information on this pastime, please see *Śrī Caitanya-caritāmṛta, Antya-līlā* 17.15–28.

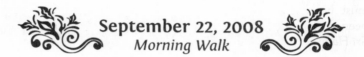

Śrī Caitanya-caritāmṛta describes that at that time Śrī Caitanya Mahāprabhu was internally seeing Rādhā and Kṛṣṇa sporting in the water or going to a cave in Govardhana. So it seems that He sees Śrī Rādhā and Kṛṣṇa together, from a distance.

Śrīla Nārāyaṇa Gosvāmī Mahārāja: Śrī Caitanya Mahāprabhu sometimes sees that Śrī Śrī Rādhā-Kṛṣṇa are meeting, and on other occasions not meeting. He sees Them in a great variety of pastimes. He is most often in *rādhā-bhāva*, sometimes in *gopī-bhāva*, and at times in *mañjarī-bhāva*. It is difficult to reveal these truths, and therefore Śrīla Kṛṣṇadāsa Kavirāja Gosvāmī has discussed them only in brief.

We have not heard about all these symptoms in Śrīmatī Rādhikā. However, if these are the symptoms of *madanākhya-bhāva*, they must be originally present in Śrīmatī Rādhikā. They have not been directly described, but they have been briefly mentioned in *Śrī Haṁsadūta* and similar books.

Śrīpāda Mādhava Mahārāja: Some hints are there.

Śrīla Nārāyaṇa Gosvāmī Mahārāja: Merely speaking about these topics will not suffice in our development of *bhakti*. It is essential to know and follow the principles of *bhakti* at its foundational stage. What is the beginning?

Śrīpāda Nemi Mahārāja: *Ādau śraddhā tataḥ sādhu-saṅgo 'tha bhajana-kriyā.*

ādau śraddhā tataḥ sādhu-
saṅgo 'tha bhajana-kriyā
tato 'nartha-nivṛttiḥ syāt
tato niṣṭhā rucis tataḥ

athāsaktis tato bhāvas
tataḥ premābhyudañcati
sādhakānām ayaṁ premṇaḥ
prādurbhāve bhavet kramaḥ

(*Bhakti-rasāmṛta-sindhu* 1.4.15–16)

In the beginning there must be faith. Then one becomes interested in associating with pure devotees. Thereafter one is initiated by the spiritual master and executes the regulative principles under his orders. Thus one is freed from all unwanted habits and becomes firmly

> fixed in devotional service. Thereafter, one develops taste and attachment. This is the way of *sādhana-bhakti*, the execution of devotional service according to the regulative principles. Gradually emotions intensify, and finally there is an awakening of love. This is the gradual development of love of Godhead for the devotee interested in Kṛṣṇa consciousness.

Śrīla Nārāyaṇa Gosvāmī Mahārāja: What kind of *śraddhā* (faith)?

Śrīpāda Nemi Mahārāja: *Pāramārthika-śraddhā* (transcendental faith).

Śrīla Nārāyaṇa Gosvāmī Mahārāja: What is the meaning?

Śrīpāda Nemi Mahārāja: One endowed with transcendental faith considers, "Kṛṣṇa is the Supreme Personality of Godhead, and I have my relationship with Him through my Gurudeva."

Śrīla Nārāyaṇa Gosvāmī Mahārāja: This is the definition of *śraddhā:*

> *śraddhā'-śabde—viśvāsa kahe sudṛḍha niścaya*
> *kṛṣṇe bhakti kaile sarva-karma kṛta haya*
>
> (*Śrī Caitanya-caritāmṛta, Madhya-līlā* 22.62)

> By rendering transcendental loving service to Śrī Kṛṣṇa, one automatically performs all subsidiary activities. This confident, firm faith, favorable to the discharge of devotional service, is called *śraddhā*.

What is the meaning?

Śrīpāda Nemi Mahārāja: This is the firm conviction that, "If I perform *bhakti* to Kṛṣṇa, all subsidiary activities are included."

Śrīla Nārāyaṇa Gosvāmī Mahārāja: That is the secondary symptom of *śraddhā*, not the first. What is the first?

Śrīpāda Mādhava Mahārāja: *Kṛṣṇa-sevā-vāsanā hi śraddhā ka mūla heih*. The desire to serve Kṛṣṇa is the internal symptom of *śraddhā*, and the other is external.

Śrīpāda Giri Mahārāja: Śrīla Gurudeva, there are two internal reasons and two external reasons for Śrīman Mahāprabhu's appearance. What are they?

Śrīla Nārāyaṇa Gosvāmī Mahārāja: There are two prominent and two secondary reasons. What are the two secondary reasons?

Śrīpāda Giri Mahārāja: One of the secondary reasons was to distribute *rāga-mārga*, the path of *rāgānugā-bhakti*. The other was to establish the *yuga-dharma*, the religious process for the age, which is the chanting of the holy name.

Śrīla Nārāyaṇa Gosvāmī Mahārāja: And what are the internal reasons?

Śrīpāda Giri Mahārāja: The primary internal reason was to fulfill Kṛṣṇa's desires to taste the three moods of Śrīmatī Rādhikā, and the secondary internal reason was to answer the prayers of Advaita Ācārya.

Śrīla Nārāyaṇa Gosvāmī Mahārāja: (To all) Do you know the Nāgapatnīs? They prayed to Kṛṣṇa in this way:

kasyānubhāvo 'sya na deva vidmahe
tavāṅghri-reṇu-sparśādhikāraḥ
yad-vāñchayā śrīr lalanācarat tapo
vihāya kāmān su-ciraṁ dhṛta-vratā

(*Śrīmad-Bhāgavatam* 10.16.36)

> O Lord, we do not know how the serpent Kāliya has attained this great opportunity of being touched by the dust of Your lotus feet. For this end, the goddess of fortune performed austerities for centuries, giving up all other desires and taking austere vows.

What is the meaning of this verse?

Śrīpāda Padmanābha Mahārāja: The Nāgapatnīs were the wives of the serpent Kāliya.

Śrīla Nārāyaṇa Gosvāmī Mahārāja: How many wives did he have?

Śrīpāda Padmanābha Mahārāja: Our book does not say.

Śrīla Nārāyaṇa Gosvāmī Mahārāja: There were thousands, but one of them was prominent.

Śrīpāda Padmanābha Mahārāja: When Kṛṣṇa subdued Kāliya by dancing on Kāliya's hoods, Kāliya lost all of his power and was dying. At that time the Nāgapatnīs approached Kṛṣṇa and began to pray.

Śrīla Nārāyaṇa Gosvāmī Mahārāja: Why did they not come to pray earlier? Why did they do so only in the end?

Prema-prayojana dāsa: At first Kāliya was fighting against Kṛṣṇa; he had no *śaraṇāgati*, no mood of surrender. Therefore his wives thought, "It is better if our husband dies, because he is not a devotee." However, when his head was trampled by Kṛṣṇa's feet, he became somewhat humble. Seeing his humility, his wives considered, "Oh, perhaps he can be a devotee." Then they prayed to Kṛṣṇa to be merciful to him.

Śrīla Nārāyaṇa Gosvāmī Mahārāja: Why did they pray to Kṛṣṇa?

Śrīpāda Nemi Mahārāja: They saw that he was now becoming a little devoted to Kṛṣṇa. For this reason they wanted Kṛṣṇa to be merciful.

Śrīla Nārāyaṇa Gosvāmī Mahārāja: Can you speak further?

Śrīpāda Padmanābha Mahārāja: They were thinking, "Maybe now he can become a pure Vaiṣṇava." And they were Vaiṣṇavīs, so now they wanted to save him.

Śrīla Nārāyaṇa Gosvāmī Mahārāja: Why?

Śrīpāda Mādhava Mahārāja: The Nāgapatnīs first prayed to Kṛṣṇa that they preferred to become widows, but now that Kāliya was surrendering they began to think, "We are women, so we do not have much physical power. If our husband is not with us, another strong serpent may come and destroy our chastity. It is good that he has now surrendered to Kṛṣṇa. If he lives with us, our chastity will be protected and we can do *bhajana* together."

Śrīla Nārāyaṇa Gosvāmī Mahārāja: Do you all understand?

The Nāgapatnīs prayed, *kasyānubhāvo 'sya na deva vidmahe*. What is the meaning?

Śrīpāda Padmanābha Mahārāja: They did not understand how Kāliya could be so fortunate to have attained the foot-dust of Kṛṣṇa on his head; how he could have received such mercy from Kṛṣṇa that even Laksmī-devī could not obtain by her severe austerities. This serpent, in spite of being so sinful, somehow became fortunate. They wondered what kind of pious activities he had performed in previous lives in order to receive this benediction.

Śrīla Nārāyaṇa Gosvāmī Mahārāja: Can you say what austerities he performed in his past lives?

Śrīpāda Dāmodara Mahārāja: In the Purāṇas it is stated that Kāliya was a king in his previous life.

Śrīpāda Mādhava Mahārāja: And Śrīla Sanātana Gosvāmī also explains this in his *Bṛhad-vaiṣṇava-toṣaṇī* commentary.

Śrīpāda Dāmodara Mahārāja: Once, when there was no rain in his kingdom, that king asked the *brāhmaṇas* what he should do. They told him to worship a *sādhu* who was living underneath a particular tree. That *sādhu* had leprosy, but they did not disclose this to the king. They simply said, "Your sins will be destroyed by this process, and rain will come as well."

Later the king saw that *sādhu*, and he brought some water to wash his feet. As the king washed the *sādhu's* feet, and seeing that the *sādhu* had leprosy, he began to think, "I cannot drink this." Hesitant to put the water in his mouth, he put it on his head instead. The *sādhu* remarked, "You are envious like a snake. Although you externally act like a very nice person, your heart contains so much poison. I therefore curse you to become a snake. However, because you put my *caraṇāmṛta* on your head, I bless you that the Supreme Lord will dance on your head."

Śrīla Nārāyaṇa Gosvāmī Mahārāja: Do you know more details?

Śrīpāda Dāmodara Mahārāja: Kāliya received the mercy of Garuḍa. Garuḍa gave him mercy by touching him as they fought, and by indirectly giving him a place in Vṛndāvana.

Śrīla Nārāyaṇa Gosvāmī Mahārāja: This is not clear. It may be told more clearly. If one takes a Vaiṣṇava as one's enemy, he will be blessed by the mercy of the enemy. The Vaiṣṇava is kind to all, merciful to all, without any cause.

Śrīpāda Mādhava Mahārāja: A Vaiṣṇava's benediction and curse yield the same result.

Śrīla Nārāyaṇa Gosvāmī Mahārāja: Garuḍa is a topmost Vaiṣṇava.

If you befriend a sense enjoyer, a person who is attached to the opposite sex or one who opposes *bhakti*, the association of that 'friend' will cause you to go to hell. On the other hand, if your enemy is a pure Vaiṣṇava, this will bestow a result similar to that which occurred with Kāliya.

There is another important point in this connection. Kāliya was in Vṛndāvana (living on an island in the Yamunā) for a very long time – since the Satya-yuga of this *manvantara's* fourth *catur-yuga*[41],

41 A *catur-yuga* is one millennium. A millennium lasts for the duration of a cycle of four *yugas*. In other words, the four *yugas* – Satya, Tretā, Dvāpara, and Kali – constitute one millennium. Each millennium, or *catur-yuga*, consists of over 4 million years. The Lord appears on schedule, namely at the end of the Dvāpara-yuga of the twenty-eighth millennium of the *manvantara* of the seventh Manu, called Vaivasvata Manu, in one day of Brahmā.

and Kṛṣṇa came to this world in this *manvantara's* twenty-eighth *catur-yuga*. Kāliya remained there until Kṛṣṇa jumped in Yamunā's water. It is stated in *śāstra*, "*Dinam ekām nivāsena karau bhaktiḥ prajāyate* – If anyone stays for even one night in Mathurā-maṇḍala, meaning Vraja-maṇḍala, he will attain *bhakti*" (*Padma Purāṇa*, *Pātāla-khaṇḍa*). Since Kāliya was living there for so many *yugas*, the effect would surely fructify.

One more thing to consider: How did Kāliya receive such mercy? Laksmī, Brahmā, and Śaṅkara desire that Śrī Kṛṣṇa place His lotus feet upon their heads, but they never attain the fruits of that desire. On the other hand, in spite of Pūtanā being inimical and wanting to kill Kṛṣṇa, He granted her the liberation of attaining a position as His nurse in Goloka; not in her present lifetime but in the next. Kāliya, however, attained Kṛṣṇa's mercy in that very lifetime.

I have explained this narration about Kāliya, which is very deep, so that you would know these truths.

Śrīpāda Mādhava Mahārāja: Śrīla Sanātana Gosvāmī explained another point as well. Kāliya left Vṛndāvana through the waterways, not the road. Why is that? He had so many wives and children. Serpents naturally look fearsome. Had Kāliya and his family used the road, everyone in the village would have been frightened.

Śrīla Nārāyaṇa Gosvāmī Mahārāja: Kāliya and his wives lived within Kāliya-daha, the lake of Kāliya. However, because snakes are not able to live in water, there must have been some land upon which they could reside. Therefore, in Kāliya-daha there must have been an island, and on that island there must have been some holes, or tunnels, in which Kāliya and his family used to live.

Because the island of Kāliya was situated in the middle of the lake, when Kṛṣṇa jumped in the lake, the water rose so high that it flooded Kāliya's tunnel. Thus, greatly angered, Kāliya came out to fight with Kṛṣṇa, calling out, "Who is He?"

Śrīpāda Dāmodara Mahārāja: Gurudeva, why did Kṛṣṇa kill Pūtanā, Aghāsura, and Bakāsura in Vṛndāvana, but He sent Kāliya and all of his wives far away. It seems that this was not a very merciful act.

Śrīla Nārāyaṇa Gosvāmī Mahārāja: If Kāliya had remained in Vṛndāvana in his lake, even if the water was pure, all the Vrajavāsīs would have been frightened to go there; no one would have gone there to use the water. Also, because he looks very frightening with all his hoods, even though he had become a devotee; the Vrajavāsīs would fear him.

Moreover, Kṛṣṇa did not send him away as one would send another person into exile. Rather, He placed His footprints on Kāliya's head, saying, "Garuḍa will not attack and eat you." Kṛṣṇa gave him a visa-stamp and passport.

Śrīpāda Padmanābha Mahārāja: You were saying that even if someone becomes the enemy of a Vaiṣṇava, that Vaiṣṇava shows mercy towards him. But in *śāstra*...

Śrīla Nārāyaṇa Gosvāmī Mahārāja: For example, Nārada Ṛṣi, a great Vaiṣṇava, a *mahā-bhāgavata* (topmost devotee), cursed Nalakūvera and Maṇigrīva. Eventually they realized that this was not a curse but a blessing. His so-called curse was actually his causeless mercy.

Similarly, Kāliya understood that he had received the causeless mercy of Kṛṣṇa and Garuḍa, and thus he prayed, "Now I realize that Garuḍa was not my enemy, even though I was inimical towards him. I have received the blessings of Your lotus feet on my head only due to his mercy."

Śrīpāda Padmanābha Mahārāja: *Śāstra* states that it is very, very dangerous to commit an offense to a Vaiṣṇava, especially to a great Vaiṣṇava. In fact, *śāstra* explains that one's creeper of devotion (*bhakti-latā*) may be destroyed by such an offense.

Śrīla Nārāyaṇa Gosvāmī Mahārāja: Yes, *śāstra* verifies this. On the other hand, although Kaṁsa showed extreme hostility towards Kṛṣṇa, in the end he was liberated, as were Pūtanā, Aghāsura, and Bakāsura.

If one knowingly commits offenses to a *mahā-bhāgavata*, his *bhakti-latā* will be destroyed. However, those who commit offenses in ignorance receive a lighter reaction. These demons never knew that they were committing offenses, or what would be the consequent reactions.

Śrīpāda Mādhava Mahārāja: Kaṁsa was always absorbed in thinking about Kṛṣṇa and dreaming about Him.

Śrīla Nārāyaṇa Gosvāmī Mahārāja: Rāvaṇa was also like that. Rāvaṇa was not an offender. He was an associate of the Lord. He came to this world only to fulfill the Lord's desire.

Śrīpāda Mādhava Mahārāja: He was always absorbed in thoughts of Rāma.

Śrīpāda Tridaṇḍī Mahārāja: But the Vaiṣṇava has no enemies.

Śrīla Nārāyaṇa Gosvāmī Mahārāja: He has no enemies. Yudhiṣṭhira Mahārāja used to address Duryodhana (meaning 'evil warrior') as Suyodhana (meaning 'pure, well-behaved warrior').

Śrīpāda Mādhava Mahārāja: And he used to address Duḥśāsana as Suḥśāsana.

Śrīla Nārāyaṇa Gosvāmī Mahārāja: Yudhiṣṭhira never regarded Duryodhana as his enemy. He used to say, "We are one-hundred-and-five brothers (the five Pāṇḍavas plus the one-hundred Kauravas headed by Duryodhana)." But Arjuna and Bhīma never thought like this. They wanted to kill Duryodhana and company.

Śrīpāda Padmanābha Mahārāja: Regarding Durvāsā Ṛṣi, the only way he could become free from his offense was to go directly to Ambarīṣa Mahārāja and beg forgiveness. So if someone commits a very heavy *vaiṣṇava-aparādha*, he must approach that Vaiṣṇava.

Śrīla Nārāyaṇa Gosvāmī Mahārāja: Durvāsā pretended to commit offenses to Mahārāja Ambarīṣa. He is an incarnation of Śiva; Śiva cannot commit any offense. Durvāsā simply wanted to establish the glories of the pure devotee, Mahārāja Ambarīṣa, throughout the world.

Śrīpāda Padmanābha Mahārāja: But still, the principle is that if someone commits *vaiṣṇava-aparādha*, he will have to go and beg forgiveness, otherwise that person will be ruined.

Śrīla Nārāyaṇa Gosvāmī Mahārāja: In my village there was a Vaiṣṇava who would take a stick and begin to pursue anyone who would say, "Rāma Rāma." Why did he do this? He considered, "Everyone will chant 'Rāma Rāma' to tease me, and then I will pursue them." This was only a trick to enthuse everyone to chant the name of Rāma; he was not against Rāma.

It is my desire that all of our discussions during these morning walks should be noted in the form of a book. (To Śrīpāda Padmanābha Mahārāja) Have you done anything in this regard? If not, then you are not able to repay me.

(To all devotees present) I am telling you all; these morning walks must be published as a book, so that in the future everyone will be able to know all these truths. This is my idea.

Śrīpāda Mādhava Mahārāja: Like *Perfect Questions, Perfect Answers.*

September 23, 2008
Morning Walk

Śrīpāda Padmanābha Mahārāja: Parjanya Prabhu (now Śrīpāda Sādhu Mahārāja) is our translator.

Śrīla Nārāyaṇa Gosvāmī Mahārāja: Are you also preaching yourself? In other words, not as a translator for other preachers?

Śrīpāda Sādhu Mahārāja: A little.

Śrīla Nārāyaṇa Gosvāmī Mahārāja: Why a little?

Śrīpāda Sādhu Mahārāja: When I go to my country, Lithuania, I give regular programs and I publish your books.

Śrīla Nārāyaṇa Gosvāmī Mahārāja: Yes, continue to organize and preach.

Śrīpāda Dāmodara Mahārāja: Gurudeva, what about Parjanya's *sannyāsa*?

Śrīla Nārāyaṇa Gosvāmī Mahārāja: I am thinking about it. That is why I am requesting him to preach alone. He is qualified. I want many Russians to become qualified for *brahmacarya* and *sannyāsa*. Be ready. I am saying this for everyone. I would like at least ten red-cloth *brahmacārīs*. Russia is a big country.

Śrīpāda Sādhu Mahārāja: There are many regions where *sannyāsīs* do not go, because there is not enough time.

Śrīla Nārāyaṇa Gosvāmī Mahārāja: There are no Russian *sannyāsīs* – only a few *brahmacārīs*. Is it because they are very lusty? Can you all not give this up?

Śrīpāda Padmanābha Mahārāja: Śrīla Gurudeva, yesterday I gave class in the late morning. After my class, your daughter Jagat-mohinī Dīdī, who is one of the translators for your books, gave a lecture to all the devotees. They were very happy to hear such *siddhānta*.

Śrīla Nārāyaṇa Gosvāmī Mahārāja: She is very qualified, and so is her daughter.

Rasa-sindhu dāsa: Gurudeva, I have a short question regarding the six limbs of *śaraṇāgati*[42]. What is the difference between *goptṛtve*

---

[42] Please see Glossary for the definition of *śaraṇāgati*.

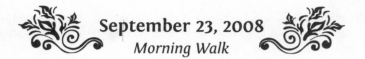

varanaṁ tathā, accepting Kṛṣṇa as one's maintainer, and *rakṣiṣyatīti viśvāso*, accepting Kṛṣṇa as one's only protector? Sometimes they appear to be the same.

Śrīla Nārāyaṇa Gosvāmī Mahārāja: (To Śrīpāda Nemi Mahārāja) Please answer this.

Śrīpāda Nemi Mahārāja: *Goptṛtve varanaṁ tathā* means that Kṛṣṇa provides all daily necessities. *Rakṣiṣyatīti viśvāso* means that Kṛṣṇa defends us in cases of emergency, when a dangerous situation comes. The first is somewhat routine. Śrīla Bhaktivinoda Ṭhākura says that *goptṛtve varanaṁ tathā* is the most fundamental mood of *śaraṇāgati*. Regarding *rakṣiṣyatīti*, if there is some danger or special situation, Kṛṣṇa will take care of you.

Śrīla Nārāyaṇa Gosvāmī Mahārāja: Do you understand?

Rasa-sindhu dāsa: Yes

Śrīpāda Mādhava Mahārāja: In the case of Ambarīṣa Mahārāja, Kṛṣṇa sent the *cakra* to protect him.

Śrīla Nārāyaṇa Gosvāmī Mahārāja: Prahlāda Mahārāja has full faith that Kṛṣṇa is his maintainer and protector, in the past, present, and future. A devotee must be like this. He should not worry, thinking, "Oh, this problem is coming; what should I do?"

Rasa-sindhu dāsa: And *goptṛtve varanaṁ tathā* is the acceptance that Kṛṣṇa will provide everything for devotional service?

Śrīla Nārāyaṇa Gosvāmī Mahārāja: Yes.

Śrīpāda Mādhava Mahārāja: In the case of Arjuna Miśra, Kṛṣṇa erased the line that scratched out His *Bhagavad-gītā* verse, thus showing, "I provide for My devotees." He brought everything required for that devotee.

Śrīpāda Sādhu Mahārāja: *Goptṛtve varanaṁ tathā* is the main point in *śaraṇāgati*.

Śrīla Nārāyaṇa Gosvāmī Mahārāja: Why? What does Śrīla Bhaktivinoda Ṭhākura say?

Śrīpāda Padmanābha Mahārāja: He says that the central limb, *goptṛtve varanaṁ tathā*, must be present in order for the other limbs to be there. In the beginning one must understand that, "Kṛṣṇa is my guardian. I cannot do anything without His mercy. He is always my guardian and maintainer." Then, coming from that, there are other moods, like doing everything favorable for advancement in *bhakti*, rejecting everything unfavorable, and so on.

Śrīla Nārāyaṇa Gosvāmī Mahārāja: And what does Śrīla Śrīdhara Mahārāja say?

Śrīpāda Padmanābha Mahārāja: He says that *goptṛtve varanaṁ tathā* means "I will accept the concept that Kṛṣṇa is my guardian at every single moment, and that I cannot do anything independent of His mercy and His will."

Śrīpāda Nemi Mahārāja: If I think that Kṛṣṇa is not maintaining me, then I would have no time for the other limbs of *śaraṇāgati* because I would have to endeavor to maintain myself. Therefore, if I have full faith that Kṛṣṇa maintains me in every respect, then I can surrender to Him. Otherwise, it is not possible.

Śrīla Nārāyaṇa Gosvāmī Mahārāja: Why is *śaraṇāgati* not *bhakti*? Giri Mahārāja?

Śrīpāda Giri Mahārāja: In *śaraṇāgati*, Kṛṣṇa says, "*Sarva-dharmān parityajya* – If you surrender unto Me, I will protect you." It's like a deal: "If you do this, I will do this." Pure *bhakti* means, "I want to do everything for Kṛṣṇa."

Śrīla Nārāyaṇa Gosvāmī Mahārāja: Anything more?

Śrīpāda Nemi Mahārāja: In *Rāya Rāmānanda Saṁvāda*, Śrī Caitanya Mahāprabhu was not satisfied until Rāya Rāmānanda began to explain *svarūpa-siddhi-bhakti*. *Śaraṇāgati* is not yet *svarūpa-siddhi-bhakti*.

Śrīla Nārāyaṇa Gosvāmī Mahārāja: Why not?

Śrīpāda Nemi Mahārāja: It does not explain the actual function of the *jīva*.

Śrīla Nārāyaṇa Gosvāmī Mahārāja: Why not? Prema-prayojana?

Prema-prayojana dāsa: *Bhakti* is the essential function (*sāra-vṛtti*) of the *svarūpa-śakti* (complete, internal potency) of Śrī Kṛṣṇa in the spiritual world. *Śaraṇāgati* is the way to open one's heart to receive that *svarūpa-śakti* that causes the living entity to engage in…

Śrīla Nārāyaṇa Gosvāmī Mahārāja: There is no *mamatā*, no sense of 'mine-ness,' in *śaraṇāgati*; so it cannot be *bhakti*. If there is *mamatā*, a true sense that "Kṛṣṇa is my son," or "Kṛṣṇa is my friend," or "Kṛṣṇa is my beloved," then *bhakti* will also be present.

There are five types of *mamatā*: *śānta*, *dāsya*, *sakhya*, *vātsalya*, and *mādhurya*. In other words, there are five kinds of relationships with Kṛṣṇa: "Kṛṣṇa is my master," "Kṛṣṇa is my friend," "Kṛṣṇa is my son," "Kṛṣṇa is my beloved," and the *mamatā* of *śānta*. Of all these relationships, *mādhurya* is the highest. In *śānta-rasa* there is only an *ābhāsa*, or shadow, of *mamatā*, and yet it has been accepted as one of these *rasas*.

Śrīpāda Padmanābha Mahārāja: When we hear the definition of *uttama-bhakti* in the verse beginning *anyābhilāṣitā-śūnyaṁ*, we understand that *ānukūlyena kṛṣṇānuśīlanam* means that we should serve Kṛṣṇa always, with our body, our mind, our emotions, our words, and with everything we possess. This definition seems to include *śaraṇāgati*. There is a mental service in *śaraṇāgati*, in the sense that one thinks, "Kṛṣṇa is my protector." There is dependency on Kṛṣṇa.

Śrīla Nārāyaṇa Gosvāmī Mahārāja: But there is no *mamatā*.

(To Śrīpāda Nemi Mahārāja) Why is the sun reddish in the morning?

Śrīpāda Nemi Mahārāja: Do you want the scientific understanding?

Śrīla Nārāyaṇa Gosvāmī Mahārāja: Yes, yes.

Śrīpāda Nemi Mahārāja: It is because there are a lot of dust particles in the air. The sun has to shine through more of this dust at sunrise. At noon the sun has to shine through less dust.

Śrīla Nārāyaṇa Gosvāmī Mahārāja: But the distance between the Sun and the Earth is the same, and the sun's rays are the same; so why is it reddish? During the daytime more people are walking and running, so there is more dust.

Śrīpāda Nemi Mahārāja: It is shining through a longer... I would have to represent it graphically, by a picture.

Śrīla Nārāyaṇa Gosvāmī Mahārāja: The distance is the same in the morning, at noon, and in the evening.

Śrīpāda Nemi Mahārāja: I have a question. Why...?

Śrīpāda Mādhava Mahārāja: First you will have to answer my question.

Śrīpāda Nemi Mahārāja: (Showing a picture) A picture is worth a thousand words, Śrīla Gurudeva. This picture demonstrates that in the morning time the sun has to penetrate a lot of atmosphere, causing it to appear red. At midday, there is less atmosphere – less dust for the sun to penetrate – and so it appears golden.

Śrīla Nārāyaṇa Gosvāmī Mahārāja: In the daytime there is much more dust, because so many people are running here and there.

Śrīpāda Dāmodara Mahārāja: The Vedas say that the Sun is moving, but Western astronomy says that it is fixed.

Śrīla Nārāyaṇa Gosvāmī Mahārāja: Our Indian science is better. *sūrya-rathasya*, the Sun's chariot, moves around the Dhruva planet, which is fixed. The Sun is moving, as is the Earth, and solar and lunar eclipses manifest because of this. In other words, at times there are solar and lunar eclipses due to the different orbits of the Sun, the Earth, and other planets such as Rāhu which also revolve in their own orbits.

Everything is correctly told in the Vedic scriptures, and therefore scientists will one day say, "We are wrong." This is certain. They continually change their opinions.

Śrīpāda Mādhava Mahārāja: First they promote a certain medicine; then, after a few years, they declare that the medicine is harmful and then they ban it.

Śrīpāda Nemi Mahārāja: They already recognize this. They do not claim any superiority of their method over the Vedic method. Einstein admitted that whether one uses the Earth or the Sun as the center, all calculations are the same.

Śrīla Nārāyaṇa Gosvāmī Mahārāja: One day the scientists are bound to declare that Indian science is perfect. Not only this; Indian science has discovered the soul and the Supersoul, whereas Western scientists have not done so. In fact, Western scientists cannot even discover what the mind is. They do not know the difference between the soul and the mind. They are fixed on the body, and all their science and research is in relation to the body.

Are there any questions about the classes?

Maheśvara dāsa: Gurudeva, if a devotee has taken initiation, but is not following *guru* in the proper way and harbors sinful desires within his heart, what is the action of *gurudeva*? Does *gurudeva* act only as a *sākṣī* (witness)?

Śrīla Nārāyaṇa Gosvāmī Mahārāja: This question is defective. Does that disciple have any faith, or not? It must be first determined whether or not the disciple has faith in *guru*.

Maheśvara dāsa: Yes, he does.

Śrīla Nārāyaṇa Gosvāmī Mahārāja: If he has faith, why would he not follow? If he has faith, he must follow his *guru*. He must at least be partially following. *Guru* knows what kind of faith the disciple has, because *guru* is an intimate friend of Kṛṣṇa. *Sākṣād-dharitvena* – he has all the qualities of Kṛṣṇa.

Rasa-sindhu dāsa: I have a question about the book, *Prema-vivarta*. What is Jagadānanda Paṇḍita's role in Mahāprabhu's *līlā*? Rāya Rāmānanda and Svarūpa Dāmodara supported Mahāprabhu's mood as Rādhikā, so what is the role of Jagadānanda Paṇḍita?

Śrīla Nārāyaṇa Gosvāmī Mahārāja: Do you know Śrīla Jagadānanda Paṇḍita?

Rasa-sindhu dāsa: No. I don't know him personally.

Śrīla Nārāyaṇa Gosvāmī Mahārāja: What is Rūpa Gosvāmī doing? What is Sanātana Gosvāmī doing? Are they not serving Him? A married man is served by his wife and son; is their service the same or is it different?

Rasa-sindhu dāsa: There is a difference.

Śrīla Nārāyaṇa Gosvāmī Mahārāja: In the same way, Mahāprabhu's associates render many different types of service.

Rasa-sindhu dāsa: My question was about the specific service of Jagadānanda Paṇḍita, because sometimes he caused Mahāprabhu to become angry.

Śrīpāda Dāmodara Mahārāja: That is his service.

Śrīpāda Mādhava Mahārāja: This is his service to Mahāprabhu. This is love.

Śrīpāda Padmanābha Mahārāja: Kolaveca Śrīdhara also served Mahāprabhu in mock argument.

Śrīla Nārāyaṇa Gosvāmī Mahārāja: There are two kinds of *bhagavat-līlā* – pastimes of the Lord performed in the mood of opulence, or awe and reverence (*aiśvaryamayi*), and those performed in the mood of a sweet human-like relationship (*mādhuryamayi*).

What is *aiśvaryamayi*?

Śrīpāda Śrautī Mahārāja: *Aiśvaryamayi* refers to those pastimes of Lord Kṛṣṇa in the mood of opulence.

Śrīla Nārāyaṇa Gosvāmī Mahārāja: What is the definition of the opulence mood?

Śrīpāda Śrautī Mahārāja: Like Dvārakā.

Śrīla Nārāyaṇa Gosvāmī Mahārāja: I want the definition.

Śrīpāda Tridaṇḍī Mahārāja: It means 'more than human pastimes.' Majestic.

Śrīla Nārāyaṇa Gosvāmī Mahārāja: It means that the activities are beyond human ability. And what is the definition of *mādhuryamayi*?

Śrīpāda Śrautī Mahārāja: Human-like pastimes.

Śrīla Nārāyaṇa Gosvāmī Mahārāja: I would like to hear the full definition.

Śrīpāda Padmanābha Mahārāja: In Vṛndāvana, Kṛṣṇa exhibits only His human-like form, as a very beautiful young boy.

Śrīpāda Mādhava Mahārāja: All opulences exist, but they are covered.

Śrīla Nārāyaṇa Gosvāmī Mahārāja: Śrī Baladeva Vidhyābhūṣaṇa has said, "*Aiśvarya prakate aprakrtane va naravata-līlā nati kramaniya iti madhurya* – Regarding the Lord's aspect of unassuming sweetness (*mādhurya*): whether divine opulence is exhibited or not, if the mood of human-like pastimes is not transgressed even slightly, then it is called *mādhurya*."

Śrīpāda Śrautī Mahārāja: The inner mood of the Vrajavāsīs is so strongly *mādhurya* that no presence of Kṛṣṇa's *aiśvarya* can change it.

Śrīla Nārāyaṇa Gosvāmī Mahārāja: Is Kṛṣṇa's killing of Pūtanā *aiśvaryamayi* or *mādhuryamayi*? [43]

[43] "For example, when Śrī Kṛṣṇa killed the demoness Pūtanā, He enacted the pastime of sucking her breast, behaving just like an ordinary human child. While smashing the terrifying and hard-hearted cart demon (Śakaṭāsura) with His extremely tender lotus feet, Kṛṣṇa maintained His human-like behavior as a small baby of only three months, lying on His back. Even when Mother Yaśodā could not bind Him with the longest rope, Kṛṣṇa appeared completely perturbed out of fear of her. In *brahma-vimohana-līlā*, having baffled Brahmā, Baladeva and everyone else, Kṛṣṇa was seen tending the cows and calves just like an ordinary human boy, even while personally remaining omniscient. Moreover, even though Kṛṣṇa's great opulence (*aiśvarya*) is present when He is seen performing the pastimes of stealing milk and yogurt and acting lustily toward the enchanting young cowherd maidens, that *aiśvarya* is not apparent.

If the Lord's child-like unawareness (*mugdhatā*) were to be called *mādhurya* simply because without displaying any divine opulence it corresponds to human activities, then the *mugdhatā* shown by any ordinary restless and playful child would also have to be called *mādhurya*. Therefore it is completely wrong to explain *mādhurya* in this way" (*Rāga-vartma-candrikā* 2.3).

Śrīpāda Śrautī Mahārāja: *Mādhurya*.

Śrīla Nārāyaṇa Gosvāmī Mahārāja: Why?

Śrīpāda Śrautī Mahārāja: Because Kṛṣṇa is playing like a child.

Śrīla Nārāyaṇa Gosvāmī Mahārāja: Yes, that is the answer.

[Śrīla Mahārāja now enters his residence and returns to his room, where the following conversation takes place.]

Śrīpāda Padmanābha Mahārāja: We have one quick question about publication. Gurudeva, yesterday you gave the instruction that you want a new book published from these morning walk conversations. In that regard I had some discussions with Śyāmarāṇī Dīdī and Vasanti Dīdī. We have some questions for you about this project.

Śrīla Nārāyaṇa Gosvāmī Mahārāja: Try to collect and publish what I have spoken.

Śyāmarāṇī dāsī: Do you want all of your morning walks and conversations published?

Śrīla Nārāyaṇa Gosvāmī Mahārāja: Yes.

Śyāmarāṇī dāsī: So it is not that you want a particular topic.

Śrīla Nārāyaṇa Gosvāmī Mahārāja: No. Whatever I have told.

Śrīpāda Padmanābha Mahārāja: There are many years of these morning walks and conversations. In that case, it will be several books.

Śrīla Nārāyaṇa Gosvāmī Mahārāja: Yes, I would expect it to be many books; one part after another, in a series. It will be very favorable for the devotees.

Śyāmarāṇī dāsī: You began giving *darśanas* way back in 1992. Do you want those included?

Śrīla Nārāyaṇa Gosvāmī Mahārāja: I want the morning walks to be in a book – while walking in Badger and everywhere else.

Śrīpāda Padmanābha Mahārāja: Previously you met with the GBC and they asked so many questions. Can we include those *darśanas*?

Śrīla Nārāyaṇa Gosvāmī Mahārāja: Yes, yes, all that I have spoken.

Brajanātha dāsa: Gurudeva has requested many times that a book of his meetings with and teachings to the GBC members be published, but no one is doing it.

September 24, 2008
Morning Walk

Śrīla Nārāyaṇa Gosvāmī Mahārāja: I do not know whether you will be able to walk when you come to my age.

Śrīpāda Nemi Mahārāja: I don't know if I will even come to your age.

Śrīla Nārāyaṇa Gosvāmī Mahārāja: My age is more than that of Śrīla Bhaktivedānta Svāmī Mahārāja when he left this world? How old was he?

Śrīpāda Padmanābha Mahārāja: Eighty-one.

Śrīla Nārāyaṇa Gosvāmī Mahārāja: I took *sannyāsa* before him...

Śrīpāda Nemi Mahārāja: And you assisted him at the time of his taking *sannyāsa* – with *ḍor-kaupīna* and shaving.

Śrīla Nārāyaṇa Gosvāmī Mahārāja: I was fortunate to serve him, even before the birth of ISKCON.

Śrīpāda Padmanābha Mahārāja: And also before the birth of ISKCON devotees.

Śrīla Nārāyaṇa Gosvāmī Mahārāja: When did you join him?

Śrīpāda Padmanābha Mahārāja: 1970.

Śrīla Nārāyaṇa Gosvāmī Mahārāja: I met him in 1946

Śrīpāda Nemi Mahārāja: Most ISKCON devotees weren't even born at that time.

Śrīla Nārāyaṇa Gosvāmī Mahārāja: Some were babies, and some were not born.

Śrīpāda Nemi Mahārāja: I was a baby.

Śrīpāda Nemi Mahārāja: Some devotees, who are here now, have a big farm in the south of Russia, with about fifty cows. They want to know if this is pleasing to you, and whether they should continue with this farm or not.

Śrīla Nārāyaṇa Gosvāmī Mahārāja: They should continue. Real milk, real butter, and real ghee can be gotten there.

Śrīpāda Nemi Mahārāja: You will be happy with this?

Śrīla Nārāyaṇa Gosvāmī Mahārāja: Yes.

Yesterday I heard that some of the devotees created a board for publications in the Russian language.

Rasa-sindhu dāsa: We met yesterday. We want to be more organized to produce your books.

Śrīla Nārāyaṇa Gosvāmī Mahārāja: Which books have been published and which have not should be noted. As a team, you should select who will do what books. Thus, all my publications should come very soon.

Śrīpāda Nemi Mahārāja: How many are there already?

Rasa-sindhu dāsa: About thirty-five.

Śrīla Nārāyaṇa Gosvāmī Mahārāja: I want *Jaiva-dharma* to come very soon, and also my *Bhagavad-gītā* and other books. I want this in English, Russian, Chinese, Spanish, German, French, and so on. Spanish is a very important language.

Śrīpāda Padmanābha Mahārāja: Chinese is the most widely spoken language in the world.

Śrīla Nārāyaṇa Gosvāmī Mahārāja: Hindi is second. Like Russia, so many devotees are coming from China. Chinese people are very polite and humble, like those in Russia. Even though China is a communist country, most of the people in general believe in God.

Śrīpāda Padmanābha Mahārāja: When our Guru Mahārāja, Śrīla Bhaktivedānta Svāmī Mahārāja, went to Moscow for the first time, he stayed for about three or four days. During that time, he examined the people of Russia and said, "Many people in the world are saying that Russians are the biggest atheists. But I say that in the future they will become the biggest theists."

Śrīla Nārāyaṇa Gosvāmī Mahārāja: The Chinese also. Before Communism became prominent in China, everyone believed in God.

Śrīpāda Nemi Mahārāja: Even Buddhists in China believe in God. They are not so atheistic. The names of Kṛṣṇa are present in the *sūtras* of the Zen Buddhists. Without their knowledge, the Buddhists are chanting Kṛṣṇa's names.

Śrīla Nārāyaṇa Gosvāmī Mahārāja: There is one very prominent Chinese Buddhist who has thousands of disciples. He took initiation from me.

Are there any questions?

Rasa-sindhu dāsa: Gurudeva, I have a question. Yesterday we spoke about *aiśvarya* and *mādhurya*. We know from you the definition of Bhagavān, as told in this verse:

> *aiśvaryasya samagrasya vīryasya yaśasaḥ śrīyaḥ*
> *jñāna vairāgyayoś caiva ṣaṇṇām bhaga itīṅganā*
>
> (*Viṣṇu Purāṇa* 6.5.47)
>
> Bhagavān, the Supreme Personality of Godhead, is thus defined by Parāśara Muni as one who is full in six opulences – who has full strength, fame, wealth, knowledge, beauty, and renunciation.

Mādhurya is not mentioned here. Why is that so?

Śrīpāda Mādhava Mahārāja: This is not the definition of Bhagavān. This verse simply enumerates the types of *bhaga* (opulence) in Bhagavān.

Śrīla Nārāyaṇa Gosvāmī Mahārāja: In *sad-aiśvarya* Bhagavān (Bhagavān, with six opulences) in Vṛndāvana, whether or not opulence is present, His activities are *naravata-līlā* (human-like pastimes). So there is no harm in Bhagavān having opulence. When He plays like a human, this is *mādhurya*.

Rasa-sindhu dāsa: *Mādhurya* is only in Svayam Bhagavān (the original Supreme Personality of Godhead)?

Śrīla Nārāyaṇa Gosvāmī Mahārāja: It is stated in *Śrīmad-Bhāgavatam*:

> *ete cāṁśa-kalāḥ puṁsaḥ kṛṣṇas tu bhagavān svayam*
>
> (*Śrīmad-Bhāgavatam* 1.3.28)
>
> All *avatāras* beginning with Rāma and Nṛsiṁha are the parts, and parts of the parts, of the Supreme Person Bhagavān. However, only Śrī Kṛṣṇa is the original Svayam Bhagavān.

Svayam Bhagavān is Śrī Kṛṣṇa, and because Kṛṣṇa is performing His *naravata-līlā*, all His pastimes are *mādhurya*. *Aiśvarya* may be present in *mādhurya*, but *mādhurya* is not present in *aiśvarya*.

Śrīpāda Padmanābha Mahārāja: Śrīla Gurudeva, I have a question about *śaraṇāgati*. Yesterday you said that *bhakti* comes only when *mamatā* is present with *śaraṇāgati*.

Śrīla Nārāyaṇa Gosvāmī Mahārāja: There is no *mamatā* in *śaraṇāgati:*

dīkṣā-kāle bhakta kare ātma-samarpaṇa
sei-kāle kṛṣṇa tāre kare ātma-sama

sei deha kare tāra cid-ānanda-maya
aprākṛta-dehe tāṅra caraṇa bhajaya

(*Śrī Caitanya-caritāmṛta, Antya-līlā* 4.192–193)

At the time of initiation, when a devotee fully surrenders unto the service of the Lord, Kṛṣṇa accepts him to be as good as Himself. When the devotee's body is thus transformed into spiritual existence, the devotee, in that transcendental body, renders service to the lotus feet of the Lord.

Even in *śānta-rasa* there is no *mamatā*. There is no *mamatā* in the *śānta-rasa* of the four Kumāras and others. Without *mamatā*, there can be no *prema*. As *mamatā* thickens, *prema* develops from *dāsya*, to *sakhya*, to *vātsalya*, and then to *mādhurya*.

Śrīpāda Padmanābha Mahārāja: But there must be some *mamatā* in *śānta-rasa*. *Śānta-rasa* is in the category of *prema*.

Śrīla Nārāyaṇa Gosvāmī Mahārāja: There is only *niṣṭhā* (firm faith) in *śānta-rasa*, not *prema*.

Śrīpāda Mādhava Mahārāja: It is called '*śānta-rasa*,' not '*śānta-prema*.'

Śrīla Nārāyaṇa Gosvāmī Mahārāja: Their *niṣṭhā* is to Kṛṣṇa, not to anything or anyone of this material world. But when they see Kṛṣṇa, they do not see *mādhurya* Kṛṣṇa, meaning the human-like form and pastimes of Kṛṣṇa. They see *nirguṇa-brahma*, and they chant prayers like this:

śāntākāraṁ bhujagaśayanaṁ padmanābhaṁ sureśam
viśvādhāraṁ gaganasadṛśaṁ meghavarṇaṁ śubhāṅgam
lakṣmīkāntaṁ kamalanayanaṁ yogīhṛddhyānagamyam
vande viṣṇuṁ bhavabhayaharaṁ sarvalokaikanātham

(*Gītābhāṣyam*, by Śrī Madhvācārya)

I bow before the God Viṣṇu, Who is the personification of peace, who rests on the snake-bed of Ananta-śeṣa, from whose navel sprouts the lotus that manifests the entire material creation, who is all-pervading like the sky, who resembles the color of a dark raincloud, who has the most beautiful limbs, whose consort is Lakṣmī, who has lotus-like eyes, who is perceived by saintly persons in their meditation, who destroys all worries and fears, and who is the Lord of all the worlds.

Śrīpāda Nemi Mahārāja: What moods do the four Kumāras have towards Śrī Kṛṣṇa?

Śrīla Nārāyaṇa Gosvāmī Mahārāja: First they were Brahmavādīs, Nirguṇavādīs, after which they became *bhaktas* by the mercy of Lord Brahmā. It may also be said that they were in *dāsya-rasa*, but not more than that.

Śrīpāda Padmanābha Mahārāja: I have one more question about *śaraṇāgati*. When does *śaraṇāgati*, which is the entrance or doorway to *bhakti*, become *bhakti*?

Śrīla Nārāyaṇa Gosvāmī Mahārāja: This occurs when the devotee has the association of high-class *sādhus*. In fact, all the stages of *bhakti* are attained by *sādhu-saṅga*. If a person has *mādhurya-rasa* in his transcendental *svarūpa*, but until now has not received any association of *sādhus* in *mādhurya-rasa*, he becomes influenced by the *bhāva* which is in the heart of his association. He may thus be attracted to *sakhya* or *vātsalya*, because the right association is not yet there for the *sadhaka* to develop his or her permanent *bhāva*. When he has attained the association of *sādhus* in *mādhurya-rasa*, at that time *mādhurya* manifests.

Śrīpāda Sādhu Mahārāja: Gurudeva, I will read a question written by Īśānī dāsī: "Some devotees do not want to observe Cāturmāsya. How does that affect spiritual progress?"

Śrīla Nārāyaṇa Gosvāmī Mahārāja: If they do not observe Cāturmāsya, they will not attain *bhakti*. Caitanya Mahāprabhu, Sanātana Gosvāmī, Rūpa Gosvāmī, and so many other *ācāryas* have personally followed Cāturmāsya. Before that, Sanaka, Sanātana, Sanandana, and Sanat Kumāra met with five-year-old Nārada Ṛṣi during Cāturmāsya. This shows that Cāturmāsya has been observed since before Satya-yuga.

In our *paramparā* we see that Śrīla Kṛṣṇadāsa Kavirāja Gosvāmī has written about Cāturmāsya in *Śrī Caitanya-caritāmṛta*, and it is also written about in the *Śrīmad-Bhāgavatam* and *Hari-bhakti-vilāsa*.

Śrīla Bhaktivinoda Ṭhākura has written that we should perform *cāturmāsya-vrata*. During that time he had a four-month beard, as did Śrīla Bhaktisiddhānta Sarasvatī Ṭhākura and my Gurudeva, Śrīla Bhakti Prajñāna Keśava Gosvāmī Mahārāja. Śrīla Bhaktivedānta

Svāmī Mahārāja did not follow it so strictly because the Westerners were newcomers.

Śrīpāda Padmanābha Mahārāja: He also told us that for four months out of the year we should not take milk, yogurt, green leaves, etc.

Śrīpāda Nemi Mahārāja: He shaved because his devotees were hippies. He did not want his disciples to grow hair during Cāturmāsya because this might revive their hippy mentality.

Śrīla Nārāyaṇa Gosvāmī Mahārāja: What they did at that time was sufficient for them, but now they are hearing more, and advancing, so they must follow. I have said not to eat tomatoes during these months. If they cannot avoid it for four months, then, as a concession, I have said to at least observe it during the month of Kārtika.

Śrīpāda Mādhava Mahārāja: And also during Puruṣottama Month.

Śrīla Bhaktivinoda Ṭhākura and Śrīla Bhakti Prajñāna Keśava Gosvāmī have written articles about Cāturmāsya. My Gurudeva once said, "In the future, people will not follow Cāturmāsya, saying that Śrīla Sarasvatī Ṭhākura and I have not followed it. So take my photo with my four-month beard." Śrīla Sarasvatī Ṭhākura and Śrīla Bhaktivinoda Ṭhākura have also taken photos like this.

Śrīpāda Padmanābha Mahārāja: Those in the Gauḍīya Vedānta Samiti have said that your Guru Mahārāja established shaving after two months, on Viśvarūpa Mahotsava.

Śrīla Nārāyaṇa Gosvāmī Mahārāja: We also do this; it is called Viśvarūpa Kshour (shaving for Viśvarūpa Mahotsava).[44]

In general, Śrīla Bhaktivinoda Ṭhākura and Śrīla Bhaktisiddhānta Sarasvatī Ṭhākura and my Gurudeva used to shave once every month. Moreover, it is not that they shaved their faces but not their heads, which is like a fashion and which is not for *sannyāsīs*, those in the renounced order. Although proper shaving is not directly *bhakti*, it is favorable for *bhakti*. It comes in the category of this verse:

> *grāmya-kathā nā śunibe, grāmya-vārtā nā kahibe*
> *bhāla nā khāibe āra bhāla nā paribe*
>
> (*Śrī Caitanya-caritāmṛta, Antya-līlā* 6.236)

> Do not talk like people in general or hear what they say. You should not eat very palatable food, nor should you dress very nicely.

44 Both are bonafide: shaving after two months and shaving after four months.

amānī mānada hañā kṛṣṇa-nāma sadā la'be
vraje rādhā-kṛṣṇa-sevā mānase karibe

(*Śrī Caitanya-caritāmṛta, Antya-līlā* 6.237)

Do not expect honor, but offer all respect to others. Always chant the holy name of Lord Kṛṣṇa, and within your mind render service to Rādhā and Kṛṣṇa in Vṛndāvana.

Those in the Śaṅkara *sampradāya* follow even more strictly than we do. If one wants *bhakti*, he should strictly follow all of these principles. These principles are very easy to follow in India, and very hard to follow in Western countries.

Śrīpāda Nemi Mahārāja: A devotee is asking this question: Those in the Nimbārka *sampradāya* are also chanting the names of Śrī Śrī Rādhā-Kṛṣṇa. What is their position?

Śrīla Nārāyaṇa Gosvāmī Mahārāja: Their mood is like *svakīya*, not *pārakīya*. They do not take into consideration the separation of Śrī Śrī Rādhā-Kṛṣṇa – only Their meeting – but meeting without separation is like an ocean without waves. Their mood is flat, like a pond with no fish, no sea animals. We Gauḍīya Vaiṣṇavas have so many fish, tortoises, *timiṅgilas*, and wales; and high waves, like in Hawaii, up to forty feet.

At first the devotees of the Nimbārka *sampradāya* worshiped Śrī Śrī Rukmiṇī-Dvārakādīśa, and after some time they saw the prominence of Śrī Śrī Rādhā-Kṛṣṇa in Vṛndāvana and began to worship Them. But their worship is without waves. They have no idea of *māna*, *prema-vaicittya*, *divyonmāda*, or *pravāsa*.[45] Śrīla Rūpa Gosvāmī has therefore remarked, "Fie on those who do not consider the separation of Śrī Śrī Rādhā-Kṛṣṇa."

Śrīpāda Nemi Mahārāja: He is asking what is the destination of the devotees in the Nimbārka *sampradāya*? What planet do they go to?

Śrīla Nārāyaṇa Gosvāmī Mahārāja: They will go to Goloka, but not to Vṛndāvana.

(To a devotee standing nearby) I see that so many Russian devotees do not have *śikhās*. I will reject those who do not wear *śikhās*.

Śrīpāda Sādhu Mahārāja: He says that he does not want to disturb the general population, and that is why he does not wear *śikhā*.

[45] Please see Glossary for the definitions of these words.

Śrīla Nārāyaṇa Gosvāmī Mahārāja: Let them be disturbed. What is the harm in that? In India, the general people do not wear *śikhās*, but we keep long *śikhās*.

Śrīpāda Sādhu Mahārāja: He says that he will definitely grow a *śikhā* from now on.

One devotee has this question: Shall we discuss philosophy with Christians and argue different points, or is it a waste of time?

Śrīla Nārāyaṇa Gosvāmī Mahārāja: If you see that they are very humble, you can discuss philosophy with them.

September 25, 2008
Morning Walk

Rasa-sindhu dāsa: In *Rāya Rāmānanda Saṁvāda*, Śrīman Mahāprabhu asked Śrī Rāya Rāmānanda, "What is the strongest pain in the material world?" Rāya Rāmānanda replied that it is separation from Vaiṣṇavas. My question is this: what do we have to do to avoid separation from *guru* and Vaiṣṇavas? What do we do to always associate with them?

Śrīla Nārāyaṇa Gosvāmī Mahārāja: *Śāstra* says that we should try to cultivate that separation mood instead of trying to avoid it. It is good for us. If there are no feelings of separation from *guru*, Vaiṣṇavas, and Kṛṣṇa, our *bhajana* is zero.

Rasa-sindhu dāsa: How is it possible to cultivate this mood of separation as another form of meeting – meeting in the heart?

Śrīla Nārāyaṇa Gosvāmī Mahārāja: Feelings of separation automatically enter the heart of a sincere devotee. For instance, if a man is in a foreign country, very far away from his dear wife, what will she think about while he is away?

Rasa-sindhu dāsa: She will always think about him and feel separation from him.

Śrīla Nārāyaṇa Gosvāmī Mahārāja: Yes, we can understand it in this way. Have you seen Śrī Kṛṣṇa or Śrī Caitanya Mahāprabhu?

Rasa-sindhu dāsa: No.

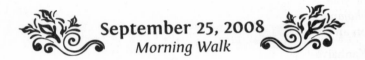

Śrīla Nārāyaṇa Gosvāmī Mahārāja: If you have not seen Them, the feeling of separation must come. If the *guru* is far away, are you meeting with him?

Rasa-sindhu dāsa: No. I meet with you only in my mind.

Śrīla Nārāyaṇa Gosvāmī Mahārāja: First we develop these feelings for our *guru*, and then for Kṛṣṇa.

Rasa-sindhu dāsa: We can experience feelings of separation only when we have established a strong relationship with you?

Śrīla Nārāyaṇa Gosvāmī Mahārāja: Both appear simultaneously. You will feel separation from your *gurudeva* according to the degree of your love for him. If you are performing an elevated level of *bhajana*, then your feelings of separation for *gurudeva* will also be on an elevated level.

Kanhaiyā-lāla dāsa: You told the history of Bharata Mahārāja and his attachment for his deer.

Śrīla Nārāyaṇa Gosvāmī Mahārāja: He wept in feelings of separation for that deer, not for Kṛṣṇa. Previously he wept for Kṛṣṇa, but later he forgot Kṛṣṇa and wept for his deer. He would call out, "Where is my deer, where is my deer?"

Kanhaiyā-lāla dāsa: What should Bharata have done in the beginning? Should he not have saved the deer?

Śrīla Nārāyaṇa Gosvāmī Mahārāja: He acted according to his level of understanding. If I were in his place, I would have also saved the deer, but I would not have been attached to it. I would have given it some water and then left it alone, saying, "You can go now." But Bharata began to give it even more love and affection than he had previously given his own child.

Śrīpāda Giri Mahārāja: Gurudeva, most of the time I try to perform *bhajana* and remember you; but sometimes I forget you, and then I become influenced by *māyā*.

Śrīla Nārāyaṇa Gosvāmī Mahārāja: Can you offer your *sāṣṭāṅga-praṇāma* (full obeisances, performed with all eight limbs of the body) to these Vaiṣṇavas?

Śrīpāda Giri Mahārāja: Yes, I can.

Śrīla Nārāyaṇa Gosvāmī Mahārāja: No. I know that you cannot. You will have real humility when the desire to offer *sāṣṭāṅga-*

praṇāma to all Vaiṣṇavas naturally enters your heart. One's *bhakti* is proportionate to one's humility. We offer *praṇāma* to all living beings, because Kṛṣṇa is in their heart.

Śrīpāda Padmanābha Mahārāja: From time to time I meet devotees who have a certain experience in their devotional life. They say, "I tried very hard to practice *bhakti*. I chanted many rounds, even sixty-four rounds every day, and I woke up early in the morning. Although I did this for eleven years, I did not get the result." Some of these people have given up chanting and practicing *bhakti*.

Śrīla Nārāyaṇa Gosvāmī Mahārāja: They did not have association with pure devotees (*sādhu-saṅga*).

Śrīpāda Padmanābha Mahārāja: They say, "I was with Gurujī and I was in Vṛndāvana so many times, but I have not achieved anything."

Śrīla Nārāyaṇa Gosvāmī Mahārāja: This is not possible. Such persons have no faith in the holy name, in *guru*, or in *bhakti*. In such circumstances, how will *bhakti* come to him?

How does one attain *bhakti*?

mārobi, rākhobi—jo icchā tohārā
nitya-dāsa prati tuwā adhikārā

(*Mānasa-deha geha*, Verse 3,
by Śrīla Bhaktivinoda Ṭhākura)

Slay me or protect me as You wish. You have this right because I am Your eternal servant.

Those who have such doubts are unable to be imbued with the mood described in this verse. They do not possess even the beginning of *śraddhā*, what to speak of *ātma-nivedana*, self-surrender. They considered, "If I take *harināma*, I will be happy because great wealth and position will come to me." Later, when this did not happen, they lost their so-called faith.

Śrīpāda Padmanābha Mahārāja: So their practice was external?

Śrīla Nārāyaṇa Gosvāmī Mahārāja: Yes.

Śrīpāda Sādhu Mahārāja: Śrīla Gurudeva, some devotees doubt that you wrote the Hindi song, *Vraja-jana-manah-sukhakārī*. Can you please confirm that you wrote this song?

Śrīla Nārāyaṇa Gosvāmī Mahārāja: Padmanābha Mahārāja will answer.

Śrīpāda Padmanābha Mahārāja: Yes, Śrīla Gurudeva personally wrote this song, a long time ago. Had he not written it, his name would not have been given as the author. His name is even in the song, where it is written, *nārāyaṇa balihārī*.

Śrīpāda Sādhu Mahārāja: Ananta Prabhu is asking if we can preach something we have not yet realized.

Śrīla Nārāyaṇa Gosvāmī Mahārāja: It is the duty of the disciple, acting as a postman who delivers a message without changing it, to distribute the words of *śrī guru* and our *guru-paramparā* to everyone. Realization will gradually come.

Śrīpāda Sādhu Mahārāja: Balabhadra Prabhu is asking: In *Brahma-vimohana-līlā* it is stated that one year after Kṛṣṇa expanded Himself as all the cowherd boys and calves, He revealed Himself to Brahmājī. Why did Brahmā see the four-armed Viṣṇu forms of Śrī Kṛṣṇa rather than two-handed Vrajendra-nandana Kṛṣṇa?

Śrīla Nārāyaṇa Gosvāmī Mahārāja: Brahmā's worshipable Deity is four-armed Viṣṇu. Viṣṇu told Brahmājī, "You should know that I, your worshipful Deity, am performing these miracles." Later on, Kṛṣṇa showed His two-armed form to Lord Brahmā in order to convince him, "I am the same Lord." This particular pastime, *Brahma-vimohana-līlā*, was a revelation of Śrī Kṛṣṇa's *aiśvarya*.[46]

Śrīpāda Sādhu Mahārāja: Dāmodara Prabhu has a question. He says that he is always seeing faults in others and his mind meditates on others' bad qualities. He is asking how he can get rid of this habit.

Śrīla Nārāyaṇa Gosvāmī Mahārāja: (To Dāmodara dāsa) Has Gurudeva told you to criticize others? You are disobeying your Gurudeva if you do so. You must not disobey. If you find that your mind is criticizing others, simply turn it away and forcibly focus it on Śrī Kṛṣṇa.

Śrīpāda Sādhu Mahārāja: Dāmodara Prabhu says that he likes to study your books, Śrīla Bhaktivedānta Svāmī Mahārāja's books, and the books of our *ācāryas*. Is it okay for him to chant only the minimum sixteen rounds so that he will have time to study these books?

Śrīla Nārāyaṇa Gosvāmī Mahārāja: Both are good, but especially give stress to chanting *harināma*.

---

46 Please see the Morning Walk of May 24, 2008 in Miami to read about this pastime in more detail.

Śrīpāda Sādhu Mahārāja: If someone is using most of his time to chant *harināma* and offer *sevā*, there will not be time to study. Is that all right? Will realization come by doing this?

Śrīla Nārāyaṇa Gosvāmī Mahārāja: There must be *sādhu-saṅga*, so that even if one cannot read so much, he can hear. Śrīla Haridāsa Ṭhākura was illiterate. Śrīla Gaura-kiśora dāsa Bābājī Mahārāja was also illiterate, but he heard from his spiritual masters Śrīla Bhaktivinoda Ṭhākura and Śrīla Jagannātha dāsa Bābājī Mahārāja, and thus he became qualified to teach all others.

Śrīla Bhaktisiddhānta Sarasvatī Ṭhākura has written about how he was accepted as a disciple by Śrīla Gaura-kiśora dāsa Bābājī Mahārāja: "My Prabhu, Śrīla Gaura-kiśora dāsa Bābājī Mahārāja, rejected me at first. I went to him so many times and asked him, 'Please accept me.' But Bābājī Mahārāja replied, 'You are a very learned scholar and the rich son of Śrīla Bhaktivinoda Ṭhākura. I will ask Śrī Śrī Gaura-Nityānanda if They will allow me to initiate you.'"

Finally, when Śrīla Bhaktivinoda Ṭhākura personally requested him to accept his son, he did so.

Śrīpāda Sādhu Mahārāja: Śrīla Gurudeva, this devotee is asking if it is necessary to chant all of his rounds on beads every day. He has a job and it is not always possible to chant on beads.

Śrīla Nārāyaṇa Gosvāmī Mahārāja: I have told the devotees that sometimes they can chant on beads, and sometimes, while walking in service, they can chant without beads. I have said this to encourage those who have no interest in chanting. When a devotee becomes truly interested in chanting, he will chant sixty-four rounds or even more than that. Śrīla Haridāsa Ṭhākura chanted three *lākhas* of holy names (one-hundred-ninety-two rounds) every day.

Rasa-sindhu dāsa: But at least sixteen rounds should be chanted on beads. Isn't that correct?

Śrīla Nārāyaṇa Gosvāmī Mahārāja: I gave that concession for those who are not at all interested in chanting – only for them, not for everyone.

Śrīpāda Sādhu Mahārāja: It is said that we will not attain *lobha* (greed) for *bhakti* unless we hear *hari-kathā* from the lotus lips of *rasika* Vaiṣṇavas. Is that correct?

Śrīla Nārāyaṇa Gosvāmī Maharaj: Yes, that is right.

Śrīpāda Sādhu Mahārāja: Is the *hari-kathā* we hear during the festivals enough to achieve *lobha*?

Śrīla Nārāyaṇa Gosvāmī Mahārāja: We will have to hear throughout our entire life.

Kamala-kānta dāsa: Śrīla Gurudeva, when you met your *guru*, Śrīla Bhakti Prajñāna Keśava Gosvāmī Mahārāja, for the very first time, what did he say to you?

Śrīla Nārāyaṇa Gosvāmī Mahārāja: The first thing I said to him was this: "I have given my life to your lotus feet. I have collected all the love and affection that I had for my father, mother, wife, and children. Having taken it from them, I am offering it at your lotus feet." Hearing this, he began to weep.

Cebu Philippines

December 26-29, 2008

[From mid-November 2008 to mid-January 2009, Śrīla Bhaktivedānta Nārāyaṇa Gosvāmī Mahārāja resided in Cebu, Philippines, on a writing retreat. After returning from his morning walks at 6.45 am, he would have short classes with the devotees in his party, teaching them verses from various Vedic scriptures and giving them 'homework' assignments to learn those verses by memory. On the next day, he would listen as they recited the verses and translations. Then he would request them to explain the meanings, after which he himself would give further explanation. The following is a few excerpts from those daily meetings:]

December 26, 2008
Darśana

Śrīla Nārāyaṇa Gosvāmī Mahārāja:

tat-prayāso na kartavyo
yata āyur-vyayaḥ param
na tathā vindate kṣemaṁ
mukunda-caraṇāmbujam
(*Śrīmad-Bhāgavatam* 7.6.4)

Endeavors merely for sense gratification or material happiness through economic development are not to be performed, for they result only in a loss of time and energy, with no actual profit. If one's endeavors are directed toward Kṛṣṇa consciousness, one can surely attain the spiritual platform of self-realization. There is no such benefit from engaging oneself in economic development.

What is the meaning?

Madhuvrata dāsa: Endeavors for sense gratification and material enjoyment should not be performed, because they are considered to be a complete waste of time and energy with no actual profit.

Śrīla Nārāyaṇa Gosvāmī Mahārāja: Why? If anything is to be obtained for our suffering or happiness, it will come of its own accord due to our past activities; so why be anxious for this? If you take shelter of Śrī Kṛṣṇa, whose lotus face is as beautiful as a *kunda* flower (*mukunda-caraṇāmbujam*), whatever you desire will be automatically available to you. All material desires will be destroyed, and whatever spiritual desires you have will be fulfilled by Kṛṣṇa, Govinda.

If someone knows all these truths, then why, when he sees a beautiful girl, would his eyes want to look at her and why would he want to talk with her? And why for that reason would he give up *sannyāsa*?

Madhuvrata dāsa: That person has no realization.

Śrīla Nārāyaṇa Gosvāmī Mahārāja: *Viṣṇu-māyā* is very powerful. One can be saved only by taking shelter of Mukunda. In this verse the word Mukunda refers to both *guru-mukunda* (God's manifestation, *śrī guru)* and *kṛṣṇa-mukunda.*

Śrīpāda Mādhava Mahārāja: *Sevaka-mukunda* (Mukunda in His manifestation as *śrī guru*, His servant) and *sevya-mukunda* (Mukunda, God himself).

December 27, 2008

Darśana

Śrīla Nārāyaṇa Gosvāmī Mahārāja: Once you are saved from attraction to the opposite sex, then you can do *bhajana*. Do you know Mohinī, Śrī Kṛṣṇa's incarnation in the form of a woman? Śaṅkara (Lord Śiva) is a pure, self-realized soul, and yet he ran after Her. Brahmā created a daughter, and then he ran after her. Saubhari Ṛṣi was engaged in austerity deep in the waters of the river Yamunā when he saw a pair of fish engaged in sexual affairs. Thus he perceived the pleasure of sex life, and induced by this desire he went to King Māndhātā and begged for one of the king's daughters.

Madhuvrata dāsa: I guess that means we shouldn't go to the zoo.

Śrīla Nārāyaṇa Gosvāmī Mahārāja: Viśvāmitra and so many others were also attracted by the opposite sex.

Offer obeisances to all ladies in the world and see them as mother. When we see any lady we should think, "She is my mother." Or, we can think, "She is my sister," or "She is my daughter." In Bengal, the men call the ladies 'Ma.' Besides meaning 'mother,' 'ma' sometimes means 'young daughter' or 'sister.' An elder sister is addressed as "Dīdī;" daughter-in-law as 'Bonma;' and so on.

Madhuvrata dāsa: In regards to Mohinī, Śrīla Bhaktivedānta Svāmī Mahārāja says in one of his purports that when Kṛṣṇa takes the form of a woman, He is more beautiful than Lakṣmī-devī.

Śrīla Nārāyaṇa Gosvāmī Mahārāja: Yes.

Madhuvrata dāsa: When Kṛṣṇa takes the form of a woman, is He more beautiful than Śrīmatī Rādhārāṇī?

Śrīla Nārāyaṇa Gosvāmī Mahārāja: No. No one can be equal to Śrīmatī Rādhikā. The beauty of Kṛṣṇa's incarnation as a woman is but a shadow of Rādhikā's beauty.

What is the next homework verse? *Rahūgaṇaitat tapasā na yāti, na cejyayā...*

Madhuvrata dāsa: I become nervous when I have to say a verse in front of you.

Śrīla Nārāyaṇa Gosvāmī Mahārāja: Don't be nervous.

Madhuvrata dāsa:

rahūgaṇaitat tapasā na yāti
na cejyayā nirvapaṇād gṛhād vā
na cchandasā naiva jalāgni-sūryair
vinā mahat-pāda-rajo-'bhiṣekam
(*Śrīmad-Bhāgavatam* 5.12.12)

My dear King Rahūgaṇa, unless one has the opportunity to smear his entire body with the dust of the lotus feet of great devotees, one cannot realize the Absolute Truth. One cannot realize the Absolute Truth simply by observing celibacy (*brahmācārya*), by strictly following the rules and regulations of householder life, by leaving home as a *vānaprastha*, by accepting *sannyāsa*, or by undergoing severe penances in winter by keeping oneself submerged in water or surrounding oneself in summer by fire and the scorching heat of the sun. There are many other processes to understand the Absolute Truth, but the Absolute Truth is only revealed to one who has attained the mercy of a great devotee.

Śrīla Nārāyaṇa Gosvāmī Mahārāja: Your recitation should have more...

Madhuvrata dāsa: Flow.

Śrīla Nārāyaṇa Gosvāmī Mahārāja: What is the translation?

Madhuvrata dāsa: "O King Rahūgaṇa, not by *tapasya*, *arcana*, or *pūjā*, not by giving up one's home or living in one's home, not by study of the Vedas, not by celibacy, not by sitting in the sun with fire all-around or sitting in water..."

Śrīla Nārāyaṇa Gosvāmī Mahārāja: This last point refers to taking *sannyāsa*.

Madhuvrata dāsa: Only by taking bath in the foot-dust of the pure devotees can one become free from material existence.

Śrīla Nārāyaṇa Gosvāmī Mahārāja: What is the meaning of *mahat-pāda-rajo-'bhiṣekam* (bathing in the foot-dust of pure devotees)?

Madhuvrata dāsa: The word 'foot-dust' implies following the instructions of the pure devotees.

Śrīla Nārāyaṇa Gosvāmī Mahārāja: Suppose someone is executing all the practices of *bhakti* and he knows no God other than Kṛṣṇa – but he has no *guru-niṣṭhā* (strong faith in *guru*). What type of *bhakti* is he performing?

Acyutānanda dāsa: It is not *bhakti*.

Śrīla Nārāyaṇa Gosvāmī Mahārāja: Not *bhakti*? After all, if he is chanting, reading scriptures, giving classes, writing books – but he has no *guru-niṣṭhā* – what is this? Is it *bhakti* or not? Is it *bhakti-ābhāsa*, a semblance of *bhakti*?

Madhuvrata dāsa: It is not *bhakti*; it is *karma*.

Śrīla Nārāyaṇa Gosvāmī Mahārāja: It is an *aparādha*, an offense. The backbone of *bhakti* is *guru-niṣṭhā*.

Suppose a man engaged in *bhakti* to Kṛṣṇa is endeavoring to have the mood a *gopī*, but he has no *guru-niṣṭhā*. This means he has no *bhakti*; He is simply engaged in *aparādha*. On the other hand, if one does not endeavor for any specific transcendental mood and he does not perform rigid disciplines and he has no *bhakti* for Kṛṣṇa, but he is serving *gurudeva* with strong faith in *guru's* lotus feet, what will happen?

yasya prasādād bhagavat-prasādo
yasyāprasādān na gatiḥ kuto 'pi
dhyāyan stuvaṁs tasya yaśas tri-sandhyaṁ
vande guroḥ śrī-caraṇāravindam

(*Śrī Gurvaṣṭaka*, Verse 8)

Only by the mercy of *śrī gurudeva* can one receive the mercy of Kṛṣṇa; without his grace the living entities

> cannot make any advancement or be delivered. Meditating three times a day on the glories to *śrī gurudeva* and reciting *stava-stuti*, I offer prayers unto his lotus feet.

All good, spiritual qualities will come to reside within him and he will become the best devotee of Kṛṣṇa. Thus, *guru-niṣṭhā* is the backbone of *bhakti*. In this verse the words *mahat-pāda-rajo-'bhiṣekam* refer to both the Vaiṣṇava and *guru*, both *śikṣā-* and *dīkṣā-gurus*. Obeying them and taking one's life in one's hands (ready to risk one's life) for serving them, one achieves all spiritual success.

What does the word *jalāgni* mean in this verse [*Śrīmad-Bhāgavatam* 5.12.12]?

Brajanātha dāsa: Sitting in cold water and performing many austerities as Saubhari Ṛṣi did – with no effect.

[Śrīpāda Mādhava Mahārāja utters many verses, one after another.]

Madhuvrata dāsa: Gurudeva, how can Mādhava Mahārāja remember so many verses? How is it possible?

Brajanātha dāsa: Perhaps Śrīla Gurudeva gave him a lemon candy for every verse he mastered, just as his own *dīkṣā gurudeva*, Śrīla Bhaktivedānta Vāmana Gosvāmī Mahārāja, was given lemon candies from his Gurudeva, Śrīla Bhakti Prajñāna Keśava Gosvāmī Mahārāja, for the verses he mastered.

Śrīla Nārāyaṇa Gosvāmī Mahārāja: I have also given lemon candies to my students as a reward for learning verses.

As soon as I left my home and came to my Gurudeva, I began to serve him totally, with my life and soul. I told him, "I have taken back all my love and affection from my father, mother, wife, wealth, and all my possessions, and now I am giving that to you. You are my soul and my everything."

I began learning Bengali, then the verses from *Gauḍīya-kaṇṭhahāra*, and then *Bhāgavata-arka-marici-mālā*, *Śrī Caitanya-caritāmṛta*, and other Vedic scriptures. I also began collecting verses from the classes of *guru* and Vaiṣṇavas. One such verse is this:

> *cintāmaṇi-prakara-sadmasu kalpa-vṛkṣa-*
> *lakṣāvṛteṣu surabhīr abhipālayantam*
> *lakṣmī-sahasra-śata-sambhrama-sevyamānaṁ*
> *govindam ādi-puruṣaṁ tam ahaṁ bhajāmi*
>
> (*Śrī Brahma-saṁhitā* 5.29)

> The transcendental realm is eternally adorned by millions of wish-fulfilling trees, by pavilions made of desire-fulfilling jewels, and by innumerable wish-fulfilling cows. There, thousands upon thousands of Lakṣmīs, or *gopīs*, are rendering services to the Supreme Personality with great affection. I worship that original Supreme Personality, Śrī Govinda.

Another verse I learned is this:

> *veṇuṁ karān nipatitaṁ skhalitaṁ śikhaṇḍaṁ*
> *bhraṣṭaṁ ca pīta-vasanaṁ vraja-rāja-sūnoḥ*
> *yasyāḥ kaṭākṣa-śara-ghāta-vimūrcchitasya*
> *tāṁ rādhikāṁ paricarāmi kadā rasena*
>
> (*Rādhā-rasa-sudhā-nidhi* 39,
> by Śrīla Prabhodānanda Sarasvatī Ṭhākura)

> When will I continually render service to Śrīmatī Kiśorījī, by whose shower of arrow-like sidelong glances Śrī Nanda-nandana faints, His flute tumbles from His hands, His crown of peacock feathers falls from His head, and His yellow cloth slips from His hips? When will the time come that I can continuously render that service with *rasa*, in accordance with the natural disposition of my *svarūpa*?

December 28, 2008
Darśana

Vṛndā-devī dāsī: So-called Christians have committed many sinful activities in the name of God. Also, the Muslims say, "God wants this holy war." In the name of God they also commit sinful activities. Is this an example of *utpāta*, a disturbance due to the discharge of devotional service that does not adhere to scripture?

Śrīla Nārāyaṇa Gosvāmī Mahārāja: This is *karma*, mundane fruitive work. They are performing fruitive work in the material modes of nature: goodness, passion, and ignorance (*sāttvika*, *rājasika*, and *tāmasika karma*). Killing others and giving problems to others are activities in the mode of ignorance (*tāmasika*).

We see this in our Indian scriptures as well. If the demon Hiraṇyakaśipu performed his abominable activities according to the will of God, why did God come and kill him?

What is the meaning of this verse?

śruti-smṛti-purāṇādi-
pañcarātra-vidhiṁ vinā
aikāntikī harer bhaktir
utpātāyaiva kalpate

(*Bhakti-rasāmṛta-sindhu* 1.2.101)

Devotional service of the Lord that ignores the authorized Vedic literatures like the Upaniṣads, Purāṇas, and *Nārada-pañcarātra* is simply an unnecessary disturbance in society.

Madhuvrata dāsa: By neglecting the rules and regulations given in scripture, the process of one's '*bhakti*' becomes a disturbance in society. Or, if one too strictly follows the rules and regulations of '*bhakti*,' not understanding the mood of the scriptures, this is also not recommended.

Śrīla Nārāyaṇa Gosvāmī Mahārāja: The word *utpāta* means 'the opposite of what is good.' That person will not have *bhakti*; rather, he will experience calamities and disturbances (*utpātas*) to his *bhakti*.

What do the Purāṇas and Upaniṣads say about the regulations of *vaidhī-bhakti*? Suppose someone is engaged in *bhakti* but he is not following the rules and regulations prescribed in scripture. He is gambling; taking betel-nut; drinking; not honoring Tulasī, thinking that she is an ordinary plant; and not honoring Vaiṣṇavas.

Rules and regulations are called *viddhi*, and it is essential that they are followed. If one does not follow them, even if he is performing activities of *bhakti*, his '*bhakti*' will disappear and so many calamities and sufferings will envelop him.

Śrīpāda Mādhava Mahārāja: He will be disturbed, and he will disturb others as well.

Śrīla Nārāyaṇa Gosvāmī Mahārāja: He will think, "What is the need of *guru*? I will engage in *rāgānuga-bhakti* with no need for *viddhi* (regulations). There is no need of *guru*. By hearing and reading *śāstra* on our own, we will follow Śrīla Bhaktivinoda Ṭhākura and other *ācāryas*." This is called *utpātāyaiva kalpate*.

Madhuvrata dāsa: Some people say that the four regulative principles (no meat-eating; no taking of intoxicants including coffee, tea, and cigarettes; no illicit sex; and no gambling) were newly introduced by Śrīla Bhaktivedānta Svāmī Mahārāja. They say that the prohibition of these vices was not an important consideration in the execution of *bhakti* until he established it.

Śrīla Nārāyaṇa Gosvāmī Mahārāja: Such prohibitions are directly discussed in *Śrīmad-Bhāgavatam*, and *Bhagavad-gītā* also refers to them. *Parama-pūjyapāda* Śrīla Bhaktivedānta Svāmī Mahārāja would never speak a word that is not from *śāstra*. One must act according to *śāstra*, as he did.

Madhuvrata dāsa: *Śrīmad-Bhāgavatam* discusses this in the chapter wherein the personality of Kali, the personification of this age of quarrel and hypocrisy, was looking for a place to reside.

Śrīpāda Mādhava Mahārāja: Yes, it is mentioned in *Śrīmad-Bhāgavatam*:

abhyarthitas tadā tasmai
sthānāni kalaye dadau
dyūtaṁ pānaṁ striyaḥ sūnā
yatrādharmaś catur-vidhaḥ
(*Śrīmad-Bhāgavatam* 1.17.38)

Mahārāja Parīkṣit, thus being petitioned by the personality of Kali, gave him permission to reside in places where gambling, drinking, prostitution, and animal slaughter were performed.

Śrīla Nārāyaṇa Gosvāmī Mahārāja: Some philosophers say that *jīva* (the infinitesimal spirit soul) and Brahman (the impersonal unlimited Supreme) are the same; there is no difference between them at all. Such persons say that when the *jīvas* are liberated, they will become one with the impersonal Brahman. Is this right or wrong?

Acyutānanda dāsa: This is completely wrong.

Śrīla Nārāyaṇa Gosvāmī Mahārāja: How is it wrong? Do you have any proof?

Acyutānanda dāsa: *Jīvera svarūpa haya nityera kṛṣṇa dāsa.*

Śrīla Nārāyaṇa Gosvāmī Mahārāja: This verse is from *Śrī Caitanya-caritāmṛta*; it is not accepted by the impersonalists as sastric evidence. Please quote something from the Upaniṣads or Vedas.

Śrīpāda Mādhava Mahārāja: *Sṛṣṭi vyāpāra varjī. Vedānta-sūtra* states that the entire universe is created by Kṛṣṇa, as are all *jīvas*. The *jīva* cannot create the universe.

Śrīla Nārāyaṇa Gosvāmī Mahārāja:

nityo nityānāṁ cetanaś cetanānām
eko bahūnāṁ yo vidadhāti kāmān

(*Kaṭha Upaniṣad* 2.2.13)

The Supreme Lord is eternal and the living beings are eternal. The Supreme Lord is cognizant and the living beings are cognizant. The difference is that the Supreme Lord is supplying all the necessities of life for the many other living entities.

mamaivāṁśo jīva-loke
jīva-bhūtaḥ sanātanaḥ
manaḥ ṣaṣṭhānīndriyāṇi
prakṛti-sthāni karṣati

(*Bhagavad-gītā* 15.7)

The eternal *jīvas* in this material world are certainly My separated parts and parcels (*vibhinnāṁśa*). Bound by material nature, they are attracted by the six senses including the mind.

He will not merge in Brahman.

Śrīpāda Mādhava Mahārāja:

apareyam itas tv anyāṁ
prakṛtiṁ viddhi me parām
jīva-bhūtāṁ mahā-bāho
yayedaṁ dhāryate jagat

(*Bhagavad-gītā* 7.5)

Besides these, O mighty-armed Arjuna, there is another, superior energy of Mine, which comprises the living entities who are exploiting the resources of this material, inferior nature.*

Śrīla Nārāyaṇa Gosvāmī Mahārāja:

bālāgra-śata-bhāgasya
śatadhā kalpitasya ca

bhāgo jīvaḥ sa vijñeyaḥ
sa cānantyāya kalpate
(*Śvetāśvatara Upaniṣad* 5.9)

When the upper point of a hair is divided into one hundred parts and again each part is further divided into one hundred parts, each such part is the measurement of the dimension of the spirit soul.

keśāgra-śata-bhāgasya
śatāṁśaḥ sādṛśātmakaḥ
jīvaḥ sūkṣma-svarūpo 'yaṁ
saṅkhyātīto hi cit-kaṇaḥ
(*Śrī Caitanya-caritāmṛta, Madhya-līlā* 19.140)

There are innumerable particles of spiritual atoms, which are measured as one ten-thousandth of the upper portion of the hair.

The *jīvas* cannot create. *Jīva* is *aṇu*, minute, whereas Brahman, the Absolute Truth, the Supreme Personality of Godhead, is *vibhu*, unlimited. The living entity is infinitesimal and the Supreme Lord is infinite. The *jīvas* are *ananta*, meaning that they are unlimited in number, whereas the Lord is one.

December 29, 2008
Darśana

Śrīla Nārāyaṇa Gosvāmī Mahārāja: Suffering with tuberculosis for six months, my god-brother Anaṅga-mohana was passing urine and stool in his bed, and he was vomiting blood. I would clean that up, make his bath, and do everything else to assist him. My Gurudeva became very happy about this.

My god-brother's illness is an example of the fact that whether or not a person is careful, due to his past activities disease may come. We should not fear death. One day, death will come.

What is the next verse?

Tamopahā dāsa:

yad advaitaṁ brahmopaniṣadi tad apy asya tanu-bhā
ya ātmāntaryāmī puruṣa iti so 'syāṁśa-vibhavaḥ

ṣaḍ-aiśvaryaiḥ pūrṇo ya iha bhagavān sa svayam ayaṁ
na caitanyāt kṛṣṇāj jagati para-tattvaṁ param iha
(*Śrī Caitanya-caritāmṛta, Ādi-līlā* 1.3)

What the Upaniṣads describe as the impersonal Brahman is but the effulgence of His body, and the Lord known as the Supersoul is but His localized plenary portion. Lord Caitanya is the Supreme Personality of Godhead, Kṛṣṇa Himself, full with six opulences. He is the Absolute Truth, and no other truth is greater than or equal to Him.

Śrīla Nārāyaṇa Gosvāmī Mahārāja: Your pronunciation is very good. What is the meaning?

Madhuvrata dāsa: That which the Upaniṣads describe as the impersonal Brahman is merely the effulgence of Kṛṣṇa's transcendental body. That Lord who is the Supersoul, Paramātmā, is merely a plenary portion of His body. Śrī Caitanya Mahāprabhu is Kṛṣṇa Himself, and no one is equal to or greater than Him. He is *para-tattva*, the Supreme Truth.

Śrīla Nārāyaṇa Gosvāmī Mahārāja: Greater than Paramātmā is Bhagavān, who is full with six opulences. He is that same Śrī Caitanya Mahāprabhu.

Tamopahā dāsa: The devotees in Navadvīpa use this verse as their evidence to show that Mahāprabhu is the highest *para-tattva* of Kṛṣṇa.

Śrīla Nārāyaṇa Gosvāmī Mahārāja: No, He is Kṛṣṇa Himself; He is not higher than Kṛṣṇa. However, His mercy is greater in the form of Mahāprabhu than when He is in the form of Kṛṣṇa.

Tamopahā dāsa: The followers of Gaurāṅga-nāgarī love this verse. Why are we opposed to the Gaurāṅga-nāgarīs?

Śrīla Nārāyaṇa Gosvāmī Mahārāja: They think that because Śrīman Mahāprabhu is Kṛṣṇa Himself, He dances and sings with ladies.

Śrīpāda Mādhava Mahārāja: They want Mahāprabhu to dance as Kṛṣṇa danced in the *rāsa* dance.

Śrīla Nārāyaṇa Gosvāmī Mahārāja: Mahāprabhu performed His pastimes only with males, not with females.

Tamopahā dāsa: They say that Mahāprabhu's associates are *gopīs* in Kṛṣṇa's pastimes – Śrī Svarūpa Dāmodara is Lalitā, Śrī Rāmānanda Rāya is Viśākhā, and Govinda dāsa is Sucitrā. Therefore they all have lady forms in which they enjoy with Śrī Caitanya Mahāprabhu, who is Kṛṣṇa.

Śrīla Nārāyaṇa Gosvāmī Mahārāja: Mahāprabhu personally said that no one should think like this.

December 29, 2008
Darśana

[Again, Śrīla Nārāyaṇa Gosvāmī Mahārāja called on all the devotees present – Tamopahā dāsa, Brajanātha dāsa, Madhuvrata dāsa, and Acuytānanda dāsa – to recite and explain their homework verses:]

Madhuvrata dāsa:

rādhā-kṛṣṇa-praṇaya-vikṛtir hlādinī śaktir asmād
ekātmānāv api bhuvi purā deha-bhedaṁ gatau tau
caitanyākhyaṁ prakaṭam adhunā tad-dvayaṁ caikyam āptaṁ
rādhā-bhāva-dyuti-suvalitaṁ naumi kṛṣṇa-svarūpam

(*Śrī Caitanya-caritāmṛta, Ādi-līlā* 1.5)

The loving affairs of Śrī Śrī Rādhā-Kṛṣṇa are transcendental manifestations of the Lord's internal pleasure-giving potency. Although Rādhā and Kṛṣṇa are one in Their identity, They separated Themselves eternally. Now these two transcendental identities have again united, in the form of Śrī Kṛṣṇa Caitanya. I bow down to Him, who has manifested Himself with the sentiment and complexion of Śrīmatī Rādhārāṇī although He is Kṛṣṇa Himself.

Śrīla Nārāyaṇa Gosvāmī Mahārāja: What is the meaning of this verse?

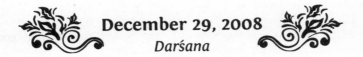

Madhuvrata dāsa: Śrīmatī Rādhikā is the transformation of *hlādinī-śakti*, Śrī Kṛṣṇa's pleasure energy. She is the manifestation of the love (*praṇaya*) between Her and Kṛṣṇa. She and Kṛṣṇa are one in *tattva* (established truth), but they have separated into two in order to perform pastimes together. This verse is saying that now these two, Rādhā and Kṛṣṇa, have become one as Śrī Caitanya Mahāprabhu.

Śrīla Nārāyaṇa Gosvāmī Mahārāja: What is the meaning of *praṇaya-vikṛtir*?

Acyutānanda dāsa: Rādhārāṇī is the transformation of *praṇaya*: *sneha, māna, praṇaya, rāga, anurāga.*[47]

Śrīla Nārāyaṇa Gosvāmī Mahārāja: Without Rādhā, who is Kṛṣṇa's *praṇaya-vikṛtir* (the transformation of His *praṇaya*), how can Kṛṣṇa exist? He is zero without Rādhā.

But the verse states *rādhā-kṛṣṇa-praṇaya-vikṛtir*, so how has She manifested? This is the question. It may be said that at first there was no Rādhikā, and then She manifested as the transformation of Kṛṣṇa's *praṇaya*, His *hlādinī-śakti*. How has She come to be Rādhikā?

The answer is that Rādhā and Kṛṣṇa cannot be separated under any circumstance. She was present with Kṛṣṇa internally, and then She manifested externally as the transformation of *kṛṣṇa-prema* (*kṛṣṇa-prema-vikāra*). *Hlādinī-śakti* is never separated from Kṛṣṇa. When They are together as two, They are Rādhā and Kṛṣṇa, and when They again become one, They are Śrī Caitanya Mahāprabhu. In this way, Caitanya Mahāprabhu is not different from Śrī Śrī Rādhā-Kṛṣṇa.

Who manifested first, Śrī Caitanya Mahāprabhu or Rādhā and Kṛṣṇa? When we 'count from' Mahāprabhu, then Mahāprabhu is first, and when we 'count from' Śrī Śrī Rādhā-Kṛṣṇa, then Rādhā-Kṛṣṇa come first and after that, Mahāprabhu.

Śrīpāda Mādhava Mahārāja: Both are eternal.

Śrīla Nārāyaṇa Gosvāmī Mahārāja: When Kṛṣṇa is together with Rādhā He is *rasa-vigraha*, the embodiment of *rasa*, or transcendental mellows. He is *viṣaya*, the enjoyer of *rasa*, the object of love.

When He is enriched with *rādhā-bhāva*, then He is Mahāprabhu, the *āśraya-vigraha*, the embodiment of love for Kṛṣṇa. When He is Mahāprabhu He is *rasarāja-mahābhāva*, the combination of Rādhā and Kṛṣṇa, and He is the *āśraya*, or abode, of *prema*.

Tamopahā dāsa: Śrīla Gurudeva, before I met you, I was visiting with Śrīla Bhakti Vaibhāva Purī Mahārāja. He said that one should recite *Upadeśāmṛta*, *Śikṣāṣṭaka*, and *Manaḥ-śikṣā* every day. Is this directly from Śrīla Bhaktisiddhānta Sarasvatī Prabhupāda?

---

[47] See glossary for the definition of the words *sneha, māna, praṇaya, rāga*, and *anurāga*.

Śrīla Nārāyaṇa Gosvāmī Mahārāja: For a *sādhaka*, these are essential. Do you know this verse?

tat te 'nukampāṁ su-samīkṣamāṇo
bhuñjāna evātma-kṛtaṁ vipākam
hṛd-vāg vapurbhir vidadhan namas te
jīveta yo mukti-pade sa dāya-bhāk

(*Śrīmad-Bhāgavatam* 10.14.8)

My dear Lord, one who earnestly waits for You to bestow Your causeless mercy upon him, all the while patiently suffering the reactions of his past misdeeds and offering You respectful obeisances with his heart, words and body, is surely eligible for liberation, for it has become his rightful claim.

And:

bhakti-yogena manasi
samyak praṇihite 'male
apaśyat puruṣaṁ pūrṇaṁ
māyāṁ ca tad-apāśrayām

(*Śrīmad-Bhāgavatam* 1.7.4)

Thus he fixed his mind, perfectly engaging it by linking it in devotional service (*bhakti-yoga*) without any tinge of materialism, and thus he saw the Absolute Personality of Godhead along with His external energy, which was under full control.

And this one?

kālaḥ kalir balina indriya-vairi-vargāḥ
śrī bhakti-mārga iha kaṅṭaka-koṭi-ruddhaḥ
hā hā kva yāmi vikalaḥ kim ahaṁ karomi
caitanyacandra yadi nādya kṛpāṁ karoṣi

(*Śrī Caitanya-candrāmṛta* 125,
by Prabodhānanda Sarasvatī)

Now it is the age of Kali. My enemies, the senses, are very strong. The beautiful path of *bhakti* is spiked with countless thorns (like *karma*, *jñāna*, and unrestricted sense enjoyment). My spirit is weak. My senses are powerful and agitated. Oh, what shall I do? Where shall I

> go? O Lord Caitanya-candra, if You do not grant me Your mercy, what shall I do to save myself?

This is *kali-kāla*, the age of Kali. In this age it is very, very difficult to perform *bhajana*. In this age there are so many varieties of preachers in this world. Some say, "There is no Kṛṣṇa, no God." Some say, "We have come from zero and we are zero." Some say, "We are Brahman, the impersonal Absolute Truth." Some say, "This world manifested from *prakṛti* (material nature) and *pradhāna* (the unmanifest material elements)." Some say, "Only *karma* exists; *karma* is Bhagavān." Some say, "*Jñāna* (impersonal knowledge) is the *sādhana* for realizing that we are Brahman." Such varieties of preachers are greater in number than the preachers of *bhakti*, and it is therefore very difficult for people to understand the truth.

Kālaḥ kalir balina indriya-vairi-vargāḥ: We have a great desire for happiness through sense gratification. Under the circumstances, how can we perform *bhakti*? *Kaṇṭaka-koṭi-ruddhaḥ*: These desires are thorns, or obstacles, on the path of *bhakti*. Our only hope is our faith that Śrī Caitanya Mahāprabhu, His name, and His *bhakti* are available. If we simply call out, "Śacīnandana Gaurahari!" *kṛṣṇa-prema* will manifest to us, pure *bhakti* will manifest, and these many varieties of thorns will not affect us at all.

Appendix

To page iv of the Foreword

[As the months went on and more and more walks and darśanas were edited, several of the editors began to consider removing the names of Śrīla Nārāyaṇa Gosvāmī Mahārāja's spiritual daughters and sons who were corrected or lovingly chastised by him, worried that those devotees would be embarrassed by 'public exposure.' They wanted to express their concerns to him personally, and did so in Delhi (March, 2010). At that time Śrīla Mahārāja (addressed as 'Śrīla Gurudeva') directed them to be transparent and not omit anything. Here is the transcription:]

Śyāmarāṇī dāsī: Śrīla Gurudeva, during some of your morning walks and *darśanas* you lovingly chastise disciples; and sometimes, out of you compassion, you tell about the faults of certain disciples and others to the devotees present with you. Some of the editors are thinking that these statements should not be in the book. They are concerned that, on one hand we are supposed to quote our Gurudeva, and on the other hand we are not supposed to criticize others. If the readers see your chastisements or apparent criticisms in the book, they might also feel comfortable to criticize those same persons – or anyone else. How do we reconcile this?

Śrīpāda Mādhava Mahārāja: If you give an example, then we can discuss.

Śyāmarāṇī dāsī: For example, in an Alachua *darśana* your disciple Rūpa-kiśora dāsa asked you about the meaning of initiation, and he also told you that initiation seems sort of regimented. In your reply you told him, "I gave you initiation, but you refused to accept its significance. You have no *śikhā*, and now you are wearing a tie. You have heard so much *hari-kathā*, but everything is now spoiled. You have entered *gṛhastha* (married) life from the life of a *brahmacārī*. All right, but you must follow the Kṛṣṇa conscious principles such as waking up early in the morning, doing *āhnika* (utterance of the *gāyatrī mantras*), reading, chanting, and also preaching. Then you are a disciple. You should take off this tie, in my presence, and be my sincere disciple. Otherwise, I will tell my daughter, your wife, to reject you."

Someone reading that quote may then tell others, "Rūpa-kiśora's life is spoiled because he has rejected Gurudeva's instructions."

Śrīla Nārāyaṇa Gosvāmī Mahārāja: What I have told, I have told. There is no need for adjustment; nothing to ask about that. By this chastisement, he will correct himself. I gave him this good instruction for himself, as well as for others.

Śyāmarāṇī dāsī: So, should we write in our Foreword to the book that the self-realized *guru* has a right to chastise, but others do not?

Śrīla Nārāyaṇa Gosvāmī Mahārāja: Yes.

Śyāmarāṇī dāsī: Suppose a disciple is doing something wrong and you instruct him or chastise him for his betterment, and after that he changes for the better. Then, although he has already changed, one or two years later people may read the Morning Walks book and think, "He is doing wrong," or "He has done wrong"?

Do we need to keep in the name of the devotee who is being corrected or chastised?

Śrīla Nārāyaṇa Gosvāmī Mahārāja: Yes. I have chastised disciples for those disciples' well-being; but others should not chastise or find fault. They have no power to do so.

Śyāmarāṇī dāsī: When you say 'no power,' do you mean that they have no power to change the person or make him Kṛṣṇa conscious, so they have no authority to criticize or chastise?

Śrīla Nārāyaṇa Gosvāmī Mahārāja: Yes.

Śyāmarāṇī dāsī: Some of the editors also say that if people who have a relationship with you, and also with ISKCON, read your criticism of ISKCON'S present leaders, they may become less favorable to you.

Śrīla Nārāyaṇa Gosvāmī Mahārāja: I don't criticize; I tell the truth.

Śyāmarāṇī dāsī: The editors are afraid that such statements might make the ISKCON leaders and their followers complain and criticize you more.

Śrīla Nārāyaṇa Gosvāmī Mahārāja: Let them do so. I have no objection.

Glossary

ācārya – preceptor, one who teaches by example. One who accepts the confidential meanings of the scriptures and engages others in proper behavior, personally following that behavior oneself.

adhibhautika-kleśa – sufferings caused by other living beings (*bhūtas*).

adhidaivika-kleśa – miseries caused by the *devas* (gods), such as disturbances in the weather.

adhyātmika-kleśa – miseries caused by the mind and body.

aiśvarya – opulence, splendor, majesty or supremacy; in regard to *bhakti*, this refers to devotion to Śrī Kṛṣṇa in a mood of awe and reverence rather than sweetness (*mādhurya*), thus restricting the intimacy of exchange between Śrī Kṛṣṇa and His devotee.

ānanda – (1) transcendental bliss; (2) the potency of the Lord which relates to His aspect of bliss. This corresponds to the *hlādinī-śakti*.

anartha – *an-artha* means 'non-value;' unwanted desires, activities, or habits that impede one's advancement in *bhakti*, or pure devotion for the Supreme Lord Śrī Kṛṣṇa.

anurāga – an intensified stage of *prema* as defined in *Ujjvala-nīlamaṇi* (14.146): "Although one regularly meets with and is well-acquainted with the beloved, the ever-fresh sentiment of intense attachment causes the beloved to be newly experienced at every moment, as if one has never before had any experience of such a person."

aparādha – the word *rādha* means 'to give pleasure' and the word *apa* means 'taking away.' Thus the word *aparādha* signifies all activities that are displeasing to the Lord and His devotees, like offenses committed against the holy name, the Vaiṣṇavas, the *guru*, the scriptures, the holy places, the Deity and so on.

āsakti – deep attachment for the Lord and His associates. It occurs when one's liking for *bhajana* leads to a direct attachment for the person who is the object of *bhajana*. It is the seventh stage in the development of the creeper of devotion, and it is awakened upon the maturing of one's taste for *bhajana*.

āśrama – (1) spiritual order; one of the four stages of life – student (*brahmacārī*), married (*gṛhastha*), retired (*vanaprastha*), or renounced (*sannyāsa*) – in which one carries out corresponding socio-religious duties in the system known as *varṇāśrama*; (2) a hermitage, usually in the association of others, which is established to facilitate spiritual practices.

Arjuna Miśra – a poor *brāhmaṇa* who, every morning after performing his *bhajana*, used to spend two hours writing a commentary on *Śrī Bhagavad-gītā*. After that he would go out to beg alms, and whatever he received he would give to his wife, who would prepare, cook, and offer to the Lord with great love.

One day while writing his commentary, the *brāhmaṇa* came across the following verse:

> *ananyāś cintayanto māṁ ye janāḥ paryupāsate*
> *teṣāṁ nityābhiyuktānāṁ yoga-kṣemaṁ vahāmy aham*
>
> (*Bhagavad-gītā* 9.22)

> However, for those who are always absorbed in thoughts of Me, and who worship Me with one-pointed devotion by every means, I Myself carry their necessities and preserve what they have.

Reading this verse, he became perplexed with a doubt: "Will the Supreme Lord, who is the only master of the universe, personally carry the progress and maintenance of those who are engaged in one-pointed *bhajana* of Him? No, this cannot be true. If this were so, then why is my situation as it is?"

He tried to resolve this difficulty by his own intelligence, but instead became more perplexed. Finally, he put three slash marks on this line of text with his red pen and went out to beg alms.

Śrī Kṛṣṇa saw that a doubt had appeared in the mind of His devotee. Taking the form of an extremely beautiful, tender, bluish-black-complexioned boy, He filled two baskets with ample rice, *dāhl*, vegetables, ghee, and so on. Putting them on either ends of a bamboo stick, He personally carried them on His shoulders to the house of that *brāhmaṇa*, where He entered the courtyard and placed His load on the floor. He told the *brāhmaṇa's* wife, "Mother, Paṇḍitajī (the *brāhmaṇa*) has sent these supplies. Please take them inside." Seating the boy in the courtyard, the *brāhmaṇī* went to the kitchen and started to cook something for Him. Kṛṣṇa then thought, "The purpose for which I personally carried these foodstuffs has been completed. Now, when the *brāhmaṇa* returns, he will immediately discover the authenticity of My words." Kṛṣṇa then disappeared.

That day, despite great effort, the *brāhmaṇa* was unable to collect any alms. When he returned home, he saw that his wife was busy cooking and he inquired, "How is it that you are cooking when I received no alms today?" His wife told him how a boy had brought so many things, and she showed him the rice, *dāhl*, flour, and other things. The *brāhmaṇa* now began to understand the whole situation, and tears flowed continuously from his eyes. He entered the Deity room and opened his *Bhagavad-gītā*. That morning he had made three slash marks with his red ink on the line: "*nityābhiyuktānāṁ yoga-kṣemaṁ vahāmy aham* – I Myself carry their necessities and preserve what they have," but now these marks were gone. He continued writing the commentary on the *Gītā* every day, and his life became full of love.

aṣṭa-sakhīs – Śrīmatī Rādhikā's eight principal *gopī* friends, namely, Lalitā, Viśākhā, Citrā, Indulekha, Campakalatā, Raṅgadevī, Sudevī, and Tuṅgavidyā.

bābājī – a renounced person; a person who is absorbed in meditation, penance, and austerity.

Bhagavān – the Supreme Personality of Godhead, Śrī Kṛṣṇa. The *Viṣṇu Purāṇa* (6.5.72–4) defines Bhagavān as follows: "The word *bhagavat* is used to describe the Supreme Spirit Whole, who possesses all opulence, who is completely pure and who is the cause of all causes. In the word *bhagavat*, the syllable *bha* has two meanings: one who maintains all living entities and one who is the support of all living entities. Similarly the syllable *ga* has two meanings: the creator and one who causes all living entities to obtain the results of *karma* and *jñāna*. Complete opulence, religiosity, fame, beauty, knowledge, and renunciation are known as *bhaga*, fortune." The suffix *vat* means possessing. Thus, one who possesses these six fortunes is known as Bhagavān.

bhajana – the performance of spiritual practices, especially the process of hearing, chanting, and meditating upon the holy name, form, qualities, and pastimes of Śrī Kṛṣṇa.

bhajana-kriyā – engagement in devotional practices such as hearing and chanting. This is the second stage in the development of the creeper of devotion, and it occurs by the influence of *sādhu-saṅga*.

bhajana-kuṭīra – a place where a devotee performs his *bhajana*.

bhakta – a devotee; one who performs *bhakti*, or devotional service.

bhakti – the primary meaning of the word *bhakti* is 'rendering service.' The performance of activities which are meant to satisfy or please the Supreme Lord, Śrī Kṛṣṇa, which are performed in a favorable spirit saturated with love, which are devoid of all desires other than the desire for His benefit and pleasure, and which are not covered by *karma* and *jñāna*.

bhakti-latā-bīja – the seed of the creeper of devotion. This refers to the inception of the desire to serve Śrī Śrī Rādhā-Kṛṣṇa in a particular capacity, which is known as *kṛṣṇa-sevā-vāsana*. Within this seed is the undeveloped conception of *bhāva*. This seed externally manifests as *śraddhā*, or faith in the instructions and goal described by the *śāstras*. When this seed is watered by the methods of hearing, chanting, and service to Vaiṣṇavas, it grows into a luxurious plant and ultimately delivers its fruit of love of God.

bhakti-yoga – the path of spiritual realization through devotional service to Lord Kṛṣṇa.

bhāva – spiritual emotions or sentiments.

bhāva-bhakti – the initial stage of perfection in devotion. A stage of *bhakti* in which *śuddha-sattva*, the essence of the Lord's internal potency consisting of spiritual knowledge and bliss, is transmitted into the heart of the practicing devotee from the heart of the Lord's eternal associates.

It is like a ray of the sun of *prema* and it softens the heart by various tastes. It is the first sprout of pure love of God (*prema*) and is also known as *rati*. In *bhāva-bhakti*, a soul can somewhat realize love for Kṛṣṇa as well as the way in which he can serve Him. After some time divine absorption and love for Him manifests, and thus the soul attains the final stage called *prema*.

bhoga – unoffered foodstuffs.

Brahman – the impersonal, all-pervading feature of the Lord, which is devoid of attributes and qualities.

brahmacāri – a celibate, unmarried student; the first *āśrama* or stage of life in the *varṇāśrama* system.

brahmacāriṇī – a female celibate, unmarried student.

brāhmaṇa – the highest of the four *varṇas* (castes) in the Vedic social system called *varṇāśrama*; one who is a member of this *varṇa*, such as a priest or teacher of divine knowledge.

brahma-jyoti – the impersonal Brahman effulgence of the Lord

Brahmavādī – one who worships the impersonal Brahman, the effulgence of Kṛṣṇa's body. He accepts the personal feature of the Lord, but thinks it inferior to Brahman.

caraṇāmṛta – nectar from the feet of Śrī Kṛṣṇa or His associates. Substances such as water, milk, honey, yoghurt, ghee, and rose water are used to bath the feet of Śrī Kṛṣṇa or His associates. The nectar that is collected from that is known as *caraṇāmṛta*.

cit – consciousness; pure thought; knowledge; spiritual cognition or perception; spirit.

dakṣiṇā – fee paid to a *brāhmaṇa* for performance of a sacrifice or other religious service.
daṇḍa – a stick carried by *sannyāsīs*, renunciates in the fourth stage of life according to the Vedic social system.
darśana – seeing, meeting, visiting or beholding, especially in regard to the Deity, a sacred place, or an exalted Vaiṣṇava.
dāsa – a male servant.
dāsī – a maidservant; a female servant.
dāsya – the mood of being a servant.
dhāma – a holy place of pilgrimage; the abode of the Lord in which He appears and enacts His transcendental pastimes; the transcendental abode.
dharma – (from the verbal root *dhṛ*, which means 'to sustain;' thus, *dharma* means 'that which sustains') (1) the natural, characteristic function of a thing (e.g., fire and its quality to give off heat and light); (2) *jaiva-dharma* or *sanātana-dharma*, the natural and eternal function of the *jīva*, or spirit soul, to love Śrī Kṛṣṇa; (3) religion in general; (4) the socio-religious duties prescribed in *śāstra* for different classes of persons in the *varṇāśrama* system, which are meant to elevate one to the platform of *bhakti*.
dhotī – a single, long piece of cloth, usually made of cotton, traditionally worn by Indian men to cover the lower half of the body.
dhyāna-yoga – meditation; the seventh stage of *aṣṭāṅga-yoga* (the eightfold process of mystic *yoga*).
dīkṣā – initiation from a spiritual master; in the *Bhakti-sandarbha* (*Anuccheda* 283) Śrīla Jīva Gosvāmī has defined *dīkṣā* as followes: "Learned exponents of the Absolute Truth declare that the process by which the spiritual master imparts divine knowledge (*divya-jñāna*) to the disciple and eradicates all sins is known as *dīkṣā*." He then explains *divya-jñāna* as "the transcendental knowledge of the Lord's form and one's specific relationship with the Lord contained within a *mantra*." This means at the time of initiation, the *guru* gives the disciple a *mantra* which, in course of time, reveals the particular form of the Lord who is the object of one's worship, and the disciple's specific relationship with the Lord in *dāsya*, *sakhya*, *vātsalya* or *mādhurya*.
dīkṣā-guru – initiating spiritual master; one who gives a *mantra* in accordance with the regulations of *śāstra* (scripture) to a qualified candidate for the purpose of worshiping the Lord and realizing Him through that *mantra* is known as a *dīkṣā-guru* or *mantra-guru*.

divyonmāda – a wonderful, divine state that resembles delusion, which is found virtually only in Śrīmatī Rādhārāṇī. One manifestation of *divyonmāda* is *citra-jalpa*, which induces Śrīmatī Rādhārāṇī to speak nonsensically.

ḍor-kaupīna – the loincloth of an ascetic.

Dvāpara-yuga – see *yuga*.

Dvārakā – the lower part of Goloka, which is the highest realm of the spiritual world (see Goloka). Dvārakādhīśa Kṛṣṇa, Kṛṣṇa who resides in Dvārakā, is a plenary expansion of the supremely complete Śrī Kṛṣṇa who resides in Vṛndāvana. In Dvārakā, Śrī Kṛṣṇa appears as a prince of the Yadu-dynasty and He performs many loving pastimes with His queens, who are all full expansions of His supremely complete pleasure potencies, the *gopīs*.

Ekādaśī – the eleventh day of the waxing or waning moon; the day on which devotees fast from grains and beans and certain other foodstuffs, and increase their remembrance of Śrī Kṛṣṇa and His associates.

Ekalavya – "Ekalavya was a hunter, who was very black and tall. He went to the school of the Pāṇḍavas and Kauravas, and approached their teacher Droṇācārya: 'O Droṇācārya, O Gurudeva, I want to learn archery from you. Please teach me.'

"Droṇācārya asked, 'Who is your father?' When Ekalavya told him, Droṇācārya replied, 'I cannot teach you. Please return home.'

"Ekalavya could not understand why Droṇācārya had said this. Droṇācārya was thinking, 'If I teach him archery, he will try to kill Arjuna. He will even try to kill Lord Kṛṣṇa.' Droṇācārya knew this because he was a perfect *guru* in both archery and devotion.

"After Droṇācārya rejected him, Ekalavya returned to the forest and created a statue of him; and there he began to practice his skills.

"One day Droṇācārya entered that part of the forest with the Kauravas and Pāṇḍavas. Suddenly a dog started barking, and in a moment they saw that the dog's mouth was full of arrows and he could no longer bark. The arrows had covered his mouth, but without leaving a single scratch or drop of blood anywhere. Everyone was wondering who had accomplished this, and then they saw a very big and black person, a hunter, practicing archery. He had done it.

"Droṇācārya asked, 'From whom have you learned to shoot arrows like this?'

"'O Gurudeva, you are my Guru I have learned it from you.'

"'If I am your *ācārya* (teacher), then give me some *dakṣiṇā*, some donation,' Droṇācārya said. 'When a student becomes perfect in his studies, he should pay his teacher some *dakṣiṇā*.'

"'Whatever you want I will give you,' the hunter said.

"'You should give me your right-hand thumb, by which an archer releases his arrows.' At once, without delay, Ekalavya cut off his thumb and gave it to Droṇācārya. Droṇācārya happily took it and left.

"Why did he do this? He knew the mood of that bogus hunter.

"Although he was now without a thumb, Ekalavya continued practicing archery and later fought against Kṛṣṇa and Arjuna; and Kṛṣṇa took His *cakra* and at once killed him" (Śrīla Bhaktivedānta Nārāyaṇa Gosvāmī Mahārāja. Badger, California, May 19, 2003).

"Don't be a disciple like Ekalavya, who gave his thumb but not his heart. He did not obey his *guru*, and that is why Droṇācārya rejected him and took his thumb. Droṇācārya knew that he was against Kṛṣṇa, and later, Kṛṣṇa cut off his head with His *cakra*" (Śrīla Bhaktivedānta Nārāyaṇa Gosvāmī Mahārāja. Hilo, Hawaii, February 8, 2005).

"In this connection, the *śraddhā*, or faith, of Ekalavya is compared to a clay pot. If one places a clay pot in fire, it will crack. The *śraddhā* of Ekalavya was like that clay. He was selfish and wanted to ruin the devotees, and because of this ulterior motive his *śraddhā* in making and worshiping a statue of Droṇācārya was really not *śraddhā* at all. Our *śraddhā* should not be like that of Ekalavya; it should be like that of Arjuna. Always remember this and do not associate with Ekalavya" (Śrīla Bhaktivedānta Nārāyaṇa Gosvāmī Mahārāja. Govardhan, India, September 4, 2005).

gaura-līlā – the divine pastimes of Śrī Caitanya Mahāprabhu.

gaura-vāṇī – the teachings of Śrī Caitanya Mahāprabhu.

gāyatrī-mantra – literally, *trī* means 'that which gives deliverance' and *gāya* means 'through singing;' it is a sacred verse, repeated by *brāhmaṇas* at the three junctions of the day. The *gāyatrī-mantra* is personified as a goddess, the wife of Brahmā and the mother of the four Vedas.

Gokula Vṛndāvana – the Vṛndāvana which is situated in the material world, where Śrī Kṛṣṇa is manifest in His original and topmost feature as a cowherd boy, surrounded by His intimate and loving servitors, the *gopas* and *gopīs* of Vraja.

Goloka Vṛndāvana – the Vṛndāvana which is situated in upper part of the highest realm of the spiritual world; the abode of Śrī Kṛṣṇa, where He is manifest in His original and topmost feature as a cowherd boy.

gopa – (1) a cowherd boy who serves Kṛṣṇa in a mood of intimate friendship; (2) an elderly associate of Nanda Mahārāja who serves Kṛṣṇa in a mood of paternal affection.

gopāla-mantra – a sacred verse that is repeated by the Gauḍīya Vaiṣṇava *brāhmaṇas* at the three junctions of the day. It is one of the *mantras* given by the *guru* at the time of initiation.

gopī – (1) one of the young cowherd maidens of Vraja, headed by Śrīmatī Rādhikā, who serve Kṛṣṇa in a mood of amorous love; (2) an elderly associate of Mother Yaśodā, who serves Kṛṣṇa in a mood of parental affection.

Gosvāmī – one who is the master of his senses; a title for those in the renounced order of life. This often refers to the renowned followers of Śrī Caitanya Mahāprabhu who adopted the lifestyle of mendicants.

gṛhastha – a householder; one who is in family life. It is the second *āśrama*, or stage of life, in the *varṇāśrama* system.

guru – a spiritual master.

gurukula – the school of the spiritual master; a school of Vedic learning.

guru-tattva – the philosophical principles relating to the spiritual master.

guru-varga – a succession of spiritual masters.

hari-kathā – narrations of the holy name, form, qualities, and pastimes of Śrī Hari (Kṛṣṇa) and His associates.

hari-nāma – the chanting of Śrī Kṛṣṇa's holy names.

hlādinī, hlādinī-śakti – the potency relating to the bliss aspect of the Supreme Lord.

ISKCON – International Society for Krsna Consciousness. ISKCON was founded in 1966 in New York by Śrīla Bhaktivedānta Svāmī Mahārāja for the purpose of spreading worldwide the practice of *bhakti-yoga* (or devotion to the Divine Couple Śrī Śrī Rādhā and Kṛṣṇa) according to the precepts of Gauḍīya Vaiṣṇavism, as taught by Śrī Kṛṣṇa Himself 500 years ago when He appeared in this world in His form of Śrī Caitanya Mahāprabhu.

Since the departure of Śrīla Bhaktivedānta Svāmī Mahārāja from this mortal world in 1979, the management of ISKCON has been overseen by a Governing Body Commission (GBC), which had been formed earlier by Śrīla Bhaktivedānta Svāmī

Mahārāja in 1970 to encourage the ISKCON members and to assist in the insurance that spiritual regulative principles were practiced within the ISKCON temples.

iṣṭagoṣṭhī – a discussion of spiritual subject matters based on questions and answers

Janmāṣṭamī – the appearance day of Lord Kṛṣṇa, which occurs on the eighth day of the dark lunar fortnight of the month of Bhādra (August-September).

japa – loud chanting or soft utterance of the holy names of Kṛṣṇa to oneself; usually refers to the practice of chanting *harināma* on *tulasī* beads.

japa-mālā – a strand of wooden beads, usually made from the *tulasī* plant, which is used like a rosary by Vaiṣṇavas for counting their chanting of *harināma*.

jīva – the eternal, individual living entity, who in the conditioned state of material existence assumes material bodies of the innumerable species of life.

jñāna – (1) knowledge in general; (2) knowledge which leads to impersonal liberation; (3) transcendental knowledge of one's relationship with Śrī Kṛṣṇa.

jñānī – one who pursues the path of *jñāna*, or knowledge, directed toward impersonal liberation.

Kali-yuga – see *yuga*.

kalpa – one day in the life of Lord Brahmā; it is equivalent to one thousand *divya-yugas*. Each *divya-yuga* is one cycle of the Satya, Dvāpara, Tretā, and Kali-yugas, altogether 4,320,000,000 years; also see *yuga*.

kaniṣṭhā, kaniṣṭha-adhikārī – a novice devotee, or neophyte practitioner of *bhakti*.

kaṇṭhī-mālā – a necklace of small beads which is composed of wood from the sacred *tulasī* plant. It is worn on the neck by Vaiṣṇavas to indicate their devotion to Śrī Kṛṣṇa and their acceptance of *dīkṣā*.

karatālas – small brass hand cymbals used in the performance of devotional songs.

karma – (1) any activity performed in the course of material existence; (2) reward-seeking activities; pious activities leading to material gain in this world or in the heavenly planets after death; (3) fate; previous actions which lead to inevitable reactions.

karma-yoga – the path of spiritual realization in which the fruit of one's work is offered to the Lord.

karmī – one who pursues the Vedic path of *karma* directed toward material gain or elevation to the heavenly planets.

Kārtika – name of the Vedic month that occurs around October-November of the solar calendar, in which the Dāmodara form of Śrī Kṛṣṇa is worshiped.

Kauravas – the descendants of King Kuru who fought together at Kurukṣetra. They are differentiated from the Pāṇḍavas by this title, but originally all of them were Kauravas.

kīrtana – one of the nine most important limbs of *bhakti*; consisting of either: (1) congregational singing of Śrī Kṛṣṇa's holy names, usually accompanied by music; (2) loud individual chanting of the holy name; or (3) oral descriptions of the glories of Śrī Kṛṣṇa's names, forms, qualities, associates, and pastimes.

kṣatriya – an administrator or warrior; the second of the four *varṇas*, or castes, in the *varṇāśrama* system.

Kumāras (four) – the four Kumāras are named Sanaka, Sanātana, Sanandana, and Sanat. Brahmā created them in the beginning of creation, from his mind (*manaḥ*). That is why they are called Brahmā's *mānasa-putra* (sons born of his mind). Because of their profound knowledge, they were completely detached from worldly attraction, and they did not give any assistance in their father's task of creation.

Brahmā was extremely displeased with this, and he prayed to Bhagavān Śrī Hari for the welfare of his sons. Śrī Bhagavān was pleased by Brahmā's prayers, and in His Haṁsa (swan) *avatāra*, He attracted their minds away from dry impersonal knowledge to the knowledge of pure devotional service on the absolute platform. Because of this, Śanaka Ṛṣi and his brothers are known as *jñānī-bhaktas*. They are the originators of the Nimbāditya disciplic succession.

kuñja – a secluded forest grove; a natural, shady retreat with a roof and walls formed by flowering trees, vines, creepers, and other climbing plants.

līlā – the divine and astonishing pastimes of the Lord and His eternal associates, which grant all auspiciousness for the *jīva*, which have no connection with this mundane world, and which lie beyond the grasp of the material senses and mind.

mādanākhya-mahābhāva – the highest spontaneous stage of *mahā-bhāva*, which is characterized by the simultaneous manifestation of all types of transcendental emotions. It is eternally and splendidly manifest only in Śrī Rādhā, and it occurs only at the time of meeting.

mādhurya – the mood of conjugal love; the highest and sweetest mood.

madhyama, madhyama-adhikārī – a practitioner of *bhakti* who has reached the intermediate stage of spiritual development.

mahā-bhāgavata – the topmost devotee, who has attained perfection in his devotion unto Śrī Kṛṣṇa; *uttama-bhāgavata.*

mahābhāva – see *mādanākhya-mahābhāva.*

mahā-mantra – the 'great *mantra,*' composed of the principal names of the Supreme Lord in their vocative forms: Hare Kṛṣṇa, Hare Kṛṣṇa, Kṛṣṇa Kṛṣṇa, Hare Hare / Hare Rāma, Hare Rāma, Rāma Rāma, Hare Hare.

mahāmāyā – there are two kinds of *māyā* : *yogamāyā* and *mahāmāyā. Mahāmāyā* is a shadow expansion of *yogamāyā. Yogamāyā* manages the spiritual worlds, causing its residents to consider themselves in various human-like relationships with Lord Kṛṣṇa; whereas *mahāmāyā* manages the material world and bewilders the conditioned souls.

māna – that stage of *prema* in which *sneha* reaches exultation, thus causing one to experience the sweetness of the beloved in ever-new varieties; when the heroine (*nāyikā*) assumes an outward demeanor of pique which turns into transcendental sulkiness and indignation arising out of jealous love. This sentiment prevents the lover and beloved from meeting freely, although they are together and are attracted to each other. *Māna* gives rise to transient emotions like anger, despondency, doubt, restlessness, pride, and jealousy.

"'When the devotee's self-conception of being extremely dear to the Lord causes *praṇaya* to assume a crooked appearance, and thus attain a surprising and unusual state, it is known as *māna.* When *māna* is present, even Śrī Bhagavān Himself becomes fearful out of love, due to the *praṇaya-kopa* of His beloved.'

"The term *praṇaya-kopa* means 'anger out of affection.' When Kṛṣṇa's beloved exhibits *māna,* He is compelled to appease her, just to savor her loving sentiment of anger aroused by their lovers' quarrel. The words *priyātva-atiśaya-abhimāna* literally mean 'the egoism of being very dear to Kṛṣṇa.' Such a feeling causes the heroine to think, 'My love for Him is so great that it has no limit. He is under the control of my *prema*'... Although the lover and beloved are present together, although they are deeply attached to one another, and although their inner longing is to embrace, to behold each other, and to exchange affectionate words, the sentiment that prevents them from doing so is known as *māna*"

(*Śrī Śikṣāṣṭaka*, Verse Seven, *Śrī Sanmodana-bhāṣya* by Śrīla Bhaktivinoda Ṭhākura).

mañjarī – (1) a bud of a flower; (2) a maidservant of Śrīmatī Rādhikā.

mantra – *man* means 'mind,' and *tra* means 'deliverance;' a spiritual sound vibration that delivers the mind from its material conditioning and illusion when repeated over and over; a Vedic hymn, prayer, or chant.

manvantara – the duration of one *manvantara* is seventy-one *yugas*, and each *yuga* lasts for 4,320,000 years.

maṭha – a monastery; a temple of the Lord with an attached *āśrama* for *brahmacārīs* and *sannyāsīs*.

Mathurā – the place where Śrī Kṛṣṇa appeared as the son of Vasudeva and Devakī in the prison of His maternal uncle, Kaṁsa. Immediately after His appearance, Vasudeva Mahārāja brought Him to the rural setting of Vṛndāvana. There He enacted His childhood pastimes. After some years He returned back to Mathurā, where He performed His pastimes as a prince. Mathurā is situated 150km south of Delhi and 14km north of Vṛndāvana.

māyā, māyā-śakti – the illusion-generating potency that is responsible for the manifestation of the material world, time, and material activities.

Māyāvāda – the doctrine of illusion and impersonalism; a theory advocated by the impersonalist followers of Śaṅkarācārya, which holds that the Lord's form, this material world, and the individual existence of the living entities are *māyā*, or false.

Māyāvādī – one who advocates the doctrine of impersonalism.

mṛdaṅga – a double-headed clay drum which is used in the performance of devotional songs (*kīrtana*).

nāma – the holy name of Śrī Kṛṣṇa, which is chanted by *bhaktas* (devotees) as part of their devotional practice or *sādhana-bhakti*.

nāma-ābhāsa – a semblance of the holy name; it is the stage of chanting in which one is becoming cleared of sins and offenses but has not yet attained pure chanting.

nāma-aparādha – offensive chanting of the holy name; chanting of the holy name that is not accompanied by the attempt to give up sinful and offensive behavior in one's life.

Navadvīpa – the sacred nine-island region about 130 kilometers north of Calcutta, where Śrī Caitanya Mahāprabhu's early pastimes were manifest. Navadvīpa consists of nine islands and resembles an eight-petalled lotus flower.

niṣṭhā – firm faith; steadiness in one's devotional practices. It is the fifth stage in the development of the creeper of devotion.

nitya-līlā – eternal pastimes of Śrī Kṛṣṇa; also see *līlā*.

pañca-tattva – the Supreme Lord, as manifested in five features: (1) *bhakta-rūpa* – the original Supreme Lord appearing as the embodiment of a devotee, Śrī Caitanya Mahāprabhu; (2) *bhakta-svarūpa* – the Lord's direct expansion appearing as a devotee, Śrī Nityānanda Prabhu; (3) *bhakta-avatāra* – the Lord's incarnation appearing as a devotee, Śrī Advaita Prabhu; (4) *bhakta* – the Lord's liberated associate manifest as a devotee, Śrīvāsa; and (5) *bhakta-śakti* – the Lord's internal potency manifest as a devotee, Śrī Gadādhara.

In *Śrī Caitanya-caritāmṛta* (*Ādi-līlā* 7.5–6) it is explained that the *pañca-tattva* in essence is one fundamental truth. There is no separation between them. They manifest in five forms simply for the purpose of tasting transcendental sentiments in reciprocal exchanges of love.

Pāṇḍavas – the five sons of Pāṇḍu: Yudhiṣṭhira, Bhīma, Arjuna, Nakula, and Sahadeva. They were great devotees of Śrī Kṛṣṇa. They are the heroes of the *Mahābhārata* and were the victorious party in the battle of Kurukṣetra.

parakīya – paramour mood; the relationship between a married woman and her paramour; particularly the relationship between the *gopīs* of Vṛndāvana and Kṛṣṇa.

parama-guru – grand-spiritual master; the *guru* of one's *guru*.

paramahaṁsa – a topmost, God-realized, swan-like devotee of Śrī Bhagavān; the fourth and highest stage of *sannyāsa*.

Paramātmā – the Supersoul situated in the hearts of all living entities as the witness and source of remembrance, knowledge, and forgetfulness.

paramparā – the system of transmission of divine knowledge from *śrī guru* to disciple through an unbroken chain of pure spiritual masters.

parikramā – circumambulation.

pralāpa – an ecstatic symptom that manifests as inconsistent talking or talking like a madman; jesting nonsense; one of the twelve verbal *anubhāvas*.

praṇāma – an obeisance; respectful obeisances.

praṇaya – "When *prema* is imbued with an exceptional feeling of intimacy known as *viśrambha*, it is called *praṇaya*. When *praṇaya* is present, there is a complete absence of awe and reverence towards the beloved even in the midst of a circumstance that would normally evoke such feelings… *Viśrambha* is defined as the feeling of being identical with the beloved. Such a feeling causes one to consider one's mind, life, intelligence, body, and possessions to be one with the mind, life, intelligence, body, and possessions of the beloved. The feeling of oneness being referred to means that out of great love one feels equally at ease with the beloved as one does with oneself, and this feeling is mutually experienced" (*Śrī Śikṣāṣṭaka*, Verse Seven, *Śrī Sanmodana-bhāṣya* by Śrīla Bhaktivinoda Ṭhākura).

prasādam – literally means 'mercy'; especially refers to the remnants of food offered to the Deity; may also refer to the remnants of other articles offered to the Deity, such as incense, flowers, garlands, and clothing.

pravāsa – one of the four divisions of separation (*vipralambha*); *pravāsa* is explained in *Ujjvala-nilamani* (*Vipralambha-prakarana* 139) as follows: "*Pravāsa* is a word used to indicate the separation of lovers who were previously intimately associated. This separation is due to their being in different places." *Pravāsa* is the obstruction or hindrance between the hero and heroine when they have been together and are now separated, either because they live in different countries or different villages, or because of a difference in mood, or because they are in different places. *Pravāsa* has two divisions: one is simply going out of sight (*pravāsa*) and the other is going to some distant place (*sudūra-pravāsa*).

prema – love for Śrī Kṛṣṇa, which is extremely concentrated, which completely melts the heart, and which gives rise to a deep sense of possessiveness in relation to Him.

prema-vaicittya – refers to a state in which even in the beloved's presence, the lover, due to intense love, fails to perceive the presence of the beloved and is thus aggrieved with feelings of separation.

priya-narma-sakhā – an intimate cowherd friend.

pūjā – offering of worship; worship of the Deity in the temple or of respected personalities such as one's *guru*, by which different paraphernalia like incense, a lighted ghee-lamp, and flowers are offered.

pūjārī – the priest who offers *pūjā* to, or worships, the Deity form of the Lord.

Purāṇas – the eighteen historical supplements to the Vedas.

Pūrṇimā – the full-moon.

Rādhāstami – the appearance day of Śrīmatī Rādhikā, which occurs on the eighth day of the bright lunar fortnight of the month of Bhādra (August-September).

rāga – (1) An intensified stage of *prema* in which an unquenchable loving thirst (*prema-mayī tṛṣṇā*) for the object of one's affection (Śrī Kṛṣṇa) gives rise to spontaneous and intense absorption in one's beloved, so much so that in the absence of the opportunity to please the beloved, one is on the verge of giving up his life; (2) When *praṇaya* is experienced in the heart as immense pleasure. If by accepting some misery there is a chance to meet with Kṛṣṇa, then that misery becomes a source of great happiness. And, where happiness affords no opportunity to meet with Kṛṣṇa, that happiness becomes the source of great distress.

rāgānuga, rāgānuga-bhakti – *bhakti* that follows in the wake of Śrī Kṛṣṇa's eternal associates in Vraja, whose hearts are permeated with *rāga*, which is an unquenchable loving thirst for Kṛṣṇa that gives rise to spontaneous and intense absorption.

rāgātmikā – one in whose heart there naturally and eternally exists a deep spontaneous desire to love and serve Śrī Kṛṣṇa. This specifically refers to the eternal residents of Vraja.

rasa – (1) the spiritual transformation of the heart which takes place when the perfectional state of love for Śrī Kṛṣṇa, known as *rati*, is converted into 'liquid' emotions by combining various types of transcendental ecstasies; (2) taste, flavor.

rasābhāsa – overlapping, contradictory *rasas*, or transcendental mellows.

rāsa-līlā – Śrī Kṛṣṇa's dance-pastime with the *vraja-gopīs*, which is a pure exchange of spiritual love between Kṛṣṇa and the *gopīs*.

rāsa-sthalī – a place where *rāsa-līlā* was performed.

rasika – one who is expert at relishing *rasa*; a connoisseur of *rasa*.

rati – (1) attachment, fondness for; (2) a stage in the development of bhakti which is synonymous with *bhāva*.

ṛṣi – a great sage, learned in the Vedas.

ruci – taste; this is the sixth stage in the development of the creeper of devotion. At this stage, with the awakening of actual taste, one's attraction to spiritual matters such as hearing, chanting, and other devotional practices exceeds one's attraction to any type of material activity.

rūpānuga, rūpānuga-bhakti – "Rūpa Gosvāmī and Sanātana Gosvāmī are the most exalted servitors of Śrīmatī Rādhikā and Lord Śrī

Caitanya Mahāprabhu. Those who adhere to their service are known as *rūpānuga* devotees" (*Śrī Caitanya-caritāmṛta*, *Madhya-līlā* 8.246, purport by Śrīla Bhaktivedānta Svāmī Mahārāja).

"We Gauḍīya Vaiṣṇavas are known as *rūpānuga*. *Rūpānuga* means the followers of Rūpa Gosvāmī. Why should we become followers of Rūpa Gosvāmī? '*Śrī-caitanya-mano-'bhīṣṭaṁ sthāpitaṁ yena bhūtale* – He wanted to establish the mission of Śrī Caitanya Mahāprabhu'" (Śrīla Bhaktivedānta Svāmī Mahārāja. Lecture on *Śrīmad-Bhāgavatam* 5.5.2, Hyderabad, April 13, 1975).

"*Rūpānuga-bhaktas* are only those who follow the same manner and mood in which Śrī Rūpa Mañjarī serves Rādhā and Kṛṣṇa. Although Śrī Rūpa Mañjarī serves both Rādhā and Kṛṣṇa, she is more inclined towards Śrīmatī Rādhikā – happy in the happiness of Śrīmatī Rādhikā and suffering like Her when She suffers. Internally, in their constitutional forms, the *rūpānuga-bhaktas* serve in the same mood as Śrī Rūpa Mañjarī, and externally they practice the same devotional activities as Rūpa Gosvāmī" (*Gaura-vāṇī Pracāriṇe*, Chapter 7).

sādhaka – practitioner; one who follows a spiritual discipline to achieve the specific goal of *bhāva-bhakti*.

sādhana – the process of devotional service; the method one adopts in order to obtain one's specific goal (*sādhya*).

sādhu – a highly realized soul, who knows life's aim.

sādhu-saṅga – the association of advanced devotees.

sahajiyā – one who considers the stages of advanced devotion to be easily and cheaply achieved, and who thus sometimes imitates the external symptoms of spiritual ecstasy associated with those stages.

sakhā – a male friend, companion, or attendant; a *gopa* (cowherd) friend.

sakhī – a female friend, companion, or attendant; a *gopī* friend.

sakhya – the mood of friendship.

śakti – (1) power; potency; energy; (2) the Lord's potencies, which are innumerable. They are generally grouped into three categories: *antaraṅga-śakti*, the internal potency; *taṭasthā-śakti*, the marginal potency; and *bahiraṅgā-śakti*, the external potency; (3) the wife of Lord Śiva, also known as Durgā, who presides over the material energy.

samādhi – (1) concentration of the mind; meditation or deep trance, either on Paramātmā or upon Kṛṣṇa's pastimes; (2) *Sama* means 'the same' and *dhi* means 'intelligence'. When the pure devotee takes *samādhi*, it means that upon departing from this world he enters the same level, position, and spiritual mood as the personal associates of his worshipful Deity. He is serving in that realm according to his own constitutional form (*svarūpa*), with equal qualities, intelligence, and beauty as those associates.

sampradāya – a particular school of religious teaching; an established doctrine transmitted from one teacher to another; a line of disciplic succession.

saṁskāras – impressions on the heart, coming from past pious or impious acts, or from reformatory procedures.

saṁvit, saṁvit-śakti – the potency by which the Supreme Lord knows Himself and causes others to know Him.

sañcārī-bhāva – thirty-three internal emotions which emerge from the nectarean ocean of *sthāyibhāva*, cause it to swell, and then merge back into it. These include emotions such as despondency, jubilation, fear, anxiety, and concealment of emotions; also known as *vyabhicāri-bhāvas*.

sandhinī, sandhinī-śakti – the potency that maintains the spiritual existence of the Supreme Lord and His associates.

saṅga – (1) association; (2) a community of devotees.

saṅkīrtana – congregational chanting of the names of God.

sannyāsa – the renounced order; the fourth *āśrama*, or stage of life, in the Vedic social system called *varṇāśrama-dharma*, which organizes society into four occupational divisions (*varṇas*) and four stages of life (*āśramas*); renounced ascetic life.

sannyāsī – a member of the renounced order.

śānta – the mood of tranquility and neutral admiration.

śaraṇāgati – In *Bhakti-sandarbha* (*Anuccheda* 236) *śaraṇāgati* is described:

> *ānukūlyasya saṅkalpa prātikūlyasya varjanam*
> *rakṣiṣyatīti viśvāso goptṛtve varaṇaṁ tathā*
> *ātma-nikṣepa kārpaṇye ṣaḍ-vidhā śaraṇāgati*

> There are six symptoms of self-surrender: (1) acceptance of that which is favorable to *bhagavad-bhajana* (*ānukūlyasya saṅkalpa*); (2) rejection of that which is unfavorable (*prātikūlyasya varjanam*); (3) firm faith in the Lord as one's protector (*rakṣiṣyatīti viśvāso*); (4) deliberate acceptance of the Lord as one's guardian and nourisher (*goptṛtve varaṇaṁ tathā*); (5) submission of the self (*ātma-nikṣepa*); and (6) humility (*kārpaṇye*).

śāstra – Vedic scripture.

sat – the potency of the Lord which relates to His existential aspect.

Satya-yuga – see *yuga*.

sāyujya-mukti – liberation in the form of becoming one with the Lord, either by merging into His body or by merging into His Brahman effulgence.

sevā – service, attendance on, reverence, devotion to.

siddha – (1) realized or perfected. (2) liberated souls who reside in the spiritual world. (3) a liberated soul who accompanies the Lord to the material world to assist in His pastimes, or (4) one who has attained the perfectional stage of *bhakti* (*prema*) in this life.

siddhānta – conclusive truth; philosophical precept; authoritative principle of the scriptures (*śāstra*).

siddha-praṇālī – the identity of the *siddha-deha* (the completely spiritual body, which is fit to render service to the transcendental couple Rādhā and Kṛṣṇa) is determined by the instructions of *śrī guru* in accordance with the *ruci*, or taste, of the *sādhaka* (spiritual practitioner). When one's own spiritual name, form, age, dress, relationship, group, specific service or instruction, residence, one's utmost summit of divine sentiment (which is the aspirant's very life breath), and the sentiment of being a maidservant is given by *śrī guru*, this is called *siddha-praṇālī*.

Some persons, prior to the actual appearance of *rāga* within the heart, make a deceitful display of solitary *bhajana* while still plagued with *anarthas*. They consider themselves *rāgānuga-bhaktas* and thus begin to practice remembrance of *aṣṭa-kālīyā-līlā*. Some ineligible persons who are also entangled in *anarthas* obtain so-called *siddha-praṇālī* from such deceitful people, and by imitation they begin to consider themselves fit to conduct the practice of *rāgānuga-bhakti*. However, without the appearance of genuine greed (*lobha*) and by pretentious means, they cannot obtain qualification.

śikhā – a 5–6 cm diameter round tuft or lock of hair on the top of the head.

śikṣā – instructions received from a teacher; as one of the limbs of *bhakti*, this specifically refers to instructions received from a *guru* about *bhakti*.

śikṣā-guru – the person from whom one receives instructions on how to progress on the path of *bhajana* is known as *śikṣā-guru*, or the instructing spiritual master.

śloka – a Sanskrit verse.

sneha – that stage in which *prema*, attaining a state of excellence, intensifies one's perception of the object of love and melts the heart. When *sneha* is enkindled in the heart, there is no quenching of the ever-new thirst for seeing the beloved.

"Only that *prema* which melts the heart to an abundant extent is called *sneha*. Due to the appearance of *sneha*, even slight contact with the beloved gives rise to a great profusion of tears. One never feels satiated in beholding the beloved; and although Śrī Kṛṣṇa is supremely competent, the devotee becomes apprehensive that some harm may come to Him" (*Śrī Śikṣāṣṭaka*, Verse Seven, *Śrī Sanmodana-bhāṣya* by Śrīla Bhaktivinoda Ṭhākura).

śraddhā – initial faith; faith in the statements of *guru*, *sādhu*, and scriptures. *Śraddhā* is awakened when one has accumulated devotional pious activities over many births, or by the association and mercy of a transcendental person who has dedicated his life to the service of Lord Kṛṣṇa. It is the first stage in the development of the creeper of devotion.

sthāyībhāva – one's eternal, fixed mode of service; the five *sthāyībhāvas* are *śānta* (tranquility), *dāsya* (service), *sākhya* (friendship), *vātsalya* (parental affection) and *mādhurya* (conjugal love); one of the five ingredients of *rasa*.

śuddha-sattva – pure existence; state of unalloyed goodness; quality of existence which is beyond the influence of material nature.

śūdra – artisans and laborers; the working class; the lowest of the four *varṇas*, or castes, in the *varṇāśrama* system.

sukṛti – past and present spiritual pious activities.

sūrya-rathasya – the Sun-god's chariot. The entire *kāla-cakra*, or wheel of time, is established on the wheel of the Sun-god's chariot. This wheel is known as Saṁvatsara. The seven horses pulling the chariot of the Sun are known as Gāyatrī, Bṛhatī, Uṣṇik, Jagatī, Triṣṭup, Anuṣṭup, and Paṅkti. They are harnessed by a demigod known as Aruṇadeva to a yoke 900,000 *yojanas* wide. Thus the chariot carries Ādityadeva, the Sun-god. Always staying in front of the Sun-god and offering their prayers are sixty thousand sages known as Vālikhilyas. There are fourteen Gandharvas, Apsarās, and other demigods, who are divided into seven parties and who perform ritualistic activities every month to worship the Supersoul through the Sun-god according to different names. Thus the Sun-god travels through the universe for a distance of 95,100,000 *yojanas* (760,800,000 miles) at a speed of 16,004 miles at every moment. (*Śrīmad-Bhāgavatam* 5.21–22, Summary by Śrīla Bhaktivedānta Svāmī Mahārāja)

svakīya – the mood of devotion wherein the devotee considers the Lord to be her lawfully wedded husband. This mood is found in the queens of Dvārakā.

Svarga – the celestial planets within this material universe.

svarūpa – constitutional nature; the eternal constitutional nature and identity of the self.

svarūpa-siddhi – the stage in which a devotee's *svarūpa*, or internal spiritual form and identity, becomes manifest in his heart. This comes at the stage of *bhāva-bhakti*.

tapasya – asceticism; austerity. Voluntary acceptance of austerity for the purpose of detaching oneself from the sense objects.

taṭasthā – marginal. The imaginary line on the bank of a river which is exactly on the boundary between land and water is called the marginal position. It may sometimes be submerged beneath the water and may sometimes be exposed to the air.

This same adjective is applied to the living entity, who is the marginal potency of Śrī Kṛṣṇa, and who may be submerged in the darkness of the material energy or may remain forever under the shelter of Kṛṣṇa's personal energy. The living entity can never remain in the marginal position, but must take shelter of the spiritual energy or be subjected to the material energy.

taṭasthā-śakti – literally: the *taṭa* (marginally) *stha* (situated) *śakti* (energy); the marginal energy of the Supreme Lord Śrī Kṛṣṇa in which the *jīvas* are situated. Although the *jīvas* are part and parcel of the internal energy (*cit-śakti*) of the Lord, they are subject to be overcome by the Lord's external energy, *māyā*, and be covered over. Thus they are known as *taṭasthā*, or marginal.

tattva – truth, reality, philosophical principle; the essence or substance of anything.

tattva-jña – one who has full knowledge of *tattva*, or the essential philosophical principles, reality, and truth.

tilaka – clay markings worn on the forehead and other parts of the body by Vaiṣṇavas, signifying their devotion to Śrī Kṛṣṇa or Viṣṇu, and consecrating the body as the Lord's temple.

Treta-yuga – see *yuga*.

Tulasī – the sacred plant whose leaves and blossoms are used by Vaiṣṇavas in the worship of Śrī Kṛṣṇa; a partial expansion of Vṛndā-devī; the wood is also used for making chanting beads and neck beads.

unnata-ujjvala rasa – *unnata* means 'highest,' *ujjvala* means 'brilliantly shining,' and *rasa* means 'the mellow taste of a specific relationship with Kṛṣṇa;' it is the most sublime and radiant mellow of conjugal love. *Unnata-ujjvala-rasa* is of two kinds. The first is called *sambhogātmikā*, which means direct enjoyment with Śrī Kṛṣṇa in an amorous relationship. This is the mood of Śrīmatī Rādhikā, Lalitā, Viśākhā, the other principal *gopīs*, and all *gopīs* like them. The other kind of *unnata-ujjvala-rasa* is called *tat-tad-bhāvecchātmikā*, which means enjoyment with Lord Kṛṣṇa that is experienced vicariously by assisting Śrī Rādhā.

Upaniṣads – 108 philosophical treatises that appear within the Vedic literatures.

uttama, uttama-adhikārī – the topmost devotee, who is perfect in his or her devotion unto Śrī Kṛṣṇa.

vaidhī, vaidhī-bhakti – devotion prompted by the regulations of the scriptures. When *sādhana-bhakti* is not inspired by intense longing, but is instigated by the discipline of scriptures, it is called *vaidhī-bhakti*.

vaijayanti-mālā – a garland made of five varieties of flowers, which reaches upto the knees.

Vaikuṇṭha – the eternal planets of the spiritual world. The majestic realm of the spiritual world, which is predominated by Lord Nārāyaṇa or His various expansions. All the residents of Vaikuṇṭha have eternal, spiritual bodies. They possess four arms and a darkish complexion like that of Bhagavān and are fully engaged in His service in pure devotional love. Their sense of intimacy with Śrī Bhagavān is somewhat hampered, however, due to their *aiśvarya-bhāva* (mood of awe and reverence). Superior to this is Goloka Vṛndāvana, the topmost planet of Śrī Kṛṣṇa, which is characterised by *mādhurya* (sweetness) and intimacy.

Vaiṣṇava – literally means one whose nature is 'of Viṣṇu,' in other words, one in whose heart and mind only Viṣṇu or Kṛṣṇa resides. Kṛṣṇa is the origin of all Viṣṇu forms. Any devotee who worships Lord Kṛṣṇa or one of His plenary manifestations (*viṣṇu-tattva*) can be called a Vaiṣṇava.

vaiṣṇava-aparādha – an offense against a person who has dedicated his life to the service of Śrī Viṣṇu or Śrī Kṛṣṇa; the greatest offense. It is called *hātī-mata* (the mad-elephant offense). Just as a mad elephant can easily uproot and destroy a plant, so an offense to a Vaiṣṇava will destroy the delicate *bhakti-lātā*. One must therefore carefully avoid such *aparādhas* by behaving with all Vaiṣṇavas according to the principle given by Śrī Caitanya Mahāprabhu, Himself: *tṛṇād api sunicena*, etc.

vaiśya – merchants and agriculturalists; the third of the four *varṇas*, or castes, in the *varṇāśrama* system.

vānaprastha – the third *āśrama* or stage of life in the *varṇāśrama* system; retired life which entails freedom from family responsibilities and the acceptance of spiritual vows.

varṇa – (1) class, occupational division, caste; (2) one of the four social orders, or castes – *brāhmaṇa* (priest), *kṣatriya* (administrator), *vaiśya* (businessman), or *śūdra* (laborer) – in which one carries out corresponding socio-religious duties in the system known as *varṇāśrama*.

varṇāśrama – Vedic social system, which organizes society into four occupational divisions (*varṇas*) and four stages of life (*āśrama*).

vastu-siddhi – the spiritual body one receives upon attaining *prema* and taking birth in Vraja.

vātsalya – the mood of parental love and affection.

Vedas – the four primary books of knowledge compiled by Śrīla Vyāsadeva, namely the *Ṛg Veda*, *Sāma Veda*, *Atharva Veda*, and *Yajur Veda*.

vijñāna – realization of divine knowledge; realization of Śrī Kṛṣṇa's *mādhurya* (sweetness).

Vraja – the eighty-four square-mile track of land where Śrī Kṛṣṇa enacted His childhood and youthful pastimes with His cowherd friends, girl-friends, parents, and well-wishers.

Vrajavāsīs – a resident of either the Vṛndāvana situated in the spiritual world (Goloka) or the Vṛndāvana situated within the material realm (Gokula).

Vṛndāvana – 'the forest of Vṛndā;' the famous place where Śrī Kṛṣṇa enacted unlimited enchanting pastimes (also see Goloka Vṛndāvana).

yoga – spiritual discipline to link one with the Supreme; to stabilize the mind so that it is not disturbed by sense objects.

yogamāyā – the internal, spiritual mystic potency of the Lord which engages in arranging and enhancing the Lord's pastimes; the personification of that potency, namely Yogamāyā.

yogī – one who practices the *yoga* system with the goal of realization of the Paramātmā (Supersoul) or of merging into the Lord's personal body.

yuga – The Vedas explain that there are four *yugas*, or ages: Satya-yuga, Tretā-yuga, Dvāpara-yuga, and Kali-yuga. These four *yugas* rotate, like calendar months. The duration of each *yuga* is different – they are said to be respectively 1,728,000; 1,296,000; 864,000; and 432,000 years.

English titles published by Śrīla Bhaktivedanta Nārāyaṇa Gosvāmī Mahārāja

Arcana-dīpikā
Bhajana-rahasya
Utkalikā-vallarī – A Vine of Intense Longings
Bhakti-rasāyana
Bhakti-tattva-viveka
Brahma-saṁhitā
Controlled by Love
Dāmodara-līlā-mādhurī
Eternal Function of the Soul
Five Essential Essays
Gauḍīya Vaiṣṇavism versus Sahajiyaism
Gaura-vāṇī Pracāriṇe
Going Beyond Vaikuṇṭha
Gopī-gīta
Guru-devatātmā
Happiness in a Fool's Paradise
Jaiva-dharma
Journey of the Soul
Letters From America
My Śikṣā-guru and Priya-bandhu
Our Gurus: One in Siddhanta, One at Heart
Pinnacle of Devotion
Raga Vartma Candrikā
Rays of the Harmonist (periodical)
Secret Truths of the Bhāgavata
Secrets of the Undiscovered Self
Shower of Love
Śiva-tattva
Śrī Bhakti-rasāmṛta-sindu-bindu
Śrī Camatkāra-candrikā – A Moonbeam of Complete Astonishment
Śrī Dāmodarāṣṭakam
Śrī Gauḍīya Gītī-Guccha
Śrī Gītā-govinda
Śrīmad Bhagavad-gītā
Śrīmad Bhakti Prajñāna Keśava Gosvāmī – His Life and Teachings
Śrī Manaḥ-śikṣa
Śrī Navadvīpa-dhāma Māhātmya
Śrī Navadvīpa-dhāma Parikramā
Śrī Prabandhāvalī
Śrī Prema-sampuṭa
Śrī Rāya Rāmānanda Saṁvāda
Śrī Saṅkalpa-kalpadrumaḥ
Śrī Śikṣāṣṭaka
Śrī Śrī Rādhā-Kṛṣṇa Gaṇoddeśa-dīpikā
Śrī Upadeśamṛta
The Butter Thief
The Essence of All Advice
The Essence of Bhagavad-gītā
Their Lasting Relation
The Nectar of Govinda-līlā
The Origin of Ratha-yātrā
The Way of Love
Veṇu-gīta
Vraja-maṇḍala Parikramā

orldwide Centers & Contacts

contact us at the address stamped or written
e first page of this book, or at the listings below:

A

Mathura - Sri Kesavaji Gaudiya Matha
Jawahar Hata, U.P. 281001 (Opp. Dist. Hospital)
Tel: 0565 250-2334, Email: mathuramath@gmail.com

- New Delhi - Sri Ramana-vihari Gaudiya Matha
  Block B-3, Janakpuri, New Delhi 110058
  (Near musical fountain park) Tel: 011 25533568, 9810192540
- New Delhi - Karol Bagh Center - Rohiṇī-nandana
  9A/39 Channa Market, WEA, Karol Bagh
  Tel.: 9810398406, 9810636370, Email: purebhakti.kb@gmail.com
- Vrndavana - Sri Rupa-Sanatana Gaudiya Matha
  Dan Gali, U.P. Tel: 0565 244-3270
- Vrndavana - Gopinath Bhavan
  Ranapat Ghat, Seva Kunja, Vrindavan 281121, U.P.
  Tel: 0565 244-3359, Email: vasantidasi@gmail.com
- Puri - Sri Damodar Gaudiya Math
  Chakratirtha. Tel: 06752-229695
- Bangalore - Sri Radha Vinodabihari Gaudiya Matha
  1244 24th Main, 25th (A) Cross, 2nd Sector, HSR Layout
  (Parangi Palya)
  Tel: 0934 148-4903, Email: venugopaldas108@gmail.com

UNITED KINGDOM & IRELAND

- Birmingham - International Distributor
  Tel: (44) 153648-1769, Email: jivapavana@googlemail.com
- London - Ganga-mata Gaudiya Matha
  Email: gangamatajis@yahoo.co.uk
- Galway - Family Center,
  Tel: 353 85-1548200, Email: loveisgod108@hotmail.com

USA

- Houston - Preaching Center
  Tel: (1) 713-984 8334, Email: byshouston@gmail.com
- Gaudiya Vedanta Publications Offices
  Tel: (800) 681-3040 ext. 108, Email: orders@bhaktiprojects.org

WORLD WIDE

www.purebhakti.com/contact-us/centers-mainmenu-60.html